FINANCIAL MARKETS

Instruments and Concepts
Second Edition

Edited by

John R. Brick
Michigan State University

H. Kent Baker
The American University

John A. Haslem
University of Maryland

Reston Publishing Company, Inc.
A Prentice-Hall Company
Reston, Virginia

Library of Congress Cataloging in Publication Data
Main entry under title:

Financial markets.

 1. Capital market--United States--Addresses, essays,
lectures. 2. Money market--United States--Addresses,
essays, lectures. 3. Finance--United States--Addresses,
essays, lectures. I. Brick, John R. II. Baker, H. Kent
(Harold Kent)   . III. Haslem, John A.
HG4523.F56 1986   332.6'0973   85-11892
ISBN 0-8359-2031-3

To Martha, Kerry, Bridget and Jeffrey
To Linda
To Jane, John, Jim and Jeffrey

© 1986 by Reston Publishing Company, Inc.
A Prentice-Hall Company
Reston, Virginia 22090

10 9 8 7 6 5 4 3 2 1

Printed in the United States of America

CONTENTS

PREFACE

A highly developed system of financial markets and institutions is characteristic of a modern market economy. These markets, institutions and their financial instruments facilitate the efficient allocation of resources and thereby contribute to society's standard of living. The financial system does this by channeling savings into their most productive uses. This requires bringing together those economic units with funds to lend and those units desiring to borrow funds.

In recent years, financial markets and institutions have been subjected to severe inflation, high and fluctuating interest rates, and even recessions. Those shocks—especially inflation—as well as rapid developments in computer and communications technology and the trend towards deregulation, have stimulated large-scale innovation in financial markets and institutions. Inflation has accelerated the pace of innovation by increasing interest rates. Higher interest rates have increased the opportunity cost of noninterest bearing deposits and stimulated development of interest-bearing, liquid instruments. The computer revolution has provided the capacity to process and communicate massive amounts of data quickly and efficiently and has encouraged the expansion and development of financial services. Changes in regulation have tended to increase competition among the increasing number and types of institutions in the financial markets.

This book attempts to relate to this dynamic environment by providing material relevant to a basic understanding of:

1. money and capital market instruments;
2. recent developments in debt, equity, and speculative market instruments;
3. selected debt and equity market relationships and concepts;
4. recent financial and regulatory developments.

The attention given to debt and equity market relationships and concepts is especially important from a decision-making standpoint in an environment characterized by high and volatile interest rates and volatile asset values.

The objectives of this book are twofold. The first is to provide an overview of contemporary financial markets with particular emphasis on instruments, their markets, and the innovations and changes that have occurred in recent years. The second objective is to improve the financial decision-making process by providing some financial market concepts and relationships.

To accomplish these objectives, the readings in this book were selected on the basis of several criteria. In addition to readability, it was essential that each article focus on an important aspect of financial markets or related conceptual issue. To reflect the changes that have occurred, it was also essential that most of the articles be relatively current. Twenty-five of the thirty-five articles have original publication dates of 1980 or later. Three additional articles were written specifically for this second edition.

The book is designed for use in courses that deal with financial markets. Because of the nature of the subject matter and the range of topics covered in the readings, the book is also an appropriate supplement in courses dealing with bank management and the management of financial institutions. On the practitioner level, the book may be used as an educational vehicle in management development programs and by managers of financial institutions, corporate financial managers, portfolio managers, individual investors, etc.

The book is divided into five parts:

 I Money Market Instruments
 II Capital Market Instruments
 III Developments in Debt, Equity, and Speculative Market Instruments
 IV Debt and Equity Market Relationships and Concepts
 V Financial and Regulatory Developments

The articles in Part I focus on individual money market instruments and their markets. The article by Hervey is an updated piece on bankers' acceptances. Part II includes sections on bond market instruments and mortgage-related instruments. The five articles on mortgage instruments are all new to this edition, including two articles specifically written for this book. This reflects the dynamic nature of mortgage securities. Part III includes articles on recent developments in debt and equity instruments, including financial futures and options contracts. Three of the five articles concerning this rapidly developing area are new to this edition, including one article specifically written for this book. Part IV contains sections on equity market and debt markets. These articles are generally more conceptual and applications oriented than those in other sections of the book. The equity section includes two articles new to this edition. Finally, Part V focuses on recent financial and regulatory developments. Three of these articles are new to this edition, reflecting the evolution of the so-called "financial services industry."

As with the first edition, a number of acknowledgements are in order. First, we are grateful to the authors and the copyright holders for granting permission to reprint their articles. Second, we are indebted to those whose assistance made possible both the previous and present editions. The encouragement of Robert F. Dame is especially appreciated. Third, we are thankful to our families for their continuing support.

Part I

MONEY MARKET
INSTRUMENTS

The readings in Part I of this book focus on the money market and the various instruments that make up this market. These instruments are characterized by their short-term, high quality, marketability, and liquidity. Because of these characteristics, money market instruments play a key role in the management of financial institutions, nonfinancial corporations, trust funds, state and local governments, universities, and mutual funds. Such instruments often constitute a large proportion of the assets of financial institutions. By their very nature, financial institutions have considerable uncertainty associated with their cash flows. The availability of a broad spectrum of money market instruments facilitates the management of short-term funds. Furthermore, when held as assets in financial institutions, many of these instruments may be used to satisfy legal reserve requirements and liquidity requirements imposed by management. In addition to being an asset, or outlet for funds, certain instruments may be issued by financial institutions as liabilities and, as such, they constitute an ongoing source of funds. For example, a commercial bank may both buy and sell federal funds, certificates of deposit, and bankers' acceptances. In this way, banks may operate on both sides of the money market.

Some nonfinancial corporations issue money market instruments, such as commercial paper, or obtain "acceptance" financing. However, in nonfinancial corporations, trust funds, universities, or other organizations with large cash flows, the primary interest in money market instruments is as short-term investments. The "double-digit" interest rates that have prevailed in recent years have resulted in considerable emphasis on the cash management process by these market participants. By collecting funds as quickly as possible and investing the proceeds in money market instruments, cash managers have been contributing significantly to the overall profitability of many firms and organizations. The investment of "lumpy" cash flows that result from tuition payments to universities and property tax collections by municipalities are other examples of how these instruments are used and their significance. The enormous growth of money market funds and other short-term investment pools that specialize in money market instruments is further testimony to the significance of these instruments in the financial system. (These specialized mutual funds and short-term investment pools are covered in Part V.)

Like so many other aspects of the financial market system, most of the money market instruments and their individual markets have undergone dramatic changes or modifications in recent years. These changes are reflected in the articles in this section.

The first article by James Parthemos provides a brief description of the money market and how it functions. The article by Charles M. Lucas, Marcos T. Jones, and Thom B. Thurston is a thorough discussion of two of the most important and yet obscure money market instruments—federal funds and repurchase agreements. The interest rates on these instruments are the most volatile and among the most closely watched in the financial markets. The article on Treasury bills by Timothy Q. Cook and Jimmie R. Monhollon summarizes the characteristics of these best known of all money market instruments. The characteristics of federally sponsored agency securities are examined in Donna Howell's article. With the passage of the Depository Institutions Deregulation and Monetary Control Act of 1980, the operations of the discount window of the Federal Reserve System were changed dramatically. For example, nonbank depository institutions such as credit unions, savings and loan associations, and mutual savings banks were allowed access to window borrowing. This and other aspects of the discount window are discussed in the article by James Parthemos and Walter Varvel. Although they are one of the safest of the private-sector money market instruments, bankers' acceptances are relatively unknown outside the banking community. In his recent article, Jack L. Hervey provides a thorough explanation of this instrument and its function as both a source and use of funds.

Negotiable certificates of deposit (CDs) are, like Treasury bills, well-known. Unlike Treasury bills, however, this instrument and its market have undergone significant changes in recent years in response to the needs of market participants. As explained in Bruce J. Summers' article, the market is no longer limited to fixed-rate CDs issued by domestic commercial banks. Yankee CDs, variable rate CDs, thrift institution CDs, and Eurodollar CDs are now integral parts of this market.

Like CDs, the commercial paper market has changed in recent years. In addition to such topics as tax-exempt paper, foreign issuers, and basic market characteristics, the relationship between the commercial paper market and bank lending is explained in Peter A. Abken's article. In the last article in this section, Marvin Goodfriend discusses the Eurodollar market. The characteristics of this market, the various types of instruments, and the risks involved in Eurodollar transactions are among the topics covered.

THE MONEY MARKET*

James Parthemos

1

Economic units, such as financial institutions, other business firms, governmental units, and even individuals, find, as a rule, that their inflow of cash receipts does not coincide exactly with their cash disbursements. The typical economic unit finds that on some days its cash holdings build up because receipts exceed outlays. On other days, it might experience a sharp reduction in cash balances because spending outstrips cash inflow.

One of the most important reasons for holding cash reserves is to bridge the gap between receipts and outlays and to insure that a planned stream of expenditures can be maintained somewhat independently of cash inflow. There are, of course, other reasons for holding reserves. In particular, depository institutions must meet legal reserve requirements.[1]

Maintenance of cash reserves involves cost, either in the form of interest paid on borrowed balances, or in the form of interest foregone on nonborrowed balances which have not been lent out. For many economic units, especially large firms, these costs can be significant, particularly in periods of high interest rates. To minimize such costs, economic units usually seek to keep their cash holdings at a minimum consistent with their working capital needs and, in the case of depository institutions, with their reserve requirements. This may be done by holding low risk and highly marketable income-bearing assets instead

*Reprinted, with deletions, from *Instruments of the Money Market*, 5th Edition, edited by Timothy Q. Cook and Bruce J. Summers, 1981, with permission of the Federal Reserve Bank of Richmond.

[1]As a result of the Depository Institutions Deregulation and Monetary Control Act of 1980, all depository institutions must meet federal reserve requirements on reservable liabilities, i.e., transactions accounts and nonpersonal time deposits. These requirements are prescribed in Regulation D of the Federal Reserve System.

3

of cash and by maintaining access to the market for short-term credit. The *money market* has evolved to meet the needs of such economic units.

THE MONEY MARKET

The term "money market" applies not to one but rather to a group of markets. In the early part of the United States' financial history, the term was frequently used in a narrow sense to denote the market for call loans to securities brokers and dealers. At other times in the past, it has been employed broadly to embrace some long-term as well as short-term markets. In current usage, the term "money market" generally refers to the markets for short-term credit instruments such as Treasury bills, commercial paper, bankers' acceptances, negotiable certificates of deposit (CDs), loans to security dealers, repurchase agreements, and Federal funds.

In general, money market instruments are issued by obligors of the highest credit rating, and are characterized by a high degree of safety of principal. Maturities may be as long as one year but usually are of 90 days or less, and sometimes span only a few days or even one day. The market for money market instruments is extremely broad and on a given day it can absorb a large volume of transactions with relatively little effect on yields. The market is also highly efficient and allows quick, convenient, and low-cost trading in virtually any volume. Unlike organized securities or commodities markets, the money market has no specific location. Like other important financial markets in this country, its center is in New York, but it is primarily a "telephone" market and is easily accessible from all parts of the nation as well as foreign financial centers. No economic unit is ever more than a telephone call away from the money market.

At the center of the money market are numerous "money market banks," including the large banks in New York and other important financial centers; about 34 Government securities dealers, some of which are large banks; a dozen odd commercial paper dealers; a few bankers' acceptance dealers; and a number of money brokers who specialize in finding short-term funds for money market borrowers and placing such funds for money market lenders. The most important money market brokers are the major Federal funds brokers in New York.

MARKET PARTICIPANTS

Apart from the groups that provide the basic trading machinery, money market participants usually enter the market either to raise short-term funds or to convert cash surpluses into highly liquid interest-bearing investments. Funds may be raised by borrowing outright, by selling holdings of money market instruments, or by issuing new instruments. The issue and sale of new money market instruments is, of course, a form of borrowing.

Generally, money market rates are below the prime lending rates of the large money market banks. Consequently, borrowers who have the ability to do so find it advantageous to tap the money market directly rather than obtaining funds through banking intermediaries. The U. S. Treasury, many commercial banks, large sales finance companies, and well-known nonfinancial corporations of the highest credit standing borrow regularly in the money market by issuing their own short-term debt obligations. Short-term loans to Government securities dealers, loans of reserves among depository institutions and Federal Reserve discount window loans to depository institutions are also money market instruments although they do not give rise to negotiable paper.

Suppliers of funds in the market are those who buy money market instruments or make very short-term loans. Potentially, these include all those economic units that can realize a significant gain through arranging to meet future cash requirements by holding interest-bearing liquid assets in place of nonbearing cash balances. The major participants on this side of the market are commercial banks, state and local governments, large nonfinancial businesses, nonbank financial institutions, and foreign bank and nonbank businesses. In recent years individuals have also become a significant supplier of funds to the money market both indirectly through investment in short-term investment pools such as money market mutual funds and directly through the purchase of Treasury bills and short-term Federal agency securities.

By far the most important market participant is the Federal Reserve System. Through the Open Market Trading Desk at the New York Federal Reserve Bank, which executes the directives of the Federal Open Market Committee, the System is in the market on a virtually continuous basis, either as a buyer or as a seller, depending on financial conditions and monetary policy objectives. The System's purpose in entering the market is quite different from that of other participants, however. As noted in greater detail below, the Federal Reserve buys and sells in certain parts of the money market not with the objective of managing its own cash position more efficiently but rather to supply or withdraw bank reserves in order to achieve its monetary policy objectives. In addition, the Federal Reserve enters the market as an agent, sometimes as a buyer and sometimes as a seller, for the accounts of foreign official institutions and for the U. S. Treasury. Overall, the operations of the Federal Reserve dwarf those of any other money market participant.

INTERRELATION AND SIZE OF THE VARIOUS MARKET SECTORS

While the various money market instruments have their individual differences, they nonetheless are close substitutes for each other in many investment portfolios. For this reason the rates of return on the various instruments tend to fluctuate closely together. For short periods of time, the rate of return on a particular instrument may diverge from the rest or "get out of line," but this sets in motion forces which tend to pull the rates back together. For example, a large supply of new commercial paper may produce a rapid run-up of commercial paper rates, resulting in a relatively large spread between these rates and rates on CDs. Sophisticated traders note the abnormal differential and shift funds from CDs into commercial paper, causing CD rates to rise and commercial paper rates to fall. In this way, a more "normal" or usual rate relation is restored. This process, known as interest arbitrage, insures general conformity of all money market rates to major interest rate movements.

THE MARKET'S SIGNIFICANCE

The money market provides an important source of short-term funds for many borrowers. In addition, since there is a continuous flow of loan funds through the market, it is possible for borrowers, through successive "rollovers," or renewals of loans, to raise funds on a more or less continuous basis and in this fashion to finance not only their immediate cash requirements but also working capital and some long-term capital needs as well. By bringing together quickly and conveniently those units with cash surpluses and those with cash deficits, the market promotes a more intensive use of the cash balances held in the economy.

The market is especially important to commercial banks in managing their money positions. Banks in the aggregate are large-scale buyers and sellers of most money market instruments, especially Federal funds. The money market permits a more intensive use of bank reserves and enhances the ability of the commercial banking system to allocate funds efficiently. By allowing banks to operate with lower excess reserves, it also makes the banking system more sensitive to central bank policy actions.[2]

Finally, conditions in the money market provide an important guide for monetary policy. The money market is an eminently free and competitive market, and the yields on money market instruments react instantaneously to changes in supply and demand. As a result, the behavior of the market provides the most immediate indication of the current relationship between credit supplies and credit demands.

THE FEDERAL RESERVE AND THE MONEY MARKET

The Federal Reserve System influences the money market not only through open market operations but also through the discount windows of the 12 Federal

---

[2]As the phase-in of required reserves for nonbank depository institutions, mandated by the Monetary Control Act of 1980, progresses, it is likely that these institutions will also become active in the market for reserve funds.

Reserve Banks. Commercial banks may borrow short-term from the Federal Reserve to meet temporary liquidity needs and to cover reserve deficiencies as an alternative to selling money market securities or borrowing Federal Funds. Similarly, banks with cash or reserve surpluses can repay outstanding borrowings at the Federal Reserve rather than invest the surpluses in money market instruments.

Reserve adjustments made by individual institutions using the discount window differ in one important respect from alternative adjustment techniques. Trading in such instruments as Federal funds, negotiable certificates of deposit, and Treasury bills among commercial banks or between banks and their customers involves no net creation of new bank reserves. Rather, existing reserves are simply shifted about within the banking system. On the other hand, net borrowings or repayments at the discount window result in a net change in Federal Reserve credit outstanding and, consequently, they affect the volume of bank reserves. Thus, the choice by individual institutions between using the discount window or alternative means of reserve adjustment may influence the supply of money and credit in the economy. Decisions to use the discount window or raise funds elsewhere in the money market depend importantly upon the relation of the Federal Reserve's discount rate to yields on money market investments and on the legal and administrative arrangements surrounding use of the discount window. Both sets of factors are determined primarily by Federal Reserve actions.

The daily operations of the Federal Open Market Trading Desk occupy a central role in the money market. For many years the Desk has conducted transactions in U. S. Government securities and in bankers' acceptances, and in December 1966 it was authorized to conduct operations in Federal Agency issues also. The Federal Reserve enters the market frequently either to provide new depository institution reserves through purchases or to withdraw reserves through sales. To a large extent, Federal Reserve operations are undertaken to compensate for changes in other factors that affect the volume of reserves, such as float, Treasury balances, and currency in circulation. Such operations are undertaken primarily to insure the smooth technical functioning of the market mechanism. But the operations of the greatest importance from the standpoint of the economy are those undertaken by the Federal Reserve to achieve its policy objectives. Since the early 1970s these objectives have centered on achieving targeted growth rates of the money supply. Thus, in addition to its other functions, the money market serves as the mechanism for implementing the Federal Reserve's objectives.

FEDERAL FUNDS AND REPURCHASE AGREEMENTS*

Charles M. Lucas, Marcos T. Jones, and Thom B. Thurston

2

The markets for Federal funds and repurchase agreements (RPs) are among the most important financial markets in the United States. Using these instruments, many banks, large corporations, and nonbank financial firms trade large amounts of liquid funds with one another for periods as short as one day. Such institutions provide and use much of the credit made available in the United States and typically manage their financial positions carefully and aggressively. The interest rate on overnight (one day) Federal funds measures the return on the most liquid of all financial assets, and for this reason is critical to investment decisions.

The Federal funds market is also important because it is related to the conduct of Federal Reserve monetary policy. The interest rate on Federal funds is highly sensitive to Federal Reserve actions that supply reserves to member commercial banks, and the rate influences commercial bank decisions concerning loans to business, individual, and other borrowers. Moreover, interest rates paid on other short-term financial assets—commercial paper and Treasury bills, for example—usually move up or down roughly in parallel with the Federal funds rate. Thus the rate also influences the cost of credit obtained from sources other than commercial banks.

Frequently, the Federal funds market is described as one in which commercial banks borrow and lend excess reserve balances held at the Federal

*Reprinted, with deletions, from the *Quarterly Review*, Summer 1977, pp. 33-48, with permission of the Federal Reserve Bank of New York and the authors.

Reserve, hence the name Federal funds. While banks often use the Federal funds market for this purpose, growth and change in the market have made this description highly oversimplified. Many active market participants do not hold balances at the Federal Reserve. These include commercial banks that are not members of the Federal Reserve System, thrift institutions, certain agencies of the United States Government, and branches and agencies of foreign banks operating on United States soil. Moreover, this broad set of market participants borrows and lends amounts far beyond the modest total of excess reserve balances.

A closely related market for short-term funds is the market for RPs involving United States Government and Federal agency securities.[1] This market includes many of the same participants that trade Federal funds, but it also includes large nonfinancial corporations, state and local governments, and dealers in United States Government and Federal agency securities. The RP market has expanded rapidly of late, and its workings are perhaps less widely known than those of the Federal funds market.

Although the Federal funds and RP markets are distinct, they share many common features. Both, for example, primarily involve transactions for one business day, although transactions with maturities of up to several weeks are not uncommon. In both markets, commercial banks that are members of the Federal Reserve System can acquire funds not subject to reserve requirements. A lesser known but nevertheless very important common element is the fact that transactions in both markets are settled in what are known as "immediately available funds." Indeed, some observers see the two markets as so closely related that they might appropriately be grouped together under a broader designation—"the markets for short-term immediately available funds." For an elaboration of the nature and uses of immediately available funds, see Box.

IMMEDIATELY AVAILABLE FUNDS

The Means of Settlement for Transactions in
Federal Funds and RPs

An essential feature of both Federal funds and RPs is that transactions are settled in "immediately available funds." Therefore it is necessary to specify precisely what such funds are. Immediately available funds are two related but distinct types of financial claims: (1) deposit liabilities of Federal Reserve Banks and (2) certain "collected" liabilities of commercial banks that may be transferred or withdrawn during a business day on the order of account holders.

---

[1]The term "Federal agency" is used here in its popular meaning, which refers both to Federal agencies, such as the Commodity Credit Corporation, and to Federally sponsored quasi-public corporations, such as the Federal National Mortgage Association.

Federal Reserve Banks, of course, are "banks for banks," and deposits are held there mainly by commercial banks that are members of the Federal Reserve System in order to satisfy the reserve requirements imposed on members. These deposits have special features, however. Along with currency and coin, they are the only form of money created directly by a Federal authority. This reflects the fact that these deposits are the direct liabilities of the Federal Reserve Banks. In addition, the Federal Reserve operates a nationwide electronic communications network over which these deposits can be transferred anywhere in the country within a business day. Deposits at Federal Reserve Banks are therefore termed immediately available funds, since they can be converted to cash or transferred anywhere in the United States within a single day on demand.

Immediately available funds also consist of certain collected liabilities of commercial banks. This group of liabilities includes a portion of a bank's demand and time deposits, as well as certain other liabilities which are used very much like deposits but which are classed separately for accounting or regulatory reasons. These liabilities are termed immediately available funds because commercial banks permit them to be withdrawn in cash or used for payment without question within a single day. The immediate and unquestioned use of these bank liabilities for payment depends on the fact that they are collected, a feature which can be illustrated by describing how an individual's checking deposit with a bank becomes collected.

Typically, an individual increases his bank balance by depositing checks payable to him drawn on the same or some other bank. When the check is drawn on some other bank, the individual is normally unable to withdraw or otherwise use the funds on the same day that the deposit is made. Frequently, several days elapse, during which time the credit to the depositor's account is only provisional and the check is in the process of being collected. That is, it is cleared and then payment is received by the depositor's bank from the bank on which the check is drawn. Payment may be received in any one of several forms: a deposit at a Federal Reserve Bank, a collected deposit at another commercial bank, or conceivably in currency or coin. Whatever the case, once collected, the individual's balance can be transferred on his order.

Alternatively, a depositor may receive payment to his account in immediately available funds. In this case, the funds can be withdrawn in cash or otherwise used on the day of receipt with no intervening period for collection. For credit to be received immediately, the deposit must be made in some form other than the common check. The most obvious alternative is cash, used frequently for small deposits but only rarely for sizable transactions because of the risk of loss.

More commonly, when the depositor wishes to receive immediately available funds, the transfer is accomplished through the Federal Reserve electronic communications network. This network is used either within or between Federal Reserve Districts. Any member bank may send or receive immediately available funds—in the form of reserve deposits—to or from any other member bank, and the entire transfer takes place within one business day. The use of the Federal Reserve network can be accomplished indirectly by individuals or institutions other than member banks. This requires the transfer of a depositor's collected balance from one member bank to another, in effect using a reserve balance at the Federal Reserve as a means of payment between banks. If the transaction results in a transfer of funds from one account to another within a single bank, only balance-sheet entries are affected since there need be no actual movement of funds over the Federal Reserve network.

Immediately available funds can be used by a customer of a commercial bank to make payment in any sort of transaction. Among the principal users are sizable financial, business, and government institutions. In practice, such funds are used only for large transactions including, for example, payment for purchase of a financial asset, for raw materials, or for a construction contract. In all these cases, immediately available funds are used as a means of payment because the parties to the transactions wish to use them. Thus, not all transactions involving the use of immediately available funds are related to either the Federal funds or the repurchase agreement markets.

The main purpose of this article is to review major recent developments in the markets for Federal funds and RPs. The most significant changes are the dramatic growth of the volume of transactions and of the number and type of institutions active in these markets. At the same time, the language of the market has been changing, mostly because of the evolution in market practices. It is, therefore, necessary to begin with definitions of some terms most frequently used by market participants.

FEDERAL FUNDS

Federal funds transactions are frequently described as the borrowing and lending of "excess reserve" balances among commercial banks.[2] This description of

---

[2]A fundamental difficulty with this notion of Federal funds borrowing is that the use of the term "excess reserves" is very imprecise. No distinction is made between the actual excess reserves held in a bank's reserve account and what might be called "potential" excess reserves. Clearly, an individual bank can control the amount of excess reserves it has available to sell in the Federal funds market most easily by selling assets and converting the proceeds into balances at a Federal Reserve Bank. In this sense, the potential excess reserves of an individual bank are nearly as large as its total earning asset portfolio.

Federal funds was accurate years ago but is now seriously deficient, even though it still appears in the financial press. While such commercial bank use of the market persists in substantial volume, Federal funds transactions are no longer confined to the borrowing and lending of excess reserve balances. Moreover— and this is a key point—a Federal funds transaction does not necessarily involve transfer of a reserve balance, even though such a transfer usually does occur. For example, a commercial bank can borrow the "correspondent balances" held with it by other banks. The execution of such a transaction involves only accounting entries on the books of both the borrower and lender.

The most useful description of Federal funds has several elements, some based on regulations, others simply on market convention. In practice, Federal funds are overnight loans that are settled in immediately available funds. Only a limited group of institutions are in a position to borrow in this fashion, mostly commercial banks and some other financial institutions such as agencies of foreign banks. If a member bank borrows Federal funds, Federal Reserve regulations do not require it to hold reserves against the borrowing, as it must for funds acquired in the form of demand or time deposits. But, under Federal Reserve regulations, member banks are permitted to borrow reserve-free funds only from a certain group of institutions. This group includes other commercial banks, Federal agencies, savings and loan associations, mutual savings banks, domestic agencies and branches of foreign banks, and, to a limited degree, Government securities dealers. Market convention has adjusted to these regulatory restrictions, and a Federal funds borrowing has come to mean an overnight loan not just between two commercial banks but between any two of the group of institutions from which member banks may borrow free of reserve requirements. A savings and loan association, for example, can lend Federal funds to an agency of a foreign bank.

This description makes it easy to see that the Federal funds market is by no means limited to the lending of excess reserves. Many of the institutions that participate in the market are not members of the Federal Reserve System and, therefore, do not have reserve accounts. Moreover, the excess reserves of individual member banks are normally very small in relation to their total reserves. The excess reserves characterization of Federal funds borrowing suggests that total activity in the market is likewise rather modest. While this was once true, it no longer is. In recent years, daily outstanding borrowings by member banks in the Federal funds market have approached $50 billion, or about 40 percent more than the total reserves they hold. Some individual banks continually borrow as much as four times their required reserves in the Federal funds market.

Fairly recently, banks have begun to borrow immediately available funds for periods longer than a single business day. This form of borrowing was developed by agencies of Canadian banks located in the United States. The transactions are arranged among the same institutions which participate in the overnight market and are similar in all respects except maturity. For these reasons, the transactions have come to be called "term Federal funds" transactions.

The Federal funds and term Federal funds transactions described above are normally "unsecured." This means that the lending institutions have no guarantee of repayment other than the promise of the borrower. For this reason, unsecured Federal funds transactions are done only by institutions that enjoy a very high degree of mutual confidence. At times, however, a lender of Federal funds will ask that the transaction be "secured." This means that the borrower must pledge an asset, usually a Government or Federal agency security, as "collateral" against the loan. The borrower may either set aside the collateral in a custody account or actually deliver it to the lender. However, secured Federal funds transactions are not very common.[3]

REPURCHASE AGREEMENTS

A repurchase agreement (RP) is an acquisition of immediately available funds through the sale of securities, together with a simultaneous agreement to repurchase them at a later date. RPs are most commonly made for one business day, though longer maturities are also frequent. The funds that a member bank acquires in this manner are free of reserve requirements so long as the securities involved are those of the United States Government or Federal agencies. When an RP is arranged, the acquirer of funds agrees to sell to the provider of funds United States Government or Federal agency securities in exchange for immediately available funds. At the maturity of the agreement, the transaction is reversed, again using immediately available funds. Market insiders use different terms to describe the RP, including "repo" and "buy back."

Those who supply or acquire funds view RPs as involving little risk. Transactions are usually arranged only among institutions enjoying a high degree of confidence in one another. In addition, contracts are usually of very short maturity. Protection against any residual risk can be incorporated in an RP contract by establishing a differential—called a margin—between the quantity of funds supplied and the market value of the securities involved. The margin can protect either party to the transaction, but not both. It protects the supplier of funds if the value of the securities exceeds the quantity of funds supplied. It protects the taker of funds if the securities are of less value than the amount of funds supplied. The supplier of funds generally considers the consequences of default by the other party to be minor, because the securities acquired are obligations either issued or guaranteed by the Federal Government. Another element of risk arises from the possibility that the price of the securities may

---

[3]Banks chartered in certain states face regulations that require collateral to be provided for the portion of an individual Federal funds transaction in excess of some proportion of the lender's combined capital and surplus.

fall between the time the RP is arranged and the time of any default. For this reason, the margin is most often set to protect the supplier of funds.

This article is concerned with RPs involving only United States Government and Federal agency securities, but it should be noted in passing that an RP can involve any sort of asset which the supplier of funds is willing to accept. RPs involving other assets are executed to a limited degree, for example using certificates of deposit of large banks.

Transactions are executed in several ways, but two approaches are most common. One approach is for the securities to be both sold and repurchased at the same price, with charges representing the agreed-upon rate of return added to the principal at the maturity of the contract. The second approach involves setting a higher price for repayment than for selling.

The term "reverse repurchase agreement" is sometimes thought to be quite different from an RP. In fact, it refers to exactly the same transaction viewed from the perspective of the supplier of funds rather than the recipient. Compare the two views of the transaction: The recipient of funds sells a security to obtain funds, and "repurchases" it at maturity by redelivery of funds. In a reverse RP, the supplier of funds buys a security by delivering funds when the agreement is made and "resells" the security for immediately available funds on maturity of the contract. From the perspective of the party acquiring funds, the term "repurchase agreement" seems apt, and from that of the supplier of funds, the transaction is exactly the "reverse." However, whether funds are acquired or supplied, the transaction is usually referred to in the marketplace simply as an RP.

THE MARKETS FOR FEDERAL FUNDS AND RPs

There is no central physical marketplace for Federal funds; the market consists of a loosely structured telephone network connecting the major participants. These participants, as already mentioned, include commercial banks and those other financial institutions from which, under Federal Reserve regulations, member banks can buy reserve-free Federal funds. The market also includes a small group of firms that act as brokers for Federal funds. These firms neither lend nor borrow but arrange transactions between borrowers and lenders in exchange for a very small percentage commission.

All major participants employ traders. These individuals make the actual telephone contact on behalf of lending or borrowing institutions, making offers to borrow or lend at specific interest rates. They also negotiate any differences between the rate bid by a borrower and that offered by a lender. Transactions are usually executed in lots of $1 million or more. Frequently, but not always, settlement of the transaction requires transfer of funds over the Federal Reserve wire transfer network, first when the agreement is reached and again the next day when repayment is made.

Many banks, particularly medium-sized and large ones, frequently borrow and lend Federal funds on the same day, thereby performing an intermediary function in the Federal funds market. Such banks channel funds from banks with lesser need for funds to banks with greater need for them, frequently borrowing from smaller banks and lending to larger ones. Over the past decade, more medium-sized regional banks have begun to act as intermediaries. In addition, many more banks during this period have come to borrow significantly more than they lend; that is, they have become continual net borrowers.

In recent years a growing portion of the market has consisted of large banks' borrowing of correspondent balances from small banks. Historically, these correspondent balances earned no interest. But both large and small banks have come to regard correspondent relationships as convenient bases for arranging Federal funds transactions. Small banks now intentionally accumulate large balances, selling off daily the excess not needed for the clearing of checks or for other purposes. In such cases, it is not necessary to transfer funds over the Federal Reserve wire transfer network, and reserve balances need not change ownership. Rather, bookkeeping entries are posted by both the borrower and lender to reflect the fact that a non-interest-bearing correspondent demand balance has been converted into a Federal funds borrowing.

No central physical marketplace for repurchase agreements exists either. Transactions are arranged by telephone, largely on a direct basis between the parties supplying and acquiring funds but increasingly through a small group of market specialists. These specialists, mostly Government securities dealers, arrange a repurchase agreement with one party to acquire funds and a reverse repurchase agreement with another party to supply funds. They earn a profit by acquiring funds more cheaply than they supply them.

Large banks and Government securities dealers are the primary seekers of funds in the RP market. Banks use the market as one among many sources of funds, but have a distinct advantage over other institutions as acquirers of funds because they hold large portfolios of United States Government and Federal agency securities. Moreover, because the supplier of funds receives securities, and because member banks acquiring funds need not hold reserves against RPs regardless of the source of funds, the RP market attracts a wider array of participants than does the Federal funds market. Government securities dealers use the market as a source of funds to finance their holdings of Government and agency securities. Many types of institutions supply immediately available funds in this market, but large nonfinancial corporations and state and local governments dominate.

Typically, participants on both sides of the RP market have lists of customers with whom they routinely do business. Each of the largest participants uses an "RP trader," an individual whose job it is to contact other traders and to negotiate the best arrangements possible. A trader begins the day with information on the amount of funds he must supply or acquire. His objective is to arrange transactions at the maximum return obtainable if he is to provide funds and at the minimum cost possible if he is to acquire funds.

With these definitions and descriptions in mind, it is possible to discuss in some detail the roles of the major institutional participants in the markets for immediately available funds. It is appropriate to begin with an examination of the role played by commercial banks, who are currently the most important of those who obtain funds in these markets. Moreover, the reserve position adjustments that banks make in the markets for immediately available funds are important links in transmitting the effects of monetary policy throughout the financial system.

COMMERCIAL BANKS AND IMMEDIATELY AVAILABLE FUNDS

Commercial banks are the largest and most active participants in the markets for immediately available funds. Banks use these markets for several purposes, among which is the day-to-day adjustment of reserve positions. Large banks have made such adjustments in the Federal funds market for over 50 years and continue to do so in substantial volume. But commercial bank use of both the Federal funds and the RP markets is best understood in the much broader context of how banks obtain and use funds. In addition, bank operations in the Federal funds and RP markets have been heavily influenced by changes in the regulations that govern bank activities.

The traditional view of banks has been that they accept deposit liabilities from customers and use the funds to lend or invest. In the process, they make a profit by earning more in interest on loans and investments than their cost of operations, including interest they pay on deposits. This approach has undergone significant modification over the past decade at least, particularly at large banks. In place of a passive stance, banks have become active solicitors of funds in the open markets. Moreover, they have developed liabilities in addition to standard demand and savings accounts. Fifteen years ago, for example, banks developed and began to exploit the negotiable certificate of deposit (CD). More recently, Eurodollars, commercial paper issued by bank holding companies, and other instruments have been developed and used as sources of funds. Large banks set a target for the total amount of liabilities they will attempt to secure, basing that target on the total of loans and investments thought to be profitable. The overall approach, summarized here in its barest outlines, is generally known as "liability management."

The spread of the practice of liability management has had two related effects on commercial bank activity in the Federal funds market. First, instead of just engaging in relatively small trades for the purpose of making daily reserve adjustments, today banks may rely on this market to meet a desired proportion of liabilities. Thus, they at times borrow amounts that are large relative to their total assets or liabilities. Second, instead of individual banks lending as often as they borrow, some banks are continual net borrowers, while others are continual lenders. The borrowers use the market both to offset the impact on their reserve holdings of day-to-day inflows and outflows of deposits and as an ongoing source of funds to finance loans and investments. The lenders, usually smaller banks, treat Federal funds as a highly liquid interest-earning short-term asset.

RECENT DEVELOPMENTS IN THE BANKING SECTOR

Some rather dramatic events occurred in the markets for immediately available funds beginning in 1973. Monetary policy was tightened that year in response to rapid inflation and a booming economy. The tightening placed severe pressure on the banking system—which had a limited supply of funds and faced strong demand for loans, particularly from businesses. Under these circumstances, banks with a strong liability management orientation turned to any and all potential sources of funds. In early 1973, large banks began to borrow heavily in the CD market. This borrowing was facilitated by the suspension in May 1973 of interest rate ceilings on all maturities of large denomination CDs. From early 1973 through mid-1974, CD borrowing jumped by about $38 billion. Large banks sought short-term open market funds to meet loan demands much more heavily than before, taking in about $18 billion of additional Federal funds and RPs during the same period.

The United States economy went through a sharp recession between late 1973 and early 1975. Demand for credit from commercial banks as well as other lenders remained strong for a time, but progressively weakened through the later stages of the downslide and into the recovery which began in mid-1975. With loans contracting, large banks gradually reduced their lending rates and also sought liabilities with lessened intensity. Their CDs dropped sharply, falling by $28 billion between early 1975 and late 1976. Commercial bank acquisition of Federal funds and RPs, however, did not follow the pattern set in the CD market. Holdings of these funds declined by only about $4 billion in late 1974 and 1975, then grew by about $17 billion in 1976. This reflected a continuing basic growth of the markets for Federal funds and RPs.

The basic growth also was manifest in the continuing entry of banks into the markets for immediately available funds. Call reports of member banks of the Federal Reserve System show that in 1969 about 55 percent of all member banks either bought or sold Federal funds. By 1976, the proportion of member banks that was in the market had climbed to 88 percent. Most of the new entrants to the market were small banks.

Thus, even in the early 1970s many commercial banks were newcomers to the markets for immediately available funds. These markets broadened and deepened in stages which typically occurred in periods of high interest rates.

The concentration of entry in such periods is due at least partially to sizable start-up expenditures for trading in immediately available funds. Start-up costs are incurred mostly by borrowers, and mainly involve expenses of finding and establishing a trading relationship with potential suppliers of funds. The expenditures are more easily justified when interest rates (and potential earnings) are high. Once established, trading relationships tend to remain active even after interest rates fall.

Other developments also contributed to the greater acquisition of Federal funds and RPs by banks during 1975 and 1976. In 1974, the Treasury changed the way it handled its deposits at commercial banks (Tax and Loan Accounts). Such accounts had been held at banks for decades. Beginning in August 1974, however, most of these balances were transferred to the twelve Federal Reserve Banks. This reduced the volume of Government and agency securities that commercial banks were required to hold as pledged collateral against Treasury deposits. Once free from this purpose, these securities were available for use in the market for repurchase agreements.

With loan demand light in 1975, commercial banks began to accumulate large amounts of additional Government and agency securities. The process was significantly aided by the large amounts of new Government securities the Treasury sold in order to finance the sizable deficits the Federal Government was running. These securities were heavily used by large banks to acquire funds in repurchase agreements since they could be financed in this way at a cost below their interest yield. At about the same time, the effects of the recession led corporations to reduce inventories and expenditures for fixed plant and equipment. This enabled corporations to begin to rebuild their liquidity, partly through the purchase of Government securities and also by supplying funds to the RP market. The use of RPs grew rapidly as corporations increasingly came to view repurchase agreements as income-generating substitutes for demand deposits at commercial banks.

Quite separately, small banks and nonbank financial institutions were also increasing their offerings of immediately available funds. Both types of institutions experienced a decline in loan demand from corporate and other borrowers with the onset of the recession. But individuals stepped up their savings in the form of deposits with small banks and with nonbank thrift institutions. With increasing deposit inflows and declining demand for loans, these institutions looked for alternative investments and became active suppliers of immediately available funds.

THE ROLE OF GOVERNMENT SECURITIES DEALERS

Government securities dealers are the second major group of participants active in the markets for immediately available funds. Dealers are in the markets primarily to acquire funds, but they also supply funds under some circ stances. In some ways dealers act as financial intermediaries, but their operations also have speculative features. Dealers earn income in two ways: "carry income" and "trading profits." Carry income (or loss) refers to the difference between the interest yield of a dealer's portfolio and the cost of the funds which support that portfolio. Trading profits refer to the gain (or loss) a dealer earns by selling securities for more (or less) than the dealer paid for them.

Government securities dealers often hold sizable positions in United States Government and Federal agency securities. These positions are highly leveraged in that the dealers borrow a very high percentage of the cost of purchasing securities. The search for low cost money to finance his position is a central part of the operations of any successful Government securities dealer. This search led the dealer community to promote the use of the repurchase agreement shortly after World War II. RPs were offered mainly to large corporations, which found them attractive because the short maturities of the RP contracts made them much like demand deposits, with the added advantage of earning income. The use of RPs by dealers has expanded ever since, in part because more corporations and others have come to accept the repurchase agreement as a reliable short-term money market instrument. Dealers have also come to vary the size of their positions much more than before, in response to the greater variability of interest rates and securities prices in recent years.

Because of greater interest rate variability, and in an effort to broaden their activities, Government securities dealers have developed new trading techniques and expanded the use of others. One of the greatly expanded techniques enables dealers to act essentially as brokers in the RP markets. They obtain funds in exchange for securities in one transaction and simultaneously release funds in exchange for securities in a separate transaction. When the maturities of the two transactions—one a repurchase agreement and the other a reverse repurchase agreement—are identical, the two are said to be "matched." The dealer profits by obtaining funds at a cost slightly lower than the return received for the funds supplied. After arranging such a pair of transactions, a dealer is exposed to credit risk (the possibility of default), but not to market risk (changes in the value of the portfolio due to changes in market prices).

A commonly used variant of the "matched" agreement gives the dealer greater opportunity to try to take advantage of movements in interest rates. A dealer may deliberately not "match" the maturity of an RP with the maturity of a reverse RP. Usually the RP is for a period shorter than the reverse RP, establishing what is called a "tail." The "tail" refers to the difference in the maturities of the two transactions. If during this period the dealer is able to refinance the reverse RP with an RP at a lower cost, he makes a profit; if not, he loses money.

Another use of the reverse RP has been developed more recently. Reverse RPs are now used frequently to facilitate "short sales" of Government and

Federal agency securities.[4] In the past, dealers wishing to establish such positions had to borrow securities from commercial banks, usually at an interest fee of 50 basis points (½ percent). Now dealers often acquire securities elsewhere under reverse RPs and frequently through this device reduce the cost of obtaining securities for the purpose of short sales.

Use of the reverse RP to facilitate the short sale has led to the appearance of a new subsector of the repurchase agreement market, known as the "specific issue market." The subsector has developed because, for purposes of a short sale, a dealer tries to obtain the exact issue whose price he expects to fall. In a usual reverse RP, the specific securities to be exchanged are rarely discussed (though their maturity should exceed that of the reverse RP), since the parties to the agreement are primarily concerned with the cost of the money involved. The placement of securities in the specific issue market is advantageous for both principals to the transaction. Since it is apparent that the dealer is interested in a particular issue, the holder of the securities is able to negotiate with the dealer and can often get funds at a slightly lower cost than if he were to place the securities in the overall RP market.

CORPORATIONS AND THE RP MARKET

Up to this point, the analysis has concentrated on the major demanders of Federal funds and RPs. The discussion of major nonbank suppliers begins with nonfinancial corporations. They have been supplying funds through RPs against Government and agency securities for about 30 years.

The principal reason corporations hold cash and other short-term liquid assets is to bridge timing gaps between receipts and expenditures. Large quantities of funds are accumulated in anticipation of payments for dividends, corporate taxes, payrolls, and other regular expenses. In addition, corporations also accumulate short-term liquid assets in anticipation of expenditures for plant and equipment. In general, corporate liquidity is related to economic conditions and expectations about the future course of the economy and interest rates. Liquidity is often low—i.e., corporations have small amounts of liquid assets and large amounts of short-term borrowing—in periods of rapid economic expansion. Liquidity is rebuilt by reducing short-term borrowings and acquiring liquid assets during an economic slowdown or the early stages of an expansion.

Corporations have traditionally held significant amounts of their liquid assets in the form of demand deposits at commercial banks. Such balances have

---

[4]The dealer does not own the securities that it promises to deliver in a short sale. It "covers" the short by buying in the open market the particular security it has promised to deliver. Trading profits can be earned during periods of falling securities prices if the securities that were sold short become available at below-contract prices prior to the agreed-upon delivery date.

not earned interest since 1933, but this was not of great significance during the low interest rate periods of the depression and just after World War II. Interest rates began to climb in the late 1950s, and the higher rates have had a significant impact on how corporations handle their liquidity positions. They constituted an inducement to develop "cash management" techniques in some ways parallel to the "liability management" techniques adopted by banks during the same period. Cash management consists of a variety of procedures designed to achieve four goals: to speed up the receipt of payments due; to slow down the disbursement of payments owed; to keep a corporation's demand deposits to a minimum because they earn no interest; and to earn the maximum return on liquid asset holdings.

Repurchase agreements are particularly useful as tools for cash management. They generate income for the supplier of funds and are generally regarded as secure. Their key advantage is flexibility, primarily because they can be arranged for periods as short as one day. Few if any other income-generating assets have this feature. Regulations prevent banks from issuing CDs with maturities of less than 30 days; commercial paper and bankers' acceptances can be obtained for shorter periods, but as a practical matter not for one day. None of these instruments are viewed as being quite as secure as repurchase agreements, where there is a margin between the amount of funds supplied and the value of the securities. Corporations can buy Government securities or other financial assets and hold them for short periods, but the transaction costs can be relatively high and the possibility of capital loss reduces the attractiveness of such alternatives. The overnight feature of RPs means that corporations treat them as if they are income-earning demand deposits.

Corporations make heavy use of a particular form of RP known as the "continuing contract." Under such a contract, a corporation will agree to provide a specific volume of funds to a bank or a dealer for a certain period of time. However, during the life of the contract the repurchase agreement is treated almost as if it were reestablished each day. That is, earnings are calculated daily often related to the prevailing overnight RP rate. Either party has the right to withdraw at any time, although this right is seldom used. The principal advantage of the continuing contract over the daily renewals of an RP is that securities and funds are exchanged only at the beginning and at the end of the contract. The continuing contract therefore significantly reduces transactions costs, compared with daily RPs. An additional feature of the continuing contract RP is the seller's right of substitution, under which securities of equal value may be used to replace those originally involved in the RP. This option does not appear in all continuing contracts but, where it does appear, it is frequently exercised.

Another RP arrangement rather similar to the continuing contract specifies neither a definite period nor a fixed amount. Arrangements are made by banks chiefly for their corporate customers. The corporation concentrates all its demand balances in a single account at that bank daily. Before the bank closes its books each day, the corporation's balance in this account is determined, and any excess over a specified minimum is automatically converted into an RP. The following morning the funds are moved from the RP back to the corporation's demand balance for use during the day. Such automatic arrangements for the conversion of demand deposits to RPs are often included in packages of services offered by banks to their corporate customers. Among the services in such packages are lines of credit, payroll administration, and the use of safekeeping facilities. Payment for such service packages is usually not made on the basis of a stated fee. Instead, average or minimum demand deposit balances—called compensating balances—are usually required.

RPs also can be used to provide liquidity for somewhat longer periods, for example, to allow the accumulation of funds for a tax or dividend payment. This option is particularly attractive to corporations if the income that can be earned on a longer RP exceeds that available on an overnight RP. One or several RPs can be written, as liquidity is accumulated over the period prior to a payment date, with the contracts maturing on the day disbursements must be made. The RP has less commanding advantages over other money market assets for longer periods, however. Commercial paper can frequently be tailored to mature on a specific day, and Treasury bills that mature very close to the desired date can often be purchased. RPs are nevertheless used very frequently for such purposes, primarily because they can be arranged easily and quickly once a corporation has established a routine trading relationship with market participants.

State and local government units have entered the RP market only in recent years but have quickly become major suppliers of funds. The RP is particularly well suited to their needs. These governments usually are required by law to hold their assets in the most secure form, generally in bank deposits or Government and Federal agency securities. The RP provides a way of meeting these requirements while earning income on short-term investments.

Tax receipts of state and local governments never match exactly the timing pattern of their expenditures, thereby creating the need for them either to borrow or to invest for short periods at various times of the year. Until recently their major investment alternative to deposits has been Treasury bills. As the advantages of the RP have become more widely recognized, these governments have switched more of their liquid investments into RPs.

THE ROLE OF NONBANK FINANCIAL INSTITUTIONS

Several types of nonbank financial institutions are active in the markets for immediately available funds. These include mutual savings banks, savings and loan associations, branches and agencies of foreign banks that operate on United States soil, and Edge Act corporations. (The latter are affiliates of United States commercial banks empowered to engage in international or foreign banking in the United States or abroad.) All of these institutions are active primarily in the market for Federal funds, and generally do not enter into repurchase agreements in volume. They generally lend Federal funds to commercial banks, although under certain circumstances agencies and branches of foreign banks will borrow from banks or other nonbank lenders.

The appearance of all these institutions in the Federal funds market has occurred relatively recently. Their entry has dramatically changed the function of the Federal funds market, allowing the banking system to draw funds from a wide array of institutions, instead of just reallocating reserves. The expanded borrowing ability of banks serves to integrate more closely the United States financial structure, and to help break down the barriers which have traditionally existed among various types of financial institutions.

The agencies and branches of foreign banks have also become active participants in the Federal funds market. These institutions deal with or represent foreign commercial banks, which trade in both the money markets of their home countries and the Euro-currency markets. Through the Federal funds market, the agencies and branches of foreign banks provide a link between the various markets abroad and the United States commercial banking system.

The participation of these institutions in United States financial markets mirrors the activities of United States commercial banks overseas. In the last three decades, overseas branch networks of United States banks have grown significantly in both the scale and range of their operations, and these networks have provided United States banks with easy access to foreign and international financial markets. Entry into the Federal funds market by agencies and branches of foreign banks, therefore, has contributed to the continuing integration of credit markets and banking in the United States and abroad.

THE ROLE OF THE FEDERAL RESERVE

The Federal Reserve is important to the markets for Federal funds and RPs for two quite different reasons. One is that Federal Reserve regulations play a very important role in the markets by limiting the type and terms of transactions member banks may undertake. A second is that actions taken by the Federal Reserve in the normal conduct of monetary policy have a major influence on the levels of interest rates in general and on the Federal funds rate in particular. Federal Reserve monetary policy is oriented toward achieving steady and sustained growth of the economy, along with reasonably stable prices. Such a sound economy depends on a multiplicity of factors, one of which is the capacity of the commercial banking system to extend loans and create deposits. These capacities, in turn, are strongly influenced by the interest rate on Federal funds and the supply of reserves to member banks.

The Federal Reserve controls the supply of reserves through open market operations, mainly via outright purchases and sales of Government and Federal agency securities. An outright purchase of securities provides reserves permanently, while a sale permanently reduces the total supply of reserves. But the Federal Reserve also needs to provide and absorb reserves for short periods, mainly to accommodate the seasonal needs of banks for reserves and to offset the effects on reserves of day-to-day changes in currency in circulation, in the Treasury's balance at Federal Reserve Banks, and in Federal Reserve float. Reserves can be supplied temporarily by use of repurchase agreements, and absorbed temporarily through "matched sale-purchase transactions," which most market participants call reverse RPs.

Federal Reserve use of RPs and matched sale-purchase transactions for temporary reserve adjustment has grown sharply in the past few years, but for generally different reasons than those which explain the increase in the use of RPs by banks and others. The increase has arisen in large part from a change in Treasury procedures for handling its cash balances. Prior to August 1974, the Treasury received payments into accounts at commercial banks, and generally moved funds into its balance at the Federal Reserve only as funds were needed to make payments on behalf of the Federal Government. Under this scheme, Treasury balances in commercial banks fluctuated widely, but the Treasury balance at the Federal Reserve was reasonably stable. In August 1974, the Treasury began to move its balances more quickly into its accounts at the Federal Reserve Banks, which climbed by several billion dollars over a period of several months. This policy has led to much wider fluctuation in these accounts. This in turn has created greater variability in the supply of reserves available to the banking system which the Federal Reserve usually offsets by temporary adjustments to reserves through RPs or matched sale-purchase transactions.

SOME MAJOR IMPLICATIONS

The Federal funds and RP markets have grown dramatically in the past few years. This growth is due in part to changes in the regulations which govern the operations of commercial banks, but is more basically due to the changing practices and behavior of all participants in these markets. The circumstances influencing each group of market participants have differed in detail, but for all, the quite high interest rates since the mid-1960s have provided the major motivation.

The growth in the Federal funds and RP markets has several implications. Most importantly, the markets have expanded to include a broader range of domestic and international financial institutions and corporations. They use the markets as a link in a worldwide network that transfers interest-sensitive dollar balances to wherever they are in great demand. To be sure, mechanisms to move funds to high-demand uses have existed for some time, but the Federal funds and RP markets help make the task easier and more efficient by bringing interest-sensitive funds into a central marketplace from a broader arena. For example, most individuals who hold deposits at thrift institutions do not move their funds quickly from one investment to another in response to small interest rate changes. But thrift institutions can lend in the Federal funds market, in effect allowing the small deposits of individuals to be combined and placed directly in the national markets for short-term credit. Similar considerations apply with respect to international credit flows.

These developments have some implications for the conduct of Federal Reserve monetary policy. Policy actions significantly influence the Federal funds and RP markets, which commercial banks now use as sources of funds more extensively than ever before. Hence any change in the availability of funds in these markets probably has a more direct impact than before on the cost to banks of making loans and on the rates they charge. Moreover, many more small banks and nonbank financial institutions have become quite active in the markets. Through this mechanism, Federal Reserve monetary policy is felt more quickly and directly by a broader range of the financial institutions, including those that provide a major portion of the total credit available in the United States economy.

United States and international financial markets have also become more closely integrated in recent years. There are multiple linkages among the various markets, but they center on the activities in this country and abroad of multinational corporations and of United States and foreign commercial banks. These institutions borrow and lend sizable amounts in both the United States and international markets, and are sensitive to the margins between borrowing and lending rates in different countries. For example, if short-term interest rates in the United States were higher than abroad, the differential would quickly draw funds from other uses abroad and channel liquidity into the United States financial markets. These flows would tend to reduce the differential between interest rates abroad and in this country.

But the flows of credit induced by such interest rate differentials may not be in keeping with Federal Reserve policy objectives at the time. For example, a restrictive monetary policy works to reduce spending by individuals and businesses, partly because it makes borrowing more expensive and difficult to obtain. The effects of such policies on the domestic economy could be dampened if large corporations and financial institutions can readily obtain credit elsewhere.

While high interest rates and inflation have encouraged growth of the Federal funds and RP markets, the evolution of technology, particularly the use of computer facilities, has also played an important part. The new and changing technology speeds the transfer of funds, reduces the cost of record keeping, and increases the availability of information concerning investment opportunities. It seems certain that technological change will continue at a rapid rate, thereby reducing further the costs of arranging and executing financial transactions and reinforcing the already strong trend toward aggressive financial management.

The rapid growth of the markets for Federal funds and RPs in recent years can be viewed as part of a pervasive trend in all United States financial markets toward more aggressive portfolio management by holders of financial assets. This trend will clearly continue to be a strong influence on the markets. Participants will no doubt devise new trading techniques, refine existing ones, and attract others into the marketplace. But the Federal funds and RP markets are only two of many markets for short-term financial claims, and their growth relative to others will be heavily influenced by the regulatory and legal framework in which they operate.

TREASURY BILLS[*]

Timothy Q. Cook and
Jimmie R. Monhollon

3

A Treasury bill is a short-term obligation of the United States Government. Treasury bills are perhaps the single most important type of money market instrument. They are a widely held liquid investment and an important tool in Federal debt management and in the execution of monetary policy. Before World War II the amount of Treasury bills outstanding rarely exceeded $2.5 billion. By 1945, however, the total had risen to over $17 billion, and by December 1980 the outstanding volume was $216.1 billion.

TREASURY BILL OFFERINGS

The Treasury sells bills at a discount through competitive biddings; the return to the investor is the difference between the purchase price of the bill and its face or par value. Treasury bills are currently sold in minimum amounts of $20,000 and multiples of $5,000 above the minimum, although at times they have been issued in smaller denominations. Treasury bills are issued only in book-entry form. Under this arrangement ownership is recorded in a book-entry account established at the Treasury and investors receive only a receipt as evidence of purchase.

Regularly scheduled offerings of 91- and 182-day bills are currently made on a weekly basis and regularly scheduled offerings of 52-week bills are made on a monthly basis. These regularly scheduled offerings are to refinance ma-

*Reprinted, with minor editorial revisions, from *Instruments of the Money Market*, 5th edition, edited by Timothy Q. Cook and Bruce J. Summers, 1981, with permission of the Federal Reserve Bank of Richmond.

turing issues and, if necessary, to help finance current Federal deficits. The Treasury also sells bills on an irregular basis to smooth out the uneven flow of revenues from corporate and individual tax receipts.

Regularly Scheduled Issues

Treasury bills were first offered in their modern form in December 1929. From then until 1934, 30-, 60-, and 90-day maturities were offered. Between February 1934 and October 1937, the Treasury experimented with maturities of 182 days to 273 days in order to reduce the frequency with which bills had to be rolled over. In 1937, largely at the insistence of commercial banks, the Treasury reverted to exclusive issue of 91-day bills. Then in December 1958 these were supplemented with six-month bills in the regular weekly auctions.

In 1959 the Treasury began to auction one-year bills on a quarterly basis. The quarterly auction of one-year bills was replaced by a monthly auction in August 1963. The Treasury added a nine-month maturity to the monthly auction in September 1966 but the sale of this maturity was discontinued in late 1972. Since then, the only regular bill cycles have been for maturities of 91 days, 6 months, and a year. The Treasury has increased the size of its weekly and monthly bill auctions as new money is needed to meet Federal borrowing requirements. In 1980 monthly sales of 52-week bills were for $4.0 billion, while the weekly auctions of 13- and 26-week bills ranged from $6.5 to $8.6 billion.

Irregularly Scheduled Issues

Prior to the mid-1970s the Treasury sold bills on an irregular basis through the use of tax anticipation bills.[1] Introduced in October 1951, tax anticipation bills were designed specifically to help smooth out the Treasury's uneven flow of tax receipts while providing corporations with an investment vehicle for funds accumulated for tax payments. These bills were accepted at par on the tax date in payment for taxes due—hence the name, tax anticipation bills. They actually matured a week later, usually on the 22nd of the month. Tax anticipation bills did not have to be used in lieu of tax payments, and some investors chose to hold them to maturity.

Tax anticipation bills were sold in periods of low Treasury revenues and scheduled to mature in periods of heavy tax receipts. Since two of the five major tax payment dates fall in the April-June quarter of the year, that quarter generally registers a budget surplus that either completely or partially offsets budget deficits in the other three quarters. Because of this pattern the great majority of the $159.4 billion of tax anticipation bills issued from 1951 through 1974 were sold in the period from July through March and were scheduled to

---

[1]Tax anticipation bills are described in more detail in [5].

mature in March, April, and June. Of the 83 tax bill auctions carried out through 1974, 19 were scheduled to mature in March, 17 in April, and 36 in June; only 9 were scheduled to mature in September and 2 in December.

No tax anticipation bills have been issued since 1974. In their place the Treasury has raised money on an irregular basis through the sale of *cash management bills*, which are usually "reopenings" or sales of additional amounts of outstanding maturities of Treasury bills. Cash management bills usually have maturities that fall after one of the five major tax dates and, like tax anticipation bills, are designed to help finance the Treasury's requirements until tax payments are received. Thirty-eight issues of cash management bills were sold in the 1975-1980 period. The maturities of these 38 issues ranged from 2 to 167 days and averaged 51 days. Annual sales of cash management bills varied from $4 billion in 1976 to $45 billion in 1980. Very short-term cash management bills are sometimes referred to as "short-dated" bills.

Auctioning New Bills

New offerings of three- and six-month bills are made each week by the Treasury. Ordinarily, an offering is announced on Tuesday and the amount of the offering is set at that time. The auction is usually conducted on the following Monday, with delivery and payment on the following Thursday.

Bids, or tenders, in the weekly auctions must be presented at Federal Reserve Banks or their branches, which act as agents for the Treasury, by 1:30 P.M., New York time, on the day of the auction. Bids may be made on a competitive or noncompetitive basis. In making a competitive bid the investor states the quantity of bills desired and the price. A subscriber may enter more than one bid indicating the various quantities willing to be taken at different prices. Competitive bids, which are usually made by large investors who are in close contact with the market, comprise the largest portion of subscriptions on a dollar basis. In making a noncompetitive bid the investor indicates the quantity of bills desired and agrees to pay the average price of accepted competitive bids. Individuals and other small investors usually enter noncompetitive bids, which are awarded in full up to $500,000 on both the 91-day and the 182-day bills. By bidding noncompetitively, small investors avoid the risks inherent in competitive bidding. In the first place, they do not risk losing their chance to buy as a result of bidding too low. Nor do they run the risk of bidding too high and paying a price near the top. The dollar amount of noncompetitive awards as a percent of total awards is generally quite small, usually less than 15 percent of the total auction amount, although it typically rises substantially in periods of high interest rates.

Subscription books at the various Federal Reserve Banks and branches close promptly at 1:30 P.M., after which the bids are tabulated and submitted to the Treasury for allocation. Allocations are first made for foreign official institutions and the Federal Reserve to roll over maturing issues. Then the

Treasury allocates whatever part of the total offering is needed to make all noncompetitive awards. The remainder is then allocated to those competitive bidders submitting the highest offers, ranging downward from the highest bid until the total amount offered is allocated. The "stop-out price" is the lowest price, or highest yield, at which bills are awarded. Usually only a portion of the total bids made at this price is accepted. The average issuing price, which is usually closer to the lowest accepted price than to the highest is then computed on the basis of the competitive bids accepted.

In the weekly auction of February 2, 1981, for example, accepted bids for the three-month bills ranged from a high of $96.319 per $100 of face amount (equivalent to an annual discount rate of 14.562 percent) to a stop-out price of $96.279 (14.729 percent). A total of $4.3 billion of bids was accepted, $859 million of which was for noncompetitive tenders accepted at the average issuing price of $96.295 (14.657 percent). The relatively high proportion (20 percent) of bills purchased on a noncompetitive basis was not unusual, given the high level of interest rates prevailing at the time of the auction.

In addition to the regular weekly auctions, 52-week bills are auctioned every fourth Thursday for issue the following Thursday and special auctions are held for cash management bills. The procedure for these auctions is similar to the weekly auctions.

Advantages of Auctions

Treasury bills are marketed by the Treasury solely through the auction technique. Treasury notes and bonds, however, can be sold either through auctions or through subscriptions. Under the subscription method the Treasury sets both the coupon and price (typically par) of a new issue, thereby determining the issue's yield prior to sale. Subscriptions may be allotted completely or may be allotted in part if aggregate subscriptions are greater than the amount of notes or bonds the Treasury wishes to sell.

In general, the auction method is simpler and less time-consuming than the subscription method. In auctions the market establishes a yield, making it unnecessary for the Treasury to second-guess market conditions, and thereby eliminating the problems associated with over-subscriptions or under-subscriptions. The Treasury merely chooses the amount of the offering and the market does the rest. For these reasons the Treasury in recent years has used the auction method exclusively not only for bills but also for notes and bonds. The last time the subscription method was used was in the Treasury's quarterly refunding operation of August 1976.

The auction technique is especially suited to the market for Treasury bills, which is enormous and can absorb billions of dollars of new bills with only minimal impact on yields. Bill auctions also provide the Treasury with a very flexible debt financing tool, since relatively small increases or decreases in the

Treasury debt can be engineered simply by changing the supply of bills in the weekly auction.

INVESTMENT CHARACTERISTICS

There are four investment characteristics of Treasury bills that distinguish them from other money market securities and that consequently influence investor decisions to purchase bills. These characteristics of bills include (1) lack of default risk, (2) liquidity, (3) favorable tax status, and (4) a low minimum denomination.

Lack of Default Risk

Because Treasury bills are an obligation of the U. S. Treasury, they are considered to be free of default risk. In contrast, even the highest grade of other money market instruments, such as commercial paper or CDs, is perceived to have some degree of default risk. Concern over default risk typically increases in times of weak economic conditions. In such periods the risk-free feature of bills increases their attractiveness to some investors.

The absence of default risk for Treasury bills not only directly but also indirectly affects the demand for bills because various laws and regulations have given Treasury bills a special role in the portfolio of some investors, especially commercial banks and state and local governments.[2] Treasury bills serve a number of purposes for commercial banks that often cannot be served by private money market instruments such as commercial paper or bankers' acceptances. For example, banks use bills to make repurchase agreements with businesses and state and local governments and banks use bills to satisfy pledging requirements on state, local and Federal government deposits. Many state and local governments invest in bills to satisfy requirements that limit the types of financial assets they can hold. Bills are always a permissible investment for state and local governments, while many other types of money market instruments frequently are not.

Liquidity

A second characteristic of bills is their high degree of liquidity. Liquidity refers to assets that may be converted to cash quickly with low transactions costs and a low degree of price risk resulting from changes in the levels of interest rates. Treasury bills have this characteristic because they are a short-term and homogeneous instrument traded in a highly organized, efficient and competitive market.

[2]Those regulations are described in more detail in [1].

Of course if an investor desires cash, the choice of whether to sell a bill or raise money through an alternative means will depend heavily on the length of time the funds are expected to be needed. The turnaround costs involved in selling bills one day and buying them back at a later date may make such sales a relatively unattractive way to cover very short-term cash need. These turnaround costs include incidental transaction costs such as phone calls and paper work and costs which arise due to the spread between bid and asked prices. Government securities dealers buy bills at a price (the bid price) slightly lower than the price at which they sell (the asked price). Thus, if interest rates do not change, an investor seeking to raise funds for only one day would sell bills at a given price and buy them back the following day at a slightly higher price. In 1980 the typical bid-asked spread on actively traded Treasury bills, such as the current three- and six-month bills, was 4 to 8 basis points. Four basis points is equivalent to about $0.01 on each $100 par value of three-month bills. Thus, for example, a bank would lose one cent per $100 by selling bills to cover a one-day reserve need. An alternative means of covering the one-day reserve need, such as borrowing Federal funds or doing repurchase agreements against the bills, would be far less costly.

Minimum Denomination

A third important investment characteristic of Treasury bills is the low minimum denomination compared to the minimum denomination of other money market instruments. Prior to 1970, the minimum denomination of bills was $1,000. In early 1970 the minimum denomination of bills was raised from $1,000 to $10,000. The stated purposes of this change were to discourage noncompetitive bids by small investors in order to retain the Treasury bill as an instrument for attracting large quantities of funds primarily from institutional investors, to reduce the costs of processing many small subscriptions yielding only a small volume of funds, and to discourage the exodus of funds from financial intermediaries and the mortgage market. As will be shown below, the increase in the minimum denomination of bills was not very successful as a deterrent to increased purchases of bills by small investors in periods of high interest rates.

Even at $10,000 the minimum denomination of Treasury bills is far below the minimum denomination required to purchase all other short-term securities, with the exception of some Federal agency securities. Typically, it takes at least $100,000 to purchase other money market instruments such as CDs or commercial paper. Consequently, for many small investors, bills have been the only security available for purchase directly in the money market.

Taxes

Unlike other money market instruments, the income earned on Treasury bills is exempt from state and local income taxes. Given a state income tax rate

(t), the relationship between, say, the commercial paper rate (or some other discount-type rate) and the bill rate that leaves an investor indifferent between the two other considerations aside[3], is given by

$$R_{cp}(1 - t) = R_{tb}.$$

From this formula it can be seen that the advantage of the tax-exempt feature for a particular investor depends on (1) the investor's state and local tax rate and (2) the current level of interest rates. For a given before-tax yield differential between bill rates and commercial paper rates, the higher the rate of state and local taxes, the more attractive bills become. Similarly, the higher the level of market interest rates, the more attractive bills become. For example, the interest rate differential at which an investor subject to a marginal state income tax rate of 6 percent is indifferent between bills and commercial paper rises from 32 basis points when the Treasury bill rate is 5 percent to 64 basis points when the Treasury bill rate is 10 percent.

This investment characteristic of bills is relevant only to those investors that pay state and local income taxes. Some investors, such as state and local governments, are not subject to state income taxes. Other investors, such as commercial banks in most states, pay a "franchise" or "excise" tax that in fact requires them to pay state taxes on interest income from Treasury bills.

INVESTORS

While comprehensive data on Treasury bill holdings does not exist, the Federal Reserve System's "Flow of Funds Accounts" uses available information to construct estimates of the amounts of marketable U. S. debt with a maturity of one year or less held by various investors.[4] These estimates are shown in Table 3-1 for the 1960 to 1980 period. The table shows that as of 1980, the largest investors in bills were individuals, commercial banks, foreigners, and the Federal Reserve.[5]

---

[3]Since the yields on Treasury bills, commercial paper, bankers' acceptances, and some Federal agency issues are quoted on a discounted basis using a 360-day year, the yields are on the same basis and thus may be directly compared. However, when analyzing Treasury bill yields relative to interest-bearing instruments such as CDs, the yields must be converted to an equivalent yield basis. Since the discounting approach and the use of a 360-day year results in an understatement of the actual yield, a procedure is presented later in this article to find the "true" yield. This yield may then be compared with the true yield on interest-bearing CDs, which is obtained by multiplying the quoted CD rate by 365/360. In 1981, some banks began issuing discounted CDs. As a result, the quoted yields on CDs may have to be converted to their true yield in order to be compared.

[4]The short-term marketable debt series in the Flow of Funds Accounts does not correspond exactly to Treasury bills because the series includes other marketable debt with a remaining maturity of less than one year. However, movement in the series is dominated by Treasury bills.

[5]The term "individuals" is used in the text to refer to the "households" sector of the Flow of Funds. The households sector also includes personal trusts and nonprofit organizations.

Table 3-1   Holdings of short-term marketable U.S. securities
(end-of-year Flow of Funds estimates in billions)

	Foreigners		Federal Reserve		Households		Commercial banks		State and local governments		Private nonbank financial institutions		Non-financial corporate business	
	$	%	$	%	$	%	$	%	$	%	$	%	$	%
1960	7.7	8.8	19.2	22.1	10.6	12.1	22.9	26.3	7.6	8.8	5.8	6.6	13.3	15.2
1961	7.1	7.2	18.3	18.7	10.8	11.0	33.5	34.3	8.0	8.2	7.6	7.8	12.5	12.8
1962	9.2	9.4	20.7	21.1	12.6	12.8	27.8	28.3	9.0	9.1	8.4	8.5	10.7	10.8
1963	8.7	8.7	25.6	25.7	16.3	16.4	24.2	24.3	9.2	9.2	7.2	7.2	8.5	8.5
1964	8.5	8.1	28.2	27.0	15.8	15.1	28.3	27.1	8.4	8.0	7.7	7.4	7.5	7.2
1965	7.6	7.1	31.9	29.6	18.0	16.8	26.2	24.4	10.5	9.7	7.3	6.8	6.0	5.6
1966	6.7	6.2	36.5	33.5	19.3	17.7	21.5	20.0	11.5	10.6	8.5	7.8	4.7	4.3
1967	7.6	6.5	39.2	33.6	18.9	16.2	27.0	23.2	12.2	10.5	8.6	7.4	3.1	2.6
1968	5.9	5.0	32.6	27.8	25.7	21.9	28.6	24.4	11.5	9.8	10.0	8.5	3.0	2.5
1969	3.7	2.9	37.6	29.6	34.7	27.3	24.3	19.1	14.1	11.1	9.0	7.1	3.8	3.0
1970	11.5	8.8	38.5	29.3	21.0	16.0	30.1	22.9	14.8	11.3	10.8	8.2	4.7	3.6
1971	25.4	19.8	39.5	30.8	8.5	6.6	25.2	19.6	13.5	10.5	7.8	6.1	8.4	6.6
1972	26.7	18.7	41.2	28.8	9.7	6.8	30.8	21.6	18.1	12.7	10.4	7.3	5.8	4.0
1973	21.0	13.8	50.6	33.3	25.7	16.9	28.3	18.6	16.2	10.6	9.7	6.3	0.9	0.6
1974	28.6	17.7	50.5	31.2	36.2	22.3	26.9	16.6	9.0	5.5	10.1	6.2	0.6	0.4
1975	35.3	16.3	52.4	24.3	41.0	19.0	48.8	22.6	12.7	5.9	15.9	7.3	10.0	4.6
1976	38.6	16.2	58.6	24.6	31.6	13.3	56.5	23.8	16.7	7.0	23.4	9.9	12.4	5.2
1977	46.7	18.0	61.7	23.8	48.4	18.7	52.0	20.0	19.6	7.6	24.3	9.4	6.7	2.6
1978	60.6	22.3	62.1	22.8	59.1	21.7	41.7	15.3	24.4	9.0	23.7	8.7	0.5	0.2
1979	38.5	13.6	55.8	19.7	64.6	22.8	56.6	20.0	24.3	8.5	29.8	10.5	13.8	4.9

Individuals

Individuals, especially since the mid-1960s, have become substantial investors in Treasury bills. Prior to developments in the late 1970s, the relatively
small minimum denomination of bills made them the only feasible money
market investment for many individual investors. The volume of investment
by individuals has varied greatly depending on the level of bill rates relative
to the rates paid on time and savings deposits at depository institutions. Until
1978 all deposit rates at Federally insured institutions were subject to fixed
ceilings that did not vary with market interest rates. Consequently, when
market rates rose above the deposit rates ceilings, many individuals reacted
by shifting funds from depository institutions into the bill market. As a result,
investment by individuals in the bill market has risen sharply in periods of
high interest rates, such as 1969, 1973, and 1974.

Two developments in the late 1970s greatly expanded the short-term investment options available to small investors. First, Regulation Q of the Federal
Reserve Act was altered to allow depository institutions to offer six-month

"money market certificates" bearing rates tied to the six-month Treasury bill rate prevailing at the time of purchase. Second, the proliferation of money market mutual funds offered investors indirect access to current money market yields. Money market funds typically require a minimum investment of only $1,000 to $5,000.

By offering small investors two additional means of earning a market yield, the availability of money market certificates and money market funds would be expected to decrease the demand for bills by individuals in high interest rate periods relative to what it would have been without these alternatives. The Flow of Funds estimates indicate that when short-term rates rose to record levels in the late 1970s, individuals again purchased very large amounts of bills. However, as a percentage of total bills outstanding, individual holdings were no greater in 1979 and 1980 than in 1974 when Treasury bill rates peaked at 9 percent. Given the extremely high level of bill rates in the 1979-1980 period, it is likely that the individual purchases of bills in that period would have been far greater were money market certificates and money market funds unavailable as investment alternatives.

Commercial Banks

The commercial banking system's holdings of total bills outstanding has trended down somewhat over the last 20 years. The Treasury bill holdings of commercial banks varies cyclically, but in the opposite direction of the holdings of individuals. In periods of strong economic activity and rising interest rates, bank investment in bills generally declines, while in periods of slack economic activity banks typically add substantially to their bill holdings.

This pattern of bank investment in bills has generally been attributed to the role of bills as "secondary reserves" for banks. According to this view, banks purchase bills to convert excess reserves into earnings assets quickly with little loss of liquidity and sell bills to acquire additional funds promptly for lending or meeting legal reserve requirements. Consequently, when loan demand is slack, banks turn to Treasury bills as a temporary investment outlet. Conversely, when loan demand is increasing, banks reduce their bill holdings in order to expand loans. Of course, banks finance increases in business loans not only through the sale of securities but also through the issue of liabilities such as CDs. Also, as discussed above, banks hold Treasury bills for other reasons in addition to their use as a buffer source of funds to finance loan expansion.

Foreign Investors

Foreign investors held about $50 billion of short-term marketable U. S. securities at the end of 1980. Bill holdings of foreigners grew sharply in the 1970s primarily due to substantial acquisitions by oil-exporting countries and foreign central bank investment of dollars obtained in exchange rate operations.

Federal Reserve System and Others

The Federal Reserve System's holdings of short-term marketable U. S. debt has generally ranged from 20 to 30 percent of the total outstanding over the last 20 years. Other investors in Treasury bills are state and local governments, nonbank financial institutions, and nonfinancial corporations. The relative holdings of both state and local governments and corporations fell in the latter half of the 1970s compared to earlier years. The decline in the share of state and local governments probably reflects the increased investment flexibility available to many of these governments.

YIELDS

Treasury bill yields are generally quoted on a discount basis using a 360-day year. Under this procedure the stated rate of return on a bill of a given maturity is calculated by dividing the discount by par and expressing this percentage at an annual rate, using a 360-day year. For example, in the weekly auction of February 2, 1981 discussed above, a price of $96.295 per $100 of face amount for a 91-day bill produced an annual rate of return on a discount basis of

$$\frac{100-96.295}{100} \times \frac{360}{91} = 14.657\%.$$

The True Yield

To calculate the true yield of a Treasury bill for comparison with other yields, the discount must be divided by the *price* and a 365-day year used. In the above example the true yield is

$$\frac{100-96.295}{96.295} \times \frac{365}{91} = 15.432\%.$$

As this example demonstrates, the yield calculated on a discount basis can seriously understate the true yield of a Treasury bill. The difference between the true yield of a bill and the discount yield is greater the longer the maturity of the bill and the higher the level of interest rates.

Yield Spreads

Most money market rates move together closely over time. Perhaps more than any other money market rate, however, the rate on Treasury bills has at times diverged substantially from other short-term rates. Figure 3-1 shows the differential between the three-month prime CD rate and the three-month Treasury bill rates. The chart shows that this differential varies greatly over

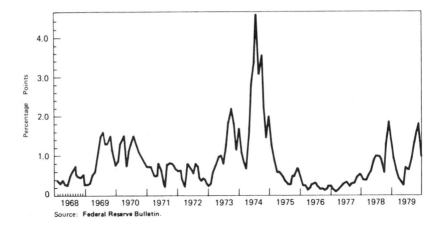

Figure 3-1 The spread between the three-month CD and Treasury bill rates

time, typically rising in high interest rate periods and falling to low levels in low interest rate periods. The spread widened to over 400 basis points in the middle of 1974. Not only does the spread vary over years but it also has a tendency to move on a seasonal basis, reaching its widest levels in the middle of the calendar year and its narrowest in February.[6]

In attempting to understand the highly variable spread between bill rates and other money market rates, it is useful to focus on the investment characteristic of bills discussed above to investigate if the effects of these cha·acteristics on short-term yield spreads might change over time. Three charac eristics that may provide insight into the behavior of the spread are default risk, taxes, and minimum denomination.

The most common explanation of the movement in the spreads between Treasury bill and other money market rates focuses on default risk. According to this explanation, the spreads between other short-term rates and bill rates vary over time due to a cyclical risk premium pushing up the yields on private sector money market instruments relative to the yields on Treasury bills in periods of weak economic activity. In fact, throughout the money and capital markets yields spreads between debt instruments of different investment quality do tend to widen in periods of economic weakness. However, yields spreads that isolate the influence of cyclical risk premiums generally do not rise much until the onset of a recession and typically peak near the end of a recession. In contrast, the spreads between private sector money market rates and bill rates have risen well before the beginning of recessions and have generally

[6]This is analyzed in [2].

fallen sharply prior to the end of recessions. This strongly suggests that cyclically varying risk premiums do not provide a complete explanation of the movement in the spreads between private money market and Treasury bill rates.

Another possible factor influencing the spread between the bill rate and other short-term rates is the exemption of Treasury bills from state and local income tax. As shown above, the higher the level of interest rates the wider the spread between bill rates and other short-term rates that is necessary to leave an investor with a given state income tax rate indifferent between bills and other money market instruments. Consequently, as interest rates rise, this tax feature of bills will induce some investors to increase their purchases of bills, thereby putting pressure on the spread between bill rates and other rates to widen.

Of course this is not to say that the tax-exempt feature of bills will necessarily cause the spread to rise with the level of interest rates. As noted above, many investors in the bill market are not subject to state and local income taxes. A widening spread between bill and CD rates could induce these investors to sell bills and buy CDs. In any case, even if investors subject to state income taxes dominated the bill market, this aspect of bills could only explain a relatively small part of the movement in the spread observed in such periods as 1969, 1973, and 1974, when the spread reached such high levels.

A third explanation for the spread focuses on the minimum denomination of bills and the behavior of individual investors in periods of disintermediation. This explanation is that massive purchases of Treasury bills by individuals that occur in periods of disintermediation have driven bill rates down relative to the rates on other money market instruments. According to this view, the inability of most individuals to meet the minimum purchase requirements necessary to acquire private-sector money market instruments prevented them from reducing the differential between bill rates and other money market rates by switching their purchases from bills to these other instruments.[7]

To the extent that this third explanation is a valid one, the spreads between bill rates and CD rates should be smaller, at a given level of interest rates, than in the past. This is because the availability of money market funds and other short-term investment polling arrangements have effectively broken down the minimum investment barriers that have prevented many individuals from acquiring money market instruments other than Treasury bills.

RELATION TO MONETARY POLICY

Treasury bills perform an important role in the implementation of monetary policy. Under its current operating procedures the Federal Reserve System manipulates the level of commercial bank reserves in order to achieve desired

---

[7]This explanation is given in more detail in [1]

growth rates of the money supply. The Federal Reserve influences the reserve positions of commercial banks primarily through the purchase and sale of bills, either outright in the bill cash market or on a temporary basis in the market for repurchase agreements (RPs). Most Federal Reserve operations are RPs, which are the purchase or sale of bills under an agreement to reverse the transaction one or more days later. Essentially, these RPs are loans collateralized by Treasury bills. RPs have a temporary effect on the supply of bank reserves and are typically used to offset temporary fluctuations in reserves arising from other sources, such as changes in Treasury deposits at the Federal Reserve Banks.

REFERENCES

1. Cook, Timothy Q. "Determinants of the Spread Between Treasury Bill and Private Sector Money Market Rates," *Journal of Economics and Business*, 33 (Spring, 1981): 177–187.
2. Lawler, T. A. "Seasonal Movements in Short-Term Yield Spreads," *Economic Review*, Federal Reserve Bank of Richmond, 64 (July/August 1978): 10-17.
3. McCurdy, Christopher J. "The Dealer Market for United States Government Securities," *Quarterly Review*, Federal Reserve Bank of New York, 2 (Winter 1977-78): 35-47.
4. Monhollon, Jimmie R. "Treasury Bills," *Instruments of the Money Market*, 4th ed. Federal Reserve Bank of Richmond, 1977.
5. Nelson, Jane F. "Tax Anticipation Bills," *Instruments of the Money Market*, 4th ed. Federal Reserve Bank of Richmond, 1977.
6. Tucker, James F. "Buying Treasury Securities at Federal Reserve Banks," Federal Reserve Bank of Richmond, 1980.

FEDERALLY SPONSORED CREDIT AGENCY SECURITIES*

Donna Howell

4

The Federally sponsored credit agencies have been one of the fastest growing components of the nation's financial system.[1] As a result, the stock of Federally sponsored agency securities grew from $13.8 billion in 1965 to $38.9 billion in 1970 and then to $78.8 billion in 1975. After a lull in growth in 1976 and 1977, agency debt exploded in the last three years of the decade to a level of $159.9 billion at the end of 1980. Over the whole period from 1965 to 1980 the outstanding debt of the Federally sponsored credit agencies grew at an annual rate of 17.7 percent.

THE ISSUING AGENCIES

Federally sponsored credit agencies are financial intermediaries established by the Federal Government to supply credit for certain economic purposes, e.g., housing and agriculture. To carry out their function, the agencies sell debt

*Reprinted, with minor editorial revisions, from *Instruments of the Money Market*, 5th Edition, edited by Timothy Q. Cook and Bruce J. Summers, 1981, with permission of the Federal Reserve Bank of Richmond.

[1] This article deals with direct debt issues of the Federally sponsored agencies. Mortgage pools are excluded from the discussion and from all numbers. Figures on total agency debt are from the Flow of Funds. Figures on short-term debt were collected by the author.

43

obligations in the financial markets and channel the proceeds to agricultural and mortgage lending institutions either through direct loans or through the purchase of loans originated by these institutions.

The five federally sponsored credit agencies are the *Federal National Mortgage Association* (FNMA), *Federal Land Banks, Federal Intermediate Credit Banks, Banks For Cooperatives*, and *Federal Home Loan Banks* (FHLB). Included with the last agency is the *Federal Home Loan Mortgage Corporation* (FHLMC), all of whose capital stock is owned by the Federal Home Loan Banks. The primary function of the FHLB, the FHLMC, and FNMA is to provide funds to the mortgage and home construction markets. The other three corporations—collectively referred to as the *Federal Farm Credit Banks*—are part of the *Farm Credit System*, which provides credit primarily to farmers.

Most of the capital stock of the Federally sponsored credit agencies was originally owned by the Treasury. All of the agencies have repaid initial Government capital and are now operated as private corporations, wholly-owned by the financial institutions and the ultimate borrowers to which they lend. The capital stock of the Federal Home Loan Banks has been owned entirely by member savings and loan associations since 1951, and the other four agencies completed the transition to private ownership following the passage of enabling legislation in the fall of 1968. Despite their independent status, the Federally sponsored credit agencies remain subject to some Congressional control.

The Farm Credit Agencies

The Federal Intermediate Credit Banks, the Banks for Cooperatives, and the Federal Land Banks are similarly organized and operated. Each Agency consists of a system composed of twelve regional banks which operate in twelve farm credit districts. The Banks for Cooperatives also have a Central Bank for Cooperatives, so all together there are thirty-seven banks in the Farm Credit System. These banks are owned by the private intermediaries through which they operate. The intermediaries, in turn, are owned by the ultimate users of the Farm Credit System, the nation's farmers and ranchers. Indirect Government supervision is maintained over the Farm Credit Banks through the Farm Credit Administration, an independent agency in the the Executive Branch of the U. S. Government.

The twelve Federal Land Banks, established in 1917, are the oldest of the Federally sponsored agencies. Through Federal Land Bank Associations, Federal Land Banks make long-term loans to farmers for a variety of purposes, including the purchase of farms, machinery, and livestock, and for the refinancing of existing debts. The loans are made with maturities ranging from 5 to 40 years and are financed primarily through the sale of long-term debt obligations.

The Federal Intermediate Credit Banks provide short- and intermediate-term loans to and discount the paper of Production Credit Associations and other agriculture financing institutions which in turn lend to farmers, commercial fishermen and other farm-related businesses. These loans are made to meet seasonal credit requirements such as production and marketing expenses. They usually mature in one year but may be extended for up to seven years.

The Banks for Cooperatives are the smallest of the Farm Credit Banks. They extend credit to agricultural and aquatic marketing, supply, and business service cooperatives to meet marketing and operating capital needs. The main function of the Central Bank for Cooperatives is to participate with the district banks in large loans that exceed their individual lending capacities.

The Housing Credit Agencies

Established in response to the financial plight of mortgage lending institutions during the depression years, the Federal Home Loan Bank System serves primarily as a source of secondary liquidity to member institutions. These institutions include Federally chartered savings and loan associations, which are required by law to belong to the system, and other eligible mortgage lending institutions such as state chartered savings and loan associations and mutual savings banks. The System is composed of twelve regional banks and a supervisory body, the Federal Home Loan Bank Board, which is an independent agency of the Executive Branch of the U. S. Government.

In performing their function, the FHLBs make loans, called advances, to member institutions. The demand for these advances is especially large during periods of disintermediation, which occur when open market interest rates are high relative to the regulatory interest rate ceilings placed on time and saving deposits. Consequently, the amount of funds raised by the FHLBs in the money and capital markets rises sharply in high interest rate periods. Advances are also made to meet seasonal mortgage demand as well as to expand overall mortgage lending consistent with the FHLBs' goal of fostering home ownership. Most of the FHLBs make advances with maturities of up to ten years.

The Federal National Mortgage Association, popularly known as "Fannie Mae," is the largest of the Federally sponsored agencies. Since its inception in 1938 under the original name of National Mortgage Association of Washington, FNMA has undergone several reorganizations on the way to its present status as a private corporation. The Federal Government maintains limited control over FNMA through the Department of Housing and Urban Development.

Under its current charter, the function of FNMA is ". . .to provide supplementary assistance to the secondary market for home mortgages by providing a degree of liquidity to mortgage investments thereby improving the distribution of investment capital for home mortgage financing. . . ." To accomplish this function, FNMA has been authorized to purchase and sell FHA, VA, and conventional loans from banks, savings and loan associations, mortgage bankers, and other organizations that meet its specified requirements. In general, FNMA increases its purchases of mortgages when the supply of funds to the mortgage market from other sources is declining. As a result, like the FHLBs, its demand for funds in the financial markets typically rises sharply in periods of high interest rates and disintermediation at the thrift institutions.

Federally Owned Agencies and the Federal Financing Bank

In addition to the Federally sponsored credit agencies, more than fifteen agencies *owned* by the Federal Government also used to borrow directly in the financial markets by placing their own individual securities. Consequently, the financial markets were faced with a wide variety of agency debt issues, with differing terms and guarantees. The *Federal Financing Bank* was established in 1974 to consolidate and streamline the borrowing activity of these Federally owned agencies and thereby lower the cost of raising agency funds.

Since the establishment of the Federal Financing Bank, all Federally owned agencies have raised funds through it rather than directly in the financial markets. Hence, there have not been any new issues of Federally owned agency debt since the mid-1970s. The Federal Financing Bank can acquire the funds it supplies to the Federally owned agencies either by borrowing in the financial market itself or by borrowing from the Treasury. With the exception of one issue of $1.5 billion of eight-month notes sold in July 1974, the Federal Financing Bank has acquired all of its funds from the Treasury.

SHORT-TERM ISSUES

As of the end of 1979 there was $31.6 billion of Federally sponsored agency debt outstanding that had an original maturity of one year or less. This was 23.5 percent of the total outstanding, which represented a substantial decline from ten years earlier because of the more rapid growth of intermediate and long-term agency debt during the 1970s. Compared to most other sectors of the money market, the agency market remains small.

Two types of short-term debt issues are sold by the Federally sponsored credit agencies: (1) bonds which carry a coupon and (2) discount notes that are sold at a discount from par and redeemed at their face value at maturity. As will be explained below, these two types of issues differ in the way they are marketed. Bonds are sold periodically through a selling group assembled by the agency's Fiscal Agent, whereas discount notes can be sold continuously on a daily basis through a small number of dealers associated with the agency. Currently, the Farm Credit Banks sell both short-term bonds and discount notes, while the FHLBs and FNMA sell only discount notes.

The Federal Intermediate Credit Banks for cooperatives and the Federal Land Banks sell their debt jointly through the use of "consolidated systemwide" issues backed by the assets of all 37 banks. The Farm Credit Banks have sold consolidated systemwide bonds since 1977 and consolidated systemwide discount notes since 1975.

Consolidated systemwide bonds are sold by the Farm Credit Banks each month with maturities of six and nine months in minimum denominations of $5,000. These securities are issued in *book-entry form,* meaning that an investor does not receive a physical certificate as evidence of purchase. Instead, computerized records are maintained at Federal Reserve Banks in the name of the purchasing institution. In turn, the purchasing institution maintains separate records of those securities they own and those maintained for other investors. Investors may choose as custodian any bank or other financial institution that maintains book-entry accounts with the Federal Reserve System.[2]

The discount notes of the Farm Credit Banks are issued daily over a maturity range of 5 to 270 days. The specific maturity date is designated by the investor at the time of purchase subject to the limitations of the issuing agency. Unlike bonds, discount notes of the Farm Credit Banks are currently sold only in certificate form.

Beginning in 1974 the FHLBs also began to sell short-term discount notes. These have maturities from 30 to 270 days and are issued in certificate form with a minimum denomination of $100,000. This high minimum denomination serves to deter small savers from withdrawing their deposits from member institutions to invest in FHLB securities.

FNMA has been selling short-term discount notes since 1960. Unlike the obligations of the other agencies, income earned on FNMA securities is subject to state and local taxes. While FNMA discount notes are issued in a relatively low minimum denomination of $5,000, FNMA has restricted minimum purchases to $50,000 in an attempt to avoid contributing to disintermediation at thrift institutions during periods of high interest rates. FNMA does not post competitive rates on its discount notes on a regular basis. It may stay out of the market for several weeks at a time but will enter aggressively when it needs to raise money. The maturity of FNMA discount notes ranges from 30 to 270 days.[3] The characteristics of the short-term Federally sponsored agency issues are summarized in Table 4-1.

The greater use of discount notes in recent years by the Federally sponsored credit agencies reflects certain advantages these notes offer compared to short-term bonds. The use of discount notes increases the ability of agencies to exercise close control over their cash balances. Unlike bond sales, which require advance announcements, discount notes can be sold as the need for funds arises. An agency wishing to sell additional notes needs only to raise its rates to be

[2]Beginning in October 1981, all depository institutions will be able to have these book-entry accounts.

[3]FNMA discount notes are also available in interest-bearing form. However, only a relative small amount of these are issued at any one time due to limited demand.

Table 4-1 Characteristics of short-term agency securities

Issuer	Type	Maturities	Form	Offering Schedule	Minimum Denomination	Tax Exemption
FCB	Consolidated system-wide bonds	6- and 9-month	Book-entry	Monthly	$ 5,000	State, local
	Consolidated system-wide discount notes	5–270 days	Certificate	Daily	$ 50,000	State, local
FHLB	Consolidated discount notes	30–270 days	Certificate	Daily	$100,000	State, local
FNMA	Discount notes	30–270 days	Certificate	Daily	$ 5,000*	None

*Minimum purchase of $50,000.

more competitive with rates on other money market instruments. Similarly, an agency wishing to use idle funds to retire debt can simply post unattractive rates on its discount notes.

Discount notes also allow the agencies greater control over the maturity structure of their short-term debt. Through selective pricing policies, the agencies can more or less confine investor demand to a desired maturity area. Rates can quickly be adjusted as necessary to obtain the desired amount of funds at the desired maturities. It is not unusual, for example, for FNMA to change rates several times within a given day.

PRIMARY MARKET

The Federally sponsored credit agencies generally sell their new debt through a Fiscal Agent in New York City. When an interest-bearing note or bond offering is to be made, the Fiscal Agent assembles the selling group of securities dealers, brokerage houses, and dealer banks. Unlike syndicates formed for the sale of a specific stock or bond issue, members of the Agent's selling group do not bid against each other. Rather, each agency offering is made through only one selling group. To establish the price or price range of the new issues, the Fiscal Agent consults with the members of the selling group, the Treasury, the Trading Desk of the Federal Reserve Bank of New York, and the issuing agency regarding maturity, amount, coupon, and price. When the sale date arrives, the price is telegraphed by the Agent to the members of the group, who then make subscriptions through the Agent. The Agent determines the allotments, which are usually a fraction of total subscriptions.

The procedure for marketing discount notes is simpler. Discount notes are typically offered on a continuous basis through a small number of dealers who, as noted above, regularly adjust their rates to meet the borrowing desires of the agencies at various maturities.

SECONDARY MARKET

Short-term obligations of the Farm Credit Banks, the Federal Home Loan Banks, and the Federal National Mortgage Associations have well-established secondary markets. Dealer's inventories usually include large amounts of these securities. The spread between the bid and offered prices is narrow in short-term issues of these agencies, and trades of several million dollars can generally be made without upsetting the market. Generally, the primary selling group of dealers for a particular agency's discount notes or long-term bonds maintains a secondary market for those instruments, as do other dealers.

In December 1966 the Federal Open Market Committee, pursuant to an act of Congress, authorized the use of repurchase agreements involving agency obligations in its open market operations. In August 1971 the Committee voted to conduct outright transactions in Federal agency securities. These developments not only increased the means available to the System for supplying and absorbing reserves but also tended to strengthen and broaden the secondary market for agency securities.

Secondary market activity in agency issues has kept pace with the growth in the outstanding supply of agency debt. Daily average gross dealer transactions in agency securities grew steadily from $140 million in 1965 to $2.72 billion in 1979. About 29 percent of the 1979 dealer transactions were accounted for by issues maturing within one year. Daily average dealer positions in agency securities rose over the same period, although more erratically, from $337 million in 1965 to $1.472 billion in 1979. The percentage of dealer positions represented by issues maturing in less than a year declined from 69 percent in 1965 to 43 percent in 1979, reflecting the relatively greater growth of longer term agency issues.

INVESTMENT CHARACTERISTICS

Although Federally sponsored credit obligations are not obligations of, or guaranteed by, the U. S. Government, the issuing agencies are considered to be instrumentalities of the U. S. Government. As such, their securities are issued under the authority of Congress and subject to the same general regulations as those governing U. S. Treasury securities. As a result, investors generally perceive agency securities as carrying almost as low a degree of default risk as Treasury securities. Another attractive feature of short-term agency securities is their well-developed secondary market, which insures liquidity and low transaction costs.

Federal agency securities have a number of other characteristics, many of which are not common to other money market instruments, with the exception of Treasury bills. Among these characteristics are: (1) they are eligible as collateral for borrowing at the Federal Reserve Banks; (2) they are public securities and eligible to be held without limit by national banks; (3) they are supported, or "backstopped" by a limited authority to borrow from the United States Treasury; (4) they are eligible as collateral for tax and loan accounts; (5) they are eligible for purchase by the Federal Open Market Committee; and (6) they are issuable and payable through the facilities of the Federal Reserve Banks.

Yield

As a result of the low perception of default risk agency issues, and perhaps also in part due to their relatively high degree of liquidity, the yield on short-term agency issues is generally below that of most private sector money market instruments of comparable maturity, and only moderately above Treasury bill rates.

Over the 20-year period from 1961 through 1980 the three- and six-month agency rates averaged 24 and 19 basis points, respectively, above Treasury bill rates of comparable maturity.[4] The spread between short-term agency and Treasury bill rates exhibits no trend over this 20-year period, although it does have a cyclical movement that is positively correlated to the level of interest rates. In particular, in 1974 the average spread between the three-month Federal agency and Treasury bill rates rose to a record level of 78 basis points. Perhaps the most common explanation for this relationship points to the relative supply of bills and short-term agency issues in high interest periods, at least prior to the late 1970s. High short-term interest rates typically have occurred in the latter phases of an expanding economy. In such periods the Treasury's demand for funds is generally small, which decreases the supply of Treasury bills coming to the market. In contrast, the supply of short-term agency securities rises sharply in such periods because of the increased activity of the housing-related agencies. In the 1978–80 period the spread between the three-month Federal agency and Treasury bill rates averaged only 34 basis points despite a rise in short-term rates to record levels. However, unlike earlier periods of high short-term interest rates, there was a large supply of Treasury bills throughout this period.

INVESTORS

Federally sponsored credit agency securities are close substitutes for U. S. Government securities and, like U. S. securities, are held by virtually all sectors of the economy. A precise breakdown of relative shares is difficult, since in the Treasury's Survey of Ownership over half of the total outstanding are included in the residual "all other" category, which includes individuals, commercial bank trust departments, and all other institutions not covered by the Survey. Undoubtedly individuals hold a significant share. Among the reporting categories, the largest holder of agency issues throughout the history of the Survey has been commercial banks, which held 18.6 percent of the total as of December 1980.[5] Next in line at that time were state and local governments (including general and pension funds) with 6.7 percent and U. S. Government accounts and Federal Reserve Banks with 5.5 percent.

In recent years the residual "other" category in the Treasury survey has grown considerably to 61.0 percent in December 1980. The growth in this category partially reflects the growing percentage of outstanding short-term agency issues purchased by short-term investment pooling arrangements, such as money market mutual funds. These funds have enabled even small investors to indirectly invest in money market instruments. As a result, the large min-

[4]The rates in this comparison are calculated on a bond equivalent basis and are from Salomon Brothers' *An Analytical Record of Yields and Yield Spreads*.

[5]Mortgage-backed bonds and certificates are excluded from these calculations.

imum purchase requirements placed on the short-term issues of FNMA and the FHLBs have become largely ineffective as a barrier to disintermediation.

REFERENCES

1. Craigie Incorporated. "Pertinent Facts for the Potential Investor in United States Federal Agency Securities," Richmond, Virginia.
2. Federal Home Loan Bank System. "Consolidated Discount Notes," Washington, D.C.
3. Federal National Mortgage Association. *Background and History*, 1973, Washington, D.C.: Federal National Mortgage Association, November 1973.
4. _____ "Debentures." Washington, D.C.
5. Fiscal Agency for the Farm Credit Banks. "An Investors Guide to Farm Credit Securities," New York.
6. _____ *Farm Credit Banks Report to Investors*, 1979, New York: Fiscal Agency for the Farm Credit Banks, 1979.
7. Nelson, Jane F. "Federal Agency Securities," *Instruments of the Money Market*, 4th ed. Edited by Timothy Q. Cook, Richmond: Federal Reserve Bank of Richmond, 1977.

THE DISCOUNT WINDOW*

James Parthemos and
Walter Varvel

5

Adjustments in bank reserve positions are accomplished through purchase and sales of financial instruments in the money market. In addition to reliance on money market instruments, member banks have long had the "privilege" of acquiring reserves by borrowing at the discount window of their regional Federal Reserve Bank. By arranging an advance at the Federal Reserve, a bank suffering an unexpected reserve loss can bring its reserve position back to the desired or required level. Similarly, an institution experiencing a temporary buildup of reserves beyond desired levels may, before placing funds in the money market, pay off any borrowings it may owe at the window. In any event, the discount window affords an additional recourse in working out reserve adjustments and may be properly viewed as an operational part of the money market.

Following passage of the *Depository Institutions Deregulation and Monetary Control Act of 1980*, or *Monetary Control Act* as it is often called, nonmember banks and thrift institutions can also choose to adjust reserve positions through the discount window. The new legislation requires nonmembers to maintain reserve balances against transaction and nonpersonal time deposits. In addition, all institutions issuing reservable deposit liabilities are authorized access to the discount window.

Reserve adjustments made by individual institutions using the discount window differ in one important respect from alternative adjustment techniques. Trading in such instruments as Federal funds, negotiable certificates of deposit,

*Reprinted, with deletions, from *Instruments of the Money Market*, 5th edition, edited by Timothy Q. Cook and Bruce J. Summers, 1981, with permission of the Federal Reserve Bank of Richmond.

and Treasury bills among commercial banks or between banks and their customers involves no net creation of new bank reserves. Rather, existing reserves
are simply shifted about within the banking system. On the other hand, net
borrowings or repayments at the discount window result in a net change in
Federal Reserve credit outstanding and, consequently, affect the volume of
bank reserves. Thus, the choice by individual institutions between using the
discount window or alternative means of reserve adjustment may influence the
availability of money and credit in the economy. Policy decisions of the Federal
Reserve affecting discount window borrowing, therefore, have ramifications for
the conduct of monetary policy.

Decisions to use the discount window relative to other segments of the
money market for making reserve adjustments depend importantly upon the
relation of the Federal Reserve's discount rate to yields on money market
investments and on legal and administrative arrangements regarding use of the
discount window. Neither of these factors are determined by the competitive
interaction of market forces, but rather by administrative decision. Adjustments
in interest rates on window borrowings are recommended by the Boards of
Directors of the regional Reserve Banks in accord with current economic and
money market conditions, with final approval required by the Board of Governors. In addition, the legal requirements and administrative guidelines for
extensions of credit through the window are embodied in Federal Reserve
Regulation A.

EARLY DISCOUNTING PRINCIPLES

An important principle underlying creation of the Federal Reserve System was
providing a pool of funds which could be drawn on by banks experiencing
reserve shortages. The ability of banks to draw on this pool, however, was not
envisaged as an absolute right. Rather, it was linked to a widely held theory
of commercial banking which is known as the commercial loan or "real bills"
doctrine. According to this doctrine, commercial banks should borrow only
against short-term, self-liquidating paper arising from the normal conduct of
production and trade. Member banks were initially permitted to borrow from
the Federal Reserve Banks only by rediscounting customer loans which met
certain carefully specified conditions based on the commercial loan theory.
Promissory notes and other credit instruments meeting these specifications
were defined as "eligible paper," that is, paper eligible for rediscount at the
Federal Reserve. By and large, the real bills doctrine dominated member bank
use of the discount window until the banking crisis of 1933.

During the 1920s, trading in such money market instruments as short-term
government debt and Federal funds was not nearly so well developed as at
present. Consequently, the discount window was a primary tool of adjustment
for member banks. While banks made extensive use of bankers' acceptances,

commercial paper, and call loans against stock exchange collateral for reserve adjustment purposes, they also relied heavily on the discount window. Many bankers made it a regular practice to hold a supply of eligible paper which would be readily available for reserve adjustment through the discount window. Throughout the 1920s, average daily borrowings at the discount window usually exceeded $500 million and at times amounted to more than twice that figure.

FROM THE 1930s TO THE ACCORD

The banking reforms of the 1930s incorporated features designed to encourage use of the discount window by banks. In some measure, these features were related to a growing conviction that the real bills doctrine and discount window eligibility requirements unduly restricted banks seeking central bank assistance in times of stress. The effect of the reforms was to sweep away the real bills basis for discounting, although the concept of eligible paper was retained in the language of Federal Reserve discount regulations.

At an early stage in Federal Reserve history, member banks were allowed to borrow on their own notes, secured by eligible paper or government securities, instead of by rediscounting customer paper. Since 1933 direct advances against government securities have accounted for most Federal Reserve lending. In addition, banking legislation of the 1930s incorporated a new section, 10(b), into the Federal Reserve Act authorizing loans to member banks against any collateral satisfactory to the lending Reserve Bank.

Despite the encouragement of these changes and low discount rates, banks used the discount window sparingly between 1933 and 1951. From 1935 to 1940 daily borrowings generally averaged below $10 million. For the most part, banks held large amounts of excess reserves and were under little pressure to borrow. Even after the business recovery of the early 1940s, borrowing remained at low levels. By that time, banks held large quantities of government securities and the Federal Reserve's practice of pegging the market for these securities, instituted in 1942, eliminated the market risk of adjusting reserve positions through sales of governments. The Treasury-Federal Reserve Accord of 1951, however, ended the pegged market for government securities and began a new chapter in the history of the discount window.

DISCOUNTING SINCE THE ACCORD

Prices of government securities fluctuated over a broader range after the Accord, and it became riskier for banks to rely on these securities as a source of reserves when adjustments were necessary. Consequently, banks began to reassess the relative attractiveness of the discount window. Partly for this reason, borrowings jumped sharply, reaching the $1 billion level in mid-1952 for the first time in more than 20 years. For most of the 1950s borrowings were at levels comparable in absolute terms (although smaller relative to required reserves) with those of the 1920s.

The renewed importance of the discount window, coming in an overall economic and credit environment quite different from that prevailing in the 1920s, suggested the need for a general review of the principles on which the discount privilege was based. In 1955, after an extended inquiry, the Board of Governors promulgated a major revision in its Regulation A. As embodied in Regulation A, administrative restrictions on use of the discount window relate to the broader aspects of the Federal Reserve's operations rather than to any particular banking theory. For example, Regulation A recognizes that discount borrowing creates new reserves and, unless subject to some restraint, could conflict with policy goals such as economic and price stability. It also recognizes the necessity for insuring that the public resources administered by the Federal Reserve are not used to support questionable banking practices, but rather to insure the continuity of banking services provided to the public.

Generally, Regulation A envisages use of the discount window primarily as a temporary expedient open to institutions requiring reserve adjustments resulting from unanticipated shortages of funds. Indeed, short-term adjustment credit represents the great bulk of window borrowings. In addition, two other categories of borrowing have been considered "appropriate." Reserve needs of smaller institutions occasioned by seasonal swings in credit demand and in deposits may give rise to appropriate borrowing. Similarly, reserve problems associated with emergency situations affecting a community or a region, or with local or regional secular change, provide appropriate reasons for borrowing. Within the constraints embodied in Regulation A, the discount window is open to depository institutions in a variety of situations that may be considered more or less normal commercial banking operations. As long as an institution demonstrates in its overall performance its intention to operate within the limits of its own resources, it can usually arrange temporary accommodation to cover a variety of needs.

Continuous borrowing at the discount window is considered "inappropriate" whatever its cause since it implies that the borrowing bank has permanent reserve difficulties that should be corrected through basic portfolio adjustments. Extended use of central bank funds would supplement an institution's capital resources as a permanent base for investment in bank assets. The Federal Reserve has enumerated specific purposes for which use of the discount window is deemed inappropriate. These include borrowing to profit from interest rate differentials, to substitute Federal Reserve credit for normal sources of short-term interest-sensitive funds, and to support increases in loan or investment portfolios [2].

In April 1973, Regulation A was revised to permit greater use of the discount window for seasonal borrowing. Short-term access to the discount window had previously been available to member banks experiencing unusually strong seasonal reserve needs. The revision in Regulation A was designed explicitly to assist those member banks, especially small institutions, that lacked access to the national money markets in meeting seasonal needs arising out of predictable patterns in deposits and loans.

Under the 1973 revision, a member bank could obtain Federal Reserve credit to meet seasonal needs exceeding 5 percent of its average annual deposits. In order to qualify for the seasonal borrowing privilege, the bank had to provide the Federal Reserve with advance evidence indicating that the seasonal need would persist for at least eight consecutive weeks. The seasonal borrowing program initiated in 1973 was available only to banks with deposits of less than $250 million. Furthermore, member banks were not permitted to use the seasonal borrowing privilege and at the same time be sellers of Federal funds.

In August 1976, Regulation A was further revised to liberalize the seasonal borrowing privilege. Under the revised regulations member banks could use the seasonal borrowing privilege to meet that part of their seasonal need for funds exceeding 4 percent of the first $100 million of the previous year's average deposits; 7 percent of the second $100 million; and 10 percent of any deposits over $200 million. The period over which the seasonal need must persist was lowered from eight weeks to four weeks, and banks with deposits up to $500 million were made eligible for the seasonal borrowing privilege. In practice, however, the increasing deductible makes it unlikely that institutions with deposits in excess of $250 million will qualify for seasonal credit. In addition, the revision permits net sales of Federal funds while banks are engaged in seasonal borrowing from the Federal Reserve, as long as the sales represent the institution's normal operating pattern of Federal funds sales—including its seasonal and cyclical variation in sales and allowance for growth. This change was made in recognition of the growing number of small banks that were continuous net sellers of Federal funds. Since the initiation of the seasonal borrowing program in 1973, seasonal borrowing has generally been heaviest in the period from July through October. The magnitude of average monthly seasonal borrowing has varied over subsequent years from a low of $18 million in 1974 to a high of $145 million in 1979.

Emergency credit assistance at the discount window has been infrequently extended to institutions facing liquidity crises. Such assistance is sometimes necessary to minimize potentially serious adverse impacts of failure on financial flows in the economy and to provide federal banking agencies sufficient time to work out a satisfactory permanent solution. In the case of Franklin National Bank in 1974, deteriorating earnings and massive withdrawals of deposits induced the Federal Reserve, in its role as "lender of last resort,"[1] to advance funds to Franklin, peaking at $1.75 billion just prior to takeover of the bulk of the bank's assets and deposits by the European American Bank. More recently,

[1] For a discussion of the classical concept of the role of the central bank as lender of last resort, see [5].

large discount window borrowings played a key role in alleviating liquidity problems at First Pennsylvania Bank. Regulation A permits emergency credit extensions to nondepository institutions when alternative sources of credit are not available and failure to obtain such credit would adversely affect the economy. Such credit, however, will be at a higher rate of interest than that applicable to depository institutions.

THE MONETARY CONTROL ACT: A NEW ERA

The *Monetary Control Act*, enacted in March 1980, gives all nonmember banks, savings and loan associations, savings banks, and credit unions holding transaction accounts or nonpersonal time deposits the same discount and borrowing privileges as member banks. The Act directs the Federal Reserve to administer the window taking into consideration "the special needs of savings and other depository institutions for access to discount and borrowing facilities consistent with their long-term asset portfolios and the sensitivity of such institutions to trends in the national money markets." The impact of this legislation on the administration of the discount window is far-reaching.

In September 1980, the Federal Reserve revised Regulation A to implement the provisions of the Act. The revision establishes an additional lending category to provide credit for an extended period for other than seasonal needs. "Other extended credit" can now be arranged for individual depository institutions experiencing financial strains due to exceptional circumstances such as sustained deposit drains, impaired access to money market funds, or sudden deterioration in loan repayment performance. Depository institutions with investment portfolios composed of primarily longer-term assets and experiencing difficulties adjusting to changing money market conditions, particularly during periods of deposit disintermediation, may also borrow under the other extended credit provision.

The revised lending provisions do not, however, alter the Federal Reserve's expectation that depository institutions are to rely primarily on their usual sources of funds before turning to the discount window for assistance. Discount window credit will generally be made available only after alternative sources have been exhausted. In the case of thrift institutions, alternative sources of funds include special industry lenders such as the Federal Home Loan Banks, the National Credit Union Administration's Central Liquidity Facility, and corporate central credit unions. Before extending credit, the Reserve Banks will consult with the borrowing institution's supervision agency to determine why funds are not available from other sources.

The September 1980 revision in Regulation A made discretionary use of a discount rate surcharge a permanent addition to the Federal Reserve's discount lending policy. Such a surcharge can be made applicable to both adjustments and extended credit. In March 1980, as part of the special credit restraint program, the System briefly instituted a 3 percent surcharge on adjustment credit of member banks with over $500 million in deposits when such borrowings occurred successively in two reserve statement weeks or more, or when the borrowing occurred in more than four weeks in a calendar quarter. The surcharge, which did not apply to seasonal borrowings or emergency loans, was designed to discourage frequent use of the discount window. The surcharge was eliminated in May but was reinstated on adjustment credit extended to frequent borrowings of large depository institutions in late 1980.

ADMINISTRATION OF THE WINDOW

Currently, most Federal Reserve loans are made under the provisions of Section 13 of the Federal Reserve Act and are in the form of direct advances secured by U. S. Government securities. Advances under Section 13 can also be made against Federal agency securities. Loans under Section 10(b) may be secured by any collateral satisfactory to the lending Reserve Bank, including State and local government securities, mortgage notes covering 1-4 family residences, and business and other customer notes. The use of these additional types of collateral has been relatively unimportant in recent discount activity, in part, because the rate charged on 10(b) loans was ½ of one percentage point higher than on Section 13 loans. Moreover, depending on the collateral offered, 10(b) loans may involve some delay before funds are made available. Banks borrowing under this Section usually offered municipal securities as collateral. The *Monetary Control Act* authorized the Federal Reserve to eliminate the ½ of one percentage point differential required on 10(b) loans, a change that became effective in September 1980. With the removal of the penalty rate, institutions may choose to increase use of municipals and residential mortgages as collateral for window borrowings.

Maturities of up to 90 days are authorized on Section 13 loans, while the statutory limit on 10(b) maturities is four months. In practice, however, Reserve Banks encourage borrowers to limit maturities to shorter periods. Large institutions with broad access to money market funds are expected to make necessary adjustments in their portfolios faster than smaller banks. Consequently, adjustment credit extended to money market banks will normally be only to the next business day. Smaller institutions may borrow with somewhat longer maturities.

Adjustment credit is available on a short-term basis to assist depository institutions "in meeting temporary requirements for funds, or to cushion more persistent outflows of funds pending an orderly adjustment of the institution's assets and liabilities."[2] It is the responsibility of the Reserve Bank discount officer to ensure that adjustment borrowing is for appropriate purposes and not

[2]Regulation A, Section 201.3(a).

simply a substitute for regular sources of funds. Borrowing requests from institutions that are not presently in the window or that have not in the recent past relied heavily on the window are normally accommodated immediately. When the size or frequency of borrowing increases, however, an institution may be asked to provide information justifying continued use of discount credit. If the borrowing is judged to be inappropriate, the borrower is asked to discontinue use of the window. Such administrative pressure represents nonprice rationing of discount credit.

To assist in the determination of the appropriateness of window borrowing, heavy reliance is placed on analysis of balance sheet trends, especially flows in loans and deposits, net positions in Federal funds, and changes in liquid assets. Balance sheets are examined to determine the extent of liquidity pressures and to see if appropriate adjustments are taking place.

An extensive review of discount window policy conducted by the Federal Reserve in the late 1960s [2] reported that some differences existed among Regional Banks in the determination of what constituted appropriate borrowing. To help achieve uniformity in discount administration, numerical guidelines for the size and frequency of borrowing by an individual institution have been established. Such guidelines, used as a secondary measure by the discount officer, provide a norm for the amount of borrowing a typical bank is likely to require, the amount of time usually needed to adjust the bank's position, and a measure of how frequently a bank is likely to need adjustment credit. Borrowing that exceeds the guidelines does not necessarily mean that the borrowing will be considered inappropriate.

Since large institutions generally have greater access to alternative sources of funds than smaller institutions, the guidelines are more stringent for large borrowers. Borrowings as a percentage of domestic deposits are generally expected to be lower than for smaller institutions, and less frequent. Some variation in the size classifications included in the guidelines exists among the regional Reserve Banks.

MECHANICS OF BORROWING

In order to borrow, an institution must furnish the Federal Reserve Bank a resolution adopted by its Board of Directors specifying which of its officers are authorized to borrow on its behalf. A *Continuing Lending Agreement* is normally executed facilitating prompt extension of discount credit upon telephone requests from borrowing institutions.

Advances secured by government obligations can be made up to the face amount of the collateral. The collateral must be held by the Federal Reserve Bank unless prior arrangements have been made permitting another institution to hold the securities under a custody receipt arrangement. Under such an arrangement, the securities may be held by a "custody" bank which in the usual course of business performs correspondent bank services, including the holding in custody of government securities, for the borrower. While institutions may also borrow on their promissory note secured by eligible paper, this procedure can be more time-consuming since the Reserve Bank must verify the eligibility of the collateral, then analyze and value it. Institutions, therefore, often submit collateral in advance of the date of the borrowing. Applications processing is prompt when municipal securities are offered as collateral, but delays may result when customer notes are offered. In addition, 10(b) collateral may be valued at less than the face amount.

Once an application for Federal Reserve credit is approved by the Reserve Bank, borrowings are normally credited directly to the institution's reserve account. Unless the Federal Reserve is notified to the contrary, the principal plus interest due on the note is automatically charged against the borrower's reserve account on the maturity date. Notes may, of course, be paid in part or in full before maturity. Nonmember institutions may (a) decide not to hold reserves directly with the Federal Reserve but hold them with a correspondent institution on a "pass-through" basis or (b) have reserve liabilities that can be met with vault cash. In these instances, three-party arrangements may be made among the Federal Reserve, borrower, and a correspondent institution providing for credits and debits to be charged against the correspondent's reserve account.

BORROWING LEVELS

The volume of borrowings at the discount window fluctuates over a wide range. Borrowings generally increase in periods of high or rising market interest rates and decline in periods of low or falling rates. To a large extent, this is because changes in the discount rate lag behind movements in money market rates. Consequently, in periods of rising rates, the cost of borrowing at the discount window frequently becomes relatively more attractive compared to the cost of raising funds in the money market.

There is a strong relationship between total member bank borrowing and the differential between the Federal funds rate and the discount rate. The 1950s and early 1960s were generally characterized by periods of relatively stable interest rates. Throughout this period, the discount rate was usually maintained at or above market rates, providing little financial incentive for discount borrowing. The latter 1960s and much of the 1970s, however, saw large swings in the interest differential. Borrowing averaged well over $1 billion throughout most of 1969 and early 1970 when the Federal funds rate exceeded the discount rate, at times, by over 3 percentage points. Throughout 1973 and 1974 member bank borrowings averaged nearly $2 billion and exceeded $3 billion in June through September 1974 when the interest differential approached 5 percent. Borrowings fell rapidly with the onset of the recession and the related drop-off in loan demand in late 1974 and early 1975. Market rates fell dramatically and were generally below the discount rate from early 1975 through mid-1977, when window borrowing was minimal.

From 1977 through most of 1979, the Federal Reserve demonstrated a desire to keep the discount rate more closely in line with increasing market rates. Discount rate increases were more frequent but still lagged behind market rates resulting in a general increase in borrowing levels. Borrowing grew rapidly, approaching a level of $3 billion following the Federal Reserve's shift to a reserve targeting procedure (described below) in October 1979 which resulted in large differentials between the funds rate and the discount rate. The imposition of the credit restraint program with its temporary three percentage point surcharge on large bank borrowings and the reduced economic activity beginning in early 1980, contributed to the subsequent sharp drop in market rates (relative to the discount rate) and the lower level of discount borrowing. Considering the low level of the discount rate relative to the cost of alternative sources of reserve adjustment funds during periods of high interest rates, the volume of borrowings would undoubtedly have been much greater without the use of discount administration as a rationing device.

During periods of high interest rates, the discount rate has usually remained below market rates and, in effect, subsidized member bank borrowing from the Federal Reserve. In such times, reduced interest expenses from borrowing at below market rates provided a partial offset to the opportunity costs associated with maintaining non-earning reserve balances with the Federal Reserve [1].

Both small and large banks use the discount window, but in most years large banks have accounted for the greater dollar volume of borrowings. Banks that manage their reserve positions closely usually meet short-run reserve deficiencies either by borrowing from the Federal Reserve or by buying Federal funds. Large banks tend to incur reserve deficiencies more frequently than small banks. Thus, they tend to rely more heavily on borrowed funds. The tendency to use both the discount window and Federal funds increases with bank size.

Since large banks are more frequent users of discount window credit than small banks, most savings on interest expenses resulting from borrowing at below-market discount rates would seem to accrue to large banks. A study analyzing member bank borrowing in the Eighth Federal Reserve District from 1974 to 1977 confirms that the dollar amounts of such benefits are disproportionately concentrated among the largest banks. Measures of the interest savings per dollar borrowed and interest savings as a percentage of average reserve balances held at the Federal Reserve, however, show that relatively small banks which borrowed heavily "benefited as much or more than the large banks" when market rates were substantially above the discount rate [4].

ROLE OF THE DISCOUNT WINDOW IN MONETARY POLICY

The role of discount rate administration in the making of monetary policy has changed somewhat since the October 1979 shift in Federal Reserve operating strategy. Prior to October 1979, the Federal Reserve attempted to achieve its money supply objectives by manipulating the Federal funds rate. Because in that policy setting the Federal Reserve chose to fix the Federal funds rate in the short-run, increases in the discount rate reduced the differential between the Federal funds rate and the discount rate, and decreased the demand for borrowed reserves. To keep the Federal funds rate steady following an increase in the discount rate, the Federal Reserve had to increase the supply of non-borrowed reserves. Consequently, increases in the discount rate did not directly affect the level of short-run interest rates; they simply changed the mix of nonborrowed and borrowed reserves. At most, under the old regime, discount rate changes were used by the monetary authorities to signal changes in policy through what was referred to as the "announcement effect."

The importance of discount window policy has been enhanced under the reserve targeting strategy adopted by the Federal Open Market Committee in October 1979. Under this strategy, the Federal Reserve attempts to achieve its money supply objectives by setting targets for nonborrowed and borrowed reserves. The demand for borrowed reserves is largely dependent on the spread between the Federal funds rate and the discount rate. Consequently, a given borrowed reserve objective will, roughly speaking, produce a particular spread between the funds rate and the discount rate. The more the Federal Reserve makes the banking system borrow, the higher the funds rate will be in relation to the discount rate. Under the new operating procedure, then, given a specific borrowed reserves objective, a rise in the discount rate is immediately trans-mitted to the Federal funds rate and to other short-term interest rates. For this reason in all instances from October 1979 through the end of 1980, increases in the discount rate resulted in increases in the Federal funds rate of at least equal magnitude.

The change in the effect of discount rate movements on short-term interest rates since the October 1979 change in operating strategy illustrates an important point, namely, that the effect of discount rate movements on market interest rates depends on the operating strategy of the Federal Reserve.

REFERENCES

1. George J. Benston, *Federal Reserve Membership: Consequences, Costs, Benefits, and Alternatives*, Association of Reserve City Bankers, 1978, p. 34.

2. Board of Governors of the Federal Reserve System, "Operation of the Federal Reserve Discount Window Under the Monetary Control Act of 1980," September 1980.

3. Board of Governors of the Federal Reserve System, *Reappraisal of the Federal Reserve Discount Mechanism: Volume I*, August 1971.

4. R. Alton Gilbert, "Benefits of Borrowing From the Federal Reserve When the Discount Rate is Below Market Interest Rates," *Review*, Federal Reserve Bank of St. Louis, March 1979, pp. 25-32.

5. Thomas M. Humphrey, "The Classical Concept of the Lender of Last Resort," *Economic Review*, Federal Reserve Bank of Richmond, January/February 1975, pp. 2-9.

BANKERS' ACCEPTANCES REVISITED*

6

Jack L. Hervey†

The ten-fold increase in world trade over the past twelve years, to more than $1.8 trillion in exports in 1982, has been accompanied by the rapid growth of short-term credit to finance the international movement of goods. The U. S. bankers' acceptance market has played an important part in providing this expansion in credit financing for both U. S. and worldwide trade.

An estimated 17 percent of the total U. S. export-import trade in 1970 was financed in the bankers' acceptance market (see Figure 6-1).[1] By 1974 only 13 percent of U. S. export-import trade was financed through acceptances. This downward trend was reversed in the last half of the 1970s when both export and import acceptances expanded rapidly. The portion of U. S. trade financed

*Reprinted from *Economic Perspectives*, May/June 1983, pp. 21-31, with permission of the Federal Reserve Bank of Chicago.

†Jack L. Hervey is a Senior Economist at the Federal Reserve Bank of Chicago. This article updates and extends "Bankers acceptances," *Business Conditions*, Federal Reserve Bank of Chicago (May 1976), pp. 3-11.

[1]The estimates are based on the average amount of export and import acceptances created and assume a 90-day average maturity. (Outstandings are from the Federal Reserve Bank of New York, "Banker's Dollar Acceptances—United States," a monthly release of the Office of Public Information, selected issues.) A shorter or longer average maturity would alter the estimates. If a 60-day average maturity were assumed, for example, the volume of export and import acceptances created in 1970 and 1982 as a proportion of total U. S. exports and imports would increase to 25 percent and 40 percent, respectively. Commercial bankers indicate that average maturity varies over time but that a 90-day average is a reasonable assumption.

by acceptances increased to about 22 percent by 1981. The proportion expanded further in 1982—to 28 percent—as a result of a continued expansion in the acceptance market that occurred at the same time that exports and imports were contracting.

International trade credit is particularly important because of the often lengthy time between shipment by the exporter and delivery to the importer. In some cases, the importer prepays prior to shipment of the goods; in others, the exporter extends credit on "open account" until delivery. Often, however, the transaction involves a third party who agrees to pay the exporter upon shipment and to receive payment from the importer at some agreed upon future date.

For this credit service, the third party receives the principal and an interest return plus a fee, or commission, associated with the services provided, including the risk of nonpayment by the importer. Open account credit continues as an important component of trade financing, especially when trading partners are well known to each other and the risk of nonperformance is low. However, when the transaction involves a relatively high degree of risk, such as when buyer and seller are not well known to each other, third party involvement (with a better information network) typically takes place.

The risk of nonperformance increases the expected costs associated with an export-import transaction and acts as a deterrent to trade. Therefore, trade can be facilitated if this risk can be shifted to a third party at a known cost. More complete information, typically through foreign correspondents, in addition to risk pooling, allows the third party, who specializes in credit, to bear

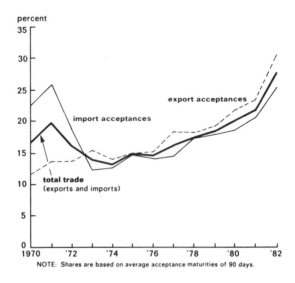

Figure 6-1   The share of U. S. international trade financed by acceptances

such risks at a lower expected cost than an exporter who specializes in goods. Historically, the desire for such risk shifting in trade arrangements led to the development of bills of exchange such as bankers' acceptances.[2]

A BANKERS' ACCEPTANCE

A bankers' acceptance originates from a draft drawn to finance the exchange or temporary storage of specified goods. It is a time draft that specifies the payment of a stated amount at maturity, typically less than six months in the future. The draft becomes a "bankers' acceptance" when a bank stamps and endorses it as "accepted."[3] For the price of its commission, the bank lends its name, integrity, and credit rating to the instrument and assumes primary responsibility for payment to the acceptance holder at maturity. The drawer of the draft retains a secondary liability to the acceptance holder, contingent upon the inability of the accepting bank to honor the claim at maturity.

The draft underlying an acceptance sometimes is preauthorized by a "letter of credit" issued by the importer's home bank. The largest dollar volume, however, are "outright" or "clean" acceptances—often arising from an agreement between a foreign bank (for their customer) and the accepting U. S. bank.

The drawer of the acceptance may extend credit to the importer by simply holding it until maturity and then collecting payment of the face amount from the accepting bank. Alternatively, the drawer can receive immediate payment by selling the acceptance at a discount, typically to the bank that created it.[4] The bank that discounts the acceptance may hold the instrument in its investment portfolio, treating it like any other loan financed from the bank's general funds. More commonly, the bank sells the acceptance in the secondary market, either to a specialized acceptance dealer or directly to an investor. At year-end 1982 about 88 percent of total bankers' acceptances created were "outstanding"—i.e., not held in the accounts of the accepting banks.

ACCEPTANCE MARKET GROWTH

Bankers' acceptances are used for two principal types of financing—for domestic trade and storage and international trade. An additional small volume of acceptances are created for the acquisition of the dollar exchange by certain countries that have periodic or seasonal shortages in their dollar foreign exchange reserves.

[2]Historians have traced the origin of these instruments to the twelfth century.

[3]Drafts drawn on and accepted by nonbank entities are called "trade acceptances."

[4]Typically the terms of the letter of credit specify whether the buyer or seller is responsible for payment of the commission (discount) due to the bank. If the responsibility for the discount is not specified in the agreement, convention dictates that the seller is liable for the charges.

Although the dollar volume of trade acceptances has grown rapidly since the early 1970s, domestic acceptances have remained a small though relatively stable proportion of total acceptances over the past decade. Domestic acceptances increased from about $200 million at year-end 1969 to more than $3 billion at the end of 1982, about 4 percent of total acceptances.

Passage of the Export Trading Company Act of 1982 may facilitate a substantial expansion in the size and relative importance of bankers' acceptances for domestic shipments. This act, effective October 8, 1982, removed a long-standing statutory requirement that title documents must accompany a bankers' acceptance originated for domestic shipments in order for such an acceptance to qualify as eligible for discount by the Federal Reserve. Because this previous requirement discouraged the use of bankers' acceptances for shipments of domestic goods, 80 percent or more of the volume of domestic acceptance creation typically has been originated to finance storage rather than trade.

International trade acceptances account for the bulk of U. S. bankers' acceptance activity, typically representing more than 90 percent of the total acceptance market. International acceptances are of three basic types: acceptances to finance U. S. exports; acceptances to finance U. S. imports; and third-country acceptances to finance trade between foreign countries or goods storage within a foreign country.

The phenomenal growth of U. S. export-import acceptances has been fostered by the increased proportion of U. S. trade financed by acceptances, which to a large degree is due to increased attention to liability management by bankers, as well as by the expanded value of U. S. trade. Gross acceptances created to finance U. S. exports increased from $1.2 billion at year-end 1969 to $16.3 billion at the end of 1982. Over the same period, acceptances to finance imports increased from $1.9 billion to $17.7 billion.

Even more impressive has been the growth in third-country acceptances which have increased from $2.3 billion at year-end 1969 to $42.3 billion at year-end 1982. Accompanying this 18-fold increase in dollar volume, third-country acceptances have captured a larger share of the (total) international acceptance market—rising from 42 percent to 53 percent of gross acceptances created in the 1970-82 period. Expansion of the third-country market largely reflects increased usage of U. S. acceptances by Japanese, South Korean, and other Asian traders, especially in the wake of higher oil import costs for these nations after the oil price increases of 1973-74 and 1979-80.

Bankers active in the acceptance market indicate that a substantial proportion of third-country acceptances are for financing oil shipments, and growth in third-country import bills appears consistent with this claim (see Figure 6-2). During 1974, third-country acceptances increased from $2.7 billion to $10.1 billion. The volume increased from $16.2 billion to $35.3 billion during the period 1979 to mid-1981.

Dollar exchange acceptances, arising from exchange shortages brought about by seasonal trade patterns in some countries, are the only acceptances not

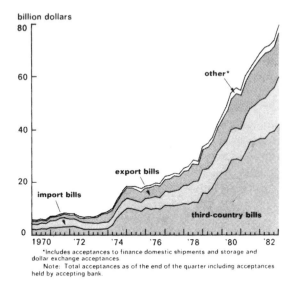

billion dollars

other*

export bills

import bills

third-country bills

1970   '72   '74   '76   '78   '80   '82

*Includes acceptances to finance domestic shipments and storage and
dollar exchange acceptances.
Note: Total acceptances as of the end of the quarter including acceptances
held by accepting bank.

Figure 6-2   U. S. bankers' acceptance market expanded rapidly over the past
decade

based on specific merchandise trade or storage. They are available only in
foreign countries designated by the Board of Governors of the Federal Reserve
System. Such acceptances are relatively minor in volume, constituting only
about 0.2 percent of total acceptances at year-end 1982.

INVESTMENT IN ACCEPTANCES

Acceptances have characteristics that are attractive to borrowers, bankers, and
investors when compared to other short-term financial instruments. This appeal
has been basic to the recent rapid growth of the acceptance market.

Borrower costs for bankers' acceptances compare favorably with the interest
and noninterest charges on conventional bank loans. In comparing interest
rates on acceptances and other bank loans, the acceptance rate must be adjusted
upward to reflect that it is quoted on a discount basis. Although typically not
quoted on a discount basis, interest rates on conventional bank loans must be
adjusted upward in cases where the loan contract requires a borrower to maintain compensating balances in excess of normal working balances at the lending
bank. Maintaining these noninterest-earning deposits increases the effective
cost of the bank loan.

Interest rates on acceptances also compare favorably with commercial paper
rates. Many borrowers lack sufficient size or credit standing to issue these

unsecured notes at competitive rates. For small borrowers, issuing costs or commissions add appreciably to the costs of commercial paper.

Bankers' acceptances have several characteristics that enhance their attractiveness to bankers and make them competitive with alternative money-market instruments. A bank earns a commission, currently from 50 to 100 basis points, simply by originating an acceptance. In the process, the bank does not commit its own funds unless it chooses to discount the acceptance. Once discounted, the acceptance can be sold in the well-developed secondary market, providing the bank with a degree of liquidity and portfolio flexibility not afforded by most conventional loans.

The amount of credit extended to an individual customer may also be expanded through bankers' acceptances. Statutory restrictions limit the amount of conventional credit extended to a single bank customer by a Federal Reserve member bank. However, by the creation, discount, and sale of acceptances in the secondary market, a bank can facilitate a further extension of credit to a single customer up to an additional 10 percent of the bank's capital, provided that the acceptances are eligible for discount by the Federal Reserve.[5]

Bank funds received by the sale of eligible-for-discount acceptances in the secondary market are not subject to reserve requirements under current Federal Reserve regulations. This practice has proved especially useful for channeling funds from the nonbank sector to bank credit customers during tight credit periods when Regulation Q ceilings have reduced the flow of funds to banks.[6]

Investors hold bankers' acceptances for yield, security, and liquidity. The rates of return on acceptances have been competitive with the returns on other money-market instruments such as commercial paper and negotiable certificates of deposit. Many investors view acceptances as one of the safest forms of investment, given the primary obligation for repayment of the accepting bank

---

[5]An outstanding acceptance of a member bank that meets the eligible for discount requirements specified in Section 13 of the Federal Reserve Act is not included in that bank's legal lending limit for conventional loans—equal to 15 percent of paid-in capital and surplus, undivided profits, subordinated debt, and 50 percent of its loan loss reserve, to any one borrower. An outstanding acceptance—which meets Section 13(7) conditions of the Federal Reserve Act—of a U. S. branch or agency of a foreign bank subject to reserve requirements under Section 7 of the International Banking Act of 1978 is also excluded from that bank's per customer limit for conventional loans. State-chartered nonmember banks and state-chartered U. S. branches and agencies of foreign banks are subject to state-imposed limitations on loans. In Illinois, for example, state-chartered nonmember U. S. banks have a legal limit for conventional loans to a single borrower of 15 percent of capital and surplus, excluding undivided profits. An Illinois-chartered nonmember bank may create acceptances for a single borrower, separate from its legal lending limit on conventional loans, in an amount up to 15 percent of capital and surplus or, if the excess is secured, up to 50 percent of capital and surplus.

[6]See Gary L. Alford, "Tight credit and the banks . . . 1966 and 1969 compared," *Business Conditions*, Federal Reserve Bank of Chicago (May 1970) pp. 4-11.

and the secondary liability of the acceptance drawer. Top quality acceptances are highly liquid in the active secondary market.

FEDERAL RESERVE ACCEPTANCE ACTIVITIES

Federal Reserve authority to regulate the creation of bankers' acceptances by depository institutions and to acquire bankers' acceptances for its own portfolio is derived from the Federal Reserve Act of 1913. Such authority has been modified by the 1915 amendments to the Act, Provisions of the Monetary Control Act of 1980, and Section 207 of the Export Trading Company Act of 1982. This legislative authority provides the basis for the bankers' acceptance regulations of the Board of Governors of the Federal Reserve System—primarily Regulations A, D, and K and regulations relating to Federal Reserve open-market operations. The regulations are augmented by published Board interpretations of rules governing creation, discount, and rediscount of acceptances.

Early Federal Reserve regulations of acceptances created by its member banks focused on assurances of the quality of the instruments and the soundness of the creating banks. The Board also placed limits on the volume of acceptances available for potential discount at the Federal Reserve. Three avenues were provided for the Federal Reserve to legally acquire bankers' acceptances. The twelve Reserve Banks in the Federal Reserve System were permitted to discount (technically rediscount) member bank acceptances deemed "eligible for discount," to advance funds secured by member bank acceptances, and finally, the Federal Reserve could purchase and sell bankers' acceptances through open-market operations. Each of these transactions affected total reserves in the banking system.

Historically, most Federal Reserve transactions in acceptances arose through open-market operations.[7] Until March 1977 the Fed's Domestic Open Market Desk, located at the Federal Reserve Bank of New York, bought and sold bankers' acceptances. Fed purchases or sales from dealers in the secondary acceptance market increased or decreased reserves, respectively, in the banking system in the same manner as its dealer purchases and sales of U. S. Treasury securities. Compared to total open market operations, however, Fed purchases and sales of acceptances were small.

---

[7] Federal Reserve System monetary policy was initially conducted through the rediscount of bankers' acceptances and other eligible paper. However, by the mid-1920s purchases of government securities exceeded holdings of discounted bills. In subsequent years open market operations of the System dominated rediscounting. For a discussion of the historical background of bankers' acceptances, see an article by Michael A. Goldberg, "Commercial Letters of Credit and Banker Acceptances," pp. 175-185, in *Below the Bottom Line: The Use of Contingencies and Commitments by Commercial Banks*, Staff Studies 113 (Board of Governors of the Federal Reserve System, 1982).

The Federal Reserve Open Market Committee in March 1977 directed the Open Market Desk to discontinue the outright purchase of bankers' acceptances for the Fed's own account. One reason for the discontinuance was that Federal Reserve direct purchases and sales were no longer deemed necessary to support the well-developed secondary market for acceptances. Acceptance activity for the Fed's own account now is confined to repurchase agreements.

The Fed also acts as an "agent" for foreign central banks wishing to acquire acceptances for investment purposes. Until the practice was discontinued in November 1974, the Federal Reserve also added its endorsement to such acceptances, thus enhancing the security of the instruments by effectively guaranteeing payment.

ACCEPTANCE ELIGIBILITY

The Federal Reserve Act (section 13.7) specifies the general conditions under which a member bank can create an acceptance and limits the dollar volume of acceptances that may be outstanding by an individual bank. Acceptances that meet the requirements specified in Section 13(7) (see Table 6-1) are *eligible for discount* at the Federal Reserve, as specified in Section 13(6). Supervision and regulation of bankers' acceptances have evolved around this concept of eligibility, thereby influencing the structure of the market. Eligibility also has served as a quality benchmark in the secondary market.

Some bankers' acceptances are *eligible for purchase* by the Federal Reserve (according to rules of the Federal Open Market Committee) under marginally less stringent conditions than are those that are eligible for discount (see Table 6-1). It should be noted that in general (see Table 6-1 for exceptions) an acceptance that is *eligible for discount,* that is, meets the conditions of 13(6) and (7) of the Federal Reserve Act, is also eligible for purchase. The reverse, however, is not true. An acceptance that meets all the conditions of 13(7), save that it has a maturity greater than six months and up to nine months, is eligible for purchase but not for discount. *Eligible for purchase* is also somewhat misleading. Under current regulations this terminology actually refers to requirements that apply to repurchase agreements between acceptance dealers and the Fed, not an outright purchase for the Fed's own account. Before the Federal Reserve will enter into a repurchase agreement for an individual acceptance, the bank creating it must have established itself in the market and must have met Federal Reserve requirements that qualify the bank as a "prime bank."[8] The prime bank requirements must be met for acceptances in each eligibility

[8]See Ralph T. Helfrich, "Trading in Bankers' Acceptances: A View from the Acceptance Desk of the Federal Reserve Bank of New York," *Monthly Review,* Federal Reserve Bank of New York (February 1976) pp. 56-57.

category-discount or purchase—before the acceptance can be used in a Fed repurchase agreement. Bankers' acceptances that do not qualify as eligible for discount or purchase by the Federal Reserve are referred to as *ineligible* acceptances. In effect, this means that all acceptances that do not meet the conditions of Section 13(7) are ineligible. Such a classification could include acceptances that are eligible for purchase but are of "long" maturities. The market treats such acceptances as ineligible.

Reserve requirements against funds obtained from the rediscount of acceptances in the secondary market are an important consideration in acceptance creation and regulation. Until 1973 member banks' funds derived from the sale of eligible as well as ineligible acceptances were free from reserve requirements. In mid-1973 the Federal Reserve Board ruled that member banks who derived funds from ineligible acceptances—those that did not meet Section 13(7) conditions—had reserve requirements on those funds.[9]

The Monetary Control Act of 1980 brought nonmember institutions under the reserve requirement authority of the Federal Reserve.[10] Regulations to implement this act also extended reserve-free treatment to funds derived from the sale of acceptances in the secondary market by these institutions. To qualify as nonreservable funds the underlying acceptances (technically eligible for purchase) were to be "of the type" specified in Section 13(7) of the Federal Reserve Act.

These rules have blurred the distinctions between acceptance eligibility for discount and for purchase. Member bank officials indicate that most acceptances created by these banks are eligible for discount. The secondary market applies a lower discount (i.e., interest rate) to acceptances that are eligible for discount and to all eligible acceptances from prime banks.

To the limited extent that nonmember depository institutions create acceptances, their instruments tend to meet the conditions of Section 13(7). Therefore, the funds obtained through rediscount in the secondary market are treated as nonreservable.

Most institutions avoid creating ineligible acceptances, because such instruments are not well received in the secondary market. In addition, reserve requirements apply when these acceptances are rediscounted in the secondary market. To the extent ineligible acceptances arise, they are usually held in the account of the bank that created them.

[9]In the early 1970s funds derived from the sale of ineligible acceptances were not subject to reserve requirements. A number of banks used this fact to advantage during periods of tight credit by creating a substantial volume of finance bills, or working capital acceptances (ineligible), and placing them in the secondary market. The Board of Governors imposed reserve requirements in mid-1973 on bank funds acquired through such instruments, sharply curtailing banks' activity in ineligibles.

[10]Prior to the Monetary Control Act of 1980, reserve requirements on nonmember bank funds acquired from the sale of ineligible bankers' acceptances in the secondary market were set by state banking laws.

Table 6-1 Bankers' acceptances—characteristics governing eligibility, reserve requirements, and aggregate acceptance limits

Bankers' acceptance categories	Federal Reserve System treatment			
	Eligible for discount[1]	Eligible for purchase[2]	Reserve requirements apply if sold[3]	Aggregate acceptance limits apply[4]
1. Specific international transactions				
a. U.S. exports or imports				
Tenor–6 months or less	yes[5]	yes	no	yes
6 months to 9 months	no	yes	yes	no
b. Shipment of goods *between* foreign countries:				
Tenor–6 months or less	yes[5]	yes	no	yes
6 months to 9 months	no	yes	yes	no
c. Shipment of goods *within* a foreign country:				
Tenor–any term	no	no	yes	no
d. Storage of goods within a foreign country—*readily marketable* staples secured by warehouse receipt issued by an independent warehouseman.[6]				
Tenor–6 months or less	yes[5]	no	no	yes
6 months to 9 months	no	no	yes	no
e. Dollar exchange–required by usages of trade in approved countries only:				
Tenor–3 months or less	yes	no	no[7]	yes
more than 3 months	no	no	yes	no
2. Specific domestic transactions (i.e., within the U.S.)				
a. Domestic shipment of goods:[8]				
Tenor–6 months or less	yes[5]	yes	no	yes
6 months to 9 months	no	yes	yes	no
b. Domestic storage–*readily marketable* staples secured by warehouse receipt issued by				

independent ware-houseman:[6]				
Tenor–6 months or less	yes[5]	yes	no	yes
6 months to 9 months	no	yes	yes	no
c. Domestic storage–*any* goods in the U.S. under contract or sale or going into channels of trade secured throughout their life by warehouse receipt:				
Tenor–6 months or less	no	yes	yes	no
6 months to 9 months	no	yes	yes	no
3. Marketable time deposits (finance bills or working capital acceptances) not related to any specific transaction				
Tenor–any term	no	no	yes	no

This table is an adaptation from a table presented in an unpublished paper from the 7th Annual CIB Conference at New Orleans, October 13, 1975 by Arthur Bardenhagen, Vice President, Irving Trust Company, New York.

[1] In accordance with Regulation A of the Board of Governors as provided by the Federal Reserve Act.

[2] Authorizations for the purchase of acceptances as announced by the Federal Reserve Act.

[3] In accordance with Regulation D of the Board of Governors as provided by the Federal Reserve Act.

[4] Member banks may accept bills in an amount not exceeding at any time 150 percent (or 200 percent if approved by the Board of Governors of (as defined by the Federal Reserve System) of unimpaired capital stock in FRB, Chicago Circular No. 2156 of April 2, 1971). Acceptances growing out of domestic transactions are not to exceed 50 percent of the total of a bank's total acceptance ceiling.

[5] The tenor of nonagricultural bills may not exceed 90 days at the time they are presented for discount with the Federal Reserve.

[6] As of May 10, 1978, the Board of Governors issued the interpretation that bankers' acceptances secured by field warehouse receipts covering readily marketable staples are eligible for discount. Readily marketable staples are defined, in general, as nonbranded goods for which a ready and open market exists. There is a regularly quoted, easily accessible, objective price setting mechanism that determines the market price of the goods.

[7] Proceeds from the sale of an eligible for discount dollar exchange acceptance are not specifically exempted from reserve requirements under Regulation D, Section 204.2 a(vii)(E) effective November 13, 1980, of the Board of Governors as are other acceptances that meet the condition of Section 13(7) of the Federal Reserve act. However, the Federal Reserve Board's legal staff issued an opinion January 15, 1981, stating that the proceeds from the sale of eligible dollar exchange acceptances are exempt from reserve requirements.

[8] Prior to the amendment to Section 13(7) of the Federal Reserve act (October 8, 1982) domestic shipment acceptances required documents conveying title be attached for eligible for discount to apply.

NOTE: Tenor refers to the duration of the acceptance from its creation to maturity. An eligible for discount acceptance must be created by or endorsed by a member bank, according to Section 13(6) of the Federal Reserve Act.

THE SECONDARY MARKET

Banks place acceptances in the secondary market through two channels—direct placements and a network of dealers who "make a market" in the instruments.

The direct sale of acceptances in-house by banks' newly established money-market and investment departments has helped these banks to satisfy customer demand for short-term investments with relatively high yields. Such direct sales allow banks to avoid the added costs of selling through acceptance dealers—still the primary outlet for acceptances.

Bankers' acceptances are sold in the secondary market by a small group of money-market dealers who act as intermediaries between banks and investors. The dealer network is centered in New York City, where about 50 percent of the dollar volume of all acceptances is created. The Open Market Desk of the Federal Reserve Bank of New York is the center of Federal Reserve acceptance activity.

The dealer market has five tiers. The first tier consists of the ten largest acceptance creating domestic banks. Because acceptances of the top-tier banks are generally viewed as the safest and most marketable, these instruments command the lowest rates (i.e., discounts) in the dealer market. Second-tier banks are the next-to-largest U. S. banks in terms of acceptance creation. By virtue of their reputation among dealers and investors, second-tier acceptances usually trade at rates very close to rates for the first tier. Third- and fourth-tier institutions are those remaining U. S. banks that are somewhat active in the dealer acceptance market. Secondary market rates on lower tier acceptances vary considerably across these instruments, but are substantially higher than rates for the top two tiers.

The fifth tier of banks consists of foreign-owned institutions. A subcategory within this tier includes acceptances originated by U. S. branches of Japanese banks. These "Yankee BAs" and others in the fifth tier trade at considerably higher rates than acceptances of comparable U. S. banks. The main reason appears to be the lack of investor recognition of the names and credit standings of these foreign banks—even those among the largest banks in the world. Presumably, rate differentials between fifth-tier acceptances and those in the upper tiers will be lower in the future if information and efficiency in the secondary market improves.[11]

---

[11] For additional details on the operation of the secondary market, see William C. Melton and Jean M. Mahr, "Bankers Acceptances," *Quarterly Review* of the Federal Reserve Bank of New York, Vol. 6, No. 2 (Summer 1981) pp. 39-55.

Acceptances in the top two tiers are eligible for discount, having been created by member banks.[12] Indeed, dealers are disinclined to trade acceptances that are ineligible for discount or that meet only minimum requirements of eligibility for Fed purchase. All dealers exclude ineligible acceptances from the conventional tier structure, and some dealers refuse to trade ineligible acceptances.

CURRENT REGULATORY ISSUES

Prior to the amendment of Section 13(7) of the Federal Reserve Act in October 1982, total outstanding acceptances of an individual bank—acceptances created but not held by the bank—were limited to an amount equal to or less than ". . . one-half of its paid-up and unimpaired capital stock and surplus." Subject to approval from the Federal Reserve Board, the limit on outstanding acceptances could be raised to an amount up to 100 percent of paid-in capital and surplus.

These ceilings posed problems for many major acceptance banks in the late 1970s, even though all major acceptance creating banks had been allowed to expand their individual limits ("aggregate ceilings") on the total volume of acceptances outstanding to 100 percent of capital stock plus surplus.[13] Rapid growth in acceptance volume outpaced the modest growth in banks' capital and threatened to slow the growth of the acceptance market or divert much of the growth to smaller regional banks and U. S. branches of foreign banks.

Legislation relaxing the ceiling on outstanding acceptances, introduced in the Congress in 1981, finally was enacted in October 1982 as part of the Export Trading Company Act of 1982. Section 207 of this act amended Section 13(7) of the Federal Reserve Act in five significant areas, including increases in the aggregate ceilings on acceptances (see box on recent legislation). For the most

---

[12]Recall that a member bank acceptance that meets the requirements of Section 13(7) is eligible for discount. For a nonmember bank, an acceptance meeting the same conditions is eligible for purchase (see Table 6-1). A member or nonmember bank may create an acceptance that is eligible for purchase but that does not meet the requirements of Section 13(7), because its original maturity is in excess of 180 days. Proceeds from the sale of such an ineligible acceptance in the secondary market would be subject to reserve requirements.

[13]Ceilings on the total amount of eligible acceptances outstanding by an individual bank may have resulted in an anomaly in the market. Suppose a member bank creates an acceptance that is eligible for discount in all respects, except the bank now exceeds its Section 13(7) aggregate ceiling. Because such an acceptance does not meet all Section 13(7) requirements, it becomes ineligible for regulatory purposes and subject to reserve requirements. However, the secondary market will treat that acceptance as eligible. It should be noted that this informal interpretation is widely, but not uniformly, accepted and, consequently, needs clarification.

part, this legislation avoided a number of fundamental issues and simply focused on relaxing the permissible ceiling for acceptances as an expedient for market expansion. Further flexibility for individual institutions was provided by permission for "covered" institutions to "participate out" acceptances with other "covered" institutions (member banks and U. S. branches of foreign banks). Through such participations, they are, in effect, permitted to pool the amount of acceptances as a percentage of their joint capital. The acceptance creating bank is allowed to remove the participated acceptance from the amount that counts against its total aggregate ceiling and the amount is added to the total that counts against the other bank's aggregate ceiling.

The debate over this legislation has prompted renewed interest in a broad range of issues, including concentration in the primary and secondary acceptance markets, application of reserve requirements to acceptances, regulatory and institutional features of the secondary market, and the more basic issue of the uniqueness of acceptances for regulatory purposes.

The provisions of the Export Trading Company Act could slow, or even reverse, the restructuring of the supply side of the market in recent years, evidenced by increased acceptance origination at regional banks and U. S. branches of foreign banks (see Figures 6-3 and 6-4). A reconcentration of the market, prompted by the increase in acceptance ceilings for large banks, actually might be favored by the secondary market. Such concentration deepens the market for the most liquid acceptances in the top tiers at the expense of growth and deepening of the market for acceptances in the lower tiers.

Banking, trade, transportation, and communications have changed drastically over the more than 50 years of acceptance legislation. It can be argued that the regulation of bankers' acceptances has failed to keep pace. Implementation of the Monetary Control Act of 1980 left little practical application for the concept of eligibility for discount as applied to member bank acceptances.

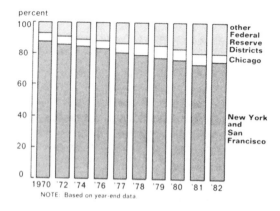

Figure 6-3   Regional banks increase their share of the acceptance market

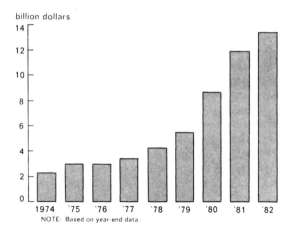

Figure 6-4 Acceptances outstanding from U. S. branches and agencies of foreign banks triple since 1978

The principal application of this concept, as specified in the amended Section 13(7) of the Federal Reserve Act, arises in outlining the administrative rules for acceptances of nonmember depository institutions.

The maturity, or tenor, of created acceptances has been a point of confusion in the market. According to the Amended Section 13(7) and subsequent legislation, member banks may create acceptances eligible for discount with maturities up to 180 days. Under current Open Market Committee regulations, depository institutions in general may create acceptances eligible for purchase with maturities up to 180 days. Neither category with a 180-day maturity is subject to reserve requirements when sold in the secondary market. However, Open Market Committee regulations also permit the creation of acceptances eligible for purchase with maturities up to 270 days. Such acceptances with maturities over 180 days are subject to reserve requirements when sold in the secondary market. Confusion sometimes arises because of the regulatory anomaly that acceptances eligible for purchase with original maturities between 180 and 270 days are subject to reserve requirements when sold in the secondary market, even if the remaining maturity at the time of such sale does not exceed 180 days.

Two regulatory and institutional aspects of the secondary acceptance market deserve careful reexamination. One such feature is the extensive paper shuffling that results from acceptances being physically transported from banks to dealers to investors. Existing technology for book-entry and electric transactions could be applied to make secondary market transactions substantially more efficient, especially for investors not located near dealers. A second feature needing reexamination is the tier structure of the market, which probably understates the quality of acceptances in the lower tiers, particularly the dollar acceptances of foreign banks.

RECENT ACCEPTANCE LEGISLATION

Section 13(7) of the Federal Reserve Act (12 U. S.C. 372), the principal statute governing acceptance creation, was amended in Section 207 of the Export Trading Company Act of 1982. Section 207 contains five modifications governing acceptances, four of which deal with ceilings on outstanding acceptances of individual financial institutions.

• The volume of outstanding acceptances—those sold in the secondary market—was raised from 50 percent to 150 percent of an individual financial institution's "paid-up and unimpaired capital stocks and surplus." This 150 percent rule applies to the maximum amount of outstanding acceptances that an individual institution can have and still qualify its acceptances as eligible for discount under Section 13(6) or purchase under Federal Open Market Committee regulations. Subject to Board approval, the 150 percent rule is relaxed. The upper limit on outstanding acceptances then becomes 200 percent of a financial institution's paid-up capital and surplus. The previous limit subject to Board approval was 100 percent.

• Member banks and U. S. branches and agencies of foreign banks ("covered institutions") now are permitted to participate an acceptance with other such institutions, provided that the participation meets Federal Reserve regulation. By "participating out" a portion of its acceptances to another institution, the creator of the acceptances does not need to count the participated portion in calculating its level of outstanding acceptances—it does not count against its aggregate ceiling—provided that the participating institution is a Federal Reserve member or a qualified U. S. branch or agency of a foreign bank.

• Any Federal or state branch or agency of a foreign bank subject to reserve requirements under Section 7 of the International Banking Act of 1980 now becomes subject to the provisions of Section 13(7) of the Federal Reserve Act. In particular, these institutions become subject to aggregate ceilings on outstanding acceptances, stated in terms of the outstanding acceptances of all U. S. branches and agencies of a given foreign bank as a percentage of the total capital and surplus of the parent institution. No Federally imposed aggregate ceilings on outstanding acceptances previously applied to foreign institutions.

• Total acceptances arising from domestic transactions (shipping and storage) may not exceed 50 percent of an individual institution's allowable outstanding acceptances, including participations. The previous ceiling for domestic acceptances was 50 percent of an institution's paid-in capital and surplus.

• Shipping documents conveying or securing title no longer must be attached at the time of origination for eligible acceptances that finance domestic shipments. This change eliminates a crucial difference in the definition of eligible acceptances between foreign and domestic acceptances in the shipments category.

BACK TO BASICS

Bankers, regulators, and economists disagree over basic issues of the uniqueness of bankers' acceptances and the appropriateness of special regulations covering these instruments. The argument for uniqueness derives from the linkage between the provision of credit and a specific trade transaction matched in maturity and amount. This linkage is considered the basic distinguishing feature of an acceptance. The opposing view, however, emphasizes that it is becoming increasingly difficult to identify many acceptances on the basis of such a linkage to trade. The importance of the linkage of an acceptance to specific imported goods derives from the traditional "self-liquidating" nature of the credit provided by an acceptance. That is, the credit obligation of the acceptance can be liquidated through the sale of the imported goods to which the acceptance is specifically tied. It can be argued, however, that the self-liquidating nature of acceptances does not provide a convincing rationale for the special regulatory status of acceptances.

To understand the funding properties of an acceptance, it is useful to compare a bank's acceptance activity to its funding of a conventional loan through the sale of a certificate of deposit (CD). Three principal differences exist for the two types of bank funding operations. The first is that under current regulations the funds obtained through the sale of an eligible banker's acceptance in the secondary market are not subject to reserve requirements. Therefore, acceptances provide a potentially cheaper source of funds than CDs on which reserve requirements are applied.

Second, theoretically an acceptance is tied to a specific transaction for a stated time period. While it is true that the importer may extinguish its liability at any time by prepaying it to the accepting bank, there is little incentive to do so because the effective cost of the credit extended would increase. In the case of CD funding of trade credit, the maturity of the loan and the maturity of the CD funding instrument in most cases would not coincide. The loan may be secured by the trade shipment, but the loan and the traded goods are not directly related to the CD. Bank funds raised through CD issuance are fungible—i.e., these funds can be used for any permissible bank investment purpose. On the other hand, an acceptance theoretically is tied to a specific transaction. The acceptance may not be "rolled over" (unless under exceptional circumstances such as the goods being tied up at dockside due to a dock strike, for example) nor may a new acceptance be created to cover the same transaction. If an extension of credit were needed to finance the transaction for a longer period than permitted under the terms of the original acceptance an alternative credit arrangement would be required. If the lending bank were to extend the customer's credit, the funding of that loan would have to incorporate some alternative liability management arrangement. Therefore, trade financing through acceptances and through loans financed by CDs have differing implications for asset-liability management.

The third difference between these funding techniques deals with the types of investor security provided by the instruments. For a bankers' acceptance acquired in the secondary market, the investor is protected by the primary liability of the acceptance bank and the secondary, or contingent, liability of the drawer of the acceptance. The CD holder has only the primary liability of the issuing bank (plus deposit insurance protection up to $100,000).

To date, the distinctions between bankers' acceptances and other funding methods have been viewed by legislators and regulators as sufficient reasons for treating acceptances as special instruments. As a result, bankers' acceptances continue to be distinct financial instruments that are growing in importance and gaining increased market approval. This view could change in the future, however, for as the size of the market increases, the issues of uniqueness and preferential regulation are likely to receive a more critical appraisal.

BIBLIOGRAPHY

Alford, Gary L. "Tight credit and the banks—1966 and 1969 compared," Federal Reserve Bank of Chicago. *Business Conditions*, (May, 1970), 4-11.

Bardenhagen, Arthur. "Bankers' Acceptances under Federal Regulation," unpublished paper presented at the seventh annual CIB Conference, New Orleans, October 13, 1975. New York: Irving Trust Bank.

Continental Illinois National Bank and Trust Company of Chicago. *Commercial Letters of Credit*. International Banking Department, Chicago.

———— *Guide to Bankers' Acceptances*. Financial Services Department, Chicago.

Federal Reserve Bank of New York. "Bankers' Dollar Acceptances—United States." Monthly statistical release, Office of Public Information.

First National Bank of Chicago. *Collections, Letters of Credit, Acceptances*. International Trade Finance Division, Chicago.

Goldberg, Michael A. "Commercial Letters of Credit and Bankers' Acceptances," *Below the Bottom Line: The Use of Contingencies and Commitments by Commercial Banks*, Staff Studies 113, Board of Governors of the Federal Reserve System, 1982.

Hackley, Howard H. *Lending Functions of the Federal Reserve Banks: A History*. Washington: Federal Reserve Board, 1973.

Harfield, Henry. *Bank Credits and Acceptances*, 5th ed. New York: Ronald Press, 1974.

Helfrich, Ralph T. "Trading in Bankers' Acceptances: A View From the Acceptance Desk of the Federal Reserve Bank of New York," Federal Reserve Bank of New York, *Monthly Review*, LVIII (February, 1976), 51-57.

Hervey, Jack L. "Bankers' acceptances." Federal Reserve Bank of Chicago, *Business Conditions* (May, 1976), 3-11.

Kvasnicka, Joseph G. "Bankers' acceptances used more widely," Federal Reserve Bank of Chicago, *Business Conditions* (May, 1965), 9-16.

Melton, William C. and Mahr, Jean M. "Bankers' Acceptances," Federal Reserve Bank of New York, *Quarterly Review*, VI No. 2 (Summer, 1981), 39-55.

U. S. Board of Governors of the Federal Reserve System. Federal Reserve Act (approved December 23, 1913) as amended. (Also, 12 USCA various sections).

NEGOTIABLE CERTIFICATES OF DEPOSIT*

Bruce J. Summers

7

Negotiable certificates of deposit (negotiable CDs) are the most important source of purchased funds to U. S. banks that are practitioners of liability management. Moreover, they have become one of the major types of liquid assets in the portfolios of many investors. Recent financial market developments, including increased competition among financial institutions, high and sometimes volatile patterns of interest rates, and regulatory changes have all led to significant changes in the money markets generally, and in the market for negotiable CDs in particular. This article describes the market for negotiable CDs, placing particular emphasis on developments that have occurred over the past decade or so.

TYPES OF ISSUERS

It is possible to distinguish between four general classes of negotiable CDs based on the type of issuer, because the characteristics of these four types of CDs, including rates paid, risk, and depth of market, can vary considerably. The most important, and the oldest of the four groups, consists of negotiable CDs, called domestic CDs, issued by U. S. banks domestically. Dollar denominated negotiable CDs issued by banks abroad are called Eurodollar CDs or

*Reprinted, with deletions and minor editorial revisions, from the *Economic Review*, July/August 1980, pp. 8-19, with permission of the Federal Reserve Bank of Richmond.

Euro CDs,[1] while negotiable CDs issued by the U. S. branches of foreign banks are known as Yankee CDs. Finally, some nonbank depository institutions, particularly savings and loan associations, have begun to issue negotiable CDs. These are referred to as thrift CDs.

DOMESTIC CDs

Negotiable CDs issued by U. S. banks domestically are large denomination (greater than $100,000) time deposit liabilities evidenced by a written instrument or certificate. The certificate specifies the amount of the deposit, the maturity date, the rate of interest, and the terms under which interest is calculated. While banks are free to offer market determined interest rates on time deposits in amounts above $100,000, negotiable CDs included, the minimum denomination acceptable for secondary market trading in domestic CDs is $1 million. The term to maturity on newly issued domestic CDs is the outcome of negotiation between a bank and its customers, the individual instrument usually tailored to fit the liquidity requirements of the purchaser. Regulations limit the minimum maturity on deposits of U. S. banks to 14 days.[2] Newly issued domestic CDs typically have maturities that run from 30 days to 12 months. The average maturity of outstanding negotiable CDs is about three months.

Interest rates on newly issued negotiable CDs, called primary market rates, are determined by market forces and sometimes are directly negotiated between the issuer and the depositor. Domestic CD rates are quoted on an interest-bearing basis; rates on most other money market instruments, such as Treasury bills, bankers acceptances, and commercial paper are calculated on a discount basis. Interest is computed for the actual number of days to maturity on a 360-day year basis and can be either fixed for the term of the instrument or variable. Interest on fixed-rate negotiable CDs with original terms to maturity of up to one year is normally paid at maturity; on longer-dated instruments, interest is normally paid semiannually. If variable, the rate usually changes every month or three months and is tied to the secondary market rate on domestic CDs having maturities equal to the variable term of the contract.

Domestic CDs may be issued in either registered or bearer form. The great majority of negotiable CDs, however, are bearer instruments. In fact, most banks automatically classify bearer CDs as negotiable instruments and classify registered CDs along with large time deposits open account as non-negotiable instruments.

---

[1] Some dollar denominated CDs are issued in foreign locations other than Europe. For example, banks in Hong Kong have issued Asian CDs, while the branches of at least two U. S. banks have issued Nassau CDs. Markets for these instruments are just developing, however.

[2] Prior to mid-1980 the minimum maturity was 30 days. (Ed. footnote.)

Domestic CDs are paid for in immediately available funds on the day of purchase. They are redeemed for immediately available funds on the maturity date. Many investors in domestic CDs prefer to purchase and settle in New York. For this reason, regional banks that are active in the CD market issue and redeem their CDs sold to national customers through a New York Correspondent bank acting as a clearing agent.

The Importance of Regulation

Unlike most other participants in the domestic money market, commercial banks are heavily regulated. Government regulation has had an important influence on the development of the market for negotiable CDs since its inception. Two Federal Reserve regulations in particular have had an influence on the negotiable CD market, namely Regulation Q, which governs interest paid on deposits by member banks, and Regulation D, which prescribes reserve requirements that must be held against deposits.

Both Regulations D and Q require that time deposits have a minimum maturity of fourteen days. Moreover, Regulation Q prohibits commercial banks from purchasing their own outstanding negotiable CDs, an action that would be interpreted under the regulation as payment of a deposit before maturity. Some investors have horizons much shorter than 14 days and might prefer to avoid having to routinely enter the secondary market to raise cash by selling negotiable CDs. Consequently, banks have had an incentive to develop alternative instruments to negotiable CDs to meet these investors' demands. The minimum maturity requirement on negotiable CDs is likely an important factor explaining the rapid growth in bank repurchase agreements, which are considered nondeposit liabilities and are therefore not subject to the 14-day minimum maturity requirement on interest-bearing deposits.

Member banks of the Federal Reserve System, a group that accounts for the largest share of negotiable CDs outstanding, have always been required to hold noninterest-bearing reserves against deposits as prescribed by Regulation D. Beginning September 1, 1980, all depository institutions having either transactions accounts or nonpersonal time deposits (which include virtually all negotiable CDs) will be required to hold reserves as specified in Regulation D. Reserve requirements increase the cost of funds to depository institutions since a portion of total assets must be set aside in noninterest-earning reserve accounts. Reserve requirements against negotiable CDs have varied over the years and have at times been graduated by both the maturity of the deposit and the amount of total balances held. The Federal Reserve varies reserve requirements primarily as an aid in achieving the objectives of monetary and credit policy. In the case of CDs, however, Regulation D has also been used to achieve a bank regulatory goal, namely the lengthening of the maturity structure of the commercial banking system's liabilities. Thus, the size of reserve requirements on CDs has at times been inversely related to maturity.

Money Center versus Regional

About one-third of domestic CDs are issued by a handful of large money center banks in New York City, while the remainder are issued by about 200 large regional banks located around the U. S. Although both the money center and regional institutions sell their newly issued instruments primarily to large national and multinational investors, the former group of banks is much more heavily involved in this market. Banks issuing negotiable CDs usually post a list of base rates, with spreads expressed in increments of five basis points, for the various maturities they are writing. These rates are adjusted upward or downward depending on the particular bank's need for funds and on market conditions. Regional banks located in cities that serve as headquarters for major corporations are often able to book a large portion of their CDs directly through the main office, without having to work through a New York correspondent. The regional issuers that are most active in the CD market, however, keep a supply of blank but signed certificates in New York so that investors not located in their area and wishing to purchase their CDs can do so conveniently. Regional banks that issue large amounts of domestic CDs but that depend heavily on purchases by investors located outside their geographic area typically employ a sales force to actively market their certificates.

Although almost all banks on occasion sell their newly issued certificates to securities dealers, most prefer to sell directly to investors. The advantages of selling directly to retail include paying a lower rate on the new issues, since the dealer intermediary is eliminated, and having more information over where certificates are ending up. Banks would prefer that their CDs be held as investments and not sold before maturity, since secondary market sales could compete with attempts to market new offerings in the future. Although dealers sometimes hold CDs for investment purposes, most of their purchases are passed through to retail investors in the secondary or resale market. Regional banks that are attempting to build a name in the domestic CD market, or that are trying to reestablish a name after a period of inactivity, generally must operate through dealers. In these cases, the dealers accept marketing responsibility for the newly issued certificates. When particularly large offerings come to market most banks, even the money center institutions, rely on dealers to help distribute the issue. A new offering of several hundred million dollars, for example, may be difficult to place directly even for a bank with a large base of regular customers.

Over the years, investors have developed preferences for the CDs of certain issuers, or groups of issuers, that are reflected in the rate structure on CDs. The rate required on the CD of a top name bank may be 5 to 25 basis points lower than that required on the CD of a lesser known institution. Historically, the rate spread on domestic CDs of the top and lesser name issuers has fluctuated with the level of interest rates, the spread widening in high interest rate periods. Prior to 1974, investors distinguished roughly between two groups of issuing banks in the domestic CD market, prime and nonprime. The prime banks included the large and well-known major money-center institutions, while the nonprime category included the smaller, lesser known regional banks. In 1974, as concerns about the liquidity of the banking system were aroused by problems at Franklin National Bank and Herstatt Bank of West Germany, investor tiering of domestic CDs by issuer became more flexible and complicated. Size remained important, but investors' perceptions of financial strength began to be formed more specifically, so that the top tier of preferred banks dropped in number and tended to vary over time. Nonetheless, investors still place the greatest emphasis in assessing risk on bank size, so that New York City banks continue to dominate the top tier. The more conventional factors used to assess risk, for example, capital ratios, asset growth rates, and earnings variability, remain of secondary importance in determining which banks are classified in the top tier. An implication of this is that portfolio managers have the opportunity to improve yield, without taking a commensurate increase in risk, by investing in the domestic CDs of regional banks that meet the traditional tests of financial soundness but that do not fall within the top tier.

EURODOLLAR CDs

Like a domestic CD, a Eurodollar CD is a dollar denominated instrument evidencing a time deposit placed with a bank at an agreed upon rate of interest for a specific period of time. Unlike a domestic CD, however, a Euro CD is issued abroad, either by the foreign branch of a U. S. bank or by a foreign bank. The market for Euro CDs is centered in London and is therefore frequently called the London dollar CD market.

This market originated in 1966 with a Eurodollar CD issue by the London branch of Citibank. The incentive to U. S. banks to start issuing CDs abroad was provided by regulations restricting their ability to raise funds in the domestic money market, especially Regulation Q. Since it is free of interest rate regulation, the Eurodollar market provides banks the opportunity to raise funds for domestic lending even when their ability to issue domestic CDs is restricted. The Euro CD market has grown rapidly since 1966. Euro CD outstandings at London banks totaled over $43 billion at year-end 1979. The foreign branches of U. S. banks dominate the London dollar CD market, accounting for about 60 percent of all CDs issued by banks located in London. Japanese banks rank second in importance, their share of the market having increased from 9 percent in 1976 to 17 percent in 1979.

Euro CD maturities run from 30 days out to 5 years, but shorter terms ranging from one month to one year are most common. By and large, the customer base is the same as that for domestic CDs, i.e., most Euro CDs are placed with the same large corporations that are active purchasers of domestic CDs in the U. S. In fact, some of the largest CD dealers in the U. S. are represented in London, where they make an active market in Euro CDs. These dealers, and many large investors as well, view their investment activity as essentially one worldwide position and manage their Euro CD and domestic CD portfolios in an integrated fashion.

Inasmuch as there is a five-hour time zone difference between London and New York, perfect synchronization of delivery and payment on Euro CDs is very difficult. Therefore, settlement for Euro CDs is normally two working days forward, which is the value date, and payment is made in clearinghouse funds. Dollar settlement is made in New York, even though the certificates themselves are issued and held in safekeeping in London. The First National Bank of Chicago has set up a Euro CD clearing center in London to smooth payment and delivery on these instruments. The clearing center, which is open to banks, dealers, and investors, operates on the clearinghouse concept, where debits and credits are cancelled by computer and only net settlement is made.

YANKEE CDs

Yankee CDs are negotiable CDs issued and payable in dollars to bearer in the U. S. (more specifically, in New York) by the branch offices of major foreign banks. They are sometimes referred to as foreign-domestic CDs. The foreign issuers of Yankee CDs are well-known international banks headquartered primarily in Western Europe, England and Japan. Investors in Yankee CDs look to the creditworthiness of the parent organization in assessing their risk, since the obligation of a branch of a foreign bank is in actuality an obligation of the parent bank. The Yankee CD market is primarily a shorter term market; most newly issued instruments have maturities of three months or less.

Foreign banks have operated branches in the U. S. for many years, most being located in New York City. These banks were initially established to provide credit services to their parent banks' multi-national business customers. Their number increased greatly during the 1970s, and the U. S. branches became more aggressive competitors for the loan business of U. S. corporations. Their major sources of funds have included borrowings from foreign parent organizations, purchases in the Federal funds market, and more recently the issuance of large time deposits to U. S. investors. At year-end 1979 the time deposits of U. S. branches of foreign banks due to private investors and public bodies totaled about $25 billion. It is estimated that about $20 billion of this amount was in the form of negotiable CDs. Some individual foreign branches have Yankee CDs outstanding well in excess of $1 billion.

The U. S. branches of foreign banks at first placed most of their Yankee CDs directly with their established loan customers, who through experience were familiar with the reputations of the issuers. Since their names were not well known outside this small group, the U. S. branches of foreign banks were forced to rely on dealers to market their CDs as reliance on this source of funds grew. The largest part of their offerings have until recently been placed through dealers, several of which are now active market makers for Yankee CDs. Foreign bank names have become much better known and acceptable in the U. S., however, so that today it is much more commonplace for foreign branches to sell their negotiable CDs directly at retail. Secondary market trading in Yankee CDs has increased greatly in just the last several years so that the liquidity of such instruments now rivals that of better rated domestic CDs.

An important institutional feature of foreign banking operations in the U. S. is that, until recently, foreign branches have been state-licensed and not subject to Federal Reserve regulations. Thus, until recently Yankee CDs have not been subject to reserve requirements under Regulation D. This exemption from regulation probably helped establish the market for Yankee CDs, because the U. S. branches of foreign banks could pay higher rates on their certificates than could domestic banks but still not incur higher costs than their U. S. banking competitors as a result of saving on reserve requirements. *The International Banking Act of 1978* provides that large foreign banks doing business in the U. S. should be subject to the same Federal Reserve regulations as domestic banks. The U. S. branches of large foreign banks become subject to Regulations D and Q as of September 4, 1980.

Yankee CDs, along with certain other managed liabilities of the U. S. branches of foreign banks, became subject to reserve requirements for the first time in October 1979. This change subjected certain managed liabilities above a base amount to an 8 percent reserve requirement, which was subsequently increased to 10 percent in March 1980, and then reduced to 5 percent in May 1980. The imposition of marginal reserve requirements on the managed liabilities of the U. S. branches of foreign banks may have had the effect of slowing the growth of Yankee CDs. This is because the market is still young, with new issuing banks entering regularly. These new banks entering the Yankee CD market typically market their negotiable CDs aggressively in an attempt to build volume and goodwill quickly. Starting from a low or zero reserve exempt base, however, the newly entering banks bear a reserve cost on all of their negotiable CDs, not just a fractional amount like established issuers. This higher cost has likely discouraged new entries into the Yankee CD market.

THRIFT INSTITUTION CDs

Thrift institutions, particularly savings and loan associations (SLAs), have become active competitors for large time deposits not subject to Regulation Q ceilings. Most of their large domestic time deposits are practically if not legally nonnegotiable, i.e., there is very little secondary market activity in thrift CDs. The large denomination CDs of FSLIC insured SLAs totaled nearly $30 billion at year-end 1979.

Recent changes in Federal Home Loan Bank Board regulations grant Federally insured savings and loans considerable broadened authority to market Euro CDs. At least one large California SLA has placed a $10 million package of unsecured CDs in the Eurodollar market. The success of such placements depends on the size and financial strength of the issuing thrift. Other thrifts have taken steps to place Euro CDs that are backed by mortgage loan collateral. Part of this process involves obtaining a credit rating from Standard & Poor's Corporation, which is now making such ratings. So far, these mortgage-backed offerings have been for longer terms, i.e., five years.

NONNEGOTIABLE CDs

Nonnegotiable CDs are an important part of total large time deposits issued by commercial banks. In fact, nonnegotiable CDs of U. S. banks have grown faster than domestic negotiable CDs in recent years and now are more important than domestic negotiable CDs as a source of funds. It is important to understand what nonnegotiable CDs are, because many investors active in the market for negotiable CDs are willing to substitute between the two types of instruments.

Nonnegotiable CDs are not considered money market instruments because they lack the liquidity of negotiable certificates. Some nonnegotiable instruments, such as time deposits open account, are legally nonnegotiable. Others, such as registered CDs, are technically negotiable but are in practice nonnegotiable because of the administrative difficulty involved in changing ownership. Some banks have ceased issuing certificates and have instead instituted book entry accounting procedures for registered CDs. This practice seems to confirm that liquidity is a secondary consideration to investors purchasing such instruments.

Among the largest investors in nonnegotiable CDs are public bodies, e.g., state and municipal governments. Often, state law requires that public bodies invest their funds locally, that all investments be registered in the name of the governmental unit, and that investments be secured. A large share of banks' total large time deposits are secured CDs issued in registered form to state and local governments. As might be expected, regional banks are more heavily dependent upon such funds than are the money center banks.

It is not just public bodies that invest in nonnegotiable certificates, however. Some corporate investors are willing to sacrifice the liquidity provided by an instrument that can be traded in the secondary market for a small increase in yield. Also, some banks have gentleman's agreements with customers who take their registered or book-entry CDs which provide that, in the event cash is needed on an emergency basis, the bank will exchange the registered CD for a bearer CD. In addition to nonfinancial corporations, some money market funds have invested in nonnegotiable CDs.

RISK AND RETURN

Negotiable CDs subject investors to two major types of risk, credit risk and marketability risk. Credit risk is the risk of default on the part of the bank issuing the CD. This is relevant even for U. S. banks which are insured by the FDIC, since domestic CDs are issued in large denominations and deposit insurance only covers up to $100,000 of a depositor's funds. Marketability risk reflects the fact that a ready buyer for a CD might not be available when the owner is ready to sell. Although the secondary market in CDs is well developed, it does not possess the depth of the U. S. Government securities market. These risks are reflected in the yields on negotiable CDs. It should be noted, however, that yields on money market instruments may vary for reasons other than differences in risk, e.g., due to changes in their relative supplies.

Figure 7-1 plots the spread between the secondary market yields on two types of 3-month CDs, domestic and Euro, and the secondary market rate on 3-month Treasury bills. The spread is positive and tends to widen in periods of high interest rates. For example, the domestic CD-Treasury bill spread was generally below 100 basis points for the periods 1971-72 and 1976-78, but widened greatly in 1973-74. The spread peaked at 458 basis points in August 1974. The chart shows that rates on Euro CDs are almost always above those on domestic CDs, typically by about 20-30 basis points, and that the Euro-domestic CD rate spread tends to widen in periods of high interest rates. The

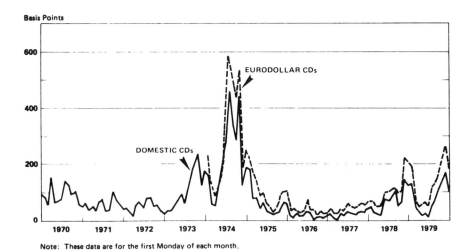

Note: These data are for the first Monday of each month.

Source: Salomon Brothers, An Analytical Record of Yields and Yield Spreads.

Figure 7-1   Spreads between secondary market rates on 3-month maturity CDs and 3-month maturity Treasury bills (bond equivalent)

higher rate on Euro CDs in part reflects the credit risk premium required by investors in these instruments; this premium tends to increase in periods of stress in the financial markets. There is no reserve requirement against such deposits, and therefore the total cost to the issuing institution is not necessarily greater than the total cost to a domestic bank issuing a CD. In fact, the reserve adjusted costs of domestic and Euro CDs tend to be very close in times of financial market normalcy.

There is no published rate series for Yankee CDs. Dealers indicate, however, that Yankee CD rates move very closely, within plus or minus 10 basis points, of Euro CD rates. These two types of CDs are good substitutes and their rates should be expected to move close together except due to technical factors, such as relative supply. On average, though, Yankee CD rates average somewhat lower than Euro CD rates. There are two reasons for this. First, Yankee CDs, unlike Euro CDs are subject to U. S. laws and regulations and therefore do not bear sovereign or foreign country risk. Second, it is easier and less costly for dealers to engage in Yankee CD transactions than in Euro CD transactions. Yankee CDs are purchased in the U. S. and positions are financed with RPs or Federal funds, while Euro CDs are purchased abroad and entail international money transfers.

Quality Ratings

One major rating firm, Moody's Investors Service, Inc., has begun to rate the CDs of banks. So far, only a small number of regional U. S. banks have received ratings and a handful of applications are in process. Foreign banks issuing Yankee CDs, however, have more actively sought formal ratings than have U. S. banks. This is understandable, since they are still attempting to establish their names with U. S. investors. The rating process used by Moody's for CDs is virtually identical to that used for rating commercial paper. It is not the particular issue that is rated but rather the issuing organization itself. The CD ratings, like those for commercial paper, are designated P-1, P-2, and P-3. Because of the closeness of the rating processes, one should never expect to see a divergence between a bank's CD rating and its commercial paper rating. It is possible, however, for a bank's CD rating to differ somewhat from the commercial paper rating of its parent holding company.

Standard & Poor's Corporation has begun rating the CDs of SLAs. Like Moody's, S&P has experience rating commercial paper issued by SLAs, but has so far applied bond rating methods to thrift CDs because of their longer terms. If asked to rate short-term thrift CDs, S&P will likely apply a variant of its commercial paper rating system.

RATES AND MATURITIES

During the first decade of their existence, negotiable CDs were written exclusively under fixed interest coupon contracts. Certificates were written specifying a particular rate of interest that would be paid for a given term to maturity. This pricing arrangement suited investors quite well, at least during the relatively stable interest rate environment of the 1960s. Those seeking a compromise between return and liquidity could invest in short-dated negotiable CDs, while those seeking extra yield could extend the maturity of their investments out to six months or perhaps even longer. So long as the upward sloping yield curve remained the norm, banks and investors had a reasonable basis for trading off higher yield against longer term.

In the latter part of the 1960s interest rate conditions changed dramatically. Interest rate fluctuations increased, and the general level of rates began to trend upward. Under such circumstances, investors can be expected to shift their preferences to shorter term instruments, and this happened in the CD market. By 1974 the average maturity of outstanding domestic CDs fell dramatically to about two months from the three-and-one-half-month length more common in the 1960s. In September 1974 the Federal Reserve provided banks an incentive to lengthen their negotiable CD maturities by restructuring reserve requirements in such a way as to raise the reserve cost of shorter term certificates. This incentive was reinforced in December 1974 when reserve requirements were set at 6 percent for negotiable CDs with an original maturity of less than six months and at 3 percent for negotiable CDs with an original maturity of six months or more. In October 1975 the reserve requirement was further lowered to 1 percent for CDs with original maturities of four years or more, and finally in January 1976 the requirement was lowered to 2½ percent on certificates with original maturities of from six months to four years. In keeping with this pattern, the marginal reserve program introduced in October 1979 exempts CDs with original maturities of one year and greater. In addition to these changes in reserve requirements, domestic banks had an incentive to increase CD maturities as a result of the deteriorating liquidity positions of their balance sheets. By the mid-1970s, therefore, the time was ripe for a fundamental change in the terms under which negotiable CDs had traditionally been offered.

Fixed-Rate Rollover CDs

Early in 1977 a large New York bank, Morgan Guaranty Trust Company, introduced to its customers on a selective basis fixed-rate rollover CDs, or "roly poly" CDs, in minimum amounts of $5 million. These instruments had full terms to maturity of from two to five years, but consisted of a series of six-month maturity instruments. Investors would sign a contract to leave a deposit with the bank for, say, four years, but instead of receiving a CD maturing in four years would receive a six-month CD. The contract obligated the investor to renew, or roll over, the six-month instrument eight consecutive times at the rate negotiated at the inception of the contract. Although the bank hoped to qualify for the four-year CD reserve requirement with these deposits, a ruling by the Federal Reserve made the rollover CDs reservable at the higher six-month maturity reserve requirement.

These instruments bore rates somewhat above the rate on Treasury notes of equal maturity, but below the rate offered on a straight two-to-five-year CD. The feeling was that an investor would earn the long-term rate but get enhanced liquidity since a single six-month issue in the series could be sold in the secondary market. This fixed-rate type of instrument proved more attractive to the issuing banks than to the investing public during a period of rising interest rates. Consequently, a sizable market in fixed-rate rollover CDs never developed.

Variable Rate CDs

Variable rate or variable coupon CDs (VRCDs or VCCDs) have the rollover feature described above but also entail periodic resettings of the coupon rate and periodic payment of interest. Interest on each component or "leg" of a VRCD is calculated according to the same rules as on conventional CDs. The dated date is the original dated date for the first leg, and for subsequent legs it is the date of the interest payment on the preceding leg. VRCDs were first offered in the Euro CD market, where floating rate instruments were an accepted method of doing business long before they were in the U. S. The VRCD was initially introduced in the domestic and Yankee CD markets by those large banks having Euro CD experience, but the new method of writing certificates was quickly adopted by the major regional banks as well. VRCDs were introduced domestically in 1975, grew in popularity in the latter 1970s, and have now become a major innovation in the market for negotiable CDs.

VRCDs range in full maturity from six months to four years, the most common full maturities being six months and one year. The rollover period for these instruments varies. For example, from 1975 to 1977, three- and six-month rollovers were common. The higher short-term interest rates of 1979 and 1980, however, have resulted in the three-month and one-month rollovers becoming standard. Investor preferences for full maturity and rollover frequency are directly related to expected interest rate patterns, periods of stable or declining rates leading to preferences for longer full maturities and longer rolls, and periods of rising rates and upward sloping yield curves leading to preferences for shorter maturities and shorter rolls. The four VRCD issues having the greatest popularity at present are (1) six-month (full maturity)/three-month (roll), (2) six-month/one-month, (3) one-year/three-month, and (4) one-year/one-month.

Coupon rates set on each new leg of VRCDs are based on the preceding day's secondary market CD rates reported daily by the Federal Reserve Bank of New York. These are averages of offered rates quoted by major dealers. Collection of interest payments, and of principal at final maturity, is made by presenting the VRCD to the issuing bank or the issuing bank's agent. When presented for collection of interest, the certificate is stamped with the amount of the previous period's interest and the new coupon rate. Payment of interest and principal is made in immediately available funds. VRCDs normally carry an interest premium over the rate one would expect to receive on a conventional CD. This premium has usually been about 15 basis points for six-month full maturities, 20 basis points for one-year full maturities, and 25 basis points for eighteen-month full maturities. As in the case of conventional CDs, VRCDs issued by the top tier banks carry somewhat lower rates than those issued by lesser name institutions.

The typical size of a VRCD issue ranges from \$50-\$200 million for large banks and \$25-\$100 million for smaller banks, but issues as large as \$400 million are not uncommon. The largest portion of VRCD issues is underwritten by dealers, who usually charge the issuing bank a small commission for underwriting and distribution services. Dealers have been willing to take larger positions in VRCDs than in longer term conventional CDs since there is less market risk involved and because retail demand has proved quite strong. So far, retail demand has been so strong that dealers have placed a major portion of newly issued VRCDs on an order basis.

Investors treat VRCDs as a conventional CD once the coupon has been set for the last time and the certificate is on its last leg. Since VRCDs carry an interest premium over the rate paid on a conventional CD, a VRCD on its last leg offers the potential for trading profits.

Estimates by market participants place the total amount of VRCDs outstanding in early 1980 at \$12 billion, about double the amount outstanding only six months earlier. Most of these are domestic CDs. Thus, in the short time since they have become popular, VRCDs have grown to equal over 10 percent of the total volume of domestic CDs outstanding. To date, money market funds have been the most active investors in VRCDs.

DEALERS

There are currently about 25 dealers in CDs, all of which are active in the domestic CDs of top tier banks and some of which specialize in regional names or Yankee CDs. The center of the dealer market is New York City but the larger dealers have branches in major U. S. cities and in London. Two main functions of the CD dealers are to distribute CDs at retail, either after first taking new issues into their own positions or by acting as brokers, and to support a secondary market in negotiable CDs. In accomplishing the latter, dealers must stand ready to make a market, i.e., buy and sell CDs. Bid and offering prices are constantly maintained and the typical spread is between 5 and 10 basis points, but narrower spreads on good names with short remaining terms to maturity are common.

The normal round-lot trade in negotiable CDs between dealers and retail customers is $1 million, but increases to $5 million for inter-dealer trades. There is, of course, a great deal of variety among the CDs being traded at any given time with respect to issuer, maturity, and other contractual terms. Consequently, dealers post bid and asked prices for certificates issued by a particular tier bank, with maturity identified as early or late in a particular month. For example, the bid and ask price for a top trading name might be for "early December" or "late January."

Financing of dealer CD positions is largely done using RPs. Since CD collateral is more risky than U. S. Government security collateral, RPs against CDs are usually slightly more expensive than RPs against, say, Treasury bills. For the same reason, it is more difficult to get term RP financing for CDs. Normal practice in the RP market is to finance the face value of a money market instrument. Since CDs bear interest, dealers must finance any accrued interest on CDs held in position from some source other than RP, e.g., from capital.

Growth in dealer activity has paralleled growth in the market for negotiable CDs. As the market expanded in the 1960s daily average transactions were in the $50-$60 million range, and the daily average dealer positions ranged from $200-$300 million. As mentioned, the secondary market nearly dried up in 1969, daily average dealer transactions falling to only $9 million and daily average positions falling to only $27 million during that year. Dealer activity burgeoned in the 1970s, when trading opportunities increased due to the more aggressive marketing of negotiable CDs by regional banks and with the development of the Yankee CD. By 1975, for example, daily average dealer positions increased about fivefold to $1.4 billion and transactions increased sixteen times to $800 million. By 1979, positions further expanded to $2.7 billion and transactions to $1.7 billion.

SUMMARY

The market for negotiable CDs issued domestically by U. S. banks grew rapidly but, due to the effects of interest rate regulation, unevenly during the 1960s. Regulation Q restrictions on rates that could be paid on domestic CDs led to the introduction of the Euro CD in 1966. After interest rate ceilings on domestic CDs were removed in the early 1970s the market grew dramatically. Regional banks became particularly active during this period, and the U. S. branches of foreign banks began issuing Yankee CDs. Most recently, savings and loan associations have also begun issuing CDs. Investors can now choose among a number of issues in selecting CDs, i.e., domestic, Euro, Yankee, and thrift.

Not only have the types of issuers multiplied, but the character of CD contracts has changed as well. The conventional fixed-rate CD, which is primarily a short-term instrument, has been modified to extend the term and float the rate. The resulting instrument, the variable rate CD, has quickly gained popularity among investors. The terms under which VRCDs are offered, however, change constantly in response to investor preferences.

The rate of change in the market for negotiable CDs has been particularly rapid in recent years. This change is the outcome of competitive forces working to redesign a financial market to better suit the needs of its major participants.

REFERENCES

1. Crane, Dwight B. "A Study of Interest Rate Spreads in the 1974 CD Market." *Journal of Bank Research* (Autumn 1976), pp. 213-224.
2. Giddy, Ian H. "Why Eurodollars Grow." *Columbia Journal of World Business* (Fall 1979), pp. 54-60.
3. Melton, William C. "The Market for Large Negotiable CDs." *Quarterly Review*, Federal Reserve Bank of New York (Winter 1977-78), pp. 22-34.
4. Slovin, Myron B., and Sushka, Marie Elizabeth. "An Econometric Model of the Market for Negotiable Certificates of Deposits." *Journal of Monetary Economics* (October 1979), pp. 551–568.
5. Stigum, Marcia. *The Money Market: Myth, Reality, and Practice.* Homewood, Illinois: Dow Jones-Irwin, 1978.

COMMERCIAL PAPER*

Peter A. Abken

8

Commercial paper is a short-term unsecured promissory note that is generally sold by large corporations on a discount basis to institutional investors and to other corporations. Since commercial paper is unsecured and bears only the name of the issuer, the market has generally been dominated by large corporations with the highest credit ratings. In recent years commercial paper has attracted much attention because of its rapid growth and its use as an alternative to short-term bank loans. The number of firms issuing commercial paper rose from slightly over 300 in 1965 to about 1,000 in 1980. Moreover, the outstanding volume of commercial paper increased at an annual rate of 12.4 percent during the 1970s to a level of $123 billion in June 1980. This article describes the commercial paper market.

MARKET CHARACTERISTICS

The principal issuers of commercial paper include finance companies, nonfinancial companies, and bank holding companies. These issuers participate in the market for different reasons and in different ways. Finance companies raise funds on a more-or-less continuous basis in the commercial paper market to support their consumer and business lending. These commercial paper sales in part provide interim financing between issues of long-term debentures. Nonfinancial companies issue commercial paper at less frequent intervals than

*Reprinted, with deletions, from the *Economic Review*, March/April 1981, pp. 11-22, with permission of the Federal Reserve Bank of Richmond.

do finance companies. These firms issue paper to meet their funding requirements for short-term or seasonal expenditures such as inventories, payrolls, and tax liabilities. Bank holding companies use the commercial paper market to finance primarily banking-related activities such as leasing, mortgage banking, and consumer finance.

Denominations and Maturities

Like other instruments of the money market, commercial paper is sold to raise large sums of money quickly and for short periods of time. Although sometimes issued in denominations as small as $25,000 or $50,000, most commercial paper offerings are in multiples of $100,000. The average purchase size of commercial paper is about $2 million. The average issuer has $120 million in outstanding commercial paper; some of the largest issuers individually have several billion dollars in outstanding paper.

Exemption from registration requirements with the Securities and Exchange Commission reduces the time and expense of readying an issue of commercial paper for sale. Almost all outstanding commercial paper meets the conditions for exemption, namely: (1) that it have an original maturity of no greater than 270 days and (2) that the proceeds be used to finance current transactions. The average maturity of outstanding commercial paper is under 30 days, with most paper falling within the 20- to 45-day range.

Placement

Issuers place commercial paper with investors either directly using their own sales force or indirectly using commercial paper dealers. The method of placement depends primarily on the transaction costs of these alternatives. Dealers generally charge a one-eighth of one percent (annualized) commission on face value for placing paper. For example, if a firm places $100 million of 45-day commercial paper using the intermediary services of a dealer, commissions would be $100 million $\times$ .00125 $\times$ (45/360) = $15,625. The annualized cost would be $125,000. There are six major commercial paper dealers.

Firms with an average amount of outstanding commercial paper of several hundred million dollars or more generally find it less costly to maintain a sales force and market their commercial paper directly. Almost all direct issuers are large finance companies. The short-term credit demands of nonfinancial companies are usually seasonal or cyclical in nature, which lessens the attractiveness of establishing a permanent commercial paper sales staff. Consequently, almost all nonfinancial companies, including large ones, rely on dealers to distribute their paper.

There is no active secondary market in commercial paper. Dealers and direct issuers may redeem commercial paper before maturity if an investor has an urgent demand for funds. However, dealers and direct issuers discourage this practice. Early redemptions of commercial paper rarely occur primarily because the average maturity of commercial paper is so short. One major commercial paper dealer estimates that only about two percent of their outstanding commercial paper is redeemed prior to maturity.

Quality Ratings

The one thousand or so firms issuing paper obtain ratings from at least one of three services, and most obtain two ratings. The three rating companies that grade commercial paper borrowers are Moody's Investors Service, Standard & Poor's Corporation, and Fitch Investor Service. Table 8-1 shows the number of companies rated by Moody's, classified by industry. This table, covering 881 issuers, gives a good indication of the industry grouping of issuers. Moody's describes its ratings procedure as follows:

> Moody's evaluates the salient features that affect a commercial paper issuer's financial and competitive position. Our appraisal includes, but is not limited to the review of factors such as: quality of management, industry strengths and risks, vulnerability to business cycles, competitive position, liquidity measurements, debt structure, operative trends, and access to capital markets. Differing weights are applied to these factors as deemed appropriate for individual situations.[1]

The other rating services use similar criteria in evaluating issuers. From highest to lowest quality, paper ratings run: P-1, P-2, P-3 for Moody's; A-1,

Table 8-1 Industry grouping of commercial paper issuers rated by Moody's (November 3, 1980)

Industry grouping	Number of firms rated	Percentage of total firms rated
Industrial	370	42.0
Public Utilities	193	21.9
Finance	155	17.6
Bank Holding	119	13.6
Mortgage Finance	9	1.0
Insurance	25	2.8
Transportation	10	1.1
Total	881	100.0

Source: *Moody's Bond Survey,* Annual Review.

[1]Sumner N. Levin, ed., *The 1979 Dow Jones-Irwin Business Almanac* (Homewood, Ill.: Dow Jones-Irwin, 1979), pp. 256-57.

A-2, A-3 for Standard & Poor's; and F-1, F-2, F-3 for Fitch. For all rating services as of mid-1980, the average distribution of outstanding commercial paper for the three quality gradations was about 75 percent for grade 1, 24 percent for grade 2, and 1 percent for grade 3. As will be discussed below, the difference in ratings can translate into considerable differences in rates, particularly during periods of financial stress.

The multifaceted rating system used by Moody's reflects the heterogeneous financial characteristics of commercial paper. Paper of different issuers, even with the same quality rating, is not readily substitutable. Consequently, commercial paper tends to be difficult to trade, and bid-asked spreads on paper of a particular grade and maturity run a wide ⅛ of a percentage point.

Backup Lines of Credit

In most cases, issuers back their paper 100 percent with lines of credit from commercial banks. Even though its average maturity is very short, commercial paper still poses the risk that an issuer might not be able to pay off or roll over maturing paper. Consequently, issuers use a variety of backup lines as insurance against periods of financial stress or tight money. These credit lines are contractual agreements that are tailored to issuers' needs. Standard credit line agreements allow commercial paper issuers to borrow under a 90-day note. So-called *swing lines* provide funds over very short periods, often to cover a shortfall in the actual proceeds of paper issued on a particular day. Revolving lines of credit establish credit sources that are available over longer periods of time, usually several years.

Noninterest Costs of Issuing Commercial Paper

There are three major noninterest costs associated with commercial paper: (1) backup lines of credit, (2) fees to commercial banks, and (3) rating services fees. Payment for backup lines is usually made in the form of compensating balances, which generally equal about 10 percent of total credit lines extended plus 20 percent of credit lines activated. Instead of compensating balances, issuers sometimes pay straight fees ranging from ⅜ to ¾ of one percent of the line of credit; this explicit pricing procedure has been gaining acceptance in recent years. Another cost associated with issuing commercial paper is fees paid to the large commercial banks that act as issuing and paying agents for the paper issuers. These commercial banks handle the paper work involved in issuing commercial paper and collect the proceeds from an issue to pay off or roll over a maturing issue. Finally, rating services charge fees ranging from $5,000 to $25,000 per year to provide ratings for issuers. Foreign issuers pay from $3,500 to $10,000 per year more for ratings depending on the rating service.

Investors

Investors in commercial paper include money center banks, nonfinancial firms, investment firms, state and local governments, private pension funds, foundations, and individuals. In addition, savings and loan associations and mutual savings banks have recently been granted authority to invest up to 20 percent of their assets in commercial paper. These groups may buy commercial paper from dealers or directly from issuers, or they may buy shares in short-term investment pools that include commercial paper. Except for scattered statistics, the distribution of commercial paper held by the various investor groups is not precisely known. At year-end 1979 all manufacturing, mining, and trade corporations held outright over $11 billion in commercial paper. A substantial but undocumented amount is held by utilities, communications, and service companies, Commercial banks held approximately $5 billion in their loan portfolios, while insurance companies had about $9 billion. Much commercial paper, about one-third of the total amount outstanding or $40 billion, is held indirectly through short-term investment pools, such as money market funds and short-term investment funds operated by bank trust departments. At year-end 1979, short-term investment pools held 32.5 percent of all outstanding commercial paper.

DEVELOPMENTS SINCE THE MID-1960s

Two events stimulated growth in commercial paper in the 1960s. First, during the last three quarters of 1966, interest rates rose above Regulation Q ceilings on bank negotiable certificates of deposit (CDs), making it difficult for banks to raise funds to meet the strong corporate loan demand existing at that time. Without sufficient funds to lend, banks encouraged their financially strongest customers to issue commercial paper and offered back-up lines of credit. Many potential commercial paper borrowers who formerly relied exclusively on bank short-term credit now turned to the commercial paper market. Consequently, the percentage increase in total outstanding commercial paper rose from 7.8 percent in 1965 to 46.6 percent in 1966.

Second, credit market tightness recurred in 1969 as open market interest rates rose above Regulation Q ceilings, again boosting growth in commercial paper. Financial innovation by banks contributed to this growth. The banking system sold commercial paper through bank holding companies, which used the funds to purchase part of their subsidiary banks' loan portfolios. This method of financing new loans resulted in rapid growth in bank-related commercial paper during late 1969 and early 1970, as is seen in Figure 8-1. The annual growth rate of total outstanding commercial paper more than doubled to 54.7 percent in 1969. In August 1970, the Federal Reserve System imposed a reserve

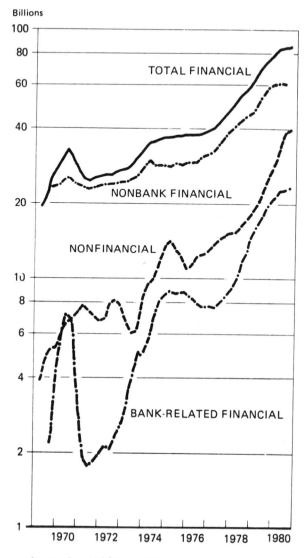

Billions

Source: Board of Governors of the Federal Reserve System.

Figure 8-1   Outstanding commercial paper

requirement on funds raised in the commercial paper market and channeled
to a member bank by a bank holding company or any of its affiliates or subsidiaries.[2] As a result, bank related commercial paper outstanding plummeted
late in 1970 and early in 1971. This episode, however, marked only the be-

[2]See footnote 3.

ginning of bank use of commercial paper, which would regain prominence by the mid-1970s.

The Penn Central Crisis

The commercial paper market grew steadily during the 1960s. Only five defaults occurred during this decade, the largest of which amounted to $35 million. In 1970, however, the commercial paper market was rocked by Penn Central's default on $82 million of its outstanding commercial paper. The default caused investors to become wary of commercial paper issuers and more concerned about their creditworthiness. In the aftermath of the Penn Central default, many corporations experienced difficulty refinancing their maturing commercial paper. Financial disruption was lessened due to a Federal Reserve action which removed Regulation Q interest rate ceilings on 30- to 89-day CDs and temporarily liberalized the discount policy for member banks. These actions insured that funds were available from commercial banks to provide alternative financing for corporations having difficulty rolling over commercial paper.

After the Penn Central episode, investors became more conscious of creditworthiness and more selective in their commercial paper purchases. During this period, the heightened concern over creditworthiness was evidenced by a widening rate spread between the financially strongest and weakest paper issuers. Although some paper had been rated long before the Penn Central crisis, paper was now rated on a widespread basis.

Interest Rate Controls

Wage and price controls imposed during the early 1970s dampened the growth of the commercial paper market. On October 15, 1971, the Committee on Interest and Dividends (CID) established voluntary restraints on "administered" rates, such as the prime rate. No restraints were placed on open market rates, however. This policy triggered flows of funds between controlled and uncontrolled credit markets as the relationship between administered rates and market rates changed. As interest rates rose in 1972, banks came under pressure from the CID to moderate their prime rate increases. By early 1973, the prime rate was held artificially below the commercial paper rate as a consequence of CID policy. Nonfinancial firms substituted short-term bank credit for funds raised through commercial paper issues. Consequently the volume of nonfinancial commercial paper outstanding fell sharply during the first and second quarters of 1973, as is seen in Figure 8-1. In April of 1973, the CID tried to stem the exodus from the commercial paper market by establishing a dual prime rate. One rate for large firms moved with open market rates, while the other for smaller firms was controlled. Despite these measures, the spread between commercial paper rates and the prime rate persisted and substitution out of paper continued. In the fourth quarter of 1973 CID controls were removed and the commercial paper rate dropped below the prime rate, causing substantial growth in commercial paper. This growth continued throughout 1975.

The 1973-75 Period

The recession of 1973-75 strained the paper market as investors became increasingly concerned about the financial strength of commercial paper issuers. Reflecting this concern, the quality rate spread (the difference between the interest rates on highest quality paper and medium quality paper) rose from about 12 basis points in January 1974 to 200 basis points in November of that year. Figure 8-2 shows movements in the quality spread from 1974 to 1980. Utility companies experienced problems selling commercial paper as their ratings were downgraded. Real Estate Investments Trusts (REITs) were another group to encounter problems in the commercial paper market. Loan defaults and foreclosure proceedings early in the recession led to financial difficulties

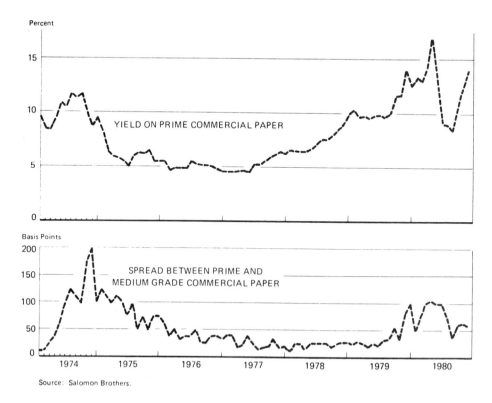

Source: Salomon Brothers.

Figure 8-2 Yields and spreads on 30-day commercial paper

and resulted in a downgrading of REIT paper. As a result, many REITs and utilities were forced to turn to bank credit.

Bank holding companies also experienced difficulty issuing commercial paper in the spring of 1974. The failure of Franklin National Bank caused widespread concern about the strength of other banking organizations. As a consequence, smaller bank holding companies in particular found it hard to place their paper. Nonetheless, the aggregate volume of outstanding bank-related commercial paper remained relatively unchanged during this period of uncertainty. In general, the strongest paper issuers with prime ratings sold their paper without problems during the 1973-75 recession, although less financially sound issuers had to pay a premium to acquire funds in the commercial paper market.

The Late 1970s

After the 1973-75 recession the commercial paper market grew rapidly. The volume of outstanding nonfinancial commercial paper expanded at a 31.9 percent compound annual rate from the first quarter of 1976 to the first quarter of 1980. Over the same period, nonbank financial paper grew at a 20.1 percent compound annual rate and bank-related paper at a 27.9 percent annual rate. The number of commercial paper issuers increased substantially as well. For example, issuers rated by Moody's Investor Service increased from 516 at year-end 1975 to 881 at year-end 1980.

The recent rapid growth in the commercial paper market owes much to the secular substitution of short-term for long-term debt, which accelerated because of the high rate of inflation in the late 1970s. Volatile interest rates due to uncertainty about the future rate of inflation make firms hesitant to structure their balance sheets with long-term, fixed rate assets and liabilities. In addition, because of inflation's debilitating effects on equity markets, debt has grown more than twice as fast as equity during the past decade. On the demand side, investors also have become wary of long-term fixed rate securities because of the uncertainty about the real rate of return on such commitments of funds. Therefore, funds have tended to flow away from the capital markets and into the money markets. A large share of these funds have been channeled into the commercial paper market.

Nonfinancial Paper

As nonfinancial firms acquired familiarity with open market finance during the 1970s, they gradually reduced their reliance on short-term bank loans. This is understandable since use of open market funds offers the potential for substantial savings to corporate borrowers compared to the cost of bank credit. Large commercial banks' primary source of funds for financing loans is the CD market, where interest rates are roughly equal to commercial paper rates. In addition, the cost of funds to commercial banks includes reserve requirements.[3] Noninterest expenses associated with lending also add to the cost of bank operations. These various costs drive a wedge between open market and bank lending rates, and the spread between the prime rate and the commercial paper rate is a good proxy for the difference in financing costs facing companies that need funds.

Large, financially sound nonfinancial firms, therefore, have relied to an increasing extent on the commercial paper market for short-term credit. The ratio of nonfinancial commercial paper to commercial and industrial (C&I) loans at large commercial banks, rose from about 11 percent in the mid-1970s to almost 25 percent in 1980. Figure 8-3 shows the movements in the ratio of paper to loans from 1972 to 1980.

Banks reacted to this loss of market share by becoming more aggressive in pricing loans. Since 1979, for example, some banks have begun making loans below the prime rate. In a Federal Reserve Board survey of 48 large banks, the percentage of below prime loans rose from about 20 percent of all com-

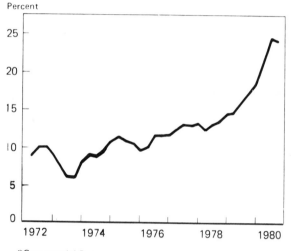

*Commercial Paper
Source: Board of Governors of the Federal Reserve System.

Figure 8-3   Ratio of nonfinancial CP* to C&I loans of large weekly reporting commercial banks

[3]The following example illustrates how reserve requirements on CDs increases the cost of funds to banks. Suppose the reserve requirement against CDs is 3 percent and a bank's CD offers a 12 percent yield. Then for every dollar obtained through the CD, only 97 cents are available to lend. The funds idled as reserves increase the effective cost of funds raised by issuing a CD. In this example the additional cost imposed by the reserve requirement is 37 basis points, i.e., 12 ÷ .97 = 12.37.

mercial loan extensions in the fourth quarter of 1978 to about 60 percent by the second quarter of 1980. Most of these loans were extended at rates determined by cost of funds formulas. In addition, the average maturity of loans over $1 billion, which make up almost half of all C&I loans in volume, fell from about three months in 1977 to a low of 1.2 months in August 1980. Loans below prime had an average maturity of well under one month. These below prime loans were in the same maturity range as the average maturity for commercial paper.

Aside from becoming more competitive with the commercial paper market, banks have tried at the same time to provide services to support their customers' commercial paper issues. Some banks have offered customers more flexible short-term borrowing arrangements to allow commercial paper issuers to adjust the timing of their paper sales. Morgan Guaranty Trust Company, which originated this service, calls its open line of credit a "Commercial Paper Adjustment Facility" and prices the service below the prime rate. Commercial banks also provide back-up lines of credit and act as issuing agents, as discussed above.

In summary, competition with the commercial paper market is changing the lending practices of commercial banks. Although banks still extend a large volume of short-term business loans, the profitability of loans to their largest customers has been reduced partly because of competition with the commercial paper market, and some commercial bank activity now focuses on supporting the issuance of their customers' commercial paper.

Financial Paper

Since the 1920s, finance companies have been important participants in the commercial paper market. They provide much of the credit used to finance consumer purchases. Historically, around 20 percent of outstanding consumer credit has come from finance companies. Finance companies also supply a large and growing amount of business credit such as wholesale and retail financing of inventory, receivables financing, and commercial and leasing financing. About half of all the credit extended by finance companies goes to businesses, predominantly to small- and medium-sized firms.

The primary source of short-term funds for finance companies is sales of commercial paper. In fact, the outstanding commercial paper liabilities of finance companies were about five times as large as their bank loans in the late 1970s. Like nonfinancial companies, finance companies since the mid-1960s gradually increased the proportion of borrowing in the commercial paper market compared to short-term borrowing from commercial banks.

As seen in Figure 8-1, nonbank financial paper constitutes the largest proportion of outstanding commercial paper. Sixty percent of all commercial paper is directly placed and the greatest proportion of this is finance company paper. Finance company paper, however, is issued by only a small fraction of the total number of finance companies. According to the Federal Reserve

Board's *Survey of Finance Companies, 1975,* 88 of the largest finance companies out of a total of about 3,400 such firms issued 97 percent of all finance company paper and extended 90 percent of total finance company credit.

The outstanding volume of bank-related financial paper has been extremely volatile compared to nonbank financial paper. As mentioned above, this market received a major jolt when the Federal Reserve imposed reserve requirements on bank-related commercial paper issues in August 1970. Growth in outstanding bank-related commercial paper resumed by mid-1971, however. This growth corresponded with record acquisitions of nonbank firms by bank holding companies, which peaked at 332 nonbank firms acquired in 1973 and 264 firms in 1974. Some of the primary activities of these newly acquired subsidiaries are commercial finance, factoring, and leasing. The 1973-75 recession curtailed the growth in bank paper, but growth resumed its upward trend by 1976 and has continued strongly since.

NEW DIRECTIONS FOR THE COMMERCIAL PAPER MARKET

Recently several new groups of issuers have entered the commercial paper market. These include foreign banks, multinational corporations, and public utilities; thrift institutions; second tier issuers relying on guarantees from supporting entities; and tax-exempt issuers. These issuers have found the commercial paper market to be a flexible and attractive way to borrow short-term funds.

Foreign Issuers

Foreign participation in the commercial paper market has been growing and will probably continue to be an important source of new growth. As of year-end 1980, Moody's rated 70 foreign issuers, which collectively had about $7 billion in outstanding commercial paper. These issuers fall into three general categories: foreign-based multinational corporations, nationalized utilities, and banks. Some large foreign multinational corporations issue paper to finance their operations in the United States. Others borrow to support a variety of activities that require dollar payments for goods and services. Nationalized utilities have been major borrowers in the commercial paper market largely because their purchases of oil require payment in dollars. Finally, foreign banks raise funds for their banking activity or act as guarantors for the commercial paper of their clients by issuing letters of credit. These banks have been among the most recent entrants into the market.

The commercial paper market is often the cheapest source of dollars for foreign issuers. A major alternative source of dollar borrowing is the Eurodollar market, where rates are generally linked to the London Interbank Offered

Rate (LIBOR). Many foreign banks, for example, obtain funds in the commercial paper market for ¼ of one percent or more below LIBOR. Aside from cost considerations, another important motivation behind foreign participation in the commercial paper market is foreign issuers' interest in obtaining ratings and gaining acceptance with the American financial community. The exposure from selling paper helps to broaden a foreign issuer's investor base and prepares the way for entering the bond and equity markets.

Two obstacles to foreign participation in the commercial paper market are obtaining prime credit ratings and coping with foreign withholding taxes on interest paid to investors outside the country. Ratings below top quality wipe out the cost advantage of raising short-term funds in the commercial paper market. To date, for example, no foreign banks have issued paper with less than top ratings.

Withholding taxes on interest paid to investors outside the country also may eliminate commercial paper's cost advantage over the Euro-dollar market. These taxes are intended to curtail short-term capital outflows and are used in France, Belgium, Australia, Canada, and other countries. For foreign issuers' commercial paper to be marketable, the issuer must bear the cost of the withholding tax. The tax therefore raises the cost of acquiring funds using commercial paper.

By taking advantage of loopholes and technicalities in the withholding tax laws, foreign issuers often circumvent these laws. For example, the nationalized French electric company, Electricite de France, one of the largest foreign or domestic paper issuers, has its commercial paper classified as long-term debt, which is not subject to France's 15 percent withholding tax on interest. The reason for this classification is that the utility backs its paper with a 10-year revolving credit facility from its banks that establishes the commercial paper borrowing as long-term debt. French banks use a different approach to take advantage of a withholding tax exemption on short-term time deposits like CDs. They set up U. S. subsidiaries to sell commercial paper and then transfer the proceeds to the French parent banks by issuing CDs to their U. S. subsidiaries.

In general, foreign issuers pay more to borrow in the commercial paper market than domestic issuers for two reasons. First, almost all foreign commercial paper issues have a sovereign risk associated with the issuer that results from additional uncertainty in the investor's mind about the probability of default on commercial paper because of government intervention, political turmoil, economic disruption, etc. This uncertainty creates a risk premium which increases the interest rate on foreign issues relative to domestic issues. The size of the premium depends on the issuer, the country, and the level of interest rates. A second source of additional costs arises when foreign issuers pay to establish and operate U. S. subsidiaries to issue paper and, in the case of foreign banks, incur reserve requirement costs on commercial paper issues. In addition, rating service fees are higher for foreign issuers than for domestic issuers, as mentioned earlier. Nevertheless, the commercial paper market is proving to be the least expensive source of short-term dollar funds for an increasing number of foreign borrowers.

Thrift Commercial Paper

Both savings and loan associations and mutual savings banks have recently been allowed to borrow funds in the commercial paper market. Mutual savings banks (MSBs) had the authority to issue commercial paper, but faced restrictions on advertising, interest payments, and minimum maturity that effectively prevented them from issuing commercial paper. On March 3, 1980, the Federal Deposit Insurance Corporation (FDIC) removed the restrictions and thereby cleared the way for MSB participation in the commercial paper market. The FDIC ruled that MSB commercial paper must be unsecured, have a maximum maturity of nine months, sell at a minimum price of $100,000, state that it is uninsured by FDIC, and bear a notice that the instrument will pay no interest after maturity. Despite the relaxation of restrictions, as of early 1981 no MSBs have issued paper. The failure of MSBs to issue commercial paper has been largely due to impaired MSB earnings, which make it difficult to obtain the high credit ratings necessary to realize the cost advantage in borrowing in the commercial paper market.

Savings and loan associations have had access to the commercial paper market since January 1979, when the Federal Home Loan Bank Board approved the first applications for S&Ls to issue commercial paper and short-term notes secured by mortgage loans. S&Ls use commercial paper principally to finance seasonal surges in loan demand and to finance secondary mortgage market operations. Commercial paper allows greater flexibility for S&Ls in managing liquidity because they can borrow large amounts of cash quickly and for periods as short as five days. Relatively few S&Ls carry commercial paper ratings. Of the 60 or so large S&Ls expected to participate in the market after the FHLBB approved the first applications, only 12 had ratings from Moody's as of mid-1980, though all were P-1. These S&Ls collectively had $327 million in outstanding commercial paper as of mid-1980.

The attractiveness of commercial paper for S&Ls and MSBs has been sharply diminished as a result of the *Depository Institutions Deregulation and Monetary Control Act of 1980*. Under the Act, commercial paper is considered a reservable liability, except when issued to certain exempt investors such as depository institutions. S&Ls and MSBs have to hold reserves in the ratio of 3 percent against outstanding commercial paper, which is classified as a nonpersonal time deposit. Reserve requirements increase the cost of funds raised through commercial paper and consequently reduce the incentive for S&Ls and MSBs to issue paper.

Support Arrangements

Many lesser known firms gain access to the commercial paper market through financial support arrangements obtained from firms with the highest credit ratings. Second tier issuers frequently issue paper by obtaining a letter of credit from a commercial bank. This procedure substitutes the credit of a bank for that of the issuer and thereby reduces the cost of issuing commercial paper. This kind of support arrangement is known as "commercial paper supported by letter of credit" and resembles bankers' acceptance financing except that the issuance of commercial paper is not associated with the shipment of goods. Because the letter of credit is appended to the commercial paper note, commercial paper supported by letter of credit is alternatively referred to as a "documented discount note." Typically, letters of credit are valid for a specific term or are subject to termination upon written notice by either party. To have a commercial bank stand ready to back up an issue of paper, an issuer must pay a fee that ranges from one-quarter to three-quarters of a percentage point.

Although commercial paper with letter of credit support reached an outstanding volume of about $2 billion by mid-1980, this segment of the market is still comparatively small. Many issuers of letter of credit commercial paper are subsidiaries of larger corporate entities. These second tier issuers include firms involved in pipeline construction, vehicle leasing, nuclear fuel supply, and power plant construction. Other commercial paper issuers also have acquired letter of credit support from commercial banks, particularly during the period of restricted credit growth in early 1980. Issuers whose ratings were downgraded faced difficulty selling their paper and paid substantial premiums over high grade paper. Buying a letter of credit from a commercial bank reduced their borrowing costs in the commercial paper market and still offered a cheaper alternative to short-term bank loans.

Other supporting entities that provide guarantees or endorsements are insurance companies, governments for government-owned companies, and parent companies for their subsidiaries. For example, the commercial paper of the nationalized French utilities, such as Electricite de France, carries the guarantee of the Republic of France. Guarantees or endorsements by parent companies for their subsidiaries are the most prevalent form of support arrangement.

Tax-Exempt Paper

One of the most recent innovations in the commercial paper market is tax-exempt paper. Except for its tax-exempt feature, this paper differs little from other commercial paper. To qualify for tax-exempt status the paper must be issued by state or municipal governments, or by qualified nonprofit organizations. Like taxable commercial paper, tax-exempt paper is also exempt from Securities and Exchange Commission registration provided the paper matures within 270 days. Most tax-exempt paper matures within 15 to 90 days. These short-term debt obligations are alternatively known as *short-term revenue bonds* or *short-term interim certificates*.

The outstanding volume of tax-exempt paper has grown rapidly, rising from an insignificant amount in 1979 to about $500 million in 1980. It will probably exceed $1 billion in 1981. Much of the demand for tax-exempt paper comes from short-term tax-exempt funds, which had assets of $1.5 billion in mid-1980, and from bank trust departments. Many mutual fund groups are setting up tax-exempt money market funds in response to the apparent increasing demands for this type of investment. A current shortage of tax-exempt commercial paper has depressed the yields on outstanding issues, making this instrument especially attractive to tax-exempt issuers. However, constraints on public agency use of short-term debt in some states may continue to limit the supply of tax-exempt commercial paper.

CONCLUSION

The commercial paper market has served the short-term financing needs of several groups of borrowers to an increasing degree in recent years. Many nonfinancial companies, especially large firms, have substituted commercial paper for short-term bank loans to satisfy their working capital requirements. Commercial paper has generally been a less costly financing alternative than bank short-term credit for these firms. Finance companies have relied to a greater extent on commercial paper than nonfinancial companies for short-term financing and have issued the greatest proportion of outstanding commercial paper. Most large finance companies realize economies of scale by placing commercial paper directly with investors. Bank holding companies also have depended on the paper market to finance their banking-related activities, which increased in size and scope during the 1970s.

Other types of issuers have been recently attracted to the commercial paper market because of the potential saving in interest costs over alternative ways of borrowing short-term funds. Foreign issuers have sold a substantial amount of commercial paper since entering the market in the mid-1970s. Foreign and domestic issuers who lack sufficient financial strength to offer commercial paper on their own have gained access to the market via support arrangements with stronger financial or corporate entities. Tax-exempt issuers are expected to increase in number and generate larger supplies of tax-exempt paper. Thrift institutions, on the other hand, probably will not make much use of the market in the future because recently imposed reserve requirements on commercial paper have reduced its cost-advantage over other sources of short-term credit.

Many investors find commercial paper to be an attractive short-term financial instrument. Although corporations and other institutional investors held most outstanding commercial paper in the past, financial intermediation by money market funds and other short-term investment pooling arrangements has given many new investors, especially individuals, indirect access to commercial paper.

REFERENCES

1. Board of Governors of the Federal Reserve System. "Short-Term Business Lending at Rates Below the Prime Rate." *Federal Monetary Policy and Its Effect on Small Business, Part 3, Hearings before a Subcommittee on Access to Equity Capital and Business Opportunities of the House Committee on Small Business.* U. S. Congress, House. Committee on Small Business, 96th Cong., 2nd sess., 1980, pp. 318-327.
2. Chell, Gretchen. "Tax-Exempt Commercial Paper Beginning to Catch on as an Investment Medium." *The Money Manager*, July 21, 1980.
3. Hurley, Evelyn M. "Survey of Finance Companies, 1975." *Federal Reserve Bulletin* (March 1976).
4. _____ "The Commercial Paper Market." *Federal Reserve Bulletin* (June 1977).
5. Judd, John P. "Competition Between the Commercial Paper Market and Commercial Banks." *Economic Review*, Federal Reserve Bank of San Francisco (Winter 1979).
6. Levin, Sumner N., ed. *The 1979 Dow Jones-Irwin Business Almanac.* Homewood, Illinois: Dow Jones-Irwin, 1979.
7. McKenzie, Joseph A. "Commercial Paper: Plugging into a New and Stable Source of Financing." *Federal Home Loan Bank Board Journal* (March 1979), pp. 2-5.
8. Puglisi, Donald J. "Commercial Paper: A Primer." *Federal Home Loan Bank Board Journal*, 13 (December 1980): 4-10.
9. Stigum, Marcia. *The Money Market: Myth, Reality, and Practice.* Homewood, Illinois: Dow Jones-Irwin, 1978.

EURODOLLARS*

Marvin Goodfriend[†]

9

Eurodollars are deposit liabilities, denominated in United States dollars, of banks located outside the United States.[1] Eurodollar deposits may be owned by individuals, corporations, or governments from anywhere in the world. The term Eurodollar dates from an earlier period when the market was located primarily in Europe. Although the bulk of Eurodollar deposits are still held in Europe, today dollar-denominated deposits are held in such places as the Bahamas, Bahrain, Canada, the Cayman Islands, Hong Kong, Japan, Panama, and Singapore, as well as in major European financial centers.[2] Nevertheless, dollar-denominated deposits located anywhere in the world outside the United States are still referred to as Eurodollars.

Banks in the Eurodollar market and banks located in the United States compete to attract dollar-denominated funds worldwide. Since the Eurodollar market is relatively free of regulation, banks in the Eurodollar market can operate on narrower margins or spreads between dollar borrowing and lending rates than banks in the United States. This allows Eurodollar deposits to com-

*Reprinted, with minor editorial revisions, from *Instruments of the Money Market*, 5th edition, edited by Timothy Q. Cook and Bruce J. Summers, 1981, with permission of the Federal Reserve Bank of Richmond.

†Dr. Goodfriend is Research Officer at the Federal Reserve Bank of Richmond.

[1] Dollar-denominated deposits at a bank located outside the U. S. are Eurodollars, even if the bank is affiliated with a bank whose home office is in the United States.

[2] See Ashby (1978) and (1979) for discussions of Europe's declining share of the global Euro-currency market. The Euro-currency market includes, along with Eurodollars, foreign currency-denominated deposits held at banks located outside a currency's home country.

pete effectively with deposits issued by banks located in the United States. In short, the Eurodollar market has grown up largely as a means of separating the currency of denomination of a financial instrument (the United States dollar) from the country of jurisdiction or responsibility for that currency (the United States), in order to reduce the regulatory costs involved in dollar-denominated financial intermediation.

THE SIZE OF THE EURODOLLAR MARKET

Measuring the size of the Eurodollar market involves looking at the volume of dollar-denominated loans and deposits on the books of banks located outside the United States. However, dollar-denominated loans and deposits may not match. Consequently, a decision must be made whether to measure the volume of Eurodollars from the asset or liability side of the balance sheet.

A liability side measure may be too broad, since it may include foreign currency liabilities incurred to fund loans to domestic residents denominated in domestic currency. Strictly speaking, this is a traditional type of international financial intermediation. Measuring Eurodollar market volume from dollar-denominated assets, however, may also overstate the size of Eurodollar volume since these assets may reflect nothing more than traditional foreign lending funded with domestic currency-denominated deposits supplied by domestic residents.

In practice, Eurodollar volume is measured as the dollar-denominated deposit liabilities of banks located outside the United States. For example, the Bank for International Settlements (BIS) defines and measures Eurodollars as dollars that have "been acquired by a bank outside the United States and used directly or after conversion into another currency for lending to a non-bank customer, perhaps after one or more redeposits from one bank to another."[3]

Under a liability side measure such as the one used by the BIS, the sum of all dollar-denominated liabilities of banks outside the United States measures the gross size of the Eurodollar market. For some purposes, it is useful to net part of interbank deposits out of the gross to arrive at an estimate of Eurodollar deposits held by original suppliers to the Eurodollar market. Roughly speaking, to construct the net size measure, deposits owned by banks in the Eurodollar market are netted out. But deposits owned by banks located outside of the Eurodollar market area are not netted out because banks located outside the Eurodollar market area are considered to be original suppliers of funds to the Eurodollar market. For still other purposes, such as comparing the volume of deposits created in the Eurodollar market with the United States monetary aggregates, it is useful to further net out all bank-owned Eurodollar deposits.

---

[3]Bank for International Settlements, *1964 Annual Report*, p. 127.

Doing so leaves only the nonbank portion of the net size measure, or what might be called the net-net size of the Eurodollar market.

The most readily accessible estimates of the size of the Eurodollar market are compiled by Morgan Guaranty Trust Company of New York and reported in the monthly bank letter *World Financial Markets*.[4] Morgan's estimates are based on a liability side measure and include data compiled by the BIS. However, Morgan's estimates are somewhat more comprehensive. Morgan reports estimates of the size of the entire Euro-currency market based roughly on all foreign-currency liabilities and claims of banks in major European countries and eight other market areas.

As of mid-1980 Morgan estimated the gross size of the Eurocurrency market at $1,310 billion.[5] The net size was put at $670 billion.[6] Morgan also reports that Eurodollars make up 72 percent of gross Euro-currency liabilities, putting the gross size of the Eurodollar market at roughly $940 billion.[7] No net Eurodollar market size is given. However, 72 percent of the net size of the Eurocurrency market yields $480 billion as an approximate measure of the net size of the Eurodollar market. Finally, Morgan reports Eurodollar deposits to nonbanks at $200 billion, and those held by United States nonbank residents as less than $50 billion.[8]

M2 is the narrowest United States monetary aggregate that includes Eurodollar deposits. M2 includes overnight Eurodollar deposits held by United States nonbank residents at Caribbean branches of United States member banks. As of June 1980, M2 measured $1,587 billion; its Eurodollar component was $2.9 billion.[9]

Even though it is conceptually appropriate to include term Eurodollar deposits held by United States nonbank residents in M3, they are only included in L, the broadest measure of money and liquid assets reported by the Federal Reserve, because the data used to estimate their volume is available with a long lag relative to other data in M3. M3 was approximately $1,846 billion in

[4]See Morgan Guaranty Trust Company of New York, *World Financial Markets* (January 1979), pp. 9-13, for a discussion of Morgan's method of measuring the size of the Eurodollar market. Other useful discussions of issues involved in measuring the Eurodollar market's size are found in Dufey and Giddy (1978), pp. 21-34, and Mayer (1976).

[5]Morgan Guaranty (December 1980), p. 15. Most of the growth of the Euro-currency market has occurred in the last two decades. Morgan reported the net size of the Euro-currency market as only $21 billion in 1966. See Dufey and Giddy (1978), Chapter III, for a discussion of the growth of the Euro-currency market.

[6]Morgan Guaranty (December 1980), p. 15.

[7]Ibid.

[8]Ibid., p. 4.

[9]Board of Governors of the Federal Reserve System, H.6 statistical release, "Money Stock Measures and Liquid Assets" (February 20, 1981), pp. 1 and 4.

June 1980, the Eurodollar component of L was $51.8 billion.[10] Eurodollar deposits owned by United States nonbank residents continue to grow rapidly, but these comparisons show clearly that such Eurodollar deposits still account for a relatively small portion of the United States nonbank resident holdings of money and liquid assets.

INCENTIVES FOR DEVELOPMENT OF THE EURODOLLAR MARKET[11]

By accepting deposits and making loans denominated in United States dollars outside the United States, banks can avoid United States banking regulations. In particular, banks located outside the United States are not required to keep non-interest bearing reserves against Eurodollar deposits. These foreign banks hold reserves with United States banks for clearing purposes only. Moreover, there is no required Federal Deposit Insurance Corporation insurance assessment associated with Eurodollar deposits. Virtually no restrictions exist for interest rates payable on Eurodollar deposits or charged on Eurodollar loans; nor are there any restrictions on the types of assets allowed in portfolio.

In most Eurodollar financial centers, entry into Eurodollar banking is virtually free of regulatory impediments. In addition, banks intending to do Eurodollar business can set up in locations where tax rates are low. For example, Eurodollar deposits and loans negotiated in London or elsewhere are often booked in locations such as Nassau and the Cayman Islands to obtain more favorable tax treatment.

Foreign monetary authorities are generally reluctant to regulate Eurodollar business because to do so would drive the business away, denying the host country income, tax revenue, and jobs. Moreover, host countries are not responsible for the United States dollar and so are relatively indifferent to what happens in dollar-denominated money markets. Even if the United States monetary authorities could induce a group of foreign countries to participate in a plan to regulate their Euromarkets, such a plan would be ineffective unless every country agreed not to host unregulated Eurodollar business. In practice,

---

[10]Ibid., pp. 1 and 5. L includes Eurodollar deposits held by U. S. nonbank residents at all banks in the U.K., Canada, and at branches of U. S. banks in other countries. These account for nearly all Eurodollar holdings of nonbank U. S. residents. Some overnight Eurodollar deposits issued to U. S. nonbank residents by banks other than Caribbean branches of member banks are only included in L because current data do not separate these overnight Eurodollars from term Eurodollars. See Board of Governors of the Federal Reserve Bulletin (February 1980), p. 98.

At present, Eurodollars held by non-U. S. residents are not included in any of the U. S. monetary aggregates. As improved data sources become available, the possible inclusion of Eurodollars held by non-U. S. residents other than banks and official institutions could be reviewed. *Federal Reserve Bulletin* (February 1980), p. 98.

[11]See Dufey and Giddy (1978), pp. 110-12, for more discussion of the conditions that made large-scale Eurodollar market growth possible.

competition for this business has been fierce, so even if a consensus should develop in the United States to regulate Eurodollar business, it would be extremely difficult to impose regulations on the entire Eurodollar market.

The worldwide competition for Eurodollar business together with lack of foreign government interference have combined to produce low cost, efficient dollar-denominated financial intermediation outside the United States.

INSTRUMENTS OF THE EURODOLLAR MARKET[12]

The overwhelming majority of money in the Eurodollar market is held in fixed-rate time deposits (TDs). The maturities of Eurodollar TDs range from overnight to several years, with most of the money held in the one-week to six-month maturity range. Eurodollar time deposits are intrinsically different from dollar deposits held at banks in the United States only in that the former are liabilities of financial institutions located outside the United States. The bulk of Eurodollar time deposits are interbank liabilities. They pay a rate of return which, although fixed for the term of the deposit, is initially competitively determined.[13]

From their introduction in 1966, the volume of negotiable Eurodollar certificates of deposit (CDs) outstanding reached roughly $50 billion at the beginning of 1980.[14] Essentially, a Eurodollar CD is a negotiable receipt for a dollar deposit at a bank located outside the United States.

On average over the past seven years, fixed-rate three-month Eurodollar CDs have yielded approximately 30 basis points below the three-month time deposit London interbank offer rate (LIBOR).[15] LIBOR is the rate at which major international banks are willing to offer term Eurodollar deposits to each other.

An active secondary market allows investors to sell Eurodollar CDs before the deposits mature. Secondary market makers' spreads for short-term fixed-rate CDs are usually 5 to 10 basis points.[16]

Eurodollar CDs are issued by banks to "tap" the market for funds. Consequently, they have come to be called *Tap CDs*. Such Tap CDs are commonly

[12]Dobbs-Higginson (1980), pp. 55-61; Dufey and Giddy (1978), pp. 228-32; and Stigum (1978), Chapters 15 and 16, contain useful surveys of Eurodollar instruments.

[13]Eurodollar deposit rates are tiered according to maturity as well as according to the perceived creditworthiness of individual issuing banks. See Stigum (1978), p. 433, and Dufey and Giddy (1978), p. 227.

[14]Bank of England, Financial Statistics Division, International Banking Group. This data only includes London dollar CDs. But until recently, virtually all Eurodollar CDs have been issued in London. See "Out-of-Towners," *The Economist* (July 12, 1980), p. 89.

[15]This spread was calculated from data in Salomon Brothers, *An Analytical Record of Yields and Yield Spreads* (1980).

[16]Dobbs-Higginson (1980), p. 59.

issued in denominations of from $250,000 to $5 million. Some large Eurodollar CD issues are marketed in several portions in order to satisfy investors with preferences for smaller instruments. These are known as *Tranche CDs*. Tranche CDs are issued in aggregate amounts of $10 to $30 million and offered to individual investors in $10,000 certificates with each certificate having the same interest rate, issue date, interest payment dates, and maturity.

In recent years *Eurodollar Floating Rate CDs* (FRCDs) or *Eurodollar Floating Rate Notes* (FRNs) have come into use as a means of protecting both borrower and lender against interest rate risk. Specifically, these "floaters" shift the burden of risk from the principal value of the paper to its coupon.

Eurodollar FRCDs and FRNs are both negotiable bearer paper. The coupon or interest rate on these instruments is reset periodically, typically every three or six months, at a small spread above the corresponding LIBOR. Eurodollar FRCDs yield, depending on maturity, between ⅛ and ¼ of one percentage point over the six-month LIBOR.[17] They are an attractive alternative to placing six-month time deposits at the London interbank bid rate. Eurodollar FRN issues have usually been brought to market with a margin of ⅛ and ¼ of one percentage point over either the three- or six-month LIBOR or the mean of the London interbank bid and offered rates.[18] To determine LIBOR for Eurodollar FRNs, "the issuer chooses an agent bank who in turn polls three or four Reference Banks—generally, the London offices of major international banks. Rates are those prevailing at 11:00 a.m. London time two business days prior to the commencement of the next coupon period."[19]

Eurodollar FRCDs have been issued in maturities from 1½ to 5 years and are employed as an alternative to short-term money market instruments. Eurodollar FRNs have been issued in maturities from 4 to 20 years, with the majority of issues concentrated in the 5- to 7-year range. Eurodollar FRNs tend to be seen as an alternative to straight fixed interest bonds, but they can in principle be used like FRCDs. Eurodollar FRNs have been issued primarily, but not exclusively, by banks.

A secondary market exists in Eurodollar FRCDs and FRNs, although dealer spreads are quite large. Secondary market makers' spreads for FRCDs are normally ¼ of one percent of the principal value.[20] The spread quoted on FRNs in the secondary market is generally ½ of one percent of the principal value.[21]

---

[17]Credit Suisse First Boston Limited, "A Description of the London Dollar Negotiable Certificate of Deposit Market" (January 1980), p. 3.

[18]Salomon Brothers, *Eurodollar Floating Rate Notes: A Guide to the Market* (1980), p. 3. The spread between interbank bid and offer rates is normally 1/8 percent, so an issue priced at 1/4 percent over the mean of the bid and offer rates would return 3/16 percent over LIBOR.

[19]Ibid., p. 7.

[20]Dobbs-Higginson (1980), p. 59.

[21]Ibid., p. 56.

INTEREST RATE RELATIONSHIPS BETWEEN EURODOLLAR DEPOSITS AND DEPOSITS AT BANKS IN THE UNITED STATES

Arbitrage keeps interest rates closely aligned between Eurodollar deposits and deposits with roughly comparable characteristics at banks located in the United States. This is illustrated in Figures 9-1 and 9-2. Figure 9-1 shows yields on Federal funds and overnight Eurodollar deposits. Figure 9-2 shows yields on Eurodollar CDs and CDs issued by banks located in the United States.

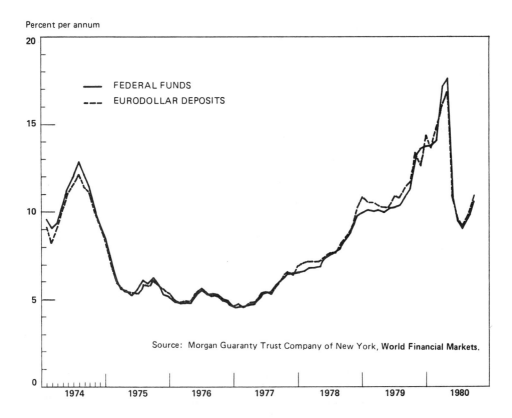

Figure 9-1   Yields on federal funds and overnight Eurodollar deposits (monthly average)

Percent per annum

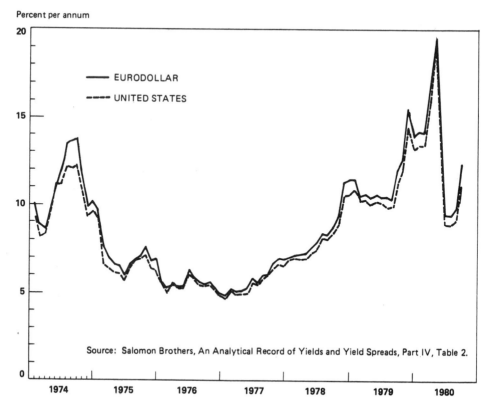

Figure 9-2   Yields on United States and Eurodollar three-month certificates of deposit (at or near the first of the month)

THE RELATIVE RISKINESS OF EURODOLLAR DEPOSITS AND DOLLAR DEPOSITS HELD IN THE UNITED STATES[22]

There are three basic sources of risk associated with holding Eurodollars. The first concerns the chance that authorities where a Eurodollar deposit is held may interfere in the movement or repatriation of interest or principal of the deposit. But this risk factor does not necessarily imply that Eurodollar deposits are riskier than dollar deposits held in the United States. The riskiness of a Eurodollar deposit relative to a dollar deposit held in the United States can depend on the deposit holder's residence. For United States residents, Eurodollars may appear riskier than domestic deposits because of the possibility

[22]See Dufey and Giddy (1978), pp. 187-90, and Tyson (July 1980) for more discussion of the riskiness of Eurodollars.

that authorities in the foreign country where the deposit is located may interfere in the movement or repatriation of the interest or principal of the deposit. Foreign residents, Iranians for example, may feel that the United States Government is more likely to block their deposits than the British Government. Consequently, Iranians may perceive greater risk from potential government interference by holding dollar deposits in the United States than by holding Eurodollar deposits in London.

A second element of risk associated with Eurodollars concerns the potential for international jurisdictional legal disputes. For example, uncertainty surrounding interaction between United States and foreign legal systems compounds the difficulty in assessing the likelihood and timing of Eurodollar deposit payment in the event of a Eurodollar issuing bank's failure.

A third type of risk associated with holding Eurodollars concerns the relative soundness *per se* of foreign banks compared to banks located in the United States. Specifically, it has been argued that Eurodollars are absolutely riskier than deposits held in the United States because deposits held in the United States generally carry deposit insurance of some kind while Eurodollar deposits generally do not. In addition, it has been argued that in event of a financial crisis banks located in the United States are more likely to be supported by the Federal Reserve System, whereas neither Federal Reserve support nor the support of foreign central banks for Eurodollar banking activities in their jurisdiction is certain.

A related factor compounding the three basic risk factors identified above is the greater cost of evaluating foreign investments compared with domestic investments. Acquiring information on the soundness of foreign banks is generally more costly than assessing the soundness of more well-known domestic banks. This means that for a given level of expenditure on information acquisition, investors must generally accept more ignorance about the soundness of a foreign bank than a domestic bank.

Two comments on this argument are relevant here. First, the fact that it is more costly to evaluate foreign than domestic investments does not imply that Eurodollar deposits are inherently riskier than deposits held in the United States. If a depositor resides in the United States the argument implies that a given expenditure on research will generally yield more information about the safety of deposits located in the United States than in the Eurodollar market. But if the depositor resides outside the United States, the reverse may be true.

Having said this, it must be pointed out that the amount of financial disclosure required by regulatory authorities abroad is generally not as great as in the United States. This fact may make it more difficult to evaluate the soundness of non-U. S. banks than U. S. banks for any depositor, regardless of his residence.

Second, to a large extent assessing the safety of Eurodollar deposits relative to deposits in banks located in the United States is made easier by the fact that many banks in the Eurodollar market are affiliated with and bear the name of a bank whose home office is in the United States. For example, a London branch of a United States bank is as closely associated with its home office as a branch located in the United States.

However, foreign offices bearing the name of a United States bank, usually in a slightly altered form, have been set up as subsidiaries. Under most legal systems, a branch can not fail unless its head office fails; but a subsidiary can fail even if its parent institution remains in business. Technically, a foreign office can bear the name of a United States bank in some form, and yet the parent institution may not be legally bound to stand fully behind the obligations of its foreign office. This suggests that a foreign office named after a parent United States bank may not be as sound as its namesake, although the parent bank, unquestionably, has great incentive to aid the foreign office in meeting its obligations in order to preserve confidence in the bank's name.

On the whole, it is difficult to assess the relative riskiness of Eurodollar deposits and dollar deposits held in the United States. Some factors affecting relative risk can be identified, but their importance is difficult to measure. What is more, perceived relative riskiness can depend on the residence of the investor. The extent to which risk-related factors affect the interest rate relationship between Eurodollar deposits and comparable deposits at banks in the United States remains unclear.

SUMMARY

From the depositor's point of view, Eurodollar deposits are relatively close substitutes for dollar deposits at banks located in the United States. Eurodollar deposits are able to compete effectively with deposits offered by banks located in the United States because Eurodollar deposits are free of reserve requirements and other regulatory burdens imposed by the United States monetary authorities on banks located in the United States. In fact, the tremendous growth of the Eurodollar market in the last two decades has largely been the result of efforts to move dollar financial intermediation outside the regulatory jurisdiction of the United States monetary authorities.

Host countries have competed eagerly for Eurodollar business by promising relatively few regulations, low taxes, and other incentives to attract a portion of the Eurodollar banking industry. Financial intermediation in United States dollars is likely to continue to move abroad as long as incentives exist for it to do so. Since these incentives are not likely to disappear soon, the Eurodollar market's share of world dollar financial intermediation is likely to continue growing.

REFERENCES

Ashby, David F. V. "Challenge from the New Euro-Centres." *The Banker*, January 1978, pp. 53–61.

——— "Changing Patterns in the $800 Billion Super-Dollar Market." *The Banker*, March 1979, pp. 21–23.

Bank of England. Personal correspondence, Financial Statistics Division, International Banking Group.

Bank for International Settlements. *1964 Annual Report*. Basle, Switzerland.

Board of Governors of the Federal Reserve System. *Federal Reserve Bulletin*, February 1980.

——— H.6 statistical release, "Money Stock Measures and Liquid Assets," February 20, 1981.

Credit Suisse First Boston Limited. "A Description of the London Dollar Negotiable Certificate of Deposit Market," January 1980.

Dobbs-Higginson, M. S. *Investment Manual for Fixed Income Securities in the International and Major Domestic Capital Markets*. London: Credit Suisse First Boston Limited, 1980.

Dufey, Gunter, and Giddy, Ian H. *The International Money Market*. Englewood Cliffs, New Jersey: Prentice-Hall, 1978.

"The London Dollar Certificate of Deposit." Bank of England *Quarterly Bulletin* 13, no. 4 (December 1973): 446–52.

Mayer, Helmut W. "The BIS Concept of the Eurocurrency Market." *Euromoney*, May 1976, pp. 60–66.

Morgan Guaranty Trust Company of New York. *World Financial Markets*. Various issues.

"Out-of-Towners." *The Economist*, July 12, 1980, p. 89.

Salomon Brothers. *An Analytical Record of Yields and Yield Spreads*. New York: Salomon Brothers, 1980.

——— *Eurodollar Floating Rate Notes: A Guide to the Market*. New York: Salomon Brothers, 1980.

Stigum, Marcia. *The Money Market: Myth, Reality, and Practice*. Homewood, Illinois: Dow Jones-Irwin, 1978.

Tyson, David O. "Fund Managers Wary of Risks in Non-Domestic CDs." *The Money Manager*, July 14, 1980, pp. 3–4.

Part II

CAPITAL MARKET
INSTRUMENTS

The Bond Market

Part II contains articles relating to capital market instruments. In contrast to their money market counterparts, most of these instruments are characterized as having greater price risk, less liquidity, and, with the exception of U. S. Treasury and agency issues, a higher degree of default risk. Not surprisingly, the expected returns on most of these instruments are higher than the expected returns on money market instruments. Because of the risks associated with these instruments, the higher expected returns are not always realized. The higher expected earnings on capital market instruments result in their use as the primary class of earning assets in the investment portfolios of most nonbank financial institutions, individuals, endowments, and other long-term investors.

Part II is divided into two sections: the bond market and mortgage-related instruments (p.185). In this first section dealing with the bond market, the article by Christopher J. McCurdy provides an overview of the market for U. S. Government securities with particular emphasis on the role of dealers and their activities. The basic structure of the corporate bond market and the dramatic changes in that market in recent years are discussed in the article by Burton Zwick. Although not well known outside investment banking and institutional investors' circles, the private placement market is an extremely important conduit for capital in the financial markets. The nature of this market, the participants, and the investors are examined in an article condensed from a Federal Reserve Board staff study. A noteworthy aspect of the study is the rapid emergence of commercial banks as agents of borrowers and, of course, as competitors of investment bankers. The article by Richard H. Rosenbloom reviews the municipal bond market. Because this market is composed of securities that are tax-exempt, it is important to understand the linkage between this market and the markets for taxable securities. As shown in the article, the nature of the linkage changes dramatically at times because of the unusual stresses imposed on the municipal market.

THE DEALER MARKET FOR U.S. GOVERNMENT SECURITIES*

Christopher J. McCurdy

10

The market for United States Government securities occupies a central position in the nation's financial system. The market helps the Treasury finance the Government debt and provides the Federal Reserve with an effective means of implementing monetary policy. While the safety of Government securities is a fundamental feature, perhaps their most vital quality to investors is their liquidity—the ability to transform them into cash quickly and at low cost. The market is an over-the-telephone one in which dealer firms stand ready to buy and sell from a wide range of public and private participants. The dynamic interaction of all participants enhances the attractiveness of Treasury securities and the importance of the market itself.

The dealer market is an effective conduit for the distribution of new Government securities to investors. Treasury financing requirements have grown significantly in recent years, owing to a series of increased Government deficits and to the need for refinancing a heavy schedule of maturities. Since 1974, dealers have initially bought slightly more than 40 percent of the securities competitively auctioned to the public by the Treasury. Moreover, the active role that the dealers have taken in making a secondary market, *i.e.*, buying and selling outstanding issues, has enabled investors to use Government securities more readily in carrying out their portfolio strategies.

*Reprinted, with deletions, from the *Quarterly Review*, Winter 1977-78, pp. 35-47, with permission of the Federal Reserve Bank of New York.

Federal Reserve open market operations are undertaken with dealers in the market to implement monetary policy. The manager of the System Open Market Account buys and sells securities on a temporary or outright basis either to augment (through purchases) or to reduce (through sales) the reserves available to member banks. These operations, conducted at the Trading Desk of the Federal Reserve Bank of New York (FRBNY), have an important bearing on overall economic activity. They help to determine the growth of monetary aggregates and the availability of credit, and they influence the trend of interest rates.

Open market operations are also used to counter sharp fluctuations in bank reserves, which arise from such factors as changes in the public's demand for currency or in the size of Treasury cash balances held at Federal Reserve Banks. The Federal Reserve serves as the fiscal agent for the Treasury and as agent for Government and foreign official institutions in the market, buying and selling Treasury securities for them. Activity at the Trading Desk has grown significantly in recent years, mainly in reflection of greater fluctuations in other factors affecting reserves and the increased participation of foreign central banks in the market. The expansion of this activity has also contributed to the growth and liquidity of the secondary market.

The Treasury and the Federal Reserve closely monitor developments in the market. The Trading Desk at the FRBNY conducts regular meetings with representatives of dealer firms and throughout the day remains in telephone contact with their trading rooms, receiving price quotations and assessments of the state of the market. Officials of the Treasury are also in frequent contact with these firms and often solicit their views on debt management. The FRBNY has recently stepped up its surveillance of dealer firms. In addition to obtaining statistical reports from them, it visits the individual firms to gain further insight into market practices and to evaluate the activities of the firms themselves.

The market has expanded sharply in the past few years, both in overall trading activity and in the number of dealer firms. The growth of trading, outright buying and selling, reflects the greater short-run variation in interest rates in the 1970s as well as the large increase in Treasury debt. The Treasury's debt management policies, especially efforts to extend the maturity of the Government debt while meeting enlarged borrowing needs, have also contributed to the market's development. There has also been a growing willingness on the part of portfolio managers to seek to anticipate interest rate movements and thus to trade more actively in the short run.

The entry of a number of new dealer firms into the market has substantially reduced the concentration of trading activity—*i.e.*, the share of trading activity accounted for by the largest firms—and has to some extent altered the trading relationships among the dealer firms. A more impersonal and even more competitive market atmosphere has developed. At times, participants, in seeking greater returns, may also have overreacted to events that could affect interest rates. This, combined with the active trading, could have contributed to short-run volatility in interest rates.

STOCK IN TRADE: UNITED STATES TREASURY DEBT

The Treasury increased its borrowing sharply following the onset of the 1973-75 recession. This mainly reflected the large increases in spending during the most severe business downturn in the post-World War II era.

The Treasury was able to float the bulk of the sizable increases in its debt without major disruptions to the financial markets, partly because the expansion of private credit demands and inflationary expectations both abated amid a more moderate pace of economic growth. At the same time, the Treasury adopted new techniques to aid its sales efforts. Initially, it concentrated debt offerings in the most liquid areas of the market, raising a substantial amount of new cash in bills during 1975. (For a discussion of the types and characteristics of Treasury debt, see Box.) It then turned heavily to the coupon sector, particularly the two- to five-year area, and also issued long-term bonds as the Congress acted to ease existing interest rate constraints on new issues of these securities. The greater reliance on the coupon sector helped make these securities more liquid by increasing the size and number of securities available for trading.

CHARACTERISTICS OF TREASURY SECURITIES

The Treasury sells two different kinds of marketable obligations: coupon-bearing securities and bills. The investor's return on a coupon-bearing security comes from semiannual interest payments plus any gain or loss in the price of the security from the time of purchase to maturity or sale if it is sold before it matures. Coupon-bearing securities are either notes or bonds. By law, notes have an original maturity of from one to ten years. Securities designated as bonds are permitted to have any maturity, but the Congress has restricted to $27 billion the amount of bonds in the hands of the public that may bear coupons exceeding $4\frac{1}{4}$ percent. As of June 30, 1977, only $13\frac{1}{2}$ billion of bonds with coupons over $4\frac{1}{4}$ percent was in private hands, *i.e.*, outside the Federal Reserve System and official United States Government accounts. There is no comparable restriction on notes. In recent years, most coupon securities have been issued in minimum denominations of $1,000 except for two- and three-year notes for which $5,000 has been the minimum.

Coupon securities are usually sold through auctions in which bidders submit competitive bids expressed as annual yields to two decimal places— 7.31 percent, for example. Noncompetitive bidders may submit tenders of up to $1 million. The Treasury allots to the noncompetitive bidders first and then allots competitive bids, beginning with those at the lowest yield. When the issue has been fully allotted, the Treasury calculates the weighted average of the yields it has accepted and then establishes a fixed coupon to the nearest eighth percent, so that the average price is usually at par or slightly below par. For example, a security sold with an average issuing yield of 7.31 percent would have a 7¼ percent coupon and an average price slightly below par. A security is sold at par when the average yield is exactly equal to the coupon. All noncompetitive bidders pay the average issuing price, and competitive bidders pay the price associated with the bids accepted by the Treasury.

Price quotations in the secondary market are expressed in points with par value equal to 100 points. Fractions of a point are expressed in 32nds. Thus, the price of a coupon security when it is below par might be expressed as 99 10/32 *i.e.*, $993.12 for a $1,000 bond. (When the price is above par, the quote might be 102 3/32, *i.e.*, $1,020.94 for a $1,000 bond.) The quoted price does not include any interest that has accrued on the security after the previous semiannual coupon payment date. The accrued interest is added to the quoted price the buyer agrees to pay the seller.

Bills do not carry coupons. They are initially sold and subsequently trade at a discount from par value. The investor's return is derived from the increase in value from the original discounted price at purchase to the par value at maturity. The Treasury auctions three- and six-month bills every week and 52-week bills every four weeks. Bills in the secondary market are quoted in terms of bank discount rates: the dollar discount is expressed as a percentage of par value computed at an annual rate until maturity (based on a 360-day year). The minimum denomination for a bill is $10,000, and noncompetitive tenders are allotted in full up to $500,000 each at the average auction price.

Another characteristic of Treasury securities is their marketability or nonmarketability. Marketable securities may be resold after issue, while nonmarketable securities are sold to designated purchasers who may not sell them to others. Official United States Government accounts hold slightly more than half the Treasury's nonmarketable securities. Among the most important accounts are the Federal employee retirement funds and the Federal old-age and survivors insurance trust fund. Savings bonds held by individuals constitute slightly less than one third of the nonmarketable debt. Other important holders of nonmarketable debt are foreign governments and state and local governments.

To facilitate its financing operations, the Treasury increased the amount of information provided to the public on the expected amount and characteristics of its financing each quarter. The Treasury began to expand the schedule of routine coupon offerings so that by 1976 it was holding monthly sales of two-year notes and quarterly sales of four- and five-year notes. Mid-quarter refundings of maturing coupon securities generally contained offerings of a three-year note, an intermediate-term note, and a long-term bond. This evolving pattern helped to extend the maturity of the debt. Starting in 1970, the Treasury came to rely increasingly on auctions to sell its coupon issues, thus letting the market set the rate competitively. This technique makes pricing easier, because it allows market participants to adjust their bidding to incorporate evaluations of last-minute developments in the credit markets. Notable exceptions to this policy occurred in 1976, when on three occasions the Treasury used a fixed price and coupon subscription method that led to successful sales of very large amounts of seven- and ten-year notes.

INVESTORS

The largest investors in Government securities are financial institutions who prefer to have very liquid and high-quality assets in their portfolios. Domestic commercial banks owned over $100 billion of Government securities in mid-1977 (Table 10-1). Banks shape their portfolio decisions in response to pronounced seasonal and cyclical flows of funds. For example, bank holdings of Government securities increased substantially in 1975 and 1976 as an offset to cyclically weak demand for loans caused by a restructuring of balance sheets on the part of bank customers in the aftermath of the 1973-75 recession. The expansion in holdings of Government securities followed many years of little or no growth while customer loan demand was heavy. Other private financial institutions—such as thrift institutions, insurance companies, and pension funds—hold somewhat less than half the amount of Government securities held by commercial banks. While they keep Treasury issues in their securities portfolios, their needs for funds are generally more predictable than those of commercial banks. They typically hold a larger proportion of mortgages and other securities that offer higher yields but are less liquid than treasury issues.

The Federal Reserve System's holdings of Government securities rival the amount held by the commercial banks. These issues constitute the great bulk of the System's assets and they support its liabilities, primarily Federal Reserve notes which constitute most of the nation's currency in circulation, member bank reserves, and Treasury deposits. The principal reason for the growth of Federal Reserve holdings of Government securities has been the expansion of Federal Reserve notes and, to a lesser extent, the increases in average Treasury cash balances at the Reserve Banks. Member bank reserves have expanded little in recent years, since the growth of member bank liabilities subject to reserve requirements has been offset by reductions in average requirements.

Table 10-1 United States Treasury debt (in billions of dollars)

Public debt	Amounts outstanding on				
	December 31, 1960	December 31, 1965	December 31, 1970	December 31, 1975	June 30, 1977
Gross public debt	290	321	389	577	674
Nonmarketable debt	101	106	140	213	242
Marketable debt	189*	215	248	363	431
Marketable by type of security:					
Bills	39	60	88	157	155
Notes	51	50	101	167	233
Bonds	80	104	59	39	43
Marketable by type of holder:†					
United States Government accounts	6	12	17	19	15
Federal Reserve System	27	41	62	88	102
Commercial banks	62	61	63	85	102
Mutual savings banks	6	5	3	5	6
Insurance companies	10	10	7	9	14
Other corporations	19	16	7	20	24
State and local governments	19	23	28	33	39
Individuals	20	22	29	24	28
Foreign and international	10	11	13	44	65
Other investors	7	16	22	36	35

Discrepancies in totals due to rounding.

*Includes $18 billion of certificates of indebtedness.

†Partially estimated.

Source: *Treasury Bulletin.*

Other governmental units, both domestic and foreign, hold substantial amounts of United States Government securities because they are bound either by law or custom to hold the safest and most liquid securities available. Foreign and international investors, primarily official institutions, held about $65 billion of marketable Treasury issues in mid-1977.[1] The growth of foreign holdings of Treasury securities mainly reflected foreign central bank investments of dollars obtained in exchange market operations as well as substantial acquisitions by oil-exporting nations. State and local governments invest in short-term Treasury securities to bridge the gap between the timing of periodic tax receipts and Federal grants-in-aid and the more continuous flow of payments for goods and services.

Individuals hold a considerable volume of marketable Treasury issues even though there are several factors tending to inhibit purchases by small investors. The transaction costs for small purchases and sales, the cost of custody, and large minimum denominations for shorter term issues have tended to restrain purchases by individuals except in periods when market yields on Treasury securities moved substantially above those on alternative liquid investments, mainly thrift and savings deposits. (The major portion of the Treasury debt held by individuals consists of savings bonds with small denominations. They are not marketable, but they are redeemable prior to maturity.)

THE DEALER MARKET

The market for United States Government securities centers on the dealers who report activity daily to the FRBNY. The dealers buy and sell securities for their own account, arrange transactions with both their customers and other dealers, and also purchase debt directly from the Treasury for resale to investors. In the normal course of these activities, they hold a substantial amount of securities. In addition to the dealer firms, there are brokers that specialize in matching buyers and sellers among the dealers in the Government securities market.

The dealer firms include dealer departments of commercial banks (bank dealers) and all others (nonbank dealers). Bank dealers call upon the custodial and other facilities of the bank and frequently obtain a portion of the financing of their securities holdings from the bank. The bank dealer often acts to meet the needs of correspondent banks of the parent. In addition to trading in Government securities, bank dealers are generally active in other money market instruments and in the market for tax-exempt general obligation securities of state and local governments. They are, however, proscribed by the Banking Act of 1933 (Glass-Steagall) from trading corporate equities and bonds, as well as tax-exempt revenue issues. The Glass-Steagall Act was intended to create a

[1]Foreign investors also held about $22 billion of nonmarketable Treasury securities in mid-1977.

legal distinction between commercial banking and investment banking. Non-bank dealers face no such proscription, and most of them trade in these other markets, although a few firms concentrate their energies on Government securities and money market instruments such as bankers' acceptances, commercial paper, and large negotiable bank certificates of deposit.

At the end of 1977, there were 36 securities dealers that reported their transactions, financing, and inventories to the FRBNY daily; twelve were commercial banks and 24 were nonbank dealers. A firm is added to the reporting list when it demonstrates that it conducts a significant amount of business with customers as well as with other dealers, that it operates in size in the major maturity areas of the market, and that it is adequately capitalized and managed by responsible personnel. If a firm's performance meets high standards in these respects for some period of time, the Manager of the System Open Market Account will generally establish a trading relationship with it. Thus, not all firms on the FRBNY reporting list necessarily trade with the System Open Market Account.

Dealers trade actively among themselves as well as with customers. Brokers facilitate this interdealer trading because they bring buyers and sellers together; the interdealer brokers themselves do not make markets or hold securities for their own account. They charge a commission on each transaction, amounting to roughly $78 per $1 million of Treasury coupon issues sold. The commission on Treasury bill transactions is generally calculated in basis points: for example, the commission on three-month bills frequently is half of 1 basis point, approximately $62 on a $5 million trade. (A basis point is 1/100 of 1 percentage point in interest rate terms.) In many cases, brokers provide their services by displaying participating dealers' bids and offers on closed circuit television screens located in the dealers' trading rooms. Other dealers then may contact the broker, respond to the quoted price, and complete the transaction. Some brokers operate completely by telephone, contacting dealers to pass along bids and offers.

In the dealer market, practically all trading is transacted over the telephone. There is no formal centralized marketplace such as an exchange; instead, the market consists of a decentralized group of firms, each willing to quote prices for purchase or sale of Treasury securities. Each firm's traders quote prices and buy from, and sell to, their counterparts at other dealer firms directly or with brokers. The firm's sales personnel use the telephone to contact customers to learn their investment needs and to arrange trades with them. The price for each block of securities traded is negotiated, and many customers will typically canvass the market to find the dealer with the best price.

The over-the-telephone organization of the Government securities market parallels that of other fixed-income securities markets. In contrast, stock exchanges largely rely on brokers to funnel orders from customers to the floor of an exchange. There, brokers called specialists attempt to match orders with designated prices from buyers and sellers in an auction market. At times, the specialists are required to act as principals and to buy and sell securities, especially when there is an imbalance of buy and sell orders.

For the most part, the delivery of Treasury bills takes place on the same business day (called "cash" delivery) while coupon issues are generally delivered on the following business day (called "regular" delivery). Delivery and safe-keeping of securities is in large part handled by a book entry system provided by the Federal Reserve Banks. At the beginning of 1977, four-fifths of the Treasury's marketable debt was in the form of bookkeeping entries on computers at the Federal Reserve Banks; the remainder was in paper certificates. The computerized system eliminates physical handling of certificates, since the securities can be transferred electronically from sellers to buyers through entries on the safekeeping accounts of commercial banks that are members of the Federal Reserve System and who act as agent for these transactions. When transactions are arranged between participants in different Federal Reserve Districts, the securities transfer is carried over the Federal Reserve wire-transfer network. Book entries and wire transfers facilitate rapid and low cost transfers of securities, especially among dealers and customers who are separated geographically.

THE ROLE OF THE DEALER

The dealer firm makes markets by purchasing and selling securities for its own account. Dealers do not typically charge commissions on their trades. Rather they hope to sell securities at prices above the ones at which they were bought. Dealers also seek to have a positive "carry" on the securities they have in position, *i.e.*, they try to earn more interest on their inventory than they must pay on the funds raised to finance that inventory.

Dealers attempt to establish positions in the various maturities of Treasury securities in light of their expectations about interest rates and then trade around that position. But the initiative often rests with customers trying to undertake specific transactions, and the dealer must be willing to bid or offer at competitive prices to retain his customer base. When traders quote prices to customers and to other dealers, they continuously make small adjustments in relation to perceived prices elsewhere in order to maintain the firm's position, its inventories of securities, within the limits laid down by the firm's management. The management relies heavily on the traders' skills to enable the firm to change its position in various maturities whenever the outlook changes. A good trader is also expected to make money from the spread between bid and offered prices in a steady market.

The spread between bid and offered prices in general depends on a variety of factors. Two basic determinants are the current state of market activity and the outlook for interest rates. Spreads are narrower for actively traded issues, because the dealer is fairly certain about the price at which the issue can be purchased or sold. Spreads are narrowest of all on Treasury bills, because they are both actively traded and involve less risk of price loss than longer term securities. Spreads for three-month bills are often as small as 2 basis points on recent issues, *i.e.*, $50 per $1 million. The spread on an actively traded coupon issue might be 2/32 to 4/32, or $625 to $1,250 per $1 million of securities. The spread is wider the longer the term to maturity and the smaller the size of a requested transaction. Spreads also widen—sometimes dramatically—when new developments generate caution or uncertainty in the market.

A substantial increase in the short-run volatility of interest rates—and thus securities prices—in the 1970s has caused dealer firms to place great emphasis on position management. Sharp, unexpected price movements can lead to profits or losses on their net position, gross long positions minus gross short positions, that can easily outweigh the gains or losses arising from other sources.[2] Consequently, they manage their positions actively, frequently altering them in response to changing economic news, the perceived supply and demand conditions for Government securities, and other factors affecting the outlook for the securities markets. In the past, when rates were reasonably steady in the short run, dealers placed somewhat more emphasis on structuring their inventories to meet customer needs.

Dealer inventories are highly leveraged. More than 95 percent of the value of their holdings is typically financed with borrowed money; the dealer's own capital furnishes the remainder. Thus, the cost and availability of funds is an important consideration in a dealer's willingness to hold securities. When interest rates on the securities themselves are higher than the cost of the funds needed to finance the position, there is a "positive" carry. A dealer will tend to hold a higher inventory than in the opposite case when "negative" carry prevails. In all but a few periods in the last several years, interest rates have generally been higher on longer maturities—*i.e.*, the yield curve, the market yield at a specific time for each available maturity outstanding, is usually upward sloping. Thus, the cost of day-today funds is usually below the yield on all but the shortest term securities in the dealer's inventory. However, the full risk of any rise in interest rates falls on the dealer. Carry profits can quickly vanish.[3]

[2]A dealer firm has a long position in a security when the firm is an owner of the security. The firm stands to gain if the price of the security rises. A firm establishes a short position by selling a security it does not own; it makes delivery to the buyer by obtaining temporary possession of the security, for example, by borrowing it from a third party. In this case, the firm stands to gain if the price falls because the firm can then purchase the security to return it to the lender at a price lower than the price at which it sold the security.

[3]Profits earned from positive carry can be rather small, compared with those resulting from buying and selling on the bid-asked spread or the profits and losses stemming from price changes. For example, a change of 1 basis point in the discount rate on a bill due in slightly more than three months is equivalent to the carry profits earned in one day if the financing cost of carrying the bill is 100 basis points (1 percentage point) lower than the rate on the bill itself. Moreover, positive carry rarely reaches magnitudes of 1 percentage point while a daily change of at least 1 basis point in bill rates is quite common.

The amount of risk a dealer is willing to take by holding a longer term portfolio is one of the distinguishing characteristics of management style.

Searching out and obtaining financing at the lowest cost is a vital ingredient in making markets and the pursuit of profit. In doing so, the dealers provide temporary investment outlets for market participants with idle cash. In addition, dealers take in funds to provide them to others who are temporarily short of cash, in effect acting as intermediaries between short-term lenders and borrowers. (See section on dealer financing and the growth of intermediation later in this article.)

Dealers also provide a service to their customers by giving their views about and advice on the market. Many dealer firms distribute market letters about recent and prospective market developments. The letters often contain assessments of Treasury financing needs, Federal Reserve actions, and prospects for the economy and interest rates. Salesmen discuss these subjects directly with participants and also seek to develop a familiarity with customers' investment objectives so that the firm's traders can provide the customers with buying and selling opportunities that mesh with their plans.

THE GROWTH OF TRADING ACTIVITY

Trading activity has grown sharply in the last few years after many years of more modest expansion. Outright trading, the total of purchases and sales, amounted to nearly $10½ billion on a daily average basis in 1976, roughly three times the level in 1974. In part, the growth of activity reflected the substantial outpouring of Treasury debt. But the efforts of all market participants in seeking superior returns on their portfolios have also been an important factor. Many investors, disenchanted by falling stock prices, have sought to obtain higher returns in the securities market by buying and selling more frequently in response to anticipated short-run movements in interest rates. Inter-dealer activity has expanded as well, particularly in the brokers' market.

While trading in bills has continued to dominate activity in the dealer market, trading in coupon securities has grown in relative importance. As recently as 1974, coupon trading accounted for 29 percent of total activity, but by 1976 it had reached 36 percent. The growing share of coupons resulted from the more rapid growth of coupon debt outstanding, and this growth in turn led to a more active secondary market for these issues. When measured by activity per dollar of debt outstanding in the hands of the public, the expansion of trading in longer term securities from 1974 to 1976 exceeded that for shorter term securities.

The growing importance of the coupon sector also stems from the increased liquidity of these issues. For several reasons, participants can make desired portfolio changes more easily than in the past. The number of coupon securities outstanding has expanded sharply, and by mid-1977 there were nearly 100 different coupon issues, over 50 percent more than in 1974. Several maturity gaps were filled in, especially in the under-five-area, thus facilitating adjustments to the maturity distribution of portfolios. Secondary market activity has been encouraged by an increase in the average size of coupon offerings from about $1.5 billion in 1974 to about $2.8 billion in 1977. Thus, dealers and other participants now have a greater variety of fairly sizable issues available with which to engage in hedge or arbitrage operations. A dealer, for example, may hedge to avoid market risk by matching a short sale in one issue with a purchase of a similar issue whose price is expected to move by about the same amount as that on the security sold short. In an arbitrage operation, a participant would attempt to profit from what is expected to be a temporary disparity in the market's pricing of two issues by selling one and buying the other. The dealer would then wait until the disparity is eliminated to reverse the transaction. If it is not eliminated, the dealer might take a loss on the operation.

The dealers' customers, who account for slightly more than half of total dealer trading activity, have expanded their trading substantially. Portfolio managers often seek to anticipate movements in interest rates and to lengthen or shorten the average maturity of their holdings to take advantage of expected rate changes. Changes in the outlook for interest rates over a day, week, or month now play an important role in portfolio decisions. In the past, such decisions were often tied to the investor's expectations of short- and long-run needs for liquidity. The profits generated by falling interest rates, *i.e.*, rising prices, in 1975 and 1976 also acted as an inducement to active trading. The annual growth in trading activity moderated through the first three quarters of 1977, compared with 1976, and trading per dollar of debt declined sharply from the highs posted at the end of 1976, as short-term interest rates rose and longer term rates fluctuated irregularly over a good part of the year.

Commercial banks account for over 40 percent of dealer trading with non-dealer customers. In recent years, banks have come to rely on their securities holdings less as a secondary source of reserves, given their emphasis on liability management, and to use securities trading more as a means of maximizing profits. The more active approach to asset management has also meant greater variability in bank holdings of coupon issues. Banks have not been the only institutions that have adopted a more aggressive approach to portfolio management and trading. In fact, the activity of other customers, including state and local governments and nonfinancial corporations, has grown even more rapidly. As a result, trading activity by dealers with customers other than banks grew from 35 percent to 57 percent of total trading with customers between 1970 and 1976.

Trading within the dealer community itself is conducted either directly between the firms themselves or indirectly through brokers. In the past few years, trading through brokers, who put together trades between dealers, has come to dominate interdealer trading, such brokering now accounts for nearly three quarters of dealer trading with other dealers, compared with about one third in 1972 (the first year for which separate data on trading through brokers are available). Using a broker provides anonymity and allows a dealer to shield information about his activity and position from other dealers and market participants. Another factor contributing to the popularity of trading through brokers is the rapid transmission of quotes to other dealers, reducing the costs of canvassing a large number of dealers to collect that information.

Still, dealers continue to arrange a portion of their trades, slightly more than 10 percent of total activity, directly with other dealers. This activity reflects established interdealer trading relationships. A dealer firm specializing in one area of the market can sometimes meet customer needs by dealing directly with a firm primarily engaged in another area of the market.

The increased emphasis on position management has contributed to a tendency for total interdealer trading to assume a larger share of total activity, since dealers will typically look first to other dealers to find bids or offers for issues they want to sell or buy. Such trading has expanded from about one third of total activity in the early 1960s to about 45 percent recently. To some extent, this reflects an increase in the number of reporting dealers. But over the longer run the expansion of the reporting list has probably not substantially distorted the measurement of the rising trend in activity. Many of the new entrants were not active in the Treasury market for very long before they became reporting dealers, and their trading volume was essentially nonexistent in the 1960s.

On the other hand, many of the newer firms are relatively more active in interdealer trading and have no doubt contributed to its measured rise. They have used trading with other dealers as a way of building up expertise and volume. (To meet the criteria for the reporting list, however, a firm must show a substantial volume of trading with customers.)

DEALERS' POSITIONS

Several important changes in the market have enabled dealers to conduct their operations with a lower level of inventories in relation to trading volume than in the 1960s and early 1970s. While dealers have placed greater emphasis on managing their positions actively, they can meet their customers' needs with inventories that are lower relative to sales than in the past. The wider range of participants in the market, the growth in the activity of brokers, the greater ease in covering short positions (as is discussed below), and possibly more caution in exposing capital have contributed to this trend. Positions were sharply cut back—in the aggregate and in relation to sales—during the 1973-74 period of steep increases in interest rates. When money market pressures later abated and rate expectations changed, inventories expanded threefold to $7½ billion by 1976, about the same as the expansion in trading activity. Even with the enlargement of inventory positions, however, dealer inventories were lower in relation to trading activity in 1976 than they had been during the years before the bear markets in bonds in 1973–74. The ratio of inventories to activity continued to fall over 1977 as a whole, when positions declined while growth of activity was rather modest.

The more performance-oriented approach of customers has generated a higher turnover of their portfolios. Dealers now find it easier to obtain issues to meet demands, especially for coupon issues. Moreover, the expansion of activity by brokers and the price quotations they provide almost continuously have probably bolstered dealers' confidence that particular issues can be found more readily than before.

The growth of the market for repurchase agreements (RPs) and reverse RPs has facilitated short sales—either to meet demands of customers or because of interest rate expectations.[4] The availability of securities in this market has made it easier for a dealer to locate the particular issue he needs to deliver by acquiring the security under a reverse RP. In fact, a market for "specific issues," with the party obtaining the securities specifying the particular issue, has developed in the RP and reverse RP markets and has become an alternative to borrowing securities. The older method of finding a holder willing to lend securities could be more costly and cumbersome. It often meant that a dealer's positioning move became obvious to others and required the borrower to put up other securities as collateral. The growth of RP markets has enabled dealers to take larger short positions than they had before during periods when interest rates were expected to rise. In other periods, dealers on average have not enlarged their long positions by as much as they had previously.

Dealers may also have become more cautious about exposing capital by assuming large short or long positions. Year-end capital relative to positions in Treasury securities at the nonbank dealers has moved somewhat higher in recent years, compared with the 1960s and early 1970s. However, capital which has reached the industry in part through the entry of additional firms did not grow so rapidly as trading volume.

DEALER FINANCING AND THE GROWTH OF INTERMEDIATION

Dealers have broadened their sources of funds significantly in recent years. Their greater participation in the money market has enabled them to reduce their reliance on borrowing from banks in money centers. The growth of the

[4]See "Federal Funds and Repurchase Agreements," this *Review* (Summer 1977), pages 33-48. In a repurchase agreement, the owner of a security sells it outright to the provider of funds and agrees to repurchase the issue at a specified future date and price. In a reverse repurchase agreement, the provider of funds purchases a security and agrees to sell it back at a specified future date and price. These terms, RPs and reverse RPs, are sometimes interchanged in market parlance, however, and RPs are often used to describe the usual transactions of an institution in the market—whether it is a provider or user of funds.

market for RPs reflects the changes in dealer financing patterns and the increasingly sophisticated cash management techniques used by many money market participants. Dealers typically raise more funds than they need to finance their positions in securities and have become important as intermediaries in the money market.

Dealers employ two basic methods of financing inventories: entering into RPs or furnishing securities as collateral for a loan. The rate of return on overnight RPs is related to the Federal funds rate but is typically below it, in part because the agreements are viewed as secured loans by many market participants. The interest rate on collateral loans to dealers by large banks in money centers is usually somewhat above the Federal funds rate since the banks view the latter rate as the cost of funding the loan.

Collateral loans have remained a significant source of dealer financing despite their higher cost. The banks are often residual suppliers of funds when money market conditions are tight and liquidity is scarce. Thus, collateral loans amounted to about one third of nonbank dealers' financings through collateral loans and RPs combined in 1973-74 but that proportion declined substantially in 1975-76. Bank loans can be obtained late in the day—and often are—after dealers have searched out other sources of funds. They can be used when a dealer agrees during the day to take delivery that same day, say, in Treasury bills, or ends up with securities that were expected to be sold but were not. Dealer departments of commercial banks do not use collateral loans. They rely on RPs and on other forms of financing and often obtain funds from their own banks.

Dealers also obtain funds to provide them to others. A dealer may raise funds through use of RPs and provide them to others by arranging a reverse RP. The growth in holdings of Government securities by many institutions over the past few years has enabled them to sell their holdings temporarily through RPs to meet short-term cash needs as an alternative to raising funds in the commercial paper market or at banks. In addition, corporations and financial institutions have also been willing to invest temporary cash surpluses in short-term RPs in preference to holding demand deposits which pay no interest.

Frequently the dealer acts as a middleman in these transactions, obtaining funds from one customer to provide them to another. While the dealers are principals in the transactions, some are essentially acting as brokers because they "match" the maturities of the RP and the reverse RP that they arrange with customers. When the maturities of such transactions are not exactly matched, the dealer shoulders some risk with respect to interest rates. There can also be some risk in that the dealer is dependent on the performance of one customer in order to ensure that he can fulfill his obligation to another customer. Dealers are often willing to finance the placement of funds under reverse RPs through a series of RPs with shorter maturities. The upward slope of the yield curve over the past few years has encouraged this pattern.

CONCLUSIONS

Recent years have witnessed substantial growth in the Government securities market, both in terms of activity and in the number of dealer firms. The market has responded well to sizable increases in Treasury financing requirements and in Federal Reserve open market operations. The liquidity of Government securities, particularly coupon issues—the fact that they can be converted into cash more quickly than other assets of similar maturity—has been enhanced in the process. Consequently, participants can carry out investment decisions readily at competitive prices.

Increased activity has both contributed to and resulted from the greater efficiency and competitiveness of the market. The market's capacity to handle large Treasury financings and Federal Reserve operations smoothly has expanded in recent years. The market is also better able to weather surges in trading activity precipitated by shifts in participants' perceptions of the economic outlook. These expanded capabilities are due in part to the increase in the number of available maturities, the enhanced ability to establish long or short positions, and the wider variety of independent decision makers active in the market. Competition has been strengthened through the large increase in the number of dealers and the resulting reduction in market concentration.

The expansion in the market and in activity has not been an unmixed benefit, however. Trading has taken on speculative overtones at times, which may well have exacerbated the volatility of prices. Participants—in searching for information about the probable course of interest rates—have increased their focus on, and reacted more to, temporary phenomena. The emphasis on trading and performance may not always have been accompanied by adequate appreciation of the increased position and credit risks that derive from this approach. Experience in 1977 seems to have served as a pertinent reminder of these risks. The dealers in the market confront a new challenge to develop and maintain activity in the more cautious but increasingly competitive market environment with which 1978 begins.

THE MARKET FOR CORPORATE BONDS*

Burton Zwick

11

The market for corporate bonds has undergone a number of major changes over the past fifteen years. Perhaps the most striking has been the increased purchase of corporate bonds by households. During the 1950s and early 1960s, households invested heavily in corporate equities. Then, as the bull market in equities ended in the mid-1960s and interest rates began rising sharply, households increased their corporate bond holdings relative to those of equities. Pension funds also began to channel large amounts of funds into the corporate bond market because of the large flows they were receiving as well as a broadening of the authority of many public pension funds (state and local government retirement funds) to include investments in corporate bonds. The increase in household and pension fund holdings of corporate bonds has meant that these investor groups now rival life insurance companies as major suppliers of funds to the corporate bond market.

On the issuer side of the market, corporations have made large adjustments in their approach to financing. From 1960 through the early 1970s, corporations increased the debt portion of their capital structures. Financial leverage—or the ratio of debt to total financing—of nonfinancial corporations rose by about one-fifth, and the ratio of bonds to total financing rose somewhat more moderately. A lower level of uncertainty or expected variability of corporations' income before interest and taxes may have encouraged corporations to increase

*Reprinted, with deletions, from the *Quarterly Review*, Autumn 1977, pp. 27-36, with permission of the Federal Reserve Bank of New York.

debt financing during the early and mid-1960s. From 1968 and into the 1970s, a new factor was at work: higher rates of inflation encouraged firms to issue debt as the real or inflation-adjusted cost of debt financing declined. In 1975, however, financial leverage declined for the first time in fifteen years. The decline occurred in part because of the reduction of short-term debt as inventories were liquidated and may also have reflected the response of corporations to greater economic uncertainty.

Borrowing and lending decisions in the corporate bond market have resulted in an 8½ percent annual growth rate since 1960 in the outstanding stock of corporate bonds. At the end of 1976, the total outstanding amounted to $323 billion, about one third more than that of the state and local government securities and about half as much as that of home mortgages and United States Treasury securities. Borrowing and lending decisions—particularly those involving substitution between corporate bonds and other instruments by both issuers and purchasers of corporate bonds—affect not only the size and rate of growth of the corporate bond market but also the effectiveness of selective credit and other public policies designed to alter the price and quantity of particular financial securities, such as home mortgages or state and local government obligations.

PURCHASERS OF CORPORATE BONDS, 1960-76

The major purchasers of corporate bonds are life insurance companies, households, private pension funds, public pension funds, and mutual savings banks. Data on the distribution of holdings among these purchasers are presented in Table 11-1. The largest and steadiest buyers of corporate bonds have been life insurance companies. The bulk of these companies' investments are confined to bonds and real estate mortgages. Inflows of life insurance premiums create actuarially determined outflows, most of which are expected to occur far in the future, and these inflows must be invested to insure that those distant liabilities are covered. Corporate bonds are attractive instruments, because they insure a specific cash flow over a long period and their yields are higher than on government bonds. Insurance companies can accept the lower marketability of most corporate bonds, compared with government bonds, since they generally expect to hold them until maturity regardless of interim movements in interest rates and bond prices. Not all corporate bonds are acceptable to life insurance companies, however. These companies are extremely averse to the provisions in some corporate bonds calling for redemption and refunding shortly after the issuance date. Such provisions create uncertainty about investment income during the period from the refunding to maturity. (Refunding provisions and other investment characteristics of corporate bonds are described in the Box.)

THE CHARACTERISTICS OF CORPORATE BONDS

A bond is a debt contract which promises its holder an amount equal to the bond's par value on a stated maturity date as well as specific interest payments at fixed intervals prior to maturity. Holders of corporate bonds that are "unsubordinated" or "senior" debt have prior claim (relative to holders of equity and "subordinated" or "junior" debt) against the issuer's income, whether generated through normal operations or through liquidation. The payments of some corporate bonds, generally called mortgage bonds, are also secured by liens on particular assets of the issuer. Corporate bonds that are unsecured by specific properties are referred to as debentures. Over the years, investors have lowered their evaluation of mortgage bonds relative to debentures. Many railroad bankrupcies have shown that a mortgage on a property is of little value unless the property produces a good flow in income. Debentures, on the other hand, have come to be very acceptable when issued by companies with good earning power. While many utilities continue to offer mortgage bonds, large and well-regarded industrial firms typically use debenture financing to avoid encumbering fixed property with liens.

Almost all bonds, whether based on a mortgage or on the general earning power of the issuing corporation, have their terms spelled out in a detailed contract called an indenture. This agreement describes the rights and obligations of both parties, mainly the rights of lenders and the obligations of the debtor. The enforcement of this indenture is usually left to a trustee who acts for the bondholders collectively. The terms of the agreement are described in the Trust Indenture Act of 1939.

To insure that bond liabilities do not exceed the value of assets financed by these liabilities, corporate bonds usually are issued with sinking fund provisions. The schedule of sinking fund payments is directly related to the estimated depreciation of the assets financed by the bonds. These provisions also name a trustee, frequently a commercial bank, who insures that funds are set aside by the issuer in a reserve account or sinking fund. The funds placed in the sinking fund generally are used to retire a portion of the outstanding bonds, and that portion of bonds scheduled for retirement can be retired or called by the trustee on behalf of the issuer, at par, even if market yields have fallen and the price of the bonds has risen above par. Some sinking fund arrangements permit the trustee to "double" or to call at par twice as many bonds as are scheduled for retirement in any particular year under the sinking fund provisions. However, this ability to double cannot be carried over and cumulated but applies only on a year-to-year basis.

For most utility bonds, the sinking fund requirement has until recently been met by applying some minimum percentage of revenues to capital improvements or to the maintenance of the assets financed by the bonds. In recent years, however, as the sharp cost increases in energy and raw mat6.7   Coset Decoders   erials were passed on in price increases and as maintenance expenditures declined as a percentage of total revenues, a part of the sinking fund requirements of utilities, as well as industrials, has been met by the retirement of a portion of outstanding bonds.

In addition to the call of bonds before maturity through sinking fund provisions, special call or "refunding" provisions have been introduced into most corporate bond issues during the past decade. The refunding provisions provide issuers an opportunity, otherwise precluded by the protection of investors against refunding, to retire bonds before maturity with funds obtained by issuing other securities at a lower rate. Refundability generally occurs after five years for utility bonds and after ten years for industrial issues, frequently at a price of 5 to 10 percent above par. Since bonds with refunding provisions will be called only if interest rates decline, the initial investors require a higher yield when purchasing securities that include refunding provisions. Issuers have been increasingly willing to offer the higher yields necessary to obtain these provisions on account of the greater uncertainty about future interest rates and capital costs due to high and variable rates of inflation.

The length of bonds, or the average period that principal is outstanding, is reduced by sinking fund or other provisions to call bonds before the final maturity date. The increased use of refunding provisions, which introduce a probability that the entire principal will be repaid before maturity, has shortened the expected length of most recently issued corporate bonds. The length of bonds may be shortened further if the increased uncertainty about future taxes makes investors as well as issuers more reluctant to commit themselves over a long period. Apart from a shortening of the length of bonds because of either call provisions or earlier final maturity dates, the length of most issued bonds—when the average timing of all payments, interest and principal, is taken into account—has been shortened as higher market rates in recent years have resulted in higher coupon rates. The investor recoups a given proportion of the purchase price of recently issued bonds with their higher coupons earlier than on bonds with similar terms to maturity issued, say, in the mid-1960s.

Table 11-1 Holdings of corporate bonds outstanding
(In billions of dollars)

Sector	1950	1960	1970	1976
Households*	$ 5	$ 10	$ 36	$ 72
Life insurance companies†	25	48	74	122
Private pension funds	3	16	30	39
Public pension funds‡	1	7	35	67
Mutual savings banks	2	4	8	20
Other	4	5	19	34
Total	$40	$90	$202	$354

While life insurance companies have remained the largest holder of corporate bonds, the amount they held relative to the total outstanding fell from 53 percent in 1960 to 35 percent in 1976. This occurred mainly because growth in the assets of life insurance companies was slower than the growth in the outstanding volume of corporate bonds. However, as revealed in Table 11-2, where each sector's corporate bond holdings are expressed as a percentage of the purchaser's portfolio of financial assets, a shift in life insurance company assets from corporate bonds to other assets also made a minor contribution to the reduction of their share of the amount outstanding.

Table 11-2 Importance of corporate bonds in purchasers' portfolios
(Corporate bonds as a percentage of total financial
assets of purchasers)

Sector	1950	1960	1970	1976
Households*	1.0%	1.0%	1.9%	2.5%
Life insurance companies†	40.0	41.0	37.0	39.0
Private pension funds	40.0	42.0	27.0	22.0
Public pension funds‡	10.0	37.0	58.0	54.0
Mutual savings banks	9.0	9.0	10.0	15.0

Corporate bond holdings include dollar-denominated bonds issued by foreign corporations in the United States market. The volume of these "Yankee bonds" increased from $6 billion in 1960 to $31 billion in 1976.

*"Households" includes funds held by commercial banks in trust accounts and funds held by nonprofit organizations.

†Includes private pension funds managed by life insurance companies.

‡State and local government retirement funds.

Source: Board of Governors of the Federal Reserve System.

Household investment portfolios are more diversified than those of life insurance companies and include large amounts of short-term securities, equities and municipal bonds, as well as corporate bonds. Since households have greater flexibility in making portfolio choices, their participation in the corporate bond market has varied a great deal over the post-World War II period. Their holdings have shown a marked increase since 1960, both as a percentage of total corporate bonds outstanding and of total household assets. The increase in long-term rates and the weak performance of the equity market contributed to this shift.

The corporate bond holdings of private and public pension funds have grown even more in value since the 1960s, almost reaching the level of life insurance company holdings. This development primarily reflects the rapid growth in total assets of pension funds. For public pension funds, corporate bonds also rose as a percentage of their total assets over the period, as the broadening in their investment authority enabled them to buy corporate bonds and so obtain the higher returns available on them in comparison with those on government bonds. By contrast, corporate bonds declined as a percentage of the total assets of private pension funds after 1960 as these funds increased the equity or variable income portion of their portfolios. Still, the corporate bond portion of both public and private pension fund assets greatly exceeds that of households. Pension funds are exempt from taxes on all forms of investment income—interest payments, dividends, and capital gains. Households are taxed at the full personal income tax rate on interest and dividends, while the tax rate on capital gains is, of course, lower. Households are, therefore, sensitive to whether income arises from interest or capital gains, whereas pension funds are not. The differential tax treatment is thus a major reason for the difference in investment choices of the two groups.

Mutual savings banks also purchase sizable amounts of corporate bonds. Their holdings have risen sharply since the 1960s, reflecting both an increase in the corporate bond portion of mutual savings bank assets (Table 11-2) and growth in the total assets of these banks. The increase in the corporate bond portion was matched by a decrease in mortgage holdings relative to total assets. Savings and loan associations, the other major group of thrift institutions, hold almost all of their assets in home mortgages.

HOW CORPORATE BONDS ARE MARKETED

New corporate bonds are sold in one of two ways. Issues are sold in the public market or they are placed directly with particular lenders. Private placements are often made by less regarded or less widely known companies. Over the 1953-64 period, about one half of new corporate bond funds was raised through public offerings. Subsequently, the proportion of funds raised through public offerings rose to about two thirds. The decline in private placements reflects the reduced share of life insurance companies in bond acquisitions, since they do most of the purchasing by this method. Apart from the long-term trend, the ratio of publicly offered to total corporate bond borrowing moves up and down with the business cycle. Public utilities are better able to pass on higher borrowing costs to their customers than are industrial firms. So during periods of high and rising interest rates, the volume of publicly offered utility issues remains fairly high while the volume of industrial issues—particularly those of weaker firms that are generally placed privately—is cut back because of the increase in borrowing costs.

During the 1920s, most public issues were handled by commercial banks. There was much concern that commercial bank underwriting and dealing in corporate securities increased financial instability, concentrated economic power, and led to conflicts of interest for banks. Therefore, bank underwriting of corporate bond issues was terminated in 1933 by passage of the Glass-Steagall Act. This legislation was passed during an era in which several important measures affecting financial markets were enacted, including the bill that created the Securities and Exchange Commission (SEC).

Since Glass-Steagall, investment banking firms have been the major underwriters of corporate bond issues. As underwriters, investment bankers purchase an issue themselves or guarantee the issuer a specific price for the bonds. Investment bankers thus bear the risk of gain or loss when the bonds are sold through competitive bidding to the particular underwriter that offers the issuer the highest price for the bonds, which of course means the lowest interest cost to the issuer. The winning underwriter then sells the bonds to the public at a price calculated to cover all costs and to provide an adequate return on the capital funds tied up in the transaction.

A large issue requires the participation of many investment banking firms, who combine under the leadership of a particular underwriter or group of underwriters to form a syndicate. The syndicate leaders must have good information about the marketability of an issue to bid aggressively for it. This information is difficult and costly to obtain if the leaders do not have close contact with the retail market. Because of the importance of accurate information about retail demand in order to bid successfully for an issue, underwriters have a strong incentive to be involved in the final sale of the bonds to retail customers. Accordingly, some large underwriting firms have recently merged with retail brokerage firms, and a number of large retail firms have increased their underwriting activities.

Many corporations maintain long-term relationships with a single underwriting firm and negotiate all of their offerings with it to encourage the underwriter to make a strong effort to sell the company's issues. The designated underwriter—who may organize a syndicate—will typically advise the corporation about the maturities, coupons, and other terms in order to attract the strongest market interest. The choice between competitive and negotiated public offerings is usually determined by the issuer's assessment of whether the benefits of competition for the issue among several groups would be offset by the increased commitment and advice of a particular underwriter. The decision may depend on how well the borrowing firm is known and how specific its borrowing needs are with regard to maturities and other terms. However, many issuers subject to regulatory authorities, such a public utilities, are required to sell their bonds through competitive bidding. In periods of high and rising rates, such as 1974, these authorities sometimes waive this requirement because of concern that strong bids will not be forthcoming.

For both negotiated and competitive offerings, the underwriter normally seeks to obtain commitments from potential buyers prior to obtaining them from the issuer. The retail purchasers will have had an opportunity to review a prospectus on the issue, prepared according to the regulations of the SEC, as well as a more detailed registration statement that must be filed with the Commission.[1] Since the actual price of the issue is not set by the syndicate until the syndicate takes ownership of the bonds the prospectus is in "red herring" form, i.e. some red printing is substituted for the final prices and other details that are not known until receipt from the issuer.

Upon receipt of the bonds from the issuer, the underwriting syndicate announces the sale of bonds by advertisement at a price reached by mutual agreements within the syndicate. Because of the prior arrangements with customers, usually most of the bonds have been sold before this announcement, particularly in the case of negotiated issues. In cases where the price set by the syndicate on the bonds is too high, the syndicate will sometimes be forced to disband. The rest of the unsold bonds will then be sold by individual members of the syndicate at prices determined by the market rather than by the initial agreement of the syndicate.

The underwriter hopes that the price of the bonds will rise by a small amount after the sale so as to satisfy the investors that they have gotten a good buy. However, too large a premium may cause issuers to believe that the interest rates they have agreed to pay are too high. On many high-quality industrial issues, the flotation cost or the spread between the public price of the bonds and the proceeds to the issuer is 7/8 percent. An underwriting commission of .2 percent is shared on a pro rata basis by all members of the underwriting syndicate, while the managers receive an additional fee of .175 percent. The remaining 1/2 percent, or $5 per $1,000 bond, is typically paid out as a selling "concession" to salesmen. On utility issues, the total spread is usually between .45 percent and .75 percent. The lower underwriting spread on utility issues is due to their greater marketability. In the case of both industrial and utility issues, the total underwriting spread does not include other flotation costs, such as legal, printing, and other costs necessary to satisfy the registration requirement of the SEC, which can run from about 1 percent

---

[1]Issues of a number of firms regulated by the Interstate Commerce Commission are exempt from registration with the SEC.

of total proceeds for issues of under $10 million to about 1/4 percent for issues over $100 million.

The most consistent purchasers of corporate bonds through private placement are life insurance companies who frequently purchase the bonds of small, lesser known companies. This method of placement saves the borrowers most of the marketing costs of a public issue, including the costs of registration with the SEC. More importantly, private placement allows these small borrowers, whose financing needs are often unusual or specialized, to sell issues that probably would meet with a poor reception in the public market. In private placements, highly complex indentures or contracts (see Box) can be included to aid the issuer and to protect the investor. Companies unable to enter the public market because the quality of their obligations is inadequate to attract large-scale public interest pay a substantially higher rate than do public offers, and they typically agree not to redeem their securities prior to maturity. The terms usually allow some prepayment of principal through retained earnings, though often with severe penalties. Prepayment to refinance at lower rates is generally prohibited.

RISK AND CORPORATE BOND YIELDS

The yields on particular bonds are partly determined by default and marketability risk. Default, or business risk, refers to the risk that payments guaranteed in the bond contract will not be made. This is not a measurable quantity, and qualitative factors—such as the quality and experience of management, the competitive position of a firm within its industry and the prospects for the industry as a whole— affect assessments or default risk. A number of quantitative financial variables, including financial leverage (the ratio of fixed to variable operating costs), and the variability of revenues, also affect default risk. Corporations that borrow sizable amounts through public offerings frequently pay one or both of the major rating agencies—Moody's or Standard & Poor's— to rate their bonds with respect to default risk. In the publication of bond ratings, the convention is that a rating by Moody's (Aaa, for example) precedes one by Standard & Poor's (AAA), *viz.*, Aaa/AAA. The agencies' rating categories differ somewhat, but in general the meaning of their ratings is similar. The first four categories—Aaa/AAA through Baa/BBB—are all of "investment grade," meaning that interest and principal are considered secure. The Baa/BBB category is said by Moody's to have some "speculative characteristics," while Standard & Poor's terms such issues as on the "borderline" between sound obligations and speculations. Ba/BB issues are far more speculative and B/Bs are even riskier. Moody's then continues through Caa, Ca and C for highly speculative issues, some of which are in default. Standard & Poor's goes down as far as DDD, DD, and D, all of which are for bonds in default but with differences in relative salvage value.

Variations in the financial condition of companies whose issues are rated by the agencies tend to be related to the ratings they receive, as summarized in Table 11-3. The rating of issues is also influenced, of course, by a number of qualitative factors affecting the outlook of individual firms. In the postwar period, no industrial or utility issue has gone into default while rated "investment grade." However, several investment-grade railroad issues went into default in the Penn Central and other railroad bankruptcies. During the Depression, 11 percent (in dollar volume) of investment-grade issues went into default.

Almost all newly issued and rated bonds carry ratings of Baa/BBB or above by Moody's, about one-third carried their Aaa rating, while about 30 percent were rated Aa, another 30 percent rated A, and about 7 percent rated Baa. About two-thirds of the dollar volume of bonds in these four highest rating categories were issued by utilities, and industrial offerings accounted for the rest. In the Aaa category, more than 75 percent of the dollar volume was offered by utilities, and telephone bonds accounted for the bulk.

The marketability risk of an issue concerns the possibility that if a holder wants to sell that issue, his inability to find a buyer may force him to take a loss unrelated to any deterioration in the corporation's financial position. Marketability (or salability) depends on the breadth of ownership of a corporation's securities—and frequently on how many securities are outstanding. The presence of a large number of potential purchasers and sellers causes dealers to become willing to buy and sell them and thus to make a secondary market. The default risk of a bond also affects marketability, insofar as issues with low ratings do not attract a wide variety of buyers.

The marketability of corporate issues is reflected in the difference— or spread—between the bid and offered prices that dealers quote (for certain minimum amounts of bonds) when they make a market in an issue. The dealer

Table 11-3   Ratings of corporate bonds and selected financial ratios

Rating*	Ratio of earnings to interest plus sinking fund obligations	Ratio of cash flow to senior debt (percent)	Ratio of long-term debt to total capitalization (percent)
Aaa/AAA	At least 5	Above 65	Below 25
Aa/AA	At least 4	45 to 65	Below 30
A/A	At least 3	35 to 45	Below 35
Baa/BBB	At least 2½	25 to 35	Below 40

*In the publication of bond ratings, the convention is that the Moody's rating comes first and Standard & Poor's uses capital letters exclusively.

Source: Irwin Ross, "Higher Stakes in the Bond Rating Game," *Fortune* (April 1976), page 136.

spread in a $500,000 to $1 million transaction for a highly marketable corporate bond is typically about 1/8 point. Spreads for less marketable issues range from about 1/4 point to 1/2 point. (The smallest spreads in the bond market are for actively traded Government securities, and these range from 1/32 point to 1/16 point.)

Since trading is generally more active immediately after new issues are brought to the market, new issues are typically quoted at narrower spreads than issues that are firmly held in investor's portfolios. The amount of uncertainty about future interest rates may also affect spreads. An increase in the degree of uncertainty or in the expected variability of rates will cause spreads to widen.

SUBSTITUTION IN THE CORPORATE BOND MARKET

The amount of corporate bonds on the balance sheets of both issuers and purchasers of corporates reflects a variety of portfolio constraints. For example, because of the pattern of their inflows and outflows, pension funds and life insurance companies are generally limited to long-term investments. On the issuer side, corporations tend to match the maturities of their liabilities with those of their assets. Nevertheless, these constraints typically permit some substitution or alteration in the bond portions of both issuer and purchaser balance sheets in response to changes in relative yields and other factors.

Bonds are issued by corporations to finance the acquisition of assets. It is convenient to look at the corporate financing process, first, as a decision about the distribution of total financing between debt and equity and, second, as a decision about the distribution of debt financing between bonds and short-term debt obligations. A number of factors affect corporations' choice between debt and equity financing, including the levels of corporate and personal income tax rates, the rate of inflation, and the level of corporations' asset risk, *i.e.*, the amount of uncertainty or expected variability of their earnings before interest and taxes.

The current tax system favors debt financing by corporations, because interest payments made by corporations are deductible from their taxable income while any dividend payments they make are not. However, the ownership of corporations resides in a collection of individuals, and the tax advantage of debt financing accruing to the owners of corporations because of taxation at the corporate level may be offset in the taxation of the owners' personal incomes. This offset may occur because interest and dividend income to the owners is taxed at the ordinary personal income tax rate, while income in the form of capital gains is taxed at half the personal tax rate—up to a maximum rate of 25 percent. The tax benefits to corporations from debt financing exceed those from equity financing except when securities are held by the small number of individuals whose personal tax rates are very high relative to the corporate tax rate. Inflation also encourages corporations to favor debt relative to equity financing if the real or inflation-adjusted cost of borrowing declines.

While the tax structure and inflation encourage firms to use debt rather than equity financing, the greater use of debt increases a firm's fixed commitments. In the case of debt financing—given the amount of asset risk—the resulting rise in fixed commitments increases the risk of bankruptcy, and bankruptcy creates two general categories of costs. The first category—direct costs—includes lawyers' and accountants' fees, other professional fees, and the value of the managerial time spent in administering the bankruptcy. Evidence in the bankruptcies of eleven large railroad firms between 1930 and 1955 suggests that these costs were small relative to the value of the firms. However, the second category—indirect costs—may be larger. These costs include lost sales, lost profits, and possibly the inability of firms to obtain credit or to issue securities except under especially onerous terms. Unless the direct and indirect costs of bankruptcy are negligible, debt financing or any other factor increasing the probability of bankruptcy may be expected to increase a firm's cost of financing or the yield required by holders of the firm's securities. The positive relation of asset risk—and the greater possibility of bankruptcy as more debt is issued—to the cost of debt relative to equity financing explains why public utilities and other firms with low asset risk maintain high debt ratios while firms with higher asset risk limit their use of financial leverage.

The inverse relation between the asset risk of individual firms and the debt ratios of the same firms should also apply over time for the corporate sector as a whole. An increase in asset risk for the corporate sector—because of an increase in the general amount of fluctuation or instability in the economy—should cause firms to reduce their debt ratios and their fixed commitments in order to reduce the risk of bankruptcy.

From 1948 through the 1950s, the debt portion of the financing of nonfinancial corporations remained stable. Subsequently, from 1960 to 1974, the ratio of debt to total financing or total assets underwent a steady and sizable increase. When the balance sheet is expressed in terms of historical costs, the ratio rose from .47 in 1960 to .50 in 1967 and then to an average of .55 during the 1972-74 period. However, the ratio of debt to assets tends to be overstated during periods of inflation. During inflationary periods the historical costs of physical assets as reported in balance sheets fall below the current value or replacement costs of these assets. There is no corresponding understatement of debt, because inflation does not increase the value of liabilities which represent dollars not physical units. When the historical costs of physical assets are replaced by the current or replacement costs of assets, the debt ratio rose from .40 in 1960 to .44 in 1967 to an average of .47 over the 1972-74 period. In 1975, the debt ratio experienced its first decline in fifteen years, as firms reduced their short-term debt. Because some of the short-term debt was replaced by bonds as well as equity, the bond proportion of total financing increased slightly during this period.

The rising debt ratios in 1960-74 should be separated into two roughly equal subperiods because of the different factors affecting debt ratios in each. Inflation remained fairly moderate until 1968 except for brief inflation episodes in the late 1940s and during the Korean war. The corporate tax burden declined slightly during the early and mid-1960s because of the investment tax credit. This behavior of inflation and the tax burden suggests that the increase in debt ratios from 1960 through 1967—after fifteen years of little change—occured because of a decrease in asset risk rather than an increase in taxes or inflation. The decrease in asset risk after 1960—or the perception that it was higher before 1960—may reflect a dimming of early postwar memories of the Great Depression during the 1930s. In contrast to the early and mid-1960s, inflation rates from 1968 on were substantially higher than during most of the 1940s and 1950s. The increase in debt ratios after 1967 seems to have resulted from this increase in inflation and a decline in the inflation-adjusted cost of debt financing.

The decrease in debt ratios during 1975 was related to the decline in short-term debt as inventories were liquidated; the moderation of inflation may also have contributed. The decline also may reflect the perceptions of both issuers and investors that corporation asset risk had increased. An increase in asset risk beginning in the mid-1960s is suggested by the deviations of corporate profits from their long-term trend. Larger deviations from trend occurred in the 1965-75 period than in the 1948-65 period, even if the 1965-75 deviations are divided by the larger values of profits in the later years. The relatively and absolutely larger deviations in the 1965-75 period indicate a higher level of profit variability—a close proxy for asset risk.

Choosing between short- and long-term debt financing is much more closely related to the business cycle and the behavior of interest rates, including short-term rates, than is the choice between debt and equity financing. During 1960-76, the ratio of long-term debt to total debt maintained a consistent and inverse relation with short-term rates. At least part of the decline in bond financing relative to short-term debt financing during periods of rising short-term rates presumably reflects large increases in inventories, which firms typically finance with short-term debt. However, the relative decline in bond financing during these intervals may also have reflected firms' efforts to substitute between short-term and long-term debt in order to reduce financing costs. This happened despite high short-term rates, both in absolute terms and relative to long-term rates. Firms may have used short-term rather than long-term financing because they expected a decline in both short- and long-term rates and they wanted to defer long-term financing until the decline in rates had occurred. Bond financing then increased relative to total debt financing, as inventories were liquidated and firms took advantage of declines in long-term rates to issue long-term debt.

SUBSTITUTION BY INVESTORS

The degree of substitution between corporate bonds and other instruments differs substantially among the major groups of holders. Households substitute freely among corporate bonds, equities, and short-term securities. During the 1920s, households owned about two thirds of the corporate bonds outstanding. After World War II, their holdings dropped sharply while their investments in equities rose substantially. As bond yields increased in the 1960s and the performance of equity investments worsened, households again became large holders of corporate bonds.

Although life insurance companies have in recent years been devoting somewhat less of their investments to obligations with very long maturities, their unique time pattern of inflows and outflows inevitably reduces their ability to substitute between corporate bonds and other instruments, particularly short-term securities. Pension funds also tend to hold most of their assets in long-term investments. The principal difference between pension funds and other corporate bondholders, however, is that all forms of investment income of pension funds are free of Federal income taxes. Since households are taxed more heavily on investment income than on capital gains and income from municipal bonds, household investment as compared with pension fund investment is more heavily concentrated in municipal bonds and growth-oriented equity issues. Pension funds invest more heavily in corporate bonds and income-oriented equity issues.

Although the differences in the tax status of households and pension funds cause relative holdings of various financial instruments to differ, these differences do not reduce their incentive or ability to substitute between different instruments in order to maximize the aftertax return on their investment portfolio. Both households and pension funds—life insurance companies do so to a lesser degree—substitute between assets on the basis of alternative aftertax yields, and this substitution does not exclude assets that are typically held by others.

There is considerable evidence that suggests such substitution by financial market participants over a wide range of financial assets including corporate bonds. Also indicative of extensive substitution is the broad similarity of interest rate movements over the 1960-76 period. Yields on corporate and government bonds moved very similarly over these years. And, although yields on commercial paper fluctuate much more than those on corporate bonds, the yields on commercial paper and corporate bonds also tended to behave alike. Parallel movements of corporate bond and stock yields also took place, though the parallelism in yield patterns of these yields was somewhat less than in the other comparisons.

Apart from the different cash flow patterns of various financial market participants, the volume and the distribution of corporate bond holdings in the economy reflect a variety of public policies. In the area of taxation, these policies include the differential treatment of interest and dividend payments in the taxation of corporate income, the differential treatment of capital gains and other investment income in the taxation on personal income, and the exemption of pension funds from taxes on all of their investment income. Statutory factors, such as prohibiting commercial banks from underwriting corporate bonds, also affect the pattern of ownership and the marketing of these bonds. However, the extensive substitution between corporate bonds and other financial instruments—by both issuers and purchasers of corporate bonds—tends to offset a part of the effects of these tax and statutory factors on the volume and distribution of corporate bond holdings. As tax and statutory factors alter the supply or the demand for corporate bonds in the market and cause prices on these bonds to change, market participants purchase corporate bonds if the new price is lower and sell them if the new price is higher. Although the substitution between assets does not reverse the desired effect of the policy on the market, the substitution does reduce the size of the effect.

Similarly, substitution between corporate bonds and other investments weakens the effect of public policies designed to alter the demand or supply of securities that are substitutes for corporate bonds. For example, the most comprehensive attempt to alter the supply of securities in a financial market has been the variety of policies designed to increase the supply or availability of mortgages in order to sustain housing expenditures. These policies include interest rate ceilings on deposits to protect mortgage lending institutions from excessive competition for funds and the creation of Federal Government agencies to raise funds in the capital markets for reinvestment in mortgages. The impact of those policies on the mortgage market was partly offset as other mortgage holders have responded to the increased purchase of mortgages by Federal agencies and mortgage lending institutions by selling mortgages and purchasing other assets. The other assets include corporate bonds, since mortgages and corporate bonds are substitutes in the portfolios of mutual savings banks, households, life insurance companies, and other investment groups. Perhaps more importantly, the moderate increase in the supply of mortgage credit that did result from selective credit policies in the mortgage market caused an even smaller reduction in yields on mortgages. Mortgage yields changed very little because the total demand for mortgage credit increased as households substituted mortgage credit for other credit in their financing of both housing and nonhousing expenditures.

This example of substitution illustrates the difficulty policymakers may have in attempting to alter supplies in particular financial markets. Financial assets are fungible, and investors in a relatively free market move their funds from one market to another on the basis of relative yields. Indeed, substitution because of yield or cost differentials—increase in corporate bond purchases by households and pension funds on the investor side and an increase in debt financing relative to equity financing on the issuer side—has accounted for the major changes in the corporate bond market over the past fifteen years. As investors and issuers of securities shift between securities and markets on the basis of relative yields, policies to steer financing into particular channels will be offset even if elaborate measures are taken to do so.

THE PRIVATE PLACEMENT MARKET*

Federal Reserve Board Staff

12

Since the mid-1960s about one-third of long-term debt and equity offerings sold by domestic businesses and foreign issuers have been placed privately rather than through public offerings. The private placement market has been a major outlet for smaller or riskier issuers. The market also has been attractive when the issuer's financial structure or the proposed transaction is relatively complex, and when factors such as speed, flexibility in financial covenants, and control of sensitive information are important. The institutional investors that purchase most private placements—life insurance companies and, to a lesser degree, pension funds—have the specialized staffs needed to handle the financing of riskier and more complex transactions. The workings of this market— the issuers, the investors, and the role of advisors—are discussed in the following sections.

*This article is excerpted and adapted, with permission, from Chapters 3 and 4 of a study entitled *Commercial Bank Private Placement Activities*, by the staff of the Federal Reserve Board, June 1977. The purpose of this study was to examine the role of commercial banks in the private placement market. The study was based on the analysis of extensive publicly available data and a Federal Reserve Board Special Survey. Since the data are now obsolete, the tabular material contained in the original paper has been deleted. For the same reason, many text references to specific statistics were also deleted. The purpose of this edited version is to provide an overview of the private placement market. Readers interested in the tabular material or the conclusion of the study are referred to the original source. (*Editor's note.*)

THE ISSUERS

From 1966 through the mid-1970s the volume of funds raised privately fluctuated considerably, ranging from as low as 15 percent to over 40 percent of the total long-term capital raised. As might be expected, domestic corporations have been the main issuers in the market, accounting for over three-fourths of the private placement volume. Most of the securities sold by these firms have been debt issues. Foreigners, mostly Canadians, have tapped the U. S. capital market increasingly since the removal in early 1974 of the interest equalization tax and quantitative restrictions on capital flows. Equity sales by foreigners, though, are rare so that the current offerings of both foreign and domestic issues are mainly debt.

Use of the private placement market varies greatly according to factors such as issuer size, reputation, and special needs. Some firms are required by regulatory commissions to offer debt through public sealed bidding and therefore are precluded from making private placements. A number of larger, more established companies may choose between public offerings and private placements as alternative sources of financing, largely on the basis of relative interest costs. In other instances, issuers may choose to offer securities privately because of the complexity of the company's business or financial structure, or because a transaction makes the standard provisions of contracts used in public offerings unsuitable and securities difficult to market to the general public. The private placement contract can be tailored so that funds can be disbursed at intervals in accord with specific financing requirements, such as for construction projects or equipment purchases, or so that funds, if need be, can be obtained on short notice. Widespread dissemination of sensitive information, moreover, is unnecessary.

In the case of smaller offerings, a private placement has great appeal because flotation costs are frequently lower than for public offerings. Many of the expenses of a public offering, such as SEC fees, listing and trustee fees, printing fees, and state taxes are relatively fixed, and can be quite high as a percent of the proceeds of a small issue. The differences in distribution, preparation, and registration costs partly explain a lower average size of private relative to public offerings.

The smaller size also reflects a market receptivity to less financially secure issues, which tend to be small- and medium-sized firms. Large institutions, which are the dominant investors in private placements, are well equipped to appraise riskier offerings. Since regulatory and legal requirements do not limit discussions of the future and since sensitive information need not be circulated widely, issuers and investors can discuss prospects in a relatively unrestricted fashion.

The covenants of a private placement agreement, moreover, can be tailormade to suit the special needs of the issuer and to control the issuer's operations and limit risk. For example, it is not uncommon for the private, long-term debt agreement to contain covenants that, among other things, restrict funded debt, dividend payouts, lease obligations, expansion or diversification, and establish a minimum level of working capital. These are, in addition to the fairly standard provisions, also found in a publicly offered debt instrument such as call protection, a sinking fund, and possibly convertibility or the attachment of warrants. Financial and protective covenants subsequently may be renegotiated regularly, in accord with the changing circumstances of the issuer. Repayments or sinking fund payments may be increased or decreased to accommodate events such as unexpectedly large or small earnings, if adjustment is thought appropriate by the lender. Such arrangements permit the lender to control the riskiness of the loan and allow the less well established borrower access to long-term funds at rates not very much greater than those paid by highly rated companies in the public market. As a result, a major share of funds raised in the private placement market goes for lower-rated securities than typically sold in the public market.

THE INVESTORS

Under Section 4(2) of the *Securities Act of 1933* and SEC Rule 146, a private sale of unregistered securities must be to a limited number of investors. The investor or offeree, under this Rule, should be known to be capable of evaluating the merits and risks of the prospective investment and capable, as well, of bearing the risk.

In practice, by far the largest portion of all directly placed securities are purchased by the 50 largest life insurance companies. Most of the remaining amounts are taken by smaller insurance companies, private and public pension funds, and other investors such as bond funds and mutual savings banks. The larger life insurance companies, which in many cases employ large, specialized staffs, use their expertise to evaluate and finance a substantial portion of the riskier and more complex transactions. Smaller insurance companies and other institutions, though they may participate with the large life insurance companies in many of these transactions, tend to be somewhat more conservative investors.

Because of the heavy reliance of the private placement market on life insurance companies, much depends on the overall availability of funds to these institutions and their allocation of funds to directly placed securities. Except for periods of unusually high interest rates that induced policyholders to borrow against their policies, life insurance companies in recent years have had record cash flows and have increased their proportion of investments in private placements. The surge in cash flows in large part can be traced to the *Employee Retirement Income Security Act of 1974* (ERISA). This legislation, which strengthened fiduciary responsibilities and increased the administrative burdens of pension fund management, led many organizations to turn the management of retirement funds over to insurance companies. Some increase in individual pension accounts at life insurance companies was stimulated by growth in *Keogh* retirement programs, which were made more attractive by ERISA, and in *Individual Retirement Accounts*, which were created by that legislation. Some life insurance companies, in addition, began offering long-term, guaranteed income contracts (or GIC's) as an investment medium for thrift or pension plans. These contracts proved attractive to many financial managers in light of their increased fiduciary responsibilities and the relatively poor performance of the stock market.

As sizable cash flows became available to life insurance companies, private placements provided an especially attractive investment outlet. In the aftermath of the severe deterioration in corporate financial positions which has occurred until around the end of 1974, there were substantial demands by businesses for long-term funds to restructure balance sheets and rebuild liquidity. Also, throughout most of the 1975-76 period, traditional outlets for life insurance companies, other than private placements, were relatively unattractive. The market for commercial and multi-family mortgages was depressed. Equity investments had little appeal, given the earlier poor performance of the stock market and the increased emphasis on meeting fiduciary responsibilities. Therefore, with ample funds available for private placements and strong business demands for long-term financing, the total value of private placements reached a new record in the mid-1970s. In 1976, the total funds raised in the public and private markets was $61.9 billion, of which $19.8 billion was in the form of private placements.[1] In 1975, private placements amounted to $12.6 billion.

ADVISED PRIVATE PLACEMENTS

The work done by an advisor includes making recommendations regarding the terms and timing of the transaction, assisting in the preparation of a financing memorandum which describes the proposed terms of the placement, contacting a limited number of institutional investors for signs of interest in the proposal, gathering together the investors' comments for the prospective issuer, arranging meetings between the client and potential investors, and often assisting in subsequent negotiations.

The issuer has responsibility for providing financial and operating data, the accuracy of which is typically subject to independent review by the investors in analyzing the issuer's financial soundness and future prospects. The final contract is signed by the investors and the issuer, and the proceeds of the sale go directly to the issuer.

---

[1] In 1979, subsequent to the publication of this study, private placements totaled $22.5 billion. In 1980, high interest rates resulted in a high volume of policy loans and thus sharply reduced the cash flows of life insurance companies. As a result, the volume of private placements fell to $16.3 billion in 1980. (*Editor's note.*)

An issuer offering placements for the first time or proposing a relatively complex transaction may find an advisor particularly valuable. When there are large or frequent offerings to be sold and saturation of a small segment of the market could be a problem, an advisor's knowledge of investors also may be highly useful. In other cases, though, a repeat borrower may find it unnecessary to use an intermediary. A small issuer, moreover, may find an advisor's fee high relative to the size of the proposed placement. In addition, outlets for the smaller or riskier placements, particularly the larger life insurance companies, are reasonably well known so that investors for such placements can be readily found without an intermediary. Accordingly, an unassisted offering tends to be much smaller than one that is assisted.

In terms of both value and number of transactions, most private placements are aided by advisors. Typically, over 75 percent of both the number and dollar volume of private placements in a given year are aided by advisors. Investment banking firms have been the main suppliers of private placement advisory services, while commercial banks have enjoyed a modest, although rapidly growing market share. The value of private placements assisted by commercial banks in 1972 was 1.8 percent of all assisted direct placements. By 1975, the commercial bank share had grown to 7.3 percent and it remained at that level in 1976. The dollar volume of business done by commercial banks rose dramatically throughout the entire 1972-76 period, as both their market share and the overall volume of advised placements reflect fairly extensive experience in lease financing.

Most of the private placement clients of commercial banks are deposit and/ or loan customers. However, the proceeds of bank-assisted placements are usually not used to repay bank loans made by the advisor bank. The advisor bank may be one of the lenders in conjunction with other banks, pension funds and life insurance companies. When acting in this capacity, banks have a preference for the short-term to intermediate-term maturities because of their short-term liability structure. On the other hand, the major nonbank investors prefer longer-term, fixed-rate loans in order to more closely match the characteristics of these assets with their actuarially based fixed-rate, longer-term liabilities.

A REVIEW OF THE MUNICIPAL BOND MARKET*

Richard H. Rosenbloom

13

Recent developments in the municipal bond market have increased public awareness of the problems state and local governments face in obtaining debt financing.[1] Of special concern to many interested observers is the recent steep rise in the yields on municipal bonds relative to those on corporate bonds with the same credit rating. This article undertakes to assess the significance of this development through an evaluation of recent trends affecting both the supply of and demand for municipal bonds and the resulting effects on the borrowing costs of state and local governments. The discussion focuses on the primary (new issue) market for municipal bonds with emphasis on market participants, market trends over the past fifteen years, recent market developments, and the probable future course of the market.

MEASUREMENT OF MUNICIPAL BOND MARKET CONDITIONS

Municipal bonds have generally the same investment characteristics and attributes as corporate bonds with one fundamental exception. The interest in-

---

*Reprinted, with deletions, from the *Economic Review*, March/April 1976, pp. 10–19, with permission of the Federal Reserve Bank of Richmond.

[1]Municipal bonds are any tax-exempt debt security of a state or local government, agency, or special authority.

come from municipal bonds is exempt from Federal income taxation.[2] This tax-exempt feature makes municipals sufficiently different from corporates that it is uncommon to find the two types of bonds together in the same portfolio. The purpose of the tax-exempt feature is to lower the borrowing costs of state and local governments by enabling them to offer investors a lower yield that is competitive with the after-tax yield available on corporate bonds.

The relationship between the yields on equal credit-rated municipal and corporate bonds differs from investors in different income brackets since the value of the tax-exempt feature, given a progressive income tax structure, increases as taxable income moves into brackets for which the tax rate is higher. The investor in tax bracket "t" would be indifferent between investment in corporates and in municipals when:

$$Rm = Rc(1 - t)$$

where Rm = the yield on municipal bonds, Rc = the yield on corporate bonds, and t = the marginal tax rate at which the after-tax yields on municipal and corporate bonds are equal. Given t and Rc, the equation determines the minimum municipal yield necessary to induce investors in tax bracket t to buy municipal rather than corporate bonds. When transposed, the equation can be solved for t as follows:

$$t = 1 - Rm/Rc.$$

This equation says simply that given the relationship between yields on municipals (Rm) and yields on corporates (Rc), the marginal tax rate at which investors are indifferent between the two types of bonds is automatically determined. The relationship between Rm and Rc can be affected, of course, by factors other than the value of the tax exemption to investors. Relative risks and call protection, for example, could be major factors. However, the risk factor has been minimized in the discussion by using both Aa-rated corporate and Aa-rated municipal bonds and by assuming the risk relationship between them has remained stable. The call protection factor has been minimized by the use of corporate and municipal bonds with approximately the same call protection.

The relationship Rm/Rc is a widely used measure of conditions in the municipal bond market relative to other capital markets and specifically to the corporate bond market. High levels of Rm/Rc are taken to indicate relatively tight credit conditions in the municipal bond market, while low levels of Rm/Rc indicate comparatively easier credit conditions for municipal borrowers.

The course of Rm/Rc over the past fifteen years is shown in Figure 13-1.

---

[2]In many cases, the interest income is also exempt from state and local taxation in the issuing state and/or locality.

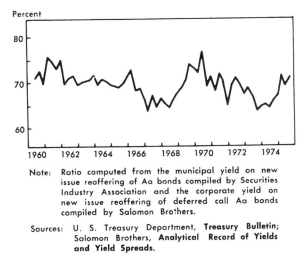

Percent

Note: Ratio computed from the municipal yield on new
issue reoffering of Aa bonds compiled by Securities
Industry Association and the corporate yield on
new issue reoffering of deferred call Aa bonds
compiled by Salomon Brothers.

Sources: U. S. Treasury Department, **Treasury Bulletin;**
Salomon Brothers, **Analytical Record of Yields
and Yield Spreads.**

Figure 13-1 Ratio of municipal bond to corporate bond yields

As can be seen, the movements are quite erratic with no long-term trends. There are, however, a number of conspicuous short-term movements that merit examination along with the general volatility of the series.

THE SUPPLY OF MUNICIPAL BONDS

Municipal bonds are issued by state and local governments and their special governmental agencies and authorities primarily to finance capital outlays that are too large to be financed out of current revenue. In many cases a new agency or authority, such as a transportation authority, is created solely to issue bonds for a specific project and, perhaps, to administer the project upon completion.[3]

There are two general types of municipal bonds—general obligation bonds and revenue bonds. General obligation bonds are "full faith and credit" obligations of the issuing body. As such, they are secured by the taxing power of the issuer. These long-term debt obligations are usually issued as serial bonds[4] with maturities from 1 to 30 years. Revenue bonds are issued primarily by governmental authorities that have no taxing power. They are secured solely by the revenue collected from the users of the particular capital project funded by the debt issue. Thus, the credit quality of a revenue bond is directly related

---

[3]In many cases special authorities are established to provide services "off-budget," thereby by-passing state constitutional requirements for balanced budgets.

[4]Serial bonds are single bond issues comprised of many different maturities, as opposed to a term bond issue in which all the bonds have the same date of maturity.

to the ability of the issuer to collect revenues from the project involved. In the case of a well established sewer authority this credit quality is likely to be high, whereas the bonds of a new mass transit authority in a low-density city, for example, might be more speculative. These obligations consist largely of one or two long-term issues with a smaller amount of serial bonds with shorter maturities. One type of revenue bond worth noting is the "moral obligation bond." This type of bond is secured by earmarked revenue and by a promise from the issuing government to appropriate funds from general revenues to cover debt service if revenues prove insufficient. The credit quality of these bonds is as good as the promise or moral obligation to redeem them.

Occasionally, state and local governments will issue short-term debt in the form of tax, revenue or bond anticipation notes which generally have a maturity of less than one year. As the name implies, tax and revenue anticipation notes are issued to aid cash flow while waiting for taxes and revenues to come in, at which time the debt is retired. Both anticipation notes are generally issued to finance a project during periods of tight credit conditions to prevent getting locked into a high rate, long-term debt obligation. When more favorable credit conditions develop, the short-term debt is refinanced by a bond issue.

The growth in the dollar amount of total state and local debt outstanding is shown in Figure 13-2. The sharp increases in the supply of municipal bonds might be explained by the acceleration in the pace of inflation in 1968 and again in late 1970, particularly the acceleration of construction costs. This development had two effects. First, as shown in Figure 13-2, inflation increased the cost of construction, thus requiring a larger bond issue to finance any given project. Second, to the extent inflation impacts on expenditures more rapidly than on revenues, it increased the costs of providing government services, which are payable out of current receipts. This reduced the availability of funds from current receipts to help finance capital projects. Consequently, more bonds were issued to help fill this gap. The growth in state and local debt may also have been affected by the entry of New York City into the long-term market to finance operating expenditures and by sharp increases in short-term debt issuance by New York City and New York State.

The stable and continued growth of the total supply of outstanding municipal securities masks some changes in the composition of the total supply that warrant examination. As shown in Figure 13-3, the percentage of total municipal debt outstanding accounted for by short-term debt is small but increasing. It is a highly volatile function but seems closely related, with a small lag, to the yield on municipal bonds. When yields are stable, little short-term financing is used. As yields rise, short-term bond anticipation notes are increasingly used while finance officers await lower rates, which sometimes fail to materialize. As yields turn lower, the short-term debt is retired by the issuance of bonds.

Another interesting development concerning the supply of municipal bonds is the increasing use of revenue bonds as opposed to general obligation bonds.

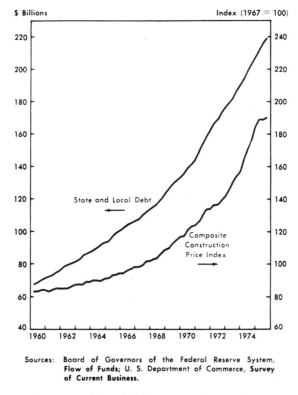

$ Billions   Index (1967 = 100)

Sources: Board of Governors of the Federal Reserve System, Flow of Funds; U. S. Department of Commerce, **Survey of Current Business.**

Figure 13-2 Total state and local debt outstanding and construction price index

In 1960 revenue bonds accounted for approximately 27 percent of total bonds issued. By 1975 this percentage increased to nearly 40 percent.

This increasing use of revenue bond financing reflects two influences. The first is the apparently growing reluctance of taxpayers to pay higher taxes for debt service and, thus, their disinclination to approve new general obligation bond issues. Accordingly, state and local governments have increasingly resorted to revenue bonds, which do not require voter approval. The second influence is the enlarged concept of what constitutes a proper government service and the growing feeling that, as much as possible, the users of particular government services should pay for them. This enlarged concept of government services is particularly evident in the growing use of tax-exempt financing to obtain funds for pollution control and industrial development projects, which are then leased or sold to private businesses. The governmental unit is, in effect, an agent of industrial tax-exempt borrowing. Ostensibly the government service is the attraction of business enterprises to provide employment. More frequently, therefore, government-sponsored corporations or authorities are created to issue bonds, provide services, and collect the revenues to retire the

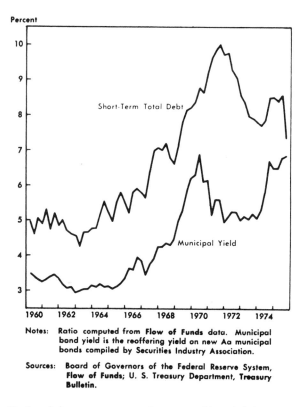

Percent

Short-Term Total Debt

Municipal Yield

Notes: Ratio computed from **Flow of Funds** data. Municipal
bond yield is the reoffering yield on new Aa municipal
bonds compiled by Securities Industry Association.

Sources: Board of Governors of the Federal Reserve System,
Flow of Funds; U. S. Treasury Department, **Treasury
Bulletin.**

Figure 13-3   Ratio of short-term to total state and local debt outstanding compared to municipal bond yield

bonds. Revenue bonds are likely to continue to be of growing importance in the municipal bond market.

To sum up, the supply of municipal bonds has grown at a steady pace with no apparent relationship to the business cycle. While there have been some structural changes in the component mix of the supply of municipal bonds, there seems to be no reason to believe that supply phenomena in the municipal market are responsible for the movements in the ratio of the yields on like-rated bonds.

THE DEMAND FOR MUNICIPAL BONDS

Due to the tax-exempt nature of municipal bonds, investors are generally those persons and institutions subject to high marginal income tax rates. Chief among these are commercial banks, individuals and individual trusts, fire and casualty insurance companies, and to a lesser extent, nonfinancial corporations and life insurance companies. Although not immediately apparent, the market for municipal bonds is rather narrow and has become more so since 1960. While all the previously mentioned groups participate in the market, individual demand and commercial bank demand are of prime importance. In 1960 individual and commercial bank holdings of municipal bonds accounted for 67 percent of the total amount outstanding; by the third quarter of 1975 this percentage had risen to 78 percent.

The nature of the demand for municipal bonds may offer a reasonable explanation for the erratic movements in municipal bond market conditions relative to other capital markets shown in Figure 13-1. An examination of the patterns of investment behavior of various types of municipal bond investors in recent years may, accordingly, prove instructive.

Commercial Banks

Of fundamental importance to the understanding of developments in the municipal bond market is the fact that the demand for municipal bonds by commercial banks is a residual demand, i.e., banks purchase municipals with any funds remaining after commitments to other borrowers have been met. The primary investment outlet for commercial banks is loans, and much of the variation in commercial bank participation in the municipal bond market can be explained by the variation in loan demand.

Figure 13-4 shows an index of loan demand pressure expressed as the ratio of commercial loans to time deposits. This ratio is intended to measure the extent to which banks have residual funds available. The relationship between the loan demand pressure and commercial bank participation in the municipal market is quite clear, particularly during the tight credit conditions of 1968–69. Generally as loan demand pressure falls, demand for municipal bonds by banks rises. As loan demand pressure rises, due to either a rise in loans or a runoff of time deposits, municipal bond demand by banks stabilizes or falls. A notable exception to this tendency, however, has developed since the third quarter of 1974. During that period both loan demand pressure and bank demand for municipals have declined. This recent experience suggests the presence of a new influence tending to reduce bank demand for municipal bonds, a development which will be discussed later.

Commercial banks are presently the primary holders of municipal bonds, although this was not always true. To maintain liquidity, banks tend to prefer short- or intermediate-term bonds. Figure 13-4 shows the municipal bond investment record of commercial banks, both absolutely and relative to the entire market. The dollar amount of bank holdings has trended generally upward, but not without interruption. Prior to 1961 the participation of commercial banks in the market was limited and erratic. From mid-1961 to late 1968 holdings grew steadily with the exception of one quarter of liquidation during the tight credit conditions of 1966. In the latter part of 1968, due to

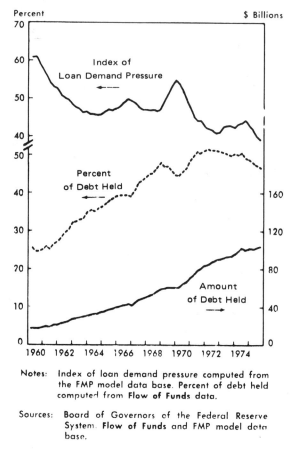

Percent $ Billions

Figure 13-4   State and local debt held by commercial banks compared to
index of loan demand pressure

increasing loan demand pressure, banks sharply curtailed new purchases of
municipal bonds and did not resume them until early 1970. As will be seen,
their departure from the market at this point was responsible for a rise in Rm/
Rc much like that experienced from the second quarter of 1974 through the
first quarter of 1975. The growth in holdings then continued from early 1970
until early 1974, when banks again essentially pulled out of the new issue
market.

Individuals and Individual Trusts

For individual investors the principal investment alternatives to the municipal bond market are the stock and corporate bond markets. The reasons

for this are that capital gains are taxed at a lower rate than regular income and corporate bonds can provide an income-producing alternative to municipals, depending, of course, on the individual's tax bracket. While there is probably a hard core of high income, risk-averse individuals who seldom seek investment alternatives to municipal bonds, changes in stock prices and the corresponding changes in opportunities for capital gains may cause other, less risk-averse individuals to alternate between stocks and municipals.

The variation in individual participation in the municipal bond market can be explained to a large degree by variations in stock prices and in the level of municipal bond yields relative to yields on other bonds (Rm/Rc). The data in Figure 13-5 indicate a pronounced inverse relationship between stock prices and individual holdings of municipals. As stock prices rise, bond holdings are increased at a slower rate or are liquidated; the reverse seems to be the case when stock prices fall. This reverse relationship is particularly evident during the periods of generally declining stock market prices from the fourth quarter of 1968 through the second quarter of 1970 and from the first quarter of 1968 through the third quarter of 1974.

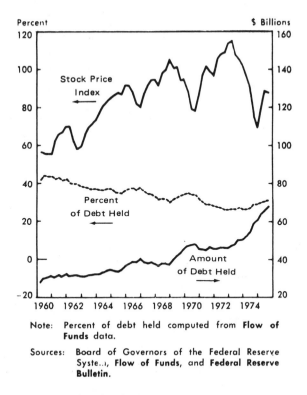

Note: Percent of debt held computed from **Flow of Funds** data.

Sources: Board of Governors of the Federal Reserve Syste.., **Flow of Funds,** and **Federal Reserve Bulletin.**

Figure 13-5 State and local debt held by households compared to Standard & Poor's stock price index

The relative level of bond yields (Rm/Rc) is important to individual demand for municipals, because as the yield ratio increases the number of potential individual investors rises. Unlike the institutional investors, most of whom face approximately the same income tax rate, individual investors face different tax rates. As Rm/Rc rises, t (the tax rate of indifference) falls, lowering the marginal tax bracket at which investment in municipals becomes attractive to individuals. For this reason when banks or other institutional investors leave the market, yields rise until t falls sufficiently to encourage enough individuals to fill the gap in the demand for municipal bonds and thereby clear the market.

Individuals and individual trusts are now the second most important source of demand for municipal bonds, having fallen from the dominant position that they held during the first half of the 1960s. These investors tend to hold the longer maturities of an issue. Figure 13-5 shows the municipal bond demand by individuals in absolute and relative terms. Although there is a general upward trend in the dollar volume of total bonds held by households, its movement is much more erratic than that displayed by bank holdings and shows many periods of liquidation.

In relative terms, household demand for municipal bonds has exhibited a general downward trend since 1960. Individual holdings declined from 43 percent of total outstandings in 1960 to a low of 26 percent in 1972–73. Recently, however, this fraction has increased to 30 percent, largely as a result of the decline in the market share of commercial banks and the introduction of municipal bond funds that facilitate investment by individuals.

Generally speaking, the high rate of inflation in recent years may be expected to have reduced the attractiveness of fixed income securities. But, combined with a progressive tax structure a high inflation rate raises the marginal tax bracket of many individuals, thereby increasing the value of the tax-exempt feature of municipal bonds through a reduction in the effective after-tax yield on taxable securities.

Fire and Casualty Insurance Companies

Fire and casualty insurance companies are ranked third in importance in the municipal bond market. These companies, like commercial banks, are subject to the standard corporate income tax rate and thus desire the tax-exempt income municipal bonds can provide. Unlike life insurance companies, fire and casualty insurance companies cannot accurately predict their probable losses; thus their net taxable income, as well as their cash needs, are highly variable. For these reasons, the demand for municipals of any fire and casualty insurance company is unstable. However, while any particular company may be highly erratic in its purchases, fire and casualty insurance companies as a group are the most stable source of demand in the market. Figure 13-6 shows a steady upward trend in holdings of this group since 1960, with no periods of liquidation.

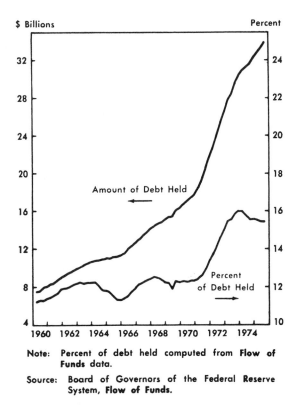

Note: Percent of debt held computed from **Flow of Funds** data.

Source: **Board of Governors of the Federal Reserve System, Flow of Funds.**

Figure 13-6 State and local debt held by fire and casualty companies

The percentage of total municipal outstandings held by fire and casualty insurance companies was remarkably stable from 1960 through 1970 at approximately 12 percent. By 1973, the market share had increased to its present level of 15 percent. Recent reductions in purchases appear to be due to lower industry profits and should prove temporary.

Nonfinancial Corporations and Life Insurance Companies

Both individually and as a group, nonfinancial corporations and life insurance companies are relatively insignificant buyers of municipal bonds. Life insurance companies buy few municipals because they are unable to take full advantage of the tax exemption due to the low effective tax rate on these companies. In 1960, nonfinancial corporations held roughly 3 percent of outstanding municipals, while life insurance companies held 5 percent. The market share of each fell to roughly 2 percent by the first quarter of 1975. The participation of these investors is the most erratic of any in the market. Nonfinancial corporations primarily buy short-term obligations to meet cash management needs. For most of the 1960s, life insurance companies were a supply factor in the secondary market rather than a demand factor in the new issue market, although their purchases of new issues have recently increased. In general, these two investor groups have little impact on the municipal bond market.

PAST EXPERIENCE IN THE MUNICIPAL BOND MARKET

Due to the residual nature of the demand for municipal bonds by the commercial banks, the overall composition of demand is highly sensitive to developments in other capital markets and in the economy generally. The participation of various investor groups changes greatly over short periods as well as over the longer term. This variation in the composition of demand for municipal bonds seems to be a major factor explaining movements in Rm/Rc.

Figure 13-7 illustrates the mechanism through which changes in demand composition affect Rm/Rc and the municipal market in general. An increase in the level of demand for municipal securities among institutions subject to high marginal tax rates (e.g., an increase in commercial bank demand triggered by a decline in loan demand pressure) causes municipal bond prices to rise, resulting in lower levels of Rm/Rc and thus higher levels of t. At the higher levels of t, the relative attractiveness of municipal bonds declines along with the value of the tax exemption. Individual demand for municipals falls as many individual investors forego purchases of municipal bonds in favor of alternative investments in stocks and corporate bonds. Under these circumstances most investors are in the same tax bracket as the marginal investors, and all receive a yield very near the after-tax yield available on corporate bonds.

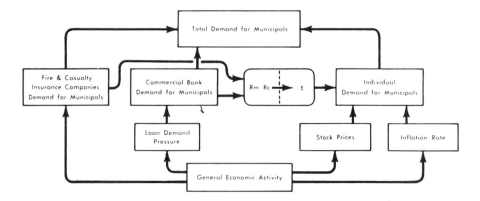

Figure 13-7

When demand for municipal bonds declines among tax-exposed institutional investors, as when loan demand pressure rises, the situation is reversed. Municipal prices fall, causing Rm/Rc to rise and t to fall. This falling level of t increases the value of the tax exemption and the demand for municipal bonds among investors in lower tax brackets, thereby inducing individuals and tax-sheltered institutions to enter the market. Due to progressive taxation, a larger number of individual investors will be in tax brackets above the marginal tax bracket (t) of the marginal investors. Thus, in this situation, many more investors receive a tax-exempt yield considerably greater than the after-tax yield available on corporate bonds.

Figure 13-8 shows the composition of demand for municipal bonds and the ratio of municipal bond to corporate bond yields since 1960. Rm/Rc generally fell from 1961 through the second quarter of 1968. This fall was due to the

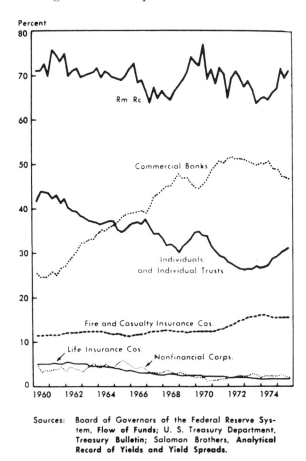

Sources: Board of Governors of the Federal Reserve System, **Flow of Funds;** U. S. Treasury Department, **Treasury Bulletin;** Salomon Brothers, **Analytical Record of Yields and Yield Spreads.**

Figure 13-8   Percent of state and local debt held by each demand sector compared to Rm/Rc

rising market participation of commercial banks (caused by generally falling or stable loan demand pressure), which also reduced the participation of individual investors. In the second quarter of 1968 Rm/Rc started a steep rise (steeper than the recent one) that lasted, with one interruption, through the second quarter of 1970. This period was one of high loan demand pressure on banks. To accommodate loan customers, commercial banks halted new purchases of municipal bonds. The departure of banks from the municipal market reduced institutional demand for municipals, causing Rm/Rc to rise and t to fall until individual demand for municipals, spurred both by rising Rm/Rc and falling stock prices, rose sufficiently to clear the market.

The rising participation of institutions caused Rm/Rc and the participation of individuals to generally decline from the second quarter of 1970 to the second quarter of 1974. Owing to easier loan demand pressure conditions, bank demand for municipals resumed in the first quarter of 1970 and rose through the first quarter of 1972. At that time a period of relative stability in bank demand for municipals began that lasted until the second quarter of 1974. Municipal bond demand by institutions was aided by the growth in municipal market participation of fire and casualty insurance companies from 1971 to 1973. This institutional demand supplanted a portion of the participation of individuals, whose market share declined from the first quarter of 1970 to the third quarter of 1972, due both to falling Rm/Rc and rising stock prices, and then stabilized until the second quarter of 1974.

SUMMARY AND CONCLUSION

The ratio of municipal bond to corporate bond yields exhibits considerable variability, part of which takes the form of explainable short-term cyclical movements. An analysis of the municipal bond market indicates that while supply is steadily rising at a stable rate, demand is continually changing in composition. These changing demand patterns are primarily due to the influence of other capital markets on municipal bond investors, i.e., to the residual nature of commercial bank demand for municipal bonds and to individuals' changing demand for municipals versus stocks and corporate bonds. The continual change in demand is responsible for the short-term volatility in the movement of Rm/Rc as well as its longer-term movements.

Mortgage-related Instruments

This second section of Part II presents recent developments in mortgage-related instruments. The residential mortgage sector has been the scene of some of the most dramatic innovations in the financial markets. For example, until recently more borrowers seeking to finance a home had little choice except a standard, fixed-payment mortgage. Such mortgages became unattractive to both lenders and borrowers during periods of high and volatile interest rates and, consequently, new home mortgage options emerged. These new mortgage instruments include adjustable rate, graduated payment, price level adjusted, shared appreciation, and wraparound mortgages. In the first article in this section, Joseph A. McKenzie describes the major characteristics of these new mortgages and the range of mortgage plans now available.

Although the proliferation of alternative mortgage instruments has enabled borrowers to find mortgages tailored to their needs, it has caused confusion for borrowers, lenders, and portfolio investors. In the second article, Richard G. Marcis contends that the diversity of current mortgage alternatives will lead to an eventual shakeout. He also indicates the factors that will be instrumental in determining what mortgage alternatives will survive.

One of the alternative mortgage instruments likely to remain after the shakeout is adjustable rate mortgages (ARMs). Despite the fact that ARMs represent a large portion of new mortgage originations, they are not without problems. For example, ARMs lack standardization because they have a number of basic features that can be combined to create a wide variety of ARMs. The article by Michael J. Lea discusses ARM features, pricing, and implications in the marketplace.

In addition to these types of mortgage loans, other developments have had a profound impact on the mortgage market. One of these events is the increased interest in second mortgages which is examined in the article by Michael Rosser. Another development is the creation of mortgage-backed securities, which has enabled mortgage lenders to tap alternative sources of funds by selling mortgage loans in the form of pass-through certificates or issuing mortgaged-backed bonds. These topics are discussed in the article by Ann J. Dougherty and Donald F. Cunningham.

A BORROWER'S GUIDE TO ALTERNATE MORTGAGE INSTRUMENTS*

14

Joseph A. McKenzie†

Five years ago, virtually all borrowers seeking to finance a home obtained a standard, fixed-payment mortgage. At the time, it was the only mortgage form that was generally available. The situation today is quite different. Borrowers now can obtain mortgages with a changing interest rate, graduated payments, or an indexed principal. Furthermore, each of the new mortgage types can have a number of options, thus the number of specific mortgage variants is almost limitless. This proliferation of new mortgage forms has made comparison shopping difficult, and it has caused confusion for borrowers and lenders. The purpose of this article is to describe the range of mortgage plans that is now available.

At the beginning, it is important to emphasize that there is no single "best" mortgage instrument. All the new mortgage instruments involve certain trade-offs. For example, most households prefer relatively stable mortgage payments, but some households might select a mortgage that has the potential for significant payment changes if the interest rate were low enough. In most cases, mortgages that involve greater risks to the borrower will have lower interest

---

*Reprinted from the *Federal Home Loan Bank Board Journal*, January 1982, pp. 16–22, with permission of the Federal Home Loan Bank Board.

†Financial Economist, Office of Policy and Economic Research, Federal Home Loan Bank Board.

rates. The development of the new mortgage forms with their many options forces borrowers to weigh the tradeoffs involved in selecting a mortgage. The large number of plans and options allows the household to find a mortgage tailored to its needs; it also provides a true opportunity for borrower and lender to negotiate the terms of the mortgage contract.

THE NEED FOR ALTERNATIVE MORTGAGE INSTRUMENTS

The standard, fixed-payment mortgage is ill-suited to a world of high and volatile interest rates for two reasons. First, a 30-year fixed-rate mortgage places all the risk of interest rate increases on the lender. Many mortgage lenders finance long-term mortgages with short-term deposits. If interest rates unexpectedly rise, the cost of the deposits can be greater than the revenues from the mortgage loan they support.

Interest rate fluctuations affect lenders and borrowers differently in a world with fixed-rate mortgages. When interest rates fall, borrowers have the option to refinance their mortgages. When interest rates rise, lenders have no way to increase the rate on their fixed-rate mortgages. This results in an asymmetric interest rate risk.

The problem of fluctuating interest rates is a serious one. The average contract rate on mortgages written in 1976 was 8.92 percent, and the average cost-of-funds to S&L's in 1976 was 6.38 percent. The average cost-of-funds for the first half of 1981 was 10.31 percent, but most of those 1976 mortgages are still on the books at the same interest rate at which they were written.

One must emphasize, however, that interest rate fluctuations *per se* are not the reason for mortgages with variable interest rates; it is the unexpected interest rate fluctuations. In setting the initial mortgage rate, the lender must forecast the cost-of-funds needed to support the mortgage for the entire term of the mortgage. The lender then sets the mortgage rate to be some mark-up over the average expected cost-of-funds over the term of the mortgage. A lender should not be concerned about the period-by-period relationship between the mortgage rate and the cost of funds; the appropriate concern is the relationship between the mortgage rate and the average cost-of-funds over the life of the mortgage.

Inflation of the magnitude experienced over the past several years had been unexpected. This unexpected inflation has resulted in unexpectedly high short-term interest rates and unexpected increases in the cost of funds to most mortgage lenders. Since existing mortgage rates, in most cases, were set with the expectation of much lower inflation rates, many lenders are not in the position of having to pay more for funds than they receive in interest income from the mortgages these funds support. Mortgages with variable rates protect lenders from future unexpected increases in interest rates; they also allow the borrower to take advantage of unexpected declines in mortgage rates without having to pay refinancing costs.

The second reason why the standard, fixed-rate mortgage is ill-suited for an inflationary environment is that the real payment—the payment in inflation-adjusted dollars—declines. This results in a high real payment burden in the early years of a mortgage and a very low payment burden in the late years of a mortgage. This declining real payment burden is illustrated in Figure 14-1. A 30-year, 12-percent mortgage for $60,000 has a payment of $617.17. At the end of 5 years the real payment, assuming a 9 percent inflation rate, is $401.12; it is $260.70 at the end of 10 years; and $110.12 at the end of 20 years.

The relatively low real payment burden in the later years of a mortgage induces many households to "trade up" houses. This trading up would be unnecessary if a mortgage had more nearly constant real payments. Such a mortgage would enable a first-time home buyer to purchase a house more in

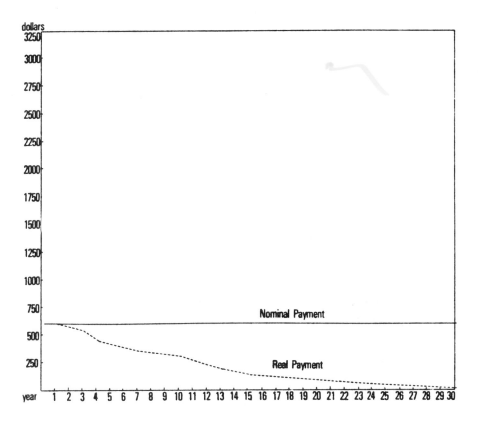

Figure 14-1   Nominal and real payments on a $60,000 conventional 30-year mortgage at 12 percent with 9 percent inflation

line with that household's long-run housing needs. Furthermore, the high initial real payment may delay home ownership for some households whose long-run income would normally qualify them for home ownership.

MORTGAGE CHARACTERISTICS

In designing a new mortgage, there are six important characteristics for which to strive. These are: yield flexibility, constant real payments, payment stability, full security, servicing simplicity, and marketability. Given the recent historical experience with extremely volatile interest rates, it is important for lenders, and borrowers, too, that the yield on the mortgage be flexible. Second, more households can purchase houses and those who do purchase may buy houses more in line with their long-run needs if the mortgage has relatively constant real payments.

Third, borrowers generally prefer a stable mortgage payment. This aids family budgeting. It also reflects the fact that most households do not receive wage adjustments more frequently than annually. Lenders also want borrowers to have relatively stable payments because excessively sharp increases in mortgage payments may lead to increased delinquencies and defaults. Fourth, lenders always want the loan to be fully secured, that is, they want the property value to exceed the loan balance. The reason is that if the loan balance exceeds the property value the borrower might default.

Unfortunately, these first four characteristics are partially contradictory in a number of mortgages. For example, one way to achieve more nearly constant real payment is to have gradually increasing payments, where the initial payments are so low that they do not cover all the interest due. In this case, that portion of the interest due but not paid is added to the loan balance. This may conflict with the goal of full security. Conversely, a mortgage with a freely variable interest rate and corresponding payment changes would never result in an increase to the loan balance, but the implied payment changes could be burdensome, in the short run, to a number of households.

The remaining two goals are servicing simplicity and marketability. All alternative mortgages are more difficult for the lender to service than the standard, fixed-payment mortgage. This is because of the possibility of changing rates, payments, and increases to the loan balance. Servicing simplicity is the reason why the interest rate and payment do not change monthly. The last goal is marketability. The mortgage must be attractive to secondary mortgage market investors, who have provided an increasing share of mortgage credit.

ADJUSTABLE MORTGAGES

The common feature of adjustable mortgages is that the interest rate is not fixed and will vary according to some interest rate index that is selected at the time the loan is originated. Lenders are not required to increase the interest rate on the mortgage if the index increases, but they are required to lower the interest rate if the index decreases. Adjustable mortgage contracts may contain limitations on the minimum and maximum size of an interest rate change.

Depending upon a particular lender's adjustable mortgage plan, a change in the interest rate may result in a change in the monthly payment, the term of the loan, the outstanding balance of the loan, or some combination of these. A number of lenders offer plans in which the interest rate can change every three or six months, but the payment changes every one, two, or three years. Under such a plan, an increase in the interest rate may mean that the monthly payment is insufficient to pay all the interest due that month. When this happens the unpaid interest will be added to the loan balance. This increase in the loan balance is known as negative amortization. Negative amortization can occur on adjustable mortgages if payments are adjusted less frequently than the interest rate.

Negative amortization can occur on a number of the new mortgage plans. It is best thought of as an additional loan to the borrower for the difference between the interest due and monthly payment. The interest rate on this loan is the same as the mortgage rate. To the extent that negative amortization arises because of low current payments, it will mean higher future payments.

The mechanics of an interest rate adjustment are as follows: The base index value is determined at the time of the closing of the loan. At an adjustment, the net difference between the then-prevailing value of the index and the base index value is either added to or subtracted from the initial contract rate, subject to the periodic and cumulative rate change limitations in the contract, if any. The index must be an interest rate series that is readily verifiable by the borrower and not under the control of the lender.

Some lenders have adjustable mortgage plans with interest rate caps, that is, limitations on the size of the periodic or cumulative interest rate changes. Other adjustable mortgage plans have limitations on the amount by which payments may change. The adjustable mortgages made by Federal savings and loan associations are known as AMLs (adjustable mortgage loans) and the adjustable mortgages made by national banks are known as ARMs (adjustable rate mortgages). Variable rate mortgages (VRMs) and renegotiable rate mortgages (RRMs) are specific types of adjustable mortgages.

GRADUATED PAYMENT MORTGAGE

The graduated payment mortgage (GPM) has a fixed interest rate, but the payments start out at a lower level than on a fixed rate mortgage. The payments on a GPM increase at a known rate during the early years of the loan. On the most popular RPM plan, the payments increase by 7½ percent each year for the first five years of the loan. Payments on a GPM ultimately rise to a level higher than on a comparable fixed-payment mortgage.

Because the payments on a GPM start out at a low level, they may be insufficient to pay all the interest owed. That portion of the monthly interest in excess of the monthly payment is added to the loan balance. The outstanding balance on most GPMs actually increases for the first several years.

PLEDGED ACCOUNT MORTGAGE

The pledged account mortgage (PAM) is a special type of GPM. On most GPM plans, the low initial payments are insufficient to pay all the interest owed. On a PAM, that portion of the interest due that is not covered by the monthly payment is deducted from a savings account pledged by the borrower. Some but not all graduated payment mortgages have the pledged account feature.

GRADUATED PAYMENT ADJUSTABLE MORTGAGE LOANS

The graduated payment adjustable mortgage loan (GPAML) combines the flexible yield feature of a mortgage with an adjustable interest rate and the low initial payment feature of a mortgage with graduated payments. The GPAML is a very complex instrument but may be thought of as a mortgage with two interest rates. The first is the debit rate, which is the rate at which the borrower is charged interest. The second is the payment rate, or the rate at which payments are computed. The common features of all GPAMLs are variable debit rates and an initial payment rate lower than the debit rate.

All GPAML variations involve a deferral of some of the interest owed during the early years of the loan. This results in some negative amortization, and the GPAML can give rise to a potentially significant amount of negative amortization if the debit rate increases during the initial period of low payments. Some GPAML plans have payments rising by a set amount each year for the first several years; other plans fix the low payments for the first three or five years. There is a limitless number of possible GPAML variations.

The regulation under which Federal savings and loan associations may write GPAMLs is extremely broad. This regulation encompasses the old GPM regulation because a GPM is simply a GPAML with a fixed interest rate. In addition, the GPAML will permit a wide variety of mortgage plans in which the borrower and lender agree to a certain pattern of payments. For example, the GPAML regulation will permit certain types of accelerated equity build-up mortgages where the payment increases by a specified amount from a level that is sufficient to amortize the loan. On such a loan, the initial payment may be based on a 30-year amortization schedule but the loan will be repaid in a much shorter period.

BALLOON MORTGAGE

A balloon mortgage is any mortgage that has not been fully paid off by the maturity of the loan. Balloon mortgages come in two basic forms. The first is known as an "interest-only" balloon, and, as the name implies, the payments cover only interest and no principal. The typical interest-only balloon has a maturity of three or five years. The second type of balloon mortgage is known as a "partially amortizing" balloon. The monthly payment on a partially amortizing balloon would be the same as on a long-term mortgage, but the loan comes due before all the principal is repaid. Partially amortizing balloon mortgages may have fixed or variable interest rates, and maturities as long as 15 years are not uncommon.

As the name implies, a borrower may still owe a large amount of money when a balloon mortgage matures. This should be of no concern if the borrower intends to sell the house before the loan matures. If the borrower does not move and does not sell the house, then the balloon mortgage typically is refinanced. The original lender is under no obligation to refinance the loan. Another consideration is that the borrower may have to pay again some or all of the costs associated with closing a loan at refinancing, even if the same lender refinances the loan.

SHARED APPRECIATION MORTGAGE

A shared appreciation mortgage (SAM) is a mortgage loan in which the borrower agrees to share the property's appreciation with the lender in return for an interest rate below that on a standard mortgage. SAMs have a "contingent interest" feature; a portion of the total interest due is contingent or dependent upon the appreciation of the property. At either the sale or transfer of the property, or the refinancing or maturity of the loan, the borrower must pay the lender a share of the appreciation of the property securing the loan. Payments on a SAM are based on a long amortization schedule, but the loan may become due at the end of five or ten years.

The borrower and lender jointly determine the size of the interest rate discount, the term of the loan, and the share of the appreciation due the lender. The amount of appreciation is unknown at the time of origination, hence the total interest due and the effective interest rate are also uncertain. Although SAMs have a relatively low initial payment, the household's mortgage payment could increase very significantly if the lender's share of the appreciation and remaining principal balance had to be refinanced at market rates.

At the present time, Federal savings and loan associations lack the specific authorization to make shared appreciation mortgages. A Federal association may make and hold shared appreciation mortgages up to five percent of assets by using its "leeway" authority found in Section 545.6–5(b) of the Rules and Regulations for the Federal Savings and Loan System.

The two key features of a shared appreciation mortgage are the deeply discounted initial payment and the refinancing at some date in the future. A GPAML can be constructed to provide these features if the payment rate is significantly below the debit rate and if the low initial payments are held fixed for three or five years. This mortgage would have two advantages over a SAM in that the interest (debit rate) would be explicitly variable and the yield to the lender would depend on interest rates and not the appreciation of a specific property.

PRICE LEVEL ADJUSTED MORTGAGE

The price level adjusted mortgage (PLAM) is different from all other mortgage types because the balance of a PLAM is indexed to account for actual inflation. Since the balance is indexed, the interest rate does not have to incorporate an inflation premium. The interest rate on a PLAM is a "real" interest, that is, an interest rate net of any inflation premium. Real interest rates typically are in the range of 3 percent.

Suppose the expected annual rate of inflation was 9 percent. This would yield a rate of 12 percent on standard mortgages. On a $60,000 loan for 30 years, this yields a payment of $617.17. The appropriate interest rate for a PLAM would be 3 percent, and the initial monthly payment would be $252.96. At the end of the first year, however, the balance on the PLAM would be adjusted upward by 9 percent to account for actual inflation. The balance then would be $64,035.34 instead of the $59,782.27 balance on a conventional loan. The payments are then recomputed on the basis of the new balance, and the second year's payment would be $275.73, which is 9 percent higher than the initial payment. In other words, a PLAM will provide for level real payments.

As Figures 14-2a and b indicate, the payments on a PLAM start out lower than on a standard mortgage and gradually rise to a higher level. The real payments on a PLAM are constant.

The maximum balance on the PLAM is $146,855 at the end of the twentieth year, but, assuming an original loan-to-value ratio of 80 percent, the property is worth $420,331 if it appreciates at the rate of inflation. Because of the low initial payment, many more households can afford homeownership with a PLAM, and first-time homebuyers can buy a much larger house. Of course, the real payments remain constant for 30 years.

There are two potential problems, however, with a PLAM. If the household's income does not grow at the same rate as the inflation rate, then the real payment burden can increase significantly during the term of the mortgage. Second, if the property value does not increase at the same rate as the inflation

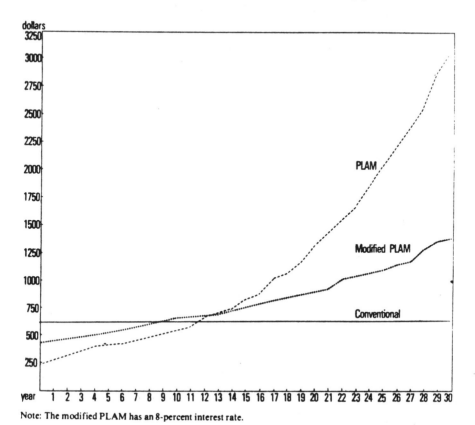

Note: The modified PLAM has an 8-percent interest rate.

Figure 14-2a Nominal payments on conventional and price level adjusted mortgages: $60,000 balance, 30-year term, 3 percent real interest rate, 9 percent inflation rate

rate, then situations could arise where the outstanding balance would exceed the value of the property. In this case, the loan would not be fully secured, and some borrowers would default.

Both problems can be remedied by developing a "modified" PLAM, in which the contract rate explicitly incorporates an inflation premium. For example, a modified PLAM could have an interest rate of 8 percent—3 percent real interest rate plus 5 percent inflation premium. If the actual inflation rate turned out to be 9 percent, the balance on the modified PLAM would increase by only 4 percent (the 9 percent inflation rate less the 5 percent inflation premium already incorporated in the interest rate) at the end of the first year. The pattern of monthly payments on this modified PLAM is shown in Figures 14-2a and 14-2b.

Although the PLAM is an attractive mortgage for the borrower, the tax code largely prevents its use. The indexing of the loan balance represents

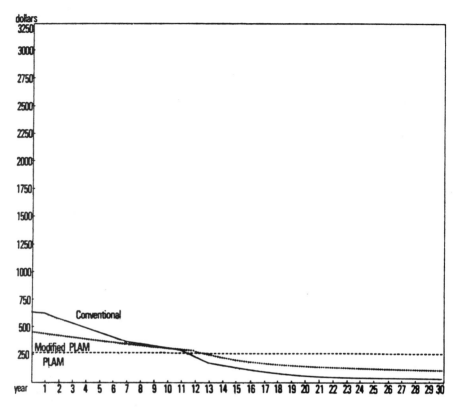

Note: The modified PLAM has an 8-percent interest rate.

Figure 14-2b   Real payments on conventional and price level adjusted mortgages: $60,000 balance, 30-year term, 3 percent real interest rate, 9 percent inflation rate

income to the lender. Since most lenders are accrual-basis taxpayers, the lender would have to pay taxes as the balance is indexed. The lender, however, does not receive an immediate cash flow when the balance is indexed. In effect, the increased loan balance is refinanced over the remaining term of the mortgage. The cash flow to the lender resulting from each indexing of the loan balance is extended over many years. The PLAM may not be attractive to the lender because of the mismatch of cash flow and tax payments.

WRAPAROUND MORTGAGE

The wraparound mortgage (WRAP) is a technique by which a homebuyer can assume a low interest rate mortgage from the seller. Suppose a buyer needs a

$50,000 mortgage and the previous owner has an assumable mortgage with a relatively low interest rate and a remaining balance of $30,000. The buyer might obtain a wraparound mortgage for $50,000. The payments to the wraparound lender must be sufficient to continue to make the payments to the assumed mortgage and to amortize the additional $20,000 loan. The advantage to the buyer is that the "blended" interest rate is lower than new mortgage rates and the payments to the wraparound lender are lower than the payments on a new $50,000 mortgage at current interest rates.

GLOSSARY OF NEW MORTGAGE TERMS

Adjustable Mortgage Loan—An AML is the broadest of the new loan categories. An AML is the fourth generation of loans with variable interest rates, and it is the designation used by Federal savings and loan associations.

Adjustable Rate Mortgage—An ARM is the third generation of mortgages with variable rates. It is the designation used by national banks. The rate on an ARM issued by a national bank may not increase by more than 1 percent each six-month period.

Balloon Mortgage—A balloon mortgage is any mortgage that is due and payable before all the principal is repaid.

Base Index Rate—The base index rate is the reference point from which all index rate changes are measured on a mortgage with a variable rate. The base index rate is known at the time of origination, and it is the most recently available value of the index series at, or within six months prior to, the date of the closing of the loan. In general, the maximum rate change from the origination of a mortgage with a variable rate may not exceed the difference between the current value of the index and the base index value.

Debit Rate—The debit rate is the rate at which the borrower is charged interest. In some mortgage plans, the debit rate and payment rate are different.

Graduated Payment Adjustable Mortgage Loan—The GPAML is any mortgage that has a variable interest rate and the initial payment is insufficient to pay all the interest due. GPAMLs involve future increased payments.

Graduated Payment Mortgage—The GPM has a fixed interest rate. The initial payment is lower than that on a standard fixed rate mortgage, and the payments gradually increase for the first five or ten years.

Index—The subsequent movement of the rate on a mortgage with a variable interest rate is governed by an index rate. Rate movements on the mortgage must correspond to movements in the index. The index rate must be an interest rate series that is readily verifiable by the borrower and not under control of the lender.

Negative Amortization—Any increase in the loan balance arising from a mortgage payment being too small to pay all the interest due that month is called negative amortization. The lender effectively makes the borrower an additional loan at the mortgage rate for the amount of unpaid interest. This loan must be repaid over the remaining term of the mortgage.

Payment Rate—The payment rate determines the size of the monthly payment. On some new mortgage plans, the payment rate is less than the debit rate, and negative amortization thus occurs.

Pledged Account Mortgage—The PAM is a special type of GPM in which the interest due in excess of the monthly payment is deducted from a savings account pledged by the borrower.

Price Level Adjusted Mortgage—The PLAM has a fixed interest rate and an indexed principal. Because repayments are in inflation-adjusted dollars, the PLAM has a real interest rate, which is in the range of three percent.

Shared Appreciation Mortgage—In return for a low initial interest rate, the SAM borrower agrees to pay the lender an amount of "contingent interest" that depends upon the appreciation of the property. The outstanding indebtedness and contingent interest are normally refinanced at the end of five or ten years.

Renegotiable Rate Mortgage—The RRM is the second generation of mortgages with variable interest rates. The rate on an RRM can change by no more than 1.5 percent every three years and by no more than 5 percent overall.

Variable Rate Mortgage—The VRM is the first generation of mortgages with variable interest rates. The rate on a VRM can change by no more than 0.5 percent annually and by no more than 2.5 percent overall.

Wraparound Mortgage—A wraparound mortgage is one method of providing the incremental financing a borrower may need when a loan is assumed. The borrower makes a single payment to the wraparound lender who, in turn, makes the payment on the underlying final trust.

THE FHLBB INDEX

Each month, the Federal Home Loan Bank Board surveys approximately 2,000 mortgage lenders and asks them to report the rate and terms on all single-family, non-farm, conventional mortgages they close during the first five working days of the month. Included in the sample are mortgages with fixed and variable rates. These results are tabulated and the national average contract mortgage rate for combined lenders (savings and loan associations, commercial banks, mutual savings banks, and mortgage companies) is published between the 10th and 15th of the following month. In addition to this five-week time lag, the rate on the loans closed usually is determined 45 to 60 days in advance. The published result, then, describes actual mortgage market conditions three to four months in the past. These lags are the reasons for possible wide divergences between the base index rate and the initial contract rate on a loan. This divergence is most likely to occur during periods of rapidly changing interest rates.

THE SHAKEOUT IN ALTERNATIVE MORTGAGE INSTRUMENTS*

Richard G. Marcis†

15

The problems associated with the long-term, fixed-rate mortgage in a volatile economic environment are by now only too well known. When high or variable rates of inflation are anticipated, the lack of payment flexibility inherent in the standard mortgage instrument adversely affects both borrowers and lenders.

Borrowers are confronted with the "tilt" problem which arises when market interest rates increase in response to upward revisions of inflationary expectations. Their monthly payments obligations may be raised dramatically by the increase in mortgage rates. Since their incomes are likely to increase less rapidly than mortgage rates, many borrowers find they cannot afford the necessarily high initial monthly payments of the standard fixed payment mortgage. Although the burden may decline through time as borrowers' incomes increase and monthly payments remain fixed, the "tilt" of the burden to the early years of the mortgage may force some potential home buyers to defer or downgrade their housing purchases, and it may force others out of the housing market entirely.

The standard fixed-rate mortgage instrument also fails to protect lenders from the interest rate risks associated with unanticipated inflation. Unexpected inflation results in higher short- and long-term interest rates which increase

*Reprinted by permission of the *Real Estate Review*, Volume 13, Spring 1983, pp. 29–33. Copyright © 1983, Warren, Gorham & Lamont, Inc., 210 South St., Boston, Mass. All rights reserved.

†Richard G. Marcis is Senior Vice-president and Chief Economist, Dallas Federal Savings. Mr. Marcis was formerly Chief Economist of the Federal Home Loan Bank Board.

costs of funds to mortgage lenders. Because their returns on long-term, fixed-rate portfolios do not keep pace with rapid increases in costs of funds, mortgage lending thrift institutions in recent years have experienced large reductions in net worth.

Because for both lenders and borrowers, the long-term, fixed-rate mortgage is largely incapable of coping with interest rate risks attributable to unanticipated inflation, a number of alternative mortgage instruments (AMIs) evolved in the marketplace in recent years. A relaxation of legislative and regulatory restrictions on mortgages and the low level of mortgage demand in recent years also promoted experimentation with alternative mortgage forms. The result was the introduction of a seemingly endless variety of alternative mortgage instruments.

However, an informal selection process is beginning to occur as the market strives for a more limited number of instruments with standardized features and options. This winnowing process should gain momentum in 1983 and 1984.

The stabilization of a market in which a limited number of alternative mortgage instruments and altered fixed rate mortgage form dominate may substantially alter the nature of and the motives for home ownership.

TYPES OF ALTERNATIVE MORTGAGES

Before examining tomorrow's home mortgage market, we will quickly review the diversity of current alternative mortgage instruments. AMIs can be clasified into the following basic categories:

1. *Adjustable rate mortgage (ARM)*. The common feature of ARMs is that the interest rate is not fixed but varies according to some preselected index or reference rate. The adjustments are made at the end of a predetermined period which may be as short as three months or as long as five years.[1]
2. *Graduated payment mortgage (GPM)*. A GPM has scheduled monthly payments that start out at a low level relative to a level-payment fixed-rate mortgage, but rise later. The graduation rate, the term of graduation, and the interest rate are fixed throughout the life of the loan.
3. *Price level adjusted mortgage (PLAM)*. In PLAMs, the interest rate is fixed, but the outstanding balance and monthly payments vary according to changes in some price index.
4. *Reverse annuity mortgage (RAM)*. A stream of monthly payments is provided to homeowners through an annuity purchased by a loan against the owner's accumulated equity in the home.

---

[1]This category includes all loans with flexible rate features such as adjustable mortgage loans, variable rate mortgages, and renegotiable rate mortgages.

5. *Shared appreciation mortgage (SAM).* Under this mortgage plan, the borrower agrees to share with the lender the appreciation in the underlying property, in return for a below-market interest rate.
6. *Growing equity mortgage (GEM).* This loan carries a fixed interest rate and a scheduled annual increase in monthly payments. Since the increase in monthly payments is applied to retirement of principal, the final maturity is shortened considerably.

The preceding categorization of AMIs may give an appearance of order to the current mortgage finance system that actually does not exist. Within each of these individual loan categories there are a variety of special features tailored to the specific needs of individual borrowers or lenders. For example, there are numerous ARM variations because of different indexes, different rate adjustment periods, and, in some cases, different limitations on the size of permitted periodic or cumulative interest rate changes. Some lenders offer plans in which a change in interest rates may be reflected in a change in the monthly payment, the term of the loan, the outstanding balance of the loan, or some combination of these. Still other plans may hold payments constant for a set period of time even if interest rates increase. Such loans involve negative amortization because the unpaid interest is added to the loan balance.[2]

The variety of terms and conditions is also evident in other types of loans. For example, GPM loans may differ because they use different graduation rates and periods of graduation. Moreover, although most GPM plans have negative amortization features, this is not always the case. Moreover, hybrid AMIs have evolved which incorporate features from two or more general loan types.

Thus, a great diversity of mortgage alternatives is currently available. The proliferation of mortgage products is a market response to the relaxation of legislative and regulatory constraints on mortgage loan terms and conditions. The depressed state of the housing market since 1979 also promoted lender inventiveness in structuring mortgages designed to increase the number of borrowers who could qualify for mortgage credit at current high levels of interest rates. These conditions are in sharp contrast to those of the past when a single, uniform mortgage instrument—the long-term, fixed-rate mortgage, dominated mortgage finance.

THE COMING SHAKEOUT OF ALTERNATIVE MORTGAGE INSTRUMENTS

The proliferation of mortgage instruments has benefited borrowers to the extent that it enables them to find mortgages tailored to their individual needs and

[2]Reflecting the diversity of ARM programs available in the market, the Federal National Mortgage Association currently has eight different ARM purchase programs. Moreover, FNMA has indicated that it will purchase on a negotiated case-by-case basis other ARM plans which do not meet existing program requirements.

requirements. On the other hand, it has probably caused some confusion for borrowers and portfolio investors as well as some lenders, and thus, it has reduced the efficiency of the mortgage process. Borrowers, for example, have probably found it hard to comparison shop because of the differences in mortgage terms and conditions. Undoubtedly some of the mortgage features have been difficult for the typical consumer to understand. Portfolio investors, especially those who do not traditionally invest in mortgages, have also probably experienced some confusion because of the diversity of current mortgage alternatives.

There is little doubt that a winnowing process can be expected, during which some of the currently available mortgage products will fall by the wayside for lack of consumer or investor acceptance. The factors that will be instrumental in determining what mortgage alternatives will survive include the degree of protection provided lenders from interest rate risk, the degree of payment stability provided borrowers, and salability in the secondary market.

Lenders' Needs

Lenders have learned the dangers of lending long at fixed rates and borrowing short. Today, lenders place a premium on mortgages with adjustable rate features that will protect them against unexpected increases in market rates of interest.

Lenders also desire servicing simplicity. Virtually all AMIs are more difficult to service than the traditional fixed-rate, level-payment mortgage. Consequently, lenders will have a bias in favor of mortgage structures in which the mix and frequency of changing rates, payments, loan balances, and other loan terms are not so cumbersome and complicated as to impose costly servicing burdens on them.

Borrowers' Needs

The needs and requirements of borrowers are also important variables in determining which mortgage instruments will survive. Although borrowers have a variety of specialized financial needs, most borrowers have in common a general requirement for some degree of stability and predictability in mortgage payments. Stability and predictability of payments not only aid family financial planning, they also eliminate the possibility of delinquencies and defaults in the event families are confronted with unexpected increases in monthly payment requirements that exceed family ability to pay.[3]

---

[3] Because of the potential for increased delinquency and default risk, lenders also would find it to their advantage to protect borrowers from such sharp increases in mortgage payments requirements.

Marketability in the Secondary Market

Finally, the relative marketability of AMIs in the secondary market is also important in determining what mortgage instruments will survive. Secondary market investors have provided an increasing share of mortgage credit in recent years. If the mortgage market is to continue to grow, the mortgage instrument should be salable not only to traditional mortgage investors such as the federally assisted housing finance agencies and savings and loan associations, mutual savings banks and commercial banks, but to nontraditional mortgage investors such as pension funds and life insurance companies as well.

Because portfolio investors have different investment needs and requirements, no one mortgage instrument or set of mortgage features is likely to appeal to all of them. Some investors emphasize investments with variable yields which are responsive to changes in inflation. Other investors place emphasis on certainty of rates of return. The former group would prefer mortgages with rate-adjustable features while the latter would emphasize investments with fixed terms and rates.

But it is generally acknowledged that standardization of mortgage terms and conditions would facilitate marketability. Portfolio investors, especially those who have not traditionally invested in mortgages, undoubtedly find the variety of mortgage products currently available confusing. Lack of familiarity with the mortgage instruments has undoubtedly hampered their willingness to purchase AMIs.

Some degree of uniformity and standardization of mortgage instruments is also desirable because it would enable AMIs to be more readily "pooled" as collateral for mortgage-backed pass-through securities which can then be sold in the secondary market. Mortgages with generally similar terms and features can be more readily pooled for sale as pass-through securities than can AMIs with varying terms and conditions. Pass-through securities promote the efficiency of the secondary market by enabling investors to buy large blocks of mortgages without having to be bothered with the loan origination and administration problems that are involved with handling individual mortgages.

The federally assisted housing finance agencies—the Federal National Mortgage Association and the Federal Home Loan Mortgage Corporation—will play an important role in determining what mortgage instruments will survive. Through their mortgage purchase requirements, FNMA and FHLMC define standards of marketability for AMIs. Even if lenders do not plan on selling AMIs to these institutions, loans originated to their purchase requirements will usually be more marketable than nonconforming loans because their purchase requirements may be adopted by other investors.

EVOLVING MORTGAGE FORMS

As the number of mortgage forms currently available diminishes, the net result should be a limited set of mortgage designs or dominant mortgage forms. Given the specific needs and requirements of market participants that we have described above, some tentative projections can be made about the likely form of the mortgage instrument that will come to serve as a standard.

The most common mortgage instrument in all likelihood will be the adjustable rate mortgage. The need for lenders to be protected against interest rate risk is critical and without such protection lenders would likely leave the mortgage market. However, the adjustable rate mortgage will also have to provide some protection for borrowers against rapid fluctuations in monthly payments. Consequently, ARMs with negative amortization features, which permit payments to be adjusted less frequently than interest rates, may become a common feature of ARMs.

GPMs will probably have only a minor role in the mortgage market. However, since ARMs do not alleviate the inflation-induced distortions of borrowers' payments burdens, the low initial payment and graduation features of the GPM will also become a standard option of ARMs in high interest rate periods.

While growing equity loans will survive the shakeout of mortgage products, they will not play a major role in the mortgage market because the benefits accrue primarily to borrowers or investors with few benefits for lenders. They, like GPMs, may be thought of as "boutique" mortgages with specialized features that appeal to a limited number of borrowers with special financing requirements.

Reverse annuity mortgages, price level adjusted mortgages, and shared appreciation mortgages are not likely to achieve any level of significance in the marketplace despite the attention these instruments have received recently in the popular press. The complexity and novelty of these mortgage forms will hamper their acceptance by not only borrowers but lenders and investors. They are also subject to unusual tax or accounting and legal considerations that may severely circumscribe their use. Furthermore, there are some unknowns associated with each of these instruments which will also limit their adoption in the marketplace. What happens, for example, if borrowers with a shared appreciation mortgage have not moved or sold their houses and their loan is approaching maturity? Will they be forced to sell the house in order to provide the lender its share of the appreciation on the property? What happens with a price level adjusted mortgage if the borrowers' incomes do not keep pace with inflation? The real payment burden on such borrowers may become excessive and may lead to delinquencies and defaults.

IS THERE A FUTURE FOR THE FIXED-RATE MORTGAGE?

What role, if any, will the fixed-rate, level payment, long-term mortgage play in the mortgage markets of the future? It is likely that the fixed-rate, level-payment mortgage will continue to be offered in the marketplace along with adjustable rate mortgages and other selected AMIs in the future.

The feature that assures the survival of the fixed-rate, level-payment mortgage is the certainty it offers borrowers with respect to their future mortgage payments regardless of interest rates. Since most borrowers are risk-averse, they will, all other things being equal, generally prefer fixed-rate loans to variable rate loans.

This does not imply that fixed-rate mortgages will be available on the same basis as in the past. Fixed-rate loans will be priced differently than they have been in the past. Lenders who originate and hold fixed-rate loans will assume all the interest rate risk, and they will require compensation for assuming that risk. Consequently, rates on long-term fixed-rate mortgages will be established at a premium relative to other mortgages by an amount sufficient to cover the interest risk inherent in making these loans.

Thus, risk-averse borrowers who desire predictability and stability in mortgage payments and are willing to pay a risk-adjusted rate, will find some lenders willing to offer fixed-rate mortgage loans. The demand for and supply of fixed-rate loans will obviously depend upon the relative attitudes of borrowers and lenders toward risk and their expectations of future levels of interest rates. Also, investor preferences for fixed-rate investments will be important in determining the availability of fixed-rate loans, since lenders will be less averse to originating fixed-rate loans if they know they can be sold to third-party investors.

In summary, adjustable rate mortgages with provisions designed to protect borrowers against abrupt changes in payments will in all likelihood become the dominant mortgage form in the future. However, there will also be some volume of activity in fixed-rate instruments such as the traditional fixed-rate mortgage instrument, as well as the graduated payment mortgage and the growing equity mortgage. However, the key to the availability of fixed-rate instruments in the future is their pricing.

IMPACT OF AMIs ON THE HOUSING MARKET

To the extent that adjustable rate mortgages have enabled lenders to remain in the mortgage lending market, the home buying public and the housing market have benefited from the introduction of alternative mortgage instruments. Given the sharp increases in their costs of funds and the reduced market value of their long-term fixed-rate mortgage portfolios, lenders would have abandoned the residential mortgage market had they not been granted the authority to originate and buy adjustable rate mortgages.

However, widespread adoption of ARM instruments will affect housing consumers in ways that will not be entirely to their benefit. These instruments will surely change the costs and investment returns from home ownership.

During the 1970s, home mortgage borrowers experienced high real investment returns from housing as inflation reduced the real costs of their mortgage payments while it increased the value of their home in both nominal and real terms. Lenders, on the other hand, were left with the problem of rolling over funds at higher rates.

ARMs redistribute the effects of inflation. With ARMs, borrowers bear the costs of inflation because these costs are reflected in higher interest rates. The more frequent and greater the rate adjustments, the greater the degree of interest rate risk shifted forward to borrowers. With future mortgage payment uncertain, home ownership becomes riskier. Because loan payments can rise, borrowers will need to budget for possible increases in monthly payments, and payments could become especially burdensome for highly leveraged borrowers.

ARMs will also reduce homeowners' investment returns from housing. Since inflation will be reflected not only in increases in housing prices but in higher mortgage rates, the appreciation in housing value should be offset by increased loan payment requirements. By increasing the costs of housing credit, ARMs reduce potential investment returns from housing.

These changes will require some tough adjustments on the part of consumers. Some consumers may find that because of the increased cost of housing credit, they can't afford to own a house, and they will either postpone their housing purchase or perhaps decide not to purchase at all. Other borrowers will have to allocate a higher percentage of their incomes to housing costs than would have been the case in the past. Others will attempt to reduce their housing outlays by purchasing smaller housing units. The increased cost of housing will also encourage greater utilization of the existing housing stock through sharing arrangements with other families.

Although consumers will adjust, the adjustments may not be easy. Consumers who have been accustomed to real low housing costs and a wide variety of housing options may find these adjustments a bitter pill to swallow.

ADJUSTABLE RATE MORTGAGES

*Michael J. Lea** *16*

As lenders recover from the balance sheet buffeting they have experienced over the years, they are increasingly turning to interest-rate-sensitive assets, like adjustable rate mortgages (ARMs), as a means to restructure their portfolios. As borrowers deal with an increasingly complex housing finance environment characterized by high house prices, volatile interest rates and a myriad of different financing programs, they are beginning to realize that ARMs can have significant advantages when compared to the standard level payment, fixed-rate mortgage (FRM).

ARMs have been allowed under Federal Home Loan Bank Board (FHLBB) regulations since 1981. However, it was not until 1983 that ARM lending took off, accounting for over 60 percent of new mortgage originations by the end of that year (Figure 16-1). Aggressive pricing by lenders has been a major factor in this upsurge, reflecting both a positively shaped yield curve during 1983, and initial period discounts given by lenders and builders to entice borrowers to take ARMs. In addition, there has been considerable experimentation with ARM features, allowing borrowers and lenders to tailor ARMs to their specific needs, thereby increasing their popularity.

The emergence of ARMs promises major changes in the nature of housing finance in the United States. Mortgage shopping used to be a simple process for borrowers, who needed only to consider the location of the lending institution and whether they qualified for the loan. Now, borrowers must choose from a large array of mortgage programs offering combinations of features at

*Michael J. Lea is a senior economist at the Federal Home Loan Mortgage Corporation. The article was written specifically for this book and is reprinted with his permission.

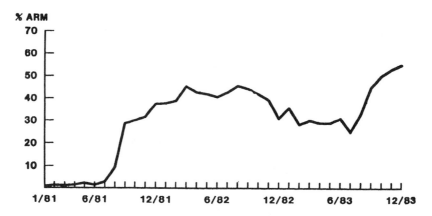

Figure 16-1   Percent of loans with adjustable rates (conventional home mortgages—all lenders)

varying prices. Adjustable rate loans offer entry to home ownership for households unable to qualify for mortgages at FRM rates, allowing them to take advantage of lower initial rates afforded by a positively sloped yield curve. However, they require assessment of key features such as the frequency of adjustment and the index used in adjusting the rate. Borrowers must also make the psychological and financial shift from fixed monthly payments to periodic changes in their mortgage payments.

Lenders, too, are learning about ARMs. These new instruments effectively shorten asset maturities and make assets sensitive to interest rate changes, presenting greater opportunities for asset-liability management and reduction of interest rate risk. The low initial rates at which ARMs can sometimes be offered allow lenders to qualify more borrowers and originate high volumes of mortgages. At the same time, ARMs raise new issues, such as the potential credit risk associated with different instrument designs and their unknown prepayment experience.

Investors accustomed to dealing with fixed-rate securities now have many new opportunities with ARMs. However, they must also assess the prepayment and default potential for these instruments, and they must make complicated pricing decisions, especially regarding ARMs with features such as rate caps and deferred interest.

The recent trend of deregulation in mortgage and financial markets suggests that ARMs are here to stay, but their ultimate design and degree of popularity will depend on a variety of factors, including the future course of interest rates and standardization of product design. The market is still undergoing a period of experimentation with ARMs; therefore, some of the features currently present in ARMs will disappear while others may be still on the horizon. This article provides a backdrop for the introduction of ARMs in their present form, describes the complex features that can be present in the instrument, and discusses the implications of continued ARM usage for the primary and secondary mortgage markets. The discussion of ARM features is based in large part on the results of a Federal Home Loan Mortgage Corporation (Freddie Mac) survey conducted in August, 1983.[1]

THE COMING OF ARMS

The development of the ARM as a major mortgage financing vehicle is due to both the deregulation of the thrift and banking industries and the interest rate volatility that the economy has experienced over the last few years. Traditionally, mortgage lenders have performed an interest rate intermediation function; borrowing short-term through various savings instruments and lending long-term by offering fixed-rate mortgages with terms of 25 years or more. As long as interest rates were relatively stable and lending institutions were protected by Regulation Q deposit ceilings, mortgage lending remained a relatively profitable business.

However, by the end of the 1970s, political pressure to give savers market rates of interest and lessen the impact of savings deposit disintermediation had led to an erosion of Regulation Q deposit ceilings and intensified institutional competition for funds. Liability deregulation came at a time in which the Federal Reserve switched its emphasis in monetary policy to control of monetary aggregates, which contributed to substantially increased volatility in interest rates. In addition, the economy was characterized by persistent inflation and rising inflationary expectations. The combination of these events led to serious earnings and net worth problems for thrift institutions by the early 1980s.

Faced with this situation, the Federal Home Loan Bank Board gave regulatory authorization to ARMs in April 1981. Although mortgage loans with provisions for rate adjustment were not new, past experiments with such mortgages, most notably the California VRM (variable rate mortgage), had not achieved widespread acceptance.[2] As interest rates climbed to historically high levels in 1981 and 1982, ARMs became a significant financing alternative to FRMs. This development was arrested during the latter part of 1982 when

---

[1]Michael J. Lea, "ARMs: The State of the Market" in *What Makes An ARM Successful*, Federal Home Loan Mortgage Corporation, January 1984.

[2]VRMs were actually introduced in California in the mid-1960s but were not promoted until 1970. State chartered S&Ls became subject to California state VRM regulations in November, 1970. VRMs were also used in Ohio and New England during the mid-1970s. Federally chartered S&Ls were authorized to originate California style VRMs in 1979. These loans contained tight interest rate caps and were not adopted on a widespread basis outside of California. For more information on different VRMs see William C. Melton and Diane L. Heidt, "Variable Rate Mortgages," *FRBNY Quarterly Review*, Summer 1979.

interest rates declined significantly. It was not until mid-1983 when aggressive pricing and marketing of ARMs, combined with a significantly upward sloping yield curve, contributed to making ARM lending the dominant factor in the mortgage market.

ARM FEATURES

There are a number of basic features that can be incorporated into ARMs. Different combinations of these features have created a wide variety of ARMs in the marketplace.

Frequency of Adjustment

Frequency of interest rate and payment adjustments are important features of ARM programs because they determine how interest rate risk is shared by the borrower and lender, as well as the magnitude of cash flow effects due to changing interest rates. The most popular ARMs have one-, three-, and five-year rate adjustment periods. At the time of the Freddie Mac survey, one-year interest rate adjustments were most common (36 percent of all programs), followed by five-year (24 percent), and three-year (21 percent) ARMs. Payment adjustment periods tend to be synchronous with rate adjustments, although recently there has been greater use of ARMs with frequent rate adjustments (e.g., annual or more frequent) and less frequent payment adjustments (e.g., every five years). Also, there has been a shift to shorter rate adjustment periods in 1984, reflecting both the gradual rise in rates during the year and the use of initial period rate discounts (described below) with frequently adjusting loans.

Index

Indexes are interest rate series that govern the rate adjustments in ARMs. Indexes vary in their volatility, which can affect both borrower budgeting and lender profitability, and the ease by which they are readily obtained and understood. The three most common types of index are Treasury indexes, FRM rates series (most commonly the FHLBB published contract rate for new or existing homes), and various industry cost-of-funds measures (national, FHLB district, or local). Cost of funds measures are usually simple ratios of interest expense on deposits to total deposits.

Treasury indexes are interest rate series whose maturity usually coincides with the term of adjustment on the ARM. They are readily available and are understood to be market rates. Their principal disadvantage is that shorter-term Treasury rates can be quite volatile. Use of FRM rates, such as the FHLBB mortgage contract rate series, adds an additional element of risk to the mortgage contract as they involve tying the rate for a short-term adjustment period to movements in long-term rates. Therefore, both the issuer and the holder are exposed to changes in the shape of the yield curve.[3] The cost-of-funds index is preferred by some lenders who, in attempting to match asset and liability durations, perceive this index to be an effective portfolio technique. This index is marketed to borrowers as being less volatile than Treasury indexes, mainly reflecting the impact of past rate regulation. However, it also exposes borrowers to the vagaries of lender portfolio policy, which may offset some of the benefits of less volatility.

The Freddie Mac survey results indicated that the majority of ARM programs utilize Treasury indices. Sixty-one percent of the ARM programs use Treasury indices as compared to 20 percent that use the Federal Home Loan Bank Board (FHLBB) contract rate and 12 percent that use some form of cost-of-funds index (Federal Home Loan Bank district or national). By mid-1984, the proportion of Treasury indexed loans had increased, primarily at the expense of loans indexed to the FHLBB contract rate.

Interest Rate Caps

Interest rate caps limit the amount the interest rate can change during the period (a per-adjustment cap) or set a maximum rate for the loan (a life-of-loan cap). By limiting the magnitude of potential rate changes, rate caps provide some protection for borrowers against payment shock. Therefore, they represent a sharing of the interest rate risk in the mortgage between borrower and lender.

At the time of the Freddie Mac survey, 36 percent of all programs contained a rate cap. Fifteen percent contained an adjustment period cap, 4 percent a life-of-loan cap, and 17 percent incorporated both types of caps. Interest rate caps were most common for instruments that are adjusted frequently (45 percent of ARM programs that adjusted annually or more frequently had such caps), and were relatively rare in longer-term instruments (12 percent of five-year programs). The incidence of rate cap ARMs has increased during 1984, reflecting greater use of shorter adjustment period ARMs as well as greater use of the feature.

Negative Amortization

Negative amortization is a term used to describe deferred interest that can be added to the outstanding mortgage loan balance. There are three major ways negative amortization can arise. Payment caps limit the amount the mortgage payment can change at the time of rate adjustment. If a payment cap is

---

[3]An additional problem with the use of this index is that it no longer reflects solely FRM rates. It is an average mortgage rate which reflects the use of ARMs. Therefore, it is based on a potentially volatile mix of long-term and short-term rates. Also, it reflects the presence of initial period discounts on ARMs.

binding so that the monthly payment is less than the full interest charge at the accrual rate on the mortgage, the unpaid monthly interest is added to the mortgage balance. Therefore, the total amount owed will increase rather than be amortized. Negative amortization can also occur with loans in which the payment adjusts less frequently than the interest rate (if rates rise) or on loans with graduated payment (GPM) options. GPM features typically occur on longer term adjustment period loans (e.g., 5-year) and are characterized by payment rates that start out less than the full interest charge on the mortgage and rise by a prescheduled amount (usually 7½ percent per year) during the adjustment period. Negative amortization can increase the default risk of a loan because an increasing loan balance may erode homeowner equity if house prices are not rising. In the Freddie Mac survey, 29 percent of the loans potentially allowed negative amortization.

Other Features

Assumability is also an important feature in ARM programs. Sixty-four percent of loans in the Freddie Mac survey were assumable. Borrowers have been sensitized to the issue of due-on-sale clauses with recent court decisions. In addition, they desire assumability to assure available financing to qualified home purchasers when they sell their houses. Lenders bear little interest rate risk with assumability on more frequently adjusting loans and have been offering the feature on ARMs, typically at no charge to the borrower.

Another feature that gives borrowers additional security is the option to convert the loan to an FRM at the existing market rate at different points in time. Given the existence of a strong secondary market in FRMs, this feature is relatively costless to lenders. The Freddie Mac survey did not collect information on the incidence of this feature.

A final feature that tends to be absent from ARMs is a prepayment penalty. With initial period discounts and rate caps, it can conceivably take several years for some ARMs to adjust to the market rate. At that point in time, a borrower could refinance and the lender would be unable to recapture the discount at a later time. Only 5 percent of loans in the Freddie Mac survey contained a prepayment penalty.

ARM PRICING

A major factor in the success of ARM programs during the last year has been their pricing. An ARM price typically refers to the interest rate, either for the initial period or for subsequent adjustment periods as determined by program features, for the loan. The interest rate on the ARM is usually arrived at by adding a margin, or spread, over the value of the underlying index used to adjust the interest rate on the loan. However, some ARM programs may have an arbitrary starting value or initial rate, with subsequent period rates deter-mined by adding the change in the index to the initial rate.

Past research has indicated that ARM price is the most important factor in generating high volume and program success.[4] ARM pricing has tended to follow the Treasury yield curve over the last two years with shorter-term ARMs having initial rates of over 200 basis points below FRM rates. One reason why price is so important is the issue of qualification. Lenders typically apply rules of thumb such as a ratio of monthly mortgage payment to gross income of 28 percent in deciding whether a household qualifies for a mortgage loan. Many households can't qualify for FRMs at rates of 13 and 14 percent but can qualify at lower ARM rates. The upward sloping yield curve that has existed since early 1983 has given lenders a window in which to successfully originate a large volume of ARMs by generating the large spreads between ARM initial rates and FRM rates. The future success of ARM programs may depend, in part, on the future course of interest rates and continued existence of a positively shaped yield curve.

Another aspect of ARM pricing that has been important in their success is the use of initial period interest rate discounts. A discount exists if the initial interest rate is less than the program rate, which is determined by the current index value plus the margin, if any, that the lender adds to the index value. Twenty-four percent of lenders in the Freddie Mac survey offered programs with discounts and 35 percent of programs had an initial period discount.

The diversity of ARM programs and the use of initial period discounts has led to a great deal of diversity in ARM pricing. Table 16-1 contains information about the program and initial rates of ARMs by program type as defined by index, frequency of rate adjustment, and presence or absence of a rate cap. While this is not an all-inclusive breakdown of ARM features, it provides some interesting insights about ARM pricing at the time of the survey. On average, ARM program rates follow the Treasury yield curve differentials with respect to frequency of adjustment. However, there is considerable variation in pro-gram rates by program type, reflecting in part features of programs not con-trolled for in this presentation. There is even more variation in the initial rates on ARM programs, reflecting the widespread practice of discounting. As ex-pected, discounting is much more common on shorter term ARMs.

One striking aspect of this table is the comparison between rate-capped and non-rate-capped versions of similar programs. For almost every program category, the initial rates on rate-capped programs are, on average, less than the initial rates on uncapped programs. In part, this finding reflects the heavier use of discounting on rate-capped programs; it also may reflect excluded features of ARMs. Even after the effect of discounting is removed, there appears to be

[4]Kent W. Colton and Michael J. Lea, "ARMing the Markets," *Secondary Mortgage Markets* 1, 2, May 1984.

Table 16-1 Program initial rates

Program	Number	Mean rate	Range (percent)	Mean spread off FRM[a]	Mean spread off program rate[b] discounted programs	Percentage of programs with discounts
Uncapped 1 year Treasury	66	11.95	9.25-13.75	1.71	0.76	29
Rate-capped 1 year Treasury	26	11.31	9.75-13.25	3.02	1.72	46
Uncapped 3 year Treasury	72	12.63	11.50-13.625	1.17	0.82	25
Rate-capped 3 year Treasury	15	12.24	11.50-13.50	1.67	1.11	53
Uncapped 5 year Treasury	120	13.15	10.90-14.00	0.61	0.65	14
Rate-capped 5 year Treasury	16	12.72	10.90-13.75	1.16	0.81	25
FHLBB 1 year uncapped	40	12.37	9.95-14.00	1.31	1.33	28
FHLBB 1 year rate capped	46	11.93	8.75-13.25	1.84	1.73	48
FHLBB 3 year uncapped	10	11.91	8.00-13.00	1.84	2.36	70
FHLBB 3 year capped	16	12.42	11.75-13.00	1.48	2.55	50

Uncapped 1 year national cost of funds	5	12.25	11.125-14.50	1.33	1.59	60
Rate-capped 1 year national cost of funds	9	12.17	11.00-13.50	1.85	1.81	67
Rate-capped[c] district 11 cost of funds	9	11.77	10.75-12.75	2.04	2.32	77

[a]FRM market rate based on Freddie Mac lender survey, August 6, 1983.

[b]Program rate equals the index value plus the margin required by the lender of the current index value, at the time of survey, depending on the method utilized for rate adjustment.

[c]District 11 Cost of Funds Programs adjusted annually or more frequently. Uncapped District 11 Cost of Funds programs were too few in number to make meaningful comparisons.

Source: Federal Home Loan Mortgage Corporation, *What Makes An ARM Successful*, p. 15.

no significant difference between the average program rates on rate-capped and non-rate-capped programs.

IMPLICATIONS

The mortgage market's brief experiment with ARMs has indicated that they can be a successful alternative to the traditional fixed-rate level payment mortgage in home finance. However, the competition among lenders for rate-sensitive assets in a deregulated environment has created a proliferation of ARM programs and a large dispersion of initial period prices. In turn, this experimentation has created much uncertainty and confusion about ARMs. Realtors, lenders, and borrowers sometimes have trouble understanding the differences between payment rates and note rates, how indexes affect rate adjustment, or the reasons for adding margins to index values for rate adjustments. In addition, the variety of programs and the often subtle differences between programs make it difficult to compare mortgage instruments.

In the short run, under favorable interest rate conditions, the complexity of ARMs has not deterred many borrowers. It is likely that these instruments will have to be adjusted at least once before the picture of their understanding and acceptance by borrowers is complete.

One area of concern about ARMs is their potential for credit risk, or risk of delinquency and default. Although ARM experience is limited, credit risk for ARMs may be greater than for FRMs, especially for programs with large initial discounts. There are two major reasons. First, the instruments themselves create more risk for the borrower. Adjustable loans introduce the potential for significant payment shock, which can lead to higher delinquency rates if borrowers' incomes do not rise with their mortgage payments. Also, for instruments with payment caps or graduated payment options, negative amortization may lead to substantially reduced net equity for the borrower if house prices do not rise at the same time or rate as increases in mortgage principal.

Second, extraordinary rates of house price inflation contributed to a decade of growing equity in the 1970s, substantially reducing the likelihood of default. In the 1980s, house prices may not increase in real terms. The combination of mortgages with negative amortization and a lack of substantial house price inflation may leave borrowers with low or negative net equity, increasing the likelihood of default. Likewise, ARM payment shock may lead to higher levels of delinquency and, combined with eroded net equity, induce mortgage default.

Judicious program design and sound underwriting will go a long way towards ameliorating concern about the credit risk of ARMs. Avoiding loans with steep initial period discounts that have no rate caps will reduce the likelihood of early payment shock. Likewise, avoiding deeply discounted loans with payment caps, which are guaranteed to generate significant amounts of negative amortization early in the loan, will reduce the default potential inherent in the instrument. Qualifying households at the true interest rate (index plus margin) on the loan, rather than an artificial discount rate, will be a safer policy for both borrowers and lenders by taking into account the fact that the mortgage payment will increase substantially early in the life of loan, even if interest rates in the underlying index do not change.

The use of interest rate caps can also reduce the potential payment shock in ARMs. Interest rate caps limit the interest rate risk to which the borrower is exposed but, conversely, expose lenders to more interest rate risk. The pricing evidence in the Freddie Mac survey indicated that rate-capped ARMs were not being priced significantly differently than non-rate-capped versions of the same program. If expected interest rate volatility or upward drift in interest rates is very small, so is the likelihood that an interest rate cap becomes binding. Therefore, it will not cost much for a lender to offer. However, such interest rate expectations may be overly optimistic given the recent monetary experience.

Another explanation for the lack of a premium for rate-capped ARMs may be their newness and the competitive pressures faced by lenders attempting to originate a large volume of loans. Saddled with large FRM portfolios—a significant portion of which have below market interest rates—and market rate liabilities, thrift institutions have been trying to restructure their asset portfolios to make them more interest rate sensitive. One way to restructure a portfolio, without incurring losses by selling below market FRMs at a discount, is to originate as large a volume of ARMs as possible. This incentive to restructure, combined with highly competitive environments in many market areas, has led to widespread use of initial period discounts and the offering of features such as rate caps in order to originate ARMs to borrowers. This strategy shifts some of the interest rate risk of mortgage lending back to the lender. While giving away rate caps may account for ARM popularity among borrowers, if interest rates remain volatile or rise significantly, thrifts may find themselves with the same earnings and net worth problems they faced prior to the explosion of ARM lending.

Will ARM lending continue at its present pace? One of the most important factors in ARM success has been the spread between FRMs and ARMs. An implication of this importance is that changes in the relationship between long- and short-term interest rates may lead to cyclical use of ARMs. For a given FRM rate, there may be a higher proportion of ARMs to fixed-rate mortgages when the yield curve is steep and a smaller proportion when the yield curve is flat.

Will ARM programs continue in their current form? In order to achieve longer term viability, there will also have to be some degree of ARM program standardization. Over time, it is likely that market pressures will lead to a reduced number of programs, with common features, at rates which will reflect capital market pricing for securities with different features and adjustment periods. The speed of the standardization process will reflect the interest rate environment governing lender portfolio policy, growing familiarity with the instrument by borrowers, lenders, and realtors, and the degree of secondary market involvement with ARMs.

Secondary market involvement in ARMs is likely to proceed slowly. Thrift institutions provide the main market for ARMs at present. Nonthrift investors will probably require more experience with ARM use in order to judge the prepayment and default potential of different designs. If ARMs remain a dominant mortgage finance vehicle, more secondary market trading in ARMs will be inevitable. More trading in ARMs, either as whole loans or in mortgage pools, will lead to more standard programs and consistent pricing of individual features. Broader disclosure regulations combined with increased mortgage insurance premiums or lack of mortgage insurance for riskier mortgage designs will reduce the potential credit risk in ARMs. The benefits that ARMs can provide to both borrowers and lenders suggest that the problems associated with their recent introduction can be worked out and, therefore, that they are here to stay.

SECOND MORTGAGES: COMING OF AGE*

Michael Rosser†

17

Mortgage bankers' interest in second mortgage lending has increased markedly during the past several years. In 1971, mortgage bankers originated only $71 million in second mortgages. While this segment of the market grew until the 1975 recession, it stood at only $84 million by 1977. Since 1977, however, the average annual second mortgage volume of mortgage bankers has risen sharply, and now stands at almost $500 million.

There are four reasons for this increasing activity in second mortgages. First is the acceptance of second mortgages by the secondary market, evidenced by the Federal National Mortgage Association's (FNMA) entrance into the market for second mortgages. According to sources at FNMA, the goal of the Association is to make available for purchase one-third to one-half of their activity in short-term seconds and adjustable rate products by the end of 1983. In addition, the rapid appreciation in property values during the late 1970s and early 1980s created a vast pool of homeowners' equity that could be used to back second mortgages.

The third reason for the popularity of second mortgages was the high level of interest rates and the deep recession in the real estate markets during 1981

*Reprinted from *Mortgage Banking*, November 1983, pp. 21-22ff., with permission of the Mortgage Bankers Association of America.

†Michael Rosser is Zone Sales Manager for PMI Mortgage Insurance Company, Denver, Colorado. He has been with the San Francisco-based company for eight years and has been responsible for the firm's marketing effort as well as the sale of its home equity loan insurance. In 1979, Rosser won the Colorado MBA's Everett C. Spellman Award for "outstanding contributions to the mortgage lending industry."

and 1982. Second mortgages and wraps were the keystones of the creative financing era, making it possible for mortgage bankers to make and sell loans despite a high interest rate environment. The second mortgage market kept loan officers busy soliciting business and underwriters and processors at their desks.

The fourth reason for the growth in second mortgage activity was the entry of the private mortgage insurance industry into the area of insuring second mortgages. This new product gave second mortgages a new respectability and safety.

SOME RESEARCH DIFFICULTIES

One of the major problems in analyzing second mortgage lending is the lack of information sources and accurate reporting systems. Inconsistent procedures from institution to institution and trade association to trade association present serious stumbling blocks to researching effectively the development of a second mortgage program.

For example, many second mortgage lenders, particularly finance companies, use terminology that is different from that customarily used in mortgage banking. Also, many lenders account for new originations, delinquencies, and foreclosures in a manner inconsistent with mortgage banking practices.

Some financial trade associations survey their membership annually, and some financial institutions conduct their own studies. Much of the information and estimates vary from one source to another. Accurate forecasts of second mortgage originations, delinquencies, or foreclosures are not available. Because of these reporting problems, the Mortgage Bankers Association could develop a research and reporting system on second mortgages. This program might include information relative to loan size, loan-to-value ratio, and payment characteristics, (i.e. whether the loans were fifteen-year amortizing, three-year interest only, or five- or three-year balloon payments). Also, the research should cover the purpose of the loans and whether the loans were for the purpose of purchase money seconds, including wraps, home improvement, or equity loans. MBA's single-family underwriting seminar should include a section on second mortgage originations, underwriting, quality control, and servicing.

A second mortgage program can provide new profit opportunities for mortgage bankers. Like any new program, however, a great deal of time and effort must be committed. Experts need to be hired and trained, and guidelines and controls must be installed before the first loan solicitation effort is made. Also, management must commit both time and resources and then continue to monitor the program's progress.

Lenders should research before starting a second mortgage program.

PRODUCT MANAGER'S ROLE

To find out more about the "state of the art" in second mortgage lending, an informal telephone survey was conducted. A total of 112 mortgage banking firms responded.

All of the firms in the survey that have successful programs hired or promoted an individual to perform the role of a product manager. The product manager has several key areas of responsibility. First, he or she must develop a corporate policy statement about the second mortgage program as well as a policy manual. The policy should state the goals and objectives of the program and the selection of various loan types and loan purposes. For example: some mortgage bankers might want to be heavily involved with the wrap and purchase money second areas, while not wanting to absorb the burdens involved in home improvement lending.

Companies originating second mortgages, whether small independents or regional or national companies, should begin by also drawing up a statement of origination philosophy. Each statement should start with a production forecast monthly and annually by number of loans and loan types: for example, three-year balloons or 15-year fixed-rate with level amortization.

The product manager also has responsibility for training of loan originators, processors, and underwriters. The product manager, further, has to coordinate with the legal department or the firm's legal counsel on various Federal and state laws and regulations. The product manager also has to develop the loan marketing program. Obviously, the product manager has to be well-versed in all aspects of second mortgage lending.

Early on in the program, the product manager has to develop a loan control and audit program to prevent the kinds of abuses in second mortgage lending that have characterized it throughout its history. The product manager continuously adapts the firm's second mortgage program to the marketplace and also helps the servicing department to understand how second mortgages are originated, processed, underwritten, and closed. That person is also responsible for making sure that servicing department personnel understand the unique characteristics of second mortgages, i.e., the necessity to check insurance policies to make sure that the second mortgage lender is the named insured.

The servicing manager must see that the first mortgage holder continues to pay the homeowners insurance, that the taxes on the property are paid, and that the first mortgage holder is notified of the position of the second mortgage holder so that in the event of default, the second mortgage holder will be given notice.

INVESTOR INTEREST

Investors in the secondary market are attracted to second mortgages for several reasons: higher yields, shorter terms to maturity, and a perception of low levels of risk. Second mortgages tended historically to yield 200 to 300 basis points more than first mortgages. Maximum maturities on seconds are about half that of the traditional 30-year fixed-rate first mortgages; the average life maturities also are shorter.

Safety has been a factor attributed to second mortgages. The safety factor, however, is attributable to the inflation pressures on housing prices and not to anything inherent in second mortgages. New investors are attracted because of the availability of insurance on second mortgages.

INCOME AND PROFITABILITY

For mortgage bankers, income and profitability comes from origination and servicing fees plus other miscellaneous charges. Institutions such as portfolio lenders that originate and hold second mortgages set a minimum required spread, normally 200 to 300 basis points over the cost of funds. Depending on interest rates, these firms adjust their origination and discount fees accordingly to obtain a maximum return.

Mortgage bankers' primary interest is in meeting their origination and servicing fee goals, while obtaining a profit from the gain on sale, if possible. In the survey, the most commonly quoted servicing fee was one-half of 1 percent. A mortgage banker should price the servicing *very* carefully, particularly because there are no escrow funds or other compensating balances.

Second mortgages require a much more intensive servicing effort than do first mortgages. For example, some second mortgage lenders recommend the borrower be called five to ten days after the payment is due, and that the borrower be visited after twenty days. In addition, intensive counseling as well as workout and restructuring of the borrower's debt structure might also be necessary. Properties must be inspected more often, and insurance policies have to be endorsed naming the second mortgage lender as an insured under the policy. All of this requires a much greater compensation for the mortgage banker. The mortgage banker also has to be prepared to advance funds to the holder of a first in the event of default.

Income derived through loan sales can be directly related to the strength of the firm's marketing department. Profits depend on the expertise of the marketing department in locating buyers of second mortgages. Many mortgage bankers that are owned by banks and S&Ls find their parent companies are a good source of funds.

In states where no discount points are allowed, lenders derive their income from excess yield and servicing fees. Depending on their required return, interest charged in these states is higher than in other states to compensate for not being able to charge points or origination fees.

MATURITIES, LOAN-TO-VALUE

Company policies vary regarding the maximum contractual maturity and required loan-to-equity ratios. Medium and large finance companies generally originate longer maturities than smaller companies. A 1980 report by the National Consumer Finance Association (NCFA) stated that 54.9 percent of second mortgages originated by consumer finance firms with $50 million in accounts receivable were for a term of five years or less. For larger firms with $50 million to $500 million in accounts receivable, one- to five-year loans made up only 27.6 percent of their portfolios. The maximum loan maturity reported was fifteen years. A five-year median maturity length was reported by the National Association of Realtors on purchase money seconds, and median maturity of just under seven years was reported by the National Second Mortgage Association (NSMA).

The most common loan-to-value ratio is 80 percent. NCFA reported loan-to-value ratios of between 70-90 percent with 80 percent being the most frequent. The NSMA reported an average ratio of 76 percent with a high of 90 percent and a low of 40 percent for 1980.

As expected, the cost of processing second mortgage loans varies from company to company. Respondents to the telephone survey were asked if the cost to process seconds is more, less, or the same as processing first mortgages. "The same" was the most common response, but a variable was acknowledged. If a lender has originated the first loan or has a close working relationship with the originator, then less work is required to credit-check the second.

Firms dealing exclusively in seconds tend to find processing more expensive because they not only have to qualify the second, but they also must verify that the first is in order.

Most firms set minimum and maximum loan limits that they will originate. The most common minimum loan value was $10,000 with $15,000 and $5,000 also mentioned. Maximum limits, especially in the West, exceeded $125,000 in some firms.

DEFAULT

Default risk appears not to represent a serious threat to investors in second mortgages. Of 60 firms responding to the NCFA study of the second mortgage market for 1980, chargeoffs only represented 0.13 percent or $14.4 million of the $10.908 billion second mortgage loans outstanding. This rate was reduced

0.11 percent with subsequent recoveries. Some of these companies reported no chargeoffs, while the maximum reported was 8.04 percent.

Additional support, although a significant difference, comes from the NSMA, which reported an average of 1.8 percent chargeoff rate to receivables and an average foreclosure rate of 1.0 percent to year's end loan balances. The NSMA average delinquency rate represented 2.48 percent of average balances of 60 days or more as compared with the average 60-day delinquency rate reported by MBA for 1980 on first mortgages of 1.48 percent.

Participants in the telephone survey cited no major problems with investing in second mortgages, although some important lessons have been learned. Respondents most frequently mentioned problems in regions that have seen a significant decrease in real estate values. Such decreases have occurred in California and Florida where rapid increases in appreciation left these areas vulnerable to devaluations of equity. One respondent explained that investors have become "regionally conscious" as a result, now preferring certain states over others.

The threat of loss to the lender increases when a homeowner takes out a second mortgage on his property; equity decreases, while the collateral backing the loan deteriorates and may not be enough to repay the loan. While not a major problem, there have been incidences where some borrowers have taken out second mortgages and simply walked on the loans. In such cases, the borrower finds this easier than trying to sell his house, and he knows the dollar value he will receive.

Despite the risks involved, certain borrowers find this route more attractive than making additional mortgage payments for an unspecified length of time and coping with the uncertainty of the final sales price and the additional deduction of commission costs. Some respondents said that this tendency to "walk" has increased since personal bankruptcy laws were relaxed in 1978.

Creditworthiness, the ability to repay, and the appraisal are the key focal points in managing the risk of a second mortgage program. Misrepresentation of home values during the recent era of "creative financing" has contributed to the increasing default risk. Buydowns of homebuyers' interest payments are offset by increased home prices. Sellers often inflate the sales price of their homes to compensate for low-interest seller financing.

Declining real home prices are weakening incentives to keep up payments for marginal borrowers who bought with small down payments and who therefore have little equity in their homes.

LOAN PURPOSE, SIZE

The purpose of the loan can fundamentally influence risk of default.

1. Home improvement loans are generally considered the least risky of second mortgages because the funds are used to increase the value of

the property securing the loan. This effectively should lower the overall loan-to-value ratio.

2. Second mortgages on non-owner-occupied housing, such as for small rental properties, are riskier because borrowers are more inclined to overextend on their investments than on their primary residence. The borrower may be investing in real estate for the tax benefits and in spite of negative cash flow resulting from mortgage payments exceeding the rental receipts. If the borrower needs the tax benefits to meet mortgage payments, the loan is of reduced security.

3. Speculative investments, such as condominiums with very high loan-to-value ratios (95 percent) gained increasing acceptance under more sophisticated underwriting methods and rapid appreciation conditions during the past several years. Real appreciation (nominal price increases adjusted for inflation) has become negative recently, resulting in greater potential for negative equity situations.

4. Debt consolidation loans—deemed among the riskiest.

The size of the second mortgage loan relative to the sum of the first and second liens (the junior lien ratio) varies inversely with the severity of losses in the event of a default, i.e., the loss per dollar of funds loaned depends on the size of the second lien relative to the size of both items combined. For a given combined loan amount and loan-to-value ratio, loss ratios are higher for second mortgages with lower junior lien ratios. This is illustrated in Table 17-1.

If net sales proceeds from a foreclosure sale fall below the combined loan amount, the second lien lender loses more per dollars loaned when the junior lien ratio is low.

Table 17-1

	Lender A	Lender B
Appraised House Value	$100,000	$100,000
First Mortgage	(70,000)	(50,000)
Second Mortgage	(10,000)	(30,000)

Assume borrower defaults, lender forecloses, acquires property, and sells.

Sales Price	$ 80,000	$ 80,000
Less 5% Commission	(4,000)	4,000)
Proceeds from Sale	76,000	76,000
Balance on First	70,000	50,000
Net Proceeds	6,000	26,000
Balance on Second	(10,000)	(30,000)
Loss	4,000	4,000
Loss Ratio	40%	13.0%
Junior Lien Ratio	12.5%	37.5%

Losses are less frequent on relatively large second mortgages, all else being the same. But losses tend to be higher on seconds secured by relatively high-priced houses. This is due to the relative volatility of market values for expensive homes, which in turn increases lender risk.

The deteriorating economy of 1980-1982 led to increasing delinquency and foreclosure rates. Ability of mortgagees to keep up with payments has been affected by:

- Unemployment, deepened by lengthy recession.
- Inflation's impact on disposable income.

The economy is expected to improve through 1984; inflation should be 5 percent or less, and interest will probably decline somewhat. This is good news for mortgage bankers interested in originating second mortgages.

Before embarking on a second mortgage program, mortgage bankers have many issues to consider and important information to assimilate. Some of this information and some of these issues are outlined in Tables 17-2–17-4.

Table 17-2 Second mortgage considerations

I. Analyzing the marketplace
    A. Size of market
    B. Customer segments
        1. Realtors
        2. Builders
        3. Seller carry
    C. Working current servicing portfolio for equity loans and home improvement loans
    D. Competitors (S&Ls, finance companies, banks, retail credit firms, credit card companies, other mortgage bankers)
    E. Legal constraints
        1. State licensing laws and regulations
        2. Agencies of jurisdiction
        3. Disclosure requirements (RESPA, Truth in Lending)

II. Assessing your company
    A. Personnel considerations
        1. Present employees' abilities
        2. Employees to be hired
        3. In-house training capabilities
    B. Documentation Requirements (See Table 17-4)
    C. Risk management and underwriting
    D. Quality control and auditing
    E. Servicing considerations
    F. Dollar value and number of loans
    G. Selecting product mix

III. Marketing
   A. Budgets (advertising, publicity, training, personal selling)
   B. Objectives of marketing program
   C. Company's current marketing and underwriting philosophy

IV. Profitability
   A. Profit objective (in dollars or percentages)
   B. Growth objective (in dollars or percentages)
   C. Potential to expand customer relationships
   D. Ability to retain current customers (both realtors and investors)

Table 17-3   Second mortgage product manager's responsibilities

1. Developing a corporate policy statement, program, and policy manual.
2. Training loan originators, processors, and underwriters.
3. Coordinating with the legal department or counsel on compliance with Federal and state laws and regulations.
4. Setting up a loan marketing program
5. Establishing and monitoring a loan control and audit program.
6. Continuously adapting the firm's plan to the marketplace.
7. Assisting the servicing department.

Table 17-4   Documentation comparison

First mortgage		Second mortgage
	Application	
	Income Verification	
	Credit Report	
	Property Appraisal and Photo	
	Preliminary Title Search	
(Purchase only)	Copy of Sales contract	(Purchase Money Second) Verification of source of down payment
	Promissory Note	(FNMA/FHLMC Uniform Instrument)
	Deed of Trust/Mortgage	
	Federal Truth in Lending Disclosure	
(Refinance Only)	Notice of Right of Rescission	(If applicable)
	Lender's Escrow/Closing Instructions	

Table 17-4   Documentation comparison

First mortgage		Second mortgage
	Tax Service	Name, address, and loan number of first mortgage holder
		Loan status report from first mortgage holder
		Request for a copy of front page of insurance policy including agent's name, address and phone number, and fire insurance endorsement showing as second loss payable.
		Request for a copy of notice of default on primary loan (included in FNMA/FHLMC Uniform Instrument Mortgage/Deed of Trust)

EVOLUTION AND INNOVATION IN THE SECONDARY MORTGAGE MARKET

Ann J. Dougherty and
Donald F. Cunningham*

18

The secondary market has always played an important role in the supply of mortgage credit to homebuyers. By providing a link between mortgage originators and capital market investors, it supplements the supply of mortgage credit to borrowers by thrifts and other depository institutions. In the past, the secondary market was particularly important during periods of high interest rates when depository institutions' ability to attract deposits to finance mortgages was constrained by deposit rate ceiling. By selling mortgages into the secondary market, capital market funds were substituted for deposit funds in financing originations.

The secondary market has also been important in providing a liquid market for trading mortgages among investors, be they thrifts or capital market investors. Thrifts in the Northeast, for example, with deposit inflows that exceed mortgage credit demand, can purchase mortgages from thrifts in capital deficit areas (e.g., the West) through the secondary market.

*Ann J. Dougherty is an economist at the Federal Home Loan Mortgage Corporation and Donald F. Cunningham is an assistant professor of finance at Baylor University. The article was specifically written for this book and is reprinted with their permission. The views expressed herein are those of the authors and do not necessarily reflect those of the sponsoring agencies. The Federal Home Loan Bank, as a matter of policy, is not responsible for the private publications or statements of its employees.

Beginning in 1980, the secondary market became increasingly important as a vehicle for restructuring thrifts' portfolios and reducing the inherent risks of mortgage-related investments. The Depository Institutions and Monetary Control Act of that year and the Garn-St Germain Depository Institutions Act of 1982 virtually transformed the thrift industry from the doldrums of regulation to the dynamic but difficult competitive arena. Deregulation, coupled with the volatile level of interest rates during this period, generated the need for creative portfolio management. The secondary market responded with explosive growth.

Mortgage sellers and investors access the secondary market in a variety of ways. For example, mortgages can be brokered among investors, and dealers stand ready to buy and sell whole loans, packages of whole loans, or mortgage-backed securities (MBSs). Mortgage-backed securities, in particular, have experienced rapid growth and refinement because of the new demands placed on the secondary markets. (Figure 18-1 shows the almost exponential growth in MBSs in recent years.) GNMA IIs, adjustable rate mortgage (ARM) MBSs, SWAPs, and *collateralized mortgage obligations* are a few of the more important developments in MBSs that are discussed below.

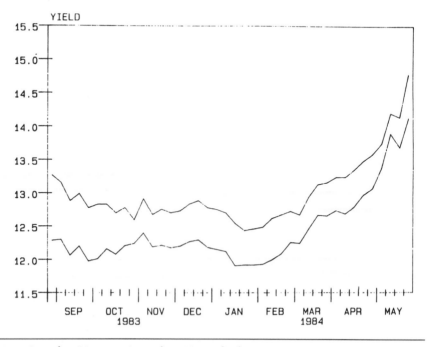

Source: *Secondary Mortgage*, September 1984, Federal Home Loan Mortgage Corp.

Figure 18-1   Yield comparison of PCS and Series A CMO

MORTGAGE-BACKED SECURITIES

A mortgage-backed security represents an investment in an underlying mortgage or pool of mortgages. Although each MBS mutation is usually relabeled with a new name, the basic product is quite similar: a security which evidences either (1) ownership (i.e., an asset sale) of an interest in a mortgage loan or pool of mortgage loans or (2) an obligation (i.e., a debt issuance) secured by a mortgage loan or pool of mortgage loans. The two types of securities are distinguishable primarily because of accounting, tax, and legal differences.

Asset sale MBSs are generally referred to as pass-through securities because their payment streams are characterized by the underlying mortgage payments that are collected and "passed-through" to investors. A straight pass-through security pays principal and interest only when collected from the borrowers. Because of the default risk inherent in mortgages, some issuers have created modified pass-through securities that provide greater repayment certainty. Investors are guaranteed to receive scheduled principal and interest payments, regardless of the actual collections received on the underlying pool. Any prepayments are passed through to investors.

Debt issuance MBSs are often referred to as pay-through or cash flow bonds because they, like the pass-through MBSs, have payment features dictated by the repayment patterns of the mortgage pool collateralizing the securities. Generally, the pay-through bond has an amortization schedule that closely tracks the scheduled collections of the collateral mortgage pool. If prepayments of principal occur on the mortgage pool, the bondholders may also receive unscheduled principal payments. However, some bond issuers have gone a step further and guaranteed specific principal prepayment schedules, in order to reduce investor's uncertainty over cash flows.

Standard Pass-Through Securities

Pass-through securities were first introduced by the Government National Mortgage Association (GNMA or Ginnie Mae) in 1970. Lenders approved by GNMA (mortgage bankers, S&Ls, etc.) form pools of FHA/VA or Farmers Home Administration mortgages and issue modified pass-through securities backed by the mortgages. They are modified pass-throughs because GNMA guarantees that investors will receive timely payment of principal and interest regardless of whether payment is received from the borrower. The GNMA guarantee is backed by the full faith and credit of the U. S. government, and as a result GNMA MBSs are in a risk class similar to U. S. Treasury obligations.

The GNMA pass-through security backed by a standard single-family fixed-rate mortgage is frequently considered the benchmark pass-through. Over $200 billion had been issued through mid-1984. The large outstanding volume, in combination with a large volume of new issues each year, make the GNMA MBS a highly marketable instrument.

There have been several new developments in GNMA pass-throughs. In 1983, GNMA II was introduced which allows multiple issuers to form jumbo pools of MBSs. GNMA I, the traditional GNMA program, allows only one issuer per pool. Multiple issuers offer several advantages over GNMA's traditional program. Small lenders can form pools faster, reducing the interest rate risk associated with loans in the pipeline. Multiple issuer pools can also lead to greater geographic diversification of mortgages within pools.

GNMA also guarantees pass-through securities backed by other types of mortgages. It guarantees pass-throughs backed by multifamily, graduated payment, and fifteen-year growing equity mortgages. All mortgages backing GNMA pass-throughs are government insured, usually by FHA/VA.

Freddie Mac has sold pass-through securities called *mortgage participation certificates* (PCs) since 1971. Unlike GNMA, Freddie Mac actually purchases the mortgages, packages them, and sells the resulting PCs to investors. PCs are modified pass-throughs in that Freddie Mac guarantees the timely payment of scheduled interest and the ultimate payment of scheduled principal to investors.

Fannie Mae began selling pass-throughs called *conventional mortgage backed securities* (CMBSs) in late 1981. Its CMBSs looks very much like Freddie Mac's PCs. The primary differences are in the guarantee (Fannie Mae guarantees timely payment of principal and interest) and the timing of cash flows collected from lenders and passed through to investors.

The sale of MBS represents an alternative financing technique for Fannie Mae. Traditionally, Fannie Mae has purchased mortgages for its own portfolio and issued debt of various maturities to finance them, in essence operating like a large S&L. Fannie Mae continues to finance the majority of its mortgage purchases this way.

Ginnie Mae, Freddie Mac, and Fannie Mae have been the dominant players in the development of the mortgage-backed securities. Recently, there has been a reemergence of private issuers. A large number of private mortgage insurance companies, bank holding companies, and financial conglomerates have either entered the secondary market conduit business, or announced plans to do so. Three of the most important are Residential Funding Corporation, a subsidiary of Norwest Mortgage, Inc., Sears Mortgage Securities Corporation, and General Electric Mortgage Securities Company, a subsidiary of General Electric Credit Corporation. All these firms issue commitments to purchase mortgages, which are pooled as insured pass-through (or pay-through) securities. Often the conduit has subsidiaries that perform all (or substantially all) the services necessary in issuing an MBS; from purchasing the mortgages to underwriting the sale.

Recently, there have been a number of regulatory and legislative initiatives to encourage further private conduits. These initiatives are aimed at reducing the costs of selling and trading private MBSs. For example, in 1983 the Department of Labor eased the requirements private pass-throughs must meet to be considered eligible investments for private pension funds. In late 1984, the Secondary Mortgage Market Enhancement Act was passed. This Act preempts state registration requirements for private pass-through securities, and eases state restrictions on the eligibility of private pass-throughs for investment by state regulated institutions. It also reduces margin requirements for dealers trading private pass-through securities. Federally related pass-through securities already enjoy similar treatment in these areas.

ARM Pass-Throughs

One of the most important stimulants to the development of new securities is the growth in alternative mortgage instruments. ARMs currently comprise two-thirds of the conventional origination market, and may prove to be an important instrument in the FHA market, given FHA's new authority to insure ARMs and GNMA's willingness to guarantee pools of these ARMs.

GNMA plans to guarantee a pass-through backed by FHA ARMs beginning in late 1984. It will be the first ARM security sold on a continuing basis. The underlying mortgages will have payments and rates that adjust annually based on movements in one-year Treasury yields. Rate caps of one percent per year, and five percent over the life of the loan, will apply.

There has been much speculation on how successful ARM pass-throughs will be. The restrictions on the rate sensitivity of the underlying mortgages could lead investors to charge premiums to hold GNMA ARM pass-throughs. More rate sensitive ARMs are being originated, but thrifts are generally holding these in portfolio in order to shorten the overall maturity of their assets. Both Freddie Mac and Fannie Mae have announced plans to issue ARM pass-throughs. However, neither has accumulated sufficient volume in one type of ARM because of the diverse nature of ARMs being originated in the primary market.

Swaps

High interest rates and the restrictions of the Federal Reserve Board's Regulation Q imposed a severe liquidity constraint on the thrift industry in 1982. In combination they effectively prevented thrift deposit accounts from competing with the newly developed money market accounts. S&Ls could only offer competitive rates on CDs with over $10,000 denominations.

S&Ls discovered an alternative to the money market accounts in the form of repurchase agreements (Repos) that could be offered in denominations as low as $1,000. Retail Repos involve the transfer of a direct obligation with the agreement to repurchase it at the end of a specified period. Because these Repos are not insured by Federal Savings and Loan Insurance Corporation (FSLIC), the FHLBB required retail Repos to be collateralized by U. S. government securities or the securities of an affiliate agency. Therefore, to be an active participant in the REPO market, an S&L would have had to liquidate a large segment of its loan portfolio and purchase government securities.

Freddie Mac's and Fannie Mae's MBSs are considered sufficiently safe to qualify as eligible collateral for retail Repos. However, unlike Ginnie Mae, Freddie Mac and Fannie Mae actually purchase mortgages daily under "cash" programs, pool them, and sell the securities through dealers. As a result, thrifts could not "securitize" their large portfolios of conventional mortgages for Repos under Freddie Mac's and Fannie Mae's standard programs without recognizing an accounting loss. Given the precarious position of thrifts' net worth during the period, this was a binding constraint.

The response of the secondary market, led by Freddie Mac, was to create the mortgage swap program that allowed S&Ls to swap new and seasoned loans for PCs backed by the exchanged pool of loans. The PCs could in turn be used as Repo (both retail and nonretail) collateral, providing the S&Ls with much needed liquidity and a method of paying depositors market rates of interest. Moreover, regulatory accounting principles did not require the recognition of losses on mortgages swapped for PCs, and if the PCs were eventually to be sold, the loss could be amortized over the expected life of the underlying mortgages rather than in a lump sum at the date of sale.

Under the deregulation initiatives of the Garn-St Germain Depository Institutions Act, S&Ls were granted the authority to offer insured money market accounts. As a result S&Ls can now compete directly with money market mutual funds and the need for retail Repos has diminished significantly. However, billions of dollars of mortgages continue to be swapped for pass-through securities. Swaps provide a low-cost alternative to lenders who wish to securitize their portfolios. As a result, lenders who want a more marketable mortgage portfolio continue to find the program attractive.

Swaps have also been used to create prototype securities. For example, Freddie Mac sold a PC backed by multifamily mortgages through a swap with American Savings and Loan Association. Currently, Freddie Mac purchases multifamily mortgages under its cash program, but either pools them with single-family loans into PCs or holds them in portfolio. Plans have been announced by both Freddie Mac and Fannie Mae to sell multifamily pass-throughs on a continuing basis through their cash program.

Collateralized Mortgage Obligations

Freddie Mac developed and brought to market a new mortgage-related security in June 1983—the collateralized mortgage obligation (CMO). The security is generally recognized as a major breakthrough in the evolution of the mortgage security market. Standard pass-through securities offer investors many advantages over holding whole mortgages. They allow investors to purchase mortgage assets without being required to service the mortgages. Modified pass-throughs provide protection against default, and eliminate the need to evaluate the underlying mortgage assets. Finally, and perhaps most importantly, pass-throughs transform relatively nonhomogeneous, illiquid mortgages into highly marketable securities. Nevertheless, investors are still confronted with an uncertain term to maturity when holding standard pass-throughs. The realized maturity of the investment depends entirely on borrowers' prepayment rates. These rates will accelerate when market rates fall below the coupon rates on the underlying mortgages, and slow when market rates rise above coupon rates. Thus not only are maturities uncertain, but they can move adversely to investor's interests.

A CMO is a pay-through security intended to increase the maturity certainty of mortgages. It is designed to partition the cash flow from the underlying mortgages among different classes of investors. It is expected to appeal to the preferences of traditional fixed income investors who have historically avoided the uncertain maturity structure of standard pass-through securities. This is particularly important given the increased role these investors are expected to play in financing home mortgages.

The Freddie Mac CMO pays cash flows semiannually (compared to monthly on PCs), and partitions the cash receipts from the underlying mortgages into different security classes. The first class is a "fast-pay" security with a short-term maturity or "tranches." All principal received from the entire mortgage pool goes to the first class until it is fully paid, thus the short maturity. Once the first class is retired, all principal goes to the second, intermediate maturity class, and so on. Finally, the last, slow-pay class is retired.

The CMO structure allows investors in mortgages to sell part of the "option" risk (i.e., the household's right to refinance) to other investors. By rebundling the cash flows, investors in the longer class and, to a lesser extent, investors in the intermediate class(es) receive greater certainty about the timing of the retirement of principal than with a standard pass-through or pay-through security. The uncertainty is passed on to investors in the first class. If prepayments accelerate (due to falling interest rates, or otherwise) the first class experiences early retirement, but the longer tranches are insulated to some extent. In effect, the rebundling of cash flows allows the CMO issuer to strip the call option from the mortgage contract and resell it to investors who are willing to incur that risk. This rebundling may allow the CMO structure to allocate risks more efficiently than a standard MBS structure.

Beyond the call protection offered by the CMO concept, Freddie Mac's CMO also differs from the PC in that it provides the investor with a guaranteed minimum repayment schedule, and an option giving the last class bondholders the right to retire their securities at par in the 25th year. These features provide greater cash flow certainty to the holders of a CMO versus a PC. They are effectively put options that reduce the penalty of slow prepayments incurred by mortgage investors in a rising rate environment. The Freddie Mac CMO also gives Freddie Mac the right to call the CMO in the 20th year.

Price premia affiliated with CMOs should equal the cost savings to individual investors vis-à-vis the cost of "homemade" methods for reallocating options risk. For example, investors can obtain call protection by restructuring their portfolios with low coupon Ginnie Mae MBSs or Freddie Mac PCs. A Freddie Mac PC with an 8 percent coupon (a Freddie Mac 8) issued in 1977 provides investors with a maturity comparable to the long tranches of the CMO. Similarly, investors can increase their call exposure by purchasing high coupon pass-through securities (e.g., GNMA 16s) with expected lives closer to the maturity of the shorter tranche CMO. Only a CMO structure that provides a more efficient or "cheaper" means of achieving a given risk distribution can explain a "richly priced" CMO package.

Figure 18-2 plots the calculated yields on the first Freddie Mac CMO and PCs sold the same day and backed by similar coupon mortgages. At the date of sale the yield spread between the two instruments appears substantial (about 100 basis points). Since the date of sale the yield spreads have diminished. Throughout September and October of 1983 the spread declined until a low of about 35 basis points occurred in late October. Subsequently the yield spread widened moderately, averaging around 50 basis points. The CMO yield has been consistently lower than the PC yield, under identical borrower prepayment assumptions. For this reason, the CMO has received high acclaim.

As of mid-1984, approximately 34 issues of CMOs have been marketed. Total volume stands at about $12 billion, of which Freddie Mac CMOs account for $2.9 billion or about one quarter.

Most non-Freddie Mac CMOs have been backed by GNMA pass-throughs in amounts that slightly exceed the face value of the bonds issued. They generally have semiannual payment schedules, although some remit interest and principal monthly. Only one other issuer besides Freddie Mac has sold CMOs with guaranteed minimum prepayment rates. CMO offerings have been divided into as many as 10 and as few as 3 tranches, sometimes with one or more segments targeted to specific investor groups. Several issuers (including Freddie Mac) have attracted retirement funds through the use of a long-term deep discount tranche on which interest accrues but is not paid until all of the shorter maturity classes have been paid in full. This "zero coupon" effect may be attractive to investors concerned about reinvestment rates. Minimum denominations of $1,000 are often set on such deep discount tranches.

In an effort to further refine the design of MBSs, changes in the tax law have been suggested that would permit the creation of a pass-through security structured like a CMO. The primary advantage of this type of MBS is that it would be classified as an asset sale by the seller and an asset purchase by the investor, rather than a debt issuance. As a result, thrifts could invest in these securities and simultaneously use them as qualifying mortgage assets for purposes of qualifying for a bad debt reserve deduction (thrifts that hold a specified percent of assets in mortgages are allowed deductions from income in the form of a bad debt reserve). This would make it one of the most appealing security designs for thrifts.

Recently, Sears Mortgage Securities Corporation sold the first pass-through security structured like a CMO. A second sale, however, was deferred by Sears

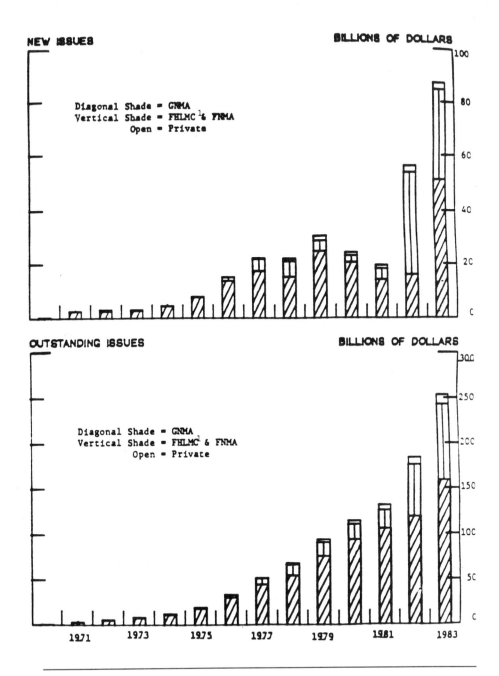

NEW ISSUES

BILLIONS OF DOLLARS

Diagonal Shade = GNMA
Vertical Shade = FHLMC[1] & FNMA
Open = Private

OUTSTANDING ISSUES

BILLIONS OF DOLLARS

Diagonal Shade = GNMA
Vertical Shade = FHLMC[1] & FNMA
Open = Private

1971   1973   1975   1977   1979   1981   1983

[1]Includes collateralized mortgage obligations.
Source: Federal Home Loan Mortgage Corp.

Figure 18-2   Issues of mortgage-backed securities

after the IRS issued proposed regulations that would have subjected the security to adverse tax treatment. Legislation to specifically allow structured pass-throughs in the form of Trusts for Investments in Mortgages (TIMs) was introduced in Congress in 1983, but never passed. Absent changes in the IRS position on legislative action, pass-throughs with structures similar to CMOs are unlikely.

Builder Bonds

Since 1979 builders and developers have utilized a new source of mortgage financing for their homebuyers. Rather than arranging the traditional block of mortgage commitments from a local lender, builders have tapped capital market investors directly. The builder issues a pay-through bond in the capital market and holds the homebuyers' mortgages as collateral. Bond issuance costs are usually less than the traditional commitment fees. Small builders may also join forces by utilizing a third party conduit to issue the bonds. The mortgage collateral is assigned to a trustee for collection, reinvestment management, and distribution of proceeds.

As with most CMOs, the issuer of builder bonds generally provides no guarantee of principal or interest payments. The investor can only look to the quality of the bond collateral for payment assurances. Often the bonds are overcollateralized or maintain a reserve fund which results in higher ratings.

Over the 1979-1983 period, the yields on GNMA pass-through MBSs have been lower than AAA rated builder bonds by a range of 50 to 135 basis points. In return for this high cost source of financing builders can capitalize on two significant advantages:

1. For tax purposes, builders can recognize the sale of properties under the installment method. Full recognition of the sales gain is deferred because income is recognized only as principal is paid down.
2. No losses are recognized on below market-rate mortgages because they are pledged as collateral rather than sold at market prices. Therefore, builders can offer buydown mortgage rates to support house prices without incurring accounting losses.

Recently, organizations have added a new twist to builder bonds by considering the possibility of "swapping" the mortgages held as collateral for federally related pass-throughs. The builder bonds would then be considered much less risky, almost akin to GNMA secured issues, resulting in much lower required yields and greater savings to builders and homebuyers. Many builders have also taken advantage of the CMO structure in issuing their bonds. CMOs issued by builders account for approximately 20 percent of all CMOs issued.

SUMMARY

Mortgage-backed securities continue to evolve with the structural changes of the housing finance system. Regulatory initiatives in particular alter the incentives of mortgage originators and investors. Lenders respond with new mortgage designs, and the secondary market reflects the response of capital market participants. In recent years this process has become increasingly dynamic as competition became the dominant market force. Growth has been explosive and security design creative, as investors have focused on the high yields but uncertain cash flow patterns of mortgage-related securities. Future developments will continue to center on the most efficient means for allocating mortgage-related risks.

Part III

DEVELOPMENTS IN DEBT, EQUITY, AND SPECULATIVE MARKET INSTRUMENTS

The growth of creative types of financial instruments has been substantial in recent years due largely to rapid changes in the economy and the desire to attract new investors. The article by Michael D. Atchison, Richard F. DeMong, and John L. Kling provides an overview of over twenty new instruments involving financial futures, options, fixed income securities, and preferred stock.

The remaining articles in this section cover the subjects of futures and options contracts in greater depth. The article by Kenneth D. Garbade and Monica M. Kaicher discusses exchange-traded options on common stock. These options have experienced remarkable growth due to their enhanced liquidity as exchange-traded instruments. They have also become important as risk-hedging as well as speculative instruments.

The article by Laurie S. Goodman discusses the "new" options market and contrasts these instruments to conventional common stock options. These new options contracts are written on stock indexes, debt instruments, foreign currencies, and gold. The new contracts take two basic forms: (1) options on actual commodities, securities, or indexes and (2) options on futures contracts.

The nature and rapid growth of exchange-traded interest rates futures is covered in the article by Marcelle Arak and Christopher J. McCurdy. These contracts are used both to hedge risk and to speculate on price movements. Futures trading includes contracts on Treasury bills, intermediate term Treasury securities, Treasury bonds, Government National Mortgage Association mortgage backed certificates, and commercial paper.

The article by K. Alec Chrystal reviews the complexities of the foreign exchange markets. The discussion includes "spot" and forward currency markets, avoidance of foreign exchange risk, and the newly emergent futures and options markets in foreign exchange.

NEW FINANCIAL INSTRUMENTS

*Michael D. Atchison, Richard F. DeMong, and John L. Kling**

19

The recent decade has witnessed a surge in the number of new financial instruments available to market participants. Increased economic uncertainty and the changes in the financial services industry account for this surge. The volatility in the financial markets during the 1970s and early 1980s was unprecedented. There have been four recessions since 1969. Interest rates climbed to historical highs, peaking no fewer than six times. The foreign currency markets experienced wide swings after exchange rates were allowed to float in 1973. Naturally, the stock market was not immune to the economic environment. After experiencing its worst one-year decline (October, 1973–October, 1974) since the Great Depression, the Dow Jones Industrial Average has fluctuated between 577.60 and 1287.20 since 1973. The period also saw the passage of the Depository Institutions Deregulation and Monetary Control Act of 1980. The Act deregulated certain aspects of the banking industry and allowed the financial markets more flexibility to adjust to the changing economic conditions.

Other reasons for changes in the traditional financial instruments included changes made to attract new investors (new markets), and to take advantage of the changes in tax laws and regulations. Further, some instruments, such as a fixed rate preferred stock issue, were no longer attractive in a period of increasing interest rates. Thus, traditional instruments had to be restructured to meet the new economic realities.

*The authors are on the faculty of the McIntire School of Commerce, University of Virginia. The research was partially funded by the Financial Analysts Research Foundation. The article was specifically written for this book and is reprinted with their permission.

This environment sent finance professionals scrambling for new ways to hedge their huge exposure to risk in the financial market place. It also encouraged companies that issue debt and equity to develop new instruments in order to find new markets. The result is a fascinating array of new financial instruments including bonds, preferred stocks, futures and options contracts. In the futures markets new contracts emerged for financial instruments, precious metals, stock market indices, and foreign currencies. In the option markets new contracts emerged for debt instruments, foreign currencies, stock market indices, and most recently, futures contracts. In the areas of fixed income securities and preferred stocks, we have seen the emergence of various adjustable rate, convertible, extendable and floating rate issues as well as "clip and strips," other innovative bonds and similarly adjustable preferred stock. In the remainder of this article we discuss all of these different instruments and give some examples of their uses.

FINANCIAL FUTURES CONTRACTS

The category of contracts known as financial futures includes contracts on financial instruments, precious monetary metals, stock indices, and foreign currencies. These contracts are merely agreements between two parties for the deferred delivery of, say, Treasury bills, gold, or British pounds. The first financial futures contracts, contracts for foreign currencies, were introduced by the Chicago Mercantile Exchange in 1972. Since then, the yearly volume of trading in financial futures has risen to over 25 percent of all futures contracts traded. The following sections describe and demonstrate uses of (1) contracts on debt and deposit instruments, (2) contracts on monetary metals, (3) contracts on currencies, and (4) contracts on stock market indices. Since different exchanges trade contracts for the same commodity or instrument, we will limit our descriptions to the contract traded on the primary (major) exchange.

Before we consider these particular contracts, it may be helpful to explain briefly the general concept of futures contracts. A futures contract is a commitment to make or take delivery, at a designated time in the future, of a specified quantity and quality of a commodity or financial instrument, at a price established through open outcry in a central, regulated marketplace. All of the futures exchanges in the U. S. are regulated by the Commodity Futures Trading Commission (CFTC), as well as by governing bodies elected by the membership of the exchange.

Since futures contracts are standardized, they allow ease of quotation and trading. Contract price is determined on an exchange trading floor and fluctuates daily as economic conditions change. (Note that the exchanges set minimum and maximum daily price fluctuations for various contracts, so as to maintain an orderly market.) A buyer who has agreed to take future physical delivery is said to be "long" and will profit by an increase in the price of the underlying commodity or financial instrument. Similarly, a seller who has agreed to make future delivery is said to be "short" and will profit by a price decline. Also, a trader who has a long (short) position in the actual commodity and a short (long) position in the associated futures contract is said to be hedged, since the profit on one position tends to offset the loss on the other. The buyer or seller may liquidate his/her contract by simply making an equal and opposite transaction for a contract of the same delivery month. Since the volume of trading for most contracts is large, market participants can enter and exit from positions without difficulty. It is worth noting that 95 percent of all contracts are closed before the last trading day of the delivery month.

The concept of margin in the futures market is considerably different from that of the stock and bond markets. Margin in the futures market must be paid by both parties to the contract and merely serves as a good faith deposit to ensure contract performance. It is not a partial payment as in the stock and bond markets. The initial minimum margin for a contract position is set by the exchange on which the contract is traded. However, individual brokerage firms may require a higher initial margin. Initial margin is quite low as a percent of the value of the underlying commodity (typically from one to ten percent). This high degree of leverage is the main reason for the extreme risk inherent in futures trading. At the end of each trading session each trader's account is "marked-to-market"—debited or credited to reflect the most recent settlement price. If the account value drops below a fixed maintenance level, the trader must deposit additional margin. Similarly, if the account value increases above the maintenance level, the trader may withdraw the excess in the form of cash profits.

Futures Contracts on Debt and Deposit Instruments

This category consists of futures contracts on the following six instruments: (1) U. S. Treasury bonds, (2) U. S. Treasury notes, (3) U. S. Treasury bills, (4) GNMA Collateralized Depository Receipts, (5) domestic Certificates of Deposit, and (6) three-month Eurodollar Time Deposits. Depending on the contract, delivery calls for instruments with face values from $100,000 to $1,000,000. Bankers, bond dealers, portfolio managers, corporate treasurers, pension fund managers, mortgage bankers, arbitrageurs, and speculators are all potential users of these contracts. These agents can use the contracts to: lock in yields on future purchases and sales; protect the value of portfolios; hedge corporate borrowing costs; profit from price differentials (arbitrage); hedge rate fluctuations in other financial instruments; and speculate with risk capital. For example, suppose a mortgage banker is making commitments for $1 million of FHA/VA mortgages to package into a GNMA certificate for sale in two months. The current price for a GNMA with 14 percent coupon is 94.16 ($945,000). Fearing a rise in interest rates in the next two months, the mortgage banker immediately sells fourteen GNMA futures contracts at 64.30 (dollar value of

$909,125). Two months later the yields on GNMAs are 14.50 percent. The GNMA certificate is sold at a price of 86.03 ($860,937) and the futures position is closed at a price of 58.30 (dollar value of $825,125). The gain on the futures position of $84,000 almost totally offsets the loss of $84,063 from the delayed sale of the GNMA certificate.

Futures Contracts on Monetary Metals

Futures contracts trade for the delivery of 100 troy ounces of gold and 5,000 troy ounces of silver. Arbitrageurs and speculators use the contracts to capitalize on price discrepancies and expected price movements. These contracts are also used by mining companies, jewelry manufacturers, electronic component manufacturers, and metal refiners to hedge against price changes. For instance, consider the following example. At the end of June, a jewelry manufacturer anticipates strong sales for the following December. However, gold for production (300 ounces) will not be needed until early October. Gold is currently selling for $364 per ounce, but is expected to be much higher by October. The company sells three contracts of November gold futures at $368 per ounce to hedge against the expected price increase. On October 1 the company closes the futures position at $392 per ounce and buys 300 ounces of gold at $389. The gain of $7,200 on the futures position offsets most of the increased cost of acquiring the gold ($7,500).

Futures Contracts on Foreign Currencies

There are currently eight futures contracts calling for delivery of the following quantities of foreign currencies: 25,000 British pounds, 100,000 Canadian dollars, 125,000 German Deutsche marks, 125,000 Dutch guilders, 250,000 French francs, 12,500,000 Japanese yen, 1,000,000 Mexican pesos, 125,000 Swiss francs. These contracts are used by arbitrageurs, speculators, international bankers, and treasurers of international corporations for the purpose of profiting from exchange rate changes and hedging risk exposure from international transactions. For example, suppose a U. S. importer has contracted to buy, five months from now, a shipment of Canadian-made coats for 500,000 Canadian dollars. Since the spot price for Canadian dollars is currently $.8095, the U. S. dollar cost of the shipment is $404,750. At this cost the importer can make a good profit, but he fears that the Canadian dollar will strengthen in the next five months. To lock in his potential profit, the importer buys five Canadian dollar futures contracts at a price of $.8045. Five months later, when the importer pays for the coats, the spot price for Canadian dollars is $.8103, while the price at which he has closed the futures position is $.8110. The increase in the shipment cost of $400 U. S. is more than offset by the futures position gain of $3,250 U. S.

Futures Contracts on Stock Market Indices

Currently, four stock index futures contracts are available, each based on a different index: the S&P 500, the S&P 100, the NYSE Composite, and the Value Line. Unlike traditional futures contracts, the settlement of index futures at maturity is by cash payment: profits and losses are credited and debited to the accounts of the position holders. The underlying value of the S&P 100 contract is equal to $200 times the S&P 100 index, while the value of the other three contracts is $500 times the respective indices.

Investors and portfolio managers can use these contracts to hedge against future declines in portfolios, and corporate treasurers can use them to protect against price decreases prior to a new issue of the corporation's stock. Speculators can also benefit from anticipated price moves. For example, consider a trader who expects the market to rise and buys one NYSE index futures contract at 80.25. If three months later he closes the contract at 84.50, his profit is $2,125. For an initial margin of $5,000, this represents an annualized return of 170 percent.

OPTION CONTRACTS ON DEBT INSTRUMENTS, FOREIGN CURRENCIES, STOCK MARKET INDICES, AND FUTURES CONTRACTS

Option contracts have existed in one form or another for hundreds of years, but only recently have contracts on financial instruments been traded on organized, federally regulated exchanges. In 1973, the Chicago Board Options Exchange became the first centralized exchange for the trading of stock options. Since then three additional exchanges (the American Stock Exchange, the Philadelphia Stock Exchange, and the Pacific Stock Exchange) have begun trading stock options, and the volume of trading has increased by over 2,000 percent. The success of stock options led to the introduction in 1982 and 1983 of exchange traded options on interest-bearing securities, stock indices, foreign currencies, and futures contracts. This section describes these most recent option contracts and give examples of their uses. The general concept of exchange traded (also known as listed) options is discussed to acquaint the reader with the terminology necessary for an understanding of their characteristics.

An option is simply an agreement between two parties, a buyer and a seller, which gives the buyer the right, through *exercise* of the option, to require the seller (or *writer*) to perform certain obligations which are specified under the contract. For example, a listed call option for common stock gives the buyer the right, but not the obligation, to purchase 100 shares of the stock during a stated period of time at a stipulated price. If the buyer decides to exercise his option to purchase, the seller is obligated to deliver the 100 shares of stock at the agreed upon price. The main difference between an option and a futures contract is that the seller of a futures contract is obligated to make delivery if the contract is held to maturity. However, the seller of an option is obligated to make delivery at any time up to expiration, but only if the buyer exercises his right. An option which is left unexercised expires worthless after a stated period of time.

Following is a list of terms needed to describe and explain the various option contracts.

1. The price of an option is called its *premium*.
2. The price of the underlying asset at which the option can be exercised is referred to as the *strike price*.
3. The last day upon which an option can be exercised is known as its *expiration date*.
4. An option which gives the buyer the right to purchase some asset at the stated strike price on or before the expiration date is known as a *call option*.
5. An option which gives the buyer the right to sell some asset at the stated strike price on or before the expiration date is known as a *put option*.
6. The amount by which the underlying asset's price is above the option's strike price, in the case of a call, or below the strike price, in the case of a put, is referred to as the option's *intrinsic value*.
7. An option without intrinsic value is *out-of-the-money*.
8. When the underlying asset's price is the same as the strike price, the option is *at-the-money*.

Given these terms, an option contract is uniquely characterized by four specifications: (1) its underlying asset; (2) its expiration date; (3) the strike price at which it may be exercised; and (4) whether the contract is a put or a call.

The mechanics of trading options are very similar to those of trading futures. Unlike futures, though, margin does not apply to the purchase of an option. Option purchases must be paid for in full. The sale of an option, however, does often require a margin deposit. As with futures, margin represents a surety bond and not a partial payment. Minimum margin requirements are set by the exchanges, the Federal Reserve Board, and other regulatory organizations, depending on the specific contract. Trading in the options contracts is regulated by the Securities and Exchange Commission, with the exception of options on futures contracts, which are regulated by the Commodity Futures Trading Commission.

Option Contracts on Debt Instruments

These are contracts which give the buyer the right to buy (call) or sell (put) a specific issue of Treasury bonds, Treasury bills, or Treasury notes. The Treasury bond contract is for a $100,000 principal amount, the Treasury bill contract for $200,000, while the Treasury note contract is for a $20,000 principal amount. The exchanges select a new Treasury issue for options trading, and the options are introduced shortly after the issue is auctioned by the Treasury.

These options can be used for protection against declines in bond portfolios or rate protection by corporations on prospective bond issues; for writing calls against holdings of bonds or notes; for "locking in" rates of return on funds that will soon become available; or for speculating on anticipated interest rate changes. Consider a corporate treasurer who is in need of cash and is forced to sell a 10 3/8 percent Treasury bond at 99.14, even though he anticipated that interest rates would fall. In order to participate in the possible rate decline, the treasurer can simultaneously purchase a March Treasury bond call with a striking price of 96 and a premium of, say, 3.30 ($3,937.50). If interest rates decline, the treasurer can make a substantial profit; but if interest rates rise, the maximum loss is the premium of $3,939.50.

Option Contracts on Foreign Currencies

These options give the holder the right to buy (for a call) or sell (for a put) a prespecified quantity of a certain foreign currency. Currently, the authorized units of trading for foreign currency options are: 12,500 British pounds, 50,000 Canadian dollars, 62,500 Deutsche marks, 6,250,000 Japanese yen, and 62,500 Swiss francs. The contracts can be used for the following purposes: hedging against foreign exchange risk for importers and exporters; controlling costs of foreign capital investment or borrowing; protecting the value of foreign dividends; hedging against foreign inflation; and hedging against balance sheet risk due to foreign subsidiaries. Following is an example of use by an exporter. An American firm exporting computers to West Germany is to be paid in Deutsche marks in late February. Deutsche marks are currently trading in the cash market for $.40. To hedge against a possible decline in the Deutsche mark (strengthening in the U. S. dollar), the exporter buys Deutsche marks with a strike price of 40. Thus, when the computers are sold, the exporter can be assured of receiving $.40/Deutsche mark, even if the American dollar has strengthened.

Option Contracts on Stock Market Indices

Index options are very similar to the options on debt instruments and currency, with one significant difference. When an index option is exercised, settlement is by payment of cash, not by delivery of an underlying instrument. The assigned writer must pay the holder cash in an amount equal to the difference between the closing level of the index on the exercise date and the striking price of the option, multiplied by $100. The indices for which options are currently traded are: S&P 500, S&P 100, NYSE Composite, AMEX Major Market, AMEX Market Value, S&P International Oils, S&P Computer and

Business Equipment, AMEX Computer Technology, AMEX Oil and Gas, Philadelphia Exchange Gaming and Hotel, Philadelphia Exchange Gold and Silver, and Pacific Exchange Technology.

These options can be used by speculators, investors, arbitrageurs, portfolio managers, pension fund managers, and corporate treasurers. Consider an investor who owns a well diversified portfolio of common stock worth $54,000. In June, he expects a short-term market decline, but wishes to hold his stocks for long-term potential. The NYSE Composite Index is currently 90.00 and the August 90 put is trading for 1 1/2. The investor buys six August 90 puts for $900. A month later the NYSE Composite Index is 85.50 and the investor sells the puts for a premium of five each. His profit of $2,100 ($3,000 − $900) at least partially offsets the decline in his portfolio value.

Option Contracts on Futures Contracts

Recently, exchanges have introduced contracts which give the holder of a call (put) the right to buy (sell) one specified futures contract at the predetermined striking price. Actually, when a contract is exercised, the exchange's clearing corporation assigns the call (put) buyer a long (short) position in the futures contract, and the call (put) writer a short (long) position in the futures contract. Futures contracts for which options currently trade are for: world sugar, gold, Treasury bonds, S&P 500, NYSE Composite, and West German marks.

These contracts can be used in the following ways: speculation on market direction; writing covered or uncovered options to earn premiums; insurance against loss on a futures position fron unanticipated market changes; locking in profits on futures position; hedging, but without having to make additional margin deposits. Consider the following example of speculative use. A speculator bought an October sugar futures contract at 11¢, and the price has since increased to 14¢ (a gain of $3,360). In order to lock in this gain, the speculator buys the October 14 put for a premium of .5 (a price of $560). If the futures price increased to 16¢ (as the speculator believes), the unrealized profit on the position would be $5,040 ($5,600 − $560). However, if prices declined, the put position would guarantee that the speculator's unrealized profit would be no less than $2,800 ($3,360 − $560).

FIXED INCOME INSTRUMENTS

The volatility of the financial markets caused fixed income securities (such as notes and bonds) to be less attractive. Their prices dropped as interest rates rose. Investors eschewed new investments without some protection for reinvestment and price risk. Reinvestment risk is the risk that the funds (such as interest payments) received during the life of the note or bond cannot be reinvested at the same rate as the original instrument. Price risk is the risk that the funds received from the investment will not be worth as much when received as when invested. Falling interest rates increase the reinvestment risk and rising inflation increases the price risk. Investors demanded some protection against these risks. The issuers responded by developing new instruments that have adjustable rates, or optional maturities. In addition, the issuers developed new instruments, such as the subordinated capital notes, that would meet the requirements of regulators.

Subordinated Capital Notes

Subordinated capital notes are issued mainly by commercial banks. These notes meet the criteria for capital of the Federal Deposit Insurance Corporation (FDIC), the Office of the Comptroller of the Currency, and the Federal Reserve Board, all of which have capital adequacy requirements. Currently, regional banks are required to have at least five percent of their total assets in primary capital, which consists of common stock, perpetual preferred stock, capital surplus, undivided profits, reserves for contingencies and other capital reserves, mandatory convertible instruments such as subordinated capital notes, and allowance for possible loan losses. Subordinated capital notes are those which have principal payments made with common stock, preferred stock, or other capital securities which are considered primary capital. The market value of the primary capital securities is equal to the maturity value of the notes. These notes are a way of selling future equity. Because they must be paid off with equity securities or primary capital, they are mandatory convertible instruments themselves which qualify as primary capital. This allows commercial banks to increase the primary capital ratio and at the same time keep the benefits of debt.

Adjustable Rate Convertible Notes

Adjustable Rate Convertible Notes (ARCN) are other new instruments classified more like equity issues than debt issues. Firms that want the advantages of debt but not the impact on their debt ratio issue ARCNs, which are notes sold at par, but redeemable at substantially less than par. These notes are convertible into common stock and the conversion ratio is based on the par value. The interest rate is pegged to the dividend rate on the issuer's common stock. For example, a firm may issue an ARCN at a par of $1,000, redeemable at $500, and convertible into 50 shares of common stock. This particular note would be booked as $500 debt and $500 equity, and the total interest payment deducted for income taxes. The issuer likes such an instrument because the debt ratio is affected less than if 100 percent debt were issued, yet the issuer still gets to deduct all of the interest. Investors like such instruments because their principal is partially protected by their conversion feature and has the higher bankruptcy claim on debt. Also, the investor participates in the growth of added earnings with the conversion feature. Even though this instrument is advantageous to both the issuer and the investor, there is some question as to whether or not the IRS will allow the tax deductibility of interest. If there is an adverse ruling, the issuer's incentive for ARCNs would diminish.

Extendable Notes and Floating Rate Extendable Notes

Extendable (also spelled extendible) notes are more flexible than traditional notes because investors can elect to have these redeemed on several predetermined dates. A typical note has a final maturity date but is repayable at three-year intervals at the option of the holder. For example, a note maturing on July 15, 1996, is repayable on July 15, 1987, 1990, and 1993, at the option of the holder, at 100 percent of the principal amount. The interest rate is indexed to some other instrument, usually a Treasury security, on the repayment date. With the extendable option, the investor has purchased a series of puts on the notes. In other words, the issuing corporation has agreed to buy back the notes at a specified price on several specified dates in the future. The investor must place a value on both the note and the puts.

Floating rate extendable notes are the same as extendable notes except that the interest rate is adjusted more often. This adjustment is made at intervals of six months or less and the rate is usually pegged to a U. S. Treasury security. Because they contain this floating rate provision, these notes are even more flexible than extendable notes, because they behave more like short-term securities.

Controlled Commercial Paper

Controlled commercial paper refers to a process by which someone with questionable credit can issue high quality commercial paper, which, of course, is more marketable for both the issuer and the investor. An issuer achieves a higher rating by setting up an independent company to issue commercial paper. This independent company uses the proceeds from the paper to buy receivables from the "true issuer." As the receivables are liquidated, the commercial paper is paid off. The high rating is warranted because the issue is backed by a line of credit from a commercial bank and by an insurance policy. Since the issue is made by an independent company without any other debt and backed by a line of credit and an insurance policy, the rates are low; however, fees on the line of credit and the insurance offset some of these savings.

Floating Rate Negotiable Certificates of Deposit

Floating rate negotiable certificates of deposits are the same as negotiable CDs except that the rates are pegged to an index. The one most commonly used is the U. S. Treasury bill rate, but the prime rate, the LIBOR (London Interbank Offered Rate), and the 30-day commercial paper rate have also been used. The floating rate provision offers the investor interest rate protection since the rates fluctuate with the market.

Clip and Strips

The clip and strip is a new instrument designed to tap new investment markets. An investment banker or brokerage house creates a clip and strip by purchasing an outstanding bond issue and formulating an instrument that will mature on a series of dates which correspond to ~~the underlying bond's annual interest dates and~~ the underlying bond's annual interest dates and maturity date. Clip and strips in which the underlying security is a Treasury note or bond are the most common. Depending on the investment banker, one of the following names is used: ETRs, CATs, TIGRs, COUGARS, or Treasury Bond Receipts. An investment banker will buy up an outstanding issue of a Treasury bond and place the bonds in trust. The banker will then issue a series of Treasury bond receipts sold at a discount and maturing either on the same dates as the underlying coupon payments (coupon Treasury bond receipts) or the underlying maturity date (principal Treasury bond receipts). The resulting instrument is the same as a zero coupon bond and has very little reinvestment risk. Because it is backed by Treasury securities and is low-risk, this instrument lends itself to IRAs and other tax deferred accounts with specific time horizons that can be matched with the maturity of the Treasury bond receipts.

Collateralized Mortgage Obligation Bonds

A CMO, which is likewise designed to attract new investment funds, is a bond backed by a fund of mortgage securities (Ginnie Mae participation certificates, mortgage backed securities, and mortgages) with semi-annual interest payments. These bonds usually comprise several classes—A, B, C and D—which designate which bonds will be paid first and which will receive interest. Interest may be paid to classes A, B, and C but not to Class D. Instead, interest will accrue to Class D bonds, and this accrual will be added to their principal. Principal payments are made in accordance with the principal payments and prepayments of the underlying mortgages. As these are paid, principal is paid to the classes according to maturity. For example, principal payments will go to Class A holders until completely paid, then Class B until paid, then Class C. Class D is the last to be paid and is very similar to a zero-coupon bond in that no interim payments are made until the other classes are completely retired. The fast pay classes, A, B, and C, are subject to reinvestment risk and some price risk while Class D is subject only to price risk. The yields on each class are priced to meet the market's required return for that expected maturity.

The advantage of a CMO over other mortgage securities is that the CMO has more maturities.

Monthly Amortizing Notes

A monthly amortizing note is a note with level principal and interest payments throughout its life. It is similar to a term loan from a commercial bank except that the funds come from the general public and thus its capital pool is larger. The investor receives level, monthly interest and principal payments. This instrument will have high reinvestment risk, but a lower price risk than a note that pays the principal at maturity since the principal is received over the term of the note.

NEW PREFERRED STOCK

Preferred stock changes have been made primarily to enhance marketability. As a result of the increased fluctuations in the financial markets, traditional preferred stock has had decreased liquidity and depressed prices. The fixed rate of dividend payments is undesirable to the potential investor in periods of increasing market rates. Thus, the fixed rate long-term preferred stock had little investor demand. Issuers were forced to find alternative ways to raise funds by designing new, more attractive instruments. The adjustable rate preferred stock is an instrument that is more flexible than the traditional preferred stock.

Adjustable Rate Preferred

Adjustable Rate Preferred Stock (ARP) is preferred stock with a dividend rate that is pegged to an underlying index rate. It is more marketable than a fixed rate preferred stock because it adjusts to changes in the investment climate. Most commonly the index used is the highest of the following rates: Treasury bill rate, the ten-year constant maturity rate, or the twenty-year constant maturity rate. The rate is stated as a certain number of basis points above or below the index. For example, the rate may be stated as 50 basis points below the highest of three indices of the Treasury bill rate, the ten-year constant maturity rate, or the twenty-year constant maturity rate, which are published by the Federal Reserve Board. It is not uncommon for ARPs to be pegged below Treasury rates, which may appear to be incongruous with risk, but with the 85 percent dividend exclusion, the after-tax yields are greater than the after-tax Treasury yields. The rate is determined for each quarterly dividend period. The index rate is usually the average of the two most recent weekly per annum rates, as published weekly by the Federal Reserve Board, immediately prior to the last ten calendar days of the dividend period. The adjustable rate preferred stock has less price risk than straight preferred stock of a company with similar risks, thus satisfying an investing corporation's desire to maintain principal (capital).

Convertible Adjustable Rate Preferred

Convertible adjustable rate preferred is an ARP with a convertible provision, convertible at the option of the purchaser to a specified number of common shares per each ARP. As in a conventional ARP, the rate is adjusted per an index, typically an index of U. S. Treasury bills. For example, a convertible ARP might be four percentage points less than the Treasury bill rate. This rate is usually lower than conventional ARPs. The issuer benefits from lower rates, as well as from the flexibility to issue common when and if it desires. If the current common price is undervalued, the issuer may consider convertible ARPs. The purchaser thus gets both the benefits of ARPs and convertible provisions.

The convertible adjustable rate preferred has less price risk than a straight preferred stock but greater return potential than an adjustable rate preferred stock. Convertible ARPs give the purchaser the 85 percent dividend exclusion, and principal protection through the convertible provision.

Multiple Adjustable Rate Preferred

The multiple adjustable rate preferred stock's dividend rate fluctuates with the highest index (like the adjustable preferred stock) and its own price. The issuer will reduce the dividend rate if the price of the multiple adjustable rate preferred stock exceeds a specified price. If the price drops below some point then the issuer will increase the dividend rate. For example, the stock is issued at $50. The dividend rate is established the same as other ARPs; however, if the price goes to $55 or more, then one percent is subtracted from the rate. If the price goes to $45 or less, then one percent is added to the dividend rate. The multiple adjustable rate preferred stocks are designed to maintain price and attract corporate investors, since the dividends are eligible for the 85 percent dividend exclusion.

Price Adjusted Rate Preferred Stock

Price adjusted rate preferred stock is similar to multiple adjustable rate preferred in that both are attempting to maintain price by adjusting the dividend rate to the highest index and its own price. However, with price adjusted preferred stock, the issuer reduces the dividend rate by a formula that includes the original price divided by the current price. So if the price adjustable preferred stock has dropped, then the dividend rate will automatically be increased. The opposite would automatically happen if the price rose. The difference between the price adjusted rate preferred stock and the multiple adjustable rate preferred stock is that the former uses a sliding scale and the latter uses a fixed adjustment. For example, stock is issued at $100. The dividend rate is established the same as other ARPs. The dividend rate is then multiplied by an applicable percentage, which is the applicable percentage of the previous dividend period times $100, divided by the current market price of the stock.

Convertible Exchangeable Preferred

Convertible exchangeable preferred is preferred stock with both a convertible and an exchangeable provision. At the option of the purchaser the stock is convertible into a specified number of shares of the issuer's common stock. The stock is also exchangeable at the option of the issuer into debentures.

The convertible provision gives the purchaser protection of the principal, and a chance to participate in increased stock prices. The exchangeable provision gives the issuer capital structure flexibility. For example, the preferred stock may be convertible at the option of the holder into common stock at the rate of one and one-half shares of common stock for each share of preferred stock, and the preferred stock is exchangeable in entirety at the option only of the corporation on any dividend date for the corporation's 9 3/4 percent convertible subordinated debentures due December 15, 2012.

SUMMARY

The rapid changes in the economy, such as the increased volatility of interest rates and stock prices, and the continued evolution of the financial services industry have caused a plethora of new financial instruments. As long as there are tax and regulation changes we expect to see this trend of new financial instruments to continue even if the economy stabilizes.

EXCHANGE-TRADED OPTIONS ON COMMON STOCK*

Kenneth D. Garbade and
Monica M. Kaicher

20

No financial instrument has aroused the enthusiasm of speculators, hedgers, and arbitrageurs—and the concern of regulatory authorities—as quickly and completely as exchange-traded stock options following their introduction in 1973 by the Chicago Board Options Exchange (CBOE). Market participants and informed observers have argued variously that options offer opportunities for speculative profits and for hedging or reducing risk, that options provide strong incentives for the manipulation of stock prices and the defrauding of investors, and that options may ultimately be the cause of a collapse comparable in magnitude to the great crash of 1929.

The explosive popularity of stock options is evident from the growth in trading volume from under 6 million call option contracts in 1974 to almost 39 million contracts in the first nine months of 1978.[1] When the CBOE first opened for business, it sponsored trading in call options of sixteen common stock issues. By the fall of 1978, four additional exchanges were sponsoring trading in options, including the American Stock Exchange, the Philadelphia Stock Exchange, the Midwest Stock Exchange, and the Pacific Stock Exchange. The five options exchanges presently sponsor trading in call options on about 220 stock issues and put options on 25 of those issues.

*Reprinted, with deletions, from the *Quarterly Review*, Winter 1978–79, pp. 26–40, with permission of the Federal Reserve Bank of New York.

[1]Exchange-traded options are traded as contracts for the purchase or sale of one round lot of stock which is 100 shares.

257

The concern of regulatory authorities with this remarkable growth became evident during the summer of 1977, when the Securities and Exchange Commission (SEC) declared an informal moratorium on additions to the list of stocks on which exchange-trade option contracts may be written. In the fall of 1977, the SEC formalized that moratorium and began an extensive study of the options market. Among the major questions being examined in that study are the adequacy of self-regulation by the options exchanges, the financial integrity of the options markets, practices in selling options to individual investors, and the relation between trading in stocks and options on those stocks.

CONTRACTUAL ASPECTS OF STOCK OPTIONS

A stock option is a contract, granting to the holder specified rights which can be exercised against the writer of the contract. There are two basic types of option contracts: puts and calls. Under the most common form of call option, the holder can purchase from the writer of the option some number of shares of a specified stock (called the *underlying stock*) at a designated *strike price* on or before an *expiration date*. Thus, an investor may hold a call option for the purchase of 100 shares of International Business Machine (IBM) stock at a strike price of $260 per share which can be exercised on or before April 21, 1979.[2]

Should the holder of a call option choose to exercise the contract rights, the holder tenders to the option writer funds sufficient to complete the purchase. If an option holder does not exercise the right to purchase on or before the expiration date, all obligations of the writer terminate and the option *expires*.

A put option is a right to sell stock. Under the most common form of put option, a holder can sell a specified number of shares of some underlying stock to the writer of the put contract, on or before an expiration date, at a designated strike price. If an option holder decides to exercise the put option, the underlying shares are tendered to the option writer. The right to sell the stock terminates after the expiration date.

---

[2]The concepts discussed in this article are illustrated with options on IBM common stock. IBM stock is widely owned and familiar to many investors, and both the stock and the options are actively traded. On December 19, 1978, IBM announced a four-for-one stock split, to take effect on or after May 10, 1979. Following the effective date of the split, each previously outstanding exchange-traded option contract for 100 shares of IBM stock will become four contracts for 100 shares each, with strike prices equal to one quarter of the original strike prices. For example, the holder of one call option contract for 100 shares at $260 per share will become the holder of four call option contracts for 100 shares each at $65 per share. The stock split will have no impact on the economic position of either writers or holders of IBM options. The stock split will also not affect any of the illustrative examples given below, since all of those examples involve options which expire on or before April 21, 1979.

Why An Option Has Value

An option will have value if a holder can profit by exercising immediately the contract rights, or if the holder thinks profits may be obtained by exercising the rights on or before the expiration date of the option.[3] If IBM stock is trading at, say, $293.50 a share, then an option to purchase IBM at a price of $240 per share is clearly a valuable right. An option to purchase IBM at $300 per share is also valuable if there is a possibility that the price of IBM stock will go over $300 before the expiration date of the option.

Tables 20-1 and 20-2 show an array of values on twelve different IBM put and call options as reflected in the closing prices on the CBOE on Friday, September 1, 1978. Table 20-1 shows that the price of a call option decreases as the strike price of the option increases. An option to purchase IBM at a price of $260 per share, for example, is more valuable than a call option with the same expiration date and a strike price of $280. Table 20-1 also shows that the price of an option increases with the futurity of the option. An option to purchase IBM stock on or before April 21, 1979 confers on the holder more rights than an option which expires on January 20, 1979. It follows that call options with more distant expiration dates will have higher prices, everything else being the same. Table 20-2 shows that the value of a put option increases with the strike price (since puts are rights to sell, a higher strike price implies a more valuable option) and increases with the futurity of the expiration date of the option.

Table 20-1 Closing prices of IBM call options on September 1, 1978*
(In dollars; per share optioned)

Strike price	Expiration date		
	October 21 1978	January 20 1979	April 21 1979
240	56.00	58.75	62.00
260	38.00	41.00	45.75
280	20.63	26.75	32.38
300	8.63	15.13	20.00

*International Business Machines stock closed at $293.50 a share on the New York Stock Exchange on September 1, 1978.

[3]It is noted in an appendix to this article that, under one theory of option pricing, the price of an option is equal to the discounted present value of the price the option is expected to have on its expiration date.

Table 20-2   Closing prices of IBM put options on September 1, 1978*
(In dollars; per share optioned)

| | Expiration date | | |
| | October 21 1978 | January 20 1979 | April 21 1979 |
Strike price			
240	.07	1.19	2.88
260	.56	3.75	8.50
280	3.63	9.00	11.63
300	11.63	17.00	20.25

*International Business Machines stock closed at $293.50 a share on the New York Stock Exchange on September 1, 1978.

EXCHANGE MARKETS FOR STOCK OPTIONS

Until 1973, stock options were bought and sold in the over-the-counter (OTC) market. In practice, a secondary market sale of an unexpired OTC option was rare. Most of the business consisted of buying options and holding them to expiration, at which time they were either exercised or allowed to expire. The strike price on an OTC option was generally set at the contemporaneous price of the underlying stock, and the expiration date was most often set at one, two, three, or six months in the future. At any point in time there typically existed a wide variety of options on a given stock, with little uniformity of either strike prices or expiration dates among different options.

The innovation in 1973 by the CBOE of an organized market for options revolutionized trading in those securities. Perhaps the single most important CBOE innovation was the standardization of option strike prices and expiration dates.

Looking again at Table 20-1, note that there were only twelve call option contracts in IBM available for trading on the CBOE on September 1, 1978. There are only four potential expiration dates for IBM options each year: the Saturday following the third Friday in January, April, July, and October.[4] Only the three nearest dates are open for trading at any one time.

Strike prices on exchange-traded options are initially selected to bracket the price of the underlying stock. Strike prices are set in intervals of $5 for stocks priced below $50, in intervals of $10 for stocks priced between $50 and $200, and in intervals of $20 for stocks priced over $200. Trading in a new

[4]This is called the January-April-July-October expiration cycle. Other options may have the same expiration cycle, or may have a February-May-August-November cycle or a March-June-September-December cycle.

strike price will be opened if the price of the underlying stock moves at least halfway through the interval bounded by the new strike price. For example, if there are options with strike prices of $80 and $90, the underlying stock must trade at or above $95 a share before trading is opened in options with a $200 strike price.

The standardization of contract terms and the limitation of the number of different contracts available for trading is a deliberate policy decision of the options exchanges. Standardization of the terms of put and call options means that trading is concentrated in a small number of contracts rather than spread out over tens or hundreds of different contracts, as was the case prior to 1973. This has resulted in more liquid markets and has facilitated trading in options.

Purchase and Sale of Exchange-Traded Options

Most investors are familiar with the mechanics of trading stock on an exchange like the New York Stock Exchange (NYSE). Brokers representing the buyer and seller meet on the Exchange's floor and agree to a mutually acceptable transaction price.[5] The seller delivers the stock to the broker, who redelivers the stock to the buyer's broker, who in turn sends it to the ultimate buyer. Payment for the stock follows the reverse path. Transactions in exchange-traded options *do not* occur the same way.

Suppose one investor wants to sell a single IBM April 280 call option contract, *i.e.*, a call option on 100 shares of IBM stock with a strike price of $280 per share and an expiration date of April 21, 1979, and a second investor wants to buy the same option. As in the case of stock trading, brokers representing the two investors will meet on the floor of the CBOE and agree to a mutually acceptable transaction price. The transaction will not, however, be completed by the delivery of a call option contract written by the seller to the buyer.

Transactions in exchange-traded stock options result in the establishment of a series of contractual relationships. Following the agreement of the two brokers in the example to a transaction price on the IBM April 280 calls, the broker representing the *seller* will give a call option contract to an organization known as The Options Clearing Corporation (OCC), agreeing to deliver 100 shares of IBM stock upon payment of $280 per share before the April expiration date. The OCC in turn gives an identical call option contract to the broker representing the *buyer* of the option. The buyer has a right to demand 100 shares of IBM stock from its broker upon payment of the strike price, and the seller's broker has a similar right to demand stock from the seller. Funds from the ultimate buyer reach the ultimate seller through the OCC and the transactors' brokers.

---

[5]The mechanics of trading stock on an exchange is discussed more completely in William Melton, "Corporate Equities and the National Market System."

The significance of these contractual relations is that the option contract does not run directly from the seller's broker to the buyer's broker, but rather runs *through* the OCC. The OCC is a contractual intermediary in all exchange-traded stock options.[6]

The importance of the OCC stems from the homogeneity of risk which it imparts to exchange-traded options. In the OTC options market that existed before 1973, an investor had to be careful not to buy an option from a financially unreliable writer. A holder certainly wanted to have confidence that the writer would deliver stock if the call was exercised, or would deliver cash if the put was exercised. A buyer of exchange-traded options does not need to know or pass judgment upon the creditworthiness of either a seller or a seller's broker, since no contract exists with either one. The contract is with the OCC, and the integrity of the contract rests solely on the creditworthiness of the OCC.

The Options Clearing Corporation

The OCC is a corporation owned by the five exchanges that sponsor trading in options. Legally, it is an *issuer* of option contracts to brokerage firms. It does not, however, act like an ordinary corporation selling securities. The OCC issues an option only when a buyer and seller have agreed, through brokers on an exchange floor, to a transaction in that option. The OCC then issues an option contract to the buyer's broker and acquires an option contract from the seller's broker. In this way, the OCC maintains a balanced book in option contracts: it writes exactly the same type and number of contracts that it holds. The number of contracts in a particular option which the OCC has written is called the *open interest* in that option.

The holder of an OCC option can sell the option by locating, through a broker, an agreeable buyer on an exchange floor. Technically, however, the sale of an option contract by an existing holder is actually a repurchase by the OCC of one of its outstanding contracts and, unless the buyer had previously written an identical contract to the OCC, the reissuance of that contract to the new buyer. Had the buyer previously written an identical contract to the OCC, a purchase would close out that earlier position. That is, a purchase would eliminate any contractual obligation to the OCC. The difference between the two sales is that in the first case the open interest in the option is unchanged while in the second case the open interest is reduced by one contract.

---

[6]The OCC deals only with brokers who are members of one of the five options exchanges and who have sufficient financial resources. Such brokers are called "clearing members" of the OCC. Any participant in the options market who is not a clearing member of the OCC must have purchases and sales booked through a clearing member. This includes other brokers and traders active on the floors of the options exchanges.

Exercising OCC Options

When a holder decides to exercise a call option the broker is informed, which in turn informs the OCC that it is exercising an option which it holds on that corporation. To complete the exercise, the OCC randomly selects a broker on whom it holds an identical option. That broker will then select one of its customers who has written call options to deliver stock according to his or her contract. The broker can select the customer randomly, or by any other reasonable method. The stock obtained from the exercise of a call option moves from the ultimate writer to the ultimate holder through their respective brokers. Put options are exercised in a similar way.

A broker who has written an option to the OCC is contractually obligated to make good on the option regardless of whether or not its customers can deliver stock (on calls) or cash (on puts). To ensure that brokers can meet their obligations, the OCC requires brokers representing option writers to maintain deposits of cash, United States Government securities, or bank letters of credit or, in the case of writers of call options, deposits of the underlying stock. In practice, the bulk of the deposits held by the OCC is in the form of letters of credit, which amounted to over $780 million on June 30, 1978. The OCC, of course, remains liable for the options that it has written to brokerage firms representing option holders.

If the price per share of some stock is greater than the strike price of a call option on that stock, the option clearly has positive value. When such an option approaches expiration, a holder will usually either sell or exercise the option, since its value will fall to zero following the expiration date. Experience with exchange-traded options has shown that most (but not all) holders of such valuable option contracts never exercise those contracts. Instead, they close out their positions by selling to other investors who are short to the OCC. If the strike price of a call option exceeds the price of the underlying stock, a holder may allow his option simply to expire.

HOW MUCH IS A CALL OPTION WORTH?

Call options have positive value because they impose obligations only on the writer and not on the holder. As Table 20-1 shows, however, the value of an option depends on its strike price and expiration date. The characteristics of this dependence illuminate the nature of a call option.[7]

---

[7]Because trading in call options is far more important at present than trading in put options, this section on option variation, and the two following sections on hedging and speculating, discuss only the former.

The Intrinsic Value of a Call Option

Consider, in Table 20-1, the October 280 call options in IBM. Since IBM was trading at $293.50 a share at the close of the markets on September 1, 1978, an investor holding that option could profitably exercise his right to buy IBM stock at a price of $280 a share. The net revenue would be the difference between the market price of the stock and the strike price of the call option, or $13.50 per share. This price difference is called the *intrinsic value* of the option.

The intrinsic value of a call option measures the value of the option to an investor who would buy and exercise the option immediately. If the stock price is greater than the option strike price, an option exercise, followed by a sale of the stock, produces a profit. Hence, the option has a positive intrinsic value, and is said to be *in-the-money*. If the stock price is less than the strike price, an exercise would not generate any revenues (it would, in fact, cause a loss), so the option has zero intrinsic value and is *out-of-the money*. The IBM October 300 call option shown in Table 20-1 was out-of-the-money and had zero intrinsic value on September 1, 1978.

The price of an unexpired option must always be greater than, or equal to, its intrinsic value. If the option price is less than intrinsic value, arbitrageurs will buy and exercise the option and simultaneously sell the underlying stock at a price greater than the cost of the option and its strike price. They will use the shares obtained from the exercise to deliver against the stock sale. Such riskless arbitrage will keep the option price from falling below the intrinsic value of the option. Table 20-3 shows the intrinsic values of the twelve call option contracts exhibited in Table 20-1. All of the option prices exceed the corresponding intrinsic values.

Table 20-3   Intrinsic values of IBM call options on September 1, 1978*
(In dollars; per share optioned)

	Expiration date		
Strike price	October 1978	January 20 1979	April 21 1979
240	53.50	53.50	53.50
260	33.50	33.50	33.50
280	13.50	13.50	13.50
300	0	0	0

*Computed as the greater of (a) zero and (b) the difference between the closing stock price of $293.50 and the strike price of the option.

The Time Value of a Call Option

Market participants will value an option at a premium over the revenue they can get from an immediate exercise if they believe they may be able to make even more money by exercising the option at some future date. When the price of an option exceeds its intrinsic value, the option is said to have a positive *time value*.

That options should have a positive time value is most easily seen by considering out-of-the-money options with zero intrinsic value. Such options are clearly not worthless because there is always the chance that the stock price will move above the option strike price before the expiration date. In Table 20-1, an IBM October 300 call option was worth $8.63 on September 1, 1978, even though the underlying stock was then trading at less than $300 a share. Investors knew it was not impossible that the stock price could exceed $300 some time during the fifty days before the October 21 expiration date.

Table 20-4 shows the time values of the twelve IBM call options contracts. Observe that the time values of options with a common strike price increase as the futurity of the expiration date increases. This shows that "time" really is a valuable aspect of an option.

The Total Value of a Call Option

Figure 20-1 shows the relation between call option prices and stock prices (both expressed as a percentage of the option strike price) for IBM options with three different expiration dates. On its expiration date, an option will have a price which lies on one of the two intrinsic value line segments. Prior to that date, the value of an option will vary with the price of the underlying stock approximately as shown in the figure. The option/stock price curve will shift

Table 20-4 Time values of IBM call options on September 1, 1978*
(In dollars; per share optioned)

	Expiration date		
Strike price	October 21 1978	January 20 1979	April 21 1979
240	2.50	5.25	8.50
260	4.50	7.50	12.25
280	7.13	13.25	18.88
300	8.63	15.13	20.00

*Computed as the difference between the closing option price in Table 20-1 and the intrinsic value of the option in Table 20-3.

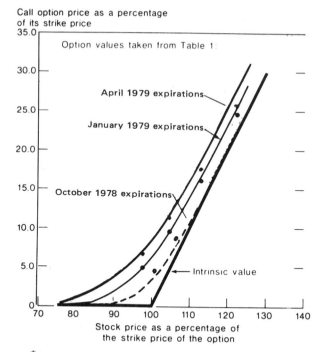

Call option price as a percentage
of its strike price

Figure 20-1   Estimated values of IBM call options as a function of the stock price on September 1, 1978*

closer to the intrinsic value line segments as the expiration date approaches. This downward shifting shows why market participants sometimes refer to an option as a *wasting asset*. As the time remaining to expiration declines, so does the value of an option when the price of the underlying stock remains unchanged.

The option/stock price curves shown in Figure 20-1 were computed from a theoretical model of option pricing derived by Fischer Black and Myron Scholes. (Their model is described in the appendix.) That model has come into general use among participants in the options markets and is available through several electronic information systems.

How Option/Stock Price Relationships are Maintained

Figure 20-1 also locates the values of the twelve IBM call option contracts shown in Table 20-1. Although the option/stock price curves exhibited in Figure 20-1 are based on a theoretical model, the proximity of the actual IBM option prices to their predicted value suggests the model is reasonably accurate. This is the result of arbitrage activity by market participants.

Suppose, for example, that the price of IBM common stock increases in trading on the NYSE but that IBM option prices remain unchanged on the CBOE. The option/stock price curves imply that the options have become "undervalued," i.e., priced below their theoretical values derived from the now higher price of the underlying stock. This may lead some market participants to buy the options and, if they want to hedge their risk, sell the stock. (Exactly how they hedge their risk is explained in the next section.) Their transactions drive up the price of the options relative to the stock price. Such arbitrage activity will continue until the predicted option/stock price relationships are reestablished.[8]

Information on the price at which an underlying stock is trading is a critically important piece of information to the market in options on that stock. Under normal circumstances, stock price information reaches the options exchanges via ticker tapes and price interrogation systems. Although these systems usually report the price of a stock trade within a minute or two after it has occurred, market participants have a substantial incentive to get even faster information. In the summer of 1976, the NYSE found some of its members were relaying information on IBM stock price changes to colleagues at the CBOE over open telephone lines. Their colleagues then bought or sold IBM options in arbitrage activities like that described above. This practice, known as *tape racing*, ended when the NYSE upgraded the speed of reporting transactions in IBM. The incident is noteworthy because it illustrates the value to the options markets of information on stock transactions and the lengths to which market participants will go to obtain and use such valuable information.[9]

It should not be assumed that causality runs only in the direction of stock price changes affecting option prices. The converse, whereby changes in option prices are reflected in subsequent stock price changes, can also occur. Indeed, since call options give an investor substantial leverage of his capital, it may sometimes make more sense to buy options instead of stock, especially if the buyer has access to favorable information about a stock issuer which has not yet been fully reflected in securities prices. Any resulting increase in option prices relative to stock prices would lead arbitrageurs to sell options and, as a hedge, buy the underlying stock. Their efforts to restore equilibrium between

---

[8]Since clearing charges and other transactions costs are incurred in trading both stock and options, an option/stock price discrepancy must be large enough to permit an arbitrageur to make a profit net of those costs. Thus, there is a region around the "equilibrium" option value within which the actual option price can fluctuate freely without inducing arbitrage activity.

[9]A related, but different, type of activity, called *front running*, involves the purchase or sale of options on the basis of *future* stock transactions. For example, if a market participant learns of the impending sale of a large block of stock, he may anticipate a price decline and hasten to sell options on that stock. Tape racing involves the use of information on transactions which occurred in the *past*, but which have not yet been reported to the options markets.

the stock and options markets will push up the stock prices, an increase which would appear as a sympathetic response of stock prices to the original increase in option prices.

The option/stock price curves of Figure 20-1 illustrate a price *level* equilibrium between the stock and options market. That figure does not, however, give any hint as to whether price *changes* will first appear in the stock market or in the options market.

Spreading

Arbitrage keeps stock prices and option prices approximately at their relative equilibrium values. A similar activity, called *spreading*, maintains the relative values of different option contracts. Suppose, for example, an influx of retail purchase orders on the floor of the CBOE was to drive up the price of IBM January 280 call options. Market professionals would quickly observe that those options had become overpriced relative to other IBM option contracts. They would then sell January 280 calls at what they perceive as a premium price and, to hedge their exposure to risk, buy other IBM call options.

Spreading, or the simultaneous purchase and sale of different option contracts, is an arbitrage of relative values between two options rather than between an option and the underlying stock. It is usually undertaken by floor traders on an options exchange, because their access to trading in options is quicker than the access of off-floor arbitrageurs.

Spreading is important to options markets, because it increases the liquidity of contracts which trade infrequently. In the absence of spreading, a relatively small public purchase or sale order in a thinly traded option could cause a large price change in that contract. Because of the opportunity to spread, however, market professionals are willing to take the other side of a public trade, thereby dampening price fluctuations, since they know they can hedge their risk in more actively traded contracts. Even though they may have to hold a position in the infrequently traded option for some time, their spread hedging removes much of their exposure to market risk.

HEDGING RISK BY WRITING CALL OPTIONS

When an investor owns common stock, there is exposure to the risk of unanticipated changes in the value of the stock. One way to avoid that risk is, of course, to sell the stock. Another, and increasingly popular, way to reduce or to eliminate risk on equity investments is to write call options.

Figure 20-1 shows that call option prices move in the same direction as stock prices. If the price of a stock declines, an investor who earlier wrote call options on his stock can recover part of the losses on that stock by buying back the same options at their new, lower, price. This method of hedging risk depends on the relation between changes in option prices and changes in stock prices, a relation known as the *hedge ratio*.

The Hedge Ratio

The hedge ratio of an option is defined as the dollar change in option value which accompanies a one-dollar change in the price of the underlying stock.[10] This ratio must lie somewhere in the interval between zero and unity. It will be zero if the option is far out-of-the-money, so that changes in the stock price hardly affect the value of the option. The hedge ratio will be unity if the option is deep-in-the-money, for the option is then tantamount to a commitment to buy the underlying stock. In that case, the stock and the option change in value dollar for dollar. In general, the hedge ratio will depend on the strike price and time to expiration of the option and on the price of the underlying stock. Table 20-5 shows estimated hedge ratios for twelve different call options on IBM common stock at the close of the markets on September 1, 1978. Note that deep-in-the-money contracts, like the April 240s, have hedge ratios near unity regardless of their expiration dates, while out-of-the-money contracts which are close to expiration (the October 300 contract) have lower hedge ratios.

Hedge Ratios and Small Price Changes

To illustrate how writing call options can reduce the risk on a stock position, consider writing January 280 calls against a position in IBM stock. As shown in Table 20-5, on September 1, 1978 a $1.00 increase (or decrease) in the price

Table 20-5 Estimated hedge ratios for IBM call options on September 1, 1978* (Change in dollar price of an option on one share per $1.00 change in the stock price)

	Expiration date		
Strike price	October 21 1978	January 20 1979	April 21 1979
240	1.00	.98	.96
260	.97	.91	.88
280	.81	.77	.77
300	.46	.56	.61

*See appendix for method of estimation.

[10]The hedge ratio of an option is also called the option delta, a reflection of its definition as the *change* in option value associated with a small change in the stock price.

of IBM stock would have been accompanied by approximately a $0.77 increase (or decrease) in the price of the January 280 call options. Suppose an investor owned 10,000 shares of IBM stock and wrote calls on 13,000 shares of the stock. If the stock decreased in value by $1.00 per share, the options would decrease in value by $0.77 per share optioned. The investor could then re-purchase the previously written option at a cost $10,000 less than the revenues received when the contracts were written ($10,000 = 13,000 shares optioned × $0.77 per share optioned). This gain just balances the decline in the value of this stock. Conversely, had the price of IBM stock increased by $1.00 a share, the investor would have gained $10,000 on the stock position and lost $10,000 on the option position. For this reason, the short position in options is a hedge against the risk of small changes in the price of the underlying stock. The decision to write calls on 13,000 shares, rather than on 14,000 shares or 12,000 shares, is based on this balancing or hedging, i.e., 13,000 = 10,000/ 0.77.

Among the most active writers of call options for hedging purposes are securities firms which provide block positioning services to their customers. When an investor wants to sell more stock than its broker can readily find buyers for, the broker may offer to purchase the remaining unsold stock for its own inventory, or to "position" the excess shares. As long as the stock remains in inventory, the broker has capital at risk. Until 1973, this risk could be eliminated only by selling the positioned stock. Because the markets in exchange-traded options have become so active, however, it is now sometimes more efficient for a broker to hedge this risk by writing call options rather than by selling the underlying stock.

It should not be assumed that simply because an investor has hedged a long stock position by writing call options, all risk has been shifted. The value of the portfolio may be insulated against small stock price changes, but it is not immune to losses which can result from sudden, large stock price changes. Moreover, the investor must monitor continually the price of the stock, because hedge ratios change with stock prices. The number of options written against the stock may have to be increased or decreased from time to time to maintain the hedge. The implications of large stock price changes for hedged positions and the consequences of changes in the hedge ratio are discussed in the box.

SPECULATING WITH CALL OPTIONS

When it is felt that there is an unusually strong likelihood of a security appreciating rapidly in price, an investor may be willing to expose capital to substantial risk by making a leveraged investment in that security. Options provide a remarkably efficient vehicle for leveraged speculation, because their values are extraordinarily sensitive to underlying stock prices. Where a stock price might increase by 5 or 10 percent on favorable news, an option can appreciate by 30 or 60 percent on the same news.

EFFECT OF CHANGES IN THE HEDGE RATIO ON A "HEDGED" POSITION

An investor can lose money on a supposedly "hedged" position because the hedge ratio of an option changes with the price of the underlying stock. The variation in the hedge ratio which follows a stock price change is illustrated in Figure 20-2. Note that the hedge ratio becomes larger when the stock price rises, and grows smaller when the stock price falls. One consequence of this behavior is that a long position in stock and a short position in call options may be hedged but it is not riskless.

As was demonstrated in the text, on September 1, 1978, an investor who was long 10,000 shares of IBM stock and short January 280 call options on 13,000 shares was hedged against the risk of small changes in the price of the stock. If the stock price began to fall, however, the hedge ratio on the options would also decrease. Were the hedge ratio to fall from 0.77 (its value on September 1) to, say, 0.72, the investor hedging 10,000 shares of stock would need to increase the short option position to call options on 13,900 shares of IBM (13,900 = 10,000/0.72). In the event of failure to sell options on an additional 900 shares, then for every additional $1.00 decrease in the stock price the loss will be $640 ($-$ $640 = 0.72 \times 13,000 - 10,000$). Were the stock price to continue to fall, the risk exposure to further price declines would become progressively larger.

A similar argument applies in the case of increases in the stock price. If the stock price increased, the hedge ratio on the January 280 options would also increase. Were the hedge ratio to increase from 0.77 to, say, 0.80, the investor hedging 10,000 shares of stock would need to maintain a short position in January 280 calls on only 12,500 shares of IBM (12,500 = 10,000/0.80). Unless the investor buys back calls on 500 shares of stock, for every additional $1.00 increase in the stock price the loss will be $400 ($-$ $400 = -0.80 \times 13,000 + 10,000$). This happens because the short position in calls on 13,000 shares now hedge 10,400 shares of IBM, yet the investor owns only 10,000 shares.

HEDGE RATIOS AND LARGE PRICE CHANGES

The loss on a hedged position which can result when stock prices change by a large amount in a short interval of time provides an extreme example of the consequences of failing to maintain the correct number of short calls against long stock. Suppose again that an investor hedged on September 1, 1978 a position in 10,000 shares of IBM stock by writing January 280 call options on 13,000 shares. The portfolio would then be insulated from small positive or negative changes in the price of IBM stock. Suppose, however, another corporation announced on Tuesday, September 5, a cash tender offer for any and all shares of IBM common stock at a price of $400 per share, *i.e.*, at a premium of 36 percent over the market price of $293.50.[1] The value of a January 280 call would rise *immediately* to about $120 a share. This implies a gain of $106.50 per share on the stock ($106.50 = $400.00 new stock price − $293.50 old stock price) and a loss of $93.25 per share optioned ($93.25 = $120.00 new option price − $26.75 old option price). The investor would incur a loss of $147,250 ($147,250 = 13,000 shares optioned × $93.25 per share optioned, minus 10,000 shares owned × $106.50 per share owned). These losses are unavoidable because the investor will be unable to repurchase the calls while the price of IBM stock is rising; the stock price will move to about $400 a share in a single, large jump as soon as the tender offer is announced.

NAKED OPTIONS AND COVERED OPTIONS

Because the hedge ratio of a call option cannot exceed unity, an investor hedging a long stock position by selling calls can be protected against unlimited losses due to stock price increases by writing calls on only as many shares of the underlying stock as are actually owned. This is called "covered" writing.

Covered option writing limits an investor's losses.[2] In the "worst case," where a stock price increase pushes the option hedge ratio almost to unity, any further losses on the short option position will be balanced by gains on the stock held long. Looked at another way, a covered option writer has just enough stock to deliver in the event his options are exercised, so he will never have to draw on any cash reserves to unwind the stock and option positions.

To hedge fully a long stock position against small stock price changes the investor must write options on more stock than is owned. In the example of an investor hedging 10,000 shares of IBM by selling January 280 calls, the investor had to write options on 13,000 shares. Call options on 3,000 shares are not covered and are called *naked* options. It is the sale of these naked options which gives rise to the investor's risk exposure on *large* price increases, even though they must be written to complete the hedge against *small* price changes.

---

[1] While an "any and all" tender offer for IBM is unlikely in view of the amount of cash which would be required, tender offer premiums of 40 percent over the market price of the target stock are hardly unusual any more, and as there is trading in options on many companies much smaller than IBM, the example is not without merit.

[2] The maximum loss the investor can experience is the original value of his stock at the time he wrote the calls, less the proceeds from writing the calls. This loss will occur if the stock price falls to zero. Because his options are fully covered, he has *no* risk exposure to stock price increases, although his gains are limited to the strike price of the options plus the proceeds from writing the calls.

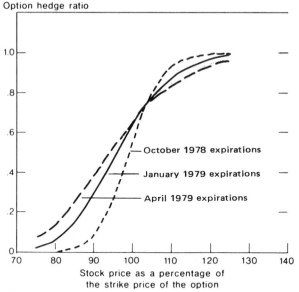

Figure 20-2 Estimated hedge ratios of IBM call options as a function of the stock price on September 1, 1978*

The Elasticity of Option Prices

The elasticity of an option is defined as the *percentage* change in the value of the option which accompanies a 1 percent change in the value of the underlying stock.[11] Thus, elasticity is a measure of the relative price sensitivity of an option contract.

The elasticity of an option depends on the strike price and time to expiration of the option and on the price of the underlying stock. Table 20-6 shows the estimated elasticities of twelve call options on IBM stock at the close of the markets on September 1, 1978. Taking, as an example, the October 240 option, if IBM had closed on that day at a price of 1 percent higher (at $296.44 = 1.01 × 293.50), then an October 240 call option would have closed approximately 5.21 percent higher (at $58.92 = 1.0521 × 56.00).

---

[11]If a call option changes in value from C_0 to C_1 while the price of the underlying stock changes from S_0 to S_1, then the elasticity of the option is e = $([C_1 - C_0]/C_0)/([S_1 - S_0])/S_0$. $[C_1 - C_0]/C_0$ measures the relative change in price of the option contract and $[S_1 - S_0]/S_0$ measures the relative change in the stock price. Note that the hedge ratio is h = $[C_1 - C_0]/[S_1 - S_0]$, so the elasticity may also be defined as e = h S_0/C_0.

Table 20-6   Estimated elasticities of IBM call options on September 1, 1978*
(Percentage change in dollar price of an option per 1 percent
change in the stock price)

| | Expiration date | | |
	October 21 1978	January 20 1979	April 1979
Strike price			
240	5.21	4.66	4.21
260	7.76	6.16	5.24
280	12.37	8.14	6.48
300	19.24	10.54	7.91

*See appendix for method of estimation.

As shown in Table 20-6, for a given strike price, option contracts close to expiration are more elastic than contracts with relatively distant expiration dates. For contracts with a common expiration date, an out-of-the-money option will be more elastic than an in-the-money option.

The foregoing comments illustrate why out-of-the-money options close to expiration are considered volatile securities: they are extremely sensitive to movements in the underlying stock price. This sensitivity is well illustrated by the behavior of IBM options during the April 1978 market rally. Table 20-7 gives the prices of IBM stock and the April 240 call option on that stock at the close of the markets each day for the two weeks preceding the April 22 expiration date of the options. On April 12, the April 240 options were out-of-the-money because IBM stock was then trading at $236.75 a share. Over the next nine days, however, the stock market enjoyed a substantial rally. The price of IBM stock rose to $253.25 a share by April 21, and the April 240 calls expired in-the-money. Between April 12 and April 21, the April 240 calls appreciated from $1.06 to $15.25 per share optioned, an increase of 1,339 percent. Over the same interval, the price of IBM common stock showed a gain of 7 percent. The April 240 options clearly provided enormous leverage for an investor prescient enough to have predicted the mid-April rally. Of course, had the market fallen during April, those same options would have expired out-of-the-money and a holder would have lost his investment.

Writing Naked Options

Investors can speculate against declines in securities prices by writing call options without owning the underlying stock, or by writing *naked* options (see Box). If an investor is primarily concerned with small price fluctuations, such naked writing will put the investor in a position comparable to that of a short seller. For example, an investor who wrote on September 1, 1978, January 280

Table 20-7 Closing IBM stock and option prices in April 1978

| | April 240 options | | |
Date	Stock price (dollars)	Price (dollars)	Hedge ratio
April 10	241.25	2.94	.60
April 11	239.88	2.56	.53
April 12	236.75	1.06	.34
April 13	238.00	1.44	.41
April 14	243.50	4.75	.75
April 17	251.13	11.75	.99
April 18	251.63	11.88	1.00
April 19	253.00	13.25	1.00
April 20	253.25	13.25	1.00
April 21*	253.25	15.25	1.00

*Trading in options on the CBOE terminates at 3:00 p.m. Eastern time on the day prior to their expiration (April 22 in the above table). The underlying stock trades on the NYSE until 4:00 p.m. Thus, the $2.00 time value of the option on April 21 may be an artifact of closing stock and option prices recorded at different times.

call options on 13,000 shares of IBM would have had a position similar to that of an investor who sold short 10,000 shares of IBM stock on the same day. A $1.00 decrease in the price of the stock would increase the wealth of both the short seller and the option writer by about $10,000. (This is obviously true for the short seller. It is true for the option writer because the hedge ratio of the January 280 calls was 0.77 on September 1, 1978, as shown in Table 20-5.)

Should the price of an underlying stock rise instead of fall, the losses incurred by a writer of naked options will accumulate more rapidly than those of a short seller. This follows because the hedge ratio of an option increases with the price of the underlying stock. (The variation of the hedge ratio of an option with respect to stock price changes is described in the Box.) January 280 calls on 13,000 shares of IBM were equivalent to 10,000 shares of stock on September 1, 1978, when IBM was trading at $293.50 a share. However, if the stock price subsequently rose, the hedge ratio would begin to increase. If it reached, say 0.80, then every additional $1.00 increase in the price of the stock would cost the naked option writer $10,400 ($10,400 = 0.80 × 13,000 shares optioned.) A short seller of 10,000 shares would still be losing $10,000 for every $1.00 increase in the stock.

An extreme example of this type of risk from writing naked options occurs when an out-of-the money option is close to expiration. Hedge ratios on such options are small. If, however, the stock price rises and the option goes in-the-money, the hedge ratio of the option will change very rapidly to almost unity and the price of the option will increase to more than its now positive intrinsic value. A writer of naked options would then face the risk of catastrophic losses from further increases in the stock price (because the hedge ratio is almost unity), and the risk can be avoided only by buying back the options at a substantial loss.

The April 1978 experience in IBM options illustrates this point. As shown in Table 20-7, on April 12, 1978, the April 240 calls on IBM had a hedge ratio of 0.34 and a price of $1.06 per share optioned. By Wednesday, April 19, the April 240 calls had gone in-the-money as a result of increases in the price of IBM stock. The price of the calls rose to $13.25 per share optioned and the hedge ratio had jumped to unity. Speculators who wrote naked calls on April 12 suffered substantial paper losses by April 19. They then faced the choice of taking those losses immediately by buying back their much appreciated options or remaining exposed to the risk of additional stock price increases.

Another difference between short selling and writing naked options is that, while a short seller eventually has to cover his borrowing of the stock sold short, a short position in options which expire out-of-the-money never has to be covered. To a writer of options who looks toward the expiration date, if there is only a small probability of an option having positive intrinsic value on its expiration date, then there is a large probability that he will be able to keep the proceeds of his option sales. Of course, as the April 1978 experience showed, there is always some finite probability that a rally will lead, unexpectedly, to options going in-the-money. The losses borne by those who wrote naked options can then become catastrophic.

DOES THE EXISTENCE OF AN OPTIONS MARKET AFFECT THE MARKETS FOR UNDERLYING STOCK ISSUES?

One of the principal concerns expressed by the SEC when it imposed its moratorium on new options was whether options affect the market for underlying stocks. This issue is important because corporations raise equity capital by selling stock, not by selling options. If options somehow reduce the willingness of investors, in the aggregate, to hold stock, regulatory authorities might conclude that restrictions on option trading may be in the public interest.

It appears that options could affect the prices of underlying stocks in three ways: (1) by affecting the *level* of stock prices; (2) by affecting the *volatility* of stock prices, and (3) by inducing *fraudulent manipulation* of stock prices.

Effects on the Level of Stock Prices

As pointed out in the previous section, call options provide a convenient vehicle for optimistic investors who want to make highly leveraged investments in a particular stock. Because they believe the stock is undervalued, optimistic investors necessarily also believe that call options on that stock are undervalued.[12] In buying options for their leverage, optimistic investors may bid option prices to a premium *relative* to the price of the stock. As the options rise to a premium, arbitrageurs will enter the markets to sell what they perceive as relatively overvalued options and to buy the underlying stock to hedge their option sales. They will continue to sell options and to buy stock as long as they continue to perceive the options as relatively overvalued. Eventually, the buying activities of arbitrageurs will push up stock prices. Thus, the purchase of call options by a group of optimistic speculators may find expression in rising stock prices through the perfectly normal activities of arbitrageurs.

The foregoing scenario suggests that call options, and especially highly elastic call options with substantial leverage, may facilitate the formation of speculative bubbles in stock prices. Such bubbles could collapse when the optimistic holders of options liquidate their positions, depressing the relative values of the options. Arbitrageurs would then reverse their former activities by buying back the options which they had previously sold and by selling the stock which they had previously bought. These stock sales may have a depressing effect on stock prices.

Effects on Stock Price Volatility

The existence of an options market may increase the short-term volatility of stock prices, especially when a particular option series is close to expiration.

When a call option is close to expiration, it will have negligible time value and its price will be only slightly greater than its intrinsic value, where the latter is defined as the excess, if any, of the stock price over the strike price of the option. If the price of an in-the-money option which is close to expiration moves significantly above its intrinsic value, arbitrageurs will sell the option and buy stock in anticipation of an imminent exercise of the option. If the price of an option falls significantly below its intrinsic value, arbitrageurs will buy the option and sell the stock. The stock needed to deliver against the sale is obtained by exercising the option.

While arbitrage plays the important role of keeping stock prices and option prices at their "correct" relative values, it also leads to purchase and sale orders for stock, which would not have appeared in the absence of an options market. An in-the-money option close to expiration is a virtually perfect substitute for

---

[12]That is, even though option prices may be in equilibrium with respect to the *existing* price of the underlying stock, optimistic investors believe that the stock price is "too low" and likely to appreciate substantially in the future. They would expect options to appreciate in value even more substantially as a consequence of the leverage of those securities.

the underlying stock.[13] The existence of geographically separated trading in stock and options thus gives rise to a type of market fragmentation not much different from the more familiar fragmentation associated with multiple markets trading identical securities.

When trading in options and underlying stocks is fragmented, arbitrageurs will send purchase and sale orders to one or both markets as they seek to take advantage of transient price discrepancies. Indeed, the very existence of arbitrage orders is evidence that the markets were not previously well integrated. While this induced order flow is beneficial to both the options market and the stock market because it keeps prices on close substitutes in line with each other, it may also have the effect of inducing transient fluctuations in stock prices which would not have been present had the options and stock markets been better integrated. In particular, market makers may not realize that the sudden appearance of selling interest in a stock is the result of an option trading below its intrinsic value and may lower their bid and offer quotations for the stock too rapidly, only to induce countervailing purchase orders from arbitrageurs. Such surges in order flow between market centers could be anticipated whenever securities trade actively in multiple, fragmented, markets, but they may be especially important in the present context in view of the now substantial size of the options markets.

Observers have generally agreed that the deleterious consequences of market fragmentation can be mitigated by enhancing the integration of competing market centers. With respect to stock and options markets, such enhancement could be obtained either by geographic concentration of trading in both stock and options on the same exchange floor or by improved communications between exchanges trading in options and exchanges trading in stocks.

Fraudulent Manipulation of Stock Prices

A third way an options market can affect the prices of underlying securities is the unusually strong incentive options give for the fraudulent manipulation of stock prices. *Capping* is a frequently cited example of such manipulation.

Suppose a market participant has a naked short position on soon-to-expire call options with a strike price only a few dollars above the contemporaneous price of the underlying stock. If the options expire out-of-the-money, the investor can keep the price received originally for writing the options. If, however, the stock price moves above the option strike price prior to expiration, the

---

[13]That is, an investor can buy the stock or he can buy an in-the-money option which is close to expiration, knowing that it is almost certain that he will want to exercise the latter on the expiration date. Conversely, a holder of the stock can either sell stock or write an in-the-money call option which is virtually certain to result in an exercise. The idea of stock and in-the-money options being close substitutes is therefore quite similar to the more familiar observation that the purchase of stock in one market is a perfect substitute for the purchase of the same stock in some other market.

investor's losses from covering his short option position could be substantial. The investor may, therefore, try to "place a cap" on the stock price by short selling the stock whenever its price approaches the strike price of his options. If the investor can defer what may be an ultimately irresistible stock price increase until after the options expire, the total loss incurred may be less than the loss if the options were to expire in-the-money.

Manipulative stock transactions can also push stock prices above the strike price of an option. If an investor has a long position in options which are only slightly out-of-the-money, an attempt may be made to push up the stock prices through the strike price by purchasing the stock and then selling the in-the-money options rather than simply allowing the options to expire out-of-the-money.

It appears that the incentives which options provide for the manipulation of stock prices are unlikely to be important except immediately before option expiration dates. Near those dates, there may be substantial rewards to a manipulator who can defer or accelerate a stock price change by a few days. At other times, the capital required to effect and maintain a prolonged change in the level of stock prices will be beyond the resources of almost all market participants. The SEC and self-regulatory organizations like the NYSE, the American Stock Exchange, and the CBOE have substantially enhanced their market surveillance programs and improved their ability to detect manipulative activities. These efforts are important for creating public confidence that the stock and options markets are fair and equitable for all participants.

CONCLUSIONS

The last five years have witnessed a remarkable growth in investor interest in options. This growth can be attributed to the much enhanced liquidity of exchange-traded option contracts. The limitation of contract terms to a modest number of expiration dates and strike prices resolved the problem of trading interest in OTC options being spread too thinly over too many different contracts to permit a viable secondary market. The creation of the OCC as a contractual intermediary eliminated the need for holders of options to evaluate the creditworthiness of ultimate writers. Greater homogeneity of both credit risks and contract terms reduced the "investigation" costs of trading in options and led to greater investor interest in those securities.

Exchange-traded options have now become important as both hedging and speculative devices. The ability to write call options against stock positions has given investors an important new way to reduce their risk exposure to price fluctuations on specific securities. On the other hand, because call option prices are extremely sensitive to the prices of underlying stocks, optimistic investors can obtain substantially leveraged returns from small capital commitments in options.

The growth of interest in option trading has also created new problems for regulators and for the securities industry in general. More frequent occurrences of manipulative practices like capping might be expected in view of the greater stake which more investors now have in options. The SEC and the self-regulatory organizations have recognized the need for much more careful scrutiny of markets and trading practices in an environment of active options markets.

Because the experience with exchange-traded options is still relatively limited, there exist additional problems whose importance is difficult to assess at present. Call options could provide a vehicle for the formation of speculative bubbles in stock prices. The collapse of such bubbles would bring losses not only to options traders but also to investors in the underlying stocks. Nor is it entirely obvious that there is adequate preparation for the possibility of catastrophic losses by writers of naked call options. History suggests, however, that, as the interests of participants in the options markets become more entrenched, the chances for an orderly appraisal of these potential problems will diminish. Moreover, any reform which follows in reaction to catastrophic losses by writers of naked options will likely be excessive. The current SEC review of the options markets is thus both timely and important.

APPENDIX: THE BLACK-SCHOLES OPTION PRICING MODEL

In 1973, Fischer Black and Myron Scholes advanced a model for valuing call options on securities such as common stock.[1] Their model has since become widely accepted and used by financial market participants. The authors showed that the value of a call option depends on five parameters: (1) the price of the underlying stock, denoted S, (2) the strike price of the option, denoted E, (3) the time remaining to the expiration of the option, denoted t, (4) the level of interest rates, denoted r, and (5) the volatility of the price of the underlying stock, denoted v. The stock price S and the option strike price E are measured in dollars per share and the time t remaining to expiration is measured in years or fractions thereof. The interest rate r is usually taken as the rate on high-quality commercial paper having a maturity comparable to the expiration date of the option. The stock price volatility v is measured as the variance per year of the natural logarithm of the stock price.

The Black-Scholes model for the dollar value C of a call option is:

$$C = S \cdot N[d_1] - E \cdot N[d_2] \cdot e^{-rt}$$

where:

$$d_1 = \{In[S/E] + (r + V/2)t\} / \{vt\}^{1/2}$$

$$d_2 = d_1 - \{vt\}^{1/2}$$

$$N[\times] = (2\Pi)^{-1/2} \int_{-\infty}^{x} e^{-u^2} du$$

Figure 20-1 shows the predicted values of call options on IBM stock computed from the Black-Scholes model for three different values of t. In that chart, option values are expressed as a percentage of the strike price of the option, *i.e.*, as the ratio C/E. The stock price is also expressed as a percentage of the strike price, or as the ratio S/E. The interest rate was set at 8.5 percent per annum, or r = 0.085. This is approximately the rate on high-quality commercial paper that prevailed at the beginning of September 1978.

The only unobservable variable in the Black-Scholes model is the stock price volatility, v. This variable can be estimated by computing the value of v which leads to a predicted option price equal to the actual market price of the option.[2] When this was done for the twelve call options on IBM on September 1,

[1]Fischer Black and Myron Scholes, "The Pricing of Options and Corporate Liabilities," *Journal of Political Economy*, 81 (May/June 1973), pages 637–54.

[2]This method of obtaining the volatility parameter is discussed by Richard Schmalensee and Robert Trippi, "Common Stock Volatility Expectations Implied by Option Premia," *Journal of Finance*, 33 (March 1978), pages 129–47.

1978, the average v came out to be .0372. This implies that there was about a 66 percent chance that the price of IBM stock would vary in one day by less than 1 percent of its previous closing price.[3] The value of v = .0372 was used to compute the option values shown in Figure 20-1. The volatility parameter can also be estimated from the historical price volatility of a stock if one is willing to assume that the future price volatility will be like the historical volatility.

Clifford Smith has pointed out that the Black-Scholes option pricing model may be interpreted as the *expected intrinsic* value of an option, on its expiration date, times a discount factor which converts that future value to a present value.[4] The expected future intrinsic value depends on the probability that the option will expire in-the-money, and hence depends on the volatility of the underlying stock. Other things being equal, options on more volatile stocks have a higher probability of expiring with a greater in-the-money value than options on more stable stocks. Thus, the value of an option increases with stock volatility.

The Black-Scholes pricing model is frequently used by market participants to estimate the hedge ratio and the elasticity of an option. The hedge ratio is defined as the ratio of simultaneous *dollar* changes in option and stock prices. It can be shown that the hedge ratio of an option is $N[d_1]$. This result was used to compute the entries of Tables 20-5 and 20-7 and the curves of Figure 20-2. The elasticity of an option is defined as the ratio of simultaneous *percentage* changes in option and stock values. From the Black-Scholes model, this ratio is $S \cdot N[d_1]/C$. This result was used to compute the entries of Table 20-6. The values of the hedge ratio and elasticity of an option both depend on the volatility parameter. Because that parameter cannot be estimated without error and because a particular estimate depends on the method of estimation, the computed hedge ratio and elasticity can only be viewed as imperfect estimates of the true values.

---

[3]The variance of the log of the price of IBM stock is 0.0372 per year, or .000102 per day (.000102 = 0.0372/365). The standard deviation of the change in the log of the stock price over a one-day interval is therefore .0101 (.0101 = (.000102)$^{1/2}$), or about 1 percent. The probability that a normally distributed variable will be less than one standard deviation from its mean is about 66 percent, so the probability that the price of IBM will change by less than 1 percent in value in one day is about 66 percent.

[4]Clifford Smith, Jr., "Option Pricing: A Review," *Journal of Financial Economics*, 3 (January/March 1976), pages 3–51, at footnote 22.

NEW OPTIONS MARKETS*

Laurie S. Goodman

21

Wide price swings have been a hallmark of financial markets in recent years. This greater volatility subjected market participants holding traditional assets to unaccustomed risks and increased their demands for instruments designed to shift risk to those better able or more willing to bear it.

This atmosphere has fostered the development of new options markets to reallocate risk. These markets offer options on Treasury bonds, notes, and bills, Treasury bond futures, gold futures, foreign currencies, stock indexes, and stock index futures. These newly established options markets, while very small at present, are potentially important. They create more flexibility in risk management than is available with existing cash and futures markets. They also provide market participants with a more efficient hedge against some contingencies that they assume in the normal course of their operations.

This article surveys the new options markets—why they have arisen, who is using them, and what purposes they serve. It also discusses how these instruments differ from conventional equity options in terms of pricing and other financial characteristics.

RISK-RETURN CHARACTERISTICS OF OPTIONS

An option is an agreement between two parties in which one party grants the other the *right* to buy or sell an asset under specified conditions while the

*Reprinted from the *Quarterly Review*, Autumn 1983, pp. 35–47, with permission of the Federal Reserve Bank of New York.

counterparty assumes an obligation to sell or buy that asset. The party who must decide whether to exercise the option is termed the option buyer since he must pay for the privilege. The party granting the right to buy or sell an asset is called the option seller or writer of the option. There are two basic types of options: calls and puts.

A *call option* gives the buyer the right to purchase, or "call away," a specified amount of the underlying security at a specified price up to a specified date. The price at which the security may be bought is the *exercise price* or the *striking price*. The last date on which the option may be exercised is called the *expiration date* or the *maturity date*. The price of this option contract is its *premium*.

A call option can best be described by means of a simple example. A December call option on Treasury bonds gives the holder of the option the right to purchase $100,000 par value of specified Treasury bonds at a price of $90,000 on or before the expiration date in December.[1] The price of these bonds on September 19, 1983 was $90,500. The price of the call option on that date was $2,094. If the market value of the bonds is greater than $90,000 on the expiration date, the option will be exercised. The rationale is that, even if the buyer does not want to hold the bonds, they can be resold at the market price. If the market value of the Treasury bonds is less than $90,000 at expiration, the option will not be exercised because the buyer can purchase the bonds at a lower cost in the market.

The price of an option consists of two components—*intrinsic value* and *time value*. The price of an option, if exercised immediately, is the maximum of either zero or the market price minus the exercise price. This is called the intrinsic value of the option. In the example above, the intrinsic value of the option is the $90,500 market price less the $90,000 exercise current price, or $500. An option must always sell for at least its intrinsic value or there will be arbitrage opportunities. Market practitioners call an option with a positive intrinsic value an "in-the-money" option. Similarly, an option with zero intrinsic value is known as an "out-of-the-money" option.

The time value of an option is the difference between the premium on the option and its intrinsic value. This is the seller's compensation for the possibility that the option will be worth more at the end of its life than if exercised immediately. In the example, the time value of the option is the difference between the total price of $2,094 and the intrinsic value, or $1,594.

A *put option* is the right to sell, or "put to" the writer, a given amount of the underlying security at a given price on or before a specific date. In the example above, the Treasury bond December/90 put option gives the buyer the right to sell $100,000 par value of Treasury bonds at a price of $90,000 on or before the expiration date. If the market value of the Treasury bonds is

---

[1] In this example, the issue used is the 10⅜ bond due 2007/12. This issue is traded on the Chicago Board Options Exchange.

greater than $90,000, the buyer will not exercise the offer, as the bonds can be sold in the open market. If the market value of the bonds is less than $90,000 at expiration, the option to sell the bonds at that price is valuable.

Some market participants purchase options for much the same reason people purchase insurance—they feel the protection they are receiving against adverse developments is worth more to them than the option premium. In the case of the call option example, the buyer of the option is purchasing protection against the price of the bonds rising above $90,000. In the case of the put option, the buyer is purchasing protection against the price of the bonds dropping below $90,000.

Other market participants purchase options as a way to speculate on asset price movements. Consider an investor who owns a Treasury bond and buys a call on a Treasury bond future. This investor is using the options market to compound his bet that interest rates will fall (bond prices will rise). Similarly, a financial institution which has liabilities of a shorter repricing period than its assets will be favorably affected if interest rates fall and unfavorably affected if interest rates rise. If this institution bought a put option on a debt security, it would clearly be hedging. If it purchased a call option, it would be compounding its current interest rate mismatch.

Why do investors write options? Their gain is limited by the premium, while their potential loss is much larger. Options writers believe that the premium is adequate compensation for their potential loss. In fact, the premium is the equilibrating price variable, equating the quantity of options supplied with the quantity of options demanded. If the option premium were too low to compensate the writer for the risk, there would be more buyers than sellers, forcing the premium to rise.

It is important to realize that option writing need not be speculative. An investor who writes call options on an equity (covered call writing) may perceive himself as hedging, as the option increases his returns in periods of poor and moderately good stock returns and reduces it in periods of very good stock returns. Similarly, if a bank that has liabilities with a shorter repricing period than its assets writes a call option on a bond or bond future, it is actually reducing its interest rate sensitivity. If interest rates rise, the option cushions the portfolio loss as the bank receives the option premium. If interest rates fall, the bank receives the premium but trades away some of its potential gain.

NEW OPTIONS MARKETS

Prior to 1982, organized markets existed only for options on common stock. These equity options are traded on four exchanges: the Chicago Board Options Exchange (CBOE), the American Stock Exchange (Amex), the Philadelphia Stock Exchange, and the Pacific Stock Exchange. Put options on the securities of the Government National Mortgage Association were traded on an over-the-counter basis.

Since the last quarter of 1982 many new options markets have opened; others are in the final planning stages (Table 21-1). These new options are written on four types of financial instruments:

- options on stock indexes
- options on debt instruments
- options on foreign currencies
- options on gold.

The new contracts take two basic forms:

- options on so-called physicals, *i.e.*, actual commodities, securities, or indexes
- options on futures contracts.

Market Participants

Since these markets are very new, it is difficult to assess who will eventually constitute the customer base. Institutions that are more conservative and less inclined to enter new markets may well turn out to be very large customers once the markets become better established.

Nevertheless, preliminary evidence indicates that the options on stock indexes and stock index futures are dominated by individuals rather than institutions. They are using the market as a method to wager bets on aggregate market movements rather than focusing attention on particular securities. Broker/dealer firms are relatively small users of options on stock indexes for their own account. Institutional money managers are just beginning to enter the market on the buy side as a hedging vehicle for their portfolio and on the sell side as a source of fee income.

By contrast, options on debt instruments appear to be dominated by institutions. Conversations with exchange officials indicate that well over half the business is generated by broker/dealer firms for their own account. The wholesale nature of the market is corroborated by evidence that almost all the transactions in the most popular of the instruments—the options on bond futures—are for ten, twenty, or fifty contracts rather than for one or two. The face value of the contracts is $100,000. Other users of options on debt instruments include savings and loan associations, commercial banks, and commodities houses.

Options on foreign currencies traded on the Philadelphia Stock Exchange appear to have generated substantial interest abroad, with more than half the business coming from Europe. Broker/dealers in the United States and abroad account for an estimated 30 percent of the business. Corporate treasurers are believed to be the largest customer group. Several banks and some professional

Table 21-1 The new options markets

Instrument	Options on physicals	Options on futures contracts
Stock indexes	**Chicago Board Options Exchange:** S&P 100 (formerly CBOE 100) S&P 500 S&P integrated international oil group S&P Computer and Business Equipment Index	**Chicago Mercantile Exchange:** S&P 500
	American Stock Exchange: Amex Major Market Index Amex Market Value Index Oil and Gas Index Computer Technology Index	**New York Futures Exchange:** NYSE Composite
	New York Stock Exchange: NYSE Composite Index	
U.S. Government debt	**American Stock Exchange:** Treasury bills Treasury notes **Chicago Board Options Exchange:** Treasury bonds	**Chicago Board of Trade:** Treasury bonds
Foreign exchange	**Philadelphia Stock Exchange:** Various currencies*	
Precious metals		**The Commodity Exchange:** Gold **Mid-American Exchange:** Gold†

S&P = Standard & Poor's Corporation.

*Canadian dollars, German marks, Japanese yen, Swiss francs, and pound sterling.

†Approved, not traded.

money managers are also using the market. The contracts have also attracted some retail interest.

Options Versus Futures as a Hedging Tool

There are established futures markets in the same instruments as the new options markets.[2] However, since options and futures have different profit profiles, options contracts can be better hedges than futures contracts for some important kinds of risk exposure. Options are ideally suited to hedge the risks of a potential transaction that is not certain to take place. Consider, for example, a U.S. firm that must submit a competitive bid in a foreign currency to provide a product but is unsure that its bid will be accepted. Here the normal business risks of competitive bidding are compounded by exchange risks. The rate of exchange is a substantial cost element in the bid price of the contract, but the firm will be reluctant to lock in these costs at the time it submits its bid—by selling its potential foreign currency receipts forward, for example—because it is uncertain about the outcome of the bidding process. However, the firm can create a perfect hedge against the contingent receivable by buying a put option in the foreign currency. If the firm's bid wins, the foreign currency can be "put" to the option seller. If the bid fails, the firm will simply not exercise the option.

In a similar vein, a bank can use options to hedge its fixed-rate loan commitments to businesses. These lines are attractive to the borrowers. If interest rates go up, the borrower will generally utilize the commitment; if rates fall, the borrower will let the commitment lapse. The bank has essentially written a put option. Banks may desire to provide this service to keep valuable customers, but they may not be so anxious to bear the full interest rate risk on their contingent liability. The bank can hedge this contingent liability by purchasing a put option on interest rates for an appropriate maturity, say, a Treasury note contract.

There are situations in which options and futures can serve similar hedging purposes. Consider a bank with a longer repricing period on its assets than on its liabilities. This institution should gain from falling interest rates and lose from rising rates. If the bank management believes that interest rates will rise more than accounted for by the term structure of interest rates, it can hedge

---

[2]An option gives its purchaser the right to buy (or sell) an asset at a specific price up to a specific time but, unlike a futures or forward contract, does not *obligate* the buyer to acquire (or provide) the underlying security. Consequently, the risk distribution for an option is quite different from that for a futures contract. Whatever the price of the underlying security, an option buyer will never lose more than the premium paid. The option seller can never gain beyond the premium charged. At best, the seller will lose nothing and retain the entire premium. With a futures or forward contract, the buyer may gain or lose, depending on the market price at maturity. The lower (higher) the price of the contract at maturity relative to the original price, the more the buyer will lose (gain) and the seller will gain (lose).

via either futures or options. Both instruments would be attractive, since the option premium and the futures prices will look cheap in terms of the protection they provide to the bank. The choice between the two will depend on the cost of the option premium, how certain management is of their prediction of future interest rates, and the risk-return trade-off preferred by management. The use of options for such a transaction is examined in Appendix 1.

Market Mechanics: Margins and Delivery Provisions

Margin requirements are a necessary protection for the clearinghouse members. On options contracts, the buyer pays the entire premium up front and is not subject to margin calls.[3] The seller of an uncovered option is subject to an initial margin requirement. If the market moves against him, he is also subject to additional or variation margin. A specific example of margin requirements on options and their calculation is given in Appendix 2.

For options on futures contracts it is customary to hold interest-bearing assets in margin accounts. Consequently, initial margin requirements do not usually represent foregone interest for these contracts. For options on physicals, initial margin requirements must be posted in cash. Alternatively, a security position can be held in lieu of the margin. For example, for an options contract on Treasury bills, Treasury bills with a par value equal to the par value on the contract can be posted instead of the margin. This is customarily done for options on debt securities. Variation margin must, in all cases, be posted in cash.

The terms of delivery for the new options contracts include cash settlement and physical delivery. Options on futures contracts require delivery of the underlying futures contracts. Options on stock indexes require cash settlement—that is, the securities which comprise the Standard & Poor's (S&P) 100, for example, do not actually have to be delivered. Rather, the difference between the exercise price and the current price must be settled in cash. Foreign currency options require delivery of a specified amount of foreign currency.

But options on debt instruments present a unique deliverability problem that arises because of the limited life of the underlying security. Other options (equities, stock indexes, foreign exchange) are written on physicals that have an infinite life and thus are not directly affected in their characteristics by the passage of time. But debt instruments get closer to maturity as the option gets closer to expiration. This feature of debt instruments requires that options on them take one of two forms: fixed deliverable or variable deliverable.

---

[3]It is interesting to note that, on futures contracts, both the buyer and seller are required to put up original margin requirements. This can be posted in interest-bearing form. If the market moves against them, either buyer or seller may be required to deposit variation margin to meet margin calls. These calls must be met in cash, as the other party can draw them out in cash.

Fixed deliverable options require that a debt instrument with specified characteristics be delivered when the option is exercised. For example, a three-month call option on a six-month Treasury bill would require that a Treasury bill with six months remaining to maturity be delivered. Contracts for fixed delivery allow for the possibility that the optioned security could have a shorter lifetime than the option itself. That is, a nine-month option on a three-month Treasury bill is possible; when the option is exercised, a three-month bill is delivered. Treasury bills on the Amex are traded on a fixed deliverable basis.

A variable deliverable option specifies the existing debt issue that is deliverable against exercise. This has been adopted for Treasury notes and bonds. For example, a one-year option on a ten-year bond spells out the specific ten-year bond to be delivered. At the expiration of the option, the bond will have nine years to maturity. Thus the maturity date of the bond must be later than the option expiration date for variable deliverable options.[4]

Market Development

Why the sudden emergence of these new markets? Increased use of futures contracts and existing equity options indicated to the management of the stock and commodities exchanges that the public desired new instruments which could serve a risk transfer function. Proposals on some of these new options contracts were submitted as early as 1980. However, questions about the division of regulatory authority between the Commodity Futures Trading Commission (CFTC) and the Securities and Exchange Commission delayed the approval process, allowing other exchanges time to design similar, slightly differentiated products. The ultimate agreement, signed into law by President Reagan in October 1982, gave the SEC jurisdiction over options contracts on physical securities traded on organized securities and commodities exchanges, and options on foreign currency when traded on a national securities exchange. The CFTC has jurisdiction over options on financial futures.

The exchanges are well aware that the first to begin trading a product has a real advantage. Liquidity will tend to develop in that market. If a second exchange enters with a similar product, even if it is slightly superior in design, it must compete with a market which has already developed liquidity. Trades can be executed with greater ease in the first market, and hence gravitate there. It is extremely difficult for the second market to develop liquidity, and it generally fails. Consequently, the competitive pressure between the exchanges induces the submission of numerous proposals on similar instruments.

[4]The difference between fixed deliverable options and variable deliverable options is discussed more fully in Walter L. Eckardt, Jr., "An Analysis of Treasury Bond and Treasury Bill Options Premiums," a paper presented at the second annual options colloquium sponsored by the Amex (New York, N.Y., March 25–26, 1982).

Yet, if there were a demand for these products, why did over-the-counter markets not develop? Regulatory approval only is necessary for options to be traded on organized exchanges. The answer is in part that the use of an organized exchange avoids the potential for abuse that is inherent in an options contract. Otherwise, the option buyer, who pays the premium up front, has very limited recourse if the writer does not uphold his obligations at the end of the contract.

Trading of standardized contracts on an organized exchange overcomes this problem because it allows for the development of a clearinghouse. On securities exchanges the clearinghouse assumes any credit risk. Thus, the option really consists of two contracts: one between the buyer and the clearinghouse and the other between the seller and the clearinghouse. On commodities exchanges, the clearinghouse member which handles the writer's account assumes the credit risk. Consequently, a buyer of an exchange-traded option does not have to pass judgment on the creditworthiness of the seller.[5]

While the clearinghouse or a clearing member thus assumes the credit risk in the contract, they can protect themselves against the risk by marking the contracts to market on a daily basis and assessing additional margin requirements as required by price movements. If the margin calls are not met, the clearinghouse can move quickly to liquidate the contracts. Two other reasons for the importance of an organized exchange is contract standardization, which allows for the development of liquidity, and a reported price, which gives option buyers and writers information on the price of the last actual trade. This information can be used to evaluate returns better on the anticipated option strategy. Since trading on an organized exchange is preferable to trading on an over-the-counter basis, regulatory approval was a crucial ingredient for market creation.

Will All These New Options Markets Survive?

There are four possible markets for any instrument: a cash market, a futures market, an option on the cash market, and an option on the futures market. But, generally, the existence of all four markets on one instrument is redundant. A cash market, a futures market, and one options market will usually be sufficient to fulfill all risk-transfer possibilities, since the option on the cash market and the option on the futures market serve very similar functions.[6]

---

[5]See Kenneth D. Garbade and Monica M. Kaicher, "Exchange-Traded Options on Common Stock," this *Quarterly Review* (Winter 1978–79), pages 26–40.

[6]This point can be made by considering the limit case: an option on a futures contract which expires the day the futures contract is delivered. The delivery on the option would be settled at once, providing the actual security. Here no distinction exists between an option on the futures contract and an option on the physical. In reality, the options contract expires before the delivery date of the futures contract. For example, for a December option on a bond future, the option would expire in November, resulting in delivery of a December futures contract. It is unlikely that this small difference is enough to sustain two independent markets.

If there is room for only one options market, what determines whether the option on the cash instrument or the option on the future wins out? Since there were only small differences in the start-up times of the various markets, technical or operational differences will make one market more desirable than the other. For example, if the cash market is more liquid than the futures market, or has lower transactions costs, an option on the cash market would be preferred. In the case of a commodity like gold, an option on the physical would involve the costs of assaying and delivery. Consequently, for gold the options market has developed on the futures contract. In the case of foreign exchange, spot markets are much deeper than the forward exchange markets.[7] The futures market is smaller still. In this case options are written on the spot currency contract.

Options on both cash instruments and futures do currently coexist in markets where the reasons to prefer one type of option over the other are not so clear-cut. But signs are already emerging to show which options will dominate. Options on Treasury bond futures appear to be generating more business than options on Treasury bond physicals. By contrast, the options market for stock indexes is more active than the market in options on stock index futures (Figure 21-1).

Many market participants believe that the contract design of options on Treasury bond futures is slightly superior for three reasons. For one, options on futures have no coupon or dividend payments. By contrast, with an options contract on a bond or note, the buyer of a call or seller of a put must compensate the other party for accrued interest when exercise occurs. Furthermore, options on bond futures are also believed to be "cleaner" instruments because of the reduced possibility of delivery squeezes. Options on bonds are written on particular issues. Since the supply of any particular issue is fixed after the date of issuance, there is always the chance of a squeeze developing that could artificially raise the price of that bond. Options on bond futures, however, are written on the underlying futures contract, which in turn, is written not on a particular bond issue but rather on a bond with particular characteristics. One bond (usually a high coupon bond) will always be cheapest to deliver against the futures contract. But, if there were a squeeze on this bond, other deliverable bonds would be available.[8] Consequently, the deliverable supply of Treasury bond futures will always prove more than adequate. Third, it is easier to learn

[7]A Federal Reserve Bank of New York turnover study showed that for April 1983 foreign exchange turnover in the United States was $702.5 billion. Of this, $451.0 billion (or roughly two thirds) was in spot transactions, $42.0 billion was in outright forwards, and $209.4 billion was in swaps. Foreign exchange futures turnover on the International Monetary Market is less than 10 percent of total foreign exchange turnover.

[8]Conceptually, options on bonds could be written on a bond with particular characteristics rather than on a particular bond. However, this would make certain option strategies, such as covered call writing, more difficult as the option would "play to a single debt issue" and the issue may change over the life of the option.

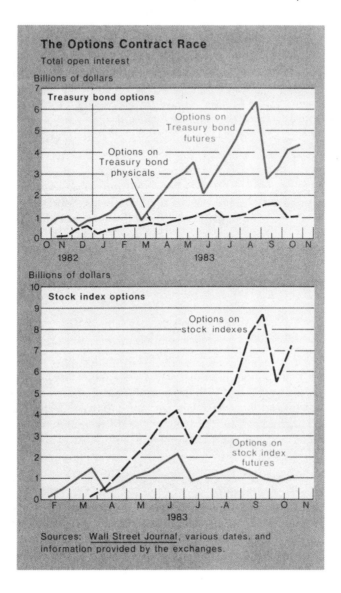

The Options Contract Race

Total open interest

Billions of dollars

Treasury bond options

Options on Treasury bond futures

Options on Treasury bond physicals

O N D 1982 J F M A M J J A S O N 1983

Billions of dollars

Stock index options

Options on stock indexes

Options on stock index futures

F M A M J J A S O N 1983

Sources: Wall Street Journal, various dates, and information provided by the exchanges.

Figure 21-1

the price of an underlying bond future rather than the bond itself. For option pricing purposes it is crucial to know the price of the underlying security. The price of the last bond futures trade is easily accessible, as bond futures and options on bond futures are traded on the same floor. This saves the investor the trouble of canvassing dealers to obtain a price on the security itself.

Options on stock indexes appear to be more popular than options on stock index futures. Of the four markets on stock indexes, the two most successful are the S&P 100 followed by the Amex Major Market. These two markets have attracted substantial retail interest as the contract sizes on these options are much smaller than those for options on the S&P 500, the Amex Market Value, or the stock index futures. Moreover, options on stock index futures can be sold only by a CFTC registered representative. Options on stock indexes can be sold by any registered representative. Thus, a stockbroker who services retail portfolios can market the S&P 100 and the Amex Major Market Index but not the options on the futures contracts.[9]

While options on the Treasury bond futures and options on the S&P 100 appear to be doing somewhat better than their competitors, the contract race is not yet over. The markets are all relatively new, and the emergence of one contract over another takes time. But weaker markets face the threat of gradually losing liquidity through a loss of customers. Participants who remain in those markets will find over time that their trades cannot be executed promptly enough or that bid-ask spreads are too wide.

FINANCIAL CHARACTERISTICS OF THE NEW OPTIONS

The new options, particularly on debt instruments, have financial characteristics that are quite different from those of the more familiar equity options. An equity is the instrument with the same characteristics over the life of the option. Unlike equities, debt instruments have finite lives and their effective maturity shortens as time passes. This creates the distinction between fixed deliverable options and variable deliverable options as discussed above. Both fixed deliverable and variable deliverable instruments attempt to capture some of the characteristics of options on equities. A fixed deliverable option tries to preserve the characteristics of a debt instrument (i.e., its sensitivity to changes in interest rates) but must move from security to security to avoid the aging problem. The variable deliverable bond option stays with a single issue, but the characteristics of the issue age over time as the bond moves to maturity.

The other major difference between the new options and traditional equity options concerns the effects of financial variables—such as the level of interest rates—on the price of the options contract. The standard theory of options pricing holds that changes in certain financial variables, including the level of interest rates, will have definite effects on the price of an equity option. For the new options, however, in some cases the effects of such factors may be

---

[9]It should be noted that options on bond futures can be sold only by a CFTC registered representative, while options on bond physicals can be sold by any registered representative. However, since there is little retail interest in the options on debt securities, this does not aid the exchange trading the options on Treasury debt securities.

ambiguous or even may go in the opposite direction to that predicted by traditional options pricing theory.

Valuation of New Options Instruments

In 1973 Black and Scholes described a formula for calculating the value of a call option on a stock.[10] This model, which has received wide recognition and attention, shows that the price of a call option depends on five factors: the price of the underlying security (S), the strike or exercise price of the option (E), the volatility of the price of the underlying security (s), the time remaining to maturity (T), and the level of interest rates (r).[11] It is useful to explore the extent to which the same factors are important in the pricing of the new options markets.[12] (The results of this section are summarized in Table 21-2, and the relationship between put and call prices is discussed in Appendix 3.)

The effect of changes in the underlying security price or the exercise price are unambiguous. For all call options, as the price of the underlying security increases or the exercise price decreases, the price of the option must increase because the intrinsic value is higher. The effect of increased volatility is similar for conventional equity options and new options instruments as described below. However, the analysis of changes in the time to expiration and the level of interest rates is different for new options instruments than for conventional equity options.

Volatility

For all options, the more volatile the underlying security price, the greater the value of the option. Consider the extreme case in which there are two securities, A and B. Security A is riskless and Security B is risky, but its mean

[10]See Fischer Black and Myron Scholes, "The Pricing of Options and Corporate Liabilities," *Journal of Political Economy* (May/June 1973).

[11]The Black-Scholes option pricing formula can be written as follows:
$$c = SN(d_1)\ Ee^{-rT}N(d_2)$$
where: $\quad d_1 = (\ln(S/E) + (r + 1/2s^2)T)/s\ \sqrt{T}$ and $d_2 = d_1 - s\sqrt{T}$.

In this formula, c is the value of the option, ln is the natural logarithm, e is the exponential and s^2 is the instantaneous variance of the stock price. $N(\cdot)$ is the normal distribution function.

[12]The Black-Scholes formula assumes that the stock's continuously compounded return follows a normal distribution with a constant variance; its expiration price will thus be "lognormally" distributed. While this may be a good approximation for stock indexes and currencies, it is not a good assumption for variable deliverable debt instruments. As mentioned previously, default-free bonds (other than "consols"), unlike common stock, do not have a perpetual life. As maturity approaches, a default-free bond will be valued closer to par, all other factors constant. Thus, even if interest rates remain unchanged, the passage of time alone will cause the price of a default-free bond to change. Consequently, it cannot be assumed that prices of debt instruments follow a random walk. Moreover, the variance of a bond will decline over time. A longer bond will move more in response to a 100 basis point change in interest rates than a shorter bond.

Table 21-2   Effects of changes in financial factors on pricing of new options instruments

Call options on instruments	Security price (S)	Exercise price (E)	Volatility of security price (s)	Time to expiration (T)	Level of Interest rates (r)
Conventional equity or stock index	+	−	+	+	+
Foreign currency	+	−	+	+	?
Fixed deliverable debt instrument	+	−	+	?	−
Variable deliverable debt instrument	+	−	+	+	−
Futures contract	+	−	+	?	−

This table should be read as follows: a plus sign indicates that an increase in the value of a factor will increase the value of a call option on an instrument; a minus sign indicates a decrease in the option value and a question mark indicates an ambiguous effect.

return is the same as the sure value of Security A. Assume further that the exercise price of the option is the same as the value of Security A at expiration. Hence, an option on Security A will be worthless, as the exercise price is the same as its current value. Security B has a probability of one half of expiring worthless, and a probability of one half of expiring with value. Its current price will reflect this, and consequently will be positive. Consider now two risky securities with the same mean value. Security B is riskier than Security A. The argument easily generalizes, as Security B will have a greater probability of a higher value at expiration than Security A. It also has a greater probability of a lower value but, since the option cuts off the lower tail of the distribution, this does not matter. Thus, the value of options on more volatile securities, holding all other factors constant, will generally be greater.

Time to Expiration

In the Black-Scholes model, an option with a longer time to expiration will be worth at least as much as another option with the same exercise price and a shorter time to expiration. The intuition is that an option with a longer time to expiration has all the attributes of an option with a shorter exercise date, as the longer option may be exercised before maturity. Once the shorter run option has expired, the longer term option can still be exercised. This is true for options on foreign currencies, options on stock indexes, and options on variable deliverable debt instruments as well.

This pricing property does not necessarily hold for options on futures and fixed deliverable options, although it will generally be the case. By way of illustration, consider the September and December call options on a futures contract. The time value of an option on a December future will, of course, be higher than that on a September future. But the September future is a different contract from the December future. Consequently, it is possible—if interest rates are currently very low and expected to rise sharply between September and December—for the option on the September future to have a positive intrinsic value, while the option on the December future has a zero intrinsic value. Thus, depending on the relative magnitudes of the time values and the intrinsic values, the option on the December future could conceivably be less valuable than the option on the September future.

Interest Rates

The Black-Scholes formula shows that, as interest rates rise, the value of a call option must rise.[13] To understand this, note that holding a call option and holding the stock itself are alternative ways for an investor to capture any gain on the security price. Consequently, as rates rise, the cost of carry on the underlying security will rise and the call option will appear more attractive vis-à-vis the underlying stock.[14] And what holds for an option on a single equity will hold for an option on a stock price index, which is just a basket of many individual equities.

For options on stock index *futures*—and on futures contracts generally— there is no opportunity cost associated with holding a futures contract, as no funds need be expended until expiration. Consequently, the interest rate effect

---

[13]The model assumes that price movements are independent of the level of interest rates.

[14]A more formal argument can be made as follows: an investor buys 100 shares of stock worth $50 per share on margin. But, instead of securing a typical margin loan, he makes an initial payment of size c, and promises $4,500 in six months. The future payment is promised on a no-recourse basis with the stock used as collateral. If the stock is worth less than $4,500 at expiration, the investor will allow the lender to claim the stock. The investor has purchased a call option with an exercise price of $45 and a time to expiration of six months; c is the premium.

If the loan were riskless, the lender would charge the investor an amount which would cover the difference between the value of the stock being delivered, S, and the present value of the future payment, Ee^{-rT} (in the example above, $4,500 is the future payment). If the loan were not riskless, the lender must charge enough to purchase an insurance premium to allow for the possibility that the stock price will be less than E dollars at expiration, leaving the lender with a loss of $E - S$. Thus the price of the premium is the present value of the levered position in the stock plus the insurance premium, or $c = S - Ee^{-rT} + I$, where I is the insurance premium. As interest rates rise, the present value of the future payment is less, hence the value of the levered position in the stock increases. Thus, the value of the call option must increase.

will be negative although very small.[15] This can best be described by considering a riskless world. The option buyer would be charged an amount equal to the present discounted value of the difference between the value of the futures contract at expiration and the exercise price. (In a risky world, this difference would be higher by the amount of an implicit insurance premium.) Then, as interest rates go up, this present discounted value, which is the price of the call option, would decline. Essentially, the purchaser of the call is forfeiting interest until contract expiration on the original call price, for which cash must be put up front. However, since the futures price and the exercise price are expected to be relatively close when the option is originally purchased, interest rate variations are only a second-order effect in the price changes of these contracts.

Assuming that the price of the underlying security is independent of the level of interest rates is a reasonable simplification in the case of equity options. However, it is an absurd assumption to make for options on debt instruments or on currencies. Major movements in the prices of debt instruments and exchange rates will occur *because* of changes in interest rates. For debt instruments, as interest rates rise, any cost of carry considerations will be dwarfed by the fall in the price of the underlying security.[16]

Interest rate increases as a rule will have a negative impact on the price of options on bond futures, as a rise in interest rates will most likely cause a fall in the price of the underlying futures contract. And this loss is compounded by the negative effect of higher interest rates on the opportunity cost of the call premium.

The effect of interest rate changes on the value of a foreign currency option will generally be ambiguous. For simplicity, consider the case where foreign interest rates are constant while dollar interest rates rise. The theory of interest rate parity holds that the forward premium or discount on foreign exchange should equal the differential between domestic and foreign interest rates. Then, as dollar interest rates rise, the forward exchange rate (expressed as dollars per unit of foreign currency) must rise relative to the spot rate. The interest rate parity linkage allows the value of the options contract to be written equivalently

---

[15]Rational optional pricing of futures contracts takes the form

$$c = e^{-rT}[FN(d_1) - EN(d_2)]$$

where: $d_2 = (\ln(F/E) + 1/2s^2 T)/s\sqrt{T}$ and $d_2 = d_1 - s\sqrt{T}.$

F is the price of the futures contract. This is the Black-Scholes option pricing formula given in footnote 11 if $F = Se^{rT}$.

[16]See, for example, George Courtadon, "The Pricing of Options on Default Free Bonds," a paper presented at a Conference on Options Pricing: Theory and Applications, sponsored by the Salomon Brothers Center for the Study of Financial Institutions (New York University, New York, N.Y., January 18–19, 1982).

in terms of either the spot or the forward exchange rate.[17] And this equivalence in the valuation formulas for the option can be used to deduce the effect of interest rate changes on the option price. There are three cases:

1. If the spot rate is unaffected by a rise in domestic interest rates, option values will rise; as in the case of a typical equity option, the cost-of-carry effect will dominate.
2. If the forward rate is unaffected by a rise in domestic interest rates, option values will fall. Intuitively, one can think of the option as being written on a futures contract that expires on the same date as the option. In this instance, the negative relationship existing between options on futures and interest rates will prevail.
3. If both the spot and forward rates change when domestic interest rates rise, the effect on option values cannot be determined without precise knowledge of how much either exchange rate moves.

Since the third case represents the typical adjustment, the effect of interest rate changes on foreign currency options values is indeterminate.

To summarize, there are three interest rate effects at work. There is a negative effect which relates to the cost of carry on the option premium—the call premium is paid when the contract is entered into and no proceeds are received until maturity or exercise. There is a positive effect which relates to the cost of carry on the underlying security. Finally, there is a negative effect of interest rates on the security price. The second effect dominates the first, and the third effect generally dominates the second. For options on futures, only the first effect is present. For options on conventional equities and equity indexes, the first two effects are present, and the impact of interest rates is positive. For options on debt instruments, all three effects are present, and the third effect dominates. For foreign currencies, the extent to which the third effect is present depends on the relative movements of spot and forward exchange rates, thus the effect of interest rates is indeterminate.

[17]See Mark B. Garman and Steven W. Kohlhagen, "Foreign Currency Option Values," unpublished working paper (School of Business Administration, University of California at Berkeley, December 1982), for a more technical discussion. The authors have shown that the price of a call option on foreign exchange may be written as

$$c = e^{-r_f T} S N(d_1) - e^{-r_D T} E N(d_2)$$

where:

$$d_1 = (\ln(S/E) + (r_D - r_f + 1/2 s^2)T)/s\sqrt{T}$$
$$d_2 = d_1 - s\sqrt{T}$$

r_D = domestic interest rates, r_f = foreign interest rate.

Alternatively,

$$c = e^{-r_D T} [F N(d_1) - E N(d_2)]$$

where:

$$d_1 = (\ln(F/E) + (1/2 s^2 T))/s\sqrt{T}$$
$$d_2 = d_1 - s\sqrt{T}$$

OPTIONS IN THE BROADER FINANCIAL CONTEXT

As risk in the financial environment has increased, many of the traditional risk bearers are no longer willing to play that role to so large an extent. Banking institutions have moved away from their conventional activity of borrowing short and lending long: instead, they are confining the calculated interest rate risks they take to the short end of the maturity spectrum. Portfolio managers who feel they have a particular expertise in picking stocks now wish to remove the market component of their risk. Corporations are looking for ways to eliminate exchange rate risk that they had normally assumed in the course of their business. Consequently, changes have emerged in the financial system that enrich the menu of risk management techniques. The new options markets are one such example. These markets allow traditional risk bearers to lay off unwanted risks and provide alternative outlets for their customers.

It must be borne in mind that, while options provide real opportunities for market participants to lay off unwanted risk, and for sophisticated market participants to earn a return by accepting these risks, they also create the potential for unsophisticated writers of options to expose themselves to much larger risks than is prudent. The bank regulatory authorities are monitoring bank participation in these markets in an effort to assess what types of activities commercial banks should be able to engage in and what limits should be placed on these activities.

The interest in these markets from the Federal Reserve System's point of view goes well beyond regulatory rules for banks. The existence of these markets may well alter the risk-taking behavior of financial intermediaries and real sector participants. If the markets become very important, they could affect the response of the economic system to real and monetary disturbances. However, it is still too early to tell even which option markets will succeed in establishing themselves and how large they will become. Time and careful study will allow us to determine the full implications for the behavior of market participants.

APPENDIX 1: AN ILLUSTRATIVE TRADE

To appreciate fully the flexibility of option instruments, it is useful to work out an illustrative example. Let us consider a depository institution—a bank, for instance—and examine how it could use options in asset-liability management. Let us assume that the financial institutions believe that interest rates will rise more than is expected in the current term structure. The bank has some long-term fixed rate commercial loans and mortgages and is funded by shorter term instruments. To hedge itself the bank wants to buy a put option on a bond future. If interest rates rise, the bank's higher funding costs will be offset or nearly offset by the gain on the options contract.

Meanwhile, a professional money manager across town has very different interest rate expectations. He believes that interest rates will fall more than is expected in the current term structure. He would like to collect the fee income from writing a put option on a bond future.* There is clearly room for a trade between the financial institution and the money manager.

We assume that it is December, the market price of a March futures is 70-00, and the strike price on the option is 70. The premium is $2,000 for $100,000 face value of bonds. The bank thinks there is a 75 percent probability the futures price in March will be 65 and there is a 25 percent probability the price will go up to 72. If the price goes above 70, the bank will not exercise the contract. Thus, the bank perceives this contract as having a positive expected value, as it has a 75 percent chance of making $5,000 and a 25 percent chance of making nothing. Thus, the expected value of the contract is $3,750 and its cost is $2,000.†

Meanwhile the money manager believes that there is a 25 percent probability the futures price in March will be 65 and a 75 percent probability the futures price in March will be 72. The expected cost of this contract to the money manager is $1,250, and he will receive the $2,000 premium. Thus, his expected profit is $750. Let us look at four scenarios at expiration (table).

Note that, while in scenario 1 the bank has lost the $2,000 option premium, interest rates have fallen or held steady. Consequently, the bank will have a gain on its portfolio. Therefore, while the bank would have been better off not buying the option, the hedge worked as it was supposed to. That is, the hedge provided insurance against rising interest rates while preserving the value of the bank's portfolio should interest rates fall.

In the example described above, the money manager writing the put leaves himself with an unlimited exposure if interest rates rise (bond prices fall). If the money manager has interest rate expectations as described above but wants to limit his downside risk, he could write a put option at 70 and buy a put option at 65. If the bond futures contract price comes in below 65, the money manager could exercise the March/65 put. The initial cost of the March/65 put is low, as it is fairly far out of the money; say it costs $250. The money manager would then collect $1,750 in net premium income but would have limited his possible loss to $5,000 on the option. This strategy is called a "bull put spread" (meaning the investor is bullish on bond prices).

The money manager may also have written the put option as part of a straddle. In a straddle, the writer anticipates that interest rates and bond prices will be relatively flat. Writing a straddle involves writing a put and a call option at the same exercise price for the same expiration. If the premium on a March/70 call option is $2,000, the money manager will have collected $4,000 in fee income. Thus, he will break even or make money if the bond futures contract price stays in the range of 66–74. If it moves outside that range, he will experience a net loss on the transaction.‡ Intuitively, if the call is in the money, the put will be out of the money. Since $4,000 in premium income has been collected, the money manager will lose money if the loss on either the put or the call is more than $4,000.

*It should be noted that the money manager could also have taken advantage of his interest rate expectations by buying a call option.

†It is plausible that a risk-averse bank would enter a contract which it believes had negative expected value because of its usefulness as a hedge.

‡It is not necessary to write a put and call option at the same strike price. The investor can modify the risk-return relationship by writing options with different strike prices. In each case, the maximum potential profit is the total of the premiums received. The downside break-even point is the put strike price less the total premium received. The upside break-even point is the call strike price plus the total premium received.

Benefits (losses) to parties in option contract

Market outcomes	Bank (buyer)	Money manager (writer)
Futures price is 70 or above March/70 put expires worthless	−2,000 premium	+2,000 premium
Futures price is 69 March/70 put expires +1	−2,000 premium +1,000 option −1,000	+2,000 premium −1,000 option +1,000
Futures price is 68 March/70 put expires +2	−2,000 premium +2,000 option breakeven	+2,000 premium −2,000 option breakeven
Futures price is 65 March/70 put expires +5	−2,000 premium +5,000 option +3,000	+2,000 premium −5,000 option −3,000

APPENDIX 2: CALCULATION OF MARGIN REQUIREMENTS

Margin requirements on options can best be illustrated by an example. Let us consider an investor who wishes to write a call option on thirteen-week Treasury bills on the American Stock Exchange (Amex). Margin requirements are governed by three rules:*

1. If the option is in the money, the writer must hold a margin equal to the premium plus a fixed amount. In the case of calls on the Amex, the fixed amount is $3,500.

Example: A customer writes an uncovered thirteen-week T-bill call option with a strike price of 88. This means the bill is at a 12 percent discount (*i.e.*, the strike price for $1,000,000 face value of the bill is roughly $970,000). The market price of the bill is 90, that is, the bill is at a 10 percent discount ($975,000 for $1,000,000 face value). The option is selling at $6,250 for $1,000,000 face value of the bill. Thus, the margin requirement is:

Option premium	$6,250
Plus fixed amount	$3,500
Total	$9,750

2. If the option is out of the money, the writer must hold a margin equal to the premium plus a fixed amount less the amount the option is out of the money.

3. The minimum margin requirement is the option premium plus $500 per contract.

Example: In the example above, the market price of the T-bill call option falls to 85. The option is selling for $1,500. Thus, the margin requirement is:

Option premium	$1,500
Plus fixed amount	$3,500
Total	$5,000
Minus out-of-the-money amount	− $7,500
Total	− $2,500

However, the minimum margin requirement is the option premium + $500 per contract. In this example, we have:

$1,500 option premium + $500 or $2,000.

Thus, the maintenance margin requirement is $2,000.

*Additionally, the initial deposit in a new margin account must total at least $2,000.

APPENDIX 3: PUT-CALL PARITY

The text discussed the relationship between various financial factors and the call option price of new options instruments. This appendix investigates the relationship between prices on put and call options.

To gain some insight into the connection between put and call prices for equity options consider the following portfolio strategy. An investor buys a security for a price of S dollars. He finances his purchase by borrowing Ee^{-rT} dollars, promising to repay E dollars at the expiration of the option. At the same time, he buys a "European" put option for a premium of p dollars. (A European option cannot be exercised before maturity, whereas an American option can.) The initial value of this portfolio is $S + p - Ee^{-rT}$.

At the expiration of the option, the security will be worth S_1. If S_1 is less than E_1 the investor will exercise the option and receive the exercise price of E with which the maturing loan will be repaid. The value of the investor's portfolio at the expiration date then is zero. If S_1 is greater than E, the investor will not exercise the put option but can sell the security in the market for S_1, repay the loan, and have $S_1 - E$ dollars left over. The payoff structure of this portfolio may be summarized as follows:

Scenario	Value of put option	Value of security	Repayment of loan	Total
$S_1 < E$	$E - S_1$	S_1	$-E$	0
$S_1 \geq E$	0	S_1	$-E$	$S_1 - E$

This portfolio strategy has been selected so that its payoff structure exactly matches that from a European call option (*i.e.*, max $(0, S_1 - E)$). To avoid arbitrage opportunities, a call option must sell for a price equal to the initial price of this equivalent portfolio. Thus, the traditional put-call parity equation:

$$c = p + S - Ee^{-rT} \qquad (1)$$

This equation holds for options on individual equities and options on stock indexes.

For bond options, a minor adjustment is needed to take into account coupon payments. Let G_0 be the accrued interest at the time of purchase of the option, and G_1 the accrued interest on the bond at the end of the life of the option. If the call is exercised, the buyer will receive $S_1 - E$. The security's value will be $S_1 + G_1$. If the put is exercised, the buyer will receive $E - S_1$. Consequently, the investor must borrow $(E + G_1)e^{-rT}$ rather than Ee^{-rT}. Put-call parity can then be rewritten:

$$c = p + S + G_0 - (E + G_1)e^{-rT}. \tag{2}$$

For futures contracts, consider a portfolio which consists of writing a call, purchasing a put, and establishing a long futures position at price F. As before, all instruments have the same expiration date and the options have the same exercise price. At expiration, the payoff where F_1 is the futures price looks like:

Scenario	Sell a call	Buy a put	Buy a futures	Total
$F_1 < E$	0	$E - F_1$	$F_1 - F$	$E - F$
$F_1 \geq E$	$E - F_1$	0	$F_1 - F$	$E - F$

The initial value of this riskless position is the cost of the put less the income received from the call. Discounting the portfolio earnings at maturity and setting them equal to the initial value gives

$$c = p + (F - E)e^{-r_D T}. \tag{3}$$

The relationship between puts and calls on currency options can be derived from this. If interest rate parity holds,

$$F = Se^{(r_D - r_f)T}, \tag{4}$$

where r_D is the domestic interest rate and r_f is the foreign interest rate. Arbitrage actions that establish interest rate parity can be conducted by borrowing the foreign currency, buying spot exchange, and investing the proceeds instead of purchasing a futures contract. Thus, equation (4) may be substituted into equation (3) to obtain:

$$c = p + Se^{-r_f T} - Ee^{-r_D T}. \tag{5}$$

A fixed deliverable option is essentially an option on a futures contract that expires on the date the option expires. Intuitively, a three-month call option on a six-month Treasury bill requires that a bill with six months to maturity be delivered at expiration. Purchasing a three-month futures on a six-month bill also requires that a bill with six months to maturity be delivered. Essentially, fixed deliverable options instruments are very similar to options on futures contracts. The same relationship between put and call prices holds as in the case of options on futures.

INTEREST RATE FUTURES*

Marcelle Arak and
Christopher J. McCurdy†

22

On a typical day in 1979, futures contracts representing about $7½ billion in three-month Treasury bills changed hands in the International Monetary Market (IMM) of the Chicago Mercantile Exchange in Chicago. This market and several other new markets for interest rate futures have very quickly become active trading arenas. For example, at the Chicago Board of Trade (CBT), futures contracts representing $820 million of long-term Treasury bonds were traded on a typical day; also, at the CBT, futures contracts representing $540 million of GNMAs (Government National Mortgage Association securities) changed hands on an average day.

Besides these three well-established interest rate futures contracts several new financial futures contracts have recently received the approval of the Commodity Futures Trading Commission (CFTC) and have begun trading. Futures contracts for intermediate-term Treasury notes commenced trading in the summer of 1979; in the fall, the Comex (Commodity Exchange, Inc.), which had traded many metals contracts, inaugurated a three-month bill futures contract, and the ACE (Amex Commodities Exchange, Inc., an affiliate of the American Stock Exchange) introduced a bond futures contract; in addition, the New York Stock Exchange is intending to start a financial futures unit.

*Reprinted from the *Quarterly Review*, Winter 1979-80, pp. 33–46, with permission of the Federal Reserve Bank of New York.

†The authors wish to thank James Kurt Dew, Ronald Hobson, and Anthony Vignola for information and helpful comments. The foregoing do not necessarily agree with the views expressed herein, nor do they bear responsibility for any errors.

What accounts for the rapid growth of interest rate futures? Who are the most active participants in these markets? Some businesses such as financial institutions and securities dealers use it to hedge or manage interest rate risk. By and large, however, participants are involved for other reasons and help provide much of the markets' liquidity. A large portion of the activity in these markets is speculative—people and institutions betting on which way interest rates will move and how the interest rate in one month will move relative to another. Others are involved in these interest rate futures markets for tax reasons.

Both the enormous size of these futures markets and the nature of the participants are a matter of concern for the regulatory authorities. The Treasury and the Federal Reserve System have become aware of potential problems for the functioning of markets in Government securities; these problems include the possibility of corners or squeezes on certain Treasury issues and the disruption of orderly cash markets for Treasury securities. In addition, the regulatory authorities have become concerned that the substantial numbers of small investors participating in the markets may not be fully aware of the risks involved.

WHAT IS A FUTURES MARKET?

For as long as mankind has traded goods and services, people have made contracts which specify that commodities and money will change hands at some future date, at a price stated in the contract. Such contracts are called "forward" contracts. A forward contract tailored to one's needs offers obvious advantages— one can pick the exact date and the precise commodity desired. On the other hand, there are disadvantages. It may be difficult to locate a buyer or seller with exactly opposite needs. In addition, there is a risk that the other party to the transaction will default.

A *futures* contract is a standardized forward contract that is traded on an exchange. Usually the type and grade of commodity is specified as well as the date for delivery. Once a bargain is struck, the clearinghouse of the futures exchange itself becomes the opposite party to every transaction. Thus, it is the soundness of the exchange's clearinghouse rather than the creditworthiness of the original buyer (or seller) that is of concern to the seller (or buyer) on the other side of the transaction. To ensure its viability, futures exchanges and their clearinghouses set up rules and regulations. These include the requirements that a clearing member firm and its customers put up "margin," that the contracts be marked-to-market daily, and that trading cease if daily price fluctuations move outside certain limits.

Among the oldest futures markets in the United States are those for wheat and corn which date back to the middle of the nineteenth century. Thereafter, futures markets for other farm products and raw materials gradually developed.

One of the major purposes was to provide producers and processors with price insurance. Suppose a farmer expects to harvest wheat in July. Nobody knows with certainty what the price will be then; it depends upon the size of the harvest and conditions elsewhere in the world. However, by selling a futures contract for July wheat, the farmer can indirectly guarantee receiving a particular price. This is illustrated in Box 1.

Futures markets for commodities not only provide a forum for hedgers, but they also provide information. This information—about prices expected to prevail on future dates—is printed in the financial section of many daily newspapers. The farmer, for example, can use these futures prices to decide whether to plant corn or wheat. The food processor can gear up to can corn or beans depending upon the expected prices and the prospective consumer demand at those prices.

Interest rate futures are a relatively new development. In the fall of 1975, the CBT inaugurated a GNMA contract. Shortly thereafter, in early 1976, the IMM introduced a contract for 90-day Treasury bills, and this was followed in 1977 by the CBT's Treasury bond futures contract. These three contracts—the CBT's original GNMA, the CBT's Treasury bond, and the IMM's three-month Treasury bill contract—have proved to be the most popular and heavily traded financial futures contracts. The amount of contracts outstanding, or open interest, in these markets has expanded significantly since their inception (Figure 22-1). Moreover, trading volume has also become quite large in relation to the underlying cash market securities. In 1979, daily average trading in the eight ninety-day Treasury bill contracts on the IMM was equivalent to about $7½ billion (at $1 million per contract), not much different from the daily volume of Treasury bills traded in the dealer market for United States Government

---

BOX 1
HEDGE IN WHEAT FUTURES

A farmer planning to harvest wheat in July sells a July wheat futures contract at $2.98 in March.

(1) Suppose the price in July turns out to be	$2.50	$3.00	$3.50
(2) Gain or loss from offsetting futures contract [$2.98 − row (1)]	.48	−.02	−.52
(3) Sales price of wheat in cash market [same as row (1)]	2.50	3.00	3.50
(4) Total earnings per bushel [row (2) + row (3)]	2.98	2.98	2.98

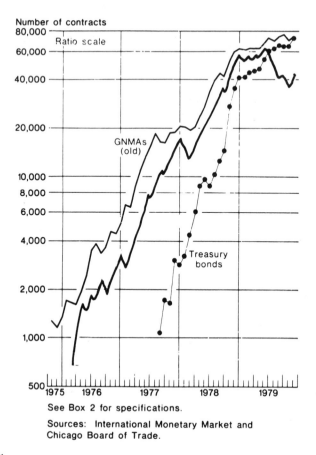

Figure 22-1

securities.[1] Some interest rate futures contracts, however, have failed to attract much trading activity. For example, activity in the ninety-day commercial paper contract has remained quite light.[2]

HOW FINANCIAL FUTURES MARKETS OPERATE

The financial futures markets operate in the same manner as other futures markets. Their terms and methods are very different from those used in the money and bond markets. One of the most active financial futures markets is

[1]The market is described in "The Dealer Market for United States Government Securities," Christopher McCurdy in this bank's *Quarterly Review* (Winter 1977–78), pages 35–47.

[2]One of the problems with this contract has been that commercial paper issuers have at times tended to sell paper with maturities much shorter than ninety days. Also, because the paper of a large number of companies is deliverable against the contract, this generates substantial uncertainty about which paper will be delivered. In addition, the original technical specifications of the contract engendered some confusion.

that for three-month Treasury bills at the IMM. Through this exchange, a customer could, for example, buy a contract to take delivery of (and pay for) $1 million of three-month Treasury bills on March 20, 1980. In all, there are eight contract delivery months on the IMM, extending at quarterly intervals for about two years into the future.

A customer places his order with a futures commission merchant—a firm registered with the CFTC and permitted to accept orders from the public—which sends the order to the trading floor of the exchange. There, a member of the exchange enters the trading pit and announces his intention to purchase the March 1980 contract. Another member who has an order to sell that contract shouts out his offer and, if the two can agree on a price, the trade is consummated. The trading in the pit is by *open outcry*, which is typical of futures exchanges and very unlike the over-the-telephone negotiations in the cash market for Treasury Securities.

The contract's price is quoted as the difference between 100 and the discount rate on the bill in question. Thus, a contract fixing a bill rate of 8.50 percent would be quoted at 91.50. This index preserves the normal futures market relationship in which the party obligated to take (make) delivery profits when the price rises (falls). The contract quote is not the price that would actually be paid for the bill at delivery. That price is computed by using the rate of discount in the standard bill price formula.

The clearinghouse interposes itself between the buyer and the seller, so that the buyer's contract is not with the seller but with the clearinghouse. (In the same fashion, the seller's contract is with the clearinghouse and not with the original buyer.)

A key ingredient in the financial viability of the clearinghouse is the margin that the clearing member firms must post on their contracts. For each outright purchase or sale of a three-month Treasury bill contract on the IMM, the firm must post margin of $1,200 per contract, which can be in the form of cash or bank letter of credit. The clearing member firm must, in turn, impose an initial margin of at least $1,500 on the customer. This may be posted in the form of cash, selected securities, or bank letters of credit. Futures firms can and often do require higher than the minimum margins of their customers. Margins formerly were more lenient, at one point down to $800 initial margin, but were raised following the greater volatility that emerged in the financial markets in the wake of the Federal Reserve System's policy actions in October 1979.

For as long as the position is outstanding, the contract will be *marked-to-market* by the clearinghouse at the end of each business day. For example a clearing member with a long position in the March contract would have its margin account credited with a profit if the price rises, or debited with a loss if it declines. The prices used in the calculations are the *final settlement prices*, which are determined by the exchange by examining the prices attached to the trades transacted at the end of trading each day.

Profits in the margin account may be withdrawn immediately. When losses occur and reduce the firm's margin below $1,200, the firm must pay the difference to the clearinghouse in cash before trading opens the next day. It is permissible for the value of a customer's margin account to fall below the initial $1,500 but, once the margin account falls below the $1,200 maintenance margin, the account must be replenished in full—brought back up to $1,500. Since the value of a 1 basis point change in the futures bill rate is $25 per contract, relatively small changes in interest rates can result in large changes in the value of a margin account.

The exchanges impose rules that prices may not change by more than a certain maximum amount from one day to the next. At the IMM, for example, no bill futures trades may be cleared if the price is more than 50 basis points above or below the final settlement price on the previous day although, if the *daily limit* restricts trading for a few days, then wider limits may be imposed on subsequent days. Margins are often temporarily increased during such periods.

When the customer wishes to get out of his contract before maturity, he must take an offsetting position. To cancel the contract he bought, he must sell another contract. His order is forwarded to the pit and a sales contract is executed, but not necessarily with the party who sold it to him in the first place. Once again, the clearinghouse interposes itself between the two parties and the latest sale will be offset against the original purchase. The customer's overall position will be canceled, and the funds in the margin account will be returned to him.

The lion's share of all contracts traded are terminated before maturity in this fashion. Only a very small percentage of contracts traded is delivered. In the case of Treasury bills, delivery takes place on the day after trading stops. The customer who has sold the contract (the short) delivers $1 million (par value) of Treasury bills that have 90, 91, or 92 days to maturity, and the customer who bought the contract (the long) pays for the bills with immediately available funds. The price paid for the bills is the settlement price on the last day of trading. (With the daily marking-to-market, almost all losses and gains have been realized before the final delivery takes place.)

Variations in procedures exist on different contracts and exchanges, but they generally adhere to the same principles: open outcry trading, interposition of the clearinghouse, posting of margin, and daily marking-to-market. Box 2 delineates the key specifications on financial futures contracts. Probably the most important difference among contracts is that some allow delivery of a variety of securities. The active Treasury bond contract, for example, permits delivery of bonds from a "market basket" of different bonds, all with maturity (or first call) beyond fifteen years. This has the effect of substantially increasing the deliverable supply of securities but generates some uncertainty among those taking delivery as to which bonds they might receive.

The formal organizational structure of futures trading stands in contrast to the informal nature of forward trading. Dealers in the market for United States Government securities often agree to transact trades that call for forward delivery of Treasury issues. These trades are negotiated in the same fashion as trades for immediate delivery. There is no standardized contract as in the futures market: the two parties must agree to the specific security involved, the exact delivery date, the size of trade, and the price. These terms are set according to the mutual convenience of the two parties. Often, there is no initial margin and no marking-to-market to account for gains and losses. Thus, each participant must size up the creditworthiness of the other. Finally, these agreements, for the most part, are designed to result in delivery. (Some GNMA forward trades among a few firms can be offset through a clearinghouse arrangement.) If either side wishes to cancel the trade, it must go back to the other side and negotiate a termination.

PARTICIPANTS IN THE INTEREST RATE FUTURES MARKET

Many types of financial institutions participate in the markets for interest rate futures, but private individuals not acting in a business capacity account for the major part of interest rate futures positions in the three most active contracts (Figure 22-2).

According to a survey by the CFTC of positions outstanding on March 30, 1979, businesses other than the futures industry, commonly called "commercial traders," accounted for only about one quarter of open interest held in the most active contracts (90-day Treasury bills on the IMM, and Treasury bonds and the original GNMA contract on the CBT). In an earlier survey, such participants had held about three-eighths of those contracts outstanding on November 30, 1977 (Table 22-1). The involvement of commercial traders is important because they are the only group that can use futures contracts for hedging cash market positions to any meaningful extent. (See next section.)

Moreover, some of the businesses who participate in these futures markets are probably not trying to eliminate risk completely. Consider securities dealers, for example, who have been very active in interest rate futures markets— they held about 7 percent of total GNMA positions and about 18 percent of total bond positions in March 1979. Securities dealers are generally risk takers, trying to benefit from interest rate change, or arbitrageurs, trying to benefit from interest rate disparities, rather than hedgers. But, in meeting customers' needs and making a market in Government securities, they do make use of interest rate futures markets to manage their risk exposure.

Among other business participants, mortgage bankers and savings and loan associations combined held about 7 percent of total positions in GNMAs. Their participation in GNMAs is to be expected in view of their involvement in generating and investing in mortgages. A total of 68 of these firms held positions on March 30, 1979, not much above the number reported in the earlier survey. Few commercial banks have been active in interest rate futures—24 had open positions in bill futures, and fourteen in bond futures on March 30, 1979—

BOX 2
FUTURES CONTRACTS ON TREASURY SECURITIES (CURRENTLY TRADING)

	Treasury bills				Intermediate-term Treasury coupon securities		Treasury bonds	
	ACE	COMEX	IMM	IMM	CBT	IMM	ACE	CBT
Deliverable items	$1 million par value of Treasury bills with 90, 91, or 92 days to maturity	$1 million par value of Treasury bills with 90, 91, or 92 days to maturity	$1 million par value of Treasury bills with 90, 91, or 92 days to maturity	$250,000 par value of Treasury bills due in 52 weeks	$100,000 par value of Treasury notes and noncallable bonds with 4 to 6 years to maturity	$100,000 par value of Treasury notes maturing between 3½ years and 4½ years	$100,000 par value of Treasury bonds with at least 20 years to maturity	$100,000 par value of Treasury bonds with at least 15 years to first call or to maturity
Initial margin* (per contract)	$800	$800	$1,500	$600	$900	$500	$2,000	$2,000†
Maintenance margin* (per contract)	$600	$600	$1,200	$400	$600	$300	$1,500	$1,600†
Daily limits‡	50 basis points	60 basis points	50 basis points	50 basis points	1 point (32/32)	3/4 point (48/64)	1 point (32/32)§	2 points (64/32)
Delivery months (each year)	January, April, July, October	February, May, August, November	March, June, September, December	March, June, September, December	March, June, September, December	February, May, August, November	February, May, August, November	March, June, September, December
Total open interest (December 31, 1979)	106	913	36,495	435	715	265	207	90,676
Date trading began	June 26, 1979	October 2, 1979	January 6, 1979	September 11, 1978	June 25, 1979	July 10, 1979	November 14, 1979	August 22, 1977

Government National Mortgage Association
(modified pass-through mortgage-backed certificates)

	CBT (old)	CBT (new)	ACE	COMEX	Commercial paper	
					CTB (30-day)	CBT (90-day)
Deliverable items	Collateralized depository receipt covering $100,000 principal balance of GNMA certificates	$100,000 principal balance of GNMA certificates	$100,000 principal balance of GNMA certificates	$100,000 principal balance of GNMA certificates	$3 million face value of prime commercial paper rated A-1 by Standard & Poor's and P-1 by Moody's	$1 million face value of prime commercial paper rated A-1 by Standard & Poor's and P-1 by Moody's
Initial margin* (per contract)	$2,000	$2,000	$2,000	$1,500	$1,500	$1,500
Maintenance margin* (per contract)	$1,500	$1,500	$1,500	$1,125	$1,200	$1,200
Daily limits‡	1½ points (48/32)	1½ points (48/32)	3/4 point (24/32)§	1 point (64/64)	50/100 point	50/100 point
Delivery months (each year)	March, June, September, December	March, June, September, December	February, May, August, November	January, April, July, October‖	March, June, September, December	March, June, September, December
Total open interest (December 31, 1979)	88,982	4,478	3,248	64	12	533
Date trading began	October 20, 1975	September 12, 1978	September 12, 1978	November 13, 1979	May 14, 1979	September 26, 1977

All specifications are as of year-end 1979.

*The speculative margin is shown where margins vary according to whether the contracts cover speculative, hedged, or spread positions.

†For all contracts but those which mature in current month. Then initial margin is increased to $2,500 and maintenance margin is raised to $2,000.

‡Exchanges frequently have rules allowing expansion of daily limits once they have been in effect for a few days (margins may change also).

§Limits in suspension as of the year-end.

‖Principal trading months; rules allow trading for current plus two succeeding months.

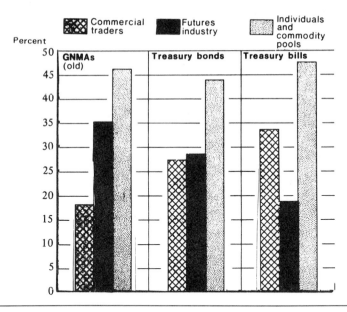

Source: Commodity Futures Trading Commission.

Figure 22-2   Futures markets participants, March 30, 1979 (shares of open interest held by various groups)

accounting for a small fraction of total positions in these markets. Their relatively low level of participation may have reflected regulatory restrictions on their involvement in the futures market or some confusion about the regulators' policies.

Futures industry personnel and firms held a significant fraction of the open positions. This group includes many who are speculating on rate movements in general or on the spread relations between rates on successive contracts. Or they might be operating in both the cash and futures markets, arbitraging differences between the two markets.

Individuals and commodity pools—funds which purchase futures contracts—are very important participants in financial futures markets. They held almost half of the open positions in 1979, a substantial increase from their already significant participation in the earlier survey. Indeed, the 1979 share of total positions in financial contracts was certainly higher than that because positions of less than five contracts were not included in the second survey and individuals tend to hold the vast majority of such small positions.[3]

---

[3]Small positions in the bill futures contracts amounted to about 8,000 contracts at the end of March 1979 and thus would raise the combined share of individuals and commodity pools to a bit more than half of the bill futures market. Comparable calculations cannot be made for the CBT's bond and GMNA contracts because some small positions are posted on a net basis (*i.e.*, long positions are offset against short positions), compared with a gross basis as in the bill contracts.

SERVICES PROVIDED BY INTEREST RATES FUTURES MARKETS

It is commonly believed that futures markets provide certain benefits—in the main, an inexpensive way to hedge risk and generate information on expected prices. Interest rate futures markets also provide these benefits.

Several observers have noted that interest rate futures markets are not necessary to provide information on future interest rates or as a hedging mechanism. They point out that one can obtain information on future interest rates by comparing yields on outstanding securities which have different maturities. However, the interest rate futures markets do provide future interest rate information in a more convenient form.

It is also true that outstanding securities could be used to hedge market risk. Again, however, the futures market can provide a less cumbersome and expensive hedge. Suppose, for example, that a firm is planning to issue short-term securities three months in the future and is worried about the prospective short-term interest rate. The short sale of a Treasury bill with more than three months to maturity is one way to hedge the risk.[4] In the futures market, the interest rate risk on this prospective issue could be hedged by selling the Treasury bill contract for the month closest to the prospective issue date. If all short rates moved up, the hedger would make a gain on the futures market transaction which would offset the loss on the higher interest rate he would have to offer.

Banks, dealers, and other such financial institutions may find futures markets helpful in achieving a particular maturity structure for their portfolios while having adequate supplies of cash securities on hand. For example, a dealer may need to hold supplies of a six-month bill to be ready for customer orders. However, he may not want the risk exposure on this particular maturity because he thinks its rate is likely to rise. Or, a mortgage banker may wish to hedge the risk on rates between the time of the mortgage loan and the time of its sale as part of a large package of loans. By selling a GNMA futures contract while assembling the mortgage package, the banker can be insured against rate changes. If rates rise, the value of the mortgage portfolio will fall, but that will be offset by the profits on the short sale of the GNMA contract. If, on the other hand, rates fall, the gain on the mortgage portfolio is offset by the loss on the sale of GNMA futures. In this hedge, the banker foregoes the possibility of additional profit (or loss) and is content to profit from the origination and servicing fees associated with assembling the mortgages.

Not every financial transaction has an exact hedge in the futures market. When the cash asset is different from the security specified in the futures

---

[4]The prospective issuer could borrow a six-month Treasury bill and sell it immediately; three months hence he would buy a bill with the same maturity date to return. If interest rates for that future time interval rise, the security would be purchased more cheaply three months hence than is currently expected. The gain on this transaction would then offset the loss connected with issuing securities at the higher interest rate.

Table 22-1 Futures markets participants, November 30, 1977 and March 30, 1979 (average open interest; number of contracts)

Type of participant	Government National Mortgage Association contract (old)				Treasury bond contract				Three-month Treasury bill contract			
	1977 amount	1977 as percentage of total	1979 amount	1977 as percentage of total	1977 amount	1977 as percentage of total	1979 amount	1979 as percentage of total	1977 amount	1977 as percentage of total	1979 amount	1979 as percentage of total
Commercial traders *(total)* ...	7,226	36.5	10,899	18.3	2,025	67.2	12,393	27.4	4,950	32.8	14,992	33.6
Securities dealers ..	3,395	17.1	4,270	7.2	1,534	50.9	8,226	18.2	2,758	18.3	5,596	12.5
Commercial banks ...	263	1.3	655	1.1	99	3.3	1,472	3.3	326	2.2	1,581	3.5
Savings and loan associations	494	2.5	2,500	4.2	–	–	394	0.9	56	0.4	136	0.3
Mortgage bankers	1,198	6.1	1,472	2.5	154	5.1	330	0.7	44	0.3	974	2.2
Other	1,875	9.5	2,003	3.4	238	7.9	1,971	4.4	1,767	11.7	6,706	15.0

Noncommercial traders (total) ...	12,588	63.5	48,705	81.7	989	32.8	32,826	72.6	10,154	67.2	29,661	66.4
Futures industry .	7,353	37.1	21,113	35.4	477	15.8	12,924	28.6	2,765	18.3	8,434	18.9
Commodity pools	2,862	14.4	11,097	18.6	254	8.4	9,484	21.0	1,520	10.1	5,640	12.6
Individual traders ..	2,373	12.0	16,495	27.7	258	8.6	10,481	23.0	5,868	38.8	15,586	34.9
Total	19,814	100	59,604	100	3,014	100	45,219	100	15,104	100	44,654	100

Because of rounding, amounts and percentages may not add to totals.

Source: Commodity Futures Trading Commission Surveys. The 1977 survey covered all positions, but the 1979 survey excluded positions of fewer than five contracts.

contract, the transaction is called a "cross hedge" and provides much less protection than an exact hedge. For example, a securities dealer might find it profitable to buy some certificates of deposit (CDs) and finance them for one month. To protect against a decline (increase) in the price (rates) of CDs over the interval, the dealer might sell Treasury bill futures contracts, assuming the movements in bill rates and CD rates will be similar over the interval. So long as the rates move in the same *direction* the dealer will be protected at least to some degree against adverse price movements. It is conceivable, however, that the rates could move in opposite directions. Thus, a cross hedge is really a speculation on the relationship between the particular cash market security held in position and the particular futures contract involved. In a cross hedge, the participants cannot deliver the cash security against the contract, so there is no threat of delivery that can be used to drive the prices on the two securities back into line as the expiration date approaches.

In contrast to financial businesses, nonfinancial businesses and private individuals are less likely to find a useful hedge in the interest rate futures market. Consider the typical nonfinancial business which is planning to issue securities to finance some capital purchase of inventory. If the rate of inflation accelerates, the firm will typically be able to sell its output at higher prices. Thus, its nominal profit and return from the investment will typically also rise.[5] This means that a rise in inflationary expectations, which is reflected in the nominal rate of interest, will tend to affect profits in the same direction as it does financing costs. Thus, to some extent, the firm is automatically hedged against inflation-induced changes in the interest rate.

A similar intrinsic hedge may be available to investors on any new funds they plan to invest. Presumably they want to be sure that their investment produces a certain real income or purchasing power in the future. If interest rates move down because anticipated inflation has fallen, then the return on any funds invested at the lower rate will be able to buy the same quantity of goods and services that they would have in the circumstances where inflation and interest rates were higher. (The real return on *past* savings, however, will move in the opposite direction as inflation.)

Thus, to the extent that interest rate changes reflect revisions in inflationary expectations, many businesses and persons will not be in a very risky position with regard to saving or investment plans. If, as some contend, the variation in interest rates is largely connected with inflationary expectations, these groups

---

[5]The firm does not, however, tend to earn nominal profits in proportion to prices because the tax structure collects more in real terms during inflation. See M. Arak, "Can the Performance of the Stock Market Be Explained by Inflation Coupled with our Tax System?" (Federal Reserve Bank of New York Research Paper).

would typically not obtain a very useful hedge in the interest rate futures market.

SPECULATION

While some participants use futures markets to hedge risk, others use them to speculate on price movements. Speculators like the high leverage obtainable and the low capital required for trades in futures markets relative to trades in cash markets. Speculation on interest rates could be accomplished in the cash markets but would typically involve greater costs than in futures markets. For example, suppose one thinks that the three-month interest rate in the June-September period will be higher than the implicit forward rate for that time interval. The short sale of a September bill in March and its repurchase in June can produce a profit if those high rates materialize. The costs involved in these transactions include the dollar value of the bid-ask spread as well as the charges for borrowing a security. In addition, one must have sufficient capital to put up collateral equivalent in value to the securities borrowed or the credit standing to borrow the securities under a reverse repurchase agreement.

In futures markets, one does not pay for or receive money for the commodity in advance. The cost of trading in the futures market is the foregone interest on the margin deposit (if in the form of cash) plus the commission fees. Assuming a $70 commission, this would amount to about $125 on a three-month bill futures contract at current interest rates, if the contract were held for three months. A change in the discount rate on the futures contract of five basis points would therefore recompense the speculator for his costs (Table 22-2).

Besides speculating on the level of rates, some futures market participants may be speculating on the relationship among interest rates. Such speculation can take the form of a "spread" trade whereby the participant buys one contract and sells another, hoping that the rate on the contract bought will fall by more than (or rise by less than) the rate on the contract sold. Also, if participants believe that the slope of the yield curve will change in a predictable way when the level of the yield curve changes, a spread transaction (which involves a lower margin) can be a less expensive way to speculate on the level of rates.

Frequently, traders will take positions in futures contracts that are related to positions in cash market securities. A trader might think that the rate in the futures market is out of line with cash Treasury bills. If he feels the futures rate is low relative to the rates on outstanding bills, he might sell the futures contract and buy the bills in the cash market. He could then carry the bill in position until the two rates move back to their more normal relationship. Then

Table 22-2   Change in discount rate on a three-month Treasury bill futures contract necessary to cover cost of a futures market transaction (in basis points)

Holding period	Commission (in dollars)		
	$30	$50	$70
One month	2.0	2.8	3.6
Three months	3.4	4.2	5.0
Six months	5.7	6.5	7.3
Twelve months	10.2	11.0	11.8

$$\text{Basis point change } = \frac{C + \dfrac{h(.01i)m}{12}}{25}$$

where h is the number of months the contract is held, i is the rate of interest obtainable over the period h, m is the cash margin, and C is the commission on the futures trade. The numbers shown are based upon i = 15 percent and m = $1,500.

the bills would be sold and the short bill futures contract off-set. These types of trades are often called "arbitrages" by participants in the cash market although they are not arbitrages in the strict sense in which a security is bought in one market and at the same time sold in another, thereby locking in an assured return. In fact, most arbitraging activity generally reflects speculation on the relationship between cash and futures rates.

USE OF FUTURES MARKETS TO REDUCE TAX LIABILITY

Individuals and institutions have also used interest rate futures markets to reduce their taxes. One means was through spread transactions.

Until November 1978, spread transactions in the Treasury bill futures market were a popular means of postponing taxes. An individual would buy one contract and sell another, both for the next calendar year. For example, in 1976, the participant might have bought the March 1977 contract and sold the September 1977 contract. An important assumption was that interest rates on all contracts would tend to move together so that the net risk was relatively small. At some point before the end of 1976, whichever position had produced a loss would be closed out. (In the above example, the short position or the sale of the September 1977 contract was the item that showed a loss during the latter part of 1976.) That loss could then be deducted from other income for 1976, reducing the 1976 tax bill. The contract for March 1977, on which the gain had accrued, was not closed out until 1977 when it no longer affected the 1976 tax liability.[6]

What made Treasury bill futures particularly attractive for such spreads was the belief of many taxpayers that, just like actual Treasury bills, they were not capital assets. In contrast, it was clear that other types of futures contracts, not held exclusively for business purposes, were capital assets.[7] If Treasury bill futures were not capital assets, then losses on them could be fully subtracted from other ordinary income (providing that *net* ordinary income did not become negative). Capital losses, in contrast, could be subtracted from ordinary income to a very limited extent.[8]

This attraction of the Treasury bill futures market for tax postponement was eliminated in November 1978 when the IRS declared that a futures contract for Treasury bills is a capital asset if neither held primarily for sale to customers in the ordinary course of business nor purchased as a hedge.[9] Further, the IRS, amplifying on an earlier ruling, stated that the maintenance of a "spread" position, in transactions involving futures contracts for Treasury bills, may not result in allowance of deductions where no real economic loss is incurred.[10]

A way that individuals can reduce taxes through the futures market is by indirectly converting part of the interest income on Treasury bills into long-term capital gains. Suppose that the discount rate on a bill is expected to fall as it matures. Since the market usually regards longer dated bills as less liquid (or as having more interest rate risk), an investor would typically expect that a bill maturing in, say, March 1981 would offer a higher annual discount rate in June 1980 than it would in February 1981. Similarly, the interest rate on futures contracts would tend to fall as they approach expiration (their price would rise). Pursuant to the November 1978 IRS ruling, the price increase in a Treasury bill futures contract should, in nonbusiness circumstances, be treated as a capital gain for an investor. In contrast, since a Treasury bill itself is not a capital asset, all the price appreciation on it—from date of purchase to date of sale—would be treated as ordinary income for tax purposes.

An investor would clearly prefer to have the price appreciation treated as a long-term gain rather than as ordinary income, since the long-term capital gains tax rate is only 40 percent of that for ordinary income. If a long position in a bill futures contract were held for more than six months, the profit would

---

[6]After the September 1977 contract was offset, another contract for 1977 would be sold to maintain a balanced position. In our example, the June 1977 contract would be sold to counterbalance the March 1977 contract that was still being held. Then sometime in early 1977, these two contracts would be closed out.

[7]*E.g.*, Faroll v. Jarecki, 231 F.2d 281 (7th Cir. 1956).

[8]Capital losses can be offset against capital gains with no limitation, but the excess of loss over gains that may be deducted from ordinary income in a single year is currently limited to $3,000.

[9]Rev. Rul. 78-414, 1978-2 C.B. 213.

[10]Rev. Rul. 77-85, 1977-1 C.B. 48.

be a long-term capital gain. (Gains and losses on short positions in futures are always treated as short-term regardless of the holding period.) Consequently, some investors who might normally purchase 52-week bills would have an incentive to purchase distant futures contracts and, as those contracts matured, sell them off to take their capital gains. They could then invest their funds in three-month bills. These activities would tend to raise the discount rate on the 52-week bill. It would also tend to reduce the required discount rate on distant futures contracts. Thus, the discount rates on futures contracts would be pushed below the implicit forward discount rate on cash bills.

There are, of course, limits on the size of the wedge that can be driven between the forward rate on cash securities and the rate on futures contracts. Financial businesses cannot treat profits in bill futures as capital gains. For them, the futures contract has no tax advantage over a cash bill. When the wedge produced by investors exceeds the cost of arbitrage, these financial businesses will buy long-term bills and sell futures contracts to profit from disparities in rates.

RELATIONSHIP BETWEEN THE CASH AND FUTURES MARKETS

For many commodities, the spot price and the futures price are very closely related. Part of the explanation is that, if a commodity is storable, it can be bought today, stored, and sold at a future date. If the futures price were to exceed the spot price by more than the costs involved, arbitrageurs would buy the commodity in the spot market—raising the spot price—and would sell it in the futures market, lowering the futures price. These activities would reduce the disparity between the future price and the current price.

The relationship between cash and futures markets for bills is somewhat different from that for other commodities. A three-month Treasury bill cannot be stored for more than three months; it matures. However, a longer term bill could be "stored" until it has three months left to run. It is the cash market for that *longer term bill* which bears a relationship to the futures market that is typical of agricultural and industrial commodities. In the case of note and bond contracts, the deliverable item exists throughout the life of the contract.

For example, consider what cash market securities correspond to the IMM's June 1980 three-month Treasury bill contract. This contract calls for delivery of bills which have 91 days to run on June 19, 1980. Treasury bills having this maturity date will be sold by the Treasury in two auctions—as six-month bills on March 17, 1980 and as three-month bills on June 16, 1980. During the first three months of its life, the six-month bill issued on March 20, 1980 is the commodity that could be "stored" for delivery on the futures contract.

The funds used to purchase the six-month bill when it is initially issued could have been invested in three-month bills which mature on the contract expiration date. One measure of the interest cost involved in storage is therefore the foregone interest on the shorter bill—this is the "opportunity cost" of the decision to invest in the longer bill which is deliverable on the futures contract. It is common to subtract that opportunity cost from the bill price to get the "forward" price and the corresponding "forward" rate; this rate can then be compared with the discount rate on the futures contract.

Because in the past only three-month and six-month bills matured on Thursdays, only bills originally issued as three-month or six-month bills could be delivered on a ninety-day bill futures contract.[11] In fact, at any date, there was only one bill issue in existence that could be delivered on an IMM bill futures contract. That particular bill had between three and six months to maturity and could be delivered on the closest three-month bill futures contract. For longer bill futures contracts, there was usually no exact correspondence. There is no cash bill in existence today that could be delivered on the September 1980, December 1980, March 1981, and subsequent contracts traded on the IMM. However, there are bills which have a maturity date that may be quite close. For example, the 52-week bill maturing on September 16, 1980 will have 89 days to run on June 19, 1980, while the June futures contract calls for bills which have 90 to 92 days to run on that date. By comparing the rate on this 52-week bill with the rate on the 52-week bill which matures twelve weeks earlier, a forward rate which covers an interval close to that of the futures contract bill can be calculated. Through this method, a rough forward rate in the period nine months prior to the contract's expiration can be obtained.

How does the rate on a three-month Treasury bill futures contract compare with the implicit forward rate in the cash market? The futures rate on the June 1979 contract and the "forward" rate on the corresponding cash bill (which matured September 1, 1979) moved very similarly in the last 91 days before the futures contract expired (Figure 22-3). Typically, the spread between the two rates was less than 25 basis points, with the forward rate somewhat higher than the futures rate. On most other futures contracts for three-month Treasury bills as well, the futures and forward rates were fairly close in the last 91 days or so before expiration.

When the contract's expiration date was far in the future, however, the link between its rate and the comparable forward rate was much weaker. In fact, spreads between forward and futures rates have at times been over 100 basis points in the three to nine months before the contract expired. Generally, in recent contracts, futures rates have been substantially below forward rates, and the spread between the two appears to have been wider than it was in earlier contracts.

Within three months of the expiration of the futures contract, futures and forward rates appear to be kept in reasonable alignment by investors and

---

[11]Now that the Treasury has begun to issue 52-week bills maturing on Thursdays, there will be some occasions on which bills issued as 52-week bills will be deliverable against the three-month bill contracts.

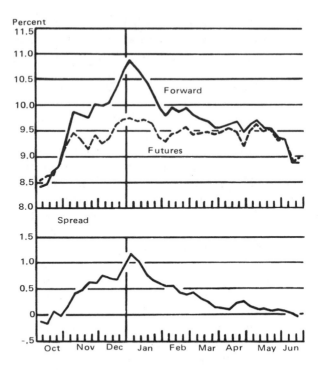

Figure 22-3   Discount rate on the June 1979 Treasury bill futures contract (IMM) and the forward rate in the cash market (spread equals forward rate minus futures rate).

arbitrageurs. An investor, for example, can on the one hand hold a sixth-month bill, or, on the other hand, hold a three-month bill plus the futures contract for the month in which the three-month cash bill matures. If the six-month bill is yielding more than the other combination, investors will tend to prefer six-month bills. And their demand will tend to reduce its discount rate, bringing the forward rate down toward the futures rate. Similarly, if investors find the three-month cash bill plus the futures contract more profitable, their buying pressure on the futures contract will tend to reduce its discount rate, bringing it down closer to the forward rate.

Another group of market participants who help keep rates in line are arbitrageurs. If they observe that the six-month bill provides a forward rate which is high relative to the futures rate, they could buy six-month bills and sell them under a repurchase agreement for three months; at the same time, they would sell a futures contract.[12] They would then have no net investment

_____

[12]A repurchase agreement specifies that the seller will rebuy at a prespecified date and price.

position: the bill returned to them in three months corresponds to the commitment to sell in the futures market. But they would earn a profit equal to the futures price minus the six-month bill price, the transaction cost, and the financing cost. As arbitrageurs conduct these activities, they put upward pressure on the six-month bill's price by buying it and put downward pressure on the futures price by selling the futures contract. These activities of the arbitrageur usually tend to keep the forward and futures rates within certain bounds.

On contracts other than the nearest, however, there is no deliverable bill as yet outstanding—that is, no security exists that can be purchased, stored, and delivered against the contract. Consequently, arbitrageurs cannot lock in a profit by taking exactly offsetting positions in the two markets. If there is an order flow in the futures market that is persistent, sizable, and at variance with the prevailing view in the cash market, it is possible for speculators to drive a wedge between the rates on futures contracts and the implicit forward rates in the cash market.

One notable example occurred in the spring of 1979. Apparently, many small speculators purchased bill futures contracts due in mid-1980, in the belief that short-term interest rates had reached a cyclical peak and would begin to fall sometime within a year or so. From the end of April to the end of June, their holdings rose from about 25 percent to 35 percent of the total open interest and their net long positions expanded sharply. As a result of this buying pressure and purchases by those trying to get out of large short positions, rates dropped sharply, with the March 1980 and June 1980 contract rates falling by nearly 1¾ percentage points from mid-May to the end of June. Rates also fell on contracts with shorter maturities—those due in the latter half of 1979.

Many other participants were net short, and some of these were firms that felt they were arbitraging between the cash and futures market, holding in this case long positions in the cash bill market against short positions in futures contracts. One of the several cash futures operations they engaged in was a long position in bills in the six-month area (*i.e.*, due in November for the most part) versus a short in the September contract (calling for delivery of the bill to mature on December 20 which had not been auctioned yet). As the rates on futures contracts fell, those with short positions faced sizable margin calls. To the extent that they then bought futures contracts to offset their short positions and also sold their cash bills, they greatly enlarged the wedge that was being driven between the rates in these two markets in late May and early June (Figure 22-4).

The widening wedge between the forward and futures rates made arbitrage involving futures contract sales even more profitable. But, after the shock of seeing large losses mount on short positions and show up in quarterly income statements, financial businesses were reluctant to expand their short positions. The futures and forward rates did not come back into alignment until late in the summer when interest rates started rising again.

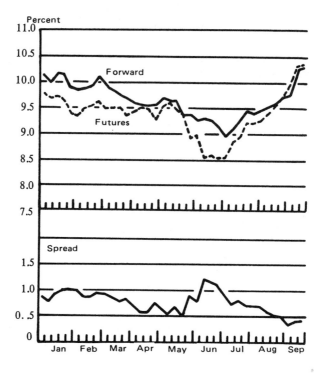

Figure 22-4   Discount rate on the September 1979 Treasury Bill futures contract (IMM) and the forward rate in the cash market (spread equals forward rate minus futures rate).

PROS AND CONS OF INTEREST RATE FUTURES MARKETS

Many observers of the new financial futures markets argue that these markets permit investors to obtain flexibility in ownership of securities at a very low cost. Someone who expects to have funds to invest in the period from mid-June to mid-September 1980, for example, can lock in an interest rate by purchasing a June Treasury bill futures contract. (For those who plan to purchase or issue other securities such as commercial paper or CDs, the links between the movements of rates in the bill futures market and the rates that obtain on these other instruments can be weak.)

By transferring the interest rate risk to those most willing to assume it, interest rate futures may increase the commitment of funds for some future time intervals. This could reduce the premium attached to funds committed for that future interval relative to funds committed for the nearer term. For example, the yield on 52-week and nine-month bills might fall. The resulting greater liquidity represents a gain to investors, while the lower interest rate on Government debt reduces the taxes necessary to service that debt.

While the provision of hedging facilities is a desirable aspect of interest rate futures markets, much of the activity appears to be speculative, and this has created some concern. One such concern is that speculation in the futures markets might push the prices of certain Treasury bills out of line with the prices of other securities. Because speculation is very inexpensive, entry into the futures market could be much more massive than entry into the cash market. Heavy demand in the futures market could be transmitted to the cash market by arbitrageurs. According to some analysts, the bill deliverable on the June 1979 contract was influenced by activities in the futures market. The June contract specified delivery on the Treasury bill due September 20 and only that bill. While the Treasury had sold $5.9 billion of bills with that maturity date, the Federal Reserve, foreign official accounts, and small investors held about one half. Thus, it appeared likely that the available trading supplies would amount to about $2 billion to $2½ billion.

However, open interest in the June 1979 contract stood at about 4,300 contracts, the equivalent of about $4.3 billion of bills at the end of May (Figure 22-5). This substantially exceeded the prospective trading supplies. During the spring, dealers reported that trading supplies in the September 20 bill were very thin and that it traded at a rate that was out of line with other bills. For example, it averaged about four basis points below the rate on the bill that was due a week earlier. Since investors usually require a higher rate when extending the maturity of their bill holdings, the four basis point difference provides a rough lower limit on the pressure that was exerted on the June contract and its spillover on the cash market.

Some observers argued that some investors were desirous of taking delivery because they thought there would be further declines in interest rates. Others pointed out that some people who had booked gains on long positions wanted to qualify for long-term capital gains. In any event, about a week before the contract expiration there was news of large increases in the money supply and industrial production which the market interpreted as indicating that a recession was not imminent and that interest rates would not fall immediately. This view probably contributed toward reducing pressure on the contract, and it was liquidated in an orderly fashion. Deliveries turned out to be a then record high of $706 million of bills due September 20, 1979, about a third of the available trading supplies of that bill. Deliveries on the September contract were somewhat lower, although still sizable (Figure 22-6), and deliveries on the December contract amounted to $1 billion.[13] Over the last month before delivery, the

---

[13]A part of the large amount of deliveries on the three 1979 contracts may reflect investor's preference for ordinary income losses instead of capital losses, a transformation that can be achieved by taking delivery on a contract on which one has booked a loss. See Arak, "Taxes, Treasury Bills, and Treasury Bill Futures."

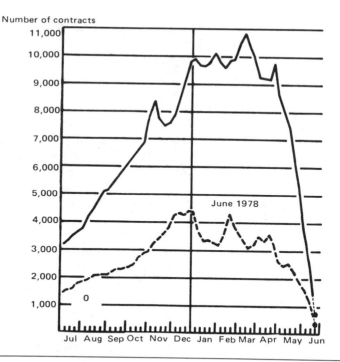

Source: International Monetary Market.

Figure 22-5   Open interest in Treasury bill futures contracts for June 1978 and June 1979 (weekly averages, week ending each Wednesday; total open interest as of last trading day is indicated by dots).

rate on the bill deliverable on the December contract averaged eight basis points below the rate on the bill due one week earlier. As a result of these events, the question arises whether supplies of the deliverable bill are sufficient to prevent pricing dislocations.

In contrast to bill futures, other future contracts, notably in notes and bonds, have adopted a market basket approach to deliverable supplies. By allowing a variety of issues to be delivered, the contracts greatly reduce the possibility of a squeeze. If, for example, the September 13 bill had also been deliverable against the June contract, then traders would have had no incentive to deliver the September 20 bill at a rate that was below that on the September 13 bill. The mere availability of the other bill would therefore have provided a floor for the rate on the September 20 bill.

This analysis of bill futures has led some to suggest that, instead of a single deliverable issue, the deliverable security should be any one of a "basket" of

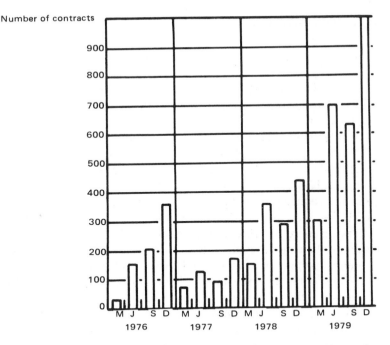

Number of contracts

Source: International Monetary Market, where M = March, J = June, S = September, and D = December.

Figure 22-6 Deliveries on three-month bill futures contracts.

Treasury bills with different maturity dates. However, others see disadvantages with the "basket" approach. In any event, the CFTC has authorized the new exchanges such as the ACE and the Comex to trade futures which involve bills maturing in a different week of the quarter than the IMM bill contracts. If these markets grow and become more active, there should be less likelihood of pressure on the one particular March, June, September, or December bill whose futures contract is traded on the IMM.

Finally, to many of the regulators, the size of the required margin deposit is a key issue. Larger margins would help insure the exchanges against possible defaults as well as discourage excessive speculation with little capital. Moreover, they might make participants more aware of the possibilities of loss inherent in trading in interest rate futures. In early October 1979, the minimum initial margin on Treasury bill futures contracts at the IMM was only $800, and a 32 basis point move in the rate on one of those contracts could have wiped out the entire margin. Now that margin is $1,500, which gives better protection to the exchange and the contract.

CONCLUDING REMARKS

Interest rate futures markets have generated much new activity within a very short time; they have also generated some apprehension on the part of those concerned with orderly marketing and trading of the United States Government debt. Thus far, neither the extreme enthusiasm nor the worst worries appear to be justified.

Interest rate futures markets can provide inexpensive hedging facilities and flexibility in investment. But, to date, participation by financial institutions that might have such a need has not been large. Rather, it appears that participants have so far been primarily interested in either speculating on interest rates or reducing tax liabilities. These participants have been encouraged by fairly low margins. Until recently, the exchanges had shown a penchant for reducing these margins, but in October 1979 when interest rates fluctuated widely following the Federal Reserve System's adoption of new operating procedures, several exchanges raised margins substantially.

Most of the time, the financial futures markets have operated fairly smoothly. In general, there has been no greater volatility in the prices of bills which are deliverable on futures contracts than in the prices of other bills. And despite the huge run-up in open interest in some of the bill futures contracts, actual deliveries have not been large enough to disrupt the operation of the cash market. However, on several bill futures contracts, the price of the deliverable bill was pushed slightly out of line with prices on other issues with adjacent maturities. The CFTC, the Treasury, the Federal Reserve, and market participants themselves will have to continue to observe futures market activities to assure that significant problems are not building up.

Interest rate futures markets have already provided an arena for some institutions to manage interest rate risk. And, as these markets mature, their economic usefulness may come to be more widely appreciated.

A GUIDE TO FOREIGN EXCHANGE MARKETS*

K. Alec Chrystal[†]

23

The economies of the free world are becoming increasingly interdependent. U.S. exports now amount to almost 10 percent of Gross National Product. For both Britain and Canada, the figure currently exceeds 25 percent. Imports are about the same size. Trade of this magnitude would not be possible without the ability to buy and sell currencies. Currencies must be bought and sold because the acceptable means of payment in other countries is not the U.S. dollar. As a result, importers, exporters, travel agents, tourists and many others with overseas business must change dollars into foreign currency and/or the reverse.

The trading of currencies takes place in foreign exchange markets whose major function is to facilitate international trade and investment. Foreign exchange markets, however, are shrouded in mystery. One reason for this is that a considerable amount of foreign exchange market activity does not appear to be related directly to the needs of international trade and investment.

*Reprinted from the *Review*, March 1984, pp. 5-18, with permission of the Federal Reserve Bank of St. Louis.

†K. Alec Chrystal, professor of economics-elect, University of Sheffield, England, is a visiting scholar at the Federal Reserve Bank of St. Louis. Leslie Bailis Koppel provided research assistance. The author wishes to thank Joseph Hempen, Centerre Bank, St Louis, for his advice on this paper.

The purpose of this paper is to explain how these markets work.[1] The basics of foreign exchange will first be described. This will be followed by a discussion of some of the more important activities of market participants. Finally, there will be an introduction to the analysis of a new feature of exchange markets—currency options. The concern of this paper is with the structure and mechanics of foreign exchange markets, not with the determinants of exchange rates themselves.

THE BASICS OF FOREIGN EXCHANGE MARKETS

There is an almost bewildering variety of foreign exchange markets. Spot markets and forward markets abound in a number of currencies. In addition, there are diverse prices quoted for these currencies. This section attempts to bring order to this seeming disarray.

Spot, Forward, Bid, Ask

Virtually every major newspaper, such as the *Wall Street Journal* or the *London Financial Times*, prints a daily list of exchange rates. These are expressed either as the number of units of a particular currency that exchange for one U.S. dollar or as the number of U.S. dollars that exchange for one unit of a particular currency. Sometimes both are listed side by side (see Table 23-1).

For major currencies, up to four different prices typically will be quoted. One is the "spot" price. The others may be "30 days forward," "90 days forward," and "180 days forward." These may be expressed either in "European Terms" (such as number of $ per £) or in "American Terms" (such as number of £ per $). (See the glossary for further explanation.)

The spot price is what you must pay to buy currencies for immediate delivery (two working days in the interbank market; over the counter, if you buy bank notes or travelers checks). The forward prices for each currency are what you will have to pay if you sign a contract today to buy that currency on a specific future date (30 days from now, etc.). In this market, you pay for the currency when the contract matures.

Why would anyone buy and sell foreign currency forward? There are some major advantages from having such opportunities available. For example, an exporter who has receipts of foreign currency due at some future date can sell those funds forward now, thereby avoiding all risks associated with subsequent adverse exchange rate changes. Similarly, an importer who will have to pay

---

[1]For further discussion of foreign exchange markets in the United States, see Kubarych (1983). See also Dufey and Giddy (1978) and McKinnon (1979).

for a shipment of goods in foreign currency in, say, three months can buy the foreign exchange forward and, again, avoid having to bear the exchange rate risk.

The exchange rates quoted in the financial press (for example, those in Table 23-1) are not the ones individuals would get at a local bank. Unless otherwise specified, the published prices refer to those quoted by banks to other banks for currency deals in excess of $1 million. Even these prices will vary somewhat depending upon whether the bank buys or sells. The difference between the buying and selling price is sometimes known as the "bid-ask spread." The spread partly reflects the banks' costs and profit margins in transactions; however, major banks make their profits more from capital gains than from spread.[2]

The market for bank notes and travelers checks is quite separate from the interbank foreign exchange market. For smaller currency exchanges, such as an individual going on vacation abroad might make, the spread is greater than in the interbank market. This presumably reflects the larger average costs—including the exchange rate risks that banks face by holding bank notes in denominations too small to be sold in the interbank market—associated with these smaller exchanges. As a result, individuals generally pay a higher price for foreign exchange than those quoted in the newspapers.

An example of the range of spot exchange rates available is presented in Table 23-2, which shows prices for deutschemarks and sterling quoted within a one-hour period on November 28, 1983. There are two important points to notice. First, all except those in the first line are prices quoted in the interbank, or wholesale, market for transactions in excess of $1 million. The sterling prices have a bid-ask spread of only 0.1 cent (which is only about 0.07 percent of the price, or $7 on $10,000). On DM, the spread per dollars worth works out to be about half that on sterling ($4 on $10,000).[3]

Second, the prices quoted by local banks for small, or retail, transactions, which serve only as a guide and do not necessarily represent prices on actual deals, involve a much larger bid-ask spread. These retail spreads vary from bank to bank, but are related to (and larger than) the interbank rates. In some cases, they may be of the order of 4 cents or less on sterling, though the prices quoted in St. Louis involved average spreads of 8 cents on sterling. The latter represents a spread of about 5 1/2 percent (about $550 per $10,000 transaction). The equivalent spread for DM was 7 percent ($700 per $10,000 transaction).

---

[2]Notice the *Wall Street Journal* quotes only a bank selling price at a particular time. The *Financial Times* quotes the bid-ask spread and the range over the day.

[3]In practice, the spread will vary during the day, depending upon market conditions. For example, the sterling spread may be as little as 0.01 cents at times and on average is about 0.05 cents. Spreads generally will be larger on less widely traded currencies.

Table 23-1 Foreign exchange rate quotations

Foreign Exchange

Wednesday, September 7, 1983

The New York foreign exchange selling rates below apply to trading among banks in amounts of $1 million and more, as quoted at 3 p.m. Eastern time by Bankers Trust Co. Retail transactions provide fewer units of foreign currency per dollar.

Country	U.S. $ equiv. Wed.	U.S. $ equiv. Tues.	Currency per U.S. $ Wed.	Currency per U.S. $ Tues.
Argentina (Peso)	.09652	.09652	10.36	10.36
Australia (Dollar)	.8772	.8777	1.1340	1.1393
Austria (Schilling)	.05296	.0560	18.88	17.84
Belgium (Franc)				
Commercial rate	.01851	.01855	54.01	53.90
Financial rate	.01844	.01846	54.21	54.15
Brazil (Cruzeiro)	.001459	.00149	685.	671.00
Britain (Pound)	1.4910	1.5000	.6707	.6666
30-Day Forward	1.4915	1.5004	.6704	.6664
90-Day Forward	1.4930	1.5010	.6697	.6662
180-Day Forward	1.4952	1.5028	.6688	.6654
Canada (Dollar)	.8120	.8123	1.2315	.2310
30-Day Forward	.8125	.8128	1.2307	1.2303
90-Day Forward	.8134	.8137	1.2293	1.2289
180-Day Forward	.8145	.8147	1.2277	1.2274
Chile (Official rate)	.01246	.01246	80.21	80.21
China (Yuan)	.50499	.50489	1.9802	1.9606
Colombia (Peso)	.01228	.01228	81.4	81.40
Denmark (Krone)	.10362	.10405	9.65	9.6100
Ecuador (Sucre)				
Official rate	.02082	.02082	48.03	48.03
Floating rate	.010917	.010917	91.60	91.60
Finland (Markka)	.17424	.17485	5.7390	5.7190
France (Franc)	.1238	.1238	8.0750	8.0750
30-Day forward	.1235	.1230	8.0955	8.1300
90-Day Forward	.1224	.1223	8.1695	8.1725
180-Day Forward	.1203	.1202	8.3100	8.3150

The Dollar Spot and Forward

Sept 7	Day's spread	Close	One month	% p.a.	Three months	% p.a.
UK†	1.4860-1.4975	1.4910-1.4920	0.02-0.07c dis	-0.36	0.17-0.22dis	-0.52
Ireland†	1.1665-1.1720	1.1710-1.1720	0.36-0.30c pm	3.39	0.88-0.78 pm	2.84
Canada	1.2305-1.2320	1.2310-1.2315	0.09-0.06c pm	0.73	0.24-0.21 pm	0.73
Nethlnd.	3.0050-3.0150	3.0050-3.0070	1.12-1.02c pm	4.26	3.00-2.90 pm	3.92
Belgium	54.06-54.20	54.06-54.08	7-6c pm	1.44	14-11 pm	0.92
Denmark	9.6400-9.6800	9.6400-9.6450	2-2½ore dis	-2.79	par-½ dis	-0.10
W. Ger.	2.6850-2.6980	2.6865-2.6875	1.07-1.02pf pm	4.66	3.00-2.95 pm	4.42
Portugal	124.20-125.00	124.40-124.70	115-290c dis	-19.51	330-790dis	-17.98
Spain	152.40-152.70	152.50-152.60	170-220c dis	-15.33	675-775dis	-18.99
Italy	1604-1608	1605-1606	10-10½lire dis	-7.65	29½-31dis	-7.53
Norway	7.4730-7.4940	7.4730-7.4780	1.90-2.20ore dis	-3.29	5.90-6.20ds	-3.23
France	8.0775-8.1225	8.0825-8.0875	2.02-2.12c dis	-3.07	9.65-9.85ds	-4.81
Sweden	7.9120-7.9265	7.9120-7.9170	0.90-1.10ore dis	-1.51	2.25-2.45ds	-1.19
Japan	245.50-246.50	245.65-245.75	0.69-0.64y pm	3.24	2.11-2.03 pm	3.36
Austria	18.89-18.95½	18.89-18.90	7.50-6.70gro pm	4.50	21.00-18.50 pm	4.17
Switz.	2.1770-2.1875	2.1800-2.1810	1.10-1.05c pm	5.91	3.10-3.05 pm	5.63

†UK and Ireland are quoted in U.S. currency. Forward premiums and discounts apply to the U.S. dollar and not to the individual currency.

Belgian rate is for convertible francs. Financial franc 54.40-54.45.

Source: *London Financial Times*, September 8, 1983.

Currency				
Greece (Drachma)	.01075	.01078	93.	92.70
Hong Kong (Dollar)	.1297	.13089	7.71	7.6400
India (Rupee)	.0980	.0980	10.20	10.20
Indonesia (Ruplah)	.001015	.001015	985.	985.
Ireland (Punt)	1.1715	1.1775	.8536	.8493
Israel (Shekel)	.0173	.0173	57.80	57.80
Italy (Lira)	.000624	.0006255	1602.	1598.50
Japan (Yen)	.004072	.004067	245.55	245.85
30-Day Forward	.004083	.004079	244.88	245.15
90-Day Forward	.004107	.004102	243.48	243.75
180-Day Forward	.004147	.004142	241.10	241.39
Lebanon (Pound)	.20618	.20618	4.85	4.85
Malaysia (Ringgit)	.42462	.42489	2.3550	2.3535
Mexico (Peso)				
Floating rate	.00665	.00666	150.25	150.00
Netherlands (Guilder) . .	.33288	.3333	3.0040	3.000
New Zealand (Dollar) . .	.6497	.6505	1.5397	1.5327
Norway (Krone)	.13368	.1340	7.48	7.4625
Pakistan (Rupee)	.07518	.07518	13.30	13.30
Peru (Sol)	.0005105	.0005105	1958.89	1958.89
Philippines (Peso)	.09085	.09085	11.007	11.007
Portugal (Escudo)	.00804	.00807	124.35	123.90
Saudi Arabia (Riyal) . .	.28735	.28735	3.48	3.48
Singapore (Dollar)	.46609	.4664	2.1455	2.1440
South Africa (Rand) . . .	.8870	.8900	1.1273	1.1236
South Korea (Won)	.001285	.001285	778.20	778.20
Spain (Peseta)	.00655	.00658	152.60	151.90
Sweden (Krona)	.12635	.12666	7.9140	7.8950

Table 23-1 Foreign exchange rate quotations

Foreign Exchange

Wednesday, September 7, 1983

The New York foreign exchange selling rates below apply to trading among banks in amounts of $1 million and more, as quoted at 3 p.m. Eastern time by Bankers Trust Co. Retail transactions provide fewer units of foreign currency per dollar.

Country	U.S. $ equiv. Wed.	Tues.	Currency per U.S. $ Wed.	Tues.
Switzerland (Franc)	.4596	.4591	2.1755	2.1780
30-Day Forward	.4619	.4615	216.46	2.1666
90-Day Forward	.4662	.4657	2.1449	2.1470
180-Day Forward	.4728	.4723	2.1150	2.1172
Taiwan (Dollar)	.02489	.02489	40.17	40.17
Thailand (Baht)	.043459	.043459	23.01	23.01
Uruguay (New Peso)				
Financial	.02798	.02798	35.73	35.73
Venezuela (Bolivar)				
Official rate	.23256	.23256	4.30	4.30
Floating rate	.07194	.07272	13.90	13.75
W. Germany (Mark)	.3726	.3726	2.6835	2.6835
30-Day Forward	.3740	.3741	2.6731	2.6728
90-Day Forward	.3767	.3768	2.6540	2.6538
180-Day Forward	.3808	.3808	2.6260	2.6259
SDR	1.04637	1.04903	.955685	.953625

Special Drawing Rights are based on exchange rates for the U.S., West German, British, French and Japanese currencies. Source: International Monetary Fund.

z—Not quoted.

Source: *Wall Street Journal*, September 8, 1983

Table 23-2 Dollar price of deutschemarks and sterling at various banks

	Deutschemark		Sterling	
	Buy	Sell	Buy	Sell
Retail				
Local (St. Louis) banks (avg.)	.3572–.3844		1.4225–1.5025	
Wholesale				
New York banks	.3681–.3683		1.4570–1.4580	
European banks (high)	.3694–.3696		1.4573–1.4583	
European banks (low)	.3677–.3678		1.4610–1.4620	
Bankers trust	.3681		1.4588	

Note: These prices were all quoted on November 28, 1983, between 2:00 p.m. and 2:45 p.m. (Central Standard Time). Prices for local banks were acquired by telephoning for their price on a $10,000 transaction. The prices quoted were reference rates and not the final price they would offer on a firm transaction. Figure for Bankers Trust is that given in the *Wall Street Journal*, November 29, 1983, as priced at 2:00 p.m. (Central Standard Time) on November 28, 1983. Other prices were taken from the Telerate information system at 2:35 p.m. New York prices were the latest available (Morgan and Citibank, respectively). European prices were the last prices quoted before close of trading in Europe by various banks. Deutschemark prices were actually quoted in American terms. The sell prices above have been rounded up. The difference between buy and sell prices for DM in the interbank market actually worked out at $0.00015.

The spread on forward transactions will usually be wider than on spot, especially for longer maturities. For interbank trade, the closing spread on one and three months forward sterling on September 8, 1983, was .15 cents, while the spot spread was .10 cents. This is shown in the top line of the *Financial Times* report in Table 23-1. Of course, like the spot spread, the forward spread varies with time of day and market conditions. At times it may be as low as .02 cents. No information is available for the size of spread on the forward prices typically offered on small transactions, since the retail market on forward transactions is very small.

HOW DOES "THE" FOREIGN EXCHANGE MARKET OPERATE?

It is generally not possible to go to a specific building and "see" the market where prices of foreign exchange are determined. With few exceptions, the vast bulk of foreign exchange business is done over the telephone between specialist divisions of major banks. Foreign exchange dealers in each bank usually operate from one room; each dealer has several telephones and is surrounded by video screens and news tapes. Typically, each dealer specializes in one or a small number of markets (such as sterling/dollar or deutschemark/

dollar). Trades are conducted with other dealers who represent banks around the world. These dealers typically deal regularly with one another and are thus able to make firm commitments by word of mouth.

Only the head or regional offices of the larger banks actively deal in foreign exchange. The largest of these banks are known as "market makers" since they stand ready to buy or sell any of the major currencies on a more or less continuous basis. Unusually large transactions, however, will only be accommodated by market makers on more favorable terms. In such cases, foreign exchange brokers may be used as middlemen to find a taker or takers for the deal. Brokers (of which there are four major firms and a handful of smaller ones) do not trade on their own account, but specialize in setting up large foreign exchange transactions in return for a commission (typically 0.03 cents or less on the sterling spread). In April 1983, 56 percent of spot transactions by value involving banks in the United States were channeled through brokers.[4] If all interbank transactions are included, the figure rises to 59 percent.

Most small banks and local offices of major banks do not deal directly in the interbank foreign exchange market. Rather they typically will have a credit line with a large bank or their head office. Transactions will thus involve an extra step (see Figure 23-1). The customer deals with a local bank, which in turn deals with a major bank or head office. The interbank foreign exchange market exists between the major banks either directly or indirectly via a broker.

FUTURES AND OPTION MARKETS FOR FOREIGN EXCHANGE

Until very recently, the interbank market was the only channel through which foreign exchange transactions took place. The past decade has produced major innovations in foreign exchange trading. On May 16, 1972, the International Money Market (IMM) opened under the auspices of the Chicago Mercantile Exchange. One novel feature of the IMM is that it provides a trading floor on which deals are struck by brokers face to face, rather than over telephone lines. The most significant difference between the IMM and the interbank market, however, is that trading on the IMM is in futures contracts for foreign exchange, the typical business being contracts for delivery on the third Wednesday of March, June, September or December. Activity at the IMM has expanded greatly since its opening. For example, during 1972, 144,336 contracts were traded; the figure for 1981 was 6,121,932.

There is an important distinction between "forward" transactions and "futures" contracts. The former are individual agreements between two parties, say, a bank and customer. The latter is a contract traded on an organized market of a standard size and settlement date, which is resalable at the market price up to the close of trading in the contract. These organized markets are discussed more fully below.

[4]See Federal Reserve Bank of New York (1983).

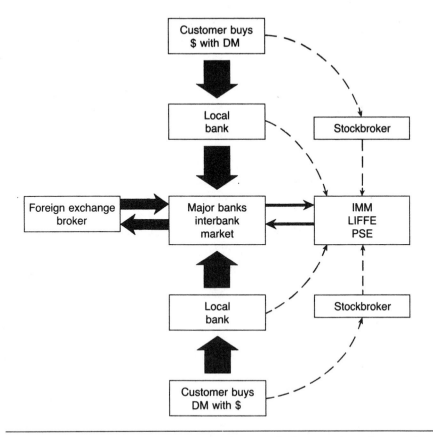

NOTE: The International Money Market (IMM) Chicago trades foreign exchange futures and DM futures options.

The London International Financial Futures Exchange (LIFFE) trades foreign exchange futures.

The Philadelphia Stock Exchange (PSE) trades foreign currency options.

Figure 23-1   Structure of foreign exchange markets

While the major banks conduct foreign exchange deals in large denominations, the IMM trading is done in contracts of standard size which are fairly small. Examples of the standard contracts at present are £25,000; DM125,000; Canadian $100,000. These are actually smaller today than in the early days of the IMM.

Further, unlike prices on the interbank market, price movements in any single day are subject to specific limits at the IMM. For example, for sterling futures, prices are not allowed to vary more than $.0500 away from the previous day's settlement price; this limit is expanded if it is reached in the same direction for two successive days. The limit does not apply on the last day a contract is traded.

Unlike the interbank market, parties to a foreign exchange contract at the IMM typically do not know each other. Default risk, however, is minor because contracts are guaranteed by the exchange itself. To minimize the cost of this guarantee, the exchange insists upon "margin requirements" to cover fluctuations in the value of a contract. This means that an individual or firm buying a futures contract would, in effect, place a deposit equal to about 4 percent of the value of the contract.[5]

Perhaps the major limitation of the IMM from the point of view of importers or exporters is that contracts cover only eight currencies—those of Britain, Canada, West Germany, Switzerland, Japan, Mexico, France and the Netherlands—and they are specified in standard sizes for particular dates. Only by chance will these conform exactly to the needs of importers and exporters. Large firms and financial institutions will find the market useful, however, if they have a fairly continuous stream of payments and receipts in the traded foreign currencies. Although contracts have a specified standard date, they offer a fairly flexible method of avoiding exchange rate risk because they are marketable continuously.

A major economic advantage of the IMM for nonbank customers is its low transaction cost. Though the brokerage cost of a contract will vary, a "round trip" (that is, one buy and one sell) costs as little as $15. This is only .04 percent of the value of a sterling contract and less for some of the larger contracts. Of course, such costs are high compared with the interbank market, where the brokerage cost on DM 1 million would be about $6.25 (the equivalent-valued eight futures contracts would cost $60 in brokerage, taking $7.50 per single deal). They are low, however, compared with those in the retail market, where the spread may involve a cost of up to 2.5 percent or 3 percent per transaction.

A market similar to the IMM, the London International Financial Futures Exchange (LIFFE), opened in September 1982. On LIFFE, futures are traded in sterling, deutschemarks, Swiss francs and yen in identical bundles to those sold on the IMM. In its first year, the foreign exchange business of LIFFE did not take off in a big way. The major provider of exchange rate risk coverage for business continues to be the bank network. Less than 5 percent of such cover is provided by markets such as IMM and LIFFE at present.

An entirely new feature of foreign exchange markets that has arisen in the 1980s is the existence of option markets.[6] The Philadelphia Exchange was the first to introduce foreign exchange options. These are in five currencies (deutschemark, sterling, Swiss franc, yen and Canadian dollar). Trades are conducted in standard bundles half the size of the IMM futures contracts. The IMM introduced an options market in German marks on January 24, 1984; this market

[5]A bank may also insist upon some minimum deposit to cover a forward contract, though there is no firm rule.

[6]For a discussion of options in commodities, see Belongia (1983).

trades options on futures contracts whereas the Philadelphia options are for spot currencies.

Futures and options prices for foreign exchange are published daily in the financial press. Table 23-3 shows prices for February 14, 1984, as displayed in the *Wall Street Journal* on the following day. Futures prices on the IMM are presented for five currencies (left-hand column). There are five contracts quoted for each currency: March, June, September, December and March 1985. For each contract, opening and last settlement (settle) prices, the range over the day, the change from the previous day, the range over the life of the contract and the number of contracts outstanding with the exchange (open interest) are listed.

Consider the March and June DM futures. March futures opened at $.3653 per mark and closed at $.3706 per mark; June opened at $.3698 per mark and closed at $.3746 per mark. Turn now to the Chicago Mercantile Exchange (IMM) futures options (center column). These are options on the futures contracts just discussed (see box for explanation of options). Thus, the line labeled "Futures" lists the settle prices of the March and June futures as above.

Let us look at the call options. These are rights to buy DM futures at specified prices—the strike price. For example, take the call option at strike price 35. This means that one can purchase an option to buy DM 125,000 March futures up to the March settlement date for $.3500 per mark. This option will cost 2.05 cents per mark, or $2,562.50, plus brokerage fees. The June option to buy June features DM at $.3500 per mark will cost 2.46 cents per mark, or $3,075.00, plus brokerage fees. The March call option at strike price $.3900 per mark costs only 0.01 cents per mark or $12.50. These price differences indicate that the market expects the dollar price of the mark to exceed $.3500, but not to rise substantially above $.3900.

Notice that when you exercise a futures call option you buy the relevant futures contract but only fulfill that futures contract at maturity. In contrast, the Philadelphia foreign currency options (right column) are options to buy foreign exchange (spot) itself rather than futures. So, when a call option is exercised, foreign currency is obtained immediately.

The only difference in presentation of the currency option prices as compared with the futures options is that, in the former, the spot exchange rate is listed for comparison rather than the futures price. Thus, on the Philadelphia exchange, call options on March DM 62,500 at strike price $.3500 per mark cost 1.99 cents per mark or $1,243.75, plus brokerage. Brokerage fees here would be of the same order as on the IMM, about $16 per transaction round trip, per contract.

We have seen that there are several different markets for foreign exchange—spot, forward, futures, options on spot, options on futures. The channels through which these markets are formed are, however, fairly straightforward (see Figure 23-1). The main channel is the interbank network, though for large interbank transactions, foreign exchange brokers may be used as middlemen.

Table 23-3 Futures and options markets

Futures prices

Open interest reflects previous trading day.

	Open	High	Low	Settle	Change	Lifetime High	Lifetime Low	Open Interest
BRITISH POUND (IMM)—25,000 pounds; $ per pound								
Mar	1.4150	1.4400	1.4150	1.4370	+.0170	1.6010	1.3930	17,694
June	1.4175	1.4435	1.4175	1.4395	+.0170	1.5520	1.3950	3,251
Sept	1.4285	1.4410	1.4220	1.4410	+.0160	1.5240	1.3980	157
Dec	1.4280	1.4435	1.4245	1.4435	+.0160	1.4650	1.3990	75
Mar85	1.4280	1.4460	1.4270	1.4470	+.0170	1.4625	1.4000	65

Est vol 10,651; vol Mon 1,987; open int 21,242, +78.

	Open	High	Low	Settle	Change	Lifetime High	Lifetime Low	Open Interest
CANADIAN DOLLAR (IMM)—100,000 dlrs.; $ per Can $								
Mar	.8010	.8024	.8010	.8020	.....	.8169	.7979	4,033
June	.8014	.8029	.8013	.8023	.....	.8168	.7983	740
Sept		.8021		.8026	.....	.8147	.7988	312
Dec	.8021	.8031	.8021	.8029	.....	.8040	.8021	152
Mar85	.8035	.8035	.8035	.8032	.....	.8035	.8023	50

Est vol 1,087; vol Mon 535; open int 5,287, −103.

	Open	High	Low	Settle	Change	Lifetime High	Lifetime Low	Open Interest
JAPANESE YEN (IMM) 12.5 million yen; $ per yen (.00)								
Mar	.4276	.4297	.4276	.4294	+.0011	.4396	.4125	25,730
June	.4315	.4337	.4312	.4334	+.0011	.4435	.4180	3,908
Sept	.4354	.4375	.4354	.4374	+.0012	.4450	.4354	974
Dec	.4416	.4420	.4400	.4415	+.0012	.4493	.4395	271

Est vol 9,133; vol Mon 3,306; open int 30,883, +534.

Futures options

W. GERMAN MARK—125,000 marks, cents per mark

Strike price	Calls—settle Mar	Jun	Puts—settle Mar	Jun
34	.....	.....	0.01	0.01
35	2.05	2.46	0.01	0.09
36	1.11	1.66	0.06	0.25
37	0.38	1.00	0.33	0.57
38	0.10	0.54	1.00	1.02
39	0.01	0.27	.....	.....
Futures	.3706	.3746		

Estimated total vol. 2,187.
Calls: Mon vol. 180: open int. 2,416.
Puts: Mon vol. 73: open int. 1,841.

Foreign currency options

Philadelphia Exchange

Option & strike underlying price	Calls—last Mar	Jun	Sep	Puts—last Mar	Jun	Sep
12,500 British Pounds-cents per unit.						
BPound 140	3.40	r	5.70	0.40	1.85	r
143.00 .145	0.70	2.40	r	3.40	r	r
50,000 Canadian Dollars-cents per unit.						
CDollar .80	r	r	0.68	r	r	r
62,500 West German Marks-cents per unit.						
DMark ..34	2.67	r	r	r	r	r
..35	1.99	2.18	r	r	r	r
36.88 ..36	1.04	1.59	r	0.05	0.35	r
36.88 ..37	0.38	1.00	r	0.37	0.56	r
36.88 ..38	0.10	0.62	0.85	r	r	r
36.88 ..39	r	0.28	s	r	r	s
36.88 ..40	0.01	0.11	s	r	r	s
6,250,000 Japanese Yen-100ths of a cent per unit.						
JYen ..42	0.95	1.49	2.04	r	r	r
..43	0.30	0.90	r	r	0.50	0.60
42.75 ..44	0.04	0.45	0.99	r	r	r
62,500 Swiss Francs-cents per unit.						
SFranc ..44	r	r	3.15	r	0.24	r
..45	0.65	r	r	r	0.26	r
45.18 ..46	0.28	1.09	1.82	r	1.00	r
45.18 ..47	0.06	r	r	r	r	r
45.18 ..48	0.02	0.28	r	r	r	r

Total call vol. 2,271   Call open int. 37,349
Total put vol. 799   Put open int. 26,173
r—Not traded. s—No option offered. o—Old.
Last is premium (purchase price).

SWISS FRANC (IMM)—125,000 francs; $ per franc

	Open	High	Low	Settle	Change	Lifetime High	Lifetime Low	Open Interest
Mar	.4495	.4556	.4486	.4549	+ .0047	.5230	.4470	24,164
June	.4564	.4629	.4557	.4622	+ .0051	.5045	.4536	3,165
Sept	.4632	.4692	.4632	.4688	+ .0052	.5020	.4598	153
Dec	.4705	.4780	.4705	.4747	+ .0049	.4880	.4665	71
Mar85	....	....	....	.4830	+ .0050	.4840	.4755	5

Est vol 30,610; vol Mon 8,466; open int 27,558, + 296.

W. GERMAN MARK (IMM)—125,000 marks; $ per mark

	Open	High	Low	Settle	Change	Lifetime High	Lifetime Low	Open Interest
Mar	.3653	.3713	.3650	.3706	+ .0036	.4100	.3537	30,974
June	.3698	.3754	.3688	.3746	+ .0037	.4002	.3568	4,911
Sept	.3743	.3790	.3743	.3780	+ .0034	.4030	.3602	362
Dec	.3780	.3825	.3780	.3825	+ .0043	.3825	.3640	204
Mar85	....	....	....	.3838	+ .0035	.3699	.3699	1

Est vol 30,248; vol Mon 9,045; open int 36,452, + 680.

Source: *Wall Street Journal*, February 15, 1984

FOREIGN EXCHANGE MARKET ACTIVITIES

Much foreign exchange market trading does not appear to be related to the simple basic purpose of allowing businesses to buy or sell foreign currency in order, say, to sell or purchase goods overseas. It is certainly easy to see the usefulness of the large range of foreign exchange transactions available through the interbank and organized markets (spot, forward, futures, options) to facilitate trade between nations. It is also clear that there is a useful role for foreign exchange brokers in helping to "make" the interbank market. There are several other activities, however, in foreign exchange markets that are less well understood and whose relevance is less obvious to people interested in understanding what these markets accomplish.

Two major classes of activity will be discussed. First, the existence of a large number of foreign exchange markets in many locations creates opportunities to profit from "arbitrage." Second, there is implicitly a market in (foreign exchange) risk bearing. Those who wish to avoid foreign exchange risk (at a price) may do so. Those who accept the risk in expectation of profits are known as "speculators."

Triangular Arbitrage

Triangular arbitrage is the process that ensures that all exchange rates are mutually consistent. If, for example, one U. S. dollar exchanges for one Canadian dollar, and one Canadian dollar exchanges for one British pound, then the U.S. dollar-pound exchange rate should be one pound for one dollar. If it differs, then there is an opportunity for profit making. To see why this is so, suppose that you could purchase two U.S. dollars with one British pound. By first buying C$1 with U.S.$1, then purchasing £1 with C$1, and finally buying U.S.$2 with £1, you could double your money immediately. Clearly this opportunity will not last for long since it involves making large profits with certainty. The process of triangular arbitrage is exactly that of finding and exploiting profitable opportunities in such exchange rate inconsistencies. As a result of triangular arbitrage, such inconsistencies will be eliminated rapidly. Cross rates, however, will only be roughly consistent given the bid-ask spread associated with transaction costs.

In the past, the possibility of making profits from triangular arbitrage was greater as a result of the practice of expressing exchange rates in American terms in the United States and in European terms elsewhere. The adoption of standard practice has reduced the likelihood of inconsistencies.[7] Also, in recent years, such opportunities for profit making have been greatly reduced by high-speed, computerized information systems and the increased sophistication of the banks operating in the market.

[7]All except U.K. and Irish exchange rates are expressed in American terms. Futures and options contracts are expressed in European terms.

Arbitrage of a slightly different kind results from price differences in different locations. This is "space" arbitrage. For example, if sterling were cheaper in London than in New York, it would be profitable to buy in London and sell in New York. Similarly, if prices in the interbank market differed from those at the IMM, it would be profitable to arbitrage between them. As a result of this activity, prices in different locations will be brought broadly into line.

Interest Arbitrage

Interest arbitrage is slightly different in nature from triangular or space arbitrage; however, the basic motive of finding and exploiting profitable opportunities still applies. There is no reason why interest rates denominated in different currencies should be equal. Interest rates are the cost of borrowing or the return to lending for a specific period of time. The relative price (exchange rate) of money may change over time so that the comparison of, say, a U.S. and a British interest rate requires some allowance for expected exchange rate changes. Thus, it will be not at all unusual to find interest rates denominated in dollars and interest rates denominated in, say, pounds being somewhat different. However, real returns on assets of similar quality should be the same if the exchange rate risk is covered or hedged in the forward market. Were this not true, it would be possible to borrow in one currency and lend in another at a profit with no exchange risk.

Suppose we lend one dollar for a year in the United States at an interest rate of r_{us}. The amount accumulated at the end of the year per dollar lent will be $1 + r_{us}$ (capital plus interest). If, instead of making dollar loans, we converted them into pounds and lent them in the United Kingdom at the rate r_{uk}, the amount of pounds we would have for each original dollar at the end of the year would be $S(1 + r_{uk})$, where S is the spot exchange rate (in pounds per dollar) at the beginning of the period. At the outset, it is not known if $1 + r_{us}$ dollars is going to be worth more than $S(1 + r_{uk})$ pounds in a year's time because the spot exchange rate in a year's time is unknown. This uncertainty can be avoided by selling the pounds forward into dollars. Then the relative value of the two loans would no longer depend on what subsequently happens to the spot exchange rate. By doing this, we end up with $\frac{S}{F}(1 + r_{uk})$ dollars per original dollar invested. This is known as the "covered," or hedged, return on pounds.

Since the covered return in our example is denominated in dollars, it can reasonably be compared with the U.S. interest rate. If these returns are very different, investors will move funds where the return is highest on a covered basis. This process is interest arbitrage. It is assumed that the assets involved are equally safe and, because the returns are covered, all exchange risk is avoided. Of course, if funds do move in large volume between assets or between financial centers, then interest rates and the exchange rates (spot and forward) will change in predictable ways. Funds will continue to flow between countries until there is no extra profit to be made from interest arbitrage. This will occur when the returns on both dollar- and sterling-denominated assets are equal, that is, when

$$(1 + r_{us}) = \frac{S}{F} (1 + r_{uk}). \tag{1}$$

This result is known as covered interest parity. It holds more or less exactly, subject only to a margin due to transaction costs, so long as the appropriate dollar and sterling interest rates are compared.[8]

Speculation

Arbitrage in the foreign exchange markets involves little or no risk since transactions can be completed rapidly. An alternative source of profit is available from outguessing other market participants as to what future exchange rates will be. This is called speculation. Although any foreign exchange transaction that is not entirely hedged forward has a speculative element, only deliberate speculation for profit is discussed here.

Until recently, the main foreign exchange speculators were the foreign exchange departments of banks, with a lesser role being played by portfolio managers of other financial institutions and international corporations. The IMM, however, has made it much easier for individuals and smaller businesses to speculate. A high proportion of IMM transactions appears to be speculative in the sense that only about 5 percent of contracts lead to ultimate delivery of foreign exchange. This means that most of the activity involves the buying and selling of a contract at *different times* and possibly different prices prior to maturity. It is possible, however, that buying and selling of contracts before maturity would arise out of a strategy to reduce risk. So it is not possible to say that all such activity is speculative.

Speculation is important for the efficient working of foreign exchange markets. It is a form of arbitrage that occurs across time rather than across space or between markets at the same time. Just as arbitrage increases the efficiency of markets by keeping prices consistent, so speculation increases the efficiency of forward, futures and options markets by keeping those markets liquid. Those who wish to avoid foreign exchange risk may thereby do so in a well-developed market. Without speculators, risk avoidance in foreign exchange markets would be more difficult and, in many cases, impossible.[9]

---

[8]Since there are many different interest rates, it obviously cannot hold for all of them. Where (1) does hold is if the interest rates chosen are eurocurrency deposit rates of the same duration. In other words, if for r_{us} we take, say, the three-month eurodollar deposit rate in Paris and for r_{uk} we take the three-month eurosterling deposit rate in Paris, then (1) will hold just about exactly. Indeed, if we took the interest rate and exchange rate quotes all from the same bank, it would be remarkable if (1) did not hold. Otherwise the bank would be offering to pay you to borrow from it and lend straight back! That is, the price of borrowing would be less than the covered return on lending. A margin between borrowing and lending rates, of course, will make this even less likely so that in reality you would lose.

[9]This is not to say that all speculative activity is necessarily beneficial.

FOREIGN EXCHANGE OPTIONS

An option is a contract specifying the right to buy or sell—in this case foreign exchange—within a specific period (American option) or at a specific date (European option). A call option confers the right to buy. A put option confers the right to sell. Since each of these options must have a buyer and a seller, there are four possible ways of trading a single option: buy a call, sell a call, buy a put, sell a put.

The buyer of an option has the right to undertake the contract specified but may choose not to do so if it turns out to be unprofitable. The seller of the option *must* fulfill the contract if the buyer desires. Clearly, the buyer must pay the seller some premium (the option price) for this privilege. An option that would be profitable to exercise at the current exchange rate is said to be "in the money." The price at which it is exercised is the "exercise" or "strike" price.

Consider a call option £1000 (although options of this size are not presently available on organized exchanges, it is used to present a simple illustration of the principles involved). Suppose this costs $0.03 per pound or $30 and the exercise price is $1.50 per pound. The option expires in three months. This means that the buyer has paid $30 for the right to buy £1000 with dollars at a price of $1.50 per pound any time in the next three months. If the current spot price of sterling is, say, $1.45, the option is "out of the money" because sterling can be bought cheaper on the spot market. However, if the spot price were to rise to, say, $1.55, the option would be in the money. If sold at that time, the option buyer would get a $50 return (1000 × $0.05), which would more than cover the cost of the option ($50 − $30 = $20 profit). In contrast, a put option at the same terms would be in the money at the current spot price of $1.45, but out of the money at $1.55.

Figure 23-2 presents a diagrammatic illustration of how the profitability of an option depends upon the relationship between the exercise price and the current spot price.[1] Figure 23-2a illustrates the profit available from buying a call option at exercise price A. At spot exchange rate A and anything lower, the option will not be exercised so the loss will equal the price of the option. At a spot exchange rate above a, the option is sufficiently in the money to more than cover its cost. Between A and a, the option is in the money but not by enough to cover cost. The profit from *selling* a call could be illustrated by reversing the + and − signs in Figure 23-2a, or by flipping the profit line about the horizontal axis.

Figure 23-2b illustrates the profit from buying a put option. At spot exchange rates below a, the option with exercise price A will show a profit.

Figure 23-2c illustrates the profit from a simultaneous purchase of a put and call at the same exercise price. This combination will show a

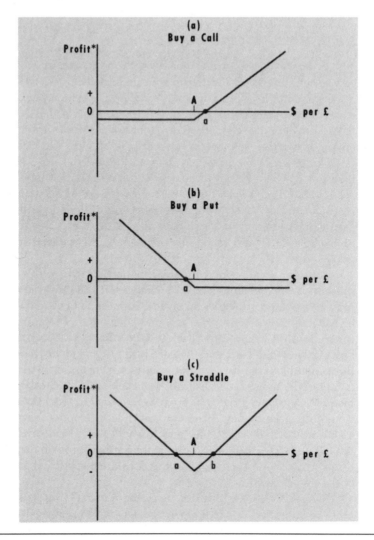

*Profit from exercise of option at current spot exchange rate.

Figure 23-2   Profit from options

profit at exercise price A if the spot price goes *either* above b or below a. .It is known as a "straddle." The straddle is of special interest because it makes clear the role of options as a hedge against risk. The price of a straddle can be regarded as the market valuation of the variability of the exchange rate. That is, the buyer of the straddle will show a profit if the spot price moves from some central value (the exercise price) by more than plus or minus some known percentage. The seller of the straddle accepts that risk for a lump sum. More complicated "multiple strategies" are also possible.[2]

[1]The pricing of options has been the subject of a large theoretical literature with a major contribution being made by Black and Scholes (1973). The Black-Scholes formula has been modified for foreign exchange options by Garman and Kohlhagen (1983) [see also Giddy (1983)], but the Black-Scholes formula is complex and beyond the scope of the present paper.

One simple relationship which is of interest may be called "option price parity." This arises because arbitrage will ensure that the difference between a call option price (per unit) and a put option price (per unit) at the same exercise price will be equal to the present value of the difference between the exercise price and the forward exchange rate at maturity of the options (if the options are marketable, it will also hold for any date to maturity). The relationship may be expressed:

$$C - P = \frac{F - E}{1 + r},$$

when C and P are the call and put option prices at exercise price E. F is the forward exchange rate and r is the interest rate per period of the contracts. This arises because the simultaneous buying of a call and selling of a put is equivalent to buying currency forward at price E. The forward contract, however, would be paid for at the end of the period, whereas the options are transacted at the beginning. Hence, the forward contract has to be discounted back to the present.

[2]See Giddy (1983).

COVERED INTEREST PARITY: AN EXAMPLE

The following interest rate and exchange rate quotations are taken from the *London Financial Times* of September 8, 1983 (Table 1).

Closing Exchange Rate: dollars per pound	Spot	3-Month forward
	1.4910 − 1.4920	.17 − .22 discount

Interest Rates: 3-Month Offer Rate	Eurosterling	Eurodollar
	9¹³⁄₁₆	10¼

The interest rate on the three-month eurodollar deposit is a little higher (.7 percent) than that on an eurosterling deposit. If the exchange rate remains unchanged, it would be better to hold dollars; if the exchange rate falls, the eurosterling deposit would be preferable. Suppose you decide to cover the exchange risk by selling the dollars forward into pounds. Let us compare the return to holding a sterling deposit with the return to holding a dollar deposit sold forward into sterling (assuming that you start with sterling).

Two important points need to be clarified about the above data. First, the interest rates are annualized so they are not what would actually be earned over a three-month period. For example, the three-month rate equivalent to an annual rate of 10¼ percent is 2.47 percent.

Second, the forward exchange rates need some explanation. The dollar is at a discount against sterling. This means the forward dollar buys less sterling. So we have to *add* the discount onto the spot price to get the forward price (because the price is the number of dollars per pound, not the reverse). Notice also that the discount is measured in fractions of a cent, not fractions of a dollar! So the bid-ask spread on the forward rate would be 1.4927 − 1.4942.

Now let us see if we would do better to invest in a three-month eurosterling deposit or a three-month eurodollar deposit where the dollars to be received were sold forward into sterling. The return per £100 invested in eurosterling is £2.369 (annual interest rate of 9¹³⁄₁₆), whereas the return on a covered eurodollar deposit is

$$£2.251 = (100 \times \frac{1.4910}{1.4942} 1.0247) - 100.$$

Thus, we could not make a profit out of covered interest arbitrage. Despite the fact that dollar interest rates are higher, the discount on forward dollars in the forward market means they buy fewer forward pounds. As a result, there is no benefit to the operation. Transaction costs for most individuals would be even greater than those above as they would face a larger bid-ask spread than that quoted on the interbank market.

Consequently, there is no benefit for the typical investor from making a covered or hedged eurocurrency deposit. The return will be at least as high on a deposit in the currency in which you start and wish to end up. That is, if you have dollars and wish to end up with dollars, make a eurodollar deposit. If you have sterling and wish to end up with sterling, make a eurosterling deposit. If you have sterling and wish to end up in dollars, there is likely to be little or no difference between holding a eurosterling deposit sold forward into dollars or buying dollars spot and holding a eurodollar deposit. Of course, if you hold an "uncovered" deposit and exchange rates subsequently change, the result will be very different.

WHY IS THE DOLLAR THE "MONEY" OF FOREIGN EXCHANGE MARKETS?

One interesting aspect of the organization of the foreign exchange markets is that the "money" used in these markets is generally the U.S. dollar. This is generally true for spot markets and universally true for foward markets. "Cross-markets" between many currencies are very thin, and future cross markets are virtually nonexistent. For example, the bulk of foreign exchange trading between £s and cruzeiro will involve dollar-£ and dollar-cruzeiro transactions instead of direct £-cruzeiro trading. The only exception to this is the transactions involving the major Organization for Economic Cooperation and Development (OECD) currencies, especially within Europe. Of the $702.5 billion turnover in foreign exchange reported by U.S. banks in April 1983, only $1.5 billion did not involve U.S. dollars.

There are two explanations for this special role of the dollar in foreign exchange markets. Both rely upon the fact that transaction costs are likely to be lower if the dollar is used as a medium. Krugman shows that the clearing of foreign exchange markets requires some "intermediary" currency.[1] Even if every country is in payments balance vis à vis the rest of the world, it will not necessarily be in bilateral balance with each other country. Because some currency has to be used to cover this residual finance, it is natural to choose the currency that has the lowest transaction costs. Chrystal shows there are economic reasons why cross-markets between many currencies do not exist.[2] It typically will be easier and cheaper to set up a deal in two steps via the dollar than in a single step (cruzeiro-dollar, dollar-drachma rather than cruzeiro-drachma). This is because these cross-markets, if they existed, would be fairly thin and hence relatively costly for such transactions. The two markets with the dollar, on the other hand, are well developed.

These analyses refer to the role of the dollar in the interbank market. In the development of the trading places such as the IMM in Chicago and LIFFE in London to date, it is also true that all currency futures are traded against the dollar.

[1]See Krugman (1980)
[2]See Chrystal (1982).

Risk Reduction

Speculation clearly involves a shifting of risk from one party to another. For example, if a bank buys forward foreign exchange from a customer, it increases its exposure to risk while the customer reduces his. However, there is not a fixed amount of risk that has to be "shared out." Some strategies may involve a net reduction of risk all around.

As a general rule, financial institutions (or other firms), operating in a variety of currencies, will try to minimize the risk of losses due to unexpected exchange rate changes. One simple way to do this is to ensure that assets and liabilities denominated in each operating currency are equal. This is known as "matching." For example, a bank that sells sterling forward to a customer may simultaneously buy sterling forward. In this event, the bank is exposed to zero exchange rate risk.

Banks often use "swaps" to close gaps in the maturity structure of their assets and liabilities in a currency. This involves the simultaneous purchase and sale of a currency for *different* maturity dates. In April 1983, 33 percent of U.S. banks' foreign exchange turnover involved swaps as compared with 63 percent spot contracts and only 4 percent outright forward contracts.[10]

Suppose a bank has sold DM to a customer three months forward and bought the same amount of DM from a different customer six months forward. There are two ways in which the bank could achieve zero foreign exchange risk exposure. It could either undertake two separate offsetting forward transactions, or it could set up a single swap with another bank that has the opposite mismatch of dollar-DM flows whereby it receives DM in exchange for dollars in three months and receives back dollars in exchange for DM in six months. Once the swap is set up, the bank's net profits are protected against subsequent changes in spot exchange rates during the next six months.

Within the limits imposed by the nature of the contracts, a similar effect can be achieved by an appropriate portfolio of futures contracts on the IMM. Thus, a bank would buy and sell futures contracts so as to match closely its forward commitments to customers. In reality, banks will use a combination of methods to reduce foreign exchange risk.

Markets that permit banks, firms and individuals to hedge foreign exchange risk are essential in times of fluctuating exchange services for their customers. In the absence of markets that permit foreign exchange risk hedging, the cost and uncertainty of international transactions would be greatly increased, and international specialization and trade would be greatly reduced.

---

[10]See Federal Reserve Bank of New York (1983).

CONCLUSION

The foreign exchange markets are complex and, for the outsider, hard to comprehend. The primary function of these markets is straightforward. It is to facilitate international transactions related to trade, travel or investment. Foreign exchange markets can now accommodate a large range of current and forward transactions.

Given the variability of exchange rates, it is important for banks and firms operating in foreign currencies to be able to reduce exchange rate risk whenever possible. Some risk reduction is achieved by interbank swaps, but some is also taken up by speculation. Arbitrage and speculation both increase the efficiency of spot and forward foreign exchange markets and have enabled foreign exchange markets to achieve a high level of efficiency. Without the successful operation of these markets, the obstacles to international trade and investment would be substantial and the world would be a poorer place.

GLOSSARY

American option—an option that can be exercised any time up to maturity.

American terms—an exchange rate expressed as number of currency units per dollar.

arbitrage—the simultaneous purchase and sale of currency in separate markets for a profit arising from a price discrepancy between the markets.

bid-ask spread—the difference between the buying (bid) and selling (ask) price.

covered interest arbitrage—buying a country's currency spot, investing for a period, and selling the proceeds forward in order to make a net profit due to the higher interest rate in that country. This act involves "hedging" because it guarantees a covered return without risk. The opportunities to profit in this way seldom arise because covered interest differentials are normally close to zero.

covered interest parity—the gap between interest rates in foreign and domestic currencies will be matched by the forward exchange rate differential, such that the "covered" interest rate differential will be close to zero.

eurodollar deposits—bank deposits, generally bearing interest and made for a specific time period, that are denominated in dollars but are in banks outside the United States. Similarly, eurosterling deposits would be denominated in sterling but outside the United Kingdom.

European option—an option that can be exercised only on a specified date.

European terms—an exchange rate expressed as number of dollars per currency unit.

floating exchange rate—an exchange rate that is allowed to adjust freely to the supply of and demand for foreign exchange.

foreign exchange speculation—the act of taking a net position in a foreign currency with the intention of making a profit from exchange rate changes.

forward exchange rate—the price of foreign currency for delivery at a future date agreed to by a contract today.

futures market—a market in which contracts are traded to buy or sell a standard amount of currency in the future at a particular price.

hedging—or covering exchange risk, means that foreign currency is sold forward into local currency so that its value is not affected by subsequent exchange rate changes. Say an exporter knows he will be paid £10,000 in two months. He can wait until he gets the money and convert it into dollars at whatever the spot rate turns out to be. This outcome is uncertain as the spot rate may change. Alternatively, he can sell £10,000 two months forward at today's two-month forward price. Suppose this is $1.5 per £. In two months, he will receive £10,000, fulfill his forward contract and receive $15,000. This export contract has been hedged or covered in the forward market.

matching—equating assets and liabilities denominated in each currency so that losses due to foreign exchange rate changes are minimized.

options market—a market in which contracts are traded that gives a purchaser the right but no obligation to buy (call) or to sell (put) a currency in the future at a given price.

spot exchange rate—the price paid to exchange currencies for immediate delivery (two business days in the interbank market, or over the counter in the retail and travelers check market).

swap—the simultaneous purchase and sale of a currency for different maturity dates that closes the gaps in the maturity structure of assets and liabilities in a currency.

REFERENCES

Belongia, Michael T. "Commodity Options: A New Risk Management Tool for Agricultural Markets," *Review* (June/July 1983), pp. 5-15.

Black, Fisher, and Myron Scholes. "The Pricing of Options and Corporate Liabilities," *Journal of Political Economy* (May/June 1973), pp. 637-54.

Chrystal, K. Alec. "On the Theory of International Money" (paper presented to U.K. International Economics Study Group Conference, September 1982, Sussex, England). Forthcoming in J. Black and G.S. Dorrance, eds., *Problems of International Finance* (London: Macmillan, 1984).

Dufey, Gunter, and Ian H. Giddy. *The International Money Market* (Prentice-Hall, 1978).

Federal Reserve Bank of New York. "Summary of Results of U.S. Foreign Exchange Market Turnover Survey Conducted in April 1983" (September 8, 1983).

Garman, Mark B., Steven W. Kohlhagen. "Foreign Currency Option Values," *Journal of International Money and Finance* (December 1983), pp. 231-37.

Giddy, Ian H. "Foreign Exchange Options," *Journal of Futures Markets* (Summer 1983), pp. 143-66.

Krugman, Paul. "Vehicle Currencies and the Structure of International Exchange," *Journal of Money, Credit and Banking* (August 1980), pp. 513-26.

Kubarych, Roger M. *Foreign Exchange Markets in the United States* (Federal Reserve Bank of New York, 1983).

McKinnon, Ronald I. *Money in International Exchange: The Convertible Currency System* (Oxford University Press, 1979).

Part IV

DEBT AND EQUITY MARKET RELATIONSHIPS AND CONCEPTS

The Equity Market

Part IV has two sections: the equity market and the debt market. This first section deals with market relationships and conceptual issues in the equity market. The article by Richard R. Simonds provides a conceptual background to this topic. It reviews modern financial theory and its applications, including portfolio theory, capital market theory, and efficient market theory. These theories represent several of the most significant academic developments in finance in recent history.

The article by Neil G. Berkman discusses one efficient market theory— the random walk model of stock price behavior. This model is defined, ex- plained, its tests reviewed, and related to traditional models of stock value.

Daniel Seligman's article also examines the efficient market hypothesis but concentrates on several "anomalies" that seem to contradict efficient market theory. Six "pockets of inefficiency" in the market are reviewed, including extraordinary records by certain high-visibility investors, superior long-run performance of the *Value Line Investment Survey* and the "small firm effect."

The impact of inflation on stock prices is discussed in the article by Douglas K. Pearce. Over the last fifteen years, the real value of common stock has fallen about 50 percent. Evidence indicates that inflation has been an important determinant of the higher rate of return required by stockholders.

MODERN FINANCIAL THEORY*

24

Richard R. Simonds†

The most significant academic developments in finance in the past 25 years have been portfolio theory, capital market theory, and efficient market theory. Portfolio theory is concerned with how a risk-averse investor should go about selecting an optimal portfolio of investment assets. Capital market theory extends portfolio theory and attempts to describe the way in which the equilibrium market price or expected return of an individual investment asset is related to the asset's risk of return. Efficient market theory deals with the relationship between information and security prices and the resulting implications for investors.

This article attempts to present the major theoretical concepts in these areas in as nontechnical a manner as possible. Several statistical terms are used along the way but only after the meaning of each is sufficiently developed. Second, empirical support for these theories is briefly summarized. Third, three applications of these theories are illustrated. Although the applications presented are by no means exhaustive, they indicate the scope of the impact of recent academic developments on financial analysis.

*Reprinted from *MSU Business Topics*, Winter 1978, No. 1, Vol. 26, pp. 54-63, by permission of the publisher, Division of Research, Graduate School of Business Administration, Michigan State University.

†Richard R. Simonds is a member of the faculty of the Graduate School of Business Administration at Michigan State University.

PORTFOLIO THEORY

The one-period return on an individual investment asset during a specified time is equal to the change in the market value of the asset plus any cash distributions received divided by the initial market value.[1] The return for the ith asset, $\tilde{R}_i$, is given by

$$\tilde{R}_i = \frac{\tilde{V}_{i1} - V_{i0} + \tilde{D}_{i1}}{V_{i0}}, \tag{1}$$

where

$\tilde{V}_{i1}$ = i^{th} asset market value at the end of the period;

V_{i0} = i^{th} asset market value at the beginning of the period; and

$\tilde{D}_{i1}$ = i^{th} asset cash distribution during the period.[2]

The return on a portfolio, $\tilde{R}_p$, is a weighted average of the returns on the individual assets in the portfolio. That is, for n assets,

$$\tilde{R}_p = A_1\tilde{R}_1 + A_2\tilde{R}_2 + \cdots + A_n\tilde{R}_n, \tag{2}$$

where A_i equals the proportion of the initial investment commited to the ith asset, and the sum of the A_i's is one.

Expected Return

Each return, $\tilde{R}_i$, is uncertain at the beginning of the period. A useful way to deal with this uncertainty is to assign subjective probabilities to possible return outcomes. Having done so, the expected return may be computed. The expected return is the weighted average of all possible returns where the weights are equal to the probabilities or relative chances of each level of return occurring. The probability of R_{ij}, where R_{ij} represents the jth level of return for the ith asset, is designated P_{ij}, and the sum of the probabilities, $P_{i1}, P_{i2}, \ldots,$ P_{im}, for m possible return levels must equal one. The expected value of $\tilde{R}_i$, $E(\tilde{R}_i)$, given the m possible outcomes shown in Figure 24-1, is

$$E(\tilde{R}_i) = \sum_{j=1}^{m} R_{ij}P_{ij} \tag{3}$$

$$= .1(.05) + .2(.06) + .4(.07) + .2(.08) + .1(.09)$$

$$= .07 \text{ or } 7\%.$$

---

[1] Although the theory is properly presented in terms of all investment assets, most applications have focused on financial assets.

[2] The tilde, ~, on $\tilde{R}_i$, $\tilde{V}_{i1}$, and $\tilde{D}_{i1}$ indicates that these quantities are uncertain at the beginning of the period and hence are random variables.

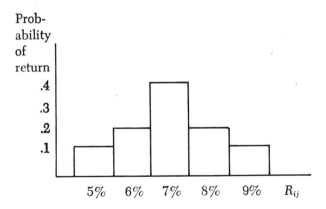

Figure 24-1   Symmetric probability distribution of return for the ith asset in portfolio p

In accordance with expression (2), the expected value of the portfolio return, $E(\tilde{R}_p)$, is equal to a weighted average of the n individual assets' expected returns,

$$E(\tilde{R}_p) = A_1 E(\tilde{R}_1) + A_2 E(\tilde{R}_2) + \cdots + A_n E(\tilde{E}_n),$$

$$= \sum_{i=1}^{n} A_i E(\tilde{R}_i). \tag{4}$$

Therefore, the contribution of each asset to the expected portfolio return is its own expected return.

Risk of Return

The risk of the portfolio return might be stated in terms of a dispersion measure which takes into account both the likelihood of $\tilde{R}_p$ being less than $E(\tilde{R}_p)$ and the size of the downside deviations. However, if the distribution for $\tilde{R}_p$ is symmetric, a measure of dispersion based on both the upside and downside deviations from the expected return level may be used even though it is only the downside deviations which leave the investor less well off than if the outcome had been the expected value. Since security returns and hence portfolio returns appear to be approximately symmetric, it is this two-sided measure of dispersion that is generally used.[3] The variance of return is just such a two-sided measure and is defined as the weighted average of squared deviations

[3]In fact, return distributions on individual securities and portfolios are approximately normal, with monthly returns better described by the normal distribution than daily returns. See Eugene Fama, *Foundations of Finance* (New York: Basic Books, 1976), Chapter 1.

from the expected return. The variance of the portfolio single-period return, designated $\sigma^2(\tilde{R}_p)$, is given by

$$\sigma^2(\tilde{R}_p) = \sum_{j=1}^{m} [R_{pj} - E(\tilde{R}_p)]^2 P_{pj}. \tag{5}$$

Correspondingly, for a single asset the variance is

$$\sigma^2(\tilde{R}_i) = \sum_{j=1}^{m} [R_{ij} - E(\tilde{R}_i)]^2 P_{ij}, \tag{6}$$

and for the security depicted in Figure 24-1

$$\sigma^2(\tilde{R}_i) = (-.02)^2 \, (.1) + (-.01)^2 \, (.2) + (0)^2 \, (.4) + (.01)^2 \, (.2) + (.02)^2 \, (.1)$$

$$= .00012.$$

The variance of the return on an n-asset portfolio with asset weights A_i, $i = 1, \ldots, n$, is also expressible as

$$\sigma^2(\tilde{R}_p) = \sum_{i=1}^{n} A_i \, \text{covariance} \, (\tilde{R}_i, \tilde{R}_p), \tag{7}$$

where the covariance $(\tilde{R}_i, \tilde{R}_p)$ measures the magnitude of the comovement of the returns on the ith asset and the returns on the portfolio, p, of which asset i is a member.[4] The covariance $(\tilde{R}_i, \tilde{R}_p)$ is expressible as

$$\text{covariance} \, (\tilde{R}_i, \tilde{R}_p) = (\text{correlation between } \tilde{R}_i \text{ and } \tilde{R}_p) \times \sqrt{\sigma^2(\tilde{R}_i) \, \sigma^2(\tilde{R}_p)}. \tag{8}$$

Expression (7) is significant because it indicates that the contribution of the ith asset to the risk of portfolio p is the covariance $(\tilde{R}_i, \tilde{R}_p)$, and the relative risk of security i in portfolio p is

$$\frac{\text{covariance} \, (\tilde{R}_i \tilde{R}_p)}{\sigma^2(\tilde{R}_p)} = \beta_{ip}. \tag{9}$$

---

[4]

$$\sigma^2(\tilde{R}_p) = \sum_{i=1}^{n} \sum_{k=1}^{n} A_i A_k \, \text{covariance} \, (\tilde{R}_i, \tilde{R}_k),$$

therefore,

$$\sigma^2(\tilde{R}_p) = \sum_{i=1}^{n} A_i \, [\sum_{k=1}^{n} \text{covariance} \, (\tilde{R}_i, A_k \tilde{R}_k)],$$

and since

$$\tilde{R}_p = \sum_{k=1}^{n} A_k \tilde{R}_k, \text{ and } \sum_{k=1}^{n} A_i = 1,$$

$$\sigma^2(\tilde{R}_p) = \sum_{i=1}^{n} A_i \, \text{covariance} \, (\tilde{R}_i \tilde{R}_p).$$

Alternatively, if one considers a portfolio of n assets in which $A_i = 1/n$, i = 1, . . . , then $\sigma^2(\tilde{R}_p)$ may be expressed as[5]

$$\sigma^2(\tilde{R}_p) = \frac{\text{average security return variance}}{n} + \left(\frac{n-1}{n}\right) \times \left(\begin{array}{c}\text{average covariance between}\\ \text{returns for pairs of securities}\\ \text{comprising portfolio } p\end{array}\right). \quad (10)$$

Two of the most important results of portfolio theory are presented in expressions (7) and (10). Expression (7) shows that the risk contribution of asset i to portfolio p is measured by the covariance $(\tilde{R}_i, \tilde{R}_p)$ and *not* the variance of its own return, $\sigma^2(\tilde{R}_i)$. Expression (10) shows that as a portfolio is expanded to include large numbers of assets, the portfolio variance may not be reduced beyond the average covariance of returns for pairs of securities comprising the portfolio.[6] Consequently, simple diversification in risky assets can be only partially effective in reducing risk.

Two-Parameter Model

Employing expressions (4) and (7), one may calculate $E(\tilde{R}_p)$ and $\sigma^2(\tilde{R}_p)$ for an n-asset portfolio with given weights, A_i. Specifically, if $n = 2$, the possible combinations of expected return and risk for different levels of A_1 and A_2, with the restriction that $A_1 + A_2 = 1$, are indicated by the curved line in Figure 24-2.

Note that it is customary to represent the risk of the portfolio as the standard deviation of the return, which is the square-root of the return variance. The less the returns for assets 1 and 2 are positively correlated, the greater is the curvature of the line representing the location attainable by combining the two assets.

Next assume that the investor has assigned subjective probability distributions to the returns for all risky investment assets. The set of possible portfolio

---

[5]See Fama, *Foundations of Finance*, p. 252. It should be emphasized that the notion that the effects of single-period risk of return tend to cancel out in the longer run is incorrect. The relationship between the future value of a security and the sequence of its n single-period return is

$$\text{Future Value} = [(1 + \tilde{R}_1)(1 + \tilde{R}_2)(1 + \tilde{R}_3) \ldots (1 + \tilde{R}_n)] \text{ (Current Value)},$$

where the subscript refers to the time period. For commonly encountered levels of security returns,

$$\text{Future Value} \simeq [1 + \tilde{R}_1 + \tilde{R}_2 + \tilde{R}_3 + \ldots + \tilde{R}_n] \text{ (Current Value)}.$$

If the returns, $\tilde{R}_i$, are independent and of constant variance, σ^2, then the variance of the future security value after n periods is equal to $\sigma^2 \times$ (current value) $\times$ (n), or n times the variance of the security value one period hence. Single-period risk effects do not cancel out in the longer run.

[6]Almost all security returns appear to be positively correlated with one another, implying positive covariances between asset returns. The average covariance of returns discussed here can therefore be presumed to be positive. See Fama, *Foundations of Finance*, pp. 251-54.

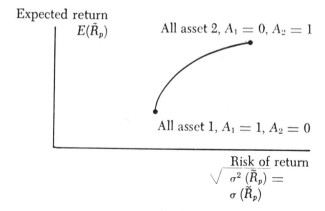

Figure 24-2   Two-parameter portfolio model with two assets

risk-return pairs resulting from different combinations of these assets would appear as the shaded area shown in Figure 24-3. (Momentarily disregard the straight line shown.) Only the darkened border of this set will be of interest to an investor, however. This so-called efficient set offers the highest expected return for a given risk level.[7] Which point on the efficient set of risky assets is best depends on the investor's willingness to accept additional risk in order to increase the level of expected portfolio returns.

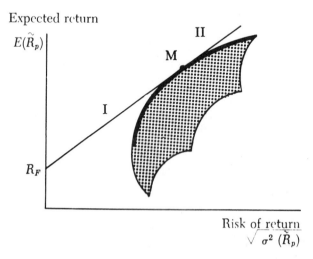

Figure 24-3   Two-parameter portfolio model with *n* assets

[7]The use of the word *efficient* here is not to be confused with its usage in describing capital markets.

CAPITAL MARKET THEORY

Equilibrium Models

Capital market theory seeks to explain the relationship between the expected equilibrium returns on investment assets and their risk of return. Although several slightly different capital market equilibrium models are derivable from two-parameter portfolio theory, depending on the assumptions imposed, only the best-known model, the Sharpe-Lintner Capital Asset Pricing Model, is discussed here.[8]

If a risk-free asset is available with a return R_F, where R_F is a certain rate at which investors may borrow or lend, the new efficient set becomes the straight line emanating from R_F tangent to the original efficient set of risky assets at point M. Anywhere along the straight line is attainable given the proper allocation of funds to the portfolio M and the risk-free asset. If the investor desires to be in region I, funds are invested in the riskless asset whereas in region II funds are borrowed at the riskless rate and invested in the portfolio M. The combination of riskless asset and portfolio M selected depends on the investor's level of desired risk exposure. Furthermore, all locations along the straight line offer returns that are perfectly positively correlated with the returns on portfolio M since R_F is a certain rate of return.

If investors' expectations regarding uncertain future returns for investment assets are homogeneous, that is, all investors perceive the same set of risk-return pairs, all investors will choose to hold the portfolio M in combination with the riskless asset.[9] Consequently, M is the market portfolio itself, which is the portfolio of all investment assets.

By referring back to expression (7) and replacing portfolio p with the market portfolio M the variance of the return on the market portfolio is seen to be

$$\sigma^2(\tilde{R}_m) = \sum_{i=1}^{n} A_i \text{ covariance } (\tilde{R}_i, \tilde{R}_m). \tag{11}$$

The relative risk of the ith asset in the market portfolio, which is referred to as the ith asset's beta coefficient is, from expression (9), seen to be equal to

$$\beta_{im} = \frac{\text{covariance } (\tilde{R}_i, \tilde{R}_m)}{\sigma^2 (\tilde{R}_m)}. \tag{12}$$

Next consider a fractional investment of A_1 in the market portfolio and $(1 - A_1)$ in the riskless asset; then the portfolio return, $\tilde{R}_p$, is

---

[8]See Michael Jensen, "Capital Markets: Theory and Evidence," *Bell Journal of Economics and Management Science* 3 (Autumn 1972):357-98, for an excellent presentation of other models.

[9]This result is frequently referred to as the separation theorem.

$$\tilde{R}_p = A_1 \tilde{R}_m + (1 - A_1)\tilde{R}_F, \tag{13}$$

and the expected portfolio return is

$$E(\tilde{R}_p) = A_1 E(\tilde{R}_m) + (1 - A_1)R_F. \tag{14}$$

Beta for the portfolio is

$$\beta_{pm} = \frac{\text{covariance } \tilde{R}_p, \tilde{R}_m)}{\sigma^2 (\tilde{R}_m)}, \tag{15}$$

which, using equation (13), may be expressed as

$$\beta_{pm} = \frac{\text{covariance } (A_1 \tilde{R}_m + (1 - A_1)R_F, \tilde{R}_m)}{\sigma^2(\tilde{R}_m)}$$

or

$$= A_1 \text{ covariance } (\tilde{R}_m, \tilde{R}_m) + \frac{(1 - A_1) \text{ covariance } (R_F, \tilde{R}_m)}{\sigma^2 (\tilde{R}_m)}. \tag{16}$$

Since R_F is a certain rate of return, then expression (16) for β_{pm} reduces to

$$\beta_{pm} = \frac{A_1 \sigma^2 (\tilde{R}_m) + (1 - A_1) (0)}{\sigma^2 (\tilde{R}_m)} = A_1. \tag{17}$$

Using this result for β_{pm} in expression (14) we arrive at

$$E(\tilde{R}_p) = \beta_{pm} E(\tilde{R}_m) + (1 - \beta_{pm})R_F. \tag{18}$$

Equation (18) is the Capital Asset Pricing Model (CAPM) developed simultaneously by William F. Sharpe and John Lintner. Although it was developed here for portfolios on the efficient set, it can be shown to hold for *each* risky asset in the market portfolio.[10] For each risky asset the relationship between expected return and risk is

$$E(\tilde{R}_i) = R_F(1 - \beta_{im}) + \beta_{im}E(\tilde{R}_m),$$

or

$$E(\tilde{R}_i) = R_F + [E(\tilde{R}_m) - R_F]\beta_{im}. \tag{19}$$

Note that it is the relative risk contribution, β_{im}, of the security to the market portfolio risk that establishes the expected return on the asset and not the total variability of asset return, $\sigma^2(\tilde{R}_i)$. This perspective of risk has dramatic consequences, as will be seen when applications of the CAPM are discussed below.

[10]The best presentation of the complete derivation of the Sharpe-Lintner CAPM is found in Fama, *Foundations of Finance*, chapter 8.

Beta Coefficients

It is common practice to use past realized data for security and market returns to estimate beta coefficients for individual securities or portfolios.[11] Employing the market-model regression equation

$$\tilde{R}_i = a_i + b_i \tilde{R}_m + \tilde{e}_i, \tag{20}$$

estimates are obtained for b_i using standard statistical techniques. Figure 24-4 shows a regression line fitted to monthly observations on $\tilde{R}_i$ and $\tilde{R}_m$.

When the error term $\tilde{e}_i$ is assumed independent of $\tilde{R}_m$, the b_i term is equal to covariance $(\tilde{R}_i, \tilde{R}_m)/\sigma^2(\tilde{R}_m)$, which is β_{im}. Therefore the estimates of b_i, denoted $\hat{b}_i$, are used as estimates of β_{im}.[12] Equation (20) also provides another description of beta. Beta reflects the sensitivity of the ith asset's returns to the returns on the market as a whole. Beta coefficients over one are deemed more risky than the market, and beta coefficients under one less risky than the market, since the market portfolio itself must have a beta coefficient of one.

If one were to consider equation (20) written separately for many individual securities it becomes clear that the return on a portfolio of n equally weighted securities may be expressed as

$$\tilde{R}_p = \frac{1}{n} \sum_{i=1}^{n} a_i + \frac{1}{n} \sum_{i=1}^{n} b_i(\tilde{R}_m) + \frac{1}{n} \sum_{i=1}^{n} \tilde{e}_i. \tag{21}$$

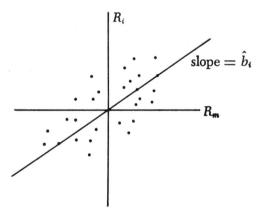

Figure 24-4 Market-model regression equation

---

[11]A surrogate for the market return, such as the return on the Standard & Poor's 500 index, is usually employed in this process.

[12]An alternative market model specification is stated in terms of excess returns, namely,

$$\tilde{R}_i - R_F = a_i + b_i(\tilde{R}_m - R_F) + \tilde{e}_i.$$

This form is also used by some investigators to obtain estimates of β_{im}.

Alternatively, equation (21) may be expressed as

$$\tilde{R}_p = \bar{a}_i + \bar{b}_i(R_m) + \frac{1}{n}\sum_{i=1}^{n} \tilde{e}_i, \tag{22}$$

or using notation to reflect that R_p is the return on a portfolio,

$$\tilde{R}_p = a_p + b_p(\tilde{R}_m) + \tilde{e}_p, \tag{23}$$

where $\bar{a}_i = a_p$ and $\bar{b}_i = b_p$ are averages for the n securities. If the $\tilde{e}_i$ terms are independent of each other then

$$\sigma^2(\tilde{R}_p) = (b_p)^2 \sigma^2(\tilde{R}_m) + \frac{1}{n}\text{(average variance of the } \tilde{e}_i\text{'s).} \tag{24}$$

Consequently, as n gets very large the risk of the portfolio can be reduced to that resulting from the comovement of the portfolio returns with the market returns. Variations independent of general market returns can be diversified away, but risk cannot be completely eliminated through diversification. This is the same conclusion we arrive at in expression (10). The standard deviation of the $\tilde{e}_p$ term has come to be called the unsystematic risk and the standard deviation of the $b_p\tilde{R}_m$ term the systematic risk. Diversification can effectively eliminate the unsystematic risk but has no such effect on the systematic risk.

Empirical Evidence

The Sharpe-Lintner CAPM was developed based on the normative idea that risk-averse investors should make portfolio choices based on the expected level and standard deviation of portfolio returns, assumed homogeneous expectations, and on the assumed presence of a risk-free rate of borrowing and lending.[13] Therefore, the model is referred to as a two-parameter market equilibrium model. Since expression (19) is stated in terms of expected returns which are unobservable, it may not be tested directly. Various researchers have, however, conducted indirect tests by using data on realized returns for New York Stock Exchange securities. Most notable of these tests are the studies by Eugene Fama and James MacBeth and by Fischer Black, Michael Jensen, and Myron Scholes.[14] Their empirical evidence suggests that the relationship between expected security returns and betas, β_{im}'s, is linear and that beta is the only required factor to explain the differences in levels of expected returns

---

[13]It is also assumed that investors do not incur transaction costs and are indifferent to capital gains or dividends.

[14]Eugene Fama and James MacBeth, "Risk, Return and Equilibrium: Empirical Tests," *Journal of Political Economy* 71 (May-June 1971): 607-36, and Fischer Black, Michael Jensen, and Myron Scholes "The Capital Asset Pricing Model: Some Empirical Tests," in Michael Jensen, ed., *Studies in the Theory of Capital Markets* (New York: Praeger, 1972), pp. 79-121.

among securities. These findings are consistent with the Sharpe-Lintner CAPM.[15] Furthermore, these findings support the proposition that securities are priced consistent with a two-parameter portfolio model used to describe how investors should select investment portfolios.

EFFICIENT CAPITAL MARKET THEORY

In an efficient capital market, individual security prices fully reflect all available information. Prices adjust completely and instantaneously to new information. Current security prices represent "correct" or unbiased assessments of all information available at the moment.

Academic researchers have attempted to test the extent to which security markets appear to behave as efficient markets.[16] Three classes of testable propositions derivable from the efficient market theory have been examined.[17] First, do current security prices fully reflect all information available in the sequences of past security prices and return data? This proposition is often referred to as the random walk hypothesis, which implies that successive security returns are not statistically associated. To examine this proposition, researchers have tested complicated buying and selling rules based on securities' past price performances. Such rules have not generated returns sufficiently greater than those available through buy-and-hold strategies to warrant investors behaving in a manner not consistent with the notion that this first efficient market proposition is correct.

A second testable proposition is that security prices adjust fully and instantaneously to *new* publicly available information. The empirical research regarding this proposition is preponderantly supportive. Studies conducted concerning earnings announcements, announced changes in accounting practices, mergers, stock splits, newly filed SEC documents, and so forth, have all supported this second proposition. It should be kept in mind, however, that even though the evidence reported would not lead one to reject this second proposition, any real market is surely not completely consistent with it either.

---

[15]It must be stated that although these findings are consistent with the Sharpe-Lintner CAPM other evidence suggests that a slightly different version of a two-parameter capital market equilibrium model which does not presume the presence of a risk-free asset is superior. Black has presented such a model in which the expected return on a riskless portfolio ($\beta_{pm} = 0$) replaces the risk-free rate in equation (19). The linearity of the relationship between $E(R_i)$ and β_{im} and the singular importance of β_{im} is not altered in any way, however. See Fama, *Foundations of Finance*, Chapter 8, for an excellent discussion of the differences between the various two-parameter capital market equilibrium models which have been developed.

[16]Most of this testing has been conducted using securities traded on the New York Stock Exchange. Caution should be exercised in generalizing these test results to all security markets.

[17]Most of the studies of market efficiency are also implicitly testing a market equilibrium model. See Fama, *Foundations of Finance*, Chapter 5, for a discussion of this point.

The important point is that the evidence suggests that individual investors are best off conducting their affairs as if the proposition were correct. Finally, if this second proposition concerning publicly available information is correct, it is only because individual investors are trying to identify securities whose current prices do not reflect their intrinsic values and are making investment decisions based on these assessments. This activity is the driving force behind market efficiency. By so behaving, investors are causing the market to behave in accordance with this second proposition.

A third testable proposition is that no sector can, through superior analysis of publicly available information or through access to nonpublicly available information, realize superior investment performance. Research by Michael Jensen in which he examined mutual fund performance strongly suggests that once returns are adjusted for risk these managers have been unable to outperform other investors.[18] On the other hand, evidence from other studies of stock trading by insiders (managers and directors) and New York Stock Exchange specialists suggests that these individuals are privy to information not reflected in current stock prices which may be used to achieve superior returns.[19] This last bit of evidence against the idea of complete market efficiency does not appear to affect the general conclusion that if investors only have access to publicly available information they are wise to act as if the market were efficient.

APPLICATIONS

Almost every facet of financial analysis has been affected by the theories described above. This pervasiveness is illustrated here by examining the impact of modern financial theory on public utility regulation, investor portfolio selection, and corporate capital budgeting. Although this examination must necessarily be brief, an effort has been made to point out several practical problems encountered when trying to apply these theories. This effort is important lest the reader get the false impression that modern financial theory has reduced many areas of financial analysis to mechanical formula manipulation.

Public Utility Regulation

Public utility rate of return regulation is based on the legal principle that "the return to the equity owner should be commensurate with returns on

---

[18]Michael Jensen, "The Performance of Mutual Funds in the Period 1945-1964," *Journal of Finance* 23 (May 1968): 389-416.

[19]Jeffrey Jaffe, "Special Information and Insider Trading," *Journal of Business* 47 (July 1974): 410-28.

investments in other enterprises having corresponding risk."[20] One concept of commensurate return is the market rate of return which investors expect when they purchase other equity shares of comparable risk. If estimates of the risk and associated expected rate of return alluded to in the legal principle above can be obtained for a utility's stock, these estimates may be used along with debt costs to determine a "fair" company rate of return on assets. This company rate of return may be applied to a rate base such as the book value of capital investment to determine utility service rates.

Portfolio theory and capital market theory may be used to estimate both the risk of the equity and the level of expected equity return. As seen in expression (12), for a well-diversified investor the relevant risk measure of a security is its beta coefficient. Expression (19) specifies the level of expected return for a security with known beta, and it also shows all securities with the same beta have the same expected return. Modern financial theory offers a conceptually sound approach to the implementation of the legal principle of "fair" return in regulatory cases and in fact has been used for this purpose.

Testimony has been offered in regulatory cases such as those involving Communications Satellite Corporation, in which experts were requested to prepare an analysis of Comsat's risk in a portfolio context and to estimate Comsat's expected return on equity capital.[21] Two major problems arise in such an analysis. First, a firm's true equity beta coefficient can only be estimated (see expression [20] for the standard statistical approach), and therefore a firm's inherent risk level may not be known exactly. Furthermore, since the "real" or inherent beta coefficient is determined by a firm's operating and financial characteristics, only if these remain constant over time will the theoretical beta remain constant. Consequently, errors may arise from two sources in predicting the future riskiness of a utility's equity shares.

Second, a major problem arises in using expression (19) to estimate the expected return on the utility's equity since values for the expected market return, $E(\tilde{R}_m)$, and risk-free rate, R_F, must be specified. These can only be specified subjectively, which, of course, means that $E(\tilde{R}_i)$, the expected equity return, is a subjective estimate. One meaningful way to proceed, however, is not to generate one estimate but to explore the range of estimates that result when different combinations of $E(\tilde{R}_m)$ and R_F are inserted. Given the limitations cited here it would not appear sensible to consider the CAPM alone a sufficient basis for regulatory decisions but rather one approach to determining the utility's required equity return which should be considered in regulatory proceedings.

[20]Supreme Court Decision in *Federal Power Commission* et al. v. *Hope Natural Gas Company*, 320 U.S. 591 (1949) at 603.

[21]Federal Communications Commission, Communications Satellite Corporation. Prepared Testimony, S.J. Meyers. F.C.C. Docket 16070; 1972.

Index Funds

An index fund is an investment fund constructed so that its rate of return behavior is approximately the same as that of a major index, such as the Standard & Poor's 500. Therefore, except for transaction costs and compositional differences, these funds offer the same return as the indices they attempt to imitate. The motivation for such funds arises from efficient market theory and portfolio theory.[22]

First, in an efficient market, investors are not able to use publicly available information to identify undervalued or overvalued securities; therefore, market prices reflect intrinsic values. Second, we have shown that the efficient set of portfolios (greatest expected return for a given risk level) is the locus of points on the straight line extending from the risk-free rate through and beyond the market portfolio. All investors should be somewhere on the straight line of efficient portfolios. By combining an investment in the market portfolio with an investment in the risk-free asset one may obtain efficient portfolios less risky than the market portfolio. An efficient portfolio riskier than the market portfolio is achieved by borrowing at the risk-free rate and investing in the market portfolio.

If the Standard & Poor's 500 index is a good surrogate for the market portfolio, investors may approximate the market portfolio by holding the index fund. If less risk is desired part of the investor's wealth can be diverted to short-term Treasury Bills, which serve as a substitute for a risk-free asset. Positions riskier than the market may also be achievable by buying on margin.[23] However, since actual margin loan rates are greater than the risk-free rate, the leveraging process is not as effective as that shown for region II in Figure 24-3. The slope of the efficient set is diminished for points past the market portfolio M.

Capital Budgeting

The two-parameter portfolio model has been applied in the capital budgeting area to develop a new market portfolio concept of project risk. This perspective suggests that the management of a publicly held firm should not be concerned with the impact a project has on the firm's total variability of return but rather with the project's relative risk. The relative risk is the incremental effect of the project on the variability of returns on a portfolio of investment assets held by a well-diversified investor holding the firm's stock. This is the same concept of risk we developed earlier for investment assets held in a portfolio and was represented by the asset's beta coefficient. It follows

---

[22]The appeal of index funds stems from efficient market and efficient portfolio considerations. However, if a majority of investors were to invest in a few index funds the market would no longer be efficient. This would destroy the underlying basis for index funds.

[23]Most institutions are legally precluded from buying on margin, however.

that product diversification by a firm for the sole purpose of reducing the variability of the firm's return is not beneficial to investors since they can achieve the same or better diversification within their own investment portfolio. The market portfolio concept of project risk shifts the emphasis away from measuring risk in the narrow context of the firm to measuring it in the context of the entire market of investment assets.

Associated with a project's relative risk measure is a required rate of return on the investment project. This rate of return is estimable using expression (19) for the Sharpe-Lintner CAPM. If the predicted internal rate of return (IRR) on the equity financed portion of a capital investment project does not exceed the project's required rate of return, the project is not acceptable. This required return is represented by the straight line of slope $E(\tilde{R}_m) - R_F$ in Figure 24-5 for a firm with a fixed capital structure.[24]

The project's expected rate of return is interpreted to be the expected return on the equity financed portion of the project. Or, stated differently, we now wish to consider the return of the project based on the generated cash flows adjusted for debt charges and the amount of the investment in the project reduced by the portion financed through debt. The project beta is considered to be the covariance between the return on the equity financed portion and the market return. Projects are positioned in Figure 24-5 by their estimated internal rates of return on the equity financed portion and their estimated betas. If a project lies above the CAPM line of slope $E(\tilde{R}_m) - R_F$ it is acceptable; otherwise it is not. Consequently, projects A and D are acceptable while C and B are not. Note that project A is acceptable even though its expected equity return is below the firm's average cost of equity capital. Apparently project A is sufficiently less risky than the firm's average project to warrant its acceptance.

Estimating betas for capital investment projects is especially difficult, much more so than for publicly traded securities. Several approaches are available, however. First, it may be possible to identify an existing firm, whose stock is publicly traded, which is involved in activities that approximate the project the firm is considering.[25] If such is the case, statistically estimated betas using historical stock return data for this firm may provide an adequate estimate of the project's beta.

Second, if the project is similar to one with which the firm has had prior experience, it may be possible to construct historical rates of return on the equity financed portion for different time periods and combine these with the

[24]Questions concerning the optimal capital structure are not considered here. See Mark Rubinstein, "Mean-Variance Synthesis," *Journal of Finance* 28 (March 1973): 167-81, and Robert Hamada, "The Effect of the Firm's Capital Structure on the Systematic Risk of Common Stocks," *Journal of Finance* 27 (May 1972): 435-52, for applications of the CAPM model to questions relating to capital structure.

[25]One should in this process adjust the beta coefficient for differences in capital structure that may exist. See Rubinstein, "Mean-Variance Synthesis."

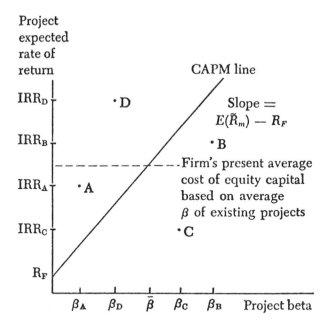

Figure 24-5   Project selection criterion

corresponding market returns (actually a surrogate such as the Standard & Poor's 500) to estimate a beta coefficient using expression (20).[26] Third, the firm might resort to constructing a simulation model of the project under consideration to help in estimating its beta.

SUMMARY

Modern financial theory and empirical evidence suggest that investors are well advised to make investment decisions assuming that security prices fully and instantaneously reflect all publicly available information. Furthermore, investors should hold efficient portfolios. Efficient portfolios offer the highest possible level of expected return for a given level of risk and represent combinations of a risk-free asset and the market portfolio.

When investors hold efficient portfolios, the risk of an individual asset is measured in terms of how much it contributes to the efficient portfolio's risk of return. This contribution is not adequately represented by the individual asset's total variability of return since a portion of this variation may be diver-

[26]See James Van Horne, *Financial Management and Policy*, 4th ed. (Englewood Cliffs: Prentice-Hall, 1977), pp. 175-78.

sified away. The proper measure of the asset's risk contribution is its beta coefficient, which is based on the covariation between the asset's returns and returns on the market portfolio. The higher this covariation, the more the asset contributes to the risk of an efficient portfolio.

The Sharpe-Lintner capital asset pricing model (CAPM) expresses the equilibrium relationship between the expected return on an individual investment asset and its risk stated as a beta coefficient. The CAPM has been used extensively to analyze theoretical and practical problems in finance. Applications of the model in public utility regulation and corporate capital budgeting were illustrated here. A particularly striking conclusion is that the risk of a capital investment project and its associated required level of return should not be judged on the basis of the project's total variability of returns. The proper basis of evaluation is to examine how the project's returns are estimated to covary with the returns on the market portfolio.

A PRIMER ON RANDOM WALKS IN THE STOCK MARKET*

Neil G. Berkman†

25

The random walk model of stock prices, often succinctly represented by the phrase "the best prediction of tomorrow's price is today's price," is probably the most controversial yet least understood result produced by economists in recent years. This model has proved to be particularly irksome to professional money managers, apparently because it is believed to undermine the claim, made implicitly or otherwise, that they can consistently pick winners. In response, technical and fundamental analyst alike, normally unable to agree on much of anything, have rallied together in the opinion that the random walk model must somehow be wrong. Faced with abundant empirical evidence in support of the model, some members of the investing public have concluded that it leads to a pure dart-throwing strategy of stock selection, others in their confusion have abandoned the market entirely. But is the random walk model really an insult to the competence of professional security analysts? Does it suggest that one cannot make money in the stock market? Does it imply that stock prices changes are unrelated to events occurring in the outside world? By examining the random walk model, by showing what it does and does not say, this paper explains why the answer to these and similar questions is "no"

*Reprinted from the *New England Economic Review*, September/October 1978, pp. 32-50, with permission of the Federal Reserve Bank of Boston.

†Economist, Federal Reserve Bank of Boston. The author wishes to thank Stephen C. Peck for his suggestions on the form of the model in Section IV and Elizabeth Berman for her research assistance.

and shows by means of an example that the model is entirely consistent with traditional approaches to stock valuation.

WHAT IS A RANDOM WALK?

Most of the confusion surrounding the implications of the random walk model of stock prices no doubt stems from a misunderstanding of precisely what is meant by a random walk. This is both unfortunate and unnecessary, since the concept may be easily explained. A convenient way to do so is by means of a simple experiment based on the outcomes of repeated throws of a pair of dice.[1] Such an experiment is particularly useful in explaining the notion of a random walk because of a well-known property of dice games. Assuming the dice are not "loaded" and thus have no "memory," knowledge of the outcome of any particular throw in no way increases one's knowledge of the likely outcome of the next throw, except insofar as it is certain to be between two and twelve. In other words, each toss of the dice is an independent event, so that the probability of any outcome on any throw is unrelated to the pattern of outcomes on all previous throws.[2] A clear understanding of the independence property is all that is needed to resolve the mystery surrounding a random walk.

The experiment is conducted as follows. Beginning with an arbitrary number of "points," 100, say, the dice are thrown and points are added or subtracted according to a schedule based on the probability of the various possible outcomes. These probabilities are stable, of course; no matter how many times the dice are thrown the chance of rolling a seven is always one in six, the chance of rolling a two is always 1 in 36.[3] Since seven is the most likely outcome, no points are awarded for this roll. A roll of two is awarded minus five points, a roll of three minus four points, a roll of four minus three points, a roll of five minus two points, and a roll of six minus one point. Analogous gains are awarded rolls of eight through twelve. By following these rules and repeatedly adding or subtracting the appropriate number of points after each roll, a series such

[1]H. Roberts was the first to use the "chance model" as a device to explain the meaning of a random walk. See Harry V. Roberts, "Stock Market 'Patterns' and Financial Analysis: Methodoligical Suggestions," *Journal of Finance*, Vol. 14, No. 1 (March 1959), pp. 1-10.

[2]Technically, independence requires that the conditional probability of any outcome equal its corresponding marginal probability.

[3]Let P(2) equal the probability of rolling two on a throw of two unloaded dice. This requires that each die come up one. Since there are six possible outcomes on a throw of a single die, the probability of a one, P(1) , equals 1/6. Since the throws are independent, the probability of rolling a second one given that a one has already been thrown (i.e., P(1/1)) is also 1/6. Therefore P(2) = P(1)P(1/1) = 1/6 × 1/6 = 1/36. To roll three on a throw of two dice requires a one on the first throw and a two on the second or a two on the first throw and a one on the second. Therefore P(3) = P(1)P(2/1) + P(2)P(1/2) =(1/6 × 1/6) + (1/6 × 1/6) = 2/36, and so on for the other possible outcomes between 4 and 12.

as that displayed in the upper panel of Figure 25-1, in this case the result of 52 throws, is obtained.

The similarities between the series in Figure 25-1 and any number of economic time series one could name are too striking to require extended comment. Compare, for example, the experimental series to the weekly values of the Standard & Poor's Composite Index for 1977 presented in the upper panel of Figure 25-2. Both series contain certain apparently repetitive patterns of fluctuation which suggest that it may be possible to predict their future course by careful study of their past behavior. Indeed, this possibility is the foundation of a technical school of stock market analysis.[4] Yet the design of the experiment that produced the series in Figure 25-1 insures that its next "step" will be determined only by the random outcome of a throw of the dice, and since the outcomes are independent, nothing in the pattern of the past behavior of the series provides any help in forecasting what the next step will turn out to be. The lower panel of Figure 25-1, which shows the number of points awarded for each of the 52 throws of the dice, illustrates this idea quite clearly. Inspection of the series reveals no discernible patterns that could be exploited to predict its future behavior. Similarly, the lower panel of Figure 25-2, showing

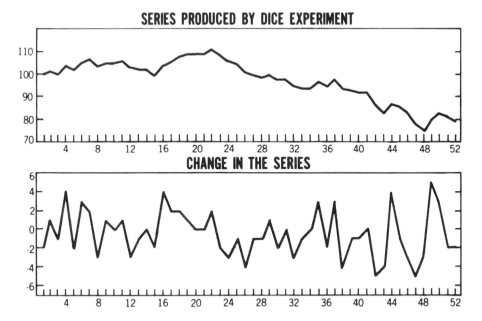

Figure 25-1

[4]Technical analysis includes all theories of stock price behavior that base forecasts solely on the past history of prices. A prominent example of technical analysis is the Dow Theory.

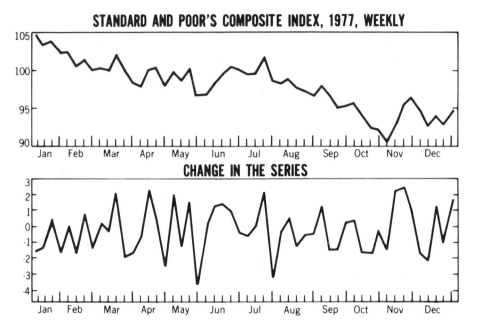

Figure 25-2

the series of successive changes in the weekly stock price index, displays none of the characteristic regularity normally associated with a series easily forecast from its behavior in the past. The movements of series such as these, where the size and the sign of each change are independent of the pattern of all previous changes, are thus very naturally described as following a random walk.

In the case of the dice experiment, the probability associated with each outcome was known a priori, as was the fact that each throw of the dice is an independent event. The latter property insured that the experimental series had no choice but to follow a random walk, the former property served only to define its allowable range of step-to-step variation. Obviously, the frequency distribution of changes of any series, whether stock prices or some other "real world" series generated by a complex economic process, may be measured from historical data and used as an estimate of the probable range of future movements.[5] On the other hand, an examination of the data evidence will not

[5]While the sample variance of a stock price series may always be computed by the formula

$$1/N \sum_{i=1}^{N} (p_i - \bar{p})^2,$$

where p_i is the i-th price change, p is the average price change and N is the number of observations, the variance of the true underlying population may not exist (e.g., if the true distribution is stable Paretian). Further, the variance of the underlying population, if it exists, may change over time, so that the sample variance must be interpreted with caution.

necessarily show that past changes in a given series are independent. The quarterly changes in nominal final sales displayed in the lower panel of Figure 25-3, for example, follow a clear cyclical pattern, with large changes tending to be followed by large changes and small changes. Thus, because successive changes in final sales are apparently related in such a way that the pattern of previous changes provides potentially useful information for forecasting the size of future changes, it is doubtful that the changes are independent or that the series follows a random walk.[6] For stock prices, however, abundant empirical research has uncovered precious little evidence of a lack of independence in successive price changes, so the random walk model has become widely accepted as a description of actual stock price behavior.

Empirical analysis of stock prices has of course also been concerned with characterizing the frequency distribution of price changes. This issue has proved surprisingly difficult to resolve, although early work generally favored a "bell-shaped" distribution centered about zero as a reasonable approximation to

Figure 25-3

<hr>

[6]Visual inspection is frequently misleading, hence the caveat "doubtful." The empirical techniques commonly used to test for independence will be described in a subsequent section.

reality.[7] Assuming this is true, then successive stock price changes may be thought of as the random outcome of independent draws from the bell-shaped distribution, just as each step in the experimental series was the result of the random outcome of independent throws of the dice. Further, just as seven is the most likely outcome of a throw of the dice, making zero points the most likely award on any throw, zero is the most likely draw from the observed frequency distribution, making zero change the most likely movement of stock prices between any two points in time.[8] Thus, since empirical analysis has shown that stock price changes are independent and that the frequency distribution of changes is approximately bell-shaped and centered near zero, the entire process is aptly summarized by the phrase, "the best prediction of tomorrow's price is today's price."

Although the pattern of observed stock price changes may be accurately described as following a random walk, this is not to say that stock prices are actually *determined* in this chance way. The common error of interpreting the random walk model as *causing* stock prices rather than as simply *describing* their behavior is the source of the misconceptions mentioned at the outset. In particular, the random walk model does not imply that stock prices are unrelated to events taking place in the economy that underlies the stock market. The model implies only that changes in the price of a stock cannot be predicted from the behavior of earlier changes in the price of that stock.

WHY DO STOCK PRICES FOLLOW A RANDOM WALK?

Hardly anyone would be surprised to learn that stock prices are a leading indicator of future economic activity, turning down in advance of recessions and turning up in advance of recoveries. Nor would many be surprised to learn the reason for this phenomenon. Stocks represent pro-rata shares to ownership of the real assets used to produce output. The market value of stock is thus intimately related to the value of this underlying capital, whose own value is

[7]The dispute has revolved around the common assumption that the distribution of price changes is normal. While convenient for statistical work (the techniques used in this area are strictly applicable only if the distribution of price changes is normal), the assumption is inconsistent with observed stock price change distributions that have "fat tails" and a peak centered near zero (i.e., that are "leptokurtic"). In addition, there is no general agreement about the appropriate transformation of the stock price data (i.e., first difference, percentage change, change in logarithm) required to induce stationarity. For some recent evidence on this issue, as well as a bibliography of previous work, see Randolph Westerfield, "The Distribution of Common Stock Price Changes: An Application of Transactions Time and Subordinated Stochastic Models,"*Journal of Financial and Quantitative Analysis*, Vol. 12, No. 5 (December 1977), pp. 743-766.

[8]The relevant unit period may range from transaction-to-transaction to year-to-year or even longer. The dispersion of possible price changes will increase as the measurement interval is lengthened, however.

in turn dependent on the profits it is expected to earn over the course of its useful life.[9] For this reason, stock prices, and the value of the capital they measure, reflect forecasts of the future course of business conditions; hence, their movements anticipate movements in the economy as a whole. Many people would be surprised, however, to learn that it is precisely because stock prices reflect forecasts that their movements follow a random walk.

Only two assumptions are required to move from the observation that stock prices reflect forecasts to the conclusion that price changes will follow a random walk. The first assumption, often referred to as the "rational expectations" hypothesis, concerns the quality of the forecasts used by investors in assessing the future course of the economy.[10] Expectations are rational if in the process of their formation, the forecaster uses all the current information he believes to be relevant for predicting the future course of the variable at hand. Naturally, both differences of opinion as to how the economy works and individual constraints on the amount of resources devoted to forecasting will influence the nature and quantity of the information incorporated in a given forecast. Idiosyncratic notions concerning the "true" casual links in the system will lead one forecaster to stress one sort of information, while others trying to predict the same variable will prefer information of some other kind.[11] The resulting forecasts may differ—witness the notorious divergence of opinion among professional economic forecasters, for example—but as long as each reflects all the information appropriate to the particular world view underlying the forecast, there is no reason to consider any one of them "irrational." Further, because information is not costless, the assumption of rational expectations requires forecasters to acquire additional data only up to the point where the value of the increase in forecast accuracy due to the marginal unit of information is just equal to the cost of acquiring and incorporating this information into the forecast. Thus, since the value of marginal improvements in forecast accuracy that presumably accompany the acquisition of additional information varies across individuals, as do the costs of acquiring the additional information itself, the amount of information incorporated in a rational forecast may vary across individuals as well.[12] Therefore, subject to the constraints imposed by the costs

[9]This is the familiar asset pricing model which holds that in equilibrium the current price of a capital good is equal to the present discounted value of the profits it is expected to earn in the future.

[10]The term "rational expectations" was introduced by Muth. See John F. Muth, "Rational Expectations and the Theory of Price Movements," *Econometrica*, Vol. 29 (July 1961), pp. 315-35.

[11]For example, in an attempt to forecast nominal GNP, a "Keynesian" might prefer information on the components of aggregate demand, while a "monetarist" might want to study money supply data.

[12]As a practical matter, however, there is little evidence that forecast accuracy is a strictly increasing function of the quantity of information used as input to the forecast.

of acquiring information and by the nature of the information required by the model implicitly or explicitly guiding the forecast, expectations are rational if no information available at the time the forecast is made that would be expected to improve its accuracy is ignored.[13] Under this assumption, the investors' expectations embody all that is knowable from available information about the future behavior of those variables believed relevant in determining the value of stocks.

Although this assumption may at first sight seem highly restrictive, it can be shown to be quite a reasonable description of investor behavior. The primary motivation for investing in stocks is to earn profits, of course, and the consistent attainment of this objective involves the early discovery of "undervalued" or "overvalued" issues.[14] The lure of trading profits available to investors who seek out information that will allow them to recognize and exploit such situations is a potent argument for rationality, as is the observation that competition among investors and their advisers has led to the development of ever more sophisticated information gathering and processing capabilities. Technological developments have also significantly reduced the cost of data collection, making the incorporation of large amounts of information into expectations economically feasible for many market participants. The concept of rationality is thus quite general, its appeal resting in the simple notion that greed should induce investors to act in this way.

The second assumption needed to develop a theoretical foundation for the random walk is that the stock market is "efficient" in the sense that available information is rapidly incorporated into current stock prices. Essentially this involves nothing more than assuming that investors attempt to earn profits from their investment in expectations formation by purchasing or selling stocks on the basis of their latest forecasts, in the perhaps mistaken belief that they have better information about the future than is already reflected in market values. This assumption follows quite naturally from the assumption of rational expectations, since investors would not bother to devote resources to processing information if they did not intend to make timely use of the forecasts they produce. In well-organized exchanges such as currently exist in the United States, where millions of investors are frequent participants, the combined effect of their transactions is to insure that stock prices at any point in time reflect all the information that is considered relevant to their value.

---

[13]In this view, rational expectations emerge simply as the outcome of constrained utility maximization, where the utility function includes "knowledge of the future" as an argument. The more common statement that a forecast is rational only if it is set equal to the conditional mathematical expectation of the variable, so that rational forecasts are always unbiased, is a special case that arises when utility functions are linear, information is costless, and everyone knows the "true" (linear) model of the economy.

[14]The terminology is loose. As used in the text, the terms refer simply to stocks whose prices, when viewed ex post, were about to exhibit significant increases or decreases.

The precise mechanism through which available information is reflected in stock prices in efficient markets may perhaps best be illustrated by means of an example. Suppose the rational processing of current information has produ   a generally held expectation that corporate profits will increase from current levels over the next few quarters. Faced with this expectation, an individual transactor might justifiably expect stock prices to rise in the near future as well. How could he profit from this expectation? Simply by purchasing stock now and waiting for the ensuing bull market to drive prices up. Clearly, however, other traders with similar expectations will act in the same fashion, and their combined purchases will drive prices up immediately.[15] Indeed, prices will rise by just enough to eliminate any further extraordinary gains that the expected increase in corporate profits had promised. This mechanism explains why stock prices lead the business cycle and defines the sense in which current prices fully reflect expectations. The profit motive provides the incentive for the stock market to behave in this way.

An important implication of the assumptions of rationality and efficiency is that one cannot consistently earn extraordinary profits by trading on the basis of generally available information, since such information is always rapidly incorporated into current stock prices. Another implication is that stock prices will change only when the arrival of "new" information causes expectations to be revised. For information to be truly new, it must of course have been unpredictable from information available previously, since it would otherwise already be reflected in expectations and stock prices by the time it is announced. The release of quarterly corporate profits data, for example, provides new information and results in an alteration of expectations only if the actual figures differ from the figures that had been expected earlier.[16] Since surprises such as these occur randomly (if they did not, they would not be surprises), the changes in stock prices that result from new information will be random as well. If expectations are rational and if the stock market is efficient, stock prices will follow a random walk.

HOW HAS THE RANDOM WALK MODEL BEEN TESTED?

The discussion up to this point has been intentionally vague regarding the precise meaning of the word "information." The random walk model defines information to include only the past history of stock prices and nothing more,

---

[15]It is not necessary for literally everyone to hold the same expectation, although the logic of the argument suggests that unless some traders disagree with the concensus view, prices will adjust without any trades taking place at all.

[16]Some traders may be surprised by the new information, while for others it may only confirm what was previously expected. The fact that shares change hands on such announcement dates merely confirms that expectations differ across individuals.

arguing that information so defined cannot be used to predict future prices.[17] The assumptions of rationality and efficiency that provide the theoretical underpinning for the random walk model implicitly allow a much broader universe of information than just past prices, however. In principle, the logic of the argument suggests that literally every conceivable bit of available information is continuously reflected in stock prices, so that neither past prices nor other information will be of any use for forecasting future prices and hence for earning extraordinary returns on stock market transactions. Whether this is true in fact is an empirical question, one which will probably never be answered completely due to the enormous amount of information that exists in the world today. Undaunted by this consideration, researchers have nevertheless devoted considerable effort to the task of testing both the simple random walk model and the broader efficient market model from which it is derived.

Tests of the Random Walk Model

Empirical analysis of the random walk model has been concerned both with testing for independence in stock price changes and with checking to see if the past history of prices provides information that can be used to predict their movements in the future and thus act as the basis for a profitable trading rule. These issues are closely related, of course; if price changes are random, then it will be impossible to predict future changes from past changes. It is nevertheless worth considering the tests separately, since the basic technique applied in trading rule tests is also widely used in tests of market efficiency generally.

The most straightforward test for independence is the "runs" test. A run is defined as a sequence of one or more price changes of the same sign. For example, replacing the numerical value of price changes by a " + " when the change is positive and by a " − " when the change is negative, the sequence " − − − + − + + − " consists of five runs. For given probabilities of a stock price increase or decrease, if positive changes tend to be followed by positive changes and negative changes by further negative changes, then the number of runs in a particular price series will be less than if the changes are independent. Similarly, if there is a tendency for positive changes to be followed by negative changes, then the number of runs will be greater than if the changes are independent. To illustrate, the case of stock price changes as measured by

---

[17]Since a pattern in a price series, like an earnings announcement, is information, the efficient market hypothesis requires that it too be continuously reflected in current prices. As an extreme example, suppose that analysis of historical data shows that the price of a particular stock has always doubled two days after it reaches a new yearly low. Assuming that this pattern is widely known, and in view of its potential profitability it certainly would be, then the price will double immediately after a new low is reached, since traders will try to buy in before the anticipated price reaction occurs. This behavior has the effect of eliminating the historical pattern, of course, so that such opportunities, if they ever exist, must be extremely short-lived.

the last day of the month closing values of the Standard & Poor's Composite Index for the 1928-1964 period, the observed probability of a price increase was .59 and of a price decrease .41.[18] Under the assumptions that these probabilities hold for the period 1965-1977 and that price changes are random, the expected number of runs in the latter period is 76.5.[19] The actual number of runs was 73, well within the expected range for standard levels of statistical significance. Thus, the result of this runs test would not allow one to reject the hypothesis that the sequence of monthly price changes between 1965 and 1977 is random.

Another popular method of analyzing stock prices is to estimate the correlation coefficient between successive price changes over a long period of time.[20] The random walk model argues that the sign and the magnitude of price changes from period to period are unrelated to each other, so that the correlation between them should be zero. Table 25-1 shows the estimated correlation coefficients between successive monthly, quarterly, and yearly changes in the Standard & Poor's Composite Index for the 1928-1977 period. As expected, the estimated coefficients are all quite small in absolute value, and none is different from zero in the statistical sense. Further, the percentage of the variability of current price change that is explained by its correlation with the previous change is virtually zero for all three differencing intervals. The correlation between successive price changes in this index therefore provides no information that would be useful for prediction, so the results of the test also support the random walk model.[21]

---

[18]Of the 442 price changes observed during this period, 259 were increases and 183 were decreases. Thus, an estimate of the probability of a price increase is $259/442 = .59$ and of a price decrease is $183/442 = .41$.

[19]This expectation was calculated as follows. There were 156 months in the 1965-1977 period. Assuming the probabilities of an increase and a decrease of .59 and .41, respectively, 92 price increases and 64 price decreases are expected. Under the null hypothesis that the changes are random, the expected number of runs is then computed as:

$$E(R) = \frac{2(92)(64)}{(92 + 64)} + 1 = 76.5$$

with a standard deviation of:

$$\sigma_R = \sqrt{\frac{2(92)(64)(2)(92)(64) - 92 - 64)}{(156)^2(155)}} = 6.02$$

[20]The correlation coefficient between successive changes in a series is $(\Sigma (p_i - \bar{p})(p_{i-1} - \bar{p}))/\Sigma (p_i - \bar{p})^2$, where p_i equals the i-th price change and $\bar{p}$ equals the average price change.

[21]Strictly speaking, the absence of correlation is sufficient for independence only if the distribution of price changes is normal. Since the available evidence suggests that the distribution may not be normal (see footnote 7), the test described in the text may be of very low power. Unfortunately, parametric statistical tests of independence for nonnormal distributions do not exist.

Table 25-1   Correlation coefficients for changes in the Standard & Poor's Composite Index

Interval	Correlation coefficient	Standard error of estimate	t-Ratio	Percentage of variance of current change in price index "explained" by its change last period[1]
Month	0.0386	.0409	0.942	0.0%
Quarter	0.0964	.0649	1.485	0.6%
Year	− 0.00535	.1020	− 0.053	0.0%

Note. These estimates were produced by an ordinary least squares regression of current change in stock price against a constant and lagged change in stock price for the period 1928-1977.

[1]These figures are the adjusted R^2s from the regression of current against lagged price change.

More sophisticated statistical techniques have been applied to price data both for individual stocks and market indices in a search for significant correlations between successive price changes or departures from randomness in sequences of runs, and price changes measured at intervals as short as transaction-to-transaction and as long as year-to-year have been analyzed, but no strong evidence inconsistent with the random walk model as a good working description of stock price behavior has been discovered. The most common conclusion is that no correlation exists, and when statistically significant correlations are reported, suggesting that the random walk model may not hold precisely, they always turn out to be too small to provide information that can be exploited as a forecasting device.[22] However, while these results indicate that at least provisional acceptance of the model is in order, they do not close the issue of the information content of a stock price series entirely because the possibility that more complex patterns exist in the data is not directly addressed by correlation and runs tests. Firm believers in the efficacy of chartist trading strategies may then justifiably argue that these tests provide unconvincing evidence against the ability of their models to predict stock prices, since chartist forecasts are typically based on intricate patterns of past behavior (the "double bottom," for example) that do not depend crucially on the presence or absence

[22]Some selected references from the vast literature on this subject are: Eugene F. Fama, "Efficient Capital Markets: A Review of Theory and Empirical Work," *Journal of Finance*, Vol. 25, No. 2 (May 1970), pp. 383-417; Clive W.J. Granger and Oskar Morgenstern, *Predictability of Stock Market Prices*, Lexington: D.C. Heath and Co., 1970; Paul Cootner, editor, *The Random Character of Stock Market Prices*, Cambridge, Ma.: MIT Press, 1964. The interested reader will find extensive bibliographies in each of these selections.

of correlation between successive movements in the price series.[23] Contrary to the implications of the efficient market hypothesis, this argument holds that the stock market does not incorporate all of the information contained in the pattern of past prices into current price. It was in an effort to counter this objection that trading rule tests were originally devised.

The goal of a trading rule test is to determine if a particular bit of information can be used to earn profits greater than could be earned without the information. The question then is can information about the past history of a stock's price be used to earn profits greater than would be earned if one just bought the stock and held it? An archetypal chartist trading scheme that has been tested in this way is the filter rule.[24] Under this rule, a stock is purchased if its price increases by x percent and held until its price declines by x percent from a subsequent high, at which time the trader simultaneously sells and goes short, covering his position when the price increases by x percent from a subsequent low. Price movements of less than x percent are ignored. For filters ranging in size from 0.5 to 1.5 percent this rule has been shown to generate greater profits than are earned if the stock is simply purchased at the beginning of the sample period and sold at the end, but *only* if the transactions costs (commissions, clearinghouse fees and the like) incurred in pursuing the strategy are not taken into account. When these costs are included, and they are substantial due to the frequent trades produced by small filters, the trader always does better under the buy-and-hold alternative. The fact that this chartist strategy can be used to earn "abnormal" returns in the absence of transactions costs is evidence against a strict random walk in stock prices, since it indicates a tendency for positive correlation in successive price changes. On the other hand, the departure from randomness is too slight to be useful as a forecasting device, since the excess profits available as a result of the observed correlation do not cover the costs involved in trying to exploit it. Indeed, although the random walk model thus appears to hold only as a very close approximation to actual price behavior, the stock market is evidently extremely efficient in incorporating the information contained in past price changes into current price. Patterns in a price series are traded upon and hence removed up to the point that any remaining patterns are not worth exploiting because of transactions costs. If transactions costs were zero, one would therefore expect stock prices to follow a random walk precisely.

Numerous runs, correlation, and trading rule tests have been conducted, none yielding results substantially different from those reviewed here. It is of

[23]Correlation is a measure of linear dependence. Technical (or chartist) analysis is based on the identification of highly *nonlinear* patterns of dependence, so that traditional statistical tests are irrelevant for analyzing the usefulness of these models.

[24]This trading strategy is very similar to the popular Dow Theory, a chartist scheme that is supposed to identify price trends. Detailed analysis of the profitability of such trading rules may be found in Sidney S. Alexander, "Price Movements in Speculative Markets: Trends or Random Walks," *Industrial Management Review*, Vol. 39 (Special Supplement, January 1966), pp. 226-41.

course impossible to analyze every stock, so that skeptics will always have reason to remain unconvinced, but the weight of the data evidence clearly favors acceptance of the random walk model and the presence of market efficiency with respect to the information contained in the history of stock prices.[25] The next step is to determine if stock prices efficiently reflect other kinds of information as well.

Tests of Broader Forms of Market Efficiency

Tests of market efficiency must begin with the selection of an appropriate bit of information from the vast universe of available data to which stock prices might react. The pragmatic approach is to narrow the search initially to a subset of information, such as that appearing in the *Wall Street Journal*, that can be reasonably expected to be available to the public at large. Even this restriction does not narrow the universe very much, of course, so the choices are ultimately made by heuristic appeal to the theory of the firm. Analyzing the market's reaction to information that on theoretical grounds should obviously be reflected in stock prices, such as earnings announcements, stock splits, or new security issues, will then show whether or not additional tests of price adjustment to more subtle information would be worthwhile.

Given a particular piece of information, for instance the announcement of a stock split, the problem is to determine if this knowledge can be used to earn profits in excess of those that could be earned without the information. In an efficient market, where stock prices continuously reflect available information, the answer is clearly "no," since the new data are impounded in market price before any trades can take place. On the other hand, evidence which reveals a consistent tendency for a slow price response, or a response that is rapid but subsequently reversed, would suggest that profitable trading rules are possible and hence that the market is not efficient. An empirical resolution of these two possibilities requires a measure of the extent and the timing of price changes in response to the arrival of new information.

A technique which has been widely used to assess price responses to new information is based on the so-called "market model."[26] This model posits a

[25]It is worth noting in this context that it is very unlikely for anyone who has discovered a profitable trading rule to ever make it public, since by doing so the profitability of the system will be quickly eliminated.

[26]See William F. Sharpe, "Capital Asset Prices: A Theory of Market Equilibrium Under Conditions of Risk," *Journal of Finance*, Vol. 20, No. 4 (December 1965), pp. 587-615; and John Lintner, "The Valuation of Risk Assets and the Selection of Risky Investments in Stock Portfolios and Capital Budgets," *Review of Economics and Statistics*, Vol. 47, No. 1 (February 1965), pp. 13-37. The seminal contributions in the development of the risk-return framework of portfolio analysis are by James Tobin, "Liquidity Preference as Behavior Towards Risk," *Review of Economic Studies*, Vol. 25, No. 1 (February 1958), pp. 65-85 and Harry Markowitz, *Portfolio Selection: Efficient Diversification of Investment*, New York: John Wiley and Sons, 1959.

stable relationship between the returns (i.e., capital gains plus dividends expressed as a percentage of purchase price) on a stock during a period of time and the returns on the "market portfolio" (generally represented by a broad-based index) during the same time period. The estimated coefficient between the returns on a stock and the returns on the market portfolio—the "beta" coefficient—is then a measure of the "riskiness" of that stock relative to movements in the market as a whole. For example, the returns on a stock with a measured beta of one tend, on average, to move in proportion to general market movements, whereas the returns on another stock with a beta of 1.5 tend to move more than in proportion to movements in the overall market. Investment advisers have found estimated betas to be useful tools for the construction of stock portfolios tailored to the individual risk tolerance of their clients. Efficient market researchers have found the model useful for another reason, however. Given the observed returns on the market portfolio during a particular time period and a set of betas for various stocks estimated from historical data, the market model can be used to estimate the "normal" returns expected to accrue to each stock on the basis of its relationship with the overall market during that period. Because returns on individual stocks are also influenced by many "firm-specific" factors not captured by returns on the market portfolio, deviations of actual returns from those predicted by the model are to be expected. The behavior of these deviations from normal returns in the period surrounding the announcement of new information provides a measure of the extent and the timing of the price reaction required for testing market efficiency.

One famous application of this technique examined the deviations from normal returns for a large sample of firms which had announced a coming stock split.[27] Examination of the cumulative deviations from normal returns for each stock for a period beginning 30 months prior to the announcement of the coming split and ending 30 months after the announcement revealed the following consistent pattern: The cumulative deviations increased *prior* to the announcement of the intended split and became flat on the announcement date and thereafter. Three important conclusions follow from this result. First, the market evidently *anticipates* the split announcement, since returns in excess of those expected from the relationship of each stock to the market are present before the information is made public. Second, the information is completely reflected in price by the time the split is announced, since deviations from normal behavior cease to accumulate on that date. Third, the adjustment of stock prices to the new information is "unbiased," since the cumulative deviations neither increase nor decrease in the 30 months after the announcement. Thus, once a coming split has been publicly announced, the stock's price fully reflects this information and no further "abnormal" returns can be expected.

---

[27] See Eugene F. Fama, Lawrence Fisher, Michael C. Jensen, and Richard Roll, "The Adjustment of Stock Prices to New Information," *International Economic Review*, Vol. X, No. 1 (February 1969), pp. 1-21.

Efficient market tests such as this have been conducted for many kinds of publicly available information, and rarely has the conclusion that published data cannot be used to earn abnormal returns been refuted.[28] Trends in the cumulative deviations from normal returns after the announcement of new information sufficient to more than cover the transactions costs required to exploit them have occasionally been detected, so that, as in the case of the random walk model, the efficient market hypothesis as applied to published information does not appear to hold absolutely. Such potentially profitable situations cannot be expected to be repeated, however, since their discovery will inevitably lead to their exploitation and hence their disappearance.[29] In any event, the weight of current evidence strongly favors market efficiency with respect to published information as a very close approximation to reality.

The fact that cumulative deviations from the market model show a strong trend prior to the announcement of new information suggests that abnormal returns are being earned by someone during this period. This in turn suggests that the market is probably not efficient with respect to information not generally available, since the transactions of those lucky few who have access to the knowledge, either directly or through forecasts, must be the source of this abnormal return behavior. Indeed, it is this group that causes the market to be efficient with respect to *available* information by impounding it in stock prices before it is made public. On theoretical grounds. price adjustments in an efficient market should be essentially instantaneous, so the observed long and gradual adjustment may be viewed as the combined result or the slow dissemination of "inside" information and the limited financial resources of those who possess it. Still, in the absence of a complete monopoly over inside information, it is unlikely that any individual or group can consistently reap these excess returns. Because reliable data on insider trading are naturally difficult to obtain, only indirect tests of this form of the efficient market hypothesis have been attempted. One study compared the returns on a sample of mutual fund portfolios with those on unmanaged but equally risky (i.e., with

[28]These studies are too numerous to cite here in toto. The volumes edited by Cootner, *op. cit.*, and James Lorie and Richard Brealey, *Modern Developments in Investment Management*, New York: Praeger, 1972 contain many early examples. In addition, nearly every issue of *The Journal of Finance*, *The Journal of Business*, and *The Journal of Financial and Quantitative Analysis* contains a new study of market efficiency. Two recent studies that fail to support the efficient market hypothesis are Stewart L. Brown, "Earnings Changes, Stock Prices, and Market Efficiency," *Journal of Finance*, Vol. 33, No. 1 (March 1978), pp. 17-28 and Peter Lloyd Davies and Michael Canes, "Stock Prices and the Publication of Second Hand Information," *Journal of Business*, Vol. 51, No. 1 (January 1978), pp. 43-56.

[29]This is a testable proposition. Since tests of market efficiency must of necessity be based on historical data (so that price adjustments can be observed both before and after the announcement of new information), those studies which uncover an apparent departure from efficiency can be performed again on more recent information as it becomes available to determine if the profitable situation still exists.

the same beta) portfolios for the period 1955-1964.[30] The idea was to determine if portfolios managed by professional investors, who as a group might reasonably be expected to have superior insight into the significance of publicly available information as well as access to information not widely known by the general public, could outperform portfolios "managed" under a naive buy-and-hold strategy. Only 26 of the 115 funds examined earned returns averaged over the entire period in excess of those produced by the naive strategy, and across all the sample funds the average return was well below that earned by the corresponding unmanaged portfolios. Further, none of the funds was consistently able to beat the market, since those which did so in one part of the sample period were unable to do so in another part. This important group of traders therefore did not appear to have continued access to information not already reflected in market prices.[31]

To summarize, extensive empirical analysis of stock price data has shown fairly convincingly that price changes follow a random walk and that new information is reflected in prices by the time it is publicly announced. The significant price adjustments that are observed to occur prior to the release of new data suggest that market participants formulate and act on forecasts of coming events, as required by the assumption underlying the efficient market hypothesis, although it is doubtful that any one group is consistently able to earn the extraordinary returns available during this anticipatory period of adjustment. Thus, the stock market is apparently efficient in the narrow sense that it removes exploitable patterns in price series themselves and in the broader sense that current prices fully reflect other publicly available information.

DOES THE RANDOM WALK MODEL REQUIRE REJECTION OF TRADITIONAL STOCK PRICING MODELS?

Despite the evidence in support of the random walk model, in the minds of many its validity remains in doubt. Perhaps this skepticism arises from the apparent anomaly that stock prices follow a random walk in a world where the progression of most economic events through time is so obviously highly correlated. The efficient market hypothesis reconciles these observations by arguing that investors exploit regularities in the data in the process of forming and acting upon their expectations, thereby fully incorporating predictable events into current stock prices and leaving only random "surprises" to produce

---

[30]See Michael C. Jensen, "The Performance of Mutual Funds in the Period 1945-64," *Journal of Finance*, Vol. 23, No. 2 (May 1968), pp. 389-416.

[31]It should be noted that these results may be sensitive to the particular definition of returns and to the form of the model used in the test. For a discussion of these issues see Norman E. Mains, "Risk, the Pricing of Capital Assets, and the Evaluation of Investment Portfolios: Comment," *Journal of Business*, Vol. 50, No. 3 (July 1977), pp. 371-384.

changes in their values. Although this theory too has been shown to be consistent with available evidence, resistance to the efficient market-cum-random walk models may persist because many fear that they must abandon more traditional models of stock price formation. The example presented in this section is designed to dispel this confusion.

Surely the most traditional of all valuation models is that the price of a stock is equal at any point in time to the present discounted value of the per share profits expected to accrue to the firm underlying the stock. Consider, then, a highly simplified economy in which nominal corporate profits depend only on past profits (a "trend" term) and the current change in nominal GNP (a "stage-of-the-business-cycle" term). Suppose in addition that changes in nominal GNP arise solely because of current and past changes in variables controlled by the government. Specifically, let these variables be the supply of money and Federal Government expenditure.[32] In such a world, one could produce "rational" corporate profit forecasts, and infer the "efficient market" level of stock prices implied by the valuation model at a particular point in time, by applying the following scheme: First, forecast the likely course of future change in money and government spending from the behavior of these variables in the past; second, use these forecasts to predict the probable path of GNP by substituting them into the historical GNP relationship; third, plug the GNP forecasts and the value of past profits into the profit relationship to predict the behavior of profits in the future; fourth, using an appropriate discount rate, compute the present value of the expected profit stream to arrive at a figure which represents the current price of stock (a "price index"). As new information becomes available, the forecasts must be updated to reflect the difference, if any, between actual and previously expected profits. If the new data turn out to equal the expected values, then a re-application of the valuation model will produce no change in stock prices. On the other hand, a surprise in figures will result in a revision of expectations, and therefore a change in stock prices.

A notable feature of this example is that the universe of relevant information has been intentionally restricted to include only past changes in money, government spending, and corporate profits. The example is also based on the assumptions that all investors know the true structure of the economy and that information gathering and processing is costless, thus insuring that everyone's expectations will be the same. These simplifications, by making operational the rather vague notions that "all available information" is included in rational forecasts and that the market "efficiently incorporates" the information into current prices, highlight the essential characteristics of the mechanism of stock price determination hypothesized by efficient market theorists and illustrates how this theory fits into the framework of traditional valuation models. The

[32]This is simply the famous St. Louis equation. See Leonall C. Andersen and Keith M. Carlson, "A Monetarist Model for Economic Stabilization," *Federal Reserve Bank of St. Louis Review*, Vol. 52, No. 4 (April 1970), pp. 7-25.

crucial question, however, is whether or not the stock price series generated by the model follows a random walk.

In an effort to answer this question, a computer simulation of the model was performed using quarterly data for the United States for the 1948-1977 period to estimate the structural relationships involved. These estimated relationships were then used to generate 25-quarter ahead profit forecasts beginning in the first quarter of 1955, updated after each quarter.[33] The discount rate required to compute present value of each of these expected profit streams was represented by the sum of the real discount rate for equity and the expected rate of price inflation, where the expected inflation rate was forecast in each quarter on the basis of its past behavior and the real discount rate was taken from a series developed by Kopcke.[34] A flow diagram of the complete model is presented in Figure 25-4, and the estimated equations themselves are reported in the Technical Appendix. The quarterly "stock price" series produced by the model is displayed in the upper panel of Figure 25-5, together with the actual quarterly values of the Standard & Poor's Composite Index for purposes of comparison. Finally, the lower panel of Figure 25-5 shows the quarter-to-quarter change in the simulated stock price series.

Inspection of Figure 25-5 shows that the model generates a surprisingly realistic-looking stock price series. Indeed, the simulated data track turning points in the actual series quite closely, with the major exception of the dramatic bear market of 1977. Further, no predictable pattern is apparent in the series of successive changes in the simulated data. The estimated correlation coefficient between these changes is only .05, reinforcing the visual impression that changes in the series are independent. In a world where stocks are capitalized at the present discounted value of expected profits, and where all available information is incorporated in profit forecasts, stock price changes evidently follow a random walk.[35]

The efficient market hypothesis thus emerges not as a radical alternative approach to the problem of stock price determination, but rather as a formalization and rationalization of the implicit axioms of asset valuation that have guided stock price models from the beginning. The efficient market hypothesis

---

[33]In theory, expected profits should be discounted over the entire life of the asset. Since the underlying corporation exists "forever," this means that the time horizon should be infinite. For positive discount rates, however, the present value of the marginal profit forecast approaches zero as the forecasting horizon increases. Experimentation revealed that for the data being considered here, the present value of profit forecasts beyond 25 quarters contributed less than 1 percent to the total value of the expected profit stream. Therefore, as a close approximation to the infinite, a 25-quarter forecasting horizon was assumed.

[34]See Richard W. Kopcke, "The Decline in Corporate Profitability," *New England Economic Review*, May/June 1978.

[35]Samuelson has proved a theorem that supports this assertion. See Paul A. Samuelson, "Proof that Properly Discounted Present Value of Assets Vibrate Randomly," *Bell Journal of Economics and Management Science*, Vol. 4, No. 2 (Autumn 1973), pp. 369-374.

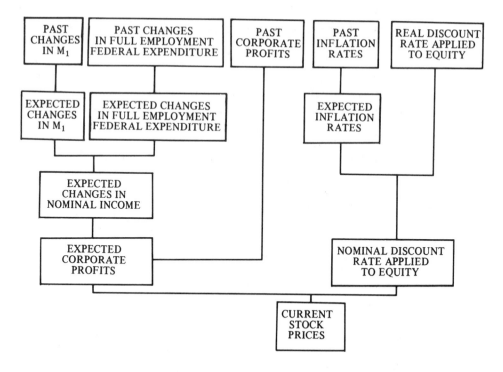

Figure 25-4   Flow diagram of stock price simulation model

makes an assumption about the nature of forecasts, but since it has always been well understood that asset values depend on expectations about events in the future, this assumption is hardly revolutionary. The efficient market hypothesis assumes that stock prices react to changes in forecasts, but this is also implied by models which set prices equal to the present value of expected profits, or to some multiple of earnings, or to a level determined by returns on alternative assets. All that is really new in the efficient market hypothesis is that it extends the logic of these familiar assumptions to reach the unfamiliar conclusion that stock prices follow a random walk.

As for the common misconceptions concerning the random walk model mentioned in the introduction, it should now be clear why the fact that stock price changes are independent does not imply that one cannot make money in the stock market, or that prices are unrelated to other economic events, or that professional security analysis is useless. While it is true that *excess* returns will not be consistently available in an efficient market, stock prices do rise in anticipation of favorable developments and fall when the outlook appears less optimistic. Success in the stock market thus involves just the same combination

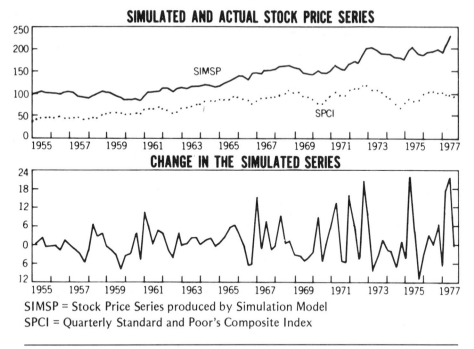

SIMSP = Stock Price Series produced by Simulation Model
SPCI = Quarterly Standard and Poor's Composite Index

SIMSP = Stock Price Series produced by Simulation Model
SPCI = Quarterly Standard and Poor's Composite Index

Figure 25-5

of forecasting skill and luck today as it did before economists began talking
about random walks. Nor does the existence of efficient markets imply the
superiority of dart-throwing strategies of stock selection, unless the riskiness
of the resulting portfolio is considered irrelevant. An investor can make use of
the fact that returns on individual stocks are systematically related to overall
market movements in the process of designing a portfolio tailored to his willingness to assume a particular degree of risk. Since such information is readily
available to professional security analysts, they have an important role to play
in a client's stock selection process. Furthermore, it is precisely because so
many analysts continually strive to improve their forecasting tools and information processing capabilities, and are willing to trade on the basis of their
knowledge, that the stock market is as efficient as it appears to be. The random
walk model is not an insult to the competence of professional money managers.
On the contrary, it is a compliment.

Figure 25-6   Technical appendix: simulation model for the "stock price" series displayed in Figure 25-5

Expected changes in the money supply and full employment Federal Expenditures are generated by:

1) $\Delta M_t = \Delta M_{t-1} + .0407 + .465\epsilon_{t-1} + .388\epsilon_{t-2}$
$\qquad\qquad\qquad (2.81) \quad (5.41) \qquad (4.47)$

$\hat{\sigma}_\epsilon = 1.0027 \quad \chi^2_{21\,D.F.} = 17.18$

2) $\Delta FEE_t = 1.0954 + .218\ \Delta FEE_{t-1} +$
$\qquad\qquad\quad (2.10) \quad (2.50)$

$\quad .205\ \Delta FEE_{t-2} + .321\ \Delta FEE_{t-3}$
$\quad (2.24) \qquad\qquad (3.47)$

$\hat{\sigma}_\epsilon = 4.178, \chi^2_{20\,D.F.} = 25.42$

The forecasts from these equations are fed into the following two equations to produce forecasts of expected corporate profits:

3) $\Delta Y_t = -.0623 + \sum\limits_{i=0}^{4} m_i \Delta M_{t-i} + \sum\limits_{i=0}^{4} e_i \Delta FEE_{t-i}$
$\qquad\quad (0.05)$

$\bar{R}^2 = .687,\ S.E. = 8.100,\ D.W. = 1.521$

Constraints: Fourth degree polynomial; $e_{+1} = m_{+1} = \ 0 = e_{-5} = m_{-5}$

Lag Weights (t-statistics)

$m_0 = 2.506\ (4.57) \qquad e_0 = 0.265\ (1.61)$
$m_1 = 1.704\ (4.94) \qquad e_1 = 0.271\ (2.18)$
$m_2 = 0.542\ (1.12) \qquad e_2 = 0.227\ (1.57)$
$m_3 = 0.343\ (0.97) \qquad e_3 = 0.218\ (1.72)$
$m_4 = 0.805\ (1.43) \qquad e_4 = 0.199\ (1.14)$
$\Sigma m_i = 5.899\ (7.97) \qquad \Sigma e_i = 1.18\ \ (3.57)$

4) $\Pi_t = \ 2.758 \ + .835\Pi_{t-1} + .226\Delta Y_t$
$\qquad\quad (2.54) \qquad (24.78) \qquad (8.29)$

$\bar{R}^2 = .907,\ S.E. = 2.681,\ D.W. = 1.878$

The discount rate applied to the expected profit stream (ρ) was computed by adding to the Kopcke real discount rate figures on expected inflation premium generated by:

5) $(\%\Delta IPD)_t = .405 + \sum\limits_{i=1}^{8} p_i(\%\Delta IPD)_{t-i}$
$\qquad\qquad\qquad (4.05)$

$\bar{R}^2 = .352,\ S.E. = .588,\ D.W. = 1.250$

Constraints: third degree polynomial; $p_{+1} = 0 = p_{-9}$

Lag Weights (t-statistics)

$$p_1 = .150\,(7.19) \qquad p_5 = .054\,(3.04)$$
$$p_2 = .207\,(7.54) \qquad p_6 = -.024\,(1.02)$$
$$p_3 = .193\,(7.94) \qquad p_7 = -.075\,(2.80)$$
$$p_4 = .134\,(7.46) \qquad p_8 = -.075\,(3.65)$$

Finally, the profit and discount rate forecasts were fed into the following equation to produce the simulated stock price series displayed in the text:

$$6)\quad SP_t = \sum_{\tau=1}^{25} \left({}_t\pi^e_{t+\tau} \Big/ (1 + {}_t\rho^e_{t+1})^\tau \right)$$

DEFINITIONS:

ΔM = quarterly change in seasonally adjusted nominal M_1;

ϵ = forecast error;

ΔFEE = quarterly change in seasonally adjusted nominal full employment Federal expenditures;

ΔY = quarterly change in seasonally adjusted nominal GNP;

Π = seasonally adjusted nominal corporate after-tax profits
(= corporate profits with capital consumption and inventory valuation adjustments less corporate profits tax liability), quarterly;

$\%\Delta IPD$ = quarterly percentage change in the implicit price deflator for GNP;

SP = simulated stock price series, quarterly;

ρ = discount rate applied to expected profit stream;

${}_t\Pi^e_{t+\tau},\ {}_t\rho^e_{t+1}$ = corporate profits (discount rate) expected as of time t to obtain in period $t + \tau$ $(t + 1)$.

DATA SOURCES: Data on the real discount rate for equity were taken from Richard W. Kopcke, "The Decline in Corporate Profitability" *New England Economic Review*, July–August 1978. All other data were taken from the NBER data base.

ESTIMATION PROCEDURES: The period of fit for all equations is 1948: II–1977: IV. The numbers in parentheses are t-statistics. Equations (1) and (2) were fit by the maximum likelihood methods of Box and Jenkins; equations (3)–(5) were fit by ordinary least squares.

CAN YOU BEAT THE STOCK MARKET?*

Daniel Seligman†

26

Most people interested in the stock market fall into one of three categories: (1) academic scholars who doubt that anybody really knows how to beat the market; (2) professional investors who indignantly reject this view of the matter; and (3) amateur investors who also believe that you can beat the market but don't realize how controversial this assumption is. I have long been a partisan of the first group, and until the last year or so had assumed that its case was airtight.

The professors seemed to have built an overwhelming case for the so-called efficient market hypothesis (EMH). If you think of the hypothesis as a literal description of the real world, the stock market cannot be beaten by mere mortals. Question: how close to reality is EMH? Having now resurveyed the basic case made for it in the business schools, and also looked at some recent findings that seem inconsistent with it, I find myself still answering that EMH is extremely useful for understanding the stock market—but doubting that it's as close to reality as I had previously assumed. It seems fairly clear that some superior investors are out there beating the market systematically.

The efficient market hypothesis says that stock prices always tend to reflect everything known about the prospects of individual companies and the economy as a whole. This simple-sounding academic proposition has some staggering

*Reprinted from *Fortune*, December 26, 1983, pp. 82-84ff. Copyright 1983, Time, Inc. All rights reserved.

†Research associate *Robert Steyer*

implications. It implies, first of all, that stock prices cannot be predicted: if all current information is already embedded in the prices, then they will be moved only by events not now foreseen—which are, by definition, unpredictable. This means in turn that all "technical analysis," and especially efforts to discern future stock price trends by examining past trends, are futile. EMH also implies that no amount of fundamental research, including the exhaustive and high-priced studies done by Wall Street for big institutional investors, will give investors an edge. It implies that if you're in the stock market, you should buy and hold rather than trade a lot; trading increases your brokerage costs without increasing your expected return. It tells you to assume that professionals, or indeed any investors, who have outperformed the market in past periods were probably just lucky, and that we have no reason to believe they will have superior results in the future. In his textbook *Foundations of Finance*, economist Eugene F. Fama of the University of Chicago asks "whether there are individuals or groups—for example, managers of mutual funds—who are adept at investment selection in the sense that their choices reliably provide higher returns than comparable choices by other investors." Answer: "If prices always fully reflect available information, this sort of investment adeptness is ruled out."

In the mid-1960s, Fama probably did more than anyone to develop the efficient market hypothesis. (Nobel laureate economist Paul Samuelson of MIT was also among those who elaborated the concept then.) Asked recently how well he thought EMH has stood up over the years, Fama replied genially: "It's done pretty well. Most economic models barely make it to the next set of data." His perspective is that publicly available information (but not all inside information) is almost certainly reflected in stock prices. This means that Fama, like most other academics, believes in the "semi-strong" form of EMH. In the so-called strong form, *all information known to anybody* is said to be built into prices; however, I never did succeed in finding anyone who accepted this proposition as literally true.

Even in the semi-strong form, however, EMH is hard for Wall Street to swallow. It implies that much of what investors hear around them every day is nonsense. Fast example: Standard & Poor's was presumably talking nonsense last June, when (like a lot of other advisory services) it said the stock market would rise further because profits were improving; the efficient market hypothesis tells us that prices in June would already be reflecting whatever was knowable about future earnings.

Having somewhat different material interests from members of the investment community, I have always found the efficient market hypothesis intuitively appealing and told myself that it had tremendous explanatory power. Indeed, it explains the single most obvious mystery about the securities business; how can it be that thousands of professional stock-pickers, including many who are plainly intelligent and industrious, are endlessly confounded by the market and embarrassed by their selections? Security analysis is one of the very few lines of work in which we take for granted that the recommendations of respected professionals will be wrong half the time or more.

EMH is intuitively appealing on several other grounds. In a world where hundreds of thousands of investors are endlessly scratching around in search of some advantageous risk-return relationship, and where professional arbitragers on exchange floors stand ready to pounce on any security that offers a marginal advantage, and where, furthermore, computers have enormously multiplied the number of investors with access to instantaneous price quotations, it would be hard to explain how market inefficiencies *could* last more than a few minutes or even seconds. These armchair arguments have been buttressed by an avalanche of empirical studies that have made EMH a solidly settled question on the campuses. Indeed, some scholars are concerned that it may be excessively settled. Michael C. Jensen of the University of Rochester, who has no doubts at all about market efficiency, nevertheless worried recently about the battle having been won so thoroughly, and added: "It's dangerously close to the point where no graduate student would dare send off a paper criticizing the hypothesis."

Among the empirical findings that make EMH noncontroversial on the campuses are any number showing that markets either anticipate or adjust instantaneously to published information and that they repeatedly see through misleading accounting practices. Studies of mutual fund managers disagree only about a minor matter: whether the managers are(a) unable to outperform the market or (b) able to do so but not by enough to give shareholders an edge after subtracting commissions and other costs. The studies agree that funds as a group do not enable investors as a group to achieve returns higher than those of the market. In the course of researching this article, I sat in on a lecture on EMH by Dean Burton G. Malkiel at the Yale Graduate School of Management. Malkiel, a lucid and witty lecturer who is a former member of the Council of Economic Advisers, had the students in stitches describing a study whose principal finding was an utter lack of correlation between mutual fund rankings from one year to the next. In this context he mentioned the Mates Investment Fund, which was ranked No. 1 among mutual funds in 1968 but never got above No. 300 in subsequent years. Malkiel's throwaway line was that Fred Mates eventually got out of the mutual fund business and took to running a singles bar in New York called, appropriately, Mates. Evidently assuming that this was a made-up detail, the Yalies groaned and hissed at the line; however, it happens to be true.

Naturally not wishing to give up on a theory that helps to explain life's mysteries, I have been distressed by some signs in recent years that the efficient market hypothesis might be in trouble, or at least in need of some updating. Like many other EMH fans, I have been shaken by the proliferation of "anomalies"—this being the professors' preferred term for stock market news that seems to confound the hypothesis. News of this kind is taken very seriously indeed on the campuses. Professor Stephen A. Ross of Yale's management school commented jovially the other day that papers on the anomalies have become "a major growth sector of the academic world."

One disturbing anomaly centers on the extraordinary records compiled by certain high-visibility investors. The records of one tightly knit group of investors, of whom Warren Buffett is the best known, are laid out in the box. Buffett, chairman of Berkshire Hathaway Inc. and the subject of a recent *Fortune* article ("Letters from Chairman Buffett," August 22), is very much aware of the extent to which his investment record constitutes a challenge to the efficient market hypothesis. He believes that there are exploitable "pockets of inefficiency" in the market, and he has several times argued his case in appearances at the Stanford business school, on whose advisory council he serves. Speaking to the council, Professor William F. Sharpe of Stanford, one of the school's academic stars and the author of a popular textbook solidly endorsing EMH, once referred to Buffett as "a five-sigma event." In business school lingo, this superlative signifies that you should think of his investment performance as being five standard deviations above the mean; if literally true—no one claims that it is— this would tell us that there was only about one chance in 3.5 million of compiling an investment record like Buffett's by chance.

The apparently superior long-run performance of the *Value Line Investment Survey* is another anomaly that efficient-market fans must come to terms with. The professors have, in fact, been worrying about the survey since 1970, when Value Line Chairman Arnold Bernhard made a presentation about its record at the University of Chicago.

Every week Value Line ranks about 1,700 stocks on a scale of 1 (most favorable) to 5. Bernhard's most compelling detail: in the five-year period beginning in April 1965, the returns to investors had corresponded precisely to the rankings. In every one of the five years, Rank 1 returns had been highest, Rank 2 returns had been next highest, and so on. For the five years as a whole, Rank 1 was up 129 percent and Rank 5 was down 41 percent; this was a period in which stocks were rising about as often as they were falling.

Bernhard's methodology in getting to those figures was challenged by Professor Fischer Black, now of MIT, a leading advocate of the efficient market hypothesis. However, Black ultimately concluded—reluctantly, I have to assume—that Value Line had indeed done well over the five years. His own figures showed annual risk-adjusted returns averaging 10 percent for Rank 1 during the period and -10 percent for Rank 5. (A risk-adjusted return is one from which you have subtracted the return expected on a randomly selected portfolio of comparable risk.) Reviewing matters three years later, Black wrote in the *Financial Analysts Journal*: "If anything, the results have been better since 1970."

However, Value Line was not yet home free. During the past decade or so, further refinements in performance evaluation techniques have led to still more pulling apart of the organization's results; the latest edition of *Financial Theory and Corporate Policy*, a textbook by Thomas E. Copeland and J. Fred

YOU ONLY SWING ON 3 AND 0

In principle, says the efficient market hypothesis, no one can systematically beat the stock market. In applying EMH to investors Warren Buffett, Charles Munger, William Ruane, and Walter Schloss, you would have three difficulties: (1) all have outperformed the market over long periods; (2) they have generally done so in both bullish and bearish environments, so it's hard to argue that their higher returns simply reflect greater risk-taking; and (3) all are pursuing strategies that reflect the ideas of the late Benjamin Graham, so it's hard to view their performance as a random event. Buffett, Ruane, and Schloss studied under Graham, and all four have been influenced by his classic *Security Analysis*, written with David L. Dodd and first published in 1934. Graham's core idea: look for companies that for some reason are undervalued and hold the stocks for as long as it takes the market to see the values. Obviously such companies are hard to find. Says Buffett: "You wait for the 3 and 0 pitch." Prize example of what you can get by waiting: the Washington Post Co. in 1974, when its market value was $80 million and its TV stations alone were worth more than that. Now its market value is about $1 billion, and Buffett's Berkshire Hathaway Inc. owns 13 percent.

Buffett himself has not formally been in the money management business since 1969, when he dissolved the Buffett Partnership Ltd. after nearly 14 years of operation. One reason for the dissolution: Buffett had stopped finding undervalued securities. During its lifetime the partnership had an average annual return of 29.5 percent, vs. 8.2 percent for the S&P 500. (Like the figures below, these assume annual reinvestment of dividends.)

Charles Munger's partnership (Wheeler Munger & Co.) operated from 1962 to 1975. It had an average return of 19.8 percent, vs. 5.3 percent for the S&P 500. Bill Ruane runs the immensely successful Sequoia Fund, which was first offered to the public in July 1970 and since then has had an average return of 18.6 percent, vs. 10.6 percent for the S&P. Sequoia now has $333 million of assets and has suspended sales to new investors because, says Ruane, "the money was coming in faster than I had ideas."

The private partnership run by Walter Schloss has had an average return of 21.3 percent, vs. 8.7 percent for the S&P (Figure 26-1, p. 410). In a recent sentimental letter to his partners, Schloss saluted Graham and *Security Analysis*, which "helped many of us along a rocky road."

Weston, offers a "partial listing" of seven serious academic papers on Value Line. The central issue in the most recent of these papers—as in much other literature about EMH anomalies—is risk adjustment. Obviously, you cannot get agreement on Value Line's providing superior risk-adjusted returns unless you first get agreement on how to measure risk.

In examining Value Line's record, a 1982 paper by Copeland and David Mayers of UCLA applied a measure of risk different from that used by Fischer Black; in addition, they extended the period under examination out to 1978. The upshot: Value Line's edge now looked much smaller, and a strategy of going long on Rank 1 and short on Rank 5 would have yielded only 6.8 percent a year in risk-adjusted returns, at which level profits would apparently have been wiped out by brokerage commissions. In a final zinger, Copeland and Mayers noted that the abnormal returns appeared to be sinking toward the end of the period. Still, any abnormal returns at all represent a challenge to EMH. The Copeland-Weston textbook concludes a detailed passage on Value Line by proclaiming that it "remains an enigma."

Several heavily studied anomalies concern the well-known discount on closed-end funds: many of the funds, which are publicly traded, sold for years at huge discounts from their underlying net asset values. After several of the heavily discounted closed-end funds went open-end a decade or so ago, the discounts began to shrink; however, no one has satisfactorily explained why they were so wide in the first place. "I've heard a hundred convoluted explanations of the discount," says Stephen Ross of Yale, "and not one that makes any sense."

In retrospect the discounts look especially disconcerting because an investor who had naively told himself that he was outfoxing the market by buying his portfolio at a discount *was* outfoxing the market, or at least outperforming it. Professor Rex Thompson of the University of British Columbia has shown that during the 32 years beginning in 1940 an investor could have consistently earned abnormal returns with a simple trading rule. The rule: maintain a portfolio of discount funds, and weight the portfolio so as to emphasize those with the largest discounts. The trading rule would have rather consistently given you a risk-adjusted rate of return of over 4 percent. Conversely, an investor who had maintained portfolios of the funds selling at a premium (which a few of the funds always did) would have racked up risk-adjusted losses of 7.9 percent a year—also an affront to EMH. Or, rather, an apparent affront. Thompson himself is inclined to think that he was looking not at a market inefficiency but at still another situation in which risk wasn't being measured properly.

Two other heavily studied anomalies pertain to the calendar. One, the "January effect," refers to a distinct, statistically significant pattern of above-average returns to investors during that month, with the gains heavily concentrated during the first five trading days of the month; in addition, the gains are concentrated in the stocks of small companies. Such seasonal happenings are supposed to be ruled out by EMH.

The other calendar-based anomaly seems even more bizarre. It is the "weekend effect," a phenomenon on which Kenneth R. French of the University of Chicago appears to be the world's leading authority. Analyzing daily returns from 1953 through 1977, French found a persistent tendency for returns on Monday to be negative even though returns for the period as a whole were positive. The data suggested the possibility of a profitable trading rule: load up on stocks on Monday, just before the close, and then sell just before Friday's close. French's data said that if you applied this rule to Standard & Poor's composite index of 500 stocks during 1953-77, you would have had an average annual return of 13.4 percent (before transaction costs), vs. 5.5 percent for the S&P.

The weekend effect seems especially mind-blowing when you focus on another detail. Why should Monday be a sick day on Wall Street? Instinct suggests that the below-average returns must have something to do with the fact that the market had been closed during the two previous days. For example, you might wonder whether companies weren't more likely to release bad news on days the market is closed. But this thought doesn't hold up. French found that when the market is closed because of a holiday (and not just a weekend), the day after the holiday is *not* sick. In other words, the weekend effect really does have something to do with weekends, and not closed markets in general.

The discovery of these calendar effects is most ironic. Over the years the academics who have developed EMH have been at pains to shoot down various Wall Street superstitions rooted in the calendar, the principal ones being belief in a summer rally and a year-end rally. In the lecture I attended at Yale, Malkiel explained why it was absurd to believe that the week between Christmas and New Year's Day tends to be bullish. If there were any foundation to the belief, he said, then investors would obviously load up on stocks just before Christmas and sell just before the New Year. If they did that, the bullish period would be moved back a day or so, the investors would then have to buy and sell still earlier, and they would be caught in an infinite regress. Against this background, it is bothersome to the academics to be in the position of discovering calendar effects that Wall Street hadn't heard about.

Furthermore, the calendar anomalies are not of the class that can be attributed to uncertainty about measuring risk. Professor G. William Schwert of the University of Rochester, who is one of the editors of the *Journal of Financial Economics*—which can claim to have published more articles about efficient market anomalies than any other periodical in the world—commented wryly the other day: "I'm willing to believe that we're mis-specifying risk in some serious way, but I have trouble believing that we only do it on certain days of the week."

The leading entry in the anomaly sweepstakes these days is none of the above. It is, instead, the "small-firm effect." Schwert contributed an article on the small-firm effect to the June 1983 issue of his journal, which also carried six other articles on the subject. Since small-company stocks are in general

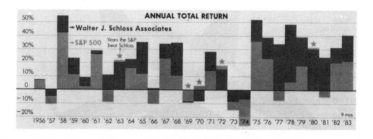

Source: Standard & Poor's, Walter J. Schloss Associates.

Figure 26-1 Could this be luck? Like his fellow Grahamites, Walter Schloss has a 28-year record that's hard to attribute to luck. His partnership's total return (unrealized gains plus distributions) exceeded that of the S&P 500 in all but five years.

riskier than blue chips, you would, of course, expect them to have higher returns on average. The news on the small-firm effect is that even after adjusting for risk, small-company stocks yield outsize returns. Marc R. Reinganum of the University of Southern California has found that for "very small capitalization firms," the risk-adjusted annual return has been running at an incredible average rate of more than 20 percent.

How can this be? If small-company stocks—or any other class of stocks, for that matter—are clearly identified as superior investments, you would expect the market to bid up their prices until they reached a level at which risk-adjusted returns to future investors would be merely normal. Why doesn't this happen?

In attempting to fathom the small-firm effect, the academics have come up with another startling finding: the small-firm effect is in part a reflection of the January effect. Donald B. Keim of the Wharton School has demonstrated that about half of that outsize return to small-company stocks is accounted for by their superior performance during January, especially during the first few days of the month. Whether this seasonal news reduces or magnifies the mystery of the small firm effect is somewhat unclear, but the finding has evidently encouraged academics to look closely at some tax-related and other institutional explanations of the anomaly.

For example, what about the possibility that small-company stocks do well early in January because they are rebounding from year-end tax-loss selling? Presumably they are especially vulnerable to such selling because, as high-risk stocks, they are more likely than blue chips to represent losses to investors. "This argument is ridiculous, of course," wrote Richard W. Roll of UCLA in a now famous article in the winter 1983 *Journal of Portfolio Management*, and he explained why: "If investors realized that such a pattern were persistent, they would bid up prices before the end of the year and there would be no significant positive returns after January 1." Roll nevertheless went ahead and ran some empirical tests of the ridiculous argument; for example, he checked to see whether the stocks that did best early in January were in fact most likely to be those with poor performances in the prior year. It turned out that they were, and for this and other reasons Roll surprised himself and concluded that the tax-selling hypothesis had something to it. (His mind-boggled attitude toward his findings is reflected in the article's Teutonic title: "Vas ist das?") This left him having to explain why traders didn't bid up the prices of small-company stocks in December and sell them in January. The likeliest explanation, he decided, was high transaction costs, especially the huge bid-asked spreads on many small stocks. Although Roll is one of the heavyweights of the efficient market fraternity, his explanation of the small-firm-cum-January phenomenon has not been accepted by all his colleagues.

Even if it were universally accepted, we would still need an explanation for the half or so of the outsize small-company returns that are not attributable to happenings in January. And we still need explanations for the other anomalies—investments that seem to have consistently offered superior risk-adjusted returns in defiance of EMH. Hopes about resolving these mysteries center on two possibilities: (a) that we will find new and better measures of risk that make the anomalies go away, and (b) that we will find quirks in the marketplace that explain the anomalies without requiring us to throw out EMH. Nobody in the academic world, so far as I know, is responding to the anomalies by saying that maybe they mean markets are much less efficient than previously supposed.

For the past 20 years or so, the preferred risk measure, both in the business schools and among portfolio managers, has been the famous beta. The logic of beta derives from the Capital Asset Pricing Model (CAPM), developed in the early Sixties by William F. Sharpe of Stanford and others. The central insight of the CAPM is that not all kinds of risk affect return. The market does not compensate you for bearing a risk associated with a given company—the risk of a strike, say, or a product failure—because you can effectively eliminate such risks by diversifying. What you cannot eliminate is the "systematic risk" that all investors share by virtue of the fact that stocks tend to rise and fall together in bull and bear markets. Beta therefore expresses only the systematic risk of a given stock and endeavors to do so by measuring the extent to which returns on the stock have been more, or less, variable than those for the market as a whole. With the market's own beta pegged at 1.0, a highly volatile stock that has historically offered extremely variable returns might have a beta of 2.0. A defensive stock with minimum swings and not too much dispersion in its returns might have a beta of 0.5. In principle, high-beta stocks have correspondingly high rates of return. So if beta works as intended, and if markets are efficient as believed, it should be impossible for scholars to find anomalies like the small-firm effect.

The fact that the anomalies nevertheless keep turning up is one reason why beta looks somewhat shaky these days. Fama's crisp judgment on beta: "It's not adequate—that's for sure." This risk measure is not in trouble just, or even mainly, because of the anomalies. It has also been hurt by (a) evidence that betas are not as stable over time as long assumed, (b) evidence that any individual stock's beta will vary considerably, depending on which index one uses as a proxy for the market as a whole, and (c) the bothersome finding of a decade ago that over one extremely long period (1931-65) the risk-return relationship wasn't quite right: actual returns were somewhat higher than predicted for low-beta stocks and lower than predicted for high-beta stocks.

The hottest current candidate to replace beta is a measure developed by Ross of Yale and Roll of UCLA. They propose to replace the whole CAPM with their APT, which stands for Arbitrage Pricing Theory. Like the CAPM the APT assumes that only systematic risk—the kind that can't be diversified away— needs to be measured. However, it also assumes that systematic risk cannot be captured adequately in a unitary measure like beta. The research thus far tells Ross and Roll that systematic risk needs to reflect several separate factors. The three mentioned most often: unanticipated changes in inflation, in industrial production, and in interest rates. Efforts to determine whether, and to what extent, the APT will get rid of the anomalies are still preliminary, but Ross believes that his model will wipe out most of them.

In any case, the APT clearly sends out messages about various stocks' riskiness quite different from what beta tells us. The beta approach casts utilities, for example, as low-risk defensive stocks, while APT shows them to be extremely risky in periods of unexpected inflation. One side effect of APT's emergence has been to give utilities a useful new tool in arguing with rate commissions about their appropriate returns. Revealing a utopian side to his character, Ross says he hopes that utilities will use APT because it is a better model and not just because it happens to serve their interests.

What about the possibility that some anomalies will ultimately be explained by quirks of the marketplace—by arrangements that might sometimes lead investors to be less rational than EMH assumes them to be? Some proposed explanations look plausible. Dean LeBaron, president of the rapidly growing Batterymarch financial management group in Boston, observes that institutional investors in general are apt to be unreasonably leery of high-risk situations because the corporate treasurer, say, doesn't want to have to explain how come the pension fund portfolio he okayed had a company in it that went bankrupt. LeBaron says that some of his institutional clients were "not enthusiastic" about a high-risk portfolio that he was assembling early in 1982 and that included such subsequent big winners as Chrysler and International Harvester.

Another cluster of quirks has to do with the sizable transaction costs (mainly in the form of outsize bid-asked spreads) and liquidity problems associated with companies that have small capitalizations. A portfolio manager would have trouble loading up on such stocks without sending their prices through the roof. Dimensional Fund Advisors, a hot new fund group, is trying to solve this problem by assembling small-company portfolios and offering them to pension funds and other institutional investors. Among DFA's advisors: Gene Fama.

On balance it seems likely that all or most of the anomalies will ultimately yield to further academic findings about risk and institutional quirks. It seems most likely that the anomalies will end up vindicating Wall Street. You have to keep reminding yourself that the Street would never have heard of most of the anomalies but for business school research, and that the puzzles still to be solved are puzzling only in relation to academic models that have long been scorned on the Street. Anyway, if the market actually was inefficient in some fundamental way, the professional stock-pickers of America wouldn't be in such chronic disarray.

The hard part is explaining the existence of such apparently superior investors as Buffett and Value Line. An EMH hard-liner would argue that it's possible such investors are just being lucky year after year after year; and since nobody knows how to run a controlled experiment decisively differentiating between luck and skill in stock selection, that argument cannot be totally excluded. But Buffett's view—that in a basically efficient market it is nevertheless possible to find occasional, exploitable pockets of inefficiency—seems much more plausible.

What Buffett's view implies for the average investor is another matter. The professors make a persuasive case for just buying and holding a diversified portfolio. And even if you accept that superior investors do exist, it could be a mistake to act as though you and your broker are among them.

The Impact of Inflation on Stock Prices[*]

Douglas K. Pearce[†]

27

The rapid and variable inflation experienced since the late 1960s has caused wealthholders to seek to protect themselves against increases in the general price level. At the beginning of this period of inflation, it is likely that common stock—which represents a claim on real capital—was recommended as such a hedge. However, those who followed such advice and placed funds in a broad portfolio of stocks in 1968 have seen the real value of their holdings fall by about 50 percent. This surprising result has spurred considerable research on the relationship between inflation and the stock market. While no consensus has yet emerged on the theoretical nexus between inflation and equity prices, several empirical studies have confirmed that inflation and stock returns have been negatively related in the postwar period.[1]

*Reprinted from the *Economic Review*, March 1982, pp. 3-18, with permission of the Federal Reserve Bank of Kansas City.

†Douglas K. Pearce is an associate professor of economics at the University of Missouri-Columbia and a visiting scholar at the Federal Reserve Bank of Kansas City. Research assistance was provided by Dan Vrabac, a research assistant with the bank.

[1]Studies reporting a negative relationship between returns and inflation include John Lintner, "Inflation and Common Stock Prices in a Cyclical Context," *NBER 53rd Annual Report*, September 1973; Zvi Bodie, "Common Stocks as a Hedge Against Inflation," *Journal of Finance*, May 1976, pp. 459-70; Jeffrey F. Jaffe and Gershon Mandelker, "The 'Fisher Effect' for Risky Assets: An Empirical Investigation," *Journal of Finance*, May 1976, pp. 447-58; Charles R. Nelson, "Inflation and Rates of Return on Common Stocks," *Journal of Finance*, May 1976, pp. 471-83; and Eugene F. Fama and G. William Schwert, "Asset Returns and Inflation," *Journal of Financial Economics*, November 1977, pp. 115-46.

It is important to investigate the reasons for this anomalous finding given the significance of the stock market. Movements in share prices are viewed as a prime indicator of the private sector's evaluation of current and future business conditions. Moreover, the stock market is thought to have a substantial influence on the consumption behavior of households and the investment decisions of business firms.[2] A fall in the real value of stocks is likely to reduce consumption demand since households hold about one-sixth of their net worth in common stock.[3] Lower stock prices should also discourage investment spending because they signal firms that the market places a lower value on their capital stock, and thus should encourage mergers rather than the purchase of new capital equipment and structures.[4] If there is a negative, causal relationship running from inflation to stock prices, inflation will reduce the growth of the corporate capital stock and thus have direct, adverse effects on productivity and output.

The purpose of this article is to analyze the possible connections between stock prices and inflation to see if such a causal link exists. The first section briefly reviews the traditonal model of stock price determination. The second section presents the historical record of stock prices, stock returns, and inflation. The third section surveys the major alternative hypotheses which have been put forth to explain the negative relationship between equity prices and inflation. The fourth section investigates the plausibility of these explanations by examining how well they accord with the empirical evidence. The final section summarizes the findings of the article.

INFLATION AND THE PRESENT VALUE MODEL OF STOCK PRICES

The effect of inflation on stock prices and stock yields can be analyzed using the traditional model for asset prices, the present value model. This model asserts that the price of a share of stock is the discounted, or present, value of

[2]For a detailed discussion of the stock market and the economy, see Barry Bosworth, "The Stock Market and the Economy," *Brookings Papers on Economic Activity*, 1975:2, pp. 257-90.

[3]The role of wealth in the consumption function is stressed in the influential life-cycle hypothesis of saving. See Franco Modigliani and Richard Brumberg, "Utility Analysis and the Consumption Function," in *Post-Keynesian Economics*, ed. by Kenneth K. Kurihara, New Brunswick, N.J.: Rutgers University Press, 1954; and Alberto Ando and Franco Modigliani, "The 'Life Cycle' Hypothesis of Savings: Aggregate Implications and Tests," *American Economic Review*, March 1963, pp. 55-84.

[4]James Tobin has emphasized the ratio of the market value of a firm to the replacement cost of its capital stock, the q ratio, as the primary determinant of investment spending. See James Tobin, "A General Equilibrium Approach to Monetary Theory," *Journal of Money, Credit, and Banking*, February 1969, pp. 15-29. A more recent paper which finds that a model emphasizing stock prices yielded forecasts superior to those from several alternative frameworks is Robert F. Engle and Duncan K. Foley, "An Asset Price Model of Aggregate Investment," *International Economic Review*, October 1975, pp. 625-47.

all future dividends. For simplicity, it is assumed that all corporate profits are paid out so that the terms profits, earnings, and dividends are interchangeable. If real dividends are expected to be constant and inflation is zero, the stock price of a debt-free (unlevered) corporation can be computed using a simple formula:[5]

$$S_t = \frac{D^e}{r} \qquad (1)$$

where

S_t = the price of the stock at the beginning of period t
D^e = the expected dividend to be received at the end of each period
r = the real rate of return required by stockholders.

For example, if the required real rate of return is 5 percent and the corporation is expected to earn $5 per share every year, the stock should sell for ($5/.05), or $100. Stock price movements, according to this model, reflect some combination of changes in the expected dividend stream or the required rate of return. This required rate is assumed to equal the real interest rate on a default-free security plus a risk premium, due to the uncertainty of dividend payments. The one-period yield on the stock is defined as

$$\text{Stock yield}_t = \frac{D^e + S_{t+1}}{S_t} - 1 \qquad (2)$$

and thus the expected yield is r, the required rate of return.[6]

In this model, inflation will cause nominal stock prices to rise at the same rate as the general price level, leaving real stock prices constant, unless inflation changes expected real dividends or the required rate of return. If inflation is neutral in the sense that all prices rise at the same rate, firms will see their revenues and costs increasing at this same rate so that nominal profits and

---

[5]The present value model for share prices is generally associated with John Burr Williams, *The Theory of Investment Value*, Cambridge: Harvard University Press, 1938. The general expression for the present value of dividends is:

$$S_t = \sum_{i=0}^{\infty} \frac{D^e_{t+1}}{(1+r)^{i+1}}$$

which can be expressed as equation (1) when all dividends are assumed to be equal.

[6]If D^e is constant,

$$\text{Stock yield}_t = \frac{D^e + \dfrac{D^e}{r}}{\dfrac{D^e}{r}} - 1$$

$$= r.$$

dividends also rise at the rate of inflation. When inflation is at rate p (and is fully anticipated), the equation for the nominal price of stock becomes:[7]

$$S_t = \frac{D^e(1 + p)^t}{r}.$$ (3)

Thus for the example above, if inflation is 10 percent per year, nominal dividends would be expected to be \$5.50 at the end of the first year, \$6.05 at the end of the second year, and so on. The initial stock price, S_0, would still be \$100, but the price at the beginning of the next year, S_1, would be (\$5.50/.05), or \$110, and S_2 would be (\$6.05/.05), or \$121. The real price of the stock would remain unchanged since the nominal stock price increases just match the increases in the general price level. The nominal one-period yield on the stock would be approximately $r + p$, leaving the real yield unaltered.[8] Hence, inflation has no real effects on stock prices or yields unless it changes the real profitability of the corporation's capital, D^e, or the return demanded by the shareholders, r.

This analysis assumes a firm which has no debt. If the firm raised some of its funds through issuing bonds or other debt, inflation might raise real equity prices. While inflation should not change the real market value of the firm—that is, the real value of all claims on the firm—if it is unexpected it will benefit shareholders (debtors) and hurt bondholders (creditors), thus raising share prices in real terms.[9] Again, this prediction is based on the assumption that inflation neither affects the profitability of capital nor raises the required rate of return.

It should be noted that the validity of the present value model is not unquestioned. Keynes, for example, considered this model of share prices only

---

[7]To see this result, note that

$$S_0 = \frac{D^e(1+p)}{(1+r)\,(1+p)} + \frac{D^e(1+p)^2}{(1+r)^2(1+p)^2} + \ldots$$

and $\quad S_1 = \dfrac{D^e(1+p)^2}{(1+r)(1+p)} + \dfrac{D^e(1+p)^3}{(1+r)^2(1+p)^2} + \ldots$

thus $\quad S_1 = (1+p)S_0 = \dfrac{(1+p)D^e}{r}.$

A similar development would show $S_2 = (1 + p)^2 S_0$ and so on.

[8]The actual yield is $r + p + rp$, but the last term is generally negligible.

[9]For a more detailed discussion of this argument, see Lintner. Support for the hypothesis that inflation raised the stock prices of net debtor firms was found by Reuben A. Kessel, "Inflation-Caused Wealth Redistribution: A Test of a Hypothesis," *American Economic Review*, March 1956, pp. 128-41.

a convention.[10] Doubting that movements in stock prices were dominated by the long-run expectations embedded in equation (1), he considered short-run speculation to be the primary force. Spectators in the stock market, Keynes asserted, spend the majority of their time guessing the preference of other speculators instead of evaluating the future earnings of firms. While other critiques of the model have also appeared, the present value model remains the predominant tool for analyzing stock prices.[11]

THE HISTORICAL PERFORMANCE OF COMMON STOCKS

The history of nominal stock prices is presented in Figure 27-1 along with the general price level for the 1901-80 period. The stock price index employed is Standard & Poor's Composite Index of 500 (S&P 500) of the largest stocks (measured by their market value) with the weights of each stock corresponding to the relative market value of the stock. The general price level is measured by the Consumer Price Index (CPI). While the two series are not closely related, they moved broadly together until the mid-1960s. From then on, however, the general price level has spurted sharply upward while nominal stock prices remained roughly constant. Figure 27-2 dramatizes this recent divergence by plotting the real value of stocks over the last 30 years.

As mentioned above, the constant purchasing power value of common stock peaked around 1968 and has since fallen to about 50 percent of that level. It is this dramatic plunge in real equity prices which has puzzled analysts.

The pattern of real stock prices is mirrored by the behavior of stock yields. Table 27-1 reports the nominal and real yields on the S&P 500 portfolio and the inflation rate for 1926-80 and subperiods. Over the entire period, investors enjoyed a 9.4 percent nominal yield and a 6.5 percent real yield on this portfolio. While similar yields occurred during the last 30 years, the last two columns of Table 27-1 indicate that there were two distinct eras. From 1951 to 1965, stocks earned high nominal returns while inflation averaged less than 2 percent per year. However, from 1966 to 1980, the nominal yield was well below the

[10]John Maynard Keynes, *The General Theory of Employment, Interest and Money*, New York: Harcourt Brace, 1936, p. 152.

[11]For recent applications of this model, see Roger E. Brinner and Stephen H. Brooks, "Stock Prices," in *How Taxes Affect Economic Behavior*, ed. by Henry J. Aaron and Joseph A. Pechman, Washington, D.C.: Brookings Institution, 1981; and William C. Brainard, John B. Shoven, and Laurence Weiss, "The Financial Valuation of the Return to Capital," *Brookings Papers on Economic Activity*, 1980: 2, pp. 453-502. For critiques of the model based on its apparent inability to account for the volatility of stock prices, see Stephen F. LeRoy and Richard D. Porter, "The Present Value Relation: Tests Based on Implied Variance Bounds," *Econometrica*, May 1981, pp. 555-74; and Robert J. Shiller, "Do Stock Prices Move Too Much to be Justified by Subsequent Changes in Dividends?" *American Economic Review*, June 1981, pp. 421-36.

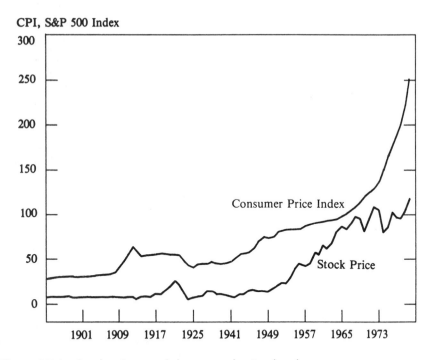

Figure 27-1   Stock prices and the general price level

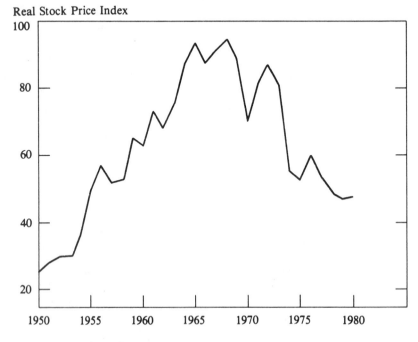

Figure 27-2   Real stock prices

Table 27-1 Nominal and real yields on common stocks
(Amounts in percent)

	1926–80	1926–50	1951–80	1951–65	1966–80
Nominal compound yield on Standard & Poor's 500 stock portfolio	9.4	7.7	10.9	15.2	6.7
Inflation rate (CPI)	2.9	1.3	4.2	1.6	6.9
Real yield on Standard & Poor's 500 stock portfolio	6.5	6.4	6.7	13.6	−0.2

Note: The yields are computed assuming all dividends are reinvested and that the portfolio was held for each period.

Source: R. G. Ibbotson and R. A. Sinquefield, *Stocks, Bonds, Bills, and Inflation: Historical Returns (1926–1978)*, Financial Analysts Research Foundation, 1979. Updated to 1980 by the authors.

historical mean while inflation was rapid, producing real returns that were negative. Thus, these data also suggest that recent inflation has had a substantial, adverse effect on the stock market.

WHY INFLATION HAS HURT THE STOCK MARKET: ALTERNATIVE VIEWS

The failure of stock prices to rise with the general price level and nominal yields to keep up with inflation during the last fifteen years has stimulated several researchers to seek an explanation for this anomaly. The present value model indicates that the fall in real stock prices signals a reduction in expected real earnings and thus real dividends, or an increase in the required rate of return on stock.

This section reviews two arguments why inflation might reduce expected earnings—namely, that inflation raises the real tax burden on corporate capital and that inflation causes investors to underestimate the returns to shareholders. Following this discussion is an examination of why inflation might raise the rate of return required by either increasing returns on alternative assets, increasing perceived risk, or confusing investors into misapplying the present value model.[12]

[12]A recent paper by Eugene F. Fama, "Stock Returns, Real Activity, Inflation and Money," *American Economic Review*, September 1981, pp. 545-54, gives a fourth explanation for the negative correlation between stock returns and inflation. Fama argues that this finding is really the result of omitting the effects of real activity from the analysis. He contends that stock returns are positively related to expected real activity, while inflation is negatively related to expected real activity. This produces the negative contemporaneous correlation between stock returns and inflation. A key assumption of his model, which many analysts may question, is that commodity prices are flexible enough to keep the money market in equilibrium even when the period of analysis is monthly.

Inflation and Expected Corporate Earnings

Tax Effects. Much of the discussion concerning the poor performance of stocks during periods of inflation has centered on the role of taxes. Several researchers believe that inflation substantially increases the real tax rate on corporate profits and, therefore, that expected inflation causes investors to revise downward their forecasts of real after-tax corporate earnings.[13]

Inflation is thought to raise the effective tax rate faced by corporate capital because of the tax treatment of depreciation charges and inventory changes. When computing its taxable profits, a corporation deducts the amount of depreciation of its physical assets. This deduction helps the firm to maintain its capital stock. During inflation, however, the replacement cost of equipment and structures rises with the general price level. Because the depreciation deductions are based on the historical cost of the assets, they no longer reflect the amount required to keep the capital stock intact. Since inflation swells nominal revenues but does not increase the depreciation charges, nominal profits rise and overstate the true profits of an ongoing firm. With taxes based on nominal income, the real tax burden on the corporation is enlarged and real after-tax earnings are reduced.

A similar argument is relevant to the treatment of inventories. During an inflationary period, firms selling goods from inventory realize nominal gains which are taxed as ordinary income. These gains arise because the firm can only deduct the original cost of buying goods rather than the current cost of replenishing the inventory. Again, an ongoing firm has made no real gains, but its real tax bill has increased. This problem is exacerbated by the still prevalent use of the first-in, first-out (FIFO) accounting method.[14] A rise in inflation will thus raise taxable profits and therefore taxes, even when real profits have not increased, with the result that real after-tax earnings fall.

Gains from Debt. It has been argued that inflation reduces real corporate debt and that such gains offset much or all of the impact of taxes on corporate earnings. However, some economists believe that shareholders ignore the gain from debt in evaluating their equity and thus underestimate true profits and undervalue the supporting stocks. This argument assumes a kind of money illusion on the part of investors because they fail to adjust reported profits adequately for all the effects of inflation.[15]

---

[13]Richard Kopcke, "Are Stocks a Bargain?" *New England Economic Review*, May-June 1979, pp. 5-24; and Martin Feldstein, "Inflation and the Stock Market," *American Economic Review*, December 1980, pp. 839-47.

[14]Firms could reduce their tax liability (assuming inflation continues) by switching to the last-in, first-out (LIFO) method, yet only about one-quarter of inventories were under LIFO accounting in 1977. See Martha S. Scanlon, "Postwar Trends in Corporate Rates of Return," in *Public Policy and Capital Formation*, Board of Governors of the Federal Reserve System, 1981, pp. 75-87.

[15]The money illusion argument is made by Franco Modigliani and Richard A. Cohn, "Inflation, Rational Valuation and the Market," *Financial Analysts Journal*, March-April 1979, pp. 24-44.

Table 27-2 illustrates why gains from debt should be added. Assume a firm initially has a net worth of $1,000 and debt of $1,000. The debt is in the form of one-period bonds paying 5 percent. Inflation is known to be zero, there are no taxes, and equity also yields a real return of 5 percent. Line one gives the initial revenues, costs, and profits, with all profits distributed as dividends. Line two shows the effect of 100 percent inflation, completely anticipated. Revenues and labor costs double, but interest expense rises to $1,100 because the nominal interest rate fully reflects expected inflation. Accounting or book profits are now negative (− $900), but the firm can still pay the same real dividend and cover the increased interest expense by borrowing $1,000. All the firm is doing is maintaining the same real debt. Thus, accounting profits provide a misleading guide to the true picture of the firm since inflation is actually neutral. There are no effects on real dividends, real debt, or the debt-equity ratio. The correct measure of profits in the last column equals accounting profit plus the gain on real debt—that is, the inflation rate times nominal debt.

Inflation and the Required Rate of Return on Stocks

Even if it had no effect on expected profits, inflation would cause real stock prices to fall if it raised the required rate of return on stocks. This might occur if inflation increased the after-tax real returns on alternative assets or if investors believed that stocks had become riskier because of inflation and thus demanded a higher risk premium. Also, investors might mistakenly use the nominal interest rate, which moves with inflation, to discount real earnings.

Return on Alternative Assets. Some analysts have attributed much of the fall in real stock prices to the exceptionally high real returns that owner-occupied housing has provided during recent inflationary times.[16] This asset enjoys two tax advantages when the general price level rises. The main return is the rental services of the house for which the owner, in effect, pays himself. Since this imputed return rises with inflation but is not taxed, the real, after-tax earnings of the house rises relative to other assets. Second, unlike common stock, realized nominal capital gains largely can be avoided by reinvestment in houses until age 55. The adjustment of portfolios by wealthholders results in housing prices being bid up and in stock prices falling, so that comparable real after-tax returns might be reestablished.

Greater Risk. An alternative reason for a rise in the required rate of return is a rise in the perceived riskiness of corporate profits. If increases in the risk premium for stocks are associated with higher inflation rates, inflation would reduce share prices even if it left expected earnings unaffected. It has been

[16]Patric H. Hendershott and Sheng Cheng Hu, "Inflation and Extraordinary Returns on Owner-Occupied Housing: Some Implications for Capital Allocation and Productivity Growth," *Journal of Macroeconomics*, Spring 1981, pp. 177-203; and Lawrence H. Summers, "Inflation, the Stock Market and Owner-Occupied Housing," *American Economic Review*, May 1981, pp. 429–34.

Table 27-2 Effect of inflation on accounting profits

Initial conditions of firm: Equity = $1,000 Debt = $1,000

Initial economic conditions: Nominal interest rate (i) = 0.05

Inflation (p) = 0

Period	Revenue	Labor cost	Interest cost	Accounting profit	Dividends	Change in debt	True profits
0 (p=0)	200	100	50	50	50	0	50
1 (p=100)	400	200	1,100	-900	100	1,000	100
2 (p=100)	800	400	2,200	-1,800	200	2,000	200
3 (p=0)	800	400	200	200	200	0	200

Note: When expected inflation is 100 percent, the nominal interest rate rises from 5 percent to 110 percent in order for the real interest rate to be unaffected. The equation for this relationship is i = r + p + r·p where i is the nominal interest rate, r is the real interest rate, and p is inflation.

argued that much of the decline in stock prices can be attributed to added uncertainty about corporate earnings and that inflation is a primary cause of this uncertainty.[17]

There are several reasons why inflation might make corporate profits less predictable. There is evidence that a rise in the level of inflation is accompanied by an increase in both the variability and the dispersion of relative price movements.[18] Either of these factors will tend to make the profits of any firm less certain. For example, an unpredictable inflation rate imposes real efficiency losses as economic agents scramble to protect themselves by using shorter contracts. In addition, a volatile inflation rate makes it more difficult to distinguish relative price movements from changes in the overall price level, possibly resulting in incorrect allocation decisions.

A high level of inflation, even without more variability, may also cause corporate earnings to be less certain if agents anticipate corrective measures by the government. Investors may fear the imposition of wage-price controls with their inherently arbitrary effects on profits. Similarly, rapid inflation is likely to bring on some form of restrictive monetary or fiscal policy which may not only dampen profit expectations but, given the unknown nature of the exact policies that will be undertaken, make planning an even more hazardous task.

Finally, energy-related inflationary jumps may add to the unpredictability of profits. Over the 1970s, the two largest jumps reflected steep increases in energy prices. Uncertainty about future energy prices and supplies coupled with the existence of production techniques and capital equipment geared to low energy prices is likely to have reduced the perceived stability of corporate earnings. Thus, the inflation rate may serve as a proxy for the riskiness assigned to returns to corporate capital. Therefore, increases in inflation may lead investors to require higher returns on stock.

Incorrect Discount Rate. A third reason why inflation could raise the required rate of return on stocks is the use by investors of a nominal interest rate rather than a real interest rate to discount future real profits.[19] This is roughly equivalent to shareholders comparing the earnings-price ratios of stocks to the nominal interest rate on bonds when making portfolio decisions. As discussed earlier in the paper, inflation should raise earnings and the price of stocks at the same rate, leaving the earnings-price ratio unchanged. In other

---

[17]See Burton G. Malkiel, "The Capital Formation Problem in the United States," *Journal of Finance*, May 1979, pp. 291-306. Increased risk has also been emphasized by William Fellner, "Corporate Asset-Liability Decisions in View of the Low Market Valuation of Equity," in *Contemporary Economic Problems 1980*, Washington, D.C.: American Enterprise Institute, 1980.

[18]For a review of this literature, see John B. Taylor, "On the Relation Between the Variability of Inflation and the Average Inflation Rate," in *The Costs and Consequences of Inflation*, Carnegie-Rochester Conference Series on Public Policy, ed. by Karl Brunner and Allan H. Meltzer, Amsterdam, Netherlands: North-Holland, 1981.

[19]This is the second part of the money illusion theory of Modigliani and Cohn.

words, the earnings-price ratio is a real yield. Thus, the correct comparison is the earnings-price ratio to the real rate of interest, the nominal rate less expected inflation. If investors do commit the error of looking at nominal interest rates, then as inflation pushes up nominal interest rates, stock prices would have to fall to provide comparable yields.

EMPIRICAL EVIDENCE ON STOCK PRICES AND INFLATION

This section reviews empirical evidence on the possible connections between inflation and stock prices. The first part examines both whether inflation has reduced the expected profitability of corporate capital through raising effective tax rates and the impact of ignoring the gains from debt on the return on equity. The second part of the section investigates the proposition that inflation has raised the required return on stock which, if true, would force stock prices down.

Inflation and Expected Corporate Earnings

Tax Effects. The tax effects hypothesis asserts that inflation reduces real after-tax corporate profits because it raises the effective tax rate. This view implies that the after-tax profitability of corporate capital should be inversely related to inflation and that the before-tax profitability should be unrelated to inflation. If inflation has little or no impact on real after-tax profitability, the tax effects theory would not account for the fall in real stock prices.

The before-tax rate of return on nonfinancial corporate capital (BTROR) is defined here as the ratio of profits plus net interest paid to the replacement cost of the nonfinancial corporate stock. The after-tax rate of return (ATROR) is similarly defined but with corporate income taxes subtracted form the numerator. The profits in both measures are adjusted for the effect of inflation on inventory and depreciation charges.[20]

Figure 27-3 plots the BTROR and the ATROR for the last 30 years. The series follow a similar pattern, peaking in 1965 and dropping sharply to lower levels thereafter. Since the difference between the two measures, which reflects

---

[20]The correction for the understatement of inventory costs is the Inventory Valuation Adjustment (IVA) which essentially removes the distortion arising from firms using FIFO accounting. The impact of inflation on depreciation allowances is measured by the Capital Consumption Adjustment (CCA) which converts reported depreciation into true depreciation by taking into account both the accelerated depreciation allowed by tax laws, which overstates depreciation, and the difference between replacement cost and historic cost. For a detailed discussion of these adjustments, see John B. Shoven and Jeremy I. Bulow, "Inflation Accounting and Nonfinancial Corporate Profits: Physical Assets," *Brookings Papers on Economic Activity*, 1975:3, pp. 557-98; and Phillip Cagan and Robert E. Lipsey, *The Financial Effects of Inflation*, National Bureau of Economic Research, Cambridge, Mass.: Ballinger, 1978.

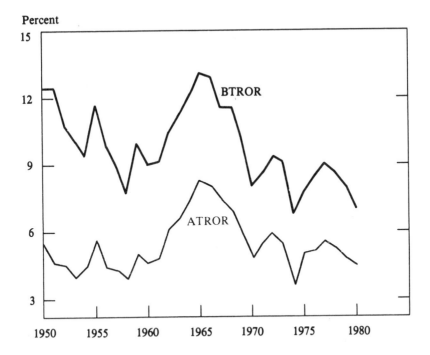

Percent

Figure 27-3 Before and after-tax returns on corporate capital

corporate income taxes, narrowed over the whole period, it would seem that inflation has not raised the tax burden on capital. However, the impression from Figure 27-3 may be misleading since other factors such as fluctuations in the economy also affect tax liabilities.

To isolate the effect of inflation on the rates of return, a model was estimated in which the rate of return depends on inflation and the level of economic activity as measured by the percentage gap of actual real GNP from full employment real GNP.[21] As expected, both the BTROR and the ATROR were found to be sensitive to movements in the real economy with the before-tax rate falling about 0.3 percent and the after-tax return about 0.17 percent for every 1 percent rise in the GNP gap. The estimated impacts of inflation on the rates of return give weak support for the tax effects theory. No statistically significant relationship was found between the BTROR and inflation, but inflation was found to have a negative effect on the ATROR, although the level of statistical significance is somewhat low. While the results are consistent with the tax effects view, the estimated reduction in the ATROR is only 0.1 percent

[21]The estimated models are reported in Table A of the Appendix. The models allow for the intercept and time trend to differ for 1951-65 and 1966-80, following the study by Richard W. Kopcke, "The Decline in Corporate Profitability," *New England Economic Review*, May-June 1978, pp. 36-60.

for a 1 percent rise in inflation. Since the ATROR has fallen about three percentage points since 1965 while inflation has risen about eight percentage points, inflation accounts for only 0.8 percentage points of the drop in the ATROR.[22]

Gains from Debt. To evaluate the proposition that inflation causes investors to underestimate the returns on equity by ignoring the gains from debt, it is necessary to look at the rate of return on stockholders' equity, with and without these gains. The rate on stockholders' equity is defined as adjusted profits divided by the net worth of the corporation (the replacement cost of the capital stock less the value of net debt). Figure 27-4 gives two measures of the return on equity. One is the after-tax return (ATROE), which includes an adjustment of profits for the effects of inflation on inventory and depreciation charges but ignores gains from debt due to inflation. The other measure is the after-tax rate of return (ATROED), which includes gains from debt. The latter measure assumes investors make all relevant adjustments for inflation while the former assumes that investors do not recognize the full effects of inflation on corporate earnings.

As Figure 27-4 illustrates, the ATROE has fallen dramatically to less than half its 1965 peak. The ATROED has also decreased substantially, but the drop is about 25-30 percent from the peak return. To assess the contribution of inflation to these decreases, the same model employed above for the return on capital was estimated.[23] While both measures of the return on equity fall significantly when the economy weakens, the impact of inflation on these returns differs. As predicted by the tax effects theory, inflation has a negative effect on the ATROE, similar to that found above for the ATROR. The ATROED, however, is positively related to inflation which suggests that the benefits inflation produces by reducing real debt outweigh the costs coming from higher taxes. If investors ignore these benefits, inflation does appear to decrease the return on equity, although the size of this effect can account for only a small portion of the observed total decline.

To sum up, the rate of return on both corporate capital and stockholders' equity was substantially lower in the 1970s compared with the mid-1960s. The poor performance of capital does not, however, appear to be due primarily to inflation since empirical evidence indicates that the tax effects hypothesis cannot account for most of the fall in the after-tax return on capital. The fall in the return on stockholders' equity, the return relevant to the determination of stock prices, can account for a little over one-half of the decrease in real stock prices,

---

[22]Nicholas J. Gonedes also found little support for the tax effects hypothesis. See his "Evidence on the 'Tax Effects' of Inflation Under Historical Cost Accounting Methods," *Journal of Business,* April 1981, pp. 227-70.

[23]The estimated models are given in Table A of the Appendix.

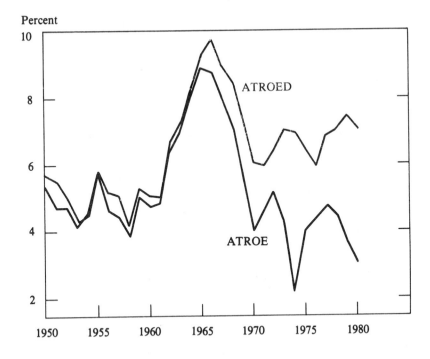

Percent

Figure 27-4   Rates of return on stockholders' equity

but this lower rate of return cannot be attributed to inflation if investors correctly compute this return.[24]

The Required Rate of Return on Stocks and Inflation

The analysis above suggests that inflation has not caused real stock prices
to fall by lowering the return on equity if shareholders include the gains from
debt in this return. Nevertheless, inflation may have depressed real share prices
by increasing the required rate of return on stocks. This argument is supported
by the pattern of the earnings-price ratio given in Figure 27-5. As discussed
in the beginning of the paper, if inflation does not raise the required rate of
return on stocks, earnings and the price of stocks should both rise at the inflation
rate, leaving the earnings-price ratio unaffected. However, as Figure 27-5
illustrates, the earnings-price ratio for the S&P 500 rose substantially as inflation

---

[24]A major negative effect of inflation is found by Richard Kopcke, "Are Stocks a Bargain?" while
a smaller impact is reported by Marcelle Arak, "Inflation and Stock Values: Is Our Tax Structure
the Villain?" *Quarterly Review*, Federal Reserve Bank of New York, Winter 1980-81, pp. 3-13.

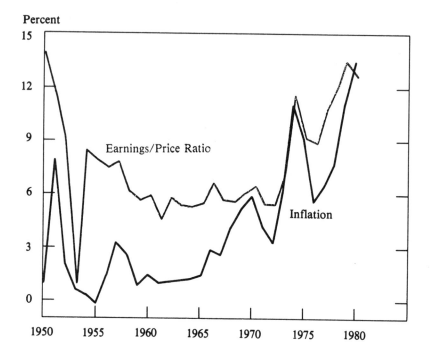

Figure 27-5   Earnings-price ratio and inflation

worsened.[25] Assuming that the gains from debt are taken into account by investors, the required rate of return on stocks has increased. This section considers evidence on the three alternative factors mentioned earlier by which inflation may have caused a rise in the required rate: higher returns on alternative assets, higher perceived risk on stock returns, and the incorrect use of the nominal interest rate to discount real earnings.

Return on Alternative Assets. Because fixed income financial assets exhibited negative real returns over the last fifteen years, they seem unlikely candidates for attracting investors away from stocks.[26] A more plausible possibility

[25]Since the earnings figure in this ratio is reported after-tax profits unadjusted for any effects of inflation, the higher ratios may have resulted from investors correcting these earnings for inflation distortions. This conjecture is not supported by a comparison of reported earnings to earnings which incorporate the IVA, CCA, and gains from debt since the two series move together quite closely, generally differing by less than $5 billion in the post-1965 period. In those years when the difference was greater, adjusted profits were greater than book profits, so earnings-price ratios should have fallen rather than increased.

[26]From 1966 to 1980, the real yield on U.S. government long-term bonds was -4.3 percent while U.S. Treasury bills had a real yield of -0.5 percent. R. G. Ibbotson and R. A. Sinquefield, *Stocks, Bonds, Bills, and Inflation: Historical Returns (1926–1978)*, Financial Analysts Foundation, 1979.

is owner-occupied housing. Imputed nominal rents rise with inflation but are untaxed, and the tax liability on nominal capital gains can generally be avoided. Hence, inflation should increase the relative return to houses, and investors should react to higher inflation by bidding up housing prices. It has been estimated that the escalating inflation rate of the 1970s reduced the real rental cost of owner-occupied housing to close to zero for higher income families and that much of the fall in real stock prices can be attributed to investors reacting to this low real cost of housing by diverting funds from the stock market to the housing market.[27] Additional support for this view comes from the finding that the return to housing, unlike that for corporate equity, rises with expected inflation.[28] This hypothesis is also consistent with the rise in the median price of existing homes by 9.8 percent per year for the 1969-80 period—over 2 percent more than inflation— which occurred while stock prices fell relative to the general price level.

Greater Risk. The second factor which may have raised the required rate of return on stocks is higher perceived risk. If corporate profits are less predictable in an inflationary environment, risk-averse wealthholders will place a lower value on them. Past work has found a statistically significant negative effect of risk on the market value of firms, although the size of the effect was generally small.[29]

Was the decade of the 1970s a period of increasing risk to investment in corporate capital? One traditional measure of risk is the actual variability experienced. Table 27-3 reports one gauge of variation: the standard deviation for the annual growth rates of three real profit measures, real GNP, and the CPI for five-year intervals, 1951-80. These data indicate that variation in these variables generally declined over the first fifteen years and then rose again over the last fifteen. However, the only dramatic rise in variability of profits was for adjusted profits excluding gains from debt for the 1971-75 interval. Moreover, the last half of the 1970s exhibited less variability than the first half, and yet real stock prices continued to fall. Thus, these data suggest that rising variability in the economy may have contributed to lowering real share values, but it cannot be the whole story.

On the other hand, actual variability may be a poor measure of perceived risk. Another suggested measure of the change in risk is the differential between medium grade bonds and U.S. government bonds.[30] More uncertainty about corporate earnings is expected to raise this differential, which has grown substantially from an average of just under 1 percent for 1951-65 to about 1.65

[27]See Hendershott and Hu.

[28]See Summers.

[29]Brainard, Shoven, and Weiss.

[30]Malkiel. The use by Malkiel of a bond series which included low yielding "flower" bonds was criticized by Patric H. Hendershott, "The Decline in Aggregate Share Values: Taxation, Valuation Errors, Risk, and Profitability," *American Economic Review*, December 1981, pp. 909–22.

Table 27-3 Variability of profits and macroeconomic activity

Variable	Standard deviations* Time period						
	1951–55	1956–60	1961–65	1966–70	1971–75	1976–80
Percentage change in real book profits	20.5	16.3	8.5	9.9	12.5	11.2
Percentage change in adjusted real profits (IVA + CCA)	20.1	19.9	9.8	11.8	39.9	15.1
Percentage change in adjusted real profits including gains from debt	21.3	17.9	11.7	9.8	11.4	11.1
Percentage growth in real GNP	3.6	2.3	1.4	2.3	3.3	2.4
Inflation (CPI)	3.3	1.0	0.2	1.4	3.3	3.3

*Standard deviation for a variable x is defined as

$$\text{S.D.} = \left[\frac{1}{n-1} \sum_{i=1}^{n} (x - \bar{x})^2 \right]^{1/2}$$

where n = number of observations
 $\bar{x}$ = arithmetic mean of x.

432

percent for 1966-80. If higher expected inflation is an important contributor to higher risk, the interest differential should be positively related to expected inflation. This proposition is supported by the data, using lagged inflation to proxy expected inflation, with a one percentage point increase in expected inflation being associated with an increased differential of about 0.16 percentage points.[31] While this evidence is supportive of the risk hypothesis, the differential, while higher in the 1970s, does not trend upward and thus cannot explain the downward trend in real share prices.

Incorrect Discount Rate. A third possible reason for a higher required rate is the comparison by investors of the earnings-price ratio with the current nominal interest rate on bonds. Since the correct comparison is with the real interest rate, use of the nominal interest rate, which rises roughly with inflation, means stock prices have to fall steeply, relative to earnings, in order for the earnings-price ratio to rise.

This hypothesis is difficult to test directly. One study of it employed a model in which stock prices depended mainly on expected earnings and the real interest rate.[32] The latter variable was measured by the nominal interest rate and expected inflation proxied by lagged inflation. Accordingly, if investors did not suffer from money illusion and thus used the real interest rate to discount real earnings, the coefficients on the nominal interest rate and expected inflation should have summed to zero. However, it was found that the coefficient on expected inflation was negative in sign and statistically insignificant from zero, which was interpreted as evidence of money illusion. Other investigators reported results which also can be construed as consistent with this view. It has been calculated that the discount rate required to equate the present value of future earnings to the market value of firms roughly doubled from 1968 to 1977.[33] This latter result is also consistent with rising risk. The unanswered

---

[31]The estimated relationship was:

$$\text{Interest Differential}_t = \underset{(4.633)}{.077} + \underset{(5.978)}{.156} \ I_t - 1$$

$R^2 = .59 \qquad \text{SEE} = .00028 \qquad \text{DW} = 1.82 \qquad \hat{\rho} = .554$

Time period 1954–80 annual observations

where $I_t - 1$ = inflation rate lagged over one period
$\hat{\rho}$ = estimated autocorrelation coefficient

t-statistics in parentheses.
Additional lagged inflation rates do not alter the results.

[32]Modigliani and Cohn. For an alternative explanation of these results, namely, that the lagged inflation rates are an inadequate proxy for expected inflation and are really picking up the negative tax effects of inflation, see Arak.

[33]Brainard, Shoven, and Weiss.

question is why investors would confuse nominal and real rates of return. Since evidence suggests that bondholders demand compensation for inflation and households see the inflation-induced benefits of homeownership, it is puzzling why investors would be confused by inflation only in the stockmarket.[34]

SUMMARY AND CONCLUSIONS

Over the last fifteen years the real value of common stock has fallen about 50 percent, coincident with a generally rising inflation rate. If inflation is to blame for the dismal performance of stocks, then it must reduce expected real corporate profits or raise the required rate of return on stocks, according to the traditional model of stock prices. This paper has examined several arguments as to why inflation may have had these consequences.

One prominent theory asserts that inflation reduces expected profits by raising the real tax burden on corporate earnings through nonindexation of inventory and depreciation charges. An alternative proposal is that inflation confuses investors, causing them to undervalue corporate profits by failing to take account of the inflation-induced fall in the real debt of corporations. On the other hand, it has been argued that inflation may have increased the required rate of return on stock by raising the return on owner-occupied housing, by creating more uncertainty about corporate profits, or by misleading investors into using too high a discount rate.

The analysis of this article indicates that the crucial issue is whether investors take into account the gains from debt which accrue to corporations when inflation occurs. The rate of return on stockholder equity when these gains are ignored has dropped by about half since the mid-1960s, consistent with the belief that lower stock prices reflect lower earnings. However, this decline in returns seems to have been due primarily to the low return on corporate capital, before as well as after taxes, reflecting perhaps the rise in energy costs and regulatory activity which characterized the period. Rising real tax burdens on corporate capital could not account for this fall in the rate of return.

Assuming investors correctly include the gains from debt when estimating corporate profits, the fall in real stock prices was caused in part by a higher rate of return required by stockholders. This conclusion is supported by the observed rise in the earnings-price ratio. Evidence indicates that inflation has been an important determinant of the increase in the required rate by producing large returns on homeownership, by increasing the perceived risk attached to

---

[34]Hendershott, "The Decline in Aggregate Share Values," argues that the inflation illusion argument of Modigliani and Cohn implies lower nominal interest rates when inflation occurs rather than lower share values, an implication which does not accord with experience.

stock, and by deceiving stockholders into using the nominal rather than the real interest rate to discount earnings. Thus, while inflation cannot account for all of the decrease in real stock prices which has occurred in the last fifteen years, it has been a significant factor in the decline.

Appendix

Table A Estimated rate of return equations: 1951–80
(Rate of return measure)

	BTROR	ATROR	ATROE	ATROED
Constant	.102	.040	.046	.034
	(10.623)	(6.130)	(4.442)	(4.380)
PCGAP	−.338	−.149	−.153	−.228
	(−4.149)	(−2.683)	(−2.228)	(−4.856)
Inflation	−.043	−.100	−.173	.123
	(−.460)	(−1.556)	(−2.177)	(2.255)
Time	.0007	.002	.002	.003
	(.793)	(3.171)	(1.900)	(3.959)
Time D66	−.002	−.003	−.003	−.004
	(−1.15)	(−2.217)	(−1.767)	(−3.037)
D66	.019	.034	.045	.055
	(.709)	(1.836)	(1.599)	(2.665)
R^2	.582	.534	.509	.623
SEE	.0087	.0059	.0074	.0051
DW	1.80	1.87	1.83	1.63
$\hat{\rho}$	.541	.548	.685	.725

Notes:
PCGAP	=	(Full employment real GNP-actual real GNP)/Actual real GNP
Inflation	=	rate of change in the CPI
Time	=	time trend with 1951 = 1
D66	=	0 for 1951–65
	=	1 for 1966–80
SEE	=	standard error of estimate
DW	=	Durbin-Watson statistic
$\hat{\rho}$	=	estimated autocorrelation coefficient

The Debt Market

This second section of Part IV deals with market relationships and conceptual issues in the debt market. The article by Kelly Price and John R. Brick examines the term structure of interest rates. The term structure of interest rates is the pattern of yields on a specific date for bonds that are identical in all respects except their terms to maturity. The discussion includes the term-structure theory and its use for forecasting interest rates and bond prices

The rediscovered concept of "duration" is discussed in the article by Frank K. Reilly and Rupinder S. Sidhu. Duration is a measure of the weighted average maturity of a bond where the weights are stated in present value terms. The discussion includes the basic concept of duration, alternative cash flow measures, and the relationships of duration to bond price volatility, bond portfolio "immunization," bond risk and common stock.

The concept of "immunization" is discussed in the article by Martin L. Leibowitz. Immunization describes the bond portfolio design which can achieve a target level of return in the face of changing reinvestment rates and bond price levels. The topics discussed include the reinvestment problem, the duration concept, multiple interest-rate changes, and portfolio rebalancing procedures.

THE TERM STRUCTURE: FORECASTING IMPLICATIONS

28

*Kelly Price and John R. Brick** *

When a corporate treasurer is faced with a financing decision or a bond portfolio manager must allocate funds to the bond market, each must address similar issues. What is the present state of the bond market? Are interest rates high or low? Should long-term bonds be issued or should short-term bonds be issued in anticipation of falling rates? Are long-term bonds more attractive from an investment standpoint than short-term bonds? What is the most likely direction of future interest rates? These are the types of questions market participants such as the corporate treasurer or the bond portfolio manager must answer on a day-to-day basis. When addressing these and related questions, many market participants rely heavily on their judgment. However, the value of such judgmental analysis may be enhanced if certain aspects of the bond market are understood. Unlike the stock and commodities markets, for example, the bond market conveys considerable information about both present and expected future conditions. The purpose of this article is to provide an overview of a conceptual framework known as the *term structure*, which enables such information to be derived by market participants. An understanding of the various shapes of the term structure and their forecasting implications provide a basis for answering the kinds of market-related questions raised above.

In the next section, an overview of the theory and rationale underlying the term structure is presented. This is followed by a section that describes how

*The authors are on the faculties of Wayne State University and Michigan State University, respectively. The article was written specifically for this book.

so-called *consensus forecasts* can be derived for both interest rates and bond prices. Then the managerial implications of the term structure are examined with particular emphasis on the problem facing the bond portfolio manager of a commercial bank. This is followed by a brief conclusion in which several caveats are discussed.

TERM STRUCTURE THEORY

The *term structure* of interest rates is described as the pattern of yields on a specific date for bonds that are identical in all respects except their terms to maturity. As such, the term structure characterizes the relationships among rates on short-, intermediate-, and long-term bonds. Graphically, it is represented by a plot of the yield-to-maturity (or internal rate of return) of the bonds on the vertical axis and the time remaining until maturity on the horizontal axis. Four typical term structures are shown in Panels A through D in Figure 28–1.

As a practical matter, few bonds exist that are identical in all respects except for their maturity dates. Most bonds differ in their quality, call provisions, coupon level or some other factor such as marketability. Thus, even if maturities are identical, such differences can result in different yields. As a result, some compromises must be made to empirically observe the term structure. The best set of bond yields for this purpose are the U.S. Treasury note and bond series. These instruments are riskless with respect to default, highly marketable, and available with similar coupons over a wide range of maturities. Their yield quotations are available daily in the financial press. Although Treasury bills may be used in conjunction with notes and bonds, their yields are quoted on a discounted basis using a 360-day year. Thus, if bills are to be included when constructing a term structure, their bond-yield equivalents should be used rather than the quoted yields.[1] Furthermore, since the coupon rate of bonds introduces subtle yield differences because of tax and call effects, a wide range of coupons for a given maturity should be avoided, especially at longer maturities. By minimizing such differences within a set of riskless bonds, a reasonably accurate description of yield-maturity relationships can be developed.

---

[1]The bond-yield equivalent for a Treasury bill is given by

$$R = \frac{365}{n} \left[\frac{1 - P}{P} \right]$$

where R = the bond-yield equivalent, n = the number of days to maturity, and P = the price of the bill in decimal form.

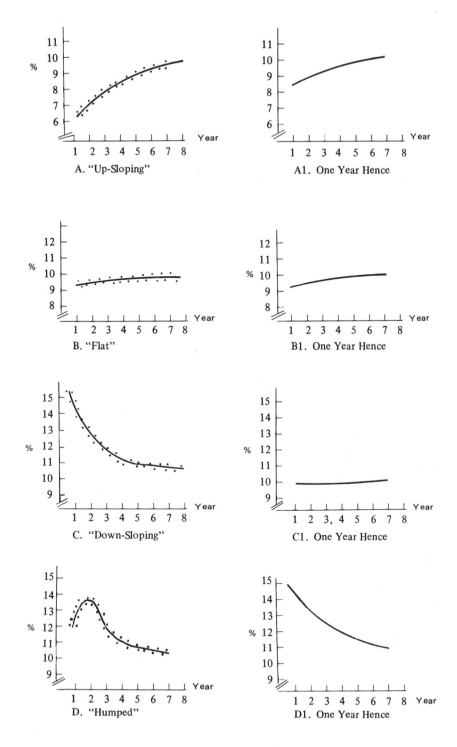

Figure 28-1 Term structure and implied forecasts

Generally, the shape of yield curves for other debt instruments, such as corporate and public utility bonds, are similar to the prevailing term structure for Treasury securities. This, coupled with a high degree of comovement among the different classes of interest rates, means that the term structure for Treasury securities characterizes the general relationship between most short-term and long-term rates.[2]

Shape of the Term Structure

The four graphs on the left side of Figure 28-1 show different term structures, referred to as *up-sloping, flat, down-sloping,* and *humped.* At one time, these four shapes were strongly associated with particular phases of the business cycle. The *upsloping* structure was associated with the cyclical trough when loan demand was slack and the Federal Reserve was following a policy of monetary ease. The *flat* structure was usually short-lived and observed during a period of transition from a cyclical trough to a cyclical peak, or vice-versa. The *down-sloping* and *humped* curves, sometimes referred to as *inverted* yield curves, were usually associated with a cyclical peak in the business cycle. Such a period was characterized by strong loan demand and tight credit conditions.

In recent years, inflationary expectations have exerted a strong influence on the term structure.[3] As a result, the traditional relationships between the various shapes of the term structure and the business cycle have become blurred. For example, during a recession, the slack loan demand that has historically characterized such a period would ordinarily result in an upward-sloping yield curve. However, because inflation has persisted during economic recessions in recent years, the effects of slack loan demand have tended to be offset by the combination of continued tight credit and investor expectations of continued inflation. The result has often been a downward-sloping or humped yield curve during the early stages of such periods. It is nevertheless important to bear in mind that the shape of the yield curve continues to characterize conditions in the credit markets and, as will be shown, conveys vital information about expected future interest rates.

---

[2]Two exceptions to this statement should be noted. When the term structure for Treasury bonds in inverted, or downward-sloping, i.e., long-term bonds yield less than shorter-term bonds, the municipal bond term structure tends to be flat or slightly upward-sloping [2]. Also, Johnson [5] noted that extremely risky corporate debt can have a down-sloping yield curve when the riskless yield curve is up-sloping.

[3]A well-known theory of the impact of inflation on interest rates, attributed to Irving Fisher [3], holds that inflation acts like negative interest. According to this view, the yield on a bond is comprised of a "real rate" and a premium equal to the inflation rate expected to prevail over the life of the bond. The theory holds that the real rate is positive. Therefore, if the economy is experiencing both a business slowdown and high inflation expectations, interest rates can still be high, reflecting a positive real rate and the inflation premium. Expectations of a sharply higher inflation rate are transmitted into correspondingly higher interest rates.

The corporate treasurer and the bond portfolio manager must contend with uncertainty that stems from the joint interaction of business cycle effects, monetary policy, and inflationary expectations. This interaction has been a major factor underlying the volatility of interest rates in recent years. In a volatile interest rate environment, the shape of the term structure can change dramatically in a short period. In 1980, for example, each of the different shapes shown in Figure 28-1 (A-D) were observed in the bond market. Thus, it is inappropriate to view the term structure shape observed on a particular day as long-lasting.

Behavior of the Bond Portfolio Manager

For the moment, assume that all bond managers have a desired holding period for interest-bearing assets. Given this holding period constraint, there are two ways to characterize portfolio managers' participation in bond markets. One way is to think of managers as being extremely risk averse, and thus unwilling to buy bonds of any maturity except those very close to their desired holding period. Purchase of a longer maturity exposes the portfolio to the risk that interest rates may rise causing the value of the longer-term bonds to be less than desired at the end of the holding period. On the other hand, an investment in shorter-term bonds carries the risk that interest rates may fall and the reinvestment of funds from maturing securities would be at a rate lower than desired. Thus, buying bonds with maturities that are too long or too short exposes the portfolio to risk. This rationale leads to the *segmented markets theory* of the term structure which hypothesizes that bond markets are segmented by maturity, and each maturity segment is independent of each other. The unique supply and demand characteristics of each market determine the yields prevailing in each. If the segmented markets theory is correct, the shape of the yield curve represents nothing more than the prevailing supply and demand characteristics in the various term-to-maturity markets. Furthermore, the theory implies no linkage among term-to-maturity segments represented by the term structure.

The second way to characterize the behavior of market participants is to view bond managers as willing to buy bonds with maturities other than their desired holding periods if they perceive an advantage in doing so. For example, a longer-term bond may be bought and then sold at the end of the holding period, or a series of shorter-term bonds could be linked together. This willingness to shift maturities in response to a perceived yield advantage underlies the *expectations theory* of the term structure. Under this rationale, the various term-to-maturity segments of the term structure are no longer independent markets. Rather, the market segments are linked together because of the participants' willingness to shift maturity preferences in response to yield opportunities. The significance of this theory is that, as will be shown shortly, the actions of bond managers who shift to a maturity other than their desired holding periods reflect an implicit interest rate forecast. From these forecasts, expected bond prices can be calculated. This will be clarified through the use of numerical examples.

Examples of Implicit Interest Rate Forecasts

In order to see how interest rate forecasts are embedded in the term structure, assume a bond manager has three bonds available at this time, as shown below. All bonds have identical characteristics except maturity.

Years to maturity	Yield to maturity
1	9.000%
2	9.312
3	9.520

If the desired holding period is two years, the portfolio manager has three options: 1) buy the two-year bond; 2) buy the three-year bond with the intention of selling it at the end of two years; or 3) buy the one-year bond, and at the end of one year, buy another one-year bond.

Suppose the manager takes the option of buying the one-year bond, with the intent of reinvesting the proceeds at the end of one year. The question arises—what yield must be obtained on the subsequent one-year bond in order to be just as well off as if the two-year bond had been purchased? The solution to this problem is to find the *forward rate*. The procedure for finding the forward rate is fairly simple. We know that a 9 percent yield can be obtained for a one-year period. When the bond matures the proceeds will be reinvested at some expected rate r for the second period. This expected rate must be sufficient to cause the wealth at the end of the second year to accumulate to the known ending wealth that would be generated by an initial investment in the two-year bond yielding 9.312 percent. That is,

$$\$1 \ (1 + .09) \ (1 + r) = \$1 \ (1 + .09312)^2$$

$$1 + r = \frac{(1 + .09312)^2}{(1 + .09)}$$

$$r = \frac{1.19491}{1.09} - 1$$

$$r = .09625 \text{ or } 9.625\%$$

Similarly, assume a three-year bond is acquired with the intention of selling the bond in two years. Then the question is—What rate must the bond be yielding at the end of two years in order for its value to exactly equal the wealth achieved by investing in the two-year bond? This problem may be formulated in the following way. We know that an investment in the two-year bond will result in an ending wealth factor of $(1 + .09312)^2 = 1.19491$. This factor must further accumulate at some rate r in order to have the accumulated three-year wealth be equal to the wealth generated by an initial investment in a three-year bond at a yield of 9.52 percent. That is,

$$(1 + .09312)^2 (1 + r) = (1 + .0952)^3.$$

Solving for r results in

$$(1 + r) = \frac{(1 + .0952)^3}{(1 + .09312)^2}$$

$$r = \frac{1.13365}{1.19491} - 1$$

$$r = .09937 \text{ or } 9.937\%.$$

The value of r is the one-year forward rate beginning two years hence. This means that after two years, the three-year bond, which will have a remaining maturity of one year, must sell in the market at an expected yield of 9.937 percent.

   If investors did not expect the subsequent yields in the above example to occur, the present yield relationships among the three bonds would not persist. That is, the yield curve would shift in response to investor expectations. To see this, assume that the two-year rate of 9.312 percent is unsustainably high and likely to fall. Furthermore, they feel that the one-year rate is relatively low. They would tend to sell the one-year bond in anticipation of a price decrease as its yield rises. The proceeds would be used to purchase two-year bonds in anticipation of a rising price. The selling pressure on one-year bonds raises one-year yields, and the buying pressure on two-year bonds decreases those yields. Equilibrium is reached when these bond managers no longer perceive an advantage in switching maturities. A term structure, therefore, implies a *consensus forecast* of future interest rates. Before examining the manner in which forecasts may be derived, it is important to understand a major variation of the expectations theory discussed above.

The Liquidity Preference Theory

   Hicks [4] noted a systematic tendency for long-term rates to be higher than short-term rates. This suggests that the forward rate should be adjusted before it is used as an estimate of the *expected* future short-term rate. The reason for this is easy to understand; most borrowers have a strong preference for longer-term funds while most lenders have strong preference to lend in the more liquid short-term sector of the market. This means that lenders must be paid a premium to lend in the longer-term market. Because of their preference, long-term borrowers are willing to pay such a premium. Thus, the predominant shape of the yield curve is upward sloping with long rates exceeding short rates. The version of the expectations theory that takes this bias into account is called the *liquidity preference theory*. It is important to note that under the liquidity preference theory, the willingness of bond managers to switch maturities remains a key underlying assumption. Now, however, portfolio managers take into account the ordinarily higher rates on longer-term bonds. The increment by which the forward rate (as calculated in the numerical examples above) differs from the expected short-term rate is called the liquidity premium. The theory holds that this liquidity premium becomes larger as the maturity increases but its rate of increase diminishes as the maturity lengthens. The liquidity preference theory underlies the remainder of this paper.

FORECASTING INTEREST RATES AND BOND PRICES

In this section, the procedure for deriving interest rate forecasts from a term structure is developed in the context of the liquidity preference theory. Once the interest rate forecasts are derived, their implications for future bond prices (and expected bond price changes) may be examined.

Even in periods of stable interest rates, it is a difficult econometric problem to measure the liquidity premium structure. In the recent high and volatile interest rate environment, this measurement problem has been made even more difficult because the volatility of recent interest rates obscures the subtle effects of the liquidity premium. Therefore, the numerical examples developed in this section and shown in Table 28-1 use a contrived liquidity premium structure rather than one that has been observed.[4] This assumed liquidity premium structure is consistent with theory in that it increases at a decreasing rate for longer maturity bonds.

A "flat" term structure, as shown in Panel B of Table 28-1, and Panel B of Figure 28-1, is defined as the term structure that predicts the same interest rate structure for future periods. If there were no liquidity premiums, this term structure would be perfectly flat, or horizontal. Reflecting the liquidity premium structure, the "flat" term structure shown here has a slight positive slope. The same liquidity premium structure that causes the "flat" term structure to have a slight upward curvature has been used in the other numerical examples shown in Panels A, C, and D of Table 28-1.

---

[4]The term structure literature indicates that the liquidity premium structure is not constant over time, but is related to the general level of interest rates. If interest rates are high according to the general perception of the market, then the liquidity premium is relatively low. This is because the prices of bonds during such a time are low, and expected to rise. The person buying a long-term bond in such a high rate period does not feel that this investment is illiquid, because as rates are expected to fall, the value of the bond is expected to rise. Similarly, when interest rates are low according to general market perceptions, longer term bond prices are high and expected to fall. Hence, buyers demand a greater premium during these times as compensation for this greater expected illiquidity. See Van Horne [8,9] for a discussion of this point. In the examples in this paper, a constant liquidity premium structure has been assumed for expository purposes.

The calculations shown in Panel B of Table 28-1 demonstrate the development of interest rate forecasts and bond price forecasts from the existing term structure shown in column 1 and the liquidity premium structure shown in column 3. Given the term structure, each one-year forward rate is derived in the same manner as discussed earlier, and placed in column 2. (A generalization of this approach is presented in the Appendix.) In the discussion that follows, forward rates are designated by r, expected rates by ρ (rho), and liquidity premiums by L. It is helpful to subscript each of these to indicate the point in time when they begin and the interval of time that they span. A *pre-subscript* (to the left of the rate or liquidity premium) indicates its beginning *point* in time, and a *post-subscript* (to the right of the rate or liquidity premium) indicates the number of periods it is to run. For example, the forward rate $_3r_1$, which begins at point in time 3 and runs one period, is calculated as:

$$_3r_1 = \frac{(1.09663)^4}{(1.09520)^3} - 1$$

$$_3r_1 = .10093 \text{ or } 10.093\%[5]$$

In order to derive the one-year *expected* rate for each one-year period in the future, each one-year liquidity premium is subtracted from its corresponding forward rate. The expected rates are placed in column 4. At this point, the reason why the flat term structure predicts the same term structure is revealed—each one-year expected rate is equal to the current one-year interest rate, and the only thing differentiating a one-year forward rate from the current one-year rate is the liquidity premium! Using the notation previously discussed,

$$_3\rho_1 = {_3r_1} - {_3L_1}$$

$$9.000\% = 10.093\% - 1.093\%$$

The next step in interest rate forecasting is to construct the one-year forward rate structure that we expect to observe one year hence. Recall that column 4 contains all the one-year rates we expect to prevail. Recall also that the difference between an expected rate and a forward rate is an appropriate liquidity premium. One year from now, our expected one-year rate that now begins at time 3 will begin at time 2, but the liquidity premium appropriate for a forward rate beginning at time 2 stays the same. Therefore, adding the liquidity premium that begins at time 2 to the forward rate that now begins at time 3, results in the expected forward rate that will then begin two years hence. Following our example, we have

$$_{2+1}r_1 = {_2L_1} + {_3\rho_1}$$

$$9.937\% = .937 + 9.000\%$$

[5]The reader should not be misled by the implied accuracy of calculations carried out to several decimal places. This was done to minimize the errors that result from cumulative rounding when working through term structure calculations.

Table 28-1 Derivation of implied forecasts

	1	2	3	4	5	6	7	8
Year	Current term structure ($_0R_n$)	Derived one-year forward rates ($_nr_1$)	One-year liquidity premiums ($_nL_1$)	One-year expected rates (w/o liq. prem.) ($_n\rho_1$)	Current bond prices ($_0V_n$)	One-year forward rates exp. one year hence ($_{n+1}r_1$)	Int. rates expected one year hence (exp. term structure) ($_1\rho_n$)	Bond prices expected one year hence ($_1V_n$)
A. "Up-sloping" Yield Curve								
1	6.500%	9.124%	.625%	8.499%	$1000.00	8.499%	8.499%	$993.47
2	7.804	9.936	.937	8.999	1000.00	9.624	9.060	990.14
3	8.510	10.095	1.093	9.002	1000.00	9.939	9.352	988.51
4	8.904	10.170	1.169	9.001	1000.00	10.094	9.537	987.57
5	9.156	10.210	1.209	9.001	1000.00	10.170	9.663	987.08
6	9.331	10.230	1.231	8.999	1000.00	10.208	9.754	986.84
7	9.459	10.237	1.240	8.997	1000.00	10.228	9.822	986.76
8	9.556	10.242	1.244	8.998	1000.00	10.238	9.874	986.83
9	9.632	10.242	1.246	8.998	1000.00	10.242	0.915	986.98
10	9.693	10.244	1.246	8.998	1000.00			
B. "Flat" Yield Curve								
1	9.000%	9.625%	.625%	9.000%	$1000.00	9.000%	9.000%	$1002.92
2	9.312	9.937	.937	9.000	1000.00	9.625	9.312	1003.72
3	9.520	10.093	1.093	9.000	1000.00	9.937	9.520	1003.66
4	9.663	10.169	1.169	9.000	1000.00	10.093	9.663	1003.29
5	9.764	10.209	1.209	9.000	1000.00	10.169	9.764	1002.87
6	9.838	10.231	1.231	9.000	1000.00	10.209	9.838	1002.49
7	9.894	10.238	1.240	8.998	1000.00	10.229	9.894	1002.14
8	9.937	10.243	1.244	8.999	1000.00	10.239	9.937	1001.85
9	9.971	10.241	1.246	8.995	1000.00	10.239	9.971	1001.58
10	9.998				1000.00			

Table 28-1 (continued)

	1	2	3	4	5	6	7	8
Year	Current term structure ($_0R_n$)	Derived one-year forward rates ($_nr_1$)	One-year liquidity premiums ($_nL_1$)	One-year expected rates (w/o liq. prem.) ($_n\rho_1$)	Current bond prices ($_0V_n$)	One-year forward rates exp. one year hence ($_{n+1}r_1$)	Int. rates expected one year hence (exp. term structure) ($_1\rho_n$)	Bond prices expected one year hence ($_1V_n$)
C. "Down-sloping" Yield Curve								
1	16.000%			9.999%	$1000.00	9.999%	9.999%	$1030.50
2	13.280	10.624%	.625%	9.001	1000.00	9.626	9.812	1041.63
3	12.155	9.938	.937	9.000	1000.00	9.937	9.854	1045.33
4	11.636	10.093	1.093	9.000	1000.00	10.093	9.914	1046.20
5	11.341	10.169	1.169	9.002	1000.00	10.171	9.965	1045.87
6	11.152	10.211	1.209	9.002	1000.00	10.209	10.006	1044.93
7	11.020	10.231	1.231	9.000	1000.00	10.229	10.038	1043.70
8	10.922	10.238	1.240	8.998	1000.00	10.236	10.063	1042.33
9	10.846	10.240	1.244	8.996	1000.00	10.245	10.083	1040.96
10	10.786	10.247	1.246	9.001	1000.00			
D. "Humped" Yield Curve								
1	12.000%			15.000%	$1000.00	15.000%	15.000%	$989.21
2	13.798	15.625%	.625%	11.999	1000.00	12.624	13.806	994.98
3	13.510	12.936	.937	9.502	1000.00	10.439	12.672	1002.48
4	12.774	10.595	1.093	8.999	1000.00	10.092	12.021	1007.05
5	12.248	10.168	1.169	9.002	1000.00	10.171	11.649	1009.54
6	11.906	10.211	1.209	8.999	1000.00	10.208	11.408	1010.95
7	11.665	10.230	1.231	9.001	1000.00	10.232	11.239	1011.75
8	11.486	10.241	1.240	8.997	1000.00	10.237	11.113	1012.19
9	11.347	10.241	1.244	8.996	1000.00	10.240	11.016	1012.36
10	11.236	10.242	1.246		1000.00			

These rates are carried in column 6. Note that there are only nine of these (and ten rates presently) because the present one-year bond will have matured in one year.

The next step is to construct the expected term structure, as shown in column 7, from the expected forward rates. This is accomplished by adding 1.0 to each expected forward rate (in decimal form) multiplying them together, taking the "kth" root and then subtracting 1.0. In our example,

$$_1\rho_3 = \sqrt[3]{(1 + \,_{1+1}r_1)\,(1 + \,_{1+2}r_1)\,(1 + \,_{1+3}r_1)} - 1$$

$$9.520\% = \sqrt[3]{(1.09)\,(1.09625)\,(1.09937)} - 1.$$

In this manner, the expected term structure one year hence (or, by appropriately "shifting" the liquidity premium structure, any number of years hence) is derived.

The last step is to analyze the expected price changes of bonds that make up the term structure. For simplicity, all bonds are assumed to be currently selling at par, as shown in column 5, and to have coupon rates equal to the yields shown in the term structure column. Recall that one year from now, a six-year bond will be a five-year bond. Even if the term structure remains constant, the yield of a bond one year from now will be shown in a different location on the term structure because of the passage of time. In our example, the six-year bond is assumed to have a coupon rate of 9.838 percent. One year from now, as a five-year bond, it is expected to yield 9.764 percent, and therefore has an expected price of $1,002.87. In this manner, the set of expected bond prices is constructed and shown in column 8.

Reference to column 8 of Panel B reveals that bond prices are expected to rise slightly when the term structure is "flat," regardless of the term to maturity of the bond chosen. The same is true of Panel C, which shows the calculations related to the "down-sloping" yield curve. Similarly, reference to column 8 of Panel A, which shows the calculations underlying the "upsloping" yield curve, indicates that all bond prices are expected to fall, regardless of the maturity chosen. The "humped" yield that is characterized by the calculations shown in Panel D is noteworthy because short-term bonds are expected to fall in price whereas longer-term bonds are expected to rise in price.

Analysis of the expected prices of bonds need not be limited to one year. The expected price of a bond can be projected in this manner throughout its life, indicating to a bond manager the times during the life of a bond when (or if) it is expected to sell for more than its current market price. This can have profound implications for a bond manager contemplating the tradeoff between risk and return.

THE BANKER'S DILEMMA

The "Low" Interest Rate Scenario

Over the course of a business cycle, commercial banks and other depository-type institutions face an on-going dilemma that is related directly to the term structure. To see this, consider the up-sloping term structure shown in Panel A of Figure 28-1. Such a term structure is usually associated with lower interest rates and excess bank liquidity stemming from deposit inflows, slack demand for new loans, run-off of old loans, and a general policy of monetary ease on the part of the Federal Reserve Board. Furthermore, bond prices tend to be high relative to prices prevailing under other shapes of the term structure. Because of the declining proportion of loans, the highest yielding and riskiest class of assets held by banks, both the risk level and gross earnings will tend to decline. Thus, it might be argued that in order to maintain the risk level and minimize the deterioration in gross earnings, investments in longer-term bonds are justified. Such a strategy is quite tempting because the current income advantage of long-term bonds relative to short-term bonds is substantial during periods when there is an upsloping yield curve. For example, in Panel A of Table 28-1, we see that ten-year bonds provide a current yield (and coupon rate) of 9.67 percent which is 317 basis points higher than the 6.5 percent yield on one-year bonds. Furthermore, management may decide to extend the same strategy to the lending area by offering longer-term, fixed-rate loans in an attempt to stimulate loan demand and obtain higher current income

If interest rates increase moderately as expected by the market and as shown in Panel A of Figure 28-1, the policy described above may be effective. The reason is that after one year the higher income of 317 basis points on the ten-year bonds would more than offset the expected loss resulting from the bond's decline in price to $986.98, as shown in Panel A of Table 28-1. But one year later, what if interest rates increased such that a down-sloping or humped yield curve prevailed as shown in Panels C or D of Figure 28-1? If the market rate is 12 percent, the bond, with its coupon rate of 9.67 percent and remaining maturity of 9 years, would sell at a price of $873.85. This represents a loss of 12.6 percent which far offsets the initial income advantage of the longer-term bond.

The main problem with this strategy is that the loss occurs at a most inappropriate time. During periods characterized by a downsloping or humped yield curve, most banks also face serious liquidity problems stemming from deposit outflows, strong demand for new loans, renewal requests on old loans, and a policy of monetary restraint on the part of the Federal Reserve Board. It is during just such a period that the bank should be able to sell bonds to help meet these cash needs. If the value of the bond portfolio is depressed, however, most banks become "locked in" because the loss on the sale of the bonds would substantially reduce earnings.[6] Thus, the funds may be unavailable to help meet the stresses that cause an inversion of the yield curve. Had the bank stayed in the short-term sector of the bond market and not succumbed to the temptation of a higher level of current income, the bank would have additional "shock absorbing" capability. Such capability is essential in a volatile interest rate environment.

The "High" Interest Rate Scenario

In a high interest rate scenario, the same temptation exists for bankers to make the wrong portfolio choices. To the extent that a bank has investable funds when the yield curve is inverted, the temptation would be to stay short in order to obtain the higher yields. In Panel C of Figure 28-1, for example, we see that one-year bonds yield 16 percent versus 11 percent on the longer-term bonds. However, *if* the bank is going to invest in longer-term bonds, this would be the most appropriate time to do so despite the lower current income on the longer-term bonds. The reason, of course, is that the *most likely* change in interest rates is downward. As a practical matter, few banks acquire long-term bonds when the yield curve is inverted because of a lack of liquidity resulting from past investment decisions, or simply a desire to be as liquid as possible.

The key point here is that failure to understand the implications of the term structure coupled with a desire for a higher level of current income leads some bankers into the revolving trap of going long when they should be going short and vice-versa. Often the same myopic policies are extended to the loan portfolio with matching results.

CONCLUSION

The shape of the term structure provides market participants with considerable information regarding present market conditions and most likely direction of future interest rate changes. However, like any other forecasting technique, caution should be used. Market expectations are formed on the basis of available information at a point in time. As new information becomes available, usually in a random fashion and with varying degrees of significance, market expectations are revised. This means that there is uncertainty associated with the forecasts implied by a term structure. Also, the fact that rates are expected to

---

[6]Some bankers would argue that earnings are only affected if the bonds are sold. However, even if the bonds are held, earnings are adversely affected because the return on the bonds is fixed while the cost of funds used to acquire the bonds increases rapidly as the yield curve becomes inverted.

decline, for example, does not necessarily mean that rates are at a peak. Rates may increase further before receding. Thus, the estimates should be used in a probabilistic or "most likely" context. Despite these caveats, term structure analysis is a useful tool for assessing present market conditions and obtaining an "acted-upon" consensus forecast.

The shape of a term structure and the conditions that give rise to a particular shape have important implications for commercial banks and other depository institutions. Failure to recognize the linkage between the various shapes of the term structure and overall operations of these institutions can lead to a sequence of inappropriate and costly decisions. For this reason, an understanding of the term structure is a prerequisite for the sound management of banks and other types of depository institutions, especially in a volatile interest rate environment.

APPENDIX
A GENERAL MODEL FOR FORWARD RATES

Term structure nomenclature designates known, observable interest rates as $_0R_n$ where the pre-subscript zero refers to the *point in time* that the rate begins and the post-subscript n refers to the number of periods until maturity which is an *interval of time*. For example, $_0R_4$ is the prevailing rate on four-year bonds. Since n is greater than one, this is a multi-period rate. In contrast to the upper-case symbols for known rates, the derived forward rates are denoted by lower-case symbols with the subscripts having the same meaning. For example, $_3r_2$ refers to the forward rate expected to prevail three years hence and span two periods.

According to the expectations theory, the multi-period rate $_0R_n$ is linked to the current single-period rate $_0R_1$, and a set of forward rates, through the formula

$$(1 + {_0R_n})^n = (1 + {_0R_1}) (1 + {_1r_1}) (1 + {_2r_1}) \ldots (1 + {_{n-1}r_1}). \tag{1}$$

Note that each side of equation (1) yields the same amount of terminal wealth. Each one-period forward rate on the right hand side of (1) begins at the end of the preceding period. The multi-period rate $_0R_n$ can be thought of as the geometric mean return of all the single-period rates over the period zero through n.

Given an existing term structure, equation (1) may be used to derive forward rates. To see this, equation (1) may be expanded for an n + 1 period bond and written as

$$(1 + {_0R_{n+1}})^{n+1} = (1 + {_0R_1}) (1 + {_1r_1}) (1 + {_2r_1}) \ldots (1 + {_{n-1}r_1}) (1 + {_nr_1}). \tag{2}$$

In expressions (1) and (2) the actual rates $_0R_n$ and $_0R_{n+1}$ are used to derive the forward rate we seek, $_nr_1$, which begins n periods from now and spans one period. Dividing (2) by (1) and cancelling terms, we have

$$\frac{(1 + {_0}R_{n+1})^{n+1}}{(1 + {_0}R_n)^n} = \frac{(1 + {_0}R_1)(1 + {_1}r_1)(1 + {_2}r_1)\ldots(1 + {_{n-1}}r_1)(1 + {_n}r_1)}{(1 + {_0}R_1)(1 + {_1}r_1)(1 + {_2}r_1)\ldots(1 + {_{n-1}}r_1)}$$

$$\frac{(1 + {_0}R_{n+1})^{n+1}}{(1 + {_0}R_n)^n} = 1 + {_n}r_1$$

therefore,

$$_nr_1 = \frac{(1 + {_0}R_{n+1})^{n+1}}{(1 + {_0}R_n)^n} - 1. \tag{3}$$

Thus, if we have two observed interest rates which differ in their terms to maturity by one period, we can use (3) to calculate the forward rate spanning their interval. For example, referring to Panel A of Table 28-1 in the text, the four-year observed rate is 8.904 percent and the observed three-year rate is 8.51 percent. The implied one-year forward rate beginning three years hence is found by substituting these rates into equation (3),

$$_3r_1 = \frac{(1 + .08904)^4}{(1 + .0851)^3} - 1 = .10095 \text{ or } 10.095\%.$$

In a similar manner, a multi-period forward rate can be derived from the relationship

$$\frac{(1 + {_0}R_{n+k})^{n+k}}{(1 + {_0}R_n)^n} = \frac{(1 + {_0}R_1)(1 + {_1}r_1)\ldots(1 + {_{n+k-1}}r_1)}{(1 + {_0}R_1)(1 + {_1}r_1)\ldots(1 + {_{n-1}}r_1)}.$$

Cancelling terms results in

$$\frac{(1 + {_0}R_{n+k})^{n+k}}{(1 + {_0}R_n)^n} = (1 + {_n}r_k)^k.$$

Taking the kth root of both sides and subtracting one from each side, the multiperiod forward rate $_nr_k$ may be found. That is,

$$_nr_k = \sqrt[k]{\frac{(1 + {_0}R_{n+k})^{n+k}}{(1 + {_0}R_n)^n}} - 1 \tag{4}$$

The term $_nr_k$ represents the k-period forward rate beginning n periods hence. Referring once again to Panel A of Table 28-1, to obtain the four-period forward rate beginning one year hence, we have

$$_1r_4 = \sqrt[4]{\frac{(1 + .09156)^5}{(1 + .065)}} - 1$$

$$_1r_4 = .0983 \text{ or } 9.83\%.$$

As can be observed from these numerical examples, implementation of these formulas is not difficult. Although cumbersome, the subscripting is necessary to position the various rates in time. Once the user is familiar with the procedure, the calculations are relatively simple. Also, recall that in the absence of a liquidity premium, a forward rate is equal to the expected rate. According to the liquidity preference theory, however, the forward rate calculated in this manner is a biased estimate of the expected rate and must be adjusted downward to reflect the presence of any liquidity premium. Such adjustments were made in the body of the text.

REFERENCES

1. Bensten, George, "Interest Rates are a Random Walk Too," *Fortune*, August 1976.
2. Cook. Timothy Q. and Jeremy G. Duffield, "Short-Term Investment Pools," *Economic Review*, Federal Reserve Bank of Richmond, September/October 1980.
3. Fisher, Irving, "Appreciation and Interest," *Publications of the American Economic Association* XI (August 1896).
4. Hicks, J. R., *Value and Capital*, 2nd edition, London: Oxford University Press, 1946.
5. Johnson, Ramon E., "Term Structures of Corporate Bond Yields as a Function of Risk of Default," *Journal of Finance*, 22 (May 1976).
6. Price, Kelly and John R. Brick, "Daily Interest Rate Relationships," *Journal of Money, Credit and Banking*, XII (May 1980)
7. Van Horne, James, "The Expectations Hypothesis, the Yield Curve, and Monetary Policy: Comment," *Quarterly Journal of Economics*, LXXIX (November 1965).
8. Van Horne, James, "Interest Rate Risk and the Term Structure of Interest Rates," *Journal of Political Economy*, 73 (August 1965).
9. Van Horne, James, *Financial Market Rates and Flows*, Englewood Cliffs, N.J.: Prentice-Hall, 1978, Chapters 3-5.

THE MANY USES OF BOND DURATION*

Frank K. Reilly and
Rupinder S. Sidhu†

29

The burgeoning interest in bond analysis over the past five to ten years has led to a rediscovery of a concept originally developed in 1938—Professor Frederick Macauley's measure of bond term known as "duration." This article explains the basic concept of duration and discusses in detail how duration is computed and how it is affected by maturity, coupon and market yield. In addition, we consider the main uses of duration in bond analysis (i.e., its relation to bond price volatility) and bond portfolio management (i.e., how it can be used to "immunize" a bond portfolio). Finally, we consider the application of duration to common stock analysis, including the computation of common stock duration and its implications for risk analysis and equity portfolio management.

AN OVERVIEW

Professor Frederick Macauley derived the basic concept of bond duration in 1938 and disseminated it in a book written for the National Bureau of Economic

*Reprinted from the *Financial Analysts Journal*, July/August 1980, pp. 58-72. Copyright by the Financial Analysts Federation, 1980. Reprinted with permission.

†The authors are the Bernard J. Frank Professor of Business Administration at the University of Notre Dame and Investment Analyst with the Prudential Insurance Company, respectively.

Research.[1] Originally, duration was conceived as a better way to summarize the timing of bond flows than maturity. Although conceded to be a better measure, duration was generally ignored for about 30 years. Duration was rediscovered in the late 1960s when academicians derived other uses for it. Specifically, Fisher and Hopewell and Kaufman discovered a direct relationship between the duration of a bond and its price sensitivity to changes in market interest rates.[2] Other authors have since demonstrated the usefulness of this relation to the active bond portfolio manager who attempts to derive superior returns by adjusting a portfolio composition to take advantage of major swings in market interest rates.[3] And Fisher and Weil have shown how the relation can be used to immunize a bond portfolio.[4]

Because of the direct relation between bond price volatility and duration, and because volatility is considered a measure of risk, some authors have attempted to use duration as a proxy for risk and to derive capital market lines that relate returns to duration.[5] (Some question remains, however, whether duration is an all-encompassing measure of risk.) Finally, since duration is basically a summary measure of the timing of an asset's cash flows, there is no reason for confining its use to bonds; an article by Boquist, Racette, and Schlarbaum examines the concepts as it applies to bonds *and* common stock.[6]

[1]Frederick R. Macauley, *Some Theoretical Problems Suggested by the Movements of Interest Rates, Bond Yields, and Stock Prices in the United States since 1865* (New York: National Bureau of Economic Research, 1938).

[2]Lawrence Fisher, "An Algorithm for Finding Exact Rates of Return," *Journal of Business*, January 1966, pp. 111-118 and Michael H. Hopewell and George C. Kaufman, "Bond Price Volatility and Term to Maturity: A Generalized Respecification," *American Economic Review*, September 1973, pp. 749-753.

[3]See, for example, Edward Blocher and Clyde Stickney, "Duration and Risk Assessments in Capital Budgeting," *The Accounting Review*, January 1979, pp. 180-188; John Caks, "The Coupon Effect on Yield to Maturity," *Journal of Finance*, March 1977, pp. 103-116; Stanley Diller, "A Three Part Series on the Use of Duration in Bond Analysis and Portfolio Management," *Money Manager*, January 29, 1979, February 5, 1979 and February 13, 1979; David Durand, "Growth Stocks and the Petersburg Paradox," *Journal of Finance*, September 1957, pp. 348-363; Robert A. Haugen and Dean W. Wichern, "The Elasticity of Financial Assets," *Journal of Finance*, September 1974, pp. 1229-1240; J. R. Hicks, *Value and Capital*, 2nd ed. (Oxford: The Clarendon Press, 1946), p. 186; Burton G. Malkiel, "Equity Yields, Growth, and the Structure of Share Prices," *American Economic Review*, December 1963, pp. 1004-1031; Richard W. McEnally, "Duration as a Practical Tool in Bond Management," *Journal of Portfolio Management*, Summer 1977, pp. 53-57; and Jess Yawitz, "The Relative Importance of Duration and Yield Volatility," *Journal of Money, Credit and Banking*, February 1977, pp. 97-102.

[4]Lawrence Fisher and Roman L. Weil, "Coping With the Risk of Interest-Rate Fluctuations: Returns to Bondholders from Naive and Optimal Strategies," *Journal of Business*, October 1971, pp. 408-431.

[5]James C. Van Horne, *Financial Market Rates and Flows* (Englewood Cliffs, NJ: Prentice-Hall, Inc., 1978), Chapter 5.

[6]John A. Boquist, George A. Racette and Gary G. Schlarbaum, "Duration and Risk Assessment for Bonds and Common Stock," *Journal of Finance*, December 1975, pp. 1360-1365.

ALTERNATIVE MEASURES

To understand the concept of duration properly, it is useful to place it in the perspective of other summary measures of the timing of an asset's cash flows. While measurement of the timing of cash flows is important to the analysis of all investments, the ability to measure it precisely is typically limited because the analyst is not certain of the timing and size of the flows. Because the cash flows from bonds are specified both as to timing and amount, however, analysts have derived a precise measure of the timing for bonds. We discuss below the principal measures and demonstrate their application for the two bonds described in Table 29-1.

Term to Maturity

The most popular timing measure is *term to maturity (TM)—the number of years prior to the final payment on the bond.* Our two sample bonds have identical terms to maturity—ten years. Term to maturity has the advantage of being easily identified and measured, since bonds are always specified in terms of the final maturity date, and it is easy to compute the time from the present to that final year. The obvious disadvantage of term to maturity is that it ignores the amount and timing of all cash flows except the final payment. In the case of the sample bonds, term to maturity ignores the substantial difference in coupon rates and the difference in the sinking funds.

A number of years ago some bond analysts and portfolio managers attempted to rectify this deficiency by computing a measure that considered the interest payments and the final principal payment. *The weighted average term to maturity (WATM)* computes the proportion of each individual payment as a percentage of all payments and makes this proportion the weight for the year (one through ten) the payment is made.[7] It equals:

$$\text{WATM} = \frac{\text{CF}_1(1)}{\text{TCF}} + \frac{\text{CF}_2(2)}{\text{TCF}} + \ldots \frac{\text{CF}_n(n)}{\text{TCF}},$$

Table 29-1 Specification of sample bonds

	Bond A	Bond B
Face value	$1,000	$1,000
Maturity	10 years	10 years
Coupon	4%	8%
Sinking fund	10% a year of face value starting at end of year 5	15% a year of face value starting at end of year 5

[7]Although it is recognized that interest payments are typically made at six-month intervals, we assume annual payments at year-end to simplify the computations.

where

$$CF_t = \text{the cash flow in year t,}$$
$$(t) = \text{the year when cash flow is received,}$$
$$n = \text{maturity, and}$$
$$TCF = \text{the total cash flow from the bond.}$$

For example, Bond A (the four percent coupon, ten-year bond) will have total cash flow payments (TCF) of $1,400 ($40 a year for ten years plus $1,000 at maturity). Thus the $40 payment in year one ($CF_1$) will have a weight of 0.02857 ($40/1,400), each subsequent interest payment will have the same weight, and the principal payment in year ten will have a weight of 0.74286 ($1,000/1,400). Table 29-2 demonstrates the specific computation of the weighted average term to maturity for each sample bond.

It is apparent from Table 29-2 that the weighted average term to maturity is definitely less than the term to maturity because it takes account of all interim cash flows in addition to the final principal payment. Furthermore, the bond with the larger coupon has a shorter weighted average term to maturity because a larger proportion of its total cash flows is derived from the coupon payments that come prior to maturity. Specifically, the interest payments constitute 28.6 percent ($400/1,400) of the total returns on Bond A, but 44.4 percent ($800/1,800) of the total flow of Bond B. Obviously, if one were to compute a measure that included sinking fund payments, the weighted average term to maturity would be even lower.

Table 29-2   Weighted average term to maturity
(assuming annual interest payments)

	Bond A				Bond B		
(1) Year	(2) Cash flow	(3) Cash flow/ TCF	(4) (1)×(3)	(1) Year	(2) Cash flow	(3) Cash flow/ TCF	(4) (1)×(3)
1	$ 40	0.02857	0.02857	1	$ 80	0.04444	0.04444
2	40	0.02857	0.05714	2	80	0.04444	0.08888
3	40	0.02857	0.08571	3	80	0.04444	0.13332
4	40	0.02857	0.11428	4	80	0.04444	0.17776
5	40	0.02857	0.14285	5	80	0.04444	0.22220
6	40	0.02857	0.17142	6	80	0.04444	0.26664
7	40	0.02857	0.19999	7	80	0.04444	0.31108
8	40	0.02857	0.22856	8	80	0.04444	0.35552
9	40	0.02857	0.25713	9	80	0.04444	0.39996
10	1,040	0.74286	7.42860	10	1,080	0.60000	6.00000
Sum	$1,400	1.00000	8.71425	Sum	$1,800	1.00000	7.99980

Weighted Average Term to Maturity = 8.71 Years   Weighted Average Term to Maturity = 8.00 Years

A major advantage of the weighted average term to maturity is that it considers the timing of all flows from the bond, rather than only the final payment. One drawback is that it does not consider the time value of the flows. The interest payment in the first year has the same weight as the interest payment in the tenth year, although the present value of the payment in the tenth year is substantially less. Also, the weighted average term to maturity would give the $1,000 principal the same weight whether payment was made in year ten or year twenty.

Duration

The duration measure is similar to the weighted average term to maturity, with the exception that *all flows are in terms of present value.* Duration equals:

$$D = \frac{\displaystyle\sum_{t=1}^{n} \frac{C_t(t)}{(1 + r)^t}}{\displaystyle\sum_{t=1}^{n} \frac{C_t}{(1 + r)^t}}$$

where

C_t = the interest and/or pricipal payment in year t,
(t) = the length of time to the interest and/or principal payment,
n = the length of time for final maturity and
r = the yield to maturity.

In the style of our equation for weighted average term to maturity, duration is:

$$D = \frac{PVCF_1(1)}{PVTCF} + \frac{PVCF_2(2)}{PVTCF} + \cdots \frac{PVCF_n(n)}{PVTCF}$$

where

$PVCF_t$ = the present value of the cash flow in year t discounted at current yield to maturity,
(t) = the year when cash flow is received and
$PVTCF$ = the present value of total cash flow from the bond discounted at current yield to maturity—obviously, the prevailing market price for the bond.

Table 29-3 shows the computations of duration for the two sample bonds. *Duration is simply a weighted average maturity, where the weights are stated in present value terms.* Specifically, the time in the future a cash flow is received is weighted by the proportion that the present value of that cash flow contributes to the total present value or price of the bond. (We assume that interest payments are made annually; use of the more realistic semiannual payments

Table 29-3   Duration (assuming eight percent market yield)

(1) Year	(2) Cash flow	(3) PV at 8%	Bond A (4) PV of flow	(5) PV as % of price	(6) $(1) \times (5)$
1	$ 40	0.9259	$ 37.04	0.0506	0.0506
2	40	0.8573	34.29	0.0469	0.0938
3	40	0.7938	31.75	0.0434	0.1302
4	40	0.7350	29.40	0.0402	0.1608
5	40	0.6806	27.22	0.0372	0.1860
6	40	0.6302	25.21	0.0345	0.2070
7	40	0.5835	23.34	0.0319	0.2233
8	40	0.5403	21.61	0.0295	0.2360
9	40	0.5002	20.01	0.0274	0.2466
10	1,040	0.4632	481.73	0.6585	6.5850
Sum			$731.58	1.0000	8.1193

Duration = 8.12 Years

			Bond B		
1	$ 80	0.9259	$ 74.07	0.0741	0.0741
2	80	0.8573	68.59	0.0686	0.1372
3	80	0.7938	63.50	0.0635	0.1906
4	80	0.7350	58.80	0.0588	0.1906
5	80	0.6806	54.44	0.0544	0.2720
6	80	0.6302	50.42	0.0504	0.3024
7	80	0.5835	46.68	0.0467	0.3269
8	80	0.5403	43.22	0.0432	0.3456
9	80	0.5002	40.02	0.0400	0.3600
10	1,080	0.4632	500.26	0.5003	5.0030
Sum			$1000.00	1.0000	7.2470

Duration = 7.25 Years

would result in the shorter duration—7.99 years versus 8.12 years and 7.07 years compared with 7.25 years.)

As with weighted average term to maturity, the duration of a bond is shorter than its term to maturity because of the interim interest payments. Obviously, a zero coupon bond yielding no interim payments would have the same duration, weighted average term to maturity and term to maturity, since 100

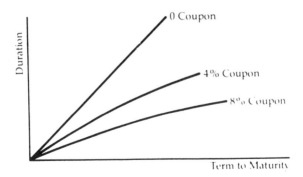

Figure 29-1 Relation between duration and term to maturity for alternative coupons

percent of the total cash flow, and 100 percent of total present value, would come at maturity. Also, like weighted average term to maturity, *duration is inversely related to the coupon for the bond*—i.e., the larger the coupon, the greater the proportion of total returns received in the interim, and the shorter the duration. Figure 29-1 graphs the relation between duration and maturity for a range of coupon rates.

One variable that does not influence weighted average term to maturity but can affect duration is the prevailing market yield (r). Market yield does not influence weighted average term to maturity because this measure does not consider the present value of flows. Market yield affects both the numerator and denominator of the duration computation, but it affects the numerator more. As a result, *there is an inverse relation between a change in the market yield and a bond's duration.* That is, an increase in the market yield will cause a decline in duration, other things being equal.

Table 29-4 demonstrates how different market yields will affect the duration of our sample bonds. The results for the case of zero market yield indicate that duration is the same as weighted average term to maturity when there is no discounting.

Table 29-4 How duration is affected by alternative market yields (assuming semiannual interest payments)

| | Market yields | | | |
	0%	4%	8%	12%
Bond A	8.60*	8.34	7.99*	7.59
Bond B	7.87*	7.50	7.07*	6.61

*The durations differ from those in Tables 29-2 and 29-3 because of the use of semiannual interest payments.

EFFECT OF SINKING FUNDS

The discussion thus far has ignored the effects of sinking funds. But a large proportion of current bond issues do have sinking funds, and these can definitely affect a bond's duration. Table 29-5 shows the computations of duration for the sample bonds with sinking funds. Inclusion of the sinking funds causes the computed durations to decline by approximately one year in both cases (i.e., from 8.12 to 7.10 for Bond A and from 7.25 to 6.21 for Bond B).

The effect of a sinking fund on the time structure of cash flows for a bond is certain to the issuer of the bond, since the firm must make the payments; they represent a legal cash flow requirement that will affect the firm's cash flow. In contrast, the sinking fund may not affect the investor. The money put into the sinking fund may not necessarily be used to retire outstanding bonds; even if it is, it is not certain that a given investor's bonds will be called for retirement.

EFFECT OF CALL

In contrast to a sinking fund, which reduces duration by only one year and may affect only a few investors, all bondholders will be affected if a bond is called, and the call feature can influence duration substantially. For example, consider a 30-year bond of eight percent coupon, selling at par and callable after ten years at 108. First, compute a cross-over yield.[8] At yields above the cross-over yield, the yield to maturity is the minimum yield. When the price of the bond rises to some value above the call price, and the market yield declines to a value below the cross-over yield, however, the yield to call becomes the minimum yield. At this price and yield, the firm will probably exercise a call option when it is available.

As Homer and Leibowitz have demonstrated, it is possible to calculate the cross-over yield by deriving the yield to maturity for a bond selling at the call price for the original maturity minus the years of call protection.[9] For the above example, this would involve deriving the yield to maturity for an eight percent coupon bond selling at $1,080 and maturing in 30 years; the implied cross-over yield is 7.24 percent. In one year's time, the bond's maturity will be 29 years, with nine years to call. Assume the market rate has declined to the point where the yield to maturity for the bond is seven percent (below the cross-over yield of 7.24 percent). At this price ($1,123.43), the bond's yield to call will be 6.2 percent.

---

[8]This discussion of cross-over yield and its computation is drawn from Sidney Homer and Martin L. Leibowitz, *Inside the Yield Book* (Englewood Cliffs, NJ: Prentice-Hall, Inc., 1972).

[9]Ibid., pp. 58-63.

Table 29-5   Impact of sinking fund on duration
(assuming eight percent market yield)

Bond A

(1) Year	(2) Cash flow	(3) PV at 8%	(4) PV of flow	(5) PV as % of price	(6) (1) × (5)
1	$ 40	0.9259	$37.04	0.04668	0.04668
2	40	0.8573	34.29	0.04321	0.08642
3	40	0.7938	31.75	0.04001	0.12003
4	40	0.7350	29.40	0.03705	0.14820
5	140	0.6806	95.28	0.12010	0.60050
6	140	0.6302	88.23	0.11119	0.66714
7	140	0.5835	81.69	0.10295	0.72065
8	140	0.5403	75.64	0.09533	0.76264
9	140	0.5002	70.03	0.08826	0.79434
10	540	0.4632	250.13	0.31523	3.15230
Sum			$793.48	1.00000	7.09890

Duration = 7.10 Years

Bond B

1	$ 80	0.9259	$ 74.07	0.06778	0.06778
2	80	0.8573	68.59	0.06276	0.12552
3	80	0.7938	63.50	0.05811	0.17433
4	80	0.7350	58.80	0.05380	0.21520
5	230	0.6806	156.54	0.14324	0.71620
6	230	0.6302	144.95	0.13264	0.79584
7	230	0.5835	134.21	0.12281	0.85967
8	230	0.5403	124.27	0.11371	0.90968
9	230	0.5002	115.05	0.10528	0.94752
10	330	0.4632	152.86	0.13987	1.39870
Sum			$1,092.84	1.00000	6.21044

Duration = 6.21 Years

If a bond portfolio manager ignored the call option and computed the duration of this bond to maturity (29 years) assuming a market yield of seven percent, the duration would work out to be 12.49 years. Recognizing the call option would mean computing the duration for a bond to be called in nine years at a price of $1,080 and using the yield to call of 6.2 percent, for a duration of 6.83 years. Table 29-6 summarizes this example.

Table 29-6   Impact of call options on duration

Original bond:	8% coupon bond sold at par with 30 years to maturity. Callable in 10 years at 108 of par. (Computed cross-over yield is 7.24%.)
One year later:	Market yields on bond decline from 8 to 7%.
	Current market price: $1,123.43 Yield to maturity (29 years): 7% Yield to call (9 years): 6.2% Call price: 108

Duration:	At 7% yield and 29 years
	  maturity—12.49 years
	At 6.2% yield, 9 years to
	  call at 108—6.83 years

The existence of a call option, which is almost universal on corporate bonds, can have a dramatic impact on the computed duration for a bond. The above example assumed a deferred call of ten years, which is currently the maximum period; five years is more typical.

Duration of GNMA Bonds

During the past several years there has been a substantial increase in investor interest in GNMA pass-through bonds because of the inherent safety of the bonds and their higher yields relative to other government securities. Without detracting from the safety and yield characteristics of these securities, a portfolio manager should recognize the extreme difference between the initial promised term to maturity, the empirical maturity and the probable duration, taking into account the form of cash flow and the empirical maturity.

An investor in a GNMA pass-through is basically purchasing a share of a pool of mortgages. The investor receives each month a payment from the mortgages that includes not only interest, but also partial repayment of the principal. Of course, homeowners may decide to pay off their mortgages in order to buy other houses (in which case prepayment penalties are usually waived). As a result, mortgage contracts are like bonds with sinking funds because they pay interest and principal over time and they are also like bonds that are freely callable because they can be paid off when the house is sold. *The empirical duration of a GNMA pass-through will thus be substantially less than the stated maturity.*

The stated maturity of most home mortgages is 25 years. Given the nature of the payment stream including principal and interest, the duration of a mortgage without prepayment is substantially less than the stated maturity. For example, assuming a 10 percent market rate and annual payments at the end of the year, a 30-year mortgage has a duration of 9.18 years, a 25-year mortgage has a duration of 8.46 years, and a 20-year mortgage has a duration of 7.51 years. (The consideration of realistic monthly payments would reduce these durations further.)

In addition, because of numerous prepayments, the empirical maturity of most mortgage pools is actually only about 12 years, rather than the stated 25. If one assumes principal and interest payments for 12 years and a prepayment at the end of 12 years (with no call premium), the mortgages have the following durations—30 years, 7.22 years; 25 years, 7.04 years; 20 years, 6.71 years. Bond portfolio managers should recognize that they are acquiring relatively short duration bonds when they invest in GNMAs.

Duration Properties

Except for very long maturity bonds selling at a discount, duration is positively related to the maturity of the bond.[10] It is inversely related to the coupon on a bond and to the market yield for the bond. Furthermore, durations can be reduced by sinking fund or call provisions.

Weighted average term to maturity and duration will be equal to a bond's term to maturity when the coupon rate is zero—that is, when there are no interim cash flows prior to maturity. But weighted average term to maturity and duration will never exceed a bond's term to maturity. In fact, Fisher and Weil suggest that insurance companies encourage some issuers (including the government) to sell long-term, zero-coupon discount bonds that would have maturities and durations of 30 or 40 years; in this way, they could match their long-term liabilities with long-duration assets.[11] Regardless of coupon size, it is nearly impossible to find bonds that have durations in excess of 20 years; most bonds have a limit of about 15 years.

As Tables 29-2 and 29-3 show, weighted average term to maturity is always longer than the duration of a bond, and the difference increases with the market rate used in the duration formula. This is consistent with the observation that there is an inverse relation between duration and the market rate. Further, this relation confirms our earlier observation that weighted average term to maturity and duration are equal when the market rate is zero.

DURATION AND BOND PRICE VOLATILITY

Hopewell and Kaufman set forth the specific form of the relation between the duration of a bond and its price volatility:[12]

---

[10]For a discussion of this point, see Van Horne, *Financial Market Rates and Flows*, p. 120.

[11]Fisher and Weil, "Coping With the Risk of Interest-Rate Fluctuations."

[12]Hopewell and Kaufman, "Bond Price Volatility and Term to Maturity."

$$\%\Delta\text{Bond Price} = -D^*(\Delta r),$$

where

$\%\Delta$ Price = the percentage change in price for the bond,

D^* = the adjusted duration of the bond in years, which is equal to $D/(1 + r)$, and

Δr = the change in the market yield in basis points divided by 100 (e.g., a 50 basis point decline would be -0.5).

Consider a bond that has a duration of 10 years and an adjusted duration of 9.259 years (10/1.08). If interest rates go from eight to nine percent, then:

$$\%\Delta \text{ Bond Price} = -9.259 \ (100/100)$$
$$= -9.259 \ (1)$$
$$= -9.259\%.$$

The price of the bond should decline by about 9.3 percent for every one percent (100 basis point) increase in market rates.

In practice, most investors use the unadjusted duration figure when computing the impact of market rate changes. At high duration figures and reasonable market prices, the difference is relatively minor.

Implications for Portfolio Management

The direct relation between duration and interest rate sensitivity is important to an active bond portfolio manager who attempts to derive superior returns by adjusting the composition of his portfolio to benefit from swings in market rates of interest. Given this portfolio rate philosophy, the manager should attempt to maximize the portfolio's interest rate sensitivity prior to an expected decline in interest rates, and to minimize it when rising rates are expected. In doing so, duration rather than term to maturity must be considered because duration is a better measure of the interest sensitivity of the portfolio. The manager will take into account coupon, call features and sinking fund provisions in addition to maturity in determining shifts in the portfolio composition.[13]

DURATION AND IMMUNIZATION

A major problem encountered in bond portfolio management is deriving a given rate of return to satisfy an ending wealth requirement for a specific future

---

[13]For a discussion of some of the practical aspects of implementing this use of duration, see Diller, "A Three Part Series on the Use of Duration in Bond Analysis and Portfolio Management."

date—i.e., the investment horizon. If the term structure of interest rates were flat and the level of the market rates never changed, the manager of a bond portfolio could deliver a known amount of wealth at the client's horizon by buying a bond maturing at the horizon. Specifically, the ending wealth position would be the beginning wealth times the compound value of a dollar at the promised yield to maturity.

Unfortunately, in the real world the term structure of interest rates is not typically flat and the level of interest rates is constantly changing. Because of the shape of the term structure and changes in the level of interest rates, the bond portfolio manager faces what is referred to as "interest rate risk" between the time of investment and the future target date. Interest rate risk can be defined as the uncertainty regarding the ending wealth position due to changes in market interest rates between the time of purchase and the target date.

Interest rate risk comprises two risks—a price risk and a coupon reinvestment risk. *Price risk* represents the chance that interest rates will differ from the rates the manager expects to prevail between purchase and target date, causing the market price for the bond (i.e., the "realized" price) to differ from his assumption. Obviously, if interest rates increase, the realized price for the bond in the secondary market will be below expectations, while if interest rates decline, the realized price will exceed expectations.

Reinvestment risk arises because interest rates at which coupon payments can be reinvested are unknown.[14] If interest rates decline after the bond is purchased, coupon payments will be reinvested at lower rates, and their contribution to ending wealth will be below expectations.

Immunization and Interest Rate Risk

Price risk and reinvestment risk have opposite effects on the investor's ending wealth position. Specifically, with an increase in market interest rates, the bond's realized price will fall below expectations, but the income from reinvesting interim cash flows will exceed expectations. A decline in market interest rates will provide a higher than expected ending price, but lower than expected ending wealth from reinvested interim cash flows.

A bond portfolio manager with a specific investment horizon will want to eliminate these two risks—i.e., to "immunize" the portfolio. According to Fisher and Weil:

> A portfolio of investments in bonds is *immunized* for a holding period if its value at the end of the holding period, regardless of the course of interest rates during the holding period, must be a least as large as it would have been had the interest rate function been constant throughout the holding period.

---

[14]For a detailed elaboration of this point, see Homer and Leibowitz, *Inside the Yield Book.*

> If the realized return on an investment in bonds is sure to be at least as large as the appropriately computed yield to the horizon, then that investment is immunized.[15]

Fisher and Weil's comparison of promised yields on bonds for the period 1925-68 with realized returns on bonds demonstrates the difference between promised yield and realized yield and indicates the importance of being able to immunize a bond portfolio.

Fisher and Weil based their portfolio immunization theory on the assumption that, if the yield curve shifts, the change in interest rates will be the same for all future rates: that is, if forward interest rates change, all rates change by the same amount. Under this assumption *a portfolio of bonds is immunized from interest rate risk if the duration of the portfolio equals the desired investment horizon.* For example, if the investment horizon of a bond portfolio is eight years, the duration of the portfolio should equal eight years. To construct a portfolio with a given duration, the manager should set the (value) weighted average duration at the desired length.

The whole point of the proof of the immunization theorem by Fisher and Weil is that a change in market rates will have opposite effects on price risk and reinvestment risk. That is, when the price change is positive the reinvestment change will be negative, and vice versa. Fisher and Weil proved that *duration is the investment horizon for which the price risk and the coupon reinvestment risk of a bond portfolio have equal magnitudes but opposite directions.*

Application of the Immunization Principle

Fisher and Weil carried out a simulation to compare the effects of applying their portfolio immunization strategy with the results for a naive strategy that set the portfolio's maturity equal to the investment horizon. This simulation computed the ending wealth ratios for the alternative portfolio strategies over 5-, 10- and 20-year investment horizons and compared them with the ending wealth ratios assuming the expected yield was realized. If a portfolio were perfectly immunized, the actual ending wealth would equal the expected ending wealth implied by the promised yield. Therefore, the comparison should indicate which portfolio strategy offered better immunization.

The duration strategy results were consistently closer to the promised yield, although the results were not perfect (i.e., the duration portfolio was not perfectly immunized). The imperfections could be traced to real-world departures from Fisher and Weil's basic assumption that, when interest rates change, all interest rates change by the same amount. The authors concluded that the naive maturity strategy removes most of the uncertainty of the expected wealth ratio from a long-term bond portfolio, and the duration strategy most of the remaining uncertainty. The authors contend that matching duration to the

---

[15]Fisher and Weil, "Coping With the Risk of Interest-Rate Fluctuations," p. 415.

investment horizon reduces the standard deviation of a bond portfolio so dramatically that the result is essentially riskless.

Alternative Definitions and Duration

Bierwag and Kaufman have pointed out that there are several specifications of the duration measure.[16] The measure derived by Macauley (the one used throughout this article) discounts all flows by the prevailing average yield to maturity on the bond being measured. Fisher and Weil use future one-period discount rates (forward rates) to discount the future flows. Depending upon the shape of the yield curve, these two definitions could give different results. Only if all forward rates are equal (so that the yield curve is flat) will the two definitions result in equal estimates and duration.

Bierwag and Kaufman note that the definition of duration used for bond portfolio immunization should be a function of the nature of the shock to the interest rate structure. It is possible to conceive of an additive shock to interest rates, where all interest rates are changed by the same nominal amount (e.g., 50 basis points), or a multiplicative shock, where all interest rates change by the same percentage (e.g., all rates decline by 10 percent). Bierwag contends that the optimal definition of duration for perfect immunization of a portfolio will depend upon the nature of the shock to the interest rate structure.[17] In the case of an additive shock, the Fisher-Weil definition is best, but a multiplicative shock requires a third measure of duration. Bierwag and Kaufman computed the duration for a set of bonds using the three definitions of duration and concluded:

> Except at high coupons and long maturities, the values of the three definitions do not vary greatly. Thus, D_1 [Macauley] may be used as a first approximation for D_2 and D_3 [Fisher-Weil and Bierwag-Kaufman, respectively]. The expression for D_1 has the additional advantage of being a function of the yield to maturity of the bond. As a result, neither a forecast of the stream of one-period forward rates over maturity of the bond nor a specific assumption about the nature of the random shocks is required.[18]

Example of Immunization

Table 29-7 demonstrates the effect of immunizing a portfolio by matching the duration of a single-bond portfolio to the investment horizon. The table

---

[16]G. O. Bierwag and George C. Kaufman, "Coping With the Risk of Interest Rate Fluctuations: A Note," *Journal of Business*, July 1977, pp. 364-370.

[17]G. O. Bierwag, "Immunization, Duration, and the Term Structure of Interest Rates," *Journal of Financial and Quantitative Analysis*, December 1977, pp. 725-742.

[18]Bierwag and Kaufman, "Coping with the Risk of Interest Rate Fluctuations: A Note," p. 367.

assumes that the portfolio manager's investment horizon is eight years and the current yield to maturity for eight-year bonds is eight percent. The ending wealth ratio for a completely immunized portfolio should therefore be 1.8509 (1.08^8).

Table 29-7 considers two portfolio strategies, one setting the term to maturity at eight years and the other setting the duration at eight years. The maturity strategy assumes that the portfolio manager acquires an eight-year, eight percent bond. In contrast, the duration strategy assumes that the portfolio manager acquires a ten-year, eight percent bond that has approximately an eight-year duration (8.12 years) assuming an eight percent yield to maturity (see Table 29-3). It is further assumed that a single shock to the interest rate structure at the end of year four causes the market yield to go from 8 to 6 percent, where it remains through year eight.

Because of the interest rate change in year four, the wealth ratio for the maturity strategy is below the desired wealth ratio, the interim coupon cash flow being reinvested at 6 rather than 8 percent. But the maturity strategy eliminates the price risk associated with interest rate volatility because the bond matures at the end of year eight. The duration strategy portfolio also suffers a shortfall in reinvestment cash flow because of the change in market rates. But this shortfall is offset by the increase in the ending value for the bond arising from the decline in market rates. That is, the bond is worth $104.06

Table 29-7   Effect of a change in market rates on a bond (portfolio) that uses the maturity strategy versus the horizon strategy

| | Expected Wealth Ratio = 1.8509 | | | | | |
| | Results with maturity strategy | | | Results with horizon strategy | | |
Year	Cash flow	Reinv. rate	End value	Cash flow	Reinv. rate	End value
1	$ 80	0.08	$ 80.00	$ 80	0.08	$ 80.00
2	80	0.08	166.40	80	0.08	166.40
3	80	0.08	259.71	80	0.08	259.71
4	80	0.08	360.49	80	0.08	360.49
5	80	0.06	462.12	80	0.06	462.12
6	80	0.06	596.85	80	0.06	596.85
7	80	0.06	684.04	80	0.06	684.04
8	1,080	0.06	1,805.08	1120.684*	0.06	1,845.72

*The bond could be sold at its market value of $1,040.64, which is the value for an 8 percent bond with two years to maturity priced to yield 6 percent.

at the end of year eight because it is an 8 percent coupon bond with two years to maturity selling to yield 6 percent.

If market interest rates had increased during this period, the maturity strategy portfolio would have experienced an excess of reinvestment income compared to the expected cash flow, and its ending wealth ratio would have exceeded expectations. In contrast, the duration portfolio would have experienced a decline in ending price that would have offset the excess cash flow from reinvestment. While the maturity strategy would have provided a higher than expected ending value under these assumptions, the whole purpose of immunization is to eliminate uncertainty (i.e., have the realized wealth position equal the expected wealth position); the duration strategy accomplishes this purpose.

The concept of duration is important to the bond portfolio manager with a specified investment horizon who wants to reduce the interest rate risk from his long-term bond portfolio. He does not want to predict future market rates, but simply to achieve a specified result irrespective of future rates.

YIELD CURVES AND BOND MARKET LINES

The typical yield curve is derived by plotting the yield to maturity (on the vertical axis) against the term to maturity (on the horizontal axis) for bonds of equal risk. Hopewell and Kaufman contend that this practice can result in abnormal curves if the bonds used have significantly different coupons.[19] The point is, of two bonds with different terms to maturity and different coupons, the longer maturity bond may have the shorter duration. For example, a 20-year bond with a large coupon could have a shorter duration than an 18-year bond with a small coupon.

Carr, Halpern and McCallum suggest that yield curves should be constructed with yield to maturity on the vertical axis and duration on the horizontal axis.[20] They further contend that forward rates (implied future short-term rates) should be computed on the basis of the duration yield curve. (Of course, the yield curves must still be derived using bonds of equal risk—e.g., all government bonds or all AAA-rated bonds).

Table 29-8 gives the durations and terms to maturity for a sample of government bonds. Figures 29-2 and 29-3 plot the yield curves using maturity and duration, respectively. The duration yield curve is clearly shorter than the maturity yield curve; any slope in the former (up or down) will be much sharper.

[19]Hopewell and Kaufman, "Bond Price Volatility and Term to Maturity."

[20]J. L. Carr, P. J. Halpern and J. S. McCallum, "Correcting the Yield Curve: A Reinterpretation of the Duration Problem," *Journal of Finance*, September 1974, pp. 1287-1294.

Table 29-8 Government bonds used to construct maturity yield curve and duration yield curve (as of November 1978)

Bond description		Yield to maturity	Maturity	Duration
Coupon	Maturity			
7⅞%	5/79	9.41%	0.5	0.500
7⅛	11/79	9.68	1	0.982
8	5/80	9.30	1.5	1.443
7⅛	11/80	9.18	2	1.897
7½	5/81	9.03	2.5	2.322
7¾	11/81	8.89	3	2.729
9¼	5/82	8.76	3.5	3.072
7⅞	11/82	8.76	4	3.499
7⅞	5/83	8.62	4.5	3.865
7	11/83	8.71	5	4.274
7⅞	5/86	8.63	7.5	5.762
7⅝	11/87	8.64	9	6.585
8¼	5/88	8.67	10	6.724
8¾	11/88	8.71	11.5	7.586
8⅝	11/93	8.71	15	8.664
7	5/98	8.41	19.5	10.278
8½	5/99	8.66	20.5	9.963
8¼	5/05	8.62	26.5	10.771
7⅞	11/07	8.80	29.0	11.061
8¾	11/08	8.97	30.0	10.845

Duration and Bond Market Line

Because bond duration indicates interest rate sensitivity, one can conceive of duration as a useful risk proxy for bonds. Specifically, an increase in duration will make a bond more sensitive to a given change in market interest rates, all else being equal. If one were to consider the computation of a "beta" for a bond (or a bond portfolio) that would indicate the percentage change in price for the bond (or portfolio) for a one percent change in price for a bond market series, one would expect a very high correlation between the beta for the bond (or portfolio) and the bond's (or portfolio's) duration.

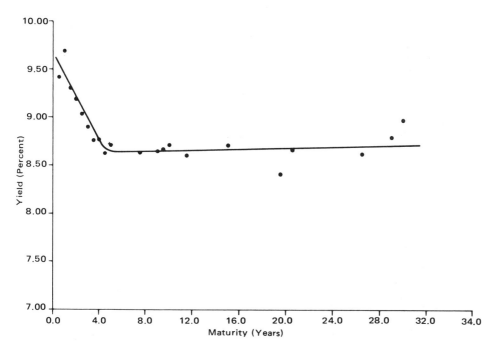

Figure 29-2 Maturity yield curve—government bonds (as of November 1978)

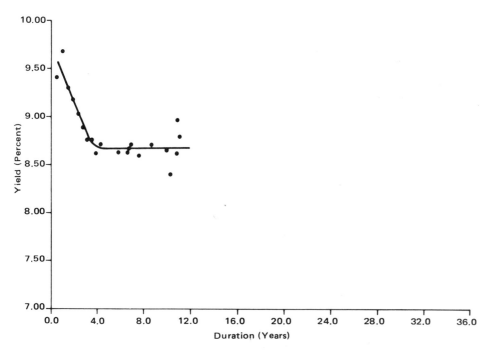

Figure 29-3 Duration yield curve—government bonds (as of November 1978)

Some investigators have suggested that investors should consider constructing a bond market line using duration as the measure of risk.[21] The vertical axis would represent the realized rate of return on bond portfolios, while the horizontal axis would specify the average duration of the portfolios being examined. The market portfolio used would be some aggregate market series like the Salomon Brothers High Grade Bond Series or the Kuhn Loeb Bond Index. Figure 29-4 displays such a market line.

While the concept of a bond market line is appealing, the specification suggested has one major drawback—it does not allow for differences in the risk of default. Because duration indicates bond price volatility caused by changes in market interest rates, duration is a good proxy for interest rate risk. Unfortunately, the bond market line constructed to take account of interest rate risk does not consider differences in default risk. Because one would expect a difference in the level of yield due to differences in default risk, one would expect a series of bond market lines—a different line for every default class (e.g., one for government bonds, another for AAA-rated bonds, a third for AAA-bonds, etc.) Figure 29-5 displays an ideal example of such a multiple set of bond market lines (although the alternative market lines would not necessarily have to be completely parallel as shown), with differences between the bond market lines reflecting the default risk premium.

Figures 29-6, 29-7, and 29-8 display a set of actual bond yield curves using rated public utility bonds. Note that the AAA-rated duration yield curve in Figures 29-6 slopes downward, as does the government bond curve. In contrast, the AA-rated and A-rated yield curves in Figures 29-7 and 29-8 have small

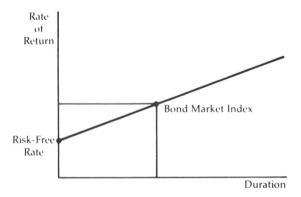

Figure 29-4   A bond market line

[21]Wayne H. Wagner and Dennis A. Tito, "Definitive New Measures of Bond Performance and Risk," *Pension World*, May 1977 and June 1977.

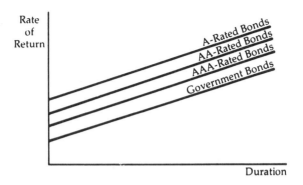

Figure 29-5 Multiple bond market lines for bonds with different default risks

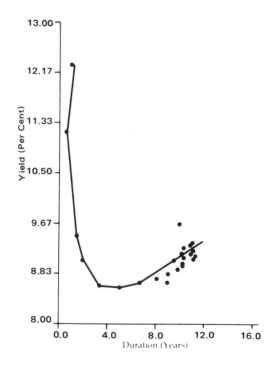

Figure 29-6 Duration yield curve—AAA public utility bonds (as of November 1978)

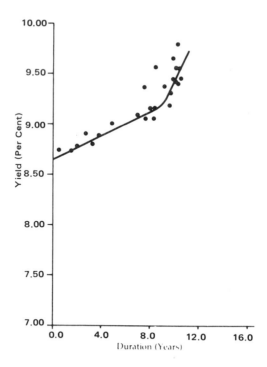

Figure 29-7   Duration yield curve—AA public utility bonds (as of November 1978)

positive slopes.[22] These differences, along with the differences in the general level of yields for the differently rated bonds, mean that attempts to evaluate the performance of portfolios with different average ratings by using one bond market line that considers only interest rate risk is very questionable.

DURATION AND COMMON STOCKS

Although the bulk of the literature of duration has applied the concept to bonds, duration can be used for any investment flow, including common stocks. Once it is acknowledged that duration can be computed for common stocks, its properties can be applied to the valuation of common stocks and the management of stock portfolios.

---

[22]Space does not permit a discussion of the reason for the differing slopes. But see Van Horne, *Financial Market Rates and Flows* and Burton G. Malkiel, *The Term Structure of Interest Rates* (Princeton, NJ: Princeton University Press, 1966).

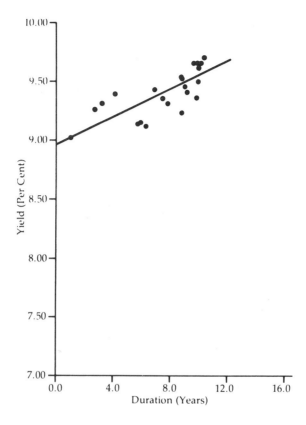

Figure 29-8   Duration yield curve—a public utility bonds (as of November 1978)

Computation of Common Stock Duration

The difficulties in computing the duration for a given common stock arise because of the several unknowns involved in the cash flows and discount rate. In the case of high-grade bonds, the analyst knows the timing and amount of interim cash flows based upon the coupon rate and the final cash flow from the principal at maturity. Also, the discount rate (using the Macauley definition) is the prevailing yield to maturity for the bond. In the case of common stocks, the interim cash flow will be the expected future dividend payments, which are uncertain in amount. The timing and amount of the final cash flow are likewise uncertain, since common stock is considered to have perpetual life. Finally, the discount rate used should be the prevailing required rate of return on the security, which in the case of stocks is an estimate based on other estimates in the stock valuation model. In the standard dividend valuation model:

$$V = \frac{d_1}{K_i - g_i} \quad,$$

where

V = the total value of the common stock,
d_1 = the next period's dividend,
K_i = the required rate of return on the stock and
g_i = the expected growth rate of dividends,

so that

$$K_i = \frac{d_1}{V} + g_i$$

Clearly, the duration for alternative stocks can differ substantially, depending on the estimates of cash flows and their timing. Still, assuming that the analyst is willing to make the necessary estimates, it is possible to compute the duration for alternative common stocks.

To gain an appreciation of the problems and effects of different characteristics on the stock's duration, consider the examples detailed in Table 29-9, which progress from short-term, stable payment investments to long-run growth investments. For simplicity, the table assumes that all dividends are paid once a year at the end of the year. The computed durations for these sample stock investments are specific to the estimates of the amount and timing of cash flows and the required rates of return. Obviously, the duration of the same investment could vary substantially between investors holding differing estimates.

The first sample stock indicates the effect on duration of a short time horizon, a reasonable dividend and a small price increase. The second has an extended horizon and some growth in dividend stream and price. The third and fourth examples both assume a 20-year holding period but differ in terms of growth in the dividend stream and ending price; the third stock has a stable dividend throughout and little price change, while the fourth has a great deal of growth in the dividend stream and price. Although both examples assume the same holding period (term to maturity), the duration of the growth stock is 23 percent longer than the stable income stock at 8 percent and 36 percent longer at 16 percent. The obvious implication is that *growth stocks have longer durations* than stable, high dividend paying securities. The longest duration stock would be a high growth, zero dividend stock that was acquired on the expectation of large future capital gains.

Because growth stocks have longer durations than other common stocks, growth stocks will be more volatile. In terms of modern portfolio theory, growth

Table 29-9   Duration for alternative common stocks (assuming all currently sell at $20/share)

	K_i		
	0.08	0.12	0.16
Example 1—Expected Dividend = $1.00/year; Expected Holding Period = 5 years; Expected Price = $25/share. Duration	4.591	4.549	4.505
Example 2—Expected Dividend = $1.00/year for first five years, $1.20/year for next five years; Expected Holding Period = 10 years; Expected Price = $30/share. Duration	8.318	7.996	7.641
Example 3—Expected Dividend = $1.00/year; Expected Holding Period = 20 years; Expected Price = $25/share. Duration	12.263	10.364	8.630
Example 4—Expected Dividend = $0.50/year for three years, $0.70/year for three years, $0.90/year for four years, $1.20/year for four years, $1.50/year for four years, $1.75/year for two years; Expected Holding Period = 20 years; Expected Price = $40/share. Duration	15.023	13.432	11.717

stocks should on average have higher betas.[23] Boquist, Racette, and Schlarbaum derived the specific relation between the duration of a security and its beta and also the formula to compute the duration for common stocks.[24] The latter employs the basic dividend valuation model to show that duration (D_i) equals:

$$D_i = \frac{1 + K_i}{K_i - g_i}$$

for discrete compounding and

$$D_i = \frac{1}{K_i - g_i}$$

[23]One of the first authors to consider the duration of common stock was Durand ("Growth Stocks and the Petersburg Paradox"), who emphasized the long duration possibilities of growth stocks. Subsequently Malkiel ("Equity Yields, Growth, and the Structure of Share Prices") likewise discussed the long duration of growth stocks and specifically noted the effect this longer duration would have on their relative price volatility. Haugen and Wichern ("The Elasticity of Financial Assets") discuss the interest rate sensitivity of numerous financial assets including common stocks.

for continuous compounding. Table 29-10 shows the effects on duration of differing combinations of K and g, given the continuous compounding formula.

Duration is determined by the spread between K and g. The larger the spread, the lower the duration. Therefore an increase in the growth rate, absent other changes, will increase the duration of a stock. In contrast, as increase in K (due, for example, to inflation) without a commensurate increase in the firm's growth rate will decrease duration.[25]

Table 29-10   Estimated duration for common stocks under alternative K and g assumptions

K	g	D*	K	g	D*
0.10	0.04	16.7	0.14	0.06	12.5
0.10	0.06	25.0	0.14	0.08	16.7
0.10	0.08	50.5	0.14	0.10	25.0
0.12	0.04	12.5	0.16	0.06	10.0
0.12	0.06	16.7	0.16	0.08	12.5
0.12	0.08	25.0	0.16	0.10	16.7
0.12	0.10	50.0	0.16	0.12	25.0

*All computations use the continuous compounding formula:

$$D_i = \frac{1}{K_i - g_i}$$

[24]Boquist, Racette and Schlarbaum, "Duration and Risk Assessment for Bonds and Common Stocks."

[25]A note by Miles Livingston ("Duration and Risk Assessment for Bonds and Common Stock: A Comment," *Journal of Finance*, March 1978, pp. 293-295) extended the Boquist results by introducing the duration of the market portfolio. The extension indicated that the risk for a stock depended, not only on the rate of growth (i.e., high growth rate, high risk), but also on the covariance between changes in the firm's growth and the market's growth (i.e., high covariance of growth, high risk).

BOND IMMUNIZATION: A PROCEDURE FOR REALIZING TARGET LEVELS OF RETURN*

Martin L. Leibowitz†

$$30$$

"Immunization" is the term coined to describe the design of bond portfolios that can achieve a target level of return in the face of changing reinvestment rates and price levels. Immunization techniques are relevant for many fixed income funds that must address the need to achieve a well-defined level of realized return over a specified investment period.

This need may arise from a variety of motivations. For example, one fund might have a lump-sum liability payment coming due at the end of the period. Another fund may need a relatively assured return for actuarial or accounting purposes. Another may have a simple desire to lock up what is thought to be a sufficiently high level of rates. Or, in yet another instance, the fund sponsor may simply wish to reduce the overall portfolio uncertainty by devoting a portion of the assets to achieving a specified return over a given period. Evidence of the growth in interest in this general form of investment can be seen in the proliferating role of the Guaranteed Investment Contract.

*This article is reprinted from memoranda dated October 10, 1979 and November 27, 1979, Salomon Brothers. Copyright 1979, by Salomon Brothers. Reprinted with permission.

†The author is a Managing Director of Salomon Brothers, Inc.

THE REINVESTMENT PROBLEM

When asked to secure such a target return over a given period such as five years, a bond portfolio manager might at first respond by selecting a portfolio of bonds having a maturity of five years. If these bonds were of sufficiently high grade, then the portfolio would indeed be assured of receiving all the coupon income due during the five years and of then receiving the redemption payments in the fifth year. However, coupon income and principal payments only constitute two of the three sources of return from a bond portfolio. The third source of return is the "interest-on-interest" derived from the reinvestment of coupon income (and/or the rollover of the maturing principal). Since this reinvestment will take place in the interest rate environments that exist at the time of the coupon receipts, there is no way to insure that one will obtain the amount of interest-on-interest required to achieve the target return.

Table 30-1 illustrates this point. A five-year 9 percent par bond will provide $450 of coupon income and $1,000 of maturing principal over its five-year life. This would amount to an added return of $450 beyond the original $1,000 investment. However, in order to achieve a 9 percent compound growth rate in asset value over the five-year period, the original $1,000 would have to reach a cumulative value of $1,553, i.e., an incremental dollar return of $553. This $103 gap in return has to be overcome through the accumulation of interest-on-interest. As Table 30-1 shows, this amount of interest-on-interest will be achieved when coupon reinvestment occurs at the same 9 percent rate as the bond's original yield-to-maturity. At lower reinvestment rates, the interest-on-interest will be less than the amount required and the growth in asset value will fall somewhat short of the required target value of $1,553.

This reinvestment problem becomes even more severe over longer investment periods. Table 30-2 shows the total dollar amount and the percentage of the target return that must be achieved through interest-on-interest for various investment periods ranging from one to 30 years.

Table 30-1 Realized return from a five-year par bond over a 5-year horizon

Reinvest-ment rate	Coupon income	Capital gain	Interest on interest	Total $ return	Realized compound yield
0%	$450	$0	$ 0	$450	7.57%
7	450	0	78	528	8.66
8	450	0	90	540	8.83
9	450	0	103	553	9.00
10	450	0	116	566	9.17
11	450	0	129	579	9.35

Table 30-2 Magnitude of interest-on-interest to achieve 9% realized compound yield from 9% par bonds of various maturities

Maturity in years	Total dollar return	Interest-on-interest at 9% reinvestment rate	Interest-on-interest as percentage of total return
1	$ 92	$ 2	2.2%
2	193	13	6.5
3	302	32	10.7
4	422	62	14.7
5	553	103	18.6
7	852	222	26.1
10	1,412	512	36.2
20	4,816	3,016	62.6
30	13,027	10,327	79.3

This "reinvestment risk" constitutes a major problem in closely achieving any assured level of target return. However, there are ways of limiting this reinvestment risk. For example, Table 30-3 shows the total return and cumulative asset value for a five-year bond over investment horizons ranging from one to five years. For the periods shorter than five years, the bond's price in Table 30-3 has been determined by the simplistic assumption that the yield-to-maturity coincides with the indicated reinvestment rate. This set of assumptions corresponds to a scenario where interest rates immediately move to a flat yield curve at the level of the indicated reinvestment rate, and then remain there throughout the entire investment period.

Table 30-3 illustrates a striking compensation effect for investment periods of less than five years. For the three-year period, at the 7 percent reinvestment rate assumption, the interest-on-interest naturally falls short of the amount required to support a target return of 9 percent. However, if the bond could be sold at the price corresponding to the assumed 7 percent yield-to-maturity rate, then a capital gain would be realized which would more than compensate for the lower value of interest-on-interest. Table 30-3 illustrates the well-known facts that over the short term, lower interest rates lead to increased returns through price appreciation while, over the longer term, lower interest rates lead to reduced returns through reduced interest-on-interest. For periods lying between the short term and the longer term, it is not surprising to find these two effects providing some compensation for each other.

This leads to the intriguing question as to whether there might be some intermediate point during a bond's life when these compensating effects precisely offset one another. Again, from Table 30-3 we can see that for a 7 percent

Table 30-3   Realized return from a five-year 9% par bond over various horizon periods

Reinvestment rate and yield-to-maturity at horizon		Horizon period			
		1 year	3 years	4.13 years	5 years
	Coupon income	$90	$270	$372	$450
7%	Capital gain	$68	$37	$16	$0
	Interest-on-interest	$2	$25	$51	$78
	Total dollar return	$160	$331	$439	$528
	Realized compound yield	15.43%	9.77%	9.00%	8.66%
9%	Capital gain	$0	$0	$0	$0
	Interest-on-interest	$2	$32	$67	$103
	Total dollar return	$92	$302	$439	$553
	Realized compound yield	9.00%	9.00%	9.00%	9.00%
11%	Capital gain	− $63	− $35	− $16	$0
	Interest-on-interest	$2	$40	$83	$129
	Total dollar return	$29	$275	$439	$579
	Realized compound yield	2.89%	8.26%	9.00%	9.36%

reinvestment rate this offset does exist and occurs at 4.13 years. That such an offset point should exist is not, of course, surprising in a situation where there are two conflicting forces—reinvestment and capital gains—with one force growing stronger and the other force growing weaker with time. What may be somewhat more surprising is that when we look at reinvestment rates of 7, 9, and 11 percent, we find that this offset point occurs at the same 4.13 years!

THE CONCEPT OF DURATION

In the context of the fund seeking an assured level of return, this finding has great significance. If we were seeking to achieve the guaranteed 9 percent return over 4.13 years, Table 30-3 tells us that we would have no problem doing so with the five-year bond, no matter what reinvestment rates existed (as long as they followed the simplistic "flat yield curve pattern" assumed in the construction of Table 30-3).

This offset effect occurs because the *duration* of a five-year 9 percent par bond is 4.13. The duration of a bond is a concept first introduced by Frederick

Macaulay in 1938.[1] Essentially, it is an average life calculation based upon the *present value* of each of the bond's cash flow payments, including coupons as well as principal. For the theoretical case of a pure discount zero-coupon bond, the duration will coincide with its maturity. Since zero-coupon bonds have no cash flows prior to maturity, they are free from the problem of coupon reinvestment. A 4.13-year zero-coupon bond priced to yield 9 percent would always provide the target 9 percent return over its maturity period—no matter what interest rates may occur over its life. Hence, the zero-coupon bond would be the ideal vehicle for the problem of achieving a target return except for one obstacle—beyond the one-year maturity range of Treasury Bills, very few such investments exist.

It would obviously be desirable if we could somehow use real coupon bonds to obtain some of the characteristics of zero-coupon bonds. Fortunately, it turns out that this can be done and that the bond's duration is similar mathematically to a zero-coupon bond having a maturity equal to that duration. For example, as shown in Table 30-3, a 9 percent target return over a 4.13-year period could be achieved by either a 4.13-year maturity zero-coupon discount bond at a 9 percent yield rate or a 5-year 9 percent par bond. Both these bonds have the same duration of 4.13 years. In fact, for the assumptions underlying Table 30-3, any other bond yielding 9 percent and having a duration of 4.13 years will achieve the 9 percent target return. Although far from obvious, this fact can be demonstrated using the mathematical analysis underlying Table 30-3. Another feature of the duration concept is that bonds having the same duration will undergo the same percentage price change for small movements in yield-to-maturity.

Table 30-4 shows the duration of various bonds. Returning to the original objective of providing an assured 9 percent target return over a five-year period, we can see that one should choose a bond having a duration of five years (as opposed to a maturity of five years).

To obtain a duration of five-years in a 9 percent par bond, it turns out that one would need a maturity of around 6.3 years. Table 30-5 shows how such a bond will indeed achieve the required growth in asset value to provide the 9 percent guaranteed return compounded semi-annually.

Using duration to select bonds would solve the problem of achieving assured returns over specified periods except for one small point: movements in the interest rate structure are not so accommodating as to provide us with permanent shifts to a flat yield curve, as assumed in Tables 30-1, 30-2, and 30-3. Different patterns of rate movement can completely unwind these carefully

[1]*The Movement of Interest Rates, Bond Yields and Stock Prices in the United States Since 1856,* Frederick R. Macaulay, NBER, 1938. (For a comprehensive discussion of *duration* see: Frank K. Reilly and Rupinder S. Sidhu, "The Many Uses of Duration," *Financial Analysts Journal,* July-August 1980, pp. 58-72. Ed. note.)

Table 30-4   Duration of various bonds all priced to yield 9%

Maturity in years	Coupon			
	0%	7.5%	9.0%	10.50%
1	1.00	0.98	0.98	0.98
2	2.00	1.89	1.87	1.86
3	3.00	2.74	2.70	2.66
4	4.00	3.51	3.45	3.38
5	5.00	4.23	4.13	4.05
7	7.00	5.50	5.34	5.20
10	10.00	7.04	6.80	6.59
20	20.00	9.96	9.61	9.35
30	30.00	11.05	10.78	10.59
100	100.00	11.61	11.61	11.61

contrived results. For example, in Table 30-5, suppose the reinvestment rate indeed moved to 7 percent and stayed there for most of the five-year period, but then jumped up to 11 percent just before the fifth year when we had to sell the bond. This scenario would mean that we would achieve the reduced level of interest-on-interest associated with the 7 percent rate together with the capital *loss* associated with the 11 percent rate. This combination would provide a total accumulated return of only $502 which is less than the $553 required to achieve the target 9 percent return.

Table 30-5   Realized return from 6-year, 4-month 9% par bond over a 5-year horizon*

Reinvestment rate and yield-to-maturity at horizon	Coupon income	Capital gain	Interest on interest	Total $ return	Realized compound yield
7%	$450	$25	$ 78	$553	9.00%
8	450	13	90	553	9.00
9	450	0	103	553	9.00
10	450	− 13	116	553	9.00
11	450	− 26	129	553	9.00

*The computations are based on a bond purchased free of accrued interest in order to obtain a categorization of the sources of return that is consistent with the preceding tables. Semi-annual compounding is assumed.

This immediately raises the following question: is there any way for the portfolio manager to go about achieving the assured return in a way that will succeed in the face of the far wilder interest rate movements that occur in the real world? One can never achieve this growth in an absolute and precise sense. However, there are techniques for periodic "rebalancing" of the portfolio that will minimize the vulnerability of the achieved return across a wide range of interest rate movements. These techniques are generally referred to as "immunization strategies" since they attempt to "immunize" the portfolio's return against the "disease" of fluctuating reinvestment rates and changing pricing yields.

There is an extensive theoretical literature in this field of "immunization strategies." Most of this research work has focused on the more academically convenient case of portfolios consisting of investments along an idealized Treasury yield curve. These portfolios are then periodically rebalanced so as to keep the portfolio's duration equal to the remaining length of the investment period.

MULTIPLE CHANGES IN RATES

In the preceding sections it was shown that it was possible to overcome the reinvestment problem and match the promised yield to maturity—*if* certain rather stringent conditions were satisfied. The key assumption was that interest rates immediately moved from their current level to some given level and remained there for the entire planning period. Under this assumption of a single move to a "flat" yield curve, the new level determines the reivestment rate for coupon income as well as the final price of the portfolio. For an initial bond investment whose duration corresponded to the length of the planning period, these conditions would result in a realized compound yield that closely matched the promised yield-to-maturity. However, this finding would be of only theoretical interest unless one could find ways to deal with more general and realistic conditions. In particular, before the immunization procedure can really be put into practice, one must come to grips with the assured fact that there will be *multiple* changes in rates during the course of the planning period. In this section, we will explore how rebalancing procedures can be used to accommodate such multiple changes in rates.

It is easy to demonstrate the problems that arise when one drops the "single-move" assumption and allows for multiple movements. In the preceding sections, we set out to achieve a 9 percent target return over a five-year planning period. To obtain a 9 percent par bond having this duration, we would need a maturity of 6.7 years.[2] If rates remained at 9 percent throughout the five-

[2]This example is based on a normal bond structure with accrued interest attached to the bond at the outset. It is in contrast to the bond purchased free of accrued interest that constituted the model for the calculations in Table 30-5.

year period, a $1,000 investment in this bond would compound to $1,552.97, thereby providing the 9 percent return that one would expect in the "no move" case. This scenario is shown in Figure 30–1A. To illustrate the effects of a "single move" in rates, suppose that rates immediately jumped to 12 percent and then stayed there for the remaining five-year period. This bond would then generate a coupon income of $436.67, interest-on-interest of $162.49, and a capital loss of $42.91. As shown in Figure 30–1B, this amounts to a total future value of $1,556.25, which produces a yield that is slightly higher than the 9 percent target return.

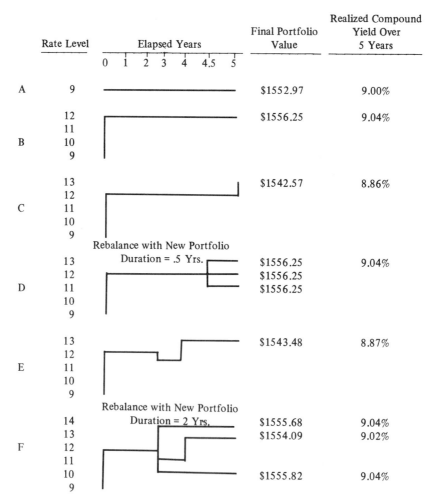

Figure 30-1   Portfolio values developed under various interest rate patterns (initial portfolio: $1,000 investment in 6.7 year, 9% par bond; initial duration: 5.00 years)

There is another way of viewing the events in Figure 30-1B. The sudden rate move generates an immediate capital loss of $131.00. In order for the remaining asset value of $869.00 to grow to the target level, a compound growth rate of 12 percent must be achieved throughout the next five years, e.g.:

$$\$869.00 \times (1.06)^{10} = \$1,556.25.$$

In this sense, the five-year return of 12 percent is needed to compensate for the immediate price loss incurred as rates jumped from 9 percent to 12 percent. In any case, the example in Figure 30-1B illustrates that, under the "single-move" assumption, even when the move is as large as 400 basis points, we still manage to realize the required target return.

Now let us examine what happens under a simple case involving a "multiple move" in rates. Suppose, as before, that the first move in rates happens immediately after purchase and changes the yield curve to 12 percent. This rate persists for the next five years. But then, just before the bond is sold at the fifth year, there is a second jump in interest rates to 13 percent (Figure 30-1C). All numbers are then the same as in the earlier example, with the exception of the capital loss which now amounts to $56.58. This greater capital loss brings the total future value down to $1,542.57, for a total realized compound yield of 8.86 percent. Thus, under this simple two-move assumption, the portfolio falls short of its target by more than fourteen basis points.

If immunization procedures could not deal with such simple "multiple movements" in rates, there would clearly be a problem in achieving any sort of application in real life. Fortunately, techniques exist involving portfolio rebalancing that can overcome this difficulty.

REBALANCING USING DURATION

The problem arising from multiple rate movements can be traced to the way that a bond ages over time. Table 30-6 illustrates how our theoretical bond, having a starting duration of five years, ages on a year-by-year basis. With each passing year, the maturity obviously gets shorter by one year, but the duration becomes shorter by less than a year. For example, over the first year, the bond's duration "ages" from 5.0 to 4.4, a drop of only .6 for the year. At the end of the fifth year, when we would clearly like to have a duration of zero, the original bond has a duration of 1.5 years. (Even when combined with the cash flow generated by coupon reinvestment, the blended duration of the portfolio becomes seriously mismatched with the passage of time.)

This "duration drift" can be overcome by periodic rebalancing of the portfolio. For example, suppose that at the end of 4.5 years, the portfolio had been "rebalanced" in the following fashion. The bond was sold at a yield-to-maturity of 12 percent, leading to a capital loss of $54.22 and a total future value of $1,468.16 (Figure 30-1D). The entire proceeds were then invested in a 12

Table 30-6   Changes in a bond's duration with the passage of time
(9% 6.7-year par bond)

Elapsed time	Maturity	Bond's duration	Target duration	Mismatch
0 yrs.	6.66 yrs.	5.00 yrs.	5.00 yrs.	0 yrs.
1	5.66	4.42	4.00	.42
2	4.66	3.79	3.00	.79
3	3.66	3.11	2.00	1.11
4	2.66	2.35	1.00	1.35
5	1.66	1.53	0.00	1.53

percent par bond, having a duration of precisely .5. Clearly, this instrument would assure us of achieving a 12 percent rate of return over the final .5-year period. In turn, this would provide a 12 percent return over the entire five years and therefore bring the total value of the portfolio up to $1,556.25. In other words, by rebalancing prior to the second movement in interest rates, we would have immunized ourselves against the effects of that movement.

As a further example, suppose that a second move to 11 percent occurred at the end of the third year, and was followed by a third move to 13 percent. Coupons from the original 9 percent bond would have been reinvested for three years at 12 percent, for one year at 11 percent, and for the remaining year at 13 percent. At the end of the fifth year, the bond would have been sold on 13 percent yield-to-maturity, engendering a sizable capital loss. This would lead to a total future value of $1,543.48, well below our target level (Figure 30-1E). However, suppose the portfolio had been rebalanced at the end of the third year, just before the interest rate jump, so as to have a duration of exactly 2.0 years. This reset in duration will help ensure that the final two years realize a 12 percent return. This lockup of the 12 percent rate over the final two years is just what is needed, together with the return achieved over the first three years, to ensure realizing the original target return of 9 percent (Figure 30-1F).

The preceding example illustrates the key idea underlying the immunization process. By rebalancing so as to continually maintain a duration matching the remaining life of the planning period, the bond portfolio is kept in an immunized state throughout the period. This guarantees that the portfolio will achieve the target return promised at the outset of every sub-period. By working backwards, this implies that the original target return of 9 percent can be met in the face of multiple movements in interest rates.

This rebalancing procedure has a dramatic immunizing power even in the face of radical changes in interest rates. This is illustrated in Table 30-7 where interest rates increase by 100 basis points at the end of each year. Through annual rebalancing (based upon duration), the total portfolio value grows to within four basis points of the original 9 percent target.

Table 30-7 Portfolio growth with duration-based rebalancing (initial investment = $1,000)

Period ending date	Rebalanced portfolio at start of period			Results over year			Realized coupon yield		
	New rate level	Duration	Maturity	Coupon flow and interest-on-interest	Capital gain	Total proceeds	Over year	Cumulative	Blended*
1 year	9%	5.00	6.66 yrs.	$ 92.02	$41.18	$1050.84	5.02%	5.02%	8.99%
2	10	4.00	5.14	107.72	−33.03	1125.52	6.98	6.00	8.99
3	11	3.00	3.66	127.22	−24.12	1228.61	8.96	6.98	8.97
4	12	2.00	2.27	151.86	−13.61	1366.87	10.95	7.97	8.97
5	13	1.00	1.00	183.47	0	1550.34	13.00	8.96	8.96

*The 5-year return that would result if the portfolio value at that date were to be compounded at the existing new rate level for all remaining periods.

REBALANCING AS PROXY FOR A ZERO-COUPON BOND OVER TIME

At first glance, the success of this rebalancing procedure in keeping the portfolio on target may seem to be somewhat magical. An insight into the rebalancing principle can be provided by thinking in terms of our old friend, the zero-coupon bond. For any change in yield level, the zero-coupon bond automatically retains sufficient asset value to provide the original return over its life. For example, in Figure 30-1B, when interest rates jump from 9 percent to 12 percent, a $1,000 investment in a five-year zero-coupon bond would decline from $1,000 to $867.17. Suppose one were to sell the zero-coupon bond immediately after this jump in rates, realize the $867.17 proceeds, and then hypothetically invest these funds into another five-year zero-coupon bond at its market yield of 12 percent. Over the remaining five years, the assured 12 percent compounding would enable the original $867.17 to grow to $1,552.97, i.e., satisfying the original 9 percent return goal.

The rebalancing process just described is, of course, equivalent to continued holding of the zero-coupon bond. The five-year zero-coupon bond purchased at 9 percent has truly locked-in the target 9 percent return over the five-year planning period. Regardless of the magnitude or frequency of subsequent rate movements, the zero-coupon bond always remains "on target." Moreover, the zero-coupon bond obviously remains *continually* "on target" even with the passage of time. In other words, it always retains the precise amount of asset value needed to realize the original target when compounded at the then yield rate for the remainder of the period.

The key idea here is that the price of the zero-coupon bond moves in lock-step with the change in the required dollar investment at the new interest rate level. Another way of saying this is that, with respect to interest rate movements, the volatility of the zero-coupon bond coincides with the volatility of the assets required to provide the promised payment in the fifth year. Thus, for a bond portfolio to retain the assets needed to stay "on target," it must have the same volatility as the five-year zero-coupon bond. Moreover, it must maintain this volatility equivalence as time passes. As noted earlier, a bond's volatility is related to its duration. In particular, the duration of a zero-coupon bond coincides with its remaining life. Thus, in order to stay "on target" with the time—as the zero-coupon bond does automatically—an "immunizing bond portfolio" must maintain the same duration as the zero-coupon bond. An "immunizing" bond portfolio can maintain this equivalence through duration-based rebalancing. Thus, duration-based rebalancing can provide a bond portfolio which mimics the automatic "immunizing" behavior of the zero-coupon bond in the face of multiple interest rate movements over time.

Part V

FINANCIAL AND
REGULATORY
DEVELOPMENTS

The pace of regulatory change and financial developments has quickened since the early 1960s. As discussed in the article by Marvin Goodfriend, James Parthemos, and Bruce J. Summers, financial innovation has been largely due to (1) high rates of inflation, (2) rapid development of computer and communications technology, and (3) changing regulatory environment. They discuss, chronologically, the innovations in payments services (e.g., NOW accounts) that have encouraged the public to reduce its dependence on demand deposits.

The article by Timothy Q. Cook and Jeremy G. Duffield discusses the various types of short-term investment pools that have emerged in recent years. Of the at least eight types of pools that exist, the most well-known is the widely publicized money market mutual fund. The emergence of these vehicles provided access to the money market to virtually all investors.

As discussed in the article by Daniel J. Vrabac, the methods used by financial intermediaries to channel funds from savers to borrowers have been affected in recent years by inflation, fluctuations in interest rates, recessions, and the trend towards deregulation. Nonetheless, the banking industry has been proven capable of adapting to an increasingly uncertain and complex environment. The basis for future competition between banks and thrift institutions lies in the continuing process of deregulation.

The article by David D. Whitehead discusses the evolution of interstate banking. While interstate banking is prohibited by law, the article describes the way banking organizations provide financial services across state lines. It is not necessary for a banking organization to maintain a physical facility for accepting demand deposits and making commercial loans to be competitive on an interstate basis.

Lastly, the article by Harvey Rosenblum, Diane Siegel, and Christine Pavel discusses the increasing competition banks face from manufacturers (e.g., General Motors), retailers (e.g., Sears, Roebuck), and diversified financial companies (e.g., Merrill Lynch). In turn, banks have sought entry into some of their new competitors' markets. While banks do not have the same geographic freedom as their nonbank competitors, they are utilizing several avenues, especially nonbank subsidiaries, to offer financial services on an interstate basis.

RECENT FINANCIAL INNOVATIONS: CAUSES, CONSEQUENCES FOR THE PAYMENTS SYSTEM, AND IMPLICATIONS FOR MONETARY CONTROL*

Marvin Goodfriend, James Parthemos, and Bruce J. Summers

31

The past two decades have been characterized by a number of significant innovations in the U. S. financial system, which today differs greatly from the system existing at the beginning of the 1960s. Today's financial intermediaries, including commercial banks, handle a much larger volume of business and generally serve broader geographic markets than their counterparts of two decades ago. They are also more competitive and more inclined to offer a greater variety of services in an effort to maintain or expand market shares. Moreover, some intermediaries, such as credit unions, now play a more important role in the nation's financial system, and entirely new types of intermediaries, such as money market funds, have emerged. Generally speaking,

*Reprinted, with deletions and minor editorial revisions, from the *Economic Review*, March/April 1980, pp. 14-27, with permission of the Federal Reserve Bank of Richmond.

both the variety of institutions offering financial services and the array of such services have increased significantly, especially in recent years.

The expanding variety of services offered by financial intermediaries has been paralleled by an increased diversity of the liabilities of these institutions. Twenty years ago, for example, the liabilities side of a typical commercial bank's balance sheet was heavily weighted with demand deposits and regular savings deposits. Today's typical bank balance sheet shows a sizable reduction in the relative importance of such deposits and a sharp increase in so-called "purchased funds," i.e., negotiable certificates of deposit, nonnegotiable certificates of deposit, repurchase agreements, Federal funds purchased, and in the case of very large banks, perhaps Eurodollar borrowings as well. Likewise, regular savings deposits (deposit shares) typified the liabilities of savings and loan associations in the 1950s but today have given way in large measure to time certificates of deposit. Much the same can be said for credit unions and mutual savings banks.

The liabilities of financial intermediaries represent indebtedness to their customers—to households, business, and governmental units for the most part. Collectively, claims on these institutions make up the predominant fraction of the public's holdings of liquid assets. Of the several types of these liquid assets, the public's holdings of demand deposit claims at commercial banks have commanded particular attention because they have traditionally been the principal means of making payment. Until recently, demand deposits possessed an advantage in that they were immediately available for spending while other liquid claims could be spent only after being converted into coin, currency, or demand deposits. For this reason, demand deposits along with coin and currency have been traditionally defined as "money" while other liquid claims at financial intermediaries have been considered to be money substitutes or "near money."

The outstanding volume of monetary assets at a given time and its rate of growth over time are important determinants of aggregate spending and inflation. Two statistical measures of the monetary aggregates, M_1 and M_2, have played an important role in the implementation of monetary policy since 1970. M_1, the measure of money narrowly defined, includes coin and currency in circulation outside the banking system and private demand deposits adjusted.[1] A broader measure, M_2, includes with M_1 time and savings deposits at commercial banks except for large denomination negotiable certificates of deposits.

FINANCIAL INNOVATION AND THE PAYMENTS SYSTEM

Recent innovations have had a direct impact on the payments system, i.e., on the types of assets and institutions involved in the consummation of payments

---

[1]The demand deposit component of M_1 consists of (1) demand deposits at commercial banks other than domestic interbank and U. S. government demand deposits, less cash items in process of collection and Federal Reserve float and (2) foreign demand balances at Federal Reserve Banks.

between individual economic units. The payments system has historically comprised the nation's 14,500 commercial banks, a system of correspondent relations between individual banks, local clearing houses, and the Federal Reserve System. This network provides the machinery for transferring demand deposit claims between individual economic units. As mentioned above, until recently payments have been made almost exclusively with demand deposits or currency and coin.

As a result of recent innovations, claims on financial institutions other than commercial banks are being used to make payments. For several years it has been possible to transfer funds from savings accounts in thrifts to bank check accounts by telephone, or to use these funds to make prearranged third-party payments. Effective in 1981, commercial banks and thrift institutions [will offer] Negotiable Order of Withdrawal (NOW) accounts. NOW accounts are a readily transferable means of payment. Share drafts at credit unions have also become a means of payment. NOW accounts and share drafts, however, differ from demand deposits at commercial banks in that they bear interest. Hence, for the first time since 1933, when interest on demand deposits was prohibited by law, what amounts to interest-bearing demand deposits comprises part of the nation's payments medium. Moreover, since November 1, 1978, commercial banks have been allowed to cover their customers' overdrafts by automatically transferring funds from savings to checking accounts. This too allows the use of interest-bearing deposits for making payments.

The emergence of new types of assets that mediate transactions—that is, serve as money—pose special monetary control problems for the Federal Reserve System. A broadened spectrum of money and near money assets complicates the problem of determining an appropriate working statistical definition of money. Moreover, growth of monetary assets issued by institutions beyond the control of the central bank can significantly weaken the Federal Reserve's ability to control the monetary aggregates. The sections that follow contain detailed discussions of major factors promoting innovation, the innovations themselves, and their implications for monetary control.

SOME FACTORS PROMOTING INNOVATION

The rapid pace of financial innovation of recent years is due largely to three major factors. The first of these is the serious inflation the economy has suffered since 1965 and especially since 1973. The second is the rapid development of computer and communications technology. The third is a change in the regulatory environment dating from the early 1960s.

Inflation has accelerated the pace of financial innovation through its impact on interest rates. Inflation is an important determinant of the level of interest rates because the level of interest rates reflects anticipation of future inflation and anticipations roughly follow recent experience with inflation. When inflation has been high anticipations of inflation are also high; and when inflation has been low so are inflationary anticipations. Inflation has continually risen in recent years, so inflationary anticipations have risen as well. In this environment lenders have sought higher interest rates as compensation for the depreciating purchasing power of their savings. Borrowers competing for funds have been willing to pay higher interest rates because they can expect corresponding increases in income from investments financed through borrowings. Consequently, rising rates of inflation have led to higher interest rates.

High interest rates increase the opportunity cost of holding noninterest-bearing assets and encourage the economizing of such assets. An example of how this leads to innovation is seen in the case of commercial banks, which are required by law to hold reserves in the form of noninterest-bearing assets.[2] The interest foregone on these reserves, and hence the cost of holding them, rises with the level of market interest rates. In a period of high rates, banks try harder to reduce the amount of reserves required by law. Banks can do this by encouraging shifts in liabilities from categories like demand deposits, which have a relatively high reserve requirement, to categories for which lower, or even no, reserves are required. For example, they might offer to enter repurchase agreements with customers holding demand deposits. This involves selling the customer government securities under agreement to buy the securities back at a somewhat higher price (determined by prevailing market interest rates on such contracts) after a stipulated period, usually one to seven days. Such repurchase agreements (RPs) are liabilities of the bank to its customers, as are demand deposits. The difference is that unlike demand deposits, there are usually no reserve requirements imposed on RPs. Consequently, the bank in effect pays interest to the customer and simultaneously reduces its required reserves.

Commercial banks can achieve these results in a variety of other ways as well. Their efforts to do so have resulted in a significant diversification of bank liabilities, hence in the claims on banks held by bank customers. As mentioned above, the liabilities side of bank balance sheets now include, in much larger proportion than in the 1960s, RPs, Federal funds purchases, negotiable and nonnegotiable CDs, consumer type CDs, and in the case of large banks, Eurodollar borrowings and other liabilities to foreign branches. These liabilities all involve lower legal reserve requirements than demand deposits. To the extent that banks can find ways to convert demand deposit liabilities into these other forms, required reserves are reduced, allowing a given reserve to support a higher volume of both earning assets and liabilities.

[2]Reserve balances of member banks held with the Federal Reserve are noninterest bearing. Nonmember banks hold reserves as specified by the individual states. A number of states allow various types of earning assets to satisfy their reserve requirements. However, during the 1980s, a uniform reserve system is currently being phased in for *all* depository institutions (see footnote 6).

High interest rates provide incentives for individuals and businesses to shift out of demand deposits and into these new types of bank liabilities. Hence, commercial banks and other financial institutions find a ready, indeed eager, market for new interest-bearing liquid substitutes for demand deposits that their ingenuity can devise. As a matter of fact, sharp-penciled corporate treasurers have been known to insist that their bankers stand ready to enter overnight repurchase agreements with them so that they can earn interest on balances that can be used rather promptly for making payments.

Arrangements allowing banks to reduce required reserves and the public to reduce its holdings of demand deposits are motivated simply by a desire to minimize individual costs of doing business. Unfortunately, however, the aggregate effect of these arrangements is the creation and rapid growth of highly liquid assets used by the public in place of demand deposits. As explained, this complicates monetary control.

The rapid development of computer and communications technology has given individual institutions the capacity to process massive amounts of data and to make transfers rapidly and efficiently. In many instances, sophisticated new equipment has resulted in sizable amounts of excess capacity, thereby creating incentives for expanding existing services and offering new kinds of services. In short, the revolution in computer and communications technology has played an important role in recent financial innovation.

Between the early 1930s and the 1960s, bank regulatory philosophy was dominated by a preoccupation with the soundness of individual institutions. Competition in banking was viewed as a double-edged sword, incorporating notable disadvantages as well as some generally accepted advantages in improving the quality of banking services to the public. Indeed, some bank regulations, such as the prohibition of the payment of interest on demand deposits and the limitation on interest payable on savings deposits, were designed explicitly to discourage competition.

In the early and middle 1960s major changes were made in Federal and state banking laws and regulations, most tending to encourage competition not only among banks but also between commercial banks and other financial institutions. With the introduction of the negotiable certificate of deposit in 1961, large commercial banks found a way to compete for short-term funds. Shortly afterwards, both large and small banks, which up to the 1960s had shown relatively little interest in consumer type savings deposits, began moving vigorously into this market. These moves ushered in an era of ever sharpening competition within the commercial banking community and between commercial banks and other financial intermediaries. Subsequent changes in bank holding company law, liberalization of regulations for thrift institutions, and a more competitive international banking climate reinforced this move to more intensive competition. In any case, there has been in the period after 1961 a more or less steady relaxation of regulatory constraints and a significant increase in competition among all types of financial institutions.[3]

The steady relaxation of regulatory constraints, however, has not always proceeded on the initiative of the regulators themselves. The NOW account case provides a simple illustration of this. The secular rise in interest rates in the late 1960s was especially troublesome for mutual savings banks. As legal ceilings on the interest they could pay became increasingly restrictive, their ability to compete for funds deteriorated and their deposit growth slowed. Federal law prohibited payment of interest on checking accounts, but the prohibition did not extend to mutual savings banks that were not insured by the FDIC. In 1970 a state-insured Massachusetts mutual savings bank, looking for a way to attract deposits, petitioned the state commissioner of banking for authority to offer NOW accounts. The petition was denied but, on appeal, the state supreme court overturned the denial on grounds that state law provided no restrictions on the form in which deposits could be withdrawn. With the public becoming increasingly aware of losses suffered by earning no interest on checking balances, Federal law authorized the issue of NOW accounts by commercial banks and thrift institutions first in the New England states, and later in all states effective in January 1981.

A REVIEW OF SPECIFIC DEVELOPMENTS

Table 31-1 is a roughly chronological listing of innovations that have permitted the public to reduce its reliance on demand deposits. The influence of each of these developments on the management of payments balances by businesses and households is described below.

Corporate Cash Management

Like other economic units, businesses have an incentive to minimize cash held for payments purposes. Doing so is a complex task, however, especially for large corporations whose operations are widely diversified geographically and by product line. A number of specialized cash management techniques have been developed to improve the efficiency with which money positions are managed. Some of these techniques, e.g., cash flow forecasting and internal accounting control systems, are available in-house or through nonbank vendors.

---

[3]An exception to this steady relaxation of regulatory constraints is the *Interest Adjustment Act* of 1966, which extended coverage of deposit rate ceilings to the thrift industry and established a differential between maximum rates that banks and thrifts could pay on deposits. This action was a direct result of the heightened competition for consumer deposits occurring in the early- and mid-1960s, which had resulted in a decline in thrift institution deposit growth relative to bank deposit growth.

Because of their central role in the payments process, however, commercial banks are the most important suppliers of corporate cash management services. Bank sponsored cash management systems are designed to accelerate collections into a large firm's regional checking accounts and then to further concentrate demand deposits into one account used to pay bills and fund short-term investments. The key elements in such a system include cash concentration, disbursement, and investment management.

The first step in cash concentration is development of a collection system for funds based on a group of local and regional banking organizations selected for their proximity either to the firm's field operations or to its customers. Customers are instructed to mail their payments to a lockbox under the control of a local bank, which collects remittances and credits the firm's checking account. Information on the amount of collected balances in these local depositories is gathered by telephone, and then a depository transfer check (DTC) is written payable to an account in a regional "concentration" bank and drawn on the various local banks. The DTC, which is a nonnegotiable check that requires no signature, is commonly used to transfer funds between a corporation's accounts held in different banks. Since the DTC can be deposited in the regional concentration bank immediately after account balances are ascertained by phone, overnight credit is available as long as the regional bank and local depositories are all located in the same Federal Reserve regional check processing area. The regional bank can then wire the collected funds to the corporation's master checking account held at a bank in the home office city.

Disbursement of corporate funds can be centralized, all checks being written from the master account, or decentralized, with separate divisions of the company making payments in their respective localities. Centralized cash control can be maintained even in a decentralized check-writing environment using zero-balance accounts. Under this system, a company's disbursing agents write checks on designated disbursing accounts maintained at regional banks and having zero balances. Debit balances accumulate in these zero-balance disbursing accounts as checks are written and are offset by charges made on the corporation's master account.

Integral to the concept of corporate cash management is a prompt reporting system that monitors, and perhaps even forecasts, cash flow. Information contained in a reporting system would consist of detailed transactions data, including transfer activity between accounts and daily bank balances. The ultimate objective of such a reporting system is to provide information on the amount of money available for short-term investment.

Negotiable CDs

As corporations became more adept at cash management during the 1950s, their investable bank balances increased significantly. Rather than holding idle demand deposits, short-term investments offering high liquidity and low risk

Table 31-1 Summary of regulatory, legislative, and technical developments enabling the public to reduce its reliance on noninterest-bearing demand deposits

Development	Date or period	Description
(1) Corporate cash management services	post-World War II	Corporate cash management services, for example, lockboxes, cash-concentration accounts, and information-retrieval systems, are technical innovations permitting more efficient management of cash balances. Their introduction by commercial banks goes back many years, although such services came to be used much more widely after World War II.
(2) Negotiable certificates of deposit (CDs)	1961	Negotiable CDs are marketable receipts for funds deposited in a bank for a specified period at a specified rate of interest. This instrument was originated in 1961 by a large money center bank.
(3) Savings accounts for state and local governments and businesses	1960s, 11/74, 11/75	Federally chartered savings and loan associations have been authorized to offer local governments and business savings accounts since the 1960s. Commercial banks were authorized to accept savings deposits from local governments starting November 1974 and from businesses (up to \$150,000) starting November 1975.
(4) Telephone transfers from savings accounts	1960s, 4/75	Telephone transfers allow savings account customers to transfer funds either to checking accounts or to third parties by phone. Federal savings and loan associations have had this authority since the 1960s, whereas banks were granted it in April 1975.
(5) Repurchase agreements (RPs)	1969	Repurchase agreements are primarily short-term contracts for the purchase of immediately available funds collateralized by securities. RPs grew rapidly beginning in 1969 after Regulation D was amended to explicitly exempt from reserve requirements RPs backed by the sale of U.S. Government or Federal agency securities.
(6) Preauthorized third-party transfers	9/70, 4/75, 9/75	Preauthorized transfers are payments made from savings accounts for recurring transactions. Savings and loan associations were permitted to make preauthorized nonnegotiable transfers from savings accounts to third parties for household-related expenditures in September 1970 and for any purpose beginning in April 1975. Commercial banks were permitted to make preauthor-

ized nonnegotiable transfers from savings accounts to third parties for any purpose in September 1975.

(7) Negotiable Order of Withdrawal (NOW) accounts	5/72, 9/72, 1/74, 3/76, 10/78, 12/79	NOW accounts are savings accounts from which payments can be made by draft. State-chartered mutual savings banks began offering NOW accounts in Massachusetts after a May 1972 state court ruling authorizing such deposits. NOWs were offered by state-chartered mutual savings banks in New Hampshire in September 1972 with the approval of the state bank commissioner. Beginning January 1974 Congress authorized NOWs at all depository institutions in Connecticut, Maine, Rhode Island, and Vermont, authority that was extended to New York in November 1978 and nationwide effective January 1981.
(8) Savings and loan remote service units (RSUs)	1/74	RSUs are machines that allow a customer to make deposits to, and withdrawals from, his savings account at stores and other places away from the institution maintaining the account. The Federal Home Loan Bank Board authorized RSUs in January 1974. Although ruled illegal in April 1979, Congress subsequently passed legislation legalizing the service until April 1, 1980.
(9) Money market funds (MMFs)	early 1974	Money market funds are mutual funds specializing in short-term investments from which shares can be redeemed by checks drawn on designated commercial banks, or by wire transfer, telephone, or mail. Use of MMFs became widespread beginning in early 1974.
(10) Credit union share drafts	10/74, 3/78	Credit union share drafts are payments made directly from share accounts. An experimental share draft program was approved for Federal credit unions in October 1974 and made permanent in March 1978. Although ruled illegal in April 1979, Congress subsequently passed legislation legalizing the service.
(11) Preauthorized savings to checking transfers	11/78	Commercial banks were allowed to offer customers automatic savings to checking transfers starting November 1978. This led to the widespread offering of automatic transfer services (ATS), which are essentially zero-balance checking accounts fed from savings accounts. Although ruled illegal in April 1979, Congress subsequently passed legislation legalizing the service.

were sought. Since few banks offered corporations interest-bearing deposits as alternatives to checking balances, businesses turned to other investment sources, particularly commercial paper, Treasury bills, and repurchase agreements with securities dealers. Consequently, there was a sharp decline in the importance of corporate deposits on the banking system's balance sheet. Large money center banks especially felt this loss of funds since they relied on corporate demand deposits to a greater extent than other, smaller banks. This situation prompted First National City Bank of New York to introduce in February 1961 the large negotiable certificate of deposit (negotiable CD), a new liability specifically designed to attract corporate funds.

Regulations limit negotiable CDs to a minimum maturity of fourteen days. Although relatively short, this maturity is still unattractive to businesses seeking an investment outlet that allows quick conversion back to demand deposits. When first introduced in 1961, therefore, it was also announced that a major government securities dealer had agreed to make a secondary market in negotiable CDs. The secondary market makes negotiable CDs an attractive substitute for demand deposits. Corporations holding CDs can sell these in the secondary market at any time to raise cash, while firms desiring investments with maturities shorter than 14 days can acquire CDs with remaining terms to maturity that fit their liquidity needs. The marketability of prime CDs issued by large well known banks is generally greater than that for those issued by lesser known regional institutions. For this reason, investment in money center bank CDs is favored by corporations.

Negotiable CDs possess some characteristics that limit their attractiveness to corporate money managers. In particular, CDs are not nearly as homogeneous (in terms of rates, denominations, and other contractual features) as are, say, Treasury bills. Also, dealers mainly trade prime CDs in denominations of $1 million and will rarely split or consolidate certificates to facilitate a secondary market transaction. For these reasons, negotiable CDs may not always exactly fit the short-term investment needs of corporations. These limitations notwithstanding, negotiable CDs have become a major source of bank funds.

Repurchase Agreements

Repurchase agreements (RPs) represent a particularly useful instrument for cash management that has become widely used only in the last few years. RPs are income-generating assets having a very low credit risk that are available in maturities as short as one day. Commercial banks became active suppliers of RPs after 1969 and now offer them as part of the cash management systems marketed to corporations.

Businesses having cash concentration systems are able to determine the amount of investable balances available in their checking accounts each morning. If funds are available to invest for only a very short period, they can be placed in the overnight or one-day RP market. To facilitate placement of idle checking balances in the RP market, an investment technique known as the continuing contract has been developed. Under this type of arrangement, a corporation agrees to provide its bank with a specific volume of funds to be automatically reinvested each day for a specified period. Continuing contracts in RPs reduce transactions costs since funds are exchanged only at the beginning and end of the contract period. Liquidity is preserved, however, since either the corporation or the bank can cancel the contract before maturity. Similar to the continuing contract is the preauthorized transfer arrangement. Under the latter arrangement, banks automatically invest a corporation's master checking account funds above a specified minimum in RPs.

The RP market has grown dramatically in recent years, especially the market for very short-term RPs. A special survey of 46 money center banks conducted in December 1977 showed RPs outstanding to nonfinancial businesses of $10.5 billion—31 percent under one-day contract, 11 percent under continuing contract, 22 percent under two- to seven-day contract. Another $3.8 billion was outstanding to state and local governments, which, like corporations, are active cash managers. The majority of state and local government RPs are either one-day or continuing contracts. Banks indicate that activity in the RP market has increased greatly since 1977.

Savings Accounts for Business

Since a fairly large minimum investment is necessary in negotiable CDs and RPs, these instruments are not generally suited to the requirements of smaller businesses. An amendment to Regulation Q, effective November 10, 1975, has permitted businesses to hold savings accounts at commercial banks, subject to a ceiling limit of $150,000. This change was made to provide an investment outlet to small businesses holding temporarily idle funds. Such balances reached $10.5 billion by June 1979.

Savings and loan associations have been able to offer savings accounts to businesses for many years. Although data on the size of such balances are not available, indications are that they do not make up a large share of savings and loan liabilities.

Telephone and Preauthorized Third-Party Transfers From Savings Accounts

Use of bank savings accounts by individuals has had the disadvantage in the past of necessitating personal trips to the bank in order to transfer funds to and from checking accounts. This inconvenience was at least partly reduced by 1975 changes in Regulation Q, allowing banks to transfer funds from savings accounts directly to checking or to third parties on the telephone-originated order of a customer, and also to pay recurring bills directly from savings accounts on a preauthorized basis. Telephone transfers to third parties have been authorized at savings and loan associations since the 1960s, while preauthorized third-party transfers for general purposes have been allowed since 1975.

The effect of these regulatory changes has probably been to increase the substitutability between checking and savings accounts. There is no way to measure directly the impact of telephone and preauthorized transfer services on cash management policies of households or businesses. Savings deposit turnover data do show signs of increasing since 1977, the first year they were collected; and it may be that telephone and preauthorized transfer services have encouraged greater use of savings accounts as payments balances.

There are two features of savings accounts that may discourage their use as demand deposit substitutes. First, in the case of direct bill paying from savings, the customer does not have a cancelled check as a record of payments. This is significant because studies of consumer attitudes toward electronic fund transfer (EFT) services have found a deep-seated reluctance to give up the record-keeping services that cancelled checks provide. Second, banks and thrift institutions typically levy charges on savings account withdrawals above some monthly or quarterly minimum. These charges can be fairly substantial, running sometimes 25 to 50 cents per transfer, thereby raising a cost barrier to heavy use of savings transfers.

NOW Accounts and Share Drafts

NOWs are negotiable drafts written on savings accounts at banks, mutual savings banks, and savings and loan associations. Share drafts are written on accounts at credit unions. The use of both NOWs and share drafts is limited by law to individuals only. While both are in practice honored as demand drafts, they are legally time drafts on which financial institutions have the right to delay payment for up to 30 days. NOWs offered by thrift institutions and share drafts are "payable through" instruments, i.e., they are cleared through normal check-clearing channels and are paid by a commercial bank with which the issuing thrift institution maintains a correspondent relationship. Federal law limits interest payments to NOW accounts to 5.25 percent for banks and 5.50 percent for thrifts with the exception of credit unions. The latter are permitted to pay the regular share account rate on balances subject to draft, currently 7 percent.

NOW accounts have been an important catalytic force causing changes in public attitudes toward cash management. This financial innovation, however, has by no means completely altered the public's money management habits. When it passed legislation in 1974 allowing NOWs throughout New England, Congress in a sense created a test of interest-bearing payment accounts. The results of this test show that the public is receptive to interest-bearing payments balances; and also that pricing policies as well as the degree of competition between financial institutions influence the spread of the new service.

Savings and Loan Remote Service Units

A remote service unit (RSU) is defined by the Federal Home Loan Bank Board as an information-processing device, and an RSU account is a savings account accessible through such a device. RSUs can be located directly on sites where frequent payments occur, e.g., the supermarket. Since RSUs are not considered branches, there are few administrative barriers to their establishment by savings and loans.

Money Market Funds

Money market funds (MMFs) were first offered to the public in 1972; but their importance, as measured by growth in number of shareholders and balances in shareholder accounts, increased rapidly only after 1974, and especially in the late 1970s and early 1980s.[4] MMFs offer individuals and businesses having relatively small amounts of funds access to open market investments that in the past were available only to large corporations.

It is reasonable to think of MMFs as being at least partial substitutes for demand deposits. Like savings accounts, they offer high liquidity, since fund shares can be purchased or sold on any business day without a sales charge. Moreover, some MMFs offer a checking option that enables shareholders to write checks in minimum amounts of $500. MMFs, however, appear to have more in common with savings than with demand deposit accounts. Evidence of this is the similarity of turnover rates in MMF accounts and bank savings accounts, both of which are very low compared to turnover rates for checking deposits.

Automatic Transfer Services

Automatic transfer services (ATS) allow depositors to arrange with their banks the automatic transfer of funds from an interest-bearing savings account to a checking account and are the functional equivalent of NOW accounts and share drafts. ATS is a direct substitute for traditional checking balances and has been authorized on a nationwide basis for all commercial banks.

A Summary Overview

Although the developments reviewed above take various forms, there are some general patterns underlying the changes in the payments system during the past several decades. As noted earlier, many changes in the payments system have resulted from a combination of regulatory and legal actions, but it appears that private initiative has been the primary force leading to financial innovation. A number of these innovations, including corporate cash management services, negotiable CDs, repurchase agreements, NOW accounts, and money market funds, came into existence without any prerequisite changes in banking regulations or law. Subsequent regulatory or legal action has been

[4]The assets of money market funds increased from about $4 billion in 1974 to over $115 billion in early 1981. (Ed. footnote)

important in encouraging the development of some of the newly introduced services, but it is not clear that such official action would have occurred without the impetus provided by private initiative.

Competition in the financial markets explains a large part of the private initiative in the payments system. Given a competitive environment for financial services, financial innovations that are demand deposit substitutes and pay interest, or that pay interest and can be quickly converted to cash, offer opportunities to aggressive banks and thrifts seeking to increase their shares of the deposit market.

The earliest innovations primarily benefited businesses, since businesses generally operate on a larger scale than do individuals and consequently maintain larger average transactions balances with a significantly greater potential gain from efficient management. Also, in the period following World War II, businesses operated with much higher ratios of transaction balances to total financial assets than did individuals. In 1950, for example, the ratio of currency plus demand deposits to total financial assets was about 60 percent for non-financial businesses compared to about 25 percent for households. Having a relatively large share of financial assets tied up in noninterest-earning form, businesses had the greater incentive to find ways of improving cash management procedures. Threatened with the loss of corporate deposits to open market debt instruments, the banking industry responded to these improved cash management practices by providing short-term investment opportunities. Thus, the 1960s witnessed the introduction of two new bank liabilities that provide businesses a positive interest return as well as high liquidity, namely negotiable CDs and RPs.

If the 1960s was the decade of business insofar as cash management is concerned, then the 1970s may have been the decade of the consumer. A number of services designed to facilitate efficient management of liquid balances by households were introduced at banks and thrift institutions in the 1970s. First in this group were telephone and preauthorized third-party transfer services from savings accounts. These were followed by NOW accounts, share drafts, ATS, and money market funds. With the exception of money market funds, all of these services rely on the use of interest-bearing savings accounts for direct third-party payments.

On the whole, the innovations which have been described here, taken both individually and collectively, are needlessly complex. For instance, RPs used by businesses and ATS accounts used by consumers entail constant switching of funds between interest-bearing accounts and non-interest-bearing demand deposit accounts. These two services facilitate the circumvention of the prohibition of interest on demand deposits, but they require a greater investment in management time and data processing than do checking accounts. The ingenuity of the financial markets in developing alternatives to demand deposits has resulted in a bewildering array of new monetary assets.

CHANGES IN BANK LIABILITIES AND THE PUBLIC'S LIQUID ASSETS

To what degree has payments system innovation affected the balance sheets of the banking system and the nonbank public? The paragraphs below present some statistical evidence indicating the extent of change in the nonbank public's total holdings of financial assets and in the composition of bank liabilities.

Changes in the Public's Financial Assets

There has been a significant reduction in the relative importance of traditional money balances in the public's holdings of liquid assets. The ratio of demand deposits plus currency and coin to this total plus time deposits and credit market instruments is shown for the household and the nonfinancial business sectors in Figure 31-1. The chart indicates a more or less steady decline in the relative importance of traditional money balances for both sectors since 1950. For the nonfinancial business sector the decline has been especially sharp since 1970, with traditional money balances falling from 56 percent of the total in that year to 39 percent in 1978.

For the household sector (including personal trusts and nonprofit organizations) the decline has been considerably less sharp. As a matter of fact, the fraction of the total in traditional money declined more sharply between 1950

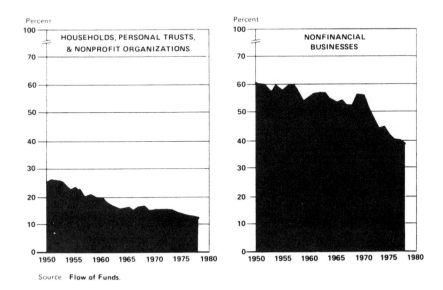

Source   **Flow of Funds.**

Figure 31-1   Demand deposits and currency as a percent of total deposits, currency, and credit market instruments

and 1965 than in the period since the latter year and remained fairly stable until 1974. Since that time, however, a noticeable downtrend appears to have developed. For households, the fraction of financial assets held in traditional money form fell from 25 percent in 1950 to 15 percent in 1965 and 12 percent in 1978. For the period since 1970, it appears that financial innovations have had a greater effect on the composition of the liquid holdings of businesses than on those of households.

Changes in Bank Liabilities

The liabilities structure of the commercial banking system has been significantly altered as a result of the public's efforts to economize on noninterest-earning cash balances. The major change has been a decline in the relative importance of demand deposits compared with net total bank liabilities.[5] For example, private demand deposits declined from 63 percent of net total liabilities in 1960 to just over 31 percent in '1978. This large drop in the ratio of private demand deposits to net total liabilities, which is shown in Figure 31-2, reflects a major shift in public preferences from noninterest-earning demand balances to time balances and other short-term liabilities such as CDs and RPs. Recalling Figure 31-1, it appears that since 1970 businesses have economized on money balances more than households. This conclusion is also supported by a comparison of the growth rates in demand deposits held by these two groups. The compound annual rate of growth of household demand deposits

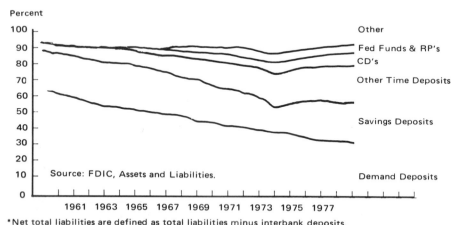

*Net total liabilities are defined as total liabilities minus interbank deposits.

Figure 31-2   Selected sources of funds as a percent of the commercial banking system's net total liabilities*

[5]Net total liabilities are defined as total liabilities exclusive of deposits due to other commercial banks.

over the eight-year period 1970-1978 was 8.3 percent, about a third greater than the 6.2 percent rate for business deposits.

Figure 31-2 shows that, as the share of demand deposits to net total liabilities has declined, the shares of time deposits other than negotiable CDs, nonnegotiable CDs, and purchased funds have all increased. From their inception in 1961, negotiable CDs have grown to nearly 10 percent of net total liabilities. Purchased funds, defined to include Federal funds and repurchase agreements, have in only ten years grown to such an extent that they equalled nearly 9 percent of the commercial banking system's liabilities in 1978. Savings deposits declined in importance as a source of funds until 1974, falling from 25 to 18 percent of net total liabilities. After the 1975 regulatory change which allowed businesses to hold savings accounts, however, savings balances gained moderately in importance, reaching 22 percent of net total liabilities in 1978.

The figure shows a steadily increasing concentration of bank liabilities in those forms not subject to Regulation Q interest rate ceilings. Negotiable CDs and purchased funds are largely free of deposit rate regulation and, therefore, offer the public particularly attractive alternatives to holding sterile demand deposit or low-earning savings deposit balances. Demand and savings deposits combined, which at one time dominated the liabilities side of bank balance sheets, have fallen in relative importance from 90 percent of total liabilities in 1960 to only 53 percent in 1978.

FINANCIAL INNOVATION AND MONETARY CONTROL

Roughly speaking, monetary control means management of the supply of money balances held by the public at depository institutions. The Federal Reserve is concerned with the management of aggregate money balances because these balances are a major determinant of aggregate spending. Aggregate expenditure by the public is, in turn, a key determinant of employment and the rate of inflation. The financial innovations described earlier appear to have interfered with the Federal Reserve's ability to control money growth. A simple view of monetary control is set out below to illustrate the channels through which this interference has been felt.

Control Problems Due to Financial Innovation

The Federal Reserve controls the money supply primarily by buying and selling Treasury securities. Payments made by the Federal Reserve when it purchases securities contribute to what is known as the monetary base. The monetary base consists of currency plus the reserves of the banking system. Since banks hold reserves that are only a fraction of their deposits, each dollar of reserves in the banking system supports several dollars' worth of deposits.

The stock of demand deposits in the banking system constitutes the bulk of what is called the basic money supply or M_1. M_1 has historically served as the nation's payments medium or transactions balances, i.e., money held for the purpose of making payments. Because of its relation to expenditure, M_1 is an important monetary aggregate for the Federal Reserve to control.

To provide a framework for analysis of monetary control, M_1 may be thought of as the product of the stock of base money times a coefficient, m, called the money multiplier, i.e., $M_1 = m \times$ [base money]. The Federal Reserve cannot control M_1 directly. Instead, it must do so indirectly by buying or selling Treasury securities to manipulate the stock of base money. For example, if the Federal Reserve wants to raise M_1 by $100 and the money multiplier, m, is 10, it would need to buy $10 worth of Treasury securities to bring about the desired $100 increase.

The Federal Reserve can exercise reasonably close control over the supply of transactions balances by operating on the stock of base money, relying on a relatively predictable money multiplier to achieve the desired results on M_1. However, the rapid pace of financial innovation has made the task more difficult. First, growth of interest-bearing substitutes for demand deposits and currency has made M_1 a less accurate measure of total transactions balances; and second, growth of these substitutes is difficult to predict. Moreover, good data coverage is not yet available because not all financial institutions offering transactions balances are required to report to the Federal Reserve. Therefore, the Federal Reserve does not know whether to interpret a change in M_1 as a change in total transactions balances or simply a substitution by the public of some newly created short-term asset for demand deposits. This means that even if the money multiplier were to remain relatively stable, it would be difficult for the Federal Reserve to know how the stock of base money should be manipulated to affect total transactions balances because M_1 has become a less reliable measure of such balances.

Unfortunately, the money multiplier is not even invariant with respect to substitutions from demand deposits into other types of liquid assets. The reason is that current law requires banks to hold reserves against demand deposits (at graduated rates of 7 to 16¼ percent) that are higher than reserve requirements on demand deposit substitutes. Reserve requirements on NOW accounts, for example, are only 3 percent. This means that if depositors shift from demand deposits to NOW accounts or RPs, excess reserves are created which enable the financial system to expand loans and increase its deposit liabilities. In other words, the money multiplier (for an appropriate measure of transactions balances) can rise with a shift from demand deposits to NOW accounts or RPs because of the different reserve requirements on these liabilities. If reserve requirements on the substituted liabilities remain low, the money multiplier will become very large. A large multiplier is likely to have greater prediction error, and therefore is likely to make controlling money growth more difficult.

Even changes in the level of interest rates can induce changes in the money multiplier. Higher interest rates, for example, provide additional incentive for individuals and corporations to take advantage of interest-bearing substitutes for demand deposits. Compounding the problem is the fact that the short-run willingness of the public to substitute into interest-earning assets or alternative transactions balances is uncertain. The speed of substitution most likely depends, for example, on the time horizon over which individuals anticipate interest rates to remain high. Because average required reserves are decreased or increased as a result of these substitutions, the M_1 money multiplier can rise and fall with interest rates. However, because the degree of substitution is uncertain, so is the relationship between interest rates and the multiplier. Greater uncertainty about the multiplier makes it more difficult for the Federal Reserve to control M_1 through control of the monetary base.

The apparent weakening of Federal Reserve control over the volume of transactions balances has spawned a number of proposals for basic reform to improve the quality of the System's money control mechanism. A brief critique of those proposals designed to improve monetary control is presented in the sections that follow.

Extending the Coverage of Legal Reserve Requirements[6]

Shifts between deposit instruments with different reserve requirements account for much of the unpredictability in the money multiplier. Extending uniform reserve requirements to all transactions balances at commercial banks would therefore be useful in improving monetary control. However, if regulators continued to impose significantly lower reserve requirements on deposits held outside commercial banks, it would be of only limited value. Deposit institutions whose transactions-type accounts are nonreservable will be able to offer interest rates above those of institutions that must hold a larger portion of their funds in noninterest-earning required reserves. Nonreservable balances would therefore tend to drive reservable balances out of use. The resulting money multiplier between the stock of transactions balances and the monetary base would consequently be much higher. Controlling the stock of transactions balances with the monetary base would be more difficult, because each dollar error in controlling the base would then have a greater effect on the stock of transactions balances.

Radical expansion in the usual coverage of reserve requirements would appear to be necessary to eliminate different reserve requirements among potential transactions balances while at the same time preventing the money multiplier from increasing. The problem is to devise a law that would allow only those deposits not used as transactions balances to qualify as nonreservable. For example, the law might state that customer orders to transfer funds be

---

[6]Subsequent to the publication of this article, the proposals discussed in this section were enacted. Under the provisions of the Depository Institutions Deregulation and Monetary Control Act of 1980, uniform reserve requirements will be imposed on transaction accounts offered by *all* depository institutions. The requirements will be phased in during the 1980s. The Act also requires that interest rate ceilings be phased out by 1986. (Ed. footnote)

delayed at least a week for an account to qualify as nonreservable. But this rule might be circumvented by setting up revolving certificates maturing every eight days, so that one-eighth of the account could be transferred on any business day. This simple example illustrates the potential difficulty in enforcing a law requiring all balances used for transactions purposes to have the same reserve requirements as demand deposits.

Removal of Regulatory Ceilings on Interest Rates

If prohibitions against offering competitive rates of interest at depository institutions were eliminated, then interest rates on deposits at these institutions would tend to move more closely with the general level of interest rates. For example, interest differentials between deposits and other liquid assets such as money market mutual funds would become more stable. This would greatly reduce the incentive to switch from transactions type deposits to higher yielding liquid assets when interest rates rise.

Monetary control would be improved for two reasons as a result of this regulatory reform. First, because there would be less switching among liquid assets with changes in the level of interest rates, a given stock of bank reserves would produce a more stable basic money supply, M_1. Second, because the incentive for use of alternative types of transactions balances would be reduced, M_1 would become a more comprehensive measure of transactions balances. The Federal Reserve's data on transactions balances would become more reliable since it would not, as it currently does, depend on an estimate of the extent to which newly created liquid assets such as RPs or MMFs are being used as transactions balances.

Financial intermediation for banks involves longer maturities on assets than liabilities. Consequently, average returns on bank assets that provide income to pay interest on demand deposits change more slowly than short-term interest rates. Therefore, even if deposits were to pay interest, deposit rates may not move perfectly together with other short-term rates. However, the level of interest rates over longer periods of time varies largely because of changes in inflationary anticipations. The effect of anticipated inflation is reflected in all interest rates. Therefore, rates paid on demand deposits would move in line with other rates on a secular basis. As a result, paying interest on demand deposits would greatly improve the secular stability of the money multiplier and facilitate long-run monetary control.

Lowering the Long-run Rate of Money Growth

Since the rate of money growth is a major determinant of the long-run rate of inflation, the secular rate of inflation can be lowered if reasonably low secular money growth is maintained. A lower rate of inflation would reduce interest rates. As a result, incentives to substitute new forms of interest-bearing transactions balances for traditional demand deposits would be reduced, even if interest payments on the latter continue to be prohibited. The consequent reduction in financial innovation would greatly facilitate monetary control.

CONCLUSION

This article has highlighted some important causes and consequences of the rapid pace of financial innovation of recent years, especially as it relates to the nation's payments system. First, high market interest rates, different reserve requirements on various types of deposits, and legal restrictions on the payment of interest on demand deposits have together provided increased incentive for the market to create and use new kinds of deposit liabilities. Second, rapid development of computer and communications technology has contributed to this outcome. Third, regulators have allowed greater competition among financial institutions, thereby promoting more rapid innovation.

Because financial innovation involves creation of money substitutes, it causes problems for monetary control. In particular, difficulty in forecasting growth of demand deposit substitutes reduces the predictability of the money multiplier. In addition, since data on demand deposit substitutes are limited, it is hard to know the extent of their use, and consequently, it is hard to estimate the total stock of money.

Fortunately, reforms can ease this monetary control problem. The most important of these include extending the coverage of legal reserve requirements to all deposits used as payments balances and removing restrictions on interest payable on deposits. Adoption of these reforms should go a long way toward improving monetary control.

REFERENCES

1. "A Proposal for Redefining the Monetary Aggregates." Study by the staff of the Board of Governors of the Federal Reserve System, *Federal Reserve Bulletin* (January 1979), pp. 13-42.
2. Cagan, Phillip. "Financial Developments and the Erosion of Monetary Controls." Reprint from American Enterprise Institute, *Contemporary Economic Problems*, 1979.
3. Cook, Timothy Q., and Duffield, Jeremy G. "Money Market Mutual Funds: A Reaction to Government Regulation or a Lasting Financial

Innovation?" *Economic Review*, Federal Reserve Bank of Richmond (July/August 1979), pp. 15-31.

4. Kimball, Ralph C. "The Maturing of the NOW Account in New England," *New England Economic Review*, Federal Reserve Bank of Boston (July/August 1978), pp. 27-42.

5. Summers, Bruce J. "Demand Deposits: A Comparison of the Behavior of Household and Business Balances." *Economic Review*, Federal Reserve Bank of Richmond (July/August 1979), pp. 2-14.

SHORT-TERM INVESTMENT POOLS*

Timothy Q. Cook and
Jeremy G. Duffield

32

Over the last decade numerous types of short-term investment pooling arrangements (STIPs) have emerged in the nation's financial system. The most well-known and widely publicized form of STIP is the money market mutual fund (MMF). However, MMFs are only one of at least eight types of STIPs that were operating in the United States at the end of 1979. While the various types of STIPs differ in some respects, such as the kind of asset held or the type of investor, they are all alike in their basic function, which is to purchase large pools of short-term financial instruments and sell shares in these pools to investors. In almost all instances discussed in this article, the pool allows participants to invest a much smaller amount of money than would be necessary to directly purchase the individual securities held by the pool. This paper examines the STIP phenomenon.

SHORT-TERM INVESTMENT POOLS

Characteristics of different STIPs are summarized in Table 32-1. While all STIPs basically function as intermediaries for short-term securities, they can differ in several ways. First, some STIPs are open to a wide variety of investors while others cater only to a narrow group. Second, some STIPs hold many different

*Reprinted, with deletions and minor editorial revisions, from the *Economic Review*, September/October 1980, pp. 3-23, with permission of the Federal Reserve Bank of Richmond.

money market instruments while others confine their investment to one type of security. Third, some STIPs are "open-end" arrangements that allow investors to purchase and redeem shares of an everchanging pool of underlying securities. In other STIPs investors buy shares of a specific pool of securities. Other features that vary among STIPs include minimum investment size, expense ratios, and methods of investing and withdrawing funds.

Money Market Mutual Funds

Because MMFs were discussed in great detail in two earlier articles in this *Review* [4, 5], the discussion here will be brief. The general operating characteristics of MMFs are fairly standard. Minimum initial investments usually range from $500 to $5,000, although a very small number of funds require no minimum and others, designed for institutional investors, require minimums of $50,000 or more. With the exception of the small number of funds that limit their investors to institutions, MMF shares are available to any type of investor. Most funds have a checking option that enables shareholders to write checks of $500 or more. Shares can also be redeemed at most MMFs by telephone or wire request, in which case payment by the MMF is either mailed to the investor or remitted by wire to the investor's bank account.

MMFs are open-end investment companies that vary considerably in both the type and average maturity of securities they hold. A large percentage of most MMFs' holdings are in domestic and Eurodollar CDs, commercial paper and Treasury bills, but various other high grade money market instruments are also commonly purchased. A small number of MMFs have restricted their investments to government securities, apparently to attract more risk-averse investors, and an equally small number have invested very heavily in Eurodollar CDs.

Because MMFs are generally "no-load" mutual funds, investors purchase and redeem MMF shares without paying a sales charge. Instead, expenses of the funds are deducted daily from gross income before dividends are declared. The difference between the yield earned on a MMF's assets and the yield earned by the shareholders is the MMF's expense ratio. (Alternatively, this can be measured as the ratio of total expenses on an annual basis to average assets.) In 1978 the expense ratio for different MMFs ranged from .4 percent to 1.4 percent [4]. The weighted average expense ratio for the industry as a whole was .55 in 1979.

The first MMF started offering shares to the public in 1972. By the end of 1974 there were 15 MMFs and by the end of 1979, 76 were in operation. Total MMF assets at the end of 1979 were $45.2 billion.[1]

---

[1]In early 1981, MMF assets exceeded $115 billion. (Ed. footnote)

Short-Term Tax-Exempt Funds

Short-term tax-exempt funds (STEFs) are the tax-exempt counterpart to MMFs. STEFs invest primarily in securities issued by state and local governments ("municipals"), which pay interest-income that is exempt from Federal income taxes. The first short-term tax-exempt fund offered shares to the public in 1977 and several others were formed in 1979. By mid-1980 there were at least 10 STEFs operating with combined assets of over one-and-a-half-billion dollars.

As a result of the type of financial assets they purchase, STEFs appeal to investors in high Federal income tax brackets. More specifically, an investor facing the choice between two investments that are alike in every respect except that one offers a yield that is subject to Federal income taxes, Y_T, while the other's yield is tax-free, Y_{TF}, will choose the alternative that offers the highest after-tax return. That is, the investor will choose the tax-free investment option if $Y_{TF} > Y_T(1-t)$, where t is the investor's marginal Federal income tax rate. Thus, by examining the ratio of short-term tax-exempt yields to short-term taxable yields it is possible to determine at what minimum marginal tax rate an investor would be better off investing in a STEF than in a MMF. While this ratio varies considerably over time, available evidence suggests that an investor probably has to have a marginal Federal tax rate of more than 50 percent to achieve a higher after-tax yield in a STEF than in a MMF.[2]

While after-tax yield comparisons might indicate that an investor with a very high marginal tax rate would be better off in a STEF than in a MMF, one major qualification must be added. Largely because of the small quantity of very short-term municipal securities available for purchase, STEF portfolios have generally been of longer average maturity than MMF portfolios. To the extent that STEF portfolios have longer maturities than MMF portfolios, the variation in the STEF's share price and in the STEF investor's principal will be somewhat greater than for MMF shares. For some investors this may lessen the relative attractiveness of STEFs.

---

[2]The ratio of short-term tax-exempt to short-term taxable yields varied from .421 to .492 in 1979 [8]. This implies that a marginal tax rate of somewhere between 50.8 percent and 57.9 percent would have been necessary to make an investor indifferent between the choice of taxable and tax-exempt instruments if no costs were associated with investment. If both the MMF and the STEF had the same expense ratio, ER, the true marginal tax rate which leaves the investor indifferent is

$$1 - \frac{Y_{TF} - ER}{Y_T - ER}$$

which implies that an even higher marginal tax bracket is necessary to make the STEF the preferable alternative.

Table 32-1 Characteristics of short-term investment pools

STIF	Year first one started	Type of investors	Minimum investment	Assets	Maturity end of 1979	Type of pool	Redemption methods	Annualized expense ratio (basis points)
Money market funds	1972	anyone	$1,000 to $5,000 is most common; some funds for institutions require $50,000 or more	wide range	weighted average maturity of 34 days	open-end	wire, check-writing, mail	weighted average ratio of .55
Short-term Tax-exempt funds	1977	investors desiring income free of Federal taxes	varies from $1,000 to $25,000	tax-exempt securities	120 to 150 days	open-end	wire, check-writing, mail	similar to MMF expenses
Short-term Investment funds	1968(?)	accounts of bank trust department	negligible	wide range; mostly commercial paper	n.a.; by regulation very short	open-end	daily transfer on request	n.a.
Local government Investment pools	1973	state and local government bodies	usually none	wide range	varies greatly (see text)	open-end	wire, checks in some cases (usually 24 hours notice needed for withdrawals of greater than $1 million)	

Name	Year	Who	Minimum	Assets	Maturity	Type	Redemption	Expense
Credit union pools	1968	credit unions	n.a.	mainly Treasury bills and Federal agencies	varies	open-end	wire, draft	n.a.
Short-term Investment trusts	1974	anyone	$1,000	primarily Eurodollar CDs	6 months	unit investment trust	funds returned at maturity; can sell prior to subject to a charge	1.40
Shares in bills	n.a.	anyone	$1,000	Treasury bills	3 or 6 months	similar to unit investment trust	funds returned at end of 3- or 6-month investment; can sell prior to maturity subject to a charge	varies inversely with maturity and with size of investment; expense ratio for a $5,000 investment in 6-month bill would be 90

In order to minimize the perceived problem of a varying price share, most STEFs have opted, like most MMFs, to maintain an average maturity of 120 days or less in order to gain exemptive orders from the Securities and Exchange Commission permitting the use of accounting policies that should enable the maintenance of a constant net asset value.

As a means of achieving shorter average maturities, some STEFs have retained the right to use a "put option" technique. Under this arrangement, the fund would purchase municipal securities, often at a higher price (lower yield) than it would normally pay for these securities, at the same time acquiring the right or option to sell the securities back to the seller at an agreed-upon price on a certain date or within a specified period in the future. The primary advantage of this technique is that it may allow the fund to tailor a shorter-term portfolio. The major disadvantage is that the fund is dependent on the ability and willingness of the seller to buy back the securities. Furthermore, there are also thorny legal issues yet to be resolved, such as the appropriate method of valuing securities purchased under put options and the tax status of securities purchased under put options.

Unlike the yield curve for taxable securities, the yield curve for municipals is almost always upward-sloping throughout the entire range of maturities, i.e., a higher yield is paid for securities of longer maturity. Consequently, the tradeoff encountered in trying to maintain a very short average maturity in a municipal portfolio is generally a lower yield on the portfolio. For this reason some STEFs retain the option of holding an average maturity of one year or over.

Short-Term Investment Funds

Short-term investment funds (STIFs) are collective investment funds operated by bank trust departments. A collective investment fund is an arrangement whereby the monies of different accounts in the trust department are pooled to purchase a certain type of security, such as common stocks, corporate bonds, or, in the case of STIFs, short-term securities. The first STIF was started no later than 1968.[3] By the end of 1974 there were over 70 STIFs with total assets of $2.7 billion. STIF assets grew rapidly in 1978 and 1979 and by the end of 1979 total STIF assets were over $32 billion.

STIFs function just like MMFs and offer the same advantages to the accounts of the trust department. In particular, the minimum investment is usually a negligible amount and funds can be put in and withdrawn without transaction fees.

That STIFs and MMFs provide virtually the same services to their customers is illustrated by the fact that many trust departments use MMFs rather

---

[3]This is the earliest date for which the authors are aware of the existence of a STIF. It is possible that other STIFs were formed prior to 1968.

than establish STIFs. The decision to set up a STIF or to use a MMF for its customers' short-term assets is largely dependent on the size of the trust department. The larger the trust department, the more likely it is to have a STIF. Most bank trust departments without STIFs use MMFs.[4]

Both the type and maturity of assets held by STIFs reflect the Comptroller of the Currency's Regulations on the portfolios of STIFs. The two key regulations are that:

1. at least 80 percent of investments must be payable on demand or have a maturity not exceeding 91 days, and
2. not less than 40 percent of the value of the fund must be cash, demand obligations, and assets that mature on the fund's next business day.

As a result of these regulations, STIFs hold a substantial amount of variable amount notes (also called master notes), which are a type of open-ended commercial paper that allows the investment and withdrawal of funds on a daily basis and pays a daily interest rate tied to the current commercial paper rate. In addition, STIFs hold a large amount of standard commercial paper and a much smaller amount of time and savings deposits and Treasury securities. A very small number of STIFs invest primarily in short-term tax-exempt securities.

Typically, only the audit expenses of STIFs are charged directly against the income earned by the STIFs and it is only this expense that appears in the STIF annual report. Other expenses are covered by fees charged to the accounts of the trust department. Consequently, it is impossible to calculate the expense ratio of STIFs from published reports.

Local Government Investment Pools

Local government investment pools (LGIPs) were in operation in eleven states by the end of 1979.[5] These pools have been set up to enable local government entities (such as counties, cities, school districts, etc., and in all but two states, state agencies) to purchase shares in a large portfolio of money market instruments. The primary purpose of state legislation establishing the pools has been to encourage efficient management of idle funds.

---

[4]Cook and Duffield [4] argue that the explanation for the use of MMFs by small- and medium-sized bank trust departments is that both MMFs and STIFs are subject to decreasing average costs as assets increase. Consequently, a small- or medium-sized bank trust department can get a higher yield net of expenses for its accounts by investing in a MMF than by setting up a relatively small STIF. It should also be noted that some agency accounts of bank trust departments are not eligible to invest in STIFs but may invest in MMFs.

[5]These states are California, Connecticut, Florida, Illinois, Massachusetts, Montana, New Jersey, Oregon, Utah, West Virginia, and Wisconsin. In addition, legislation was recently passed in Oklahoma providing for the creation of a LGIP.

Since many local government bodies have relatively small sums of money to invest, they would seem to benefit most from LGIPs. However, in many LGIPs the majority of assets represent state funds. Surprisingly, through 1979 only a small percentage of eligible local government bodies were investing in the pools. Duncan [6] reports that in July 1979 the percentage of eligible participants contributing to LGIPs ranged from less than 1 percent in Illinois to 35 percent in Massachusetts.

Except for the LGIPs of Massachusetts and Illinois, the pools are administered by the state treasurer's office, often in conjunction with the state investment board and a local government advisory council. The Illinois pool is administered by a bank trust department, while the Massachusetts LGIP is run by an investment management firm.

In most respects, the operating characteristics of LGIPs are identical to those of MMFs. Funds may be invested by wire or check and withdrawn either by telephone request, with payment sent by wire, or in some cases by check. Funds may generally be invested and withdrawn on a daily basis, although several LGIPs require 24 hours' notice prior to the withdrawal of $1 million or more. While there are usually no minimum investment or withdrawal constraints, small transactions are often informally discouraged. Interest is earned daily, except in one LGIP which distributes income quarterly.

The pools invest in a broad range of securities many of which would not be legally available to the participants if they invested their funds individually. That is, many LGIP participants are legally prohibited from directly investing in some of the types of securities which the pool is authorized to purchase.

LGIPs in different states have followed widely different maturity strategies. Whereas at the end of December 1979, the longest average maturity of any MMF was less than three months, several LGIP portfolios had average maturities in the one- to three-year range. Others maintained average maturities as short as those of MMFs.

Credit Union Pools

Two short-term pools have been established for the investment of surplus funds of credit unions. The government securities pool of the Credit Union National Association (CUNA), a service organization representing more than 90 percent of the 22,000 credit unions in the U. S., represents one of the nation's earliest short-term pooling arrangements, having commenced operations in 1968. This pool had over $1 billion in assets and more than 10,000 participating credit unions at year-end 1979. The other pool was created in 1976 by the National Association of Federal Credit Unions (NAFCU).

Both pools are operated as common trust funds by bank trust departments. In most respects they are identical to other open-end STIPs. Investments and withdrawals may be made daily. Participating credit unions may request withdrawals by telephone with funds remitted by wire or they may write a draft on their pool account and deposit it at their commercial bank. Drafts may not be used for third-party payment.

CUNA's pool invests solely in U. S. Government and Federal agency securities. The average maturity of its portfolio was seven-and-one-half-months at the end of 1979. The NAFCU pool can invest in any type of security eligible for purchase by a Federal credit union. Thus, in addition to U. S. Government securities, the pool may purchase domestic certificates of deposit but is prohibited from investing in Eurodollar CDs, commercial paper and bankers acceptances. The NAFCU pool has maintained a very short average maturity, 30 days at the end of 1979.

Short-Term Investment Trusts

Short-term investment trusts (STITs), or short-term income trusts, are a type of unit investment trust that invests exclusively in short-term financial instruments. These funds are put together by groups of brokers that sell shares in units of $1,000 to their retail customers. Unlike MMF shares, these shares represent a claim to part of a specific set of securities. Hence, when these securities mature, the fund is terminated. The first eight series of STITs were sold in 1974, all by one broker group. No more STITs were sold until September 1978 when the same broker group again began to offer STITs. A second broker group began to market STITs in January 1979. From September 1978 through the end of 1979, 47 separate series of STITs totalling $6.1 billion were sold to the public. At the end of 1979 there were 35 series of STITs outstanding with total assets of $4.6 billion.

The maturity of all but two of the STIT series sold through 1979 was six months. The assets of the STITs put together by the first broker group have been composed of (1) CDs of foreign branches of U.S. Banks, (2) CDs of foreign banks, (3) CDs of U.S. branches of foreign banks, and (4) CDs of domestic banks. Of these, the first two categories, which are "Eurodollar CDs," comprised 72.1 percent of the total assets of the STITs offered by this group in 1979. The second broker group has generally included in their STITs only CDs of foreign branches (specifically, London branches) of domestic banks.

On an annualized basis the expense ratios of the STIT series sold in 1979 generally ranged from 140 to 150 basis points.[6] (This is calculated as the sales charge plus expenses of the Fund divided by the offering price and annualized.) This calculation assumes that the STIT share is held to maturity. The share

---

[6]The term "expense ratio" is used broadly here to encompass all expenses, including sales charges, that lower the investor's net yield. There are two possible reasons why the STIT expense ratio is higher than the MMF expense ratio. First, the labor expenses of a STIT may be greater because it requires a large network of dealers to actively market the STIT shares. Second, the size of the average STIT is much smaller than the size of the average MMF, so that MMFs may benefit more from economies of scale.

can be sold prior to maturity subject to an additional charge, in which case the investor's effective ratio would be somewhat higher.

Other Types of STIPS

In addition to the six types of STIPs discussed so far, there are a small number of STIPs for which data were not collected for this article. These fall into two categories.

Shares-in-bills.   One organization of brokers and dealers has established a program whereby investors can purchase shares in specific three- and six-month Treasury bills. From the investor's point of view, this program is similar to a unit investment trust that invests exclusively in bills. The minimum purchase requirement is $1,000. According to the program's advertising literature, it has been in operation since 1969. However, only recently has the program been widely advertised, suggesting that it was relatively insignificant prior to 1979.[7]

The annualized expense ratio of a bill purchased through the program is inversely related to the size and maturity of the investment. An investment of $5,000 in a three-month bill has an annualized expense ratio of 120 basis points while a $5,000 investment in a six-month bill has an expense ratio of 90 basis points.

Other-open-end-STIPs.   Lastly, at least one other type of financial intermediary—life insurance companies—is already operating open-end STIPs and a second—savings and loan associations—will probably begin to do so in the early 1980s. Life insurance companies provide investment services of various types of thrift and pension plans. In the past, insurance companies have offered these plans such alternatives as investing in commingled bond or stock accounts. Recently, some life insurance companies have also begun to offer short-term investment commingled accounts.[8]

The Depository Institutions Deregulation and Monetary Control Act of 1980 gives federal savings and loan associations the authority to provide trust services. As noted above, most small- and moderate-sized bank trust departments use MMFs while large trust departments generally set up their own STIFs. The savings and loan associations who compete in the market for trust services will have these same options. It is probable that some of the larger

---

[7]Interestingly, unlike a STIT, the shares-in-bills program is not organized as an investment company. Hence, no prospectus or annual report is published and no information on the size of the program is readily available. The authors were unable to get this information from the sponsor.

[8]The authors became aware of the existence of life insurance company STIPs late in the preparation of this article. Consequently, no attempt was made to gather data for this type of STIP.

associations will establish their own short-term investment pooling arrangements.

STIP Growth and Percentage Holdings of Various Money Market Instruments

The growth of assets of each type of short-term investment pool and the growth of aggregate STIP assets from 1974 through 1979 is shown in Table 32-2. Total STIP assets grew rapidly in the high interest rate period of 1974. Asset growth leveled off in 1976, when interest rates reached a cyclical trough, and accelerated sharply from 1977 through 1979, a period of rising interest rates. Almost all types of STIPs participated in this rapid growth. Assets of the six types of STIPs for which data were available totaled $88.5 billion at the end of 1979. MMFs held slightly over half of this total. Table 32-2 confirms the fact that STIPs have become a significant intermediary in the financial system.

FINANCIAL MARKET IMPLICATIONS OF STIPS

Before considering the financial market implications of STIPs, it is necessary to review the three short-term investment options available to investors prior to the emergence of STIPs. First, they could hold deposits in a bank or other financial intermediary. These deposits generally required little or no minimum investment, but were subject to Regulation Q interest rate ceilings that were frequently below market interest rates. The second option was purchase of Treasury bills, which has required a minimum of $10,000 since early 1969. The third option was purchase of private sector money market instruments, such as CDs, commercial paper, or bankers acceptances. These securities are generally only available in minimum denominations of $100,000, although a few issuers will sell commercial paper in amounts as small as $25,000 and bankers acceptances less than $100,000 are sometimes issued.

In this environment investors could be divided into three groups by the amount of funds they had to invest in short-term financial instruments. One group with less than $10,000 had access only to small denomination time and savings deposits. A second group with $10,000 but less than $100,000 had the additional option of purchasing Treasury bills. The final group with at least $100,000 could also invest in private sector money market instruments.

The fundamental importance of STIPs is that they have made this distinction among investors largely meaningless. Because all forms of STIPs have minimum purchase requirements as low as $1,000 and sometimes lower, all three investment options are effectively available to all types of investors, regardless of the amount of short-term funds at their disposal. This increased access to the money market through STIPs has several implications for the financial markets which are discussed below.

Table 32-2 Assets and numbers of various forms of STIPs (end-of-year)

	Money market funds		Short-term tax-exempt funds		Short-term investment funds[1]		Local government investment pools		Credit union pools		Short-term investment trusts		Total assets
	Assets ($ mil.)	Number (funds)	Assets ($ mil.)	Number (funds)	Assets ($ mil.)	Number (funds)	Assets ($ mil.)	Number (states)	Assets ($ mil.)	Number (pools)	Assets ($ mil.)	Number (sponsors)	($ mil.)
1974	1,715	15			2,660	73	394	4	1,224	1	846	1	6,839
1975	3,696	36			3,986	102	890	4	1,947	1		0	10,519
1976	3,686	48			3,427	92	2,034	6	1,816	2		0	10,963
1977	3,888	50	2	1	8,409	136	3,044	10	1,151	2		0	16,494
1978	10,858	61	30	1	25,125	na	3,845	11	1,074	2	665	1	41,597
1979	45,214	76	350	3	32,227	251[2]	4,779	11	1,237	2	4,614	2	88,471
Sources:	Investment Company Institute		data gathered by authors from funds		Common Trust Fund Surveys; ABA Collective Investment Funds Survey Report (1978)		data gathered by authors from funds		data gathered by authors from funds		prospectuses		

[1] The STIF data for 1978 is year-end data from a special American Bankers Association, Collective Investment Funds Survey Report. The STIF data for 1974–77 is from the Common Trust Fund Survey. Prior to 1979, the Survey was conducted by the Comptroller of the Currency. Banks that were not national banks reported on a voluntary basis and there appear to be a number of large trust departments not reporting in those years. In addition, assets were reported prior to year-end by some banks. Hence, the 1974–77 data should be regarded as estimates which are on the low side. In 1979 the Common Trust Fund Survey was incorporated into the Trust Assets of Insured Commercial Banks survey conducted jointly by the Comptroller of the Currency, the Federal Deposit Insurance Corporation, and the Federal Reserve Board. The 1979 data is year-end and covers all trust departments.

[2] These 251 STIFs were operated by a total of 155 bank trust departments and 5 trust companies owned by bank holding companies.

The Impact of STIPs on the Administration
of Regulation Q Interest Rate Ceilings

Deposit rate ceilings under Regulation Q originated with the Banking Act of 1933 and were initially applied only to rates paid on commercial bank time and savings deposits. The purpose was to prevent "excessive" rate competition for deposits among banks that might encourage risky loan and investment policies, thereby leading to bank failures. The passage of the Interest Adjustment Act in 1966 expanded the coverage of deposit interest rate ceilings to thrift institutions.

The implicit assumptions underlying Regulation Q through the mid-1970s was that most deposit holders were relatively small investors who were locked into deposits as the only available short-term investment option. As a result, if market rates were to rise above fixed Regulation Q ceilings rates, there would not be a massive flight of funds out of the deposit institutions in 1973 and 1974, when short-term market interest rates rose to levels over twice as high as the Regulation Q ceiling rate on these deposits. While the growth of savings deposits slowed markedly during this period, total savings deposits actually increased despite the huge positive differential between market rates and Regulation Q ceiling rates.

The emergence of STIPs, by providing *access* to money market yields to virtually all investors, severely damaged the ability of the deposit institutions to raise funds at below market interest rates. As a result, after interest rates began to rise above Regulation Q ceiling rates in 1977, regulators fundamentally altered the application of Regulation Q. This alteration came in June 1978 when the Regulation Q ceiling rate on six-month deposit certificates ("money market certificates") was tied to the six-month Treasury bill rate. Subsequently, Regulation Q ceiling rates on four-year and then 2½-year deposit certificates were also tied to market rates of comparable maturity U. S. Government securities.

One suggested response to the emergence of STIPs as a competitor to the deposit institutions was to expand the coverage of Regulation Q ceiling rates to MMFs. That response ignores the many other forms of STIPs that are either perfect or close substitutes to MMFs. If binding Regulation Q ceiling rates were placed on MMFs, the major effect would probably simply be to shift funds from MMFs to other forms of STIPs. For instance, for bank trust departments STIFs are virtually perfect substitutes for MMFs. If Regulation Q ceilings were placed on MMFs, many bank trust departments that now use MMFs would start STIFs. Similarly for many individuals STITs are close substitutes for MMFs. If Regulation Q ceilings were imposed on MMFs, many individuals would undoubtedly shift their funds out of MMFs into STITs. As a result STITs would probably develop for additional types of money market instruments, such as commercial paper.

The Depository Institutions Deregulation and Monetary Control Act of 1980 calls for a total phase-out of deposit interest rate ceilings over a six-year period. Developments other than the growth of STIPs, such as changing regulatory attitudes, may have also played a part in the decision to end fixed deposit interest rate ceilings. However, the view taken here is that even without these other factors, STIPs would have led to the termination of deposit rate ceilings.

The Impact of STIPs on Short-Term Yield Spreads

Figure 32-1 shows the spread between the three-month prime CD rate and the three-month Treasury bill rate. The figure shows that the spread between the CD rate and the bill rate has risen in periods when market interest rates have been high relative to Regulation Q ceiling rates, such as 1969, 1973, and 1974.

To understand this relationship it is useful to focus on the three investor categories described above, especially the group with sufficient funds to buy bills but not other money market instruments. When interest rates are above Regulation Q ceilings, many deposit holders with sufficient funds withdraw these funds from deposit institutions (i.e., "disintermediate") to invest them directly in higher-yielding money market instruments. Prior to the late 1970s the bulk of such investment was directed towards Treasury bills, because of the much larger minimum amounts of funds required to purchase private-sector money market instruments such as CDs and commercial paper.

The massive purchases of Treasury bills by individuals in periods of disintermediation has driven down bill rates relative to the rates on other money market instruments. This phenomenon had its peak effect in mid-1974 when the spread between private sector money market rates and bill rates reached

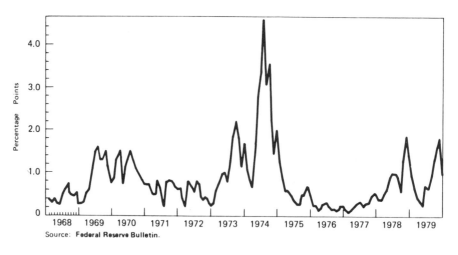

Figure 32-1   The spread between the three-month CD and Treasury bill rates

a level as high as 400 basis points. The inability of most individuals to meet the minimum purchase requirements necessary to acquire private-sector money market instruments prevented them from reducing this large differential by switching their purchases from bills to these instruments.[9]

The rapid growth of STIPs in the late 1970s (along with the introduction of floating Regulation Q ceiling rates on 6-month money market certificates) has fundamentally changed this situation, because STIPs have effectively broken down the minimum investment barriers that have prevented many individuals from acquiring money market instruments other than Treasury bills. In periods of rising spreads between private sector rates and bill rates, the yields earned by most STIPs will rise relative to the yield on bills. In these circumstances households and all other investors have the option of switching out of bills into STIPs. Furthermore, most STIPs are highly sensitive to yield spreads. Consequently, the aggregate substitution of private-sector money market instruments for bills in periods of rising spreads should be greater than in the past. As a result the presence of STIPs should prevent the spread between bill rates and private sector money market rates from ever again reaching the levels of 1974. The evidence to date provides some support for this view. As shown in Figure 32-1, in the 1978-79 period of rising interest rates the spread between the CD and Treasury bill rates rose only moderately despite a high increase in the spread between market rates and the passbook savings ceiling rate.

SUMMARY

Over the last decade numerous types of short-term investment pooling arrangements have emerged in the nation's financial system. These pooling arrangements allow participants to invest a much smaller amount of money than would be necessary to directly purchase the individual securities held by the pool. While the first STIPs were started as early as 1968, rapid growth in STIPs did not occur until 1974. Aggregate assets of STIPs surged from a small amount at the beginning of 1974 to $88 billion by the end of 1979.

---

[9]This explanation for the spread between bill rates and other money market rates prior to the late 1970s along with data on Treasury bill purchases is given in detail in Cook [3]. The explanation rests critically on the fact that sectors other than household—such as commercial banks and state and local governments—have been willing to hold bills despite large spreads between bill and other money market rates. This willingness occurs because for numerous reasons other money market instruments are not viewed as perfect substitutes for bills by these sectors. For instance, banks have used bills to (1) satisfy pledging requirements for state and Federal deposits, (2) satisfy reserve requirements in some cases, (3) make repurchase agreements with businesses and state and local governments, and (4) influence the ratio of equity to risky assets, a ratio used by bank regulators to judge a bank's capital adequacy. Private sector money market instruments, such as commercial paper, are not perfect substitutes for bills for any of these purposes.

Because STIPs generally have minimum purchase requirements of $1,000 or even lower, they provide access to the money market to virtually all investors. This increased access to the money market has had several implications for the financial markets. First, by providing small investors an alternative to deposits, STIPs have played a major role in forcing the termination of Regulation Q deposit rate ceilings. Second, STIPs have increased the liquidity associated with a given volume of outstanding money market instruments. As a result the shares of one type of STIP—MMFs—were included in a redefinition of the monetary aggregates in 1980. For consistency, the shares of other types of STIPs should also be included in the monetary aggregates. Third, the presence of STIPs has increased the aggregate substitution from Treasury bills to other money market instruments in periods of widened differentials between private money market rates and bill rates. This increased substitution should prevent the spread between private money market rates and bill rates from rising to past peak levels.

REFERENCES

1. American Bankers Association. *Trust Software Buyers Guide*. Washington, D.C., 1979.
2. Benston, George J., and Smith, Clifford W., Jr. "A Transactions Cost Approach to the Theory of Financial Intermediation." *Journal of Finance*, XXXI (May 1976): 215–231.
3. Cook, Timothy. "The Determinants of Spreads Between Treasury Bill and Other Money Market Rates." *Journal of Economics and Business*, forthcoming.
4. _____ , and Duffield, Jeremy G. "Average Costs of Money Market Mutual Funds." *Economic Review*, Federal Reserve Bank of Richmond (July/August 1979).
5. _____ , "Money Market Mutual Funds: A Reaction to Government Regulations or a Lasting Financial Innovation?" *Economic Review*, Federal Reserve Bank of Richmond (July/August 1979).
6. Duncan, Harley T. "Local Government Investment Pools: Potential Benefits for Texas Local Governments." *Public Affairs Comment*, Lyndon B. Johnson School of Public Affairs, The University of Texas at Austin (August 1978).
7. Dunham, Constance. "The Growth of Money Market Funds." *New England Economic Review* (September/October 1980).
8. Public Securities Association. *Municipal Market Developments*. New York, February 6, 1980.

RECENT DEVELOPMENTS AT BANKS AND NONBANK DEPOSITORY INSTITUTIONS*

Daniel J. Vrabac†

33

The methods used by financial intermediaries to channel funds from savers to borrowers have been affected significantly in recent years by inflation, fluctuations in interest rates, two recessions, and the ongoing deregulation of depository institutions. During this time, the banking industry has shown itself capable of adapting to an increasingly uncertain and complex operating environment. This article describes developments in the industry that allowed it to achieve reasonable success despite the generally unfavorable economic environment.

The article first reviews the economic environment of the past several years, with particular emphasis on the 1979-82 period. Against this backdrop, the changes in commercial bank deposits, earning assets, and profitability are discussed. These changes are then compared with changes that have occurred at thrift institutions. The article concludes by discussing some possible explanations for the relatively better performance of banks, and then examines the outlook for banks and thrifts.

*Reprinted from the *Economic Review*, July/August 1983, pp. 33–45, with permission of the Federal Reserve Bank of Kansas City.

†Daniel J. Vrabac was a research associate with the Economic Research Department at the Federal Reserve Bank of Kansas City when this article was written. The author wishes to thank Karlyn Mitchell for her helpful comments during preparation of the article.

THE ENVIRONMENT

The financial environment that affected the strategies of all depository institutions during 1979-82 was shaped primarily by macroeconomic conditions, monetary policy, and the deregulation of depository institutions.

Macroeconomic Conditions

The turbulent 1979-82 period was characterized by recession, double-digit inflation, and high and volatile interest rates. January 1980 and July 1981 marked the beginnings of the seventh and eighth recessions since World War II. The first was the shortest recession in the postwar era, while the second was much longer and more severe. Adjusted for inflation, GNP did not grow at all between 1979 and 1982. Industrial production increased only slightly and at times declined. Inflation, which reached 13.3 percent in 1979 after the second OPEC price shock, averaged 9.6 percent for the period as a whole. Interest rates, which tend to decline during recessions and rise with expectations of higher inflation, fluctuated widely between 1979 and 1982. As Figure 33-1 shows, interest rates declined sharply in the second quarter of 1980 following the onset of the recession. The economy recovered quickly, however, and by the fourth quarter of 1980 interest rates had climbed above their prerecession

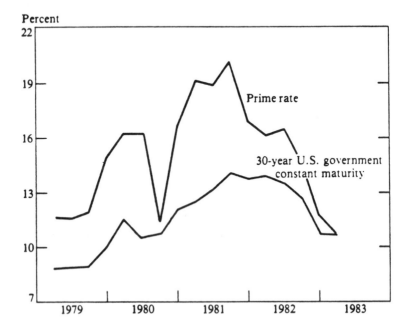

Figure 33-1 Selected interest rates

peaks, where they remained at double-digit levels until the third quarter of 1982. Deepening recession and lower expected inflation then combined to bring interest rates back to somewhat more normal levels.

The turbulence of this four-year period stands in marked contrast to the previous four years when economic conditions were generally more stable. The economy turned upward after the severe recession of 1973-75 and the impact of the first OPEC oil price shock was absorbed. Industrial production increased at an annual average rate of nearly 7.5 percent in the 1975-78 period as long-term borrowing for durable good purchases and capital expenditures increased. Inflation averaged less than 7 percent a year, while short-term Treasury rates averaged 5.8 percent and long-term Treasury rates averaged 8.1 percent.

Monetary Policy

Throughout most of the 1979-82 period, monetary policy sought to achieve a reduction in inflation. To meet this objective, the Federal Reserve switched its operating procedure in October 1979 from targeting short-term interest rates to targeting reserves. Controlling reserves to gradually reduce the growth of the monetary and credit aggregates, it was reasoned, would lead to a reduction in inflation. The new operating procedures facilitated better monetary control, and by mid-1982 there was a substantial lowering of inflation.

The new operating procedure, however, lent an element of uncertainty to the financial environment. Under the old procedure, the Federal Reserve influenced market interest rates by limiting movements in the federal funds rate. Stability of the federal funds rate, in turn, led to stability in both short and long-term interest rates and to more certainty in financial markets. Under the new procedure, close control of reserves can lead to wide shifts in interest rates. Greater volatility in interest rates, in turn, complicates the management of asset and liability portfolios for depository institutions by making future rates of return on financial assets less predictable.

Deregulation

Commercial banks traditionally have been the primary suppliers of short- and medium-term credit to businesses, while thrift institutions have been the primary suppliers of long-term housing credit to consumers. This specialization worked well when prices were stable, yield curves were upward sloping, and the economy was growing. The turbulence of the 1970s, however, revealed the weaknesses of such specialized institutions. The need for change in financial institutions was first put forth by the Commission on Money and Credit and by the Heller Committee in the early 1960s, followed by the Hunt Commission report in the early 1970s, and the Financial Institutions Act (FIA) of 1975. Few changes were made, however, until passage of the Depository Institutions Deregulation and Monetary Control Act (DIDMCA) in 1980. The DIDMCA included many of the provisions first recommended by the Hunt Commission and the FIA. Table 33-1 provides a brief history of deregulatory actions.

The DIDMCA altered the competitive balance between depository institutions by changing the rules of the game for all institutions. First, reserve requirements, previously imposed only on banks that were members of the Federal Reserve System, were imposed on all institutions accepting deposits. Reserve ratios for member banks were to be gradually reduced while ratios for

Table 33-1   Regulatory developments

1972	NOW accounts were authorized for thrift institutions in Massachusetts. In the next few years, all New England thrifts were allowed to issue NOWs.
1973	The wild card experiment: The first use of ceiling-free, small denomination certificates of deposit. The certificate had a minimum maturity of four years; the experiment lasted four months. All depository institutions were allowed to participate.
1975	California state-chartered savings and loans were authorized to issue variable-rate mortgages. At the same time, a few national banks in California began to issue variable-rate mortgages.
1978	6-month money market certificates were authorized nationally for all depository institutions. California federally chartered savings and loans were authorized to issue variable-rate mortgages.
1980	Authorization of the 2 1/2-year small saver certificate for all depository institutions. Passage of the DIDMCA: Extension of reserve requirements to all depository institutions. Creation of the DIDC. Allowed thrifts to invest 20 percent of assets in consumer loans. Allowed mutual savings banks to make business loans and accept business deposits.
1981	Introduction of nationwide NOW accounts. Introduction of the ceiling-free Individual Retirement Account. Introduction of the tax-exempt All Savers certificate of deposit.
1982	Several new accounts paying market-related rates were introduced: 91-day money market certificate 3 1/2-year ceiling-free deposit. 7-to-31 day time deposit. Passage of the Garn-St. Germain Act: Capital assistance for ailing thrifts. Authorization of the money market deposit account. Increase allowable consumer loan percentage at thrifts to 30 percent. Authorized savings and loans to issue business loans and accept business deposits.
1983	Introduction of the Super NOW accounts. Lowering of minimum deposit on short-term certificates of deposit to $2,500. Elimination of ceiling rates on remaining time deposits.

other depository institutions were to be increased until reserve ratios at all institutions were equal. By imposing uniform reserve requirements on all depository institutions, the Act removed the penalty member banks pay by having to keep more of their assets in noninterest-earning reserves.

The Act also called for the gradual phasing out of interest-rate ceilings on deposits and the creation of the Depository Institutions Deregulation Committee (DIDC) to oversee the phaseout. The committee was charged with administering differences between banks and thrifts, determining the rates that could be paid on existing accounts, and establishing new types of accounts.

To help prop up the ailing thrift industry, the DIDMCA gave thrifts broader asset powers. They were authorized to invest up to 20 percent of their assets in consumer loans, commercial paper, and corporate debt securities. Mutual savings banks could make business loans up to 5 percent of their assets and accept business deposits.

The Garn-St. Germain Act passed in the fall of 1982 further broadened the asset powers of thrifts. Authorization to make business loans and accept business deposits was extended to savings and loans. Beginning in 1984, thrifts can increase business loans from 5 percent of assets to 10 percent. The percentage of consumer loans allowed at thrift institutions was increased from 20 percent of assets to 30 percent. Most important, the Act authorized a new deposit account at banks and thrifts, the money market deposit account, to compete with the money market mutual funds.

THE BANKING INDUSTRY

Against the background of turbulent financial developments, a number of important changes took place in commercial bank deposits, earning assets, and profits during the 1979-82 period. Moreover, the comparative performance of banks and other depository institutions varied widely.

Deposits at Commercial Banks

Total deposits at commercial banks grew from $870 billion at the end of 1978 to $1,210 billion at the end of 1982 (Figure 33-2), an average annual increase of 8.7 percent.[1] Although less than the 9.2 percent average increase for 1975-78, deposit growth held up remarkably well considering the volatility of the economic environment. As interest rates began rising in 1978, commercial banks faced tremendous competition for deposit funds from nondepository institutions, especially money market mutual funds. The competition centered on savings and demand deposits, traditionally the main sources of funds at

---

[1]Total deposits include demand deposits, other checkable deposits, overnight repurchase agreements, term repurchase agreements, regular savings accounts, small time deposits, large time deposits, and money market deposit accounts.

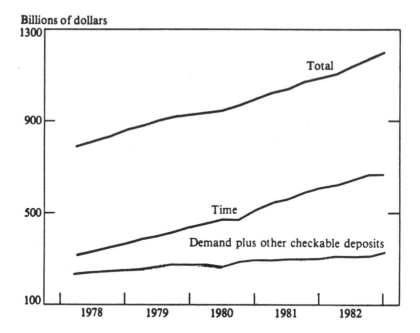

Figure 33-2   Deposit growth at commercial banks

commercial banks. That total deposit growth slowed as little as it did between 1979 and 1982 is due partly to banks having restructured their deposits. Banks came to depend less on demand and savings deposits and more on time deposits paying market-related interest rates. Changes in the composition of bank deposits can be seen in Table 33-2.

Because interest rates were comparatively low in the 1975-78 period, holders of demand deposits were not penalized unduly for keeping their transactions balances in noninterest-bearing accounts. Also, since the maximum rate allowed on fixed-ceiling passbook savings accounts was similar to the yields on other financial assets, savers had little incentive to withdraw funds from insured accounts. This situation changed dramatically beginning in 1979, as interest rates rose generally and short-term rates climbed above long-term rates. As a result, depositors began to keep transactions balances in noninterest-bearing demand deposits to a minimum, and growth in demand deposits was brought to a halt. In addition, money either flowed out of savings deposits into higher yielding time deposits, or flowed out of banks entirely into money market mutual funds. The growth of demand and savings deposits was further affected after 1981 by the nationwide introduction of NOW accounts which, by combining the most important features of demand and savings deposits into one account, attracted funds away from both types of deposits.

Table 33-2 Composition of deposits at commercial banks

	End of year holdings as a percent of total deposits			Average annual growth rates	
	1974	1978	1982	1975–78	1979–82
Demand deposits	34.4	30.9	22.7	6.3	0.7
Demand and other checkables	34.4	31.5	29.3	6.8	6.7
Savings deposits	22.1	24.6	15.4	12.5	(2.4)
Time deposits	43.5	43.9	55.3	9.7	15.2
Large time	23.6	22.8	24.1	9.8	10.2
Small time	19.9	21.1	31.2	10.8	20.1
Total deposits	100.0	100.0	100.0	9.2	8.7

Note: Demand deposits include overnight RPs.

Savings deposits include money market deposit accounts.

Large time deposits include term RPs.

Other checkables, overnight RPs, term RPs, and MMDAs are not seasonally adjusted.

Time deposits became the main source of deposit growth at commercial banks in the 1979-82 period.[2] As savings deposits declined, growth in time deposits increased, especially time deposits with variable ceilings. Large time deposits, which has become a fairly stable source of deposit funds in the early 1970s, continued to grow at about the same pace into the 1980s. Most of the growth in time deposits came from the proliferation of small time deposits, which increased in both amount and number.[3] Small time deposits grew from the least important source of funds at the end of 1978 to the most important source at the end of 1982. They also grew nearly twice as fast as any other deposit category (Table 33-2).

The two accounts responsible for growth in small time deposits were the six-month money market certificate and the 2½ year small saver certificate. The six-month CD, introduced in June 1978, increased to $220 billion by the end of 1982. The 2½ year CD, introduced in January 1980, increased to $87 billion by the end of 1982. Together, these two accounts represented 25 percent of total deposits at the end of 1982 and 77 percent of small time deposits at commercial banks. The introduction of these CD's gave banks and thrift insti-

[2]Growth in time deposits was due entirely to growth in variable-ceiling certificates. Fixed-ceiling certificates declined as a percentage of small time deposits from 100 percent at the end of 1977 to 12 percent at the end of 1982.

[3]The six-month money market certificate was the only variable-ceiling account at the end of 1978. It then accounted for less than 3 percent of all deposits. By the end of 1982, there were nine such accounts and many of them offered both fixed and variable rates.

tutions an account that savers could use in shifting funds from lower yielding fixed ceiling accounts, and thus prevented disintermediation and its costly effects.

Deposit Comparison of Depository Institutions

Although the growth rate of deposits at commercial banks totaled only slightly less in 1979-82 than in 1975-78, the growth rate of deposits at thrift institutions was less than half what it had been in the previous period (Table 33-3). In the earlier period, when interest rates were generally lower and more stable, savings deposits were the most important source of deposit growth at all depository institutions. But as interest rates went higher and became more volatile, savers began seeking higher returns. All depository institutions lost savings deposits in 1979-82, but the effect on total deposit growth was greater at thrifts than at banks because thrifts depended on savings deposits more than banks.

As savings deposits declined, time deposits became the most important source of funds for banks and thrifts. Time deposits grew at an annual rate of less than 12 percent at thrifts, compared with more than 15 percent at banks. While large time deposits at commercial banks grew at about the same rate in both periods, the growth of these deposits at thrifts was sizable in the second period. Even so, large time deposits accounted for less than 10 percent of deposits at thrifts by the end of 1982.

Table 33-3 Deposit growth at commercial banks and thrift institutions (Four-year average annual growth rates)

	Total depository institutions	Commercial banks	Thrift institutions
1975–78			
Total deposits	11.0	9.2	13.8
1979–82			
Total deposits	7.6	8.7	6.0
Demand and other checkables	8.1	6.7	69.5
Savings deposits	(3.7)	(2.4)	(4.8)
Time deposits	13.6	15.2	11.8
Large time	14.0	10.2	40.0
Small time	13.5	20.1	9.3

Note: Demand and other checkables at commercial banks includes overnight RPs. Savings deposits for banks and thrifts include MMDAs. Large time deposits for banks and thrifts include term RPs.

The competition for funds between banks and thrifts in 1979-82 centered mainly on small time deposits and, to a less extent, on savings deposits. Banks fared well in the competition. Where banks had held about 40 percent of the small time savings deposits at the end of 1978, they held 45 percent at the end of 1982 (Figure 33-3). Small time deposits grew at an annual average rate of over 20 percent at banks, compared with less than 9 percent at thrifts. Although banks and thrifts both lost savings deposits, the decline at banks was only half as rapidly at thrifts, with the result that banks increased their share of the market.

Earning Assets at Commercial Banks

Earning assets at commercial banks grew from $1,000 billion at the end of 1978 to $1,400 billion at the end of 1982 (Figure 33-4), an average annual growth of 8.7 percent compared with 9.7 percent in 1975-78. This slower growth in assets reflected the slower growth in deposits.

All categories of bank assets increased between 1979 and 1982, but the rates of increase were not uniform and they differed from the rates in the 1975-78 period (Table 33-4). Loan growth between 1975 and 1978 was greatest in

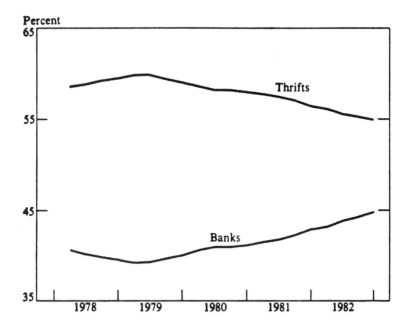

Figure 33-3   Market share of savings and small time deposits at commercial banks and thrift institutions

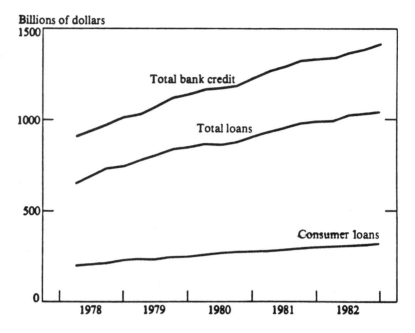

Figure 33-4 Earning asset growth at commercial banks (seasonally adjusted)

Table 33-4 Distribution of earning assets at commercial banks

	End of year holdings as a percent of total asset			Average annual growth rates	
	1974	1978	1982	1975–78	1979–82
Total loans	72.9	73.7	73.8	9.7	8.7
Commercial and industrial	27.6	24.3	27.8	6.0	12.5
Consumer	14.4	16.2	13.6	12.8	4.0
Real estate	18.2	20.8	21.5	12.9	9.6
All other	12.7	12.4	11.0	8.8	5.3
Investments	27.1	26.3	26.2	8.5	8.6
U.S. Treasuries	7.5	9.3	9.3	17.2	9.0
Other	19.6	17.0	16.9	5.5	8.5
Total earning assets	100.0	100.0	100.0	9.2	8.7

consumer loans for housing.[4] The relative importance of these two categories increased as the proportion of commercial and industrial loans declined. The situation was reversed in the 1979-82 period, however, as growth in consumer-oriented loans declined significantly and growth of commercial and industrial loans increased.

The composition of earning assets shifted as banks adjusted the distribution of their portfolios in response to the changing economic environment. Household incomes rose during the 1975-78 economic upswing and consumers became more willing to incur debt. As a result, consumer borrowing at banks increased. With interest rates relatively low, nonfinancial business firms preferred to borrow in long-term capital markets instead of taking short-term loans from banks. The result was an increase in the relative importance of consumer-oriented loans in banks' portfolios. Over the next four years, however, household incomes declined and, with substantially higher interest rates, demand for consumer loans declined. Growth in real estate loans dropped to 10 percent a year as loans for one- to four-family housing declined. The recessionary environment and rising interest rates also reduced corporate cash flow and profitability, causing nonfinancial corporations to rely more on bank loans. Part of the increase in bank loans to business was to finance unwanted inventories, but nonfinancial corporations also were reluctant to issue bonds at double-digit interest rates, preferring instead to borrow short term from banks until interest rates declined.

Earning Asset Comparison of Depository Institutions

Earning assets grew significantly faster at commercial banks than at thrift institutions during the 1979–82 period (Tables 33-4 and 33-5). The difference represented a reversal from the previous four years, when earning assets grew faster at thrifts than at banks.

The divergence was due to changes in the composition of assets. Regulations allowed banks to make a greater variety of loans than thrift institutions. The effect of the restrictions on thrifts can be seen from a comparison of the composition of earning assets at banks and thrifts. Over the whole period from 1975 through 1982, banks as a group never held more than 28 percent of their assets in any one type of loan or security. In the same period, thrifts as a group held over 65 percent of their assets in mortgage loans and mortgage-backed securities. As consumer mortgage lending waned in 1979–82, the traditional lending base of thrifts was eroded. And as mortgage loan demand declined, funds deposited at thrifts had to be invested in lower yielding securities. In contrast,

---

[4]Real estate loans with a consumer orientation are loans on one- to four-unit family housing, which had average annual growth during the 1975-78 and 1979-82 periods of 14.9 percent and 8.3 percent, respectively.

Table 33-5   Distribution of earning assets at savings and loans and mutual savings banks

	End-of-year holdings as a percent of total assets			Average annual growth rates	
	1974	1978	1982	1975–78	1979–82
Savings and loans					
Mortgage loans	87.1	85.0	73.9	14.9	3.0
Mortgage-backed securities	2.0	3.2	9.7	31.5	42.4
Nonmortgage loans	2.0	2.3	3.6	19.3	20.1
Cash and investments	8.9	9.5	12.8	17.7	15.1
Total earning assets	100.0	100.0	100.0	15.6	6.5
Mutual savings banks					
Mortgage loans	70.1	61.8	56.7	6.2	−0.1
Mortgage-backed securities	2.1	6.5	8.5	46.8	9.4
Nonmortgage loans	3.6	4.7	10.1	17.5	23.9
Cash and investments	24.3	27.0	24.7	13.0	−0.2
Total earning assets	100.0	100.0	100.0	9.6	2.0

banks were able to respond to the change in loan demand by diverting funds from mortgages and consumer loans to short-term business loans.

Profitability Comparison of Depository Institutions

Banks have been substantially more profitable than thrifts since 1979. The differences in profitability can be seen by a comparison of the returns on assets (ROA) at banks and thrifts (Table 33-6). Return on assets is defined as net income for a year expressed as a percentae of average assets for the year. Profitability was about the same at banks and at thrifts in the 1975–78 period, an bank profitability remained about the same through 1982. At thrifts, however, ROA declined sharply after 1979 and then turned negative.

One reason banks were more profitable after 1979 is that their loans were shorter term. Because thrifts had concentrated their lending on long-term mortgages, only a small percentage of their loans matured during an accounting period. And as most of these loans were made at fixed rates, an unexpected rise in interest rates caused a significant proportion of the assets of thrifts to earn below-market rates.

The shorter terms of bank loans caused a much larger percentage of their loans to mature during a given period. Many bank loans also were made at floating rates. Following a rise in interest rates, banks were able to adjust loan

Table 33-6 Profitability comparison of depository institutions*
(percent)

	1975	1976	1977	1978	1979	1980	1981
Commercial banks	0.69	0.70	0.71	0.76	0.80	0.79	0.76
Savings and loans	0.47	0.63	0.77	0.82	0.67	0.14	−0.73
Mutual savings banks	0.38	0.45	0.55	0.58	0.46	−0.12	−0.83

*Profitability is the return on assets, or ROA. ROA is defined as net income as a percentage of the average of beginning and end of year assets.

Source: Commercial Banks—"Profitability of Insured Commercial Banks," *Federal Reserve Bulletin*, August 1982, Table 9. Savings and Loans and Mutual Savings Banks—"Thrift Institutions in Recent Years," *Federal Reserve Bulletin*, December 1982, Table 1.

rates closer to the current market rate. The result was that bank profitability was affected less by unexpected changes in interest rates. Banks could keep more of their assets earning at or near market rates.

The contractual features of loans by thrifts combined with the less favorable economic environment of the 1979-82 period put thrifts in a profit squeeze. As interest rates rose and deregulation led to the introduction of new accounts paying market-related interest rates, the cost of funds at all depository institutions rose. Banks were able to maintain their profitability, however, by earning market rates of return on a significant part of their earning assets. Thrifts, able to earn market rates of interest on only a small proportion of their earning assets, saw their profitability decline both absolutely and relatively to banks.

PERFORMANCE AND OUTLOOK

Bank and Thrift Performance

Commercial banks were able to maintain deposit growth better than thrifts in the 1979-82 period, primarily because they were more successful in attracting consumer-type deposits. One explanation for the difference in deposit growth after 1979 is that banks were more profitable than thrifts. Their greater profitability probably made banks more aggressive in seeking deposits to invest in earning assets. Another explanation is the phasing out of regulatory interest rate differentials that allowed thrifts to pay more than banks on certain time and savings deposits. The purpose of this interest rate differential had been to allow thrifts to compete for deposits with banks, which offered a wider variety of services. As thrifts began losing the advantage of the interest ceiling differential, customers lost some of the incentive to hold deposits with thrifts instead of banks. Also, because several large thrift institutions had failed or been merged into other institutions, there may have been a perceived risk difference between banks and thrifts that hastened deposit withdrawal from thrifts and increased deposits at banks.

Continued stable deposit growth at commercial banks contributed to stable growth in earning assets. Similarly, the decline in deposit growth at thrifts in the 1979-82 period contributed to a decline in earning asset growth. Another factor that contributed to differences in asset growth at banks and thrifts was differences in their regulation that worked to the detriment of the profitability of thrift institutions. Where asset restrictions on thrifts caused them to be geared to making consumer-oriented loans, primarily mortgages, banks were more able to diversify their assets. When consumer borrowing declined in the 1979-82 period, thrifts were forced to invest in mortgage-backed or money market securities (Table 33-5). In contrast, banks—especially large banks—were able to respond to the decline in consumer loan demand and the rise in business loan demand by shifting from consumer loans to business loans. Because the yield on business loans was higher than the yield on mortgage-backed and money market securities, banks had a distinct profit advantage over thrifts.[5] Given the differences in profitability, it is hardly surprising that asset growth was faster at banks than thrifts.

Bank and Thrift Outlook

The basis for more competition among depository institutions lies in their continued deregulation, as provided for the DIDMCA and the Garn-St. Germain Act. The two major facets of the deregulation movement are the removal of interest rate ceilings from deposit accounts at banks and thrifts and the broadening of the asset powers of thrifts. The removal of interest rate ceilings began in late 1981 with the introduction of the ceiling-free IRAs. The real impact of ceiling removal was felt, however, when money market deposit accounts (MMDAs) were introduced in December 1982. More than $367 billion was accumulated in MMDAs by the end of June 1983, a growth unparalleled by any other deposit account at any time. Super NOW accounts, checking accounts paying market-related rates, were introduced in early January 1983. Although they have not grown as fast as MMDAs, Super NOWs totaled more

[5]The following shows the average annual rate of return on prime rate loans, GNMAs and 3-month Eurodeposits:

	1978	1979	1980	1981	1982
Prime	9.06	12.67	15.27	18.87	14.86
GNMAs	8.98	10.22	12.55	15.29	14.68
3-month Eurodeposits	8.78	11.96	14.00	16.79	13.12

Source: Federal Reserve Board *Annual Statistical Digest*.

than $31 billion by the end of June. In the short run, MMDAs and Super NOWs will raise the cost of funds at banks and thrifts, possibly causing profitability to decline. This is because most of the funds being deposited in these accounts are coming from the banks' and thrifts' own deposit bases. Although the long-run effect of these accounts on the profitability of banks and thrifts is as yet undetermined, the greater stability in deposits that comes from the ability to pay market-related rates should allow both banks and thrifts to shift more of their assets into longer term, higher yielding loans.

Broader asset powers for thrifts should help narrow the divergence in bank and thrift profitability that arises when interest rates shift unexpectedly. Thrifts, however, will now have to determine their own area of lending expertise and identify the markets in which they want to participate. This will be a break from the past, when their markets were determined by legislation. Competition between banks and thrifts will certainly increase, but the allocation of credit in the economy will be more efficient.

CONCLUSION

Depository institutions have faced numerous challenges in the past few years, including unfavorable macroeconomic trends, a monetary policy geared to the reduction of inflation, and a definitive move toward the deregulation of all depository institutions. Despite the challenges, commercial banks have fared well compared with other depository institutions. Part of the success of banks has been due to their ability to profit from a rise in business loan demand. Lending to business was an avenue of growth open to them when consumer loan demand was declining. Under previous regulation, this avenue was not open to thrifts. Whether the banking industry continues to outperform the thrift industry will depend on how each responds to the challenges and opportunities brought by further deregulation.

INTERSTATE BANKING: TAKING INVENTORY*

David D. Whitehead[†]

34

Although interstate banking is prohibited by the McFadden Act and the Douglas amendment to the Bank Holding Company Act, the fact is that banking organizations are providing financial services across state lines and have been doing so for some time. Four gateways allow commercial banking organizations to offer financial services on an interstate basis. First, "grandfather" provisions of banking legislation allow some banking organizations to maintain full-service commercial banks in more than one state. Second, the Garn-St Germain Depository Institutions Act of 1982 allows banks and savings and loan associations to acquire failing institutions across state lines. Third, and perhaps more importantly, the 4(c)8 provisions of the Bank Holding Company Act allow bank holding companies to establish or acquire nonbank subsidiaries that are not subject to the prohibitions on interstate banking. And fourth, other nonbank subsidiaries may establish offices across state lines, i.e., loan production offices and Edge Act corporations, allowing their parent organization to provide financial services on an interstate basis.

*Reprinted from the *Economic Review*, May 1983, pp. 4-20, with permission of the Federal Reserve Bank of Atlanta.

†Pam Frisbee contributed valuable research assistance in the preparation of this article. The author also wishes to thank the other District Federal Reserve Banks for their vital contributions. A longer, more detailed version of this study is available from the Information Center, Federal Reserve Bank of Atlanta.

In addition, the BHC Act allows bank holding companies to acquire or establish banking subsidiaries in states which explicitly permit such entry. This article will describe various ways in which bank holding companies provide interstate financial services and will inventory their activities on a state-by-state basis. This should give us some idea of the extent to which bank holding companies are actively supplying interstate financial services. The numbers presented in this inventory represent the best available information but may not include all activities or offices. Therefore, the figures represent activities and offices documented by our inventory and should be viewed as a minimum.

GRANDFATHERED INTERSTATE BANKING

Legislation and regulation tend to follow actual events in the marketplace. This is especially true in banking. Market participants first become creative in terms of supplying financial services, and then legislators and regulators react to the evolving market circumstance. Reacting to changing market conditions means that legislators are constantly faced with restricting given activities after innovative organizations have engaged in the activity. In some cases it would be detrimental or impossible to require the organization to cease the activity even though a general prohibition is deemed desirable. In such cases, one equitable approach is to allow the innovative organization to continue but not expand the activity in question. Such a clause is then written into the legislation and is termed a "grandfather provision." A number of domestic and international banking organizations enjoy such grandfather provisions with respect to prohibitions on interstate banking.

We were able to identify 21 domestic bank holding companies that controlled banking subsidiaries in more than one state. One of these organizations controlled banking subsidiaries in eleven states, one had banking subsidiaries in seven states, two had subs in five states, four had banking subsidiaries in three states and the remainder were represented in only two states (Table 34-1). In total these 21 banking organizations control 138 banks and 1,369 branch offices in 22 states. This means that almost half of our states house banks controlled by out-of-state holding companies.

In addition to domestic holding companies controlling interstate banks, seven international banking organizations control banks in more than a single state. Table 34-1 identifies and locates these organizations. Prior to the Bank Holding Company Act of 1956, international organizations could establish banks in more than one state. Following 1956, however, any international organization controlling more than one U.S. bank fell under the Holding Company Act and became subject to the Douglas Amendment. Grandfather provisions allowed these organizations to continue their interstate system but restricted the organization from expanding outside its declared home state. In total, seven international bank holding companies control seven banks in states other than

Table 34-1   Foreign and domestic bank holding companies with subsidiary banks in more than one state

Bank holding company	Home state	Number of states	States in which banks are located
First Interstate Bancorporation	CA	11	AZ, CA, CO, ID, MT, NM, OR, NV, WA, WY, UT
First Bank System, Inc	MN	5	MN, MT, ND, SD, WI
Northwest Bancorporation	MN	7	IA, MN, MT, NE, ND, SD, WI
Otto Bremer Foundation	MN	3	MN, ND, WI
Financial General Bancshares, Inc.	DC	5	DC, MD, NY, TN, VA
General Bancshares Corporation	MO	3	IL, MO, TN
First Security Corporation	UT	3	ID, WY, UT
Citicorp	NY	3	DE, NY, SD
Bank of Montreal*	NY	2	CA, NY
Canadian Imperial Bank of Commerce*	NY	2	CA, NY
The Bank of Tokyo, Ltd*	CA	2	CA, NY
Barclays Bank Limited*	NY	2	CA, NY
The Sumitomo Bank, Ltd.*	CA	2	CA, HI
The Royal Bank of Canada	NY	2	NY, PR
Banco Central, S.A.*	NY	2	NY, PR
J. P. Morgan & Company	NY	2	DE, NY
The Girard Company	PA	2	DE, PA
NCNB Corporation	NC	2	FL, NC
Chase Manhattan Corporation	NY	2	DE, NY
Provident National Corporation	PA	2	DE, PA
Northern Trust Corporation	IL	2	FL, IL
Maryland National Corporation	MD	2	DE, MD
Philadelphia National Corporation	PA	2	DE, PA
First Maryland Bancorp	MD	2	DE, MD
Equitable Bancorporation	MD	2	DE, MD
Chemical New York Corporation	NY	2	DE, NY
Manufacturers Hanover Corporation	NY	2	DE, NY
Pittsburg National Corporation	PA	2	DE, PA

*Foreign banking organizations

Source: Federal Reserve Board as of 12/31/82

the state in which they are based. Of the seven foreign holding companies controlling banks in more than one state, five declared New York as their state of residence and two declared California (Table 34-2).

Fifty-three international banks have interstate branches, 25 of which are home officed in New York and 24 in California. As Table 34-2 shows, 71 percent of their interstate branches (73 in number) are located in either New York or Illinois. As would be expected, most of the interstate branches of foreign banks are located in our larger cities and trade centers. These organizations then have established an interstate presence of full service banks in some of our most attractive markets.

Table 34-2   Foreign banking organizations controlling interstate offices

State	Number of foreign banking organizations controlling interstate offices by state of residence	Number and type of interstate office locations by type of office				Total number of interstate offices controlled by foreign banking organizations headquartered outside the state
		Banks	Branches	Edge Acts	Agencies	
California	26	8	2	2	63	75
District of Columbia	—	—	1	—	—	1
Florida	1	—	—	6	22	28
Georgia	—	—	—	—	10	10
Hawaii	—	1	—	—	2	3
Illinois	1	1	36	3	—	40
Louisiana	—	—	—	—	1	1
Massachusetts	1	—	4	—	—	4
New York	58	3	37	2	18	60
Oregon	—	—	7	—	—	7
Pennsylvania	—	—	6	—	—	6
Texas	—	—	—	9	—	9
Washington	—	—	10	—	—	10
	103*	13	103	22	116	254

*16 of these organizations that have offices in more than one state are international organizations having no resident state—i.e. agency offices of international banks.

Source: Federal Reserve Bank of New York as of 6-30-82.

In addition to the 103 interstate branches established by foreign banks, they have established 116 interstate agency offices and 22 interstate Edge Act offices. This brings the total number of interstate offices of foreign banks and holding companies to 254 (Table 34-2).

The door to interstate banking is not completely closed. The Douglas Amendment allows bank holding companies to acquire banks on an interstate basis if the target state passes legislation that specifically allows out-of-state holding companies to acquire instate banks. To date, five states have passed such legislation.[1] Two other states, Delaware and South Dakota, allow entry through limited purpose banks, and both have actually experienced entry by

[1] Utah passed reciprocal legislation in 1981 but repealed same in 1983.

out-of-state holding companies. In addition, Iowa, Illinois, and Florida allow expansion by out-of-state banking organizations that operate banks or trust companies under grandfather provisions.

Although interstate deposit-taking is prohibited, many interstate banking services exist, and more could develop in the future even without changes in the federal laws prohibiting interstate banking. Three recent avenues for establishing an interstate banking presence or position are through the purchase of up to 5 percent of voting stock, preferred convertible stock, and franchise agreements among banks.

The Bank Holding Company Act specifies that it "shall be unlawful, except with the prior approval of the Board, . . . for any bank holding company to acquire directly or indirectly ownership or control of any voting shares of any bank, if after such acquisition, such company will directly or indirectly own or control more than 5 percent of the voting shares of such bank, ..."[2] This clause leaves the door open for bank holding companies to acquire up to 5 percent of the voting shares of a bank without Board approval. As a result, some bank holding companies have taken the opportunity to invest in banks across state lines, establishing associations of banks that may work together for their common benefit. These investments have taken the form of 4.9 percent voting stock ownership, nonvoting preferred stock that automatically converts to voting stock should the prohibition on interstate banking be removed, or simple franchise agreement among banks.

Whatever the path, the result is a potential interstate network of banks large enough and geographically dispersed enough to offer products and services no one bank may have been capable of offering separately. These formal and informal agreements represent a form of geographic positioning for the day when interstate powers are granted. Texas Commerce Bankshares, for example, has investments in banks in Wyoming, Colorado, Arizona, Oklahoma and Louisiana.[3] While no comprehensive list of these investments and agreements was available, we are aware of these methods to establish an interstate presence. To date the Federal Reserve Board has approved two preferred stock deals, has disapproved one which is being restructured and has at least seven others pending.

The Bank Holding Company Act does not prohibit individuals from acquiring more than one bank. Neither does it require individuals to file an application with the Board regarding the acquisition of bank stock either within a given state or on an interstate basis.[4] We know that interstate banking groups controlled by individuals exist, but we have no accurate measure of the number

---

[2]Section 3(a) Bank Holding Company Act of 1956.

[3]*United States Banker*, January 1983, p. 15.

[4]See "Change in Bank Control Act," Title VI of the Financial Institutions Regulatory and Interest Rate Control Act of 1978.

of these groups or the number and geographic dispersion of the banks involved. To this extent, our inventory again is understated.

Another avenue for interstate expansion was opened by the emergency provisions of the Depository Institutions Act of 1982 allowing out-of-state organizations to acquire troubled banks and insured mutual savings banks under certain circumstances.[5] Although these provisions have not been used to allow interstate bank acquisitions to date, they do provide an avenue for interstate expansion.[6] The Federal Home Loan Bank Board began allowing interstate mergers of savings and loans in 1981, allowing only four that year. In 1982, however, 16 such mergers were allowed and today 29 interstate savings and loan systems exist (Table 34-3). Although these cases are limited, the provisions of the Garn-St Germain Depository Institutions Act and the fact that the Federal Home Loan Bank Board is actively allowing S&Ls to merge across state lines indicates increasing pressure for further relaxation of the prohibition on interstate banking.

Commercial banks are the only financial services suppliers effectively constrained geographically today, and even these constraints do not apply to all commercial banks under all conditions. The fact that a commercial banking organization in one state may acquire a failing institution in another state inevitably will result in commercial banks facing competition from interstate banking organizations.[7] Because of the criteria for such acquisitions, the degree of competition may be limited at first; yet as the failing institution recovers and takes advantage of its association with an interstate parent, local bank competitors will resent such relationships. Geographically constrained banking organizations will feel that a two way competitive street is necessary. As the number of such acquisitions across state lines increases, support for repeal of interstate bank prohibitions will also increase. The emergency provisions of the Depository Institutions Act of 1982 may in fact be unlocking the door to full interstate banking.

Given the number of interstate banking organizations, the extent of their geographic coverage, the other unmeasured forms of interstate banking, and the potential avenues for still further expansion, the actual extent of interstate

---

[5]See footnote 1.

[6]The Depository Institution Act of 1982 allows closed insured commercial banks with assets of $500 million or more and insured mutual savings banks with assets of $500 million or more and in danger of failing to be acquired by an out-of-state bank or bank holding company with priority given in the following order: acquisition of similar institutions in the same state; acquisition by same type of institution in different states; acquisition by different types of institutions in the same state; and acquisition by different types of institutions in different states.

[7]The degree of interstate expansion through the emergency provisions will be limited by the requirement that the failing institution must have at least $500 million in assets. It may be possible, however, for a number of weak institutions to be consolidated in order to meet this requirement. An organization in Tennessee is currently attempting such a consolidation.

Table 34-3   Interstate savings and loan associations and their geographic coverage (March 7, 1983)

Parent	Home office locations	Interstate locations
1. Northeast Savings, F.A.	CT	CT, MA, NY
2. City FS & LN	NJ	NJ, FL
3. Empire of America, FSA	MI	MI, FL, NY, TX
4. Carteret S & LA, FA	NJ	NJ, FL
5. Perpetual American FS & LA	VA	VA, DC, MD
6. Home Savings of America, FS & Los Angeles	CA	CA, FL, IL, MO,
7. Glendale FS & LA	CA	TX
8. First Nationwide Savings FS & LA	CA	CA, FL
9. California FS & LA	CA	CA, NY, FL
10. World S & LA, A, FS & LA	CA	CA, GA, FL, NV
11. First FS & LA of Arizona	AZ	CA, KS, CO
12. Bay Savings Bank	MI	AZ, TX
13. National Permanent FS & LA	DC	MI, VA
14. First FS & LA of Puerto Rico	PR	DC, MD
15. Charter FS & LA	GA	PR, VI
16. Equitable FS & LA	MD	GA, AL
17. Union FS & LA of Evansville	IN	MD, DC
18. Farm and Home SA	MO	IN, KY
19. Mountainwest S & L	UT	MO, TX
20. The Benj Franklin FS & LA	OR	UT, WY
		OR, ID, WA, UT

Source: Federal Home Loan Bank Board

banking is probably far greater than might be assumed given the laws prohibiting it.

NONBANK SUBSIDIARIES

For purposes of the Bank Holding Company Act, a bank is defined as ". . . an institution . . . which (1) accepts deposits that the depositor has a legal right to withdraw on demand, and (2) engages in the business of making commercial loans."[8] Therefore an organization that offers both demand deposits and commercial loans may be defined as a commercial bank, and, hence, would fall under the interstate banking restrictions. The laws prohibiting interstate banking limit the ability of a formal banking organization to offer both demand deposits and commercial loans at a single location in more than one state. But by separating the demand deposit and commercial lending functions it is pos-

[8]Section 2(c) of the Bank Holding Company Act of 1956.

sible for banking organizations to circumvent the interstate restrictions and provide interstate financial services. Indeed, nothing prevents a commercial bank in one state from advertising and accepting demand deposits or savings deposits from consumers in another state. Many large commercial banks aggressively sell large certificate of deposits on an interstate basis. They employ calling officers to seek out major accounts nationwide, and they market their credit cards nationwide. In addition, commercial banks are offering such financial services as cash management, electronic funds transfer accounts, loan participations and a variety of correspondent banking services that know no state boundary. These are all examples of services offered across state lines that do not require the bank to establish a physical presence.

By separating the demand deposits and commercial lending functions, however, a banking organization can establish a physical presence across state lines. One way for bank holding companies to accomplish this is through the creation or acquisition of nonbank subsidiaries. The nonbank subsidiaries do not constitute a commercial bank and, hence, are free to open offices on an interstate basis. National banks may undertake a number of the same 4(c)8 type activities allowed to bank holding companies (Table 34-4). For the most part, however, these activities are constrained to the state in which the parent bank is located.

IDENTIFYING INTERSTATE 4(c)8 OFFICES

With the assistance of the eleven other Federal Reserve District Banks, we were able to piece together a composite picture of holding companies throughout the nation that controlled interstate 4(c)8 subsidiaries and the number of interstate offices each controlled. Although an application is required prior to a 4(c)8 subsidiary opening a new office, no consolidated records were available. Each district Federal Reserve Bank compiled a list of holding companies with interstate 4(c)8 offices and provided the office locations on a state-by-state basis. In a few instances it was necessary to contract holding companies directly to obtain the desired information. This article presents the best information available on 4(c)8 interstate activity, but the data may not be 100 percent inclusive. The numbers represent an actual count of those institutions and office locations of those institutions we identified as being involved in 4(c)8 services on an interstate basis. Therefore, the numbers may understate the extent of interstate activity.

In total there are 3,201 one-bank holding companies and 430 multibank holding companies in the United States (Table 34-5). Of the 3,631 holding companies capable of establishing or acquiring interstate offices of 4(c)8 subsidiaries, only 139 or approximately four percent elected to do so. Of those 139, 68 were one-bank and 71 were multibank holding companies. One common characteristic of holding companies electing to go interstate through their (4c)8

Table 34-4 Permissible nonbank activities for bank holding companies under Section 4(c)8 of Regulation Y, February, 1983

Activities permitted by regulation	Activities permitted by order	Activities denied by the Board
1. Extensions of credit[2] Mortgage banking Finance companies: consumer, sales, and commercial Credit cards Factoring 2. Industrial bank, Morris Plan bank, industrial loan company 3. Servicing loans and other extensions of credit[2] 4. Trust company[2] 5. Investment or financial advising[2] 6. Full-payout leasing of personal or real property 7. Investments in community welfare projects[2] 8. Providing book-keeping or data processing services[2] 9. Acting as insurance agent or broker primarily in connection with credit extensions[2] 10. Underwriting credit life, accident and health insurance 11. Providing courier services[2] 12. Management consulting for all depository institutions	1. Issuance and sale of travelers checks[2,6] 2. Buying and selling gold and silver bullion and silver coin[2,4] 3. Issuing money orders and general-purpose variable denominated payment instruments[1,2,4] 4. Futures commission merchant to cover gold and silver bullion and coins[1,2] 5. Underwriting certain federal state and municipal securities[1,2] 6. Check verification[1,2,4] 7. Financial advice to consumers[1,2] 8. Issuance of small denomination debt instruments[1] 9. Arranging for equity financing of real estate[1] 10. Acting as futures commissions merchant[1] 11. Discount brokerage[1] 12. Operating a distressed savings and loan association[1] 13. Operating an Article XII Investment Co.[1] 14. Executing foreign banking unsolicited purchases and sales of securities 15. Engaging in commercial banking acitivities abroad through a limited purpose Delaware bank[1] 16. Performing appraisal of real estate and real estate advisor and real estate brokerage on nonresidential properties.[1]	1. Insurance premium funding (combined sales of mutual funds and insurance) 2. Underwriting life insurance not related to credit extension 3. Sale of level-term credit life 4. Real estate brokerage (residential) 5. Armored car 6. Land development 7. Real estate syndication 8. General management consulting 9. Property management consulting 10. Computer output microfilm services 11. Underwriting mortgage guaranty insurance[3] 12. Operating a savings and loan association[1,5] 13. Operating a travel agency[1,2] 14. Underwriting property and casualty insurance[1] 15. Underwriting home loan life mortgage insurance[1] 16. Investment note issue with transactional characteristics[1] 17. Real estate advisory services[1]

Activities permitted by regulation	Activities permitted by order	Activities denied by the Board
13. Sale at retail of money orders with a face value of not more than $1000, travelers checks and savings bonds[1,2]	17. Operating a Pool Reserve Plan for loss reserves of banks for loans to small businesses[1]	
14. Performing appraisals of real estate[1]	18. Operating a thrift institution in Rhode Island	
15. Issuance and sale of travelers checks[1]	19. Operating a guarantee savings bank in New Hampshire[1]	
	20. Offering informational advice and transactional services for foreign[1] exchange services	

[1]Added to list since January 1, 1975.

[2]Activities permissible to national banks.

[3]Board orders found these activities closely related to banking but denied proposed acquisitions as part of its "go slow" policy.

[4]To be decided on a case-by-case basis.

[5]Operating a thrift institution has been permitted by order in Rhode Island, Ohio, New Hampshire and California.

[6]Subsequently permitted by regulation.

Source: Federal Reserve Board

subsidiaries was their absolute size. Of the 50 largest banking organizations in the country, 42 have interstate 4(c)8 subsidiaries. Of the 100 largest banking organizations, 70 have 4(c)8 subsidiaries that control interstate offices; of the top 150 organizations, 102 have interstate 4(c)8 subsidiaries. Therefore, as a generalization, large bank holding companies are the most likely to provide interstate financial services through offices of their 4(c)8 subsidiaries. They are also the organizations most likely to undertake interstate banking if or when the prohibitions are lifted.

Table 34-5 also indicates that these 139 holding companies control 382 4(c)8 subsidiaries which collectively have at least 5,500 offices outside the state in which the parent holding company resides. Map 1 indicates that 56 of these holding companies (41 percent of the total) with interstate 4(c)8 subsidiaries reside in 10 northeastern states (Maine, New York, Massachusetts, Rhode Island, Connecticut, Pennsylvania, New Jersey, Delaware, Maryland and Virginia). The highest concentration of holding companies controlling 4(c)8 subsidiaries with interstate offices is in the northeastern portion of the nation.

Table 34-5 Bank holding companies, number with interstate 4(c)8 subsidiaries and offices of interstate 4(c)8 subsidiaries by state

Home state of holding company	Total number of holding companies home officed in state			Interstate Companies		
	One-bank	Multi bank	Total	Number of holding companies	Number of subsidiaries	Number of offices
Alabama	16	9	25	4	5	12
Alaska	3	1	4	—	—	—
Arizona	5	0	5	0	—	—
Arkansas	47	2	49	1	1	1
California	42	6	48	5	28	636
Colorado	104	22	126	1	1	1
Connecticut	7	3	10	2	5	13
D.C.	7	3	10	—	—	—
Delaware	12	1	13	1	3	1,171
Florida	48	29	77	3	4	50
Georgia	49	22	71	4	7	157
Hawaii	3	0	3	—	—	—
Idaho	6	1	7	1	1	2
Illinois	316	7	323	5	24	70
Indiana	66	1	67	3	11	38
Iowa	268	16	284	2	2	3
Kansas	323	8	331	2	2	2
Kentucky	43	1	44	1	1	5
Louisiana	47	1	48	—	—	—
Maine	2	4	6	1	1	1
Maryland	3	4	7	6	18	102
Massachusetts	14	13	27	4	10	34
Michigan	18	24	42	1	3	6
Minnesota	286	15	301	3	21	585
Mississippi	26	0	26	1	1	2
Missouri	175	40	215	7	7	7
Montana	34	7	41	—	—	—
Nebraska	283	0	283	2	2	2
Nevada	2	0	2	—	—	—
New Hampshire	6	4	10	—	—	—
New Jersey	8	11	19	4	7	17

Home state of holding company	Total number of holding companies home officed in state			Interstate companies		
	One-bank	Multi-bank	Total	Number of holding companies	Number of subsidiaries	Number of offices
New Mexico	19	4	23	—	—	—
New York	19	11	30	19	96	1,593
North Carolina	9	1	10	4	9	226
North Dakota	51	4	55	—	—	—
Oklahoma	250	6	256	1	1	1
Ohio	16	17	33	11	12	12
Oregon	3	5	8	2	8	27
Pennsylvania	32	3	35	11	28	283
Rhode Island	11	0	11	3	16	167
South Carolina	5	0	5	3	7	86
South Dakota	41	4	45	—	—	—
Tennessee	40	10	50	6	8	14
Texas	283	59	342	2	2	2
Utah	17	5	22	2	10	37
Vermont	4	1	5	—	—	—
Virginia	5	9	14	5	7	86
Washington	7	1	8	4	10	42
West Virginia	9	1	10	—	—	—
Wisconsin	82	28	110	2	3	7
Wyoming	29	6	35	—	—	—
TOTAL	3,201	430	3,631	139	382	5,500

Note: Data on holding companies with interstate subsidiaries is based on data from the District Federal Reserve Banks except in the 11th and 12th Federal Reserve Districts where we contacted the holding companies. This data based on December 31, 1981, figures, is a snapshot of a constantly changing situation and is not intended as an exhaustive listing.

Source: Federal Reserve Board Data Base as of December 31, 1981.

Total: 139

Map 1   Resident state of bank holding companies controlling interstate 4(c)8 subsidiaries

---

ALLOWABLE NONBANK ACTIVITIES

The Bank Holding Company Act of 1956 as amended in 1970 defines a bank holding company as "—any company which has control over any bank or over any company that is or becomes a bank holding company by virtue of this Act." The term company includes all legal entities except individuals—that is, corporations, partnerships, trusts or associations. Individuals are excluded and consequently may own any number of banks or other financial institutions in any number of states without coming under the provisions of the act. For purposes of the act, the term "control" was defined as controlling directly or indirectly 25 percent or more of any class of voting securities of the bank or company, or controlling the election of a majority of directors or trustees of the bank or company, or the Board of Governors of the Federal Reserve System determines that the company directly or indirectly exercises a controlling influence over the management or policies of the bank or company.[9] This latter provision gives the Board of Governors wide latitude in determining what constitutes control, and hence, what is or is not a holding company.

Section 4(c)8 of the Bank Holding Company Act states the criteria the Board must apply before allowing bank holding companies to engage in certain nonbank activities. Some of those nonbank activities are prohibited to individual banks, but the majority are activities in which nationally chartered banks may engage.[10] Under 4(c)8, a bank holding company may be exempted from the general prohibition against acquiring or establishing nonbank activities and allowed to acquire.

> shares of any company the activity of which the Board after due notice and opportunity for hearing has determined (by order or regulation) *to be so closely related to banking or managing or controlling banks as to be a proper incident thereto.* In determining whether a particular activity is a proper incident to banking or managing or controlling banks the Board shall consider whether its performance by an affiliate of a holding company can reasonably be expected to produce benefits to the public, such as greater convenience, increased competition or gains in efficiency, that outweigh possible adverse effects, such as undue concentration of resources, decreased or unfair competition, conflicts of interest, or unsound banking practices.

To be considered a permissible nonbank activity for bank holding companies, the activity must pass two tests. First, it must be closely related to the activities in which banks engage. This is a rather vague criterion in light of the "incidental powers" accorded banks through Section 8 of the National Bank Act of 1864 which states that banks may "exercise . . . all such incidental powers as shall be necessary to carry on the business of banking . . . ." Given this vagueness it is not surprising that the Board of Governors has no published statement of the criteria it uses to determine activities closely related to banking. Researchers have observed, however, that the Board has approved activities in which banks have historically engaged, or activities complementing services normally provided by banks or activities in which banks clearly possess technical skills.[11] If the activity satisfies at least one of these criteria, it may be proclaimed a permissible activity if it also passes the second test: that providing the service through a nonbank subsidiary may reasonably be expected to produce net public benefits.

The Board may approve a nonbank activity either by order or by regulation—adding the activity to the "laundry list" of approved activities as set forth in Regulation Y, Section 4(c)8. If the activity is approved by order, then every future applicant wishing to undertake that activity must justify the activity to the Board. Effectively, this amounts to a case-by-case review and opinion. On the other hand, if the activity is approved and added to approved activities listed in the regulation, a future applicant need not justify the activity and an application may be approved under delegated authority at the Reserve Bank level if all other conditions for delegated authority are met.

To date, the Board has approved and added to the "laundry list" 17 activities in which bank holding companies may engage by either establishing *de novo* nonbank subsidiaries or acquiring nonbank subsidiaries. The approved activities are set forth in Table 34-4.

Through an application process, one bank and multibank holding companies may gain approval to establish a nonbank subsidiary to engage in any or a combination of activities. By definition, a nonbank subsidiary is not a bank and, hence, does not fall under regulations or laws that apply only to banks. The nonbank entities are, therefore, capable of unrestricted geographic expansion both intrastate and interstate.[12] Since the vast majority of the approved nonbank activities are activities in which banks may engage, i.e. "activities which are closely related to banking or managing or controlling banks . . .", the 4(c)8 provisions effectively allow bank holding companies to provide financial services similar to those provided by banks but on an interstate basis.

[9]See Statutory Appendix to Regulation Y.

[10]See Dale S. Drum, "Nonbanking Activities of Bank Holding Companies," *Economic Perspectives*, Federal Reserve Bank of Chicago March/April, 1977.

[11]See for example, Harvey Rosenblum, "Bank Holding Companies: An Overview," *Business Conditions*, Federal Reserve Bank of Chicago, August, 1973; or Samuel H. Talley: "Developments in the Bank Holding Company Movement," Proceedings of a Conference on Bank Structure and Competition, 1972, Federal Reserve Bank of Chicago.

[12]In two cases, bank holding companies have received approval to acquire troubled S&Ls with the condition that bank branching laws would apply to the acquired S&Ls.

Map 2 shows the number of 4(c)8 subsidiaries controlled by holding companies home officed in a given state. In total the 139 holding companies control 382 4(c)8 subsidiaries with interstate offices. Approximately fifty percent of the 4(c)8 subsidiaries (191) have parent holding companies that reside in the Northeast, specifically the northeastern coastal states from Virginia to Maine plus Pennsylvania (Maine, New York, Massachusetts, Rhode Island, Connecticut, Pennsylvania, New Jersey, Delaware, Maryland and Virginia). And as Map 3 shows, these 191 subsidiaries controlled better than 64 percent (3,472) of all interstate 4(c)8 offices. Therefore, the vast majority of holding companies controlling 4(c)8 subsidiaries with interstate offices are based in the Northeast. In fact, New York and Pennsylvania alone accounted for 22 percent (30) of all holding companies with interstate 4(c)8 subsidiaries. Holding companies in those two states controlled 124 separate interstate subsidiaries, 33 percent of the total, and 1,874 (34 percent) of the total interstate offices. This is not surprising given the number of large holding companies in this area. If interstate

Total: 382

Map 2   Number of interstate subsidiaries of holding companies home officed in the state

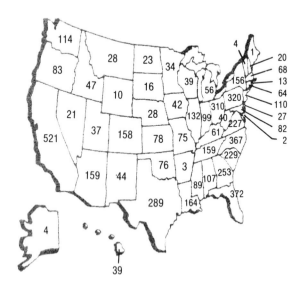

Total: 5,500

Map 3   Total number of offices: all 4(c)8 subsidiaries

positioning through 4(c)8 subsidiaries is any indication, large organizations, especially those in the Northeast, are the most likely to become active in interstate banking if and when the laws permit.

TYPES OF FINANCIAL SERVICES PROVIDED

A nonbank subsidiary may provide more than one 4(c)8 activity at a given location. For instance, a nonbank subsidiary primarily engaged in consumer finance activity may also provide credit life insurance and leasing activities. Therefore, there is a difference between the number of 4(c)8 services provided and the number of 4(c)8 subsidiaries and the number of offices of 4(c)8 subsidiaries. Table 34-6 summarizes the number of 4(c)8 activities provided through interstate offices of nonbank subsidiaries by section of the country. At least 4,613 offices of nonbank subsidiaries of out-of-state bank holding companies provide consumer finance services, by far the most popular type of interstate 4(c)8 activity for bank holding companies to engage in. The second most popular is the insurance agency activity (provided through 2,440 offices), followed by underwriting credit life (1,118 offices), servicing loans (1,995 offices), mortgage banking (623 offices) and leasing (580 offices).[13] Interstate offices that provide check verification, audit services, and credit cards are the least popular. Although these services are provided on an interstate basis, they don't require permanent physical presence.

The geographic distribution of these services is interesting. The South Atlantic (Census Region) states lead the nation in the number of activities provided through nonbank subsidiaries belonging to out-of-state holding companies. These South Atlantic states house 1,327 offices of out-of-state holding companies providing consumer finance services, 214 offices offering mortgage banking and 21 offices offering trust services. The Pacific states are the second most popular target for most 4(c)8 activities, but these states house less than half the number of activities provided through offices in the South Atlantic region. Quite obviously, a region's size plays a part in these statistics, but generally the primary targets for 4(c)8 activities appear to be the faster growing states with substantial populations. In terms of total number of activities offered through nonbank subsidiaries of out-of-state holding companies, California leads the way with 907, followed by Florida with 824, North Carolina with 769, Pennsylvania with 640, Ohio with 614, South Carolina with 558, Georgia with 557 and Texas with 542. The remaining 42 states house approximately the same number of activities offered through offices of nonbank subsidiaries of out-of-state holding companies as the total offered in these 8 states.

---

[13]Any location at which a customer may obtain credit life insurance which is reinsured by a holding company subsidiary is included in the 1,118 offices providing underwriting credit life.

Table 34-6   Interstate nonbank subsidiaries: location of activities by region

Type of activity										Total
Mortgage banking	19	27	214	47	61	74	32	80	69	623
Finance company	149	536	1,327	466	389	565	208	652	321	4,613
Credit cards	0	0	5	0	0	0	1	0	0	6
Factoring	1	5	10	9	3	3	1	12	4	48
Industrial bank	2	0	29	1	1	2	18	23	49	125
Servicing loans	47	140	334	83	32	105	45	106	103	995
Trust company	0	4	21	0	2	1	13	7	20	68
Financial advisor	2	2	29	17	1	17	1	12	11	92
Leasing	30	86	167	53	14	114	23	49	44	580
Investment in community welfare	0	0	0	0	0	4	0	4	4	12
Data processing	2	3	6	4	1	9	16	3	10	54
Insurance agent	72	230	836	253	236	251	97	273	192	2,440
Underwriting credit life	21	45	407	106	83	78	65	159	154	1,118
Management consulting	0	0	2	3	0	0	1	2	2	10
Money orders, travelers checks	0	0	113	2	42	12	0	4	4	177
Check verification	0	0	2	0	1	0	0	0	0	3
Audit services	0	0	0	0	0	0	4	0	1	5
Total per region	345	1,078	3,502	1,044	866	1,235	525	1,386	988	
Total for U.S.										10,969

Source: Federal Reserve Bank of Atlanta

INTERSTATE OFFICES BY PRIMARY ACTIVITY

As noted above, more than one 4(c)8 activity may be provided through a single subsidiary office. Many activities are low profile and normally provide a complementary service to some other 4(c)8 activity. For example, as Table 34-6 indicates, the insurance agent activity is provided at 2,440 locations, although the interstate offices of 4(c)8 subsidiaries primarily engaged in this activity number only 40. The same is true for underwriting credit life insurance; while credit life insurance is provided at 1,118 offices of 4(c)8 subsidiaries, only 56 are primarily engaged in this activity. Therefore, to assess the geographic extent to which bank holding companies are establishing a physical presence on an interstate basis, one should focus on the number of 4(c)8 offices by primary activity. A table detailing the number of these offices by primary activity and by region is available from the Atlanta Fed.

At least 5,500 offices of 4(c)8 subsidiaries are located outside the state in which the parent company resides. Four of the primary activities are what may be considered high profile activities: finance company, mortgage banking, industrial banking and trust services. While offices of some of the other primary activities establish the holding company's presence in an area, they are less visible to the public. In addition, these four highly visible activities accounted for 5,189 of the interstate 4(c)8 offices, or 95 percent of the total. Finance companies dominate as the most popular type of primary 4(c)8 activity. In total, subsidiaries of bank holding companies control 4,442 finance company offices outside the state in which the parent company resides. This one activity accounts for better than 80 percent of all interstate 4(c)8 offices.

A look at the geographic distribution of interstate offices of 4(c)8 subsidiaries may indicate which states or areas of the country will be the primary targets for interstate expansion if the prohibition on interstate banking is lifted. Map 3 shows by state the number of 4(c)8 offices controlled by out-of-state holding companies. In terms of total office locations, California has attracted more activity than any other state with 521 offices. Florida is a distant second with 372 offices, closely followed by North Carolina (367), Pennsylvania (320), Ohio (310) and Texas (289).[14] Five southeastern Atlantic coast states have attracted a good deal of the attention of out-of-state holding companies—Virginia, North Carolina, South Carolina, Georgia and Florida. Combined, these states constitute a land mass half again as large as California but house almost three times the number of 4(c)8 offices, 1,447 offices of out-of-state holding companies (27 percent of the total). Indeed, these five states and Pennsylvania, Ohio, Texas and California have been the most attractive for interstate expansion through 4(c)8 subsidiaries and, if we may use this as any indication, will probably be the most attractive targets for interstate bank expansion should the prohibition be removed.

Map 4, again, reveals that most interstate 4(c)8 activity has been consumer finance oriented. Over 83 percent of all interstate 4(c)8 offices in the nine states mentioned above as attractive targets were finance companies. In fact, 93 percent of all 4(c)8 offices in Pennsylvania are finance companies. This may be interpreted as evidence that these states would be especially attractive for consumer-oriented banks.

---

[14]Pennsylvania has very attractive usury laws which may explain at least in part the degree of nonbank entry.

Total: 4,442

Map 4   By major 4(c)8 activity and number of offices located in each state: Finance companies

Map 5 shows a more or less consistent pattern for mortgage banking offices with the exception that Tennessee and Illinois should be added to our list of attractive states.

Footnote 15 lists the number of office locations of all 4(c)8 subsidiaries engaged primarily in offering trust services.[15] Florida is obviously the prime target for such activities—again a consumer or retail-oriented service. Part of this pattern, however, may be due to the relative leniency of restrictions that states place on entry via the trust route. Florida, for example, has no restrictions on out-of-state organizations establishing trust companies in the state.

State laws restricting industrial banks also play a part in the geographic distribution of this 4(c)8 activity.[16] Although there is some activity in the Carolinas and Georgia, many states prohibit such organizations. A number of midwestern and western states do allow industrial banks, and that is where most such offices are located.

[15]Trust companies (number of offices in each state)—Florida (20), Arizona (9), Montana (8), North Dakota (6), South Dakota (4), New York (3), Nebraska (2), Pennsylvania (1), Hawaii (1), California (1), Illinois (1), and Tennessee (1).

[16]Industrial Banks (number of offices in each state)—Colorado (40), North Carolina (12), Kansas (12), California (10), Georgia (9), South Carolina (7), Washington (8), Utah (20), Hawaii (2), Arizona (10), Nebraska (1), and Florida (1).

Total: 584

Map 5 By major 4(c)8 activity and number of offices located in each state: Mortgage banking

To the extent that offices primarily engaged in the leasing activity may be used to indicate the wholesale banking function, it appears that California, Texas and Ohio will be prime targets for wholesale banking should the laws permit. Each of these states houses at least 10 offices of out-of-state holding companies' 4(c)8 subsidiaries. North Carolina, Illinois, Missouri and Florida also would appear to be desirable targets from this perspective.[17]

OTHER NONBANK SUBSIDIARIES

In addition to 4(c)8 subsidiaries, banking organizations are permitted to establish loan production offices and Edge Act corporations on an interstate basis. Loan production offices can do little more than a calling officer, but they are useful in establishing a wholesale presence in an area. Edge Act offices are also aimed at wholesale customers but are limited to dealing with organizations engaged in international trade.

Since regulatory agencies do not track data on loan production offices, it was necessary to survey banking organizations directly. Only the largest banking

[17]Leasing activities (number of offices in each state)—Texas (11), California (10), Ohio (10), Illinois (8), North Carolina (8), New Jersey (5), Missouri (5), Florida (5), New York (4), Colorado, Michigan, Kentucky, Tennessee, Pennsylvania (3 each), Delaware, Washington, Minnesota (2 each), Montana, Arizona, New Mexico, Nebraska, Louisiana, Georgia, South Carolina, Connecticut (1 each).

Total: 202

Map 6   Interstate loan production offices located in each state

organizations are likely to commit resources to loan production offices, especially in light of the fact that calling offices may provide the same services without a physical presence in an area. Therefore we surveyed the top 200 banking organizations in the country and found that they controlled a total of 202 loan production offices.

Table 34-7 shows the number of banking organizations in each state that have established out-of-state loan production offices, the number of offices established and the number of states in which these offices have been placed. Map 6 shows that California, Illinois, Texas, New York, Colorado and Tennessee have attracted more loan production offices than other states.

Following the same logic, Edge Act corporations are established in order to follow the geographic distribution of one's customers engaged in international trade. There are 143 interstate Edge Act offices of domestic organizations located in the United States. Map 7 shows their geographic distribution. Predictably, states with international trade centers have attracted the most Edge Act offices. New York attracted the largest number, 31, closely followed by Florida with 25 offices. California follows with 23, Texas with 17 and Illinois is a distant fifth with 11 Edge Act offices. New York, Florida, California and Texas are prime targets for this type of wholesale banking. Since only the largest banks may offer services needed by international corporations, banking

Table 34-7 Interstate loan production offices

Parent state	Number of organizations establishing loan production offices	Number of interstate loan production offices maintained	Number of states entered by LPOs
California	5	36[a]	14
District of Columbia	1	7	7
Florida	1	1	1
Illinois	4	31	13
Kentucky	2	8	7
Maryland	1	3	3
Massachusetts	3	14	12
Michigan	1	1	1
Minnesota	2	5	5
Missouri	2	22[b]	6
New Jersey	1	2	2
New York	8	31[c]	13
North Carolina	2	4	2
Oklahoma	1	1	1
Pennsylvania	2	4	2
Rhode Island	2	6	5
Texas	2	5	3
Virginia	2	12	5
Washington	2	9	7
TOTAL	44	202	34

Notes: [a]Only 3 LPOs from California are in New York

[b]General Bancshares Corporation of St. Louis, MO has full service banks in Missouri, Illinois, and Tennessee. They have 13 LPOs in Tennessee and 4 LPOs in Illinois.

[c]10 of the 31 are in California

Source: FRB—Atlanta Survey of Largest 200 Banking Organizations; data as of December 31, 1982.

organizations in the money centers have already located offices to serve these needs. For example, New York banks have established 15 Edge Act offices in California and California organizations have established five such offices in New York. Interstate banking would allow these organizations to provide little more wholesale services than they are providing today.

Source: Federal Reserve Bank of New York
(As of Oct. 1982)   Total: 143

Map 7   Interstate Edge Act office domestic banking organization

SUMMARY OF INTERSTATE ACTIVITY

Table 34-8 summarizes by state the number of interstate offices of out-of-state banking organizations. The most impressive aspect is the fact that domestic banking organizations control at least 7,383 interstate offices and, if we include interstate offices of foreign banking organizations, the total reaches 7,840. This compares to a total of 55,440 banking offices in the nation. Almost 1,500 of the identified interstate offices supply all banking services. The remaining offices are nonbank subsidiaries offering a more limited number of banking type services. The sheer number of interstate offices controlled by holding companies is impressive, given the prohibition on interstate banking.

Holding companies may use a number of avenues to serve both interstate retail and wholesale customers. The only area in which they cannot effectively compete for consumer accounts is in the convenience area—providing brick-and-mortar offices to attract small and medium sized consumer accounts.

On the wholesale side, holding companies are providing a wide array of interstate financial services, some of which require a physical presence but many of which do not. Many of these corporate services may be provided through nonbank subsidiaries, which are free to establish interstate offices. In addition, large banking organizations are providing large corporate customers with banking services not requiring physical interstate offices. These banking organizations appear to be competitively handicapped only in providing certain wholesale banking services to medium and especially small business customers. These customers still depend to a large extent on locally controlled banks.[18]

It appears, however, that as time goes by more and more of the financial services required by medium and small businesses will be targets for large banking organizations supplying these services through 4(c)8 provisions. It simply is not necessary for a banking organization to maintain a facility that both accepts deposits and makes loans to be competitive across state lines. The larger holding companies have already established their nonbank interstate presence.

Some of the smaller banking organizations having a regional scope are moving quickly to establish formal and informal agreements to form interstate networks if the interstate prohibitions are removed. Their rationale seems to be a perceived need to become large enough to compete with the money center banks on an equal footing. Although the smaller banking organizations make the assumption, the question is whether larger banking organizations are under any strong pressure to establish a nationwide interstate banking network involving brick-and-mortar offices. The answer must be a modified no.

First, the removal of Regulation Q means that banks will be required to pay money market rates for a large proportion of their small and medium size deposits. The day of bank deposit customers subsidizing banks through low interest is over. Take this subsidy away and add in the expense of operating distant offices and one conclusion is clear: large banks have no great incentive to use brick and mortar facilities to collect deposits except possibly in the most attractive high growth markets.

From the consumer's standpoint the idea of interstate networks is also questionable. As banks are required to pay money market rates for more of their funds, they necessarily will have to pass the costs along to consumers through direct pricing on services. Since an interstate banking network will be expensive to maintain, will customers be willing to pay for the marginal benefits associated with "unlimited" geographic access to their accounts? The answer is probably "no," given the number of less costly alternatives available that do not require an interstate network. For these reasons it does not appear that the consumer will lead the way to interstate banking. Supply in this case will definitely follow demand—and little demand exists for this type of service.

Too many avenues allow banking organizations to provide interstate financial services on a less costly basis to believe that nationwide interstate brick-and-mortar expansion is inevitable.

Interstate bank expansion will occur in the absence of the interstate prohibition, but, because of the prodigious amount of interstate activity already in place, it will evolve slowly and will be geographically limited to the more

---

[18]David Whitehead. "Sixth District Survey of Small Business Credit," *Economic Review*, Federal Reserve Bank of Atlanta (April 1982), pp. 42-48.

Table 34-8 Summary of interstate activity

| LOCATION | GRANDFATHERED | | | | | | | | | States* with reciprocal agreement | Preferred* stock deals filed with board | Interstate* S&Ls | Offices of 4(c)8 subs | Loan production offices | Edge Act corporation | Total offices per state |
| | DOMESTIC | | | FOREIGN | | | FOREIGN BANKS | | | | | | | | | |
	Holding* companies	Banks	Branches	Holding companies	Banks	Branches	Agency	Edge	Branch							
Alabama											1	1	107	1		108
Alaska		1											4	1		5
Arizona	1	1	161							✓			159			321
Arkansas													3			3
California	1			8	8	148	63	2	2			2	521	22	23	787
Colorado		3	7									1	158	14		182
Connecticut											1		64	1		65
Delaware	12	12	40						1	○		2	27	3	5	87
District of Columbia												2	2	3		6
Florida	2	2	188				22	6		□	1	7	372	6	25	621
Georgia							10				1	2	253	8	5	276
Hawaii				1	1		2					2	39			57
Idaho	2	2	107									1	47			156
Illinois	1	3	4	1	1	1		3	36	□		1	132	21	11	212
Indiana													99	1		100
Iowa	1	11	50							□	1		42	2		105
Kansas												1	78			78
Kentucky												1	61			61
Louisiana							1						164	4	1	170
Maine										✓	1		1			1
Maryland	1	2	30									2	82	7		121
Massachusetts									4	✓	2	1	68	6	3	81
Michigan													56	2		58
Minnesota											1		34	5	4	43
Mississippi													89			89
Missouri												1	75	6	2	83
Montana	3	25	48									2	28	1		102
Nebraska	1	5	39									28	2		74	
Nevada	1	1	66									1	21			88
New Hampshire													20	1		21

State	1	2	3	4	5	6	7	8	9	10	11	12	13	14	15	Total
New Jersey	1	5	35										110	2		112
New Mexico	1	2	27										44			84
New York				3	3	39	18	2	37				156	16	31	331
North Carolina				3									367	3		370
North Dakota	3	34	110										23	1	4	168
Ohio									2	1			310	8	4	322
Oklahoma													76	3		79
Oregon	1	1	169						7			4	83	7	3	270
Pennsylvania									6			2	320	7	2	335
Rhode Island													13			13
South Carolina								1					229			229
South Dakota	3	12	80							○			16	14		108
Tennessee	2	2	27										159	19		202
Texas								9			√	5	289	19	17	334
Utah			35	1							√		37	1		74
Vermont													4			4
Virginia	1	6	63									1	227	1		297
Washington	1	1	85						10			2	114	3	6	219
West Virginia													40			40
Wisconsin	3	8	22										39		1	68
Wyoming	2	4	4									1	10			18
TOTALS	45	141	1,397	13	13	203	116	22	103	10	20	45	5,500	202	143	7,840

Notes:

○ —These states allow entry of limited-purpose banks

□ —These states allow expansion of interstate grandfathered banks

* —These columns are not included in total number of offices

A —Six of the foreign bank holding companies own only one bank, but the bank is located outside the home state of the foreign banking organization.

attractive markets. There is some danger that small and medium sized banking organizations might be panicked into building interstate banking systems large enough to fend off money center banks. In the short run this may create some inefficient organizations. Taking a longer view, however, market forces will correct these inefficiencies. The larger money center banks, on the other hand, quite obviously will become active in the more attractive markets—but are unlikely to establish comprehensive nationwide interstate networks because they have already established themselves through nonbank subsidiaries.

BANKS AND NONBANKS: A RUN FOR THE MONEY*

Harvey Rosenblum, Diane Siegel, and Christine Pavel†

35

For many years, commercial banks have competed in some product lines with other financial institutions such as S&Ls, mutual savings banks, and credit unions. Recently, commercial banks have increasingly found themselves faced with new competitors—manufacturers such as General Motors Corporation, retailers such as Sears, Roebuck and Company, and diversified financial concerns such as Merrill Lynch and American Express. This new mixed breed of nonbank financial companies and even nonfinancial companies has been encroaching on banks' "turf" over the last decade. And banks, though constrained by regulations, have not willingly shared their traditional business of lending and deposit-taking; rather, they have sought footholds in some of their new competitors' markets.

This article examines the expanded competition in the financial services industry first by quantifying the extent and impact of competition against depository institutions, especially commercial banks, by nonbank companies and

*Reprinted from *Economic Perspectives*, May/June 1983, pp. 3-12, with permission of the Federal Reserve Bank of Chicago.

†Harvey Rosenblum is vice president and economic advisor in the Research Department, Federal Reserve Bank of Chicago. Diane Siegel was a summer intern with the Research Department during 1982 and is now completing her MBA studies at the University of Chicago. Christine Pavel is a research assistant at the Chicago Fed.

then by looking at what depository institutions have done to meet their new competition.

NONBANK COMPETITION—AN HISTORICAL OVERVIEW

Two decades ago the only significant nonfinancial-based firms dealing in financial services were Sears and General Motors with 1962 respective net incomes from financial services of $50.4 million and $40.9 million.[1]

But nonfinancial-based companies have taken a major competitive position in financial services in the past ten years. Such companies have been offering credit and other financial services not as loss leaders to attract additional business, but as profit-making products.[2]

A sample of ten nonfinancial-based companies with impressive earnings from financial services in 1972 is presented in Table 35-1. During 1972, these companies had net profits from financial activities that totaled $662.2 million. By year-end 1981, their earnings from financial services had reached $1.7 billion, more than 2½ times the 1972 total and certainly more than can be accounted for by inflation. Only two of these companies had lower percentages of earnings attributable to financial services in 1981 than in 1972. The others had higher percentages; in fact, were it not for its finance subsidiary, General Motors would have posted a net loss in 1981.

General Motors and Sears, with 1981 earnings from financial activities of $365 million and $385 million respectively, each had approximately the same financial service earnings as J. P. Morgan & Co., the holding company for the nation's fifth largest bank. Among the nation's largest banking firms, only Citicorp, BankAmerica Corporation, and Chase Manhattan Corporation had earnings that exceeded the financial service earnings of these nonbank giants.

Many of the manufacturers listed in Table 35-1 originally financed only their own products and therefore did not effectively compete with commercial banks. But by 1972, many of these so-called "captive" finance companies were engaged in financial activities unrelated to the sale of their parents' products.

---

[1]Cleveland A. Christophe, *Competition in Financial Services*, New York: First National City Corporation, 1974. In this study of eleven companies, Christophe provides an in-depth view of the relative importance of banks and nonfinancial firms in the extension of consumer credit. Rosenblum and Siegel, *Competition in Financial Services: The Impact of Non-bank Entry* Staff Study 83-1 from which this article is adapted, updates Christophe's work and elaborates upon new competition in other segments of the banking business such as business credit and retail deposits.

[2]As pointed out in "Banking's New Competition: Myths and Realities," *Economic Review*, Federal Reserve Bank of Atlanta, January 1982, pp. 4-11, by William F. Ford, many nonbank firms have sought to enter the product lines of commercial banks because banking appears to be more profitable relative to their traditional lines of business. Yet, despite the entry of these nonbank firms, commercial banks have remained more profitable than their new competitors.

This trend has continued. In 1981, over 90 percent of Borg-Warner Acceptance Corporation's income and assets came from financing *other* companies' products, and less than 1 percent of Westinghouse Credit Corporation's financing volume was related to Westinghouse products. For General Electric Credit Corporation, this trend toward financing non-G.E. products began in the mid-to-late 1960s; by 1972, less than 10 percent of General Electric Credit's receivables represented G.E. products, and in 1981 only about 5 percent of General Electric Credit's financing was for its parent's products.

Thus, not only have the earnings from financial activities increased as a percent of total earnings for the majority of the companies listed in Table 35-1, but many of those companies which were originally captive have evolved to compete increasingly with commercial banks and others in the financial services industry.

Table 35-1   Financial service earnings of nonfinancial-based companies (estimated)

	1972		1981	
	Million dollars	Percent of total earnings	Million dollars	Percent of total earnings
Borg-Warner	$6.3	10.6%	$31	18.0%
Control Data	55.6	96.2	50	29.2
Ford Motor	44.1	5.1	186	n.a.[1]
General Electric	41.1	7.8	142	8.6
General Motors	96.4	4.5	365	109.6[2]
Gulf & Western	29.3	42.1	71	24.5
ITT	160.2	33.6	387	57.2
Marcor	9.0	12.4	110	n.a.[1]
Sears	209.0	34.0	385	51.1
Westinghouse	15.2	7.6	34	7.8
	662.2		1,732	

[1]Not available because parent company had a net loss for 1981.

[2]General Motors and consolidated subsidiaries had a loss of $15 million after taxes; however, after adding $348 million of equity in earnings of such nonconsolidated subsidiaries as GMAC, General Motors had after-tax net income of $333 million.

Source: Harvey Rosenblum and Diane Siegel, *Competition in Financial Services: The Impact of Nonbank Entry*, Staff Study 83-1 (Federal Reserve Bank of Chicago, 1983), Table 1, p. 12.

CONSUMER LENDING

Over the last decade, some nonfinancial-based companies have made quite remarkable inroads in the area of consumer lending; nonetheless, banks have gained ground in some areas, most notably in credit cards. At year-end 1972, for example, the three largest banks held less consumer installment credit than the three largest nonfood retailers. These, in turn, held less consumer installment credit than three large consumer durable goods manufacturers (see Figure 35-1a). As shown in Figure 35-1b, these rankings had changed by year-end 1981. Within this sample of nine companies, bank holding companies experienced the highest growth rate since 1972, in large part due to their credit card operations.

The incursion of nonbank firms in the area of consumer lending is illustrated dramatically in the narrower field of auto loans. As shown in Figure 35-2, banks have the largest share in auto lending—47 percent at year-end 1981—but this share is down 13 percentage points from its peak in 1978. Over this same three-year period, the share of auto loans held by the captive finance companies of General Motors, Ford, and Chrysler had increased by 12 percentage points to 33 percent of the market. GMAC alone, in 1981, held $28.5 billion of auto

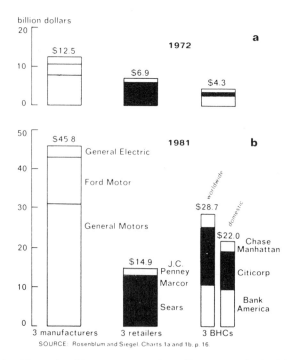

Figure 35-1   How the big consumer installment credit holders stacked up: 1972 and 1981

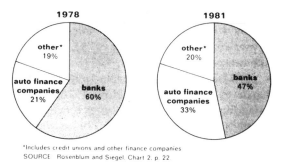

*Includes credit unions and other finance companies
SOURCE Rosenblum and Siegel. Chart 2. p. 22

Figure 35-2 Car loans: auto finance companies take a bigger slice of outstanding loans

loans outstanding and double its share of just three years earlier. Bank of America, the largest auto lender among commercial banks, held $2.2 billion of auto loans at year-end 1981, a mere one-thirteenth of the total held by GMAC, far and away the largest consumer lender in the United States and probably the world.

These figures, however, may be somewhat biased by recent events. The soaring cost of funds, binding usury ceilings in many states, and use by General Motors, Ford, and Chrysler of below-market financing rates in an attempt to boost sluggish sales have caused many lenders to exit the auto lending business in recent years.

As shown in Table 35-2, commercial banks, in 1978, made 58 percent of net new auto loans (new loans extended less liquidations); in 1981, banks' extensions of net auto loans were negative; and in 1982, banks made only 16 percent of the net new auto loans that year. Finance companies, however, made only 25 percent of the net new auto loans in 1978 but accounted for 72

Table 35-2 Sources of net new automobile credit by holder

	1978		1981		1982	
	Dollar billion	Percent	Dollar billion	Percent	Dollar billion	Percent
Commercial banks	10.9	58	−3.5	*	.8	16
Finance companies	4.7	25	4.0	*	3.5	72
Credit unions			.9			
	3.1	17		*	.6	12
	18.7	100	8.4	*	4.9	100

*Percentages not shown because market shares cannot be negative.

Sources: U.S. Board of Governors of the Federal Reserve System. *Federal Reserve Bulletin* 69 (May 1982), pp. A42-A43 and *Consumer Installment Credit* G.19 (March 1983).

percent of such loans in 1982. The sharp drop-off in new business volume is also particularly noteworthy as it demonstrates a market in a state of flux, a condition conducive to large—even massive—shifts in market shares.

The shift in the consumer lending market away from commercial banks toward finance companies can also be seen Figure 35-3. In 1978, commercial banks issued 55 percent of net new installment debt (new loans less liquidations) to households; finance companies accounted for only 22 percent. By 1981, however, these relative shares had more than reversed themselves as commercial banks moved away from consumer installment lending over the 1978-1981 period. In fact, in 1978 commercial banks extended almost $1.20 in new consumer installment credit for every one dollar of consumer installment loans liquidated, but by 1980, they extended only 95 percent for every one dollar of consumer installment loans that were repaid or liquidated. Over this same period, finance companies increasingly entered the consumer lending market; thus, by 1981, finance companies issued 72 percent of net new consumer installment debt while commercial banks issued only 3 percent.

These shifts in market shares may be somewhat distorted by the fact that finance company subsidiaries of bank holding companies are included with finance companies. Further complicating interpretation of the data is the tendency of some banks to sell consumer loans to their finance company affiliates and vice versa. The division between finance companies and banks, however,

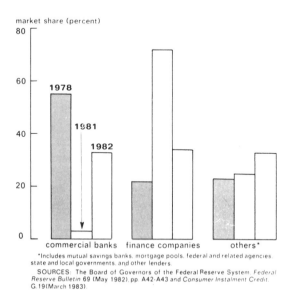

Figure 35-3 Consumer loans: banks take a beating

is correct because banks are regulated very differently than finance companies, regardless of their affiliations.

Also, the shifts in market shares in consumer installment lending are not necessarily permanent but probably reflect cyclical as well as secular forces working simultaneously. As can be seen in Figure 35-3, commercial banks recovered some market share in 1982, as did S&Ls and all other lenders at the expense of finance companies. In fact, finance companies lost almost 38 percentage points in only one year. Furthermore, the comeback of commercial banks and S&Ls in the consumer lending market is likely to continue through 1983 as banks and other depository institutions that have been flooded with new funds in response to the success of money market deposit accounts (MMDAs), Individual Retirement Accounts (IRAs), and other deregulated deposit instruments become more willing to offer consumer installment loans. Further, S&Ls are likely to maintain a more significant presence in consumer lending than they did in the past as they continue to take advantage of the broader lending powers given them under the Depository Institutions Deregulation and Monetary Control Act of 1980 and the Garn-St Germain Depository Institutions Act of 1982.

Just as the shift in market share in consumer installment lending has been dramatic, so too has the decline in net *new* loan volume, falling by more than half—to less than $20 billion in 1981 from over $43 billion in 1978. Even more significant was the decline in volume of net new consumer installment loans at commercial banks—down to $0.6 billion in 1981 from $23.6 billion three years earlier. During this same period, auto loans outstanding at commercial banks declined by $2.4 billion; in the prior three-year period (year-end 1978 vs. year-end 1975), auto loans at commercial banks grew by $29 billion.

While commercial banks held less in auto loans in 1981 than they held in 1978, their outstanding credit card receivables remained relatively constant at about $17.5 billion over this same three-year period. In fact, it is in the area of charge cards that banks have done best against their nonfinancial-based competitors. In 1972, Sears had the leading credit card in the United States in terms of number of active accounts, charge volume, and customer account balances. By 1981, Visa was the undisputed leader by all three measures with MasterCard not far behind and Sears a distant third except in number of active accounts (see Figure 35-4). Beginning in 1980 Visa and MasterCard began displacing the cards issued by many retailers such as J. C. Penny and Montgomery Ward.

Whether the success of Visa and MasterCard relative to the Sears card implies a victory for banks over a nonbank competitor is unclear since neither Visa nor MasterCard are banks. They are franchising companies that license a product to franchisees. The original franchisees were banks, but several hundred savings and loan associations, mutual savings banks, and credit unions have become franchisees during the last few years. Indeed, some of Visa's recent

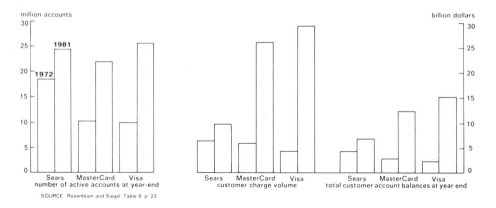

SOURCE: Rosenblum and Siegel. Table 9, p 23

Figure 35-4   The bank cards ace out the biggest retailer on balance and volume

growth is attributable to the popularity of Merrill Lynch's Cash Management Account, which includes a Visa card.

BUSINESS LENDING

Commercial banks remain the predominant source of credit to all businesses, large and small. As can be seen in Table 35-3, banks have the lion's share of short-term commercial and industrial loans (C&I loans) in the United States. The 15 largest bank holding companies held $141.6 billion of domestic C&I loans at year-end 1981, more than triple the total held by a selected group of 32 nonbank companies, most of whom have made forays into banks' traditional commercial lending activities.[3]

The importance of nonbank lenders should not be underestimated. With $39.4 billion in C&I loans the 15 selected industrial companies were an important factor in the C&I loan market, holding almost three-tenths as much in loans as were booked domestically by the 15 largest bank holding companies. In addition, funds that large firms raise from banks and from the money and capital markets are used to provide loans to many small businesses. This trade credit, although an imperfect substitute for bank credit because it cannot be used to pay other creditors or meet employee payrolls, is the most widely used source of credit for small businesses, both in terms of the percentage of firms utilizing it and in dollar volume. Moreover, at year-end 1981 nonfinancial firms had $53.7 billion of commercial paper outstanding and nonbank financial firms

---

[3]These 32 companies were chosen on the basis of their being the most frequently listed nonbanking-based competitors of commercial banks. Many financial-based companies have been excluded because they have demonstrated little or no inclination to invade the turf of commercial banks.

had $77.4 billion of commercial paper outstanding; some portion of this was used to provide credit to businesses.

Banks are also an important source of funds for commercial mortgages and lease financing, but nonbank firms again should not be overlooked in these areas. As shown in Table 35-3, four insurance-based companies held more commercial mortgage loans at year-end 1981 than did the 15 largest bank holding companies.[4] The 32 selected nonbank firms also held more lease receivables at that time than did the top 15 bank holding companies on a worldwide basis and more lease receivables than did domestic offices of the nation's more than 14,000 insured commercial banks. If the sum of C&I loans, commercial mortgage loans, and business lease financing can be used as a *rough* proxy for total business credit, then it would appear that the 32 selected nonbanking-based firms have made significant inroads into the commercial lending activities of commercial banks.

Table 35-3   Business lending by selected nonbanking-based firms and bank holding companies at year-end 1981

Commercial and industrial loans	Commercial and industrial loans	Commercial mortgage loans	Lease financing	Total business lending
	(------------------------------$ million------------------------------)			
15 Industrial/communications/transportation†	39,365	1,768	14,417*	55,550
10 Diversified financial†	3,602	3,054	1,581*	8,237
4 Insurance-based	399	35,506	892*	35,797
3 Retail-based	606	—	—	606
	43,972	40,328	16,890*	101,190
15 Largest BHCs				
domestic	141,582	19,481	14,279*	175,342
international	118,021	5,046	—	123,067
Total, top-15 BHCs	259,603	24,527	14,279	298,409
Domestic offices, all insured commercial banks	327,101	120,333**	13,168	460,602

*Includes domestic and foreign lending and may include leasing to household or government entities.

**Includes all real estate loans except those secured by residential property.

†Financing by banking and savings and loan subsidiaries has been subtracted.

Source: Harvey Rosenblum and Diane Siegel, *Competition in Financial Services: The Impact of Nonbank Entry*, Staff Study 83-1 (Federal Reserve Bank of Chicago, 1983), Table 10, p. 26.

[4]Insurance companies have played a major role in commercial mortgage lending for many years. Further, many banks do not have the ability to hold long-term commercial mortgages because of the short-term nature of their funds.

DEPOSIT-TAKING

Not only are banks experiencing competition from nonbanking-based firms in lending areas, but they are also witnessing the same phenomenon in the area of deposit-taking. Substitutes for bank deposits have been around as long as there has been a reasonably efficient secondary market for government and private securities. Treasury bills and repurchase agreements, for example, are close substitutes for bank deposits, including demand deposits.

In 1973 a closer substitute for bank deposits emerged—money market mutual funds (MMFs). While not a big threat to banks when interest rates were relatively low, MMFs became very successful when rates rose, growing from only a few billion dollars in "deposits" in 1975 to over $230 billion by December 1982 when they reached their peak. At that time, Merrill Lynch alone managed $50.4 billion in MMF assets, and the Dreyfus Corporation managed $18.5 billion. Originally offered by nonbank financial firms such as Dreyfus and the Fidelity Group, MMFs attracted nonfinancial-based firms as well. Sears began offering the Sears U.S. Government Money Market Trust in late 1981 and later acquired Dean Witter Reynolds, a brokerage firm managing five MMFs.

Although MMFs do compete with bank deposits, few nonbank companies rely to any significant extent upon deposits as a source of funds to finance the loans extended to their customers. Mostly, their funds are raised in the money and capital markets at competitive rates; consequently, the profit margins of most nonbank companies which have financial activities are not, and have never been, dependent upon the Regulation Q franchise. It has been estimated that roughly half of the 1980 profits of 31 of the 50 largest U.S. banks could be attributed to their ability to pay below-market rates on savings accounts.[5] Thus, the continued phase-out of Q-ceilings is unlikely to damage the market position of nondepository firms in lending.

THE BANKS' RESPONSES TO NONBANK COMPETITION

Commercial banks, as well as other depository institutions, have attempted to meet the nonbank challenge by offering some products and services—such as MMFs and discount brokerage services—that had become the domain of nonbank financial firms (see box, chronology 1). In addition, banks and other depository institutions have tried to circumvent regulatory geographic barriers to compete on an even keel with their nonbank rivals (see box, chronology 2).

---

[5]Alex J. Pollock. "The Future of Banking: a National Market and Its Implications," in *Proceedings of a Conference on Bank Structure and Competition*, Federal Reserve Bank of Chicago, 1982, pp. 31-36.

CHRONOLOGIES OF CHANGE

1. Banks Fight Back

Apr 1981   Citibank and Northwestern National Bank allow their customers to borrow money on their six-month money market certificates through a checking account.

May 1981   The Bank of California NA, San Francisco, introduces a new account to compete with money market funds. Because the account is housed in the bank's London branch, BanCal says it is not subject to interest rate ceilings and reserve requirements, but the Fed disagrees.

May 1981   J. P. Morgan & Co. forms a subsidiary to trade financial futures for Morgan Guaranty's account. In July 1981, the Federal Reserve Board allows Morgan Guaranty to execute trades for its customers; in December 1982, the Commodity Futures Trading Commission approves.

Sep 1981   Dreyfus Service Corp. sweeps excess cash from bank accounts into its money market funds, and other firms follow Dreyfus' lead.

Nov 1981   BankAmerica Corp. plans to acquire Charles Schwab & Company, the nation's largest discount brokerage firm; the Federal Reserve Board approves the acquisition early in 1983.

Jan 1982   Banks and thrifts collaborate with brokerage firms to offer discount brokerage services to customers of the banks and thrifts.

Mar 1982   Orbanco Financial Services Corp., a Portland, Oregon holding company, proposes a note with a minimum denomination of $5,000, which bears market interest rates, and which has transactions features. The Federal Reserve Board, however, disallows the note.

May 1982   Three S&Ls receive permission to start a joint securities brokerage service that S&Ls nationwide can use to offer investment services to their customers. The service, known as Invest, begins operations in November.

Jun 1982   Citicorp purchases two transponders on the Westar V satellite in preparation for global banking.

Jul 1982   The Federal Reserve Board allows Citicorp to offer various data processing and data transmission services nationwide through a new subsidiary, Citishare Corp.

Aug 1982 The Comptroller of the Currency allows First National Bank of Chicago to form a subsidiary to trade in the futures market for its customers. In January 1983, the Commodity Futures Trading Commission approves.

Sep 1982 Talman Home Federal Savings and Loan Association introduces its Instant Cash Account to compete with money market funds. The account requires a $5,000 minimum balance and pays the rate of a 6-month CD.

Sep 1982 North Carolina National Bank's NCNB Futures Corp. receives final approval from the Commodity Futures Trading Commission to act as a futures commission merchant.

Sep 1982 The Federal Reserve Board allows Bankers Trust New York Corp. to buy and sell futures contracts for its customers through a new subsidiary, BT Capital Markets Corp. In January 1983, the Commodity Futures Trading Commission approves.

Sep 1982 Poughkeepsie Savings Bank applies to the FHLBB to acquire Investors discount Corp., a Poughkeepsie Discount brokerage firm.

Oct 1982 The Comptroller of the Currency allows Security Pacific, Los Angeles, to acquire Kahn & Co., a Memphis-based discount brokerage firm.

Oct 1982 The DIDC authorizes an account which federal depository institutions can offer and which is "directly equivalent to and competitive with money market funds."

Nov 1982 Security Pacific National Bank forms a subsidiary, Security Pacific Brokers Inc., to provide back office support for other banks which offer discount brokerage services.

Dec 1982 The DIDC authorized a Super-NOW account which federal depository institutions can offer on January 5, 1983.

2. Interstate Barriers Crumble

Mar 1980   South Dakota passes legislation which allows out-of-state bank holding companies to move credit card operations to South Dakota. Three years later, the state passes a new bill that allows out-of-state bank holding companies to own state chartered banks which can own insurance companies.

Feb 1981   Delaware passes an out-of-state banking bill which opens the state to major money center banks.

Jun 1981   Citibank establishes Citibank (South Dakota) NA in Sioux Falls to handle its credit card operations.

Aug 1981   Marine Midland Banks, Inc. Buffalo, New York, infuses $25 million into Industrial Valley Bank and Trust Company, Philadelphia, by buying newly issued common stock and nonvoting preferred stock with warrants to buy an additional 20 percent of Industrial Valley's common stock should interstate banking be permitted.

Sep 1981   United Financial Corp., San Francisco, a subsidiary of National Steel and parent of Citizens Savings and Loan, acquires an S&L in New York and one in Miami Beach. The Combined S&Ls later become First Nationwide Savings.

Nov 1981   Casco-Northern Corp., Portland, Maine, parent of Casco Bank and Trust Company, sells First National Boston Corp. 56,250 shares of its convertible preferred stock and warrants to buy additional common shares. In March 1983, first National Bank of Boston Corp. agrees to acquire Casco-Northern.

Dec 1981   J. P. Morgan & Company establishes Morgan Bank (Delaware), to engage in wholesale commercial banking.

Dec 1981   Home Savings and Loan Association, Los Angeles, acquires one Florida thrift and two in Missouri. In connection with the acquisitions, Home Savings and Loan becomes Home Savings of America.

Jan 1982   North Carolina National Bank Corp. acquires First National Bank of Lake City, Florida, by using a legal loophole in a grandfather clause.

Jan 1982   AmSouth Bancorp. of Alabama, South Carolina National Bank Corp. and Trust Company of Georgia plan to merge into a single holding company if and when interstate banking is permitted. Until then, each is buying $2 million of nonvoting preferred stock in the other two.

Jan 1982   Home Savings of America, Los Angeles, acquires five Texas savings associations and one in Chicago.

Mar 1982   Marine Midland Banks, New York, invests $10 million in Centran Corp., Cleveland, in the form of newly issued nonvoting preferred stock and warrants to buy over 2 million shares of Centran's common stock should interstate banking be permitted.

Jun 1982   Alaska's new banking law permits out-of-state banks to acquire Alaskan banks without the states of those banks enacting reciprocal legislation.

Jul 1982   New York legislation amends the state's banking law to allow out-of-state bank holding companies to acquire control of New York banks provided that the states of these banks reciprocate.

Aug 1982   The Federal Reserve Board and the shareholders of Gulfstream Banks Inc., Boca Raton, Florida, approve the acquisition of Gulfstream Banks by North Carolina National Bank Corp.

Sep 1982   In the first reciprocal interstate bank acquisition between New York and Maine, Key Banks Inc. of Albany agrees to acquire Depositors Corp. of Augusta; the acquisition is expected to be completed by the end of 1983.

Dec 1982   The Federal Reserve Board allows Exchange Bancorp., Florida, to merge into North Carolina National Bank Corp., and the Fed approves the merger of Downtown National Bank of Miami into NCNB/ Gulfstream Banks Inc.

Dec 1982   Both houses of the Massachusetts State legislature pass an interstate banking bill which allows Massachusetts banks to expand into other New England states on a reciprocal basis. The law is effective in 1983.

PRODUCTS AND SERVICES

Banks and other depository institutions have not stood idle while deposits left their low-yielding accounts for MMFs. As shown in chronology 1, banks and thrifts have designed various products to compete with MMFs and, at the same time, to skirt a number of competition-inhibiting or cost-raising regulations. The Bank of California, for example, tried to shield an MMF-like account from interest rate ceilings by housing it in Bancal's London branch, and Orbanco proposed a note that would pay market rates and have transaction features. These two schemes were stopped by the Federal Reserve Board, but other innovations have met with more success. Northwestern National Bank, for instance, began allowing its customers to borrow money on their six-month money market certificates through checking accounts in April 1981, and Talman Home, Chicago, introduced its Instant Cash Account in September 1982.

While some depository institutions created products to compete with MMFs, others decided to join them rather than try to beat them. Banks and thrifts began collaborating with money fund managers like Dreyfus and Federated Securities to offer sweep accounts—accounts that sweep idle cash balances exceeding some predetermined level into high-yielding MMFs.

Finally, banks and thrifts no longer had to try to circumvent regulations by linking up with money fund managers in order to offer their customers MMF-like products. In early October 1982, the Congress passed, as part of the Garn-St Germain Depository Institutions Act of 1982, new legislation which permits banks and other depository institutions to offer the Money Market Deposit Account, and in December 1982, the DIDC authorized the Super NOW account. Both are designed to compete directly with MMFs.[6]

Another area dominated by nonbank financial firms which banks have sought to enter is discount brokerage services. Generally, banks have taken one of three paths in offering these services: collaborating with discount brokerage firms, acquiring existing brokerage firms, or establishing discount brokerage subsidiaries of their own.

As shown in chronology 1, many banks and thrifts have taken the first route, hooking up with brokers such as Fidelity Brokerage Services and Quick & Reilly. Some, however, have opted for one of the other two routes. For example, Security Pacific National Bank, which at first offered discount brokerage services through Fidelity, acquired Kahn & Company, a Memphis-based discount brokerage, in October 1982. In November 1982, Security Pacific formed a subsidiary to provide back office support for other banks entering the discount

---

[6]Both the MMDA and the Super NOW account require an initial deposit of $2,500, are free of interest rate ceilings, and are federally insured; however, depositors can write only three checks per month on an MMDA whereas they can write an unlimited number of checks on a Super NOW. Super NOW accounts are restricted to individuals, certain nonprofit corporations, and governmental units, whereas MMDAs can be offered to any entity.

brokerage field. More recently, BankAmerica Corporation acquired Charles Schwab & Company, the nation's largest discount broker. Taking the third path, in November 1982, three S&Ls started Invest, a brokerage service which S&Ls nationwide can offer.

In addition, since mid-1981 when J. P. Morgan & Co. formed a subsidiary to trade financial futures for Morgan Guaranty's account, banks have increasingly been seeking to trade in the financial futures market for their own accounts as well as for their customers. Before they can act as brokers for third parties, however, banks must first get approval from the Comptroller of the Currency or, in the case of bank holding companies, from the Federal Reserve Board. Then they must apply to the Commodity Futures Trading Commission (CFTC) for registration as brokers. Among those that have cleared both stages of the regulatory process are J. P. Morgan & Co., North Carolina National Bank, Bankers Trust, and First National Bank of Chicago.

Banks are also expanding into less finance-related fields such as data processing and telecommunications. For example, Citicorp was recently given permission to offer an expanded range of data processing and transmission services and, in June 1982, it purchased two transponders on the Westar V satellite, thus becoming the first financial institution to own transponders in space.[7]

GEOGRAPHIC BARRIERS

Banks seem to be meeting the challenges of nonbank competition in many of their new rivals' product lines, but banks do not yet enjoy the same geographic freedom as their nonbank competitors. Although many of the products and services which banks and bank holding companies provide are offered nationwide, such as those provided through nonbank subsidiaries like consumer finance and mortgage banking companies, the interstate expansion of a *bank's* physical facilities is still generally prohibited. Nonetheless, as shown in chronology 2, banks and thrifts are preparing for the legalization of interstate banking, and—through mergers, acquisitions, affiliations, relaxations of some state laws, and technological advances—interstate banking is slowly becoming a reality.

Agreements to merge are the most common way in which banks and thrifts have been preparing for interstate banking. Usually, one institution agrees to invest in another by purchasing nonvoting preferred stock with warrants to buy additional shares of common stock should interstate banking be allowed. Although Citicorp was the first to use such a maneuver, many others have followed. In this manner, for example, Marine Midland Banks, New York City,

---

[7]*Federal Reserve Bulletin*, August 1982, p. 505.

invested $25 million in Industrial Valley Bank and Trust Company, Philadelphia, and $10 million in Centran Corporation, Cleveland.[8]

Some interstate mergers and acquisitions, however, have already taken place. In January 1982, Home Savings of America, Los Angeles, acquired five ailing savings associations in Texas and one in Chicago after acquiring a troubled Florida thrift and two in Missouri. Also in January 1982, North Carolina National Bank Corporation acquired First National Bank of Lake City, Florida, through a loophole in a grandfather clause, and later expanded further in that state. Although the acquisitions by Home Federal and those by North Carolina Bank Corporation are different in nature and purpose, five or ten years from now their effects will be the same.

In some instances, interstate banking has been encouraged by individual states. In early 1980, South Dakota passed a law which allows out-of-state bank holding companies to establish banks to house credit card operations, and in June 1981, Citicorp moved its credit card operations to the newly established Citibank (South Dakota). In March 1983, South Dakota passed another law which allows out-of-state bank holding companies to acquire or charter state banks, which could own insurance companies. Delaware passed its out-of-state banking law in February 1981 to encourage banks to relocate certain activities in the state; since then twelve institutions have established banks in Delaware, including five from New York, four from Maryland, and three from Pennsylvania. However, these new banks do not compete with Delaware banks in general banking operations. In June 1982, Alaska enacted legislation that allows out-of-state banks to acquire Alaskan banks without reciprocal legislation on the part of the states of those banks. New York, Massachusetts, and Maine enacted similar legislation but require reciprocity. Out-of-state banks, therefore, can compete with banks in Alaska, New York, Massachusetts, and Maine, but Massachusetts limits interstate banking to the New England states.

Interstate banking also occurs through banks' and thrifts' affiliations with nationwide brokers and investment firms. Alliances that would have been termed "unholy" not long ago are commonplace today. Through its network of some 475 offices, Merrill Lynch has marketed All Savers Certificates for Bank of America, Crocker National Bank, and two S&Ls, one in Florida and the other in Washington. Merrill Lynch also maintains a secondary market for retail CDs issued by banks and S&Ls and acts as a broker in the placement of retail CDs issued by more than 20 banks and thrifts, thus giving each of them a nationwide reach. Merrill Lynch is not alone in this regard but is joined by several other companies including Sears/Dean Witter, Shearson/American Express, and E. F. Hutton. Together these four firms operate roughly 1,325 offices throughout

---

[8]The Federal Reserve Board permits these limited interstate banking activities if the acquiring company holds no more than 24.9 percent of the nonvoting shares, holds no more than 5 percent of the voting stock, and exercises no control over the bank in which the investment is being made.

the United States. Thanks to these and other firms like them, a comparatively small depository institution such as City Federal Savings and Loan of Elizabeth, New Jersey, can now compete toe-to-toe on a nationwide basis with Bank of America in the sale of federally insured retail CDs.

The importance of the cooperative affiliations between brokers and depository institutions should not be underestimated, for it may represent one of the most significant reductions in entry barriers into the financial services business. No longer is deposit and loan growth of a de novo bank or S&L constrained by its ability to generate deposits from its local customers. To the extent that it has profitable lending opportunities, a new depository institution can engage in liability management through the sale of brokered, insured *retail* deposits by paying above the going market rate. The availability of federal deposit insurance should make depositors virtually indifferent to the identity of the institution they deal with. It is now conceivable that a de novo bank or S&L could develop a billion-dollar deposit base within a year or two of its opening.

CONCLUSION

Over the last decade, competition in financial services has increased as the number of firms grew and the geographic market became more and more national. Furthermore, deregulation tends to be accompanied by unbundling of products, and this has been the case in the financial services industry. Nonbank firms have been able to target and successfully enter the major and minor product lines of commercial banks. Thus the preeminent position of commercial banks has been eroded somewhat in consumer lending, business lending, and deposit-taking. But as nonbank rivals encroached upon banks' traditional territory, banks responded where possible by invading some of their new competitors' product lines and by attempting to compete on a nationwide basis as do these competitors.

Thus, by 1983, the line of commerce that was once called commercial banking has evolved into a new line of commerce, the provision of financial intermediation services. Yet, the courts have continued to delineate commercial banking as a distinct line of commerce, separate from other financial services. In the eyes of the courts, banks compete only with other banks, but not with S&Ls, credit unions, finance companies, mutual savings banks, insurance companies and so forth. This has been the prevailing view of the courts for two decades, having been decided in *Philadelphia National Bank* in 1963.[9]

The evidence provided in this article illustrates quite clearly that technological advances and long overdue statutory and regulatory changes have

[9]*United States* v. *The Philadelphia National Bank* et al., 374 U.S. 321, 915 (1963).

blurred the distinctions between financial intermediation services offered by old-line, traditional financial institutions such as banks and S&Ls and the services offered by the financing arms of manufacturers, retailers, and diversified financial conglomerates. In the longer run, the survivors will be the low cost producers—irrespective of their charters. Perhaps then the line of commerce definition will be judicially or legislatively revised.